Finding Justice

A conjectural painting of Margaret Brent arguing in front of the Maryland General Assembly by Louis S. Glanzman, 1976.

Courtesy of the National Geographic Creative.

Finding Justice

A History of Women Lawyers in Maryland since 1642

Edited by the Honorable Lynne A. Battaglia

WITH CONTRIBUTIONS BY

Chancellor Phoebe A. Haddon,
the Honorable Diane O. Leasure,
Andrea Leahy,
Michelle R. Mitchell,
Professor Jane C. Murphy, and
the Honorable Julie R. Rubin

GEORGE F. THOMPSON PUBLISHING
in association with the
Maryland Women's Bar Association Foundation
and University of Baltimore Foundation
and distributed by the University of Virgina Press

CONTENTS

The Honorable Lynne A. Battaglia, Chair of the Finding Justice Project Editorial Committee

The mission of the Finding Justice Project has been, since its inception:

Today, women in Maryland serve in the legal profession with distinction at all levels, whether as lawyers, judges, professors, or elected officials. The fact that some women have achieved prominence in the law obscures the significant barriers that still remain and disconnects us from the struggles faced by women historically. By understanding and embracing the history of women in the law, including the recent past, we can determine what forces bridged the legal system from exclusion to inclusion. Knowing how individual women in their professional and personal lives contributed to this societal change will help forge a secure foundation for future women in the law. This project will showcase these women's achievements, lives, and goals in an historical context; it will describe and preserve the efforts that ensured the place that women lawyers enjoy today; and the project will illuminate the goals that have yet to be achieved by future generations of women in the law.

Our efforts really began more than 300 years ago, when Margaret Brent advocated for herself and others. The story of Margaret Brent the attorney is well known: she was appointed attorney to Lord Baltimore and administatrix to the deceased Governor Leonard Calvert in 1647. At that time, the role of a woman was determined by her marital status. Margaret Brent never married, and as *feme sole*, or single woman, she could sell property and transact business in her own right. Her role as an attorney enabled Margaret Brent to independently sell and manage property, transact business, and participate in the colony's government (largely in cases before the Provincial Court of St. Mary's County). So important was the contribution of Margaret Brent to women and the practice and profession of law that the American Bar Association annually honors "the accomplishments of women lawyers who have excelled in their field and have paved the way to success for other women lawyers" with the Margaret Brent Women Lawyers of Achievement Award.[1]

Margaret Brent may be best known for her petition before Maryland's assembly in January 1648, when she sought two votes, one for herself as a landowner and one as Lord Baltimore's attorney. When the request was denied, she purportedly exclaimed, "Where is justice?" The question's refrain can be heard throughout the next two hundred plus years.

In 1878, after women had been admitted to the Bars of eleven other states and U.S. territories, a judge in Prince George's County denied Belva Lockwood's admission to practice law in that county, even though she was already licensed to practice law in the District of Columbia.[2] The judge exclaimed, "I pray to God that the day will never come when the women of Maryland will be admitted to the bar."[3] The 1901 petition of Etta Haynie Maddox was similarly denied by the Court of Appeals of Maryland.

It was not until the next year, 1902, that the path toward justice was undertaken when Etta Maddox lobbied tirelessly in the General Assembly to remove gender as a qualification for bar admission. She succeeded and became the first woman to pass the bar examination and sign the testbook for attorneys, signifying her formal admission to the Maryland Bar. By Etta Maddox's admission, the door opened for women to practice law in Maryland, the thirty-sixth state to formally admit women (of forty-eight states).[4] Another forty-four years would pass before the Maryland State Bar Association finally admitted its first female member, becoming the last state bar association to do so. It was not until 1974 that women at the Bar became a significant force that "mushroomed" when ninety women were admitted. That number has been exceeded in every year since then.

Finding Justice attempts to explore what propelled women to pursue legal careers and achieve admission to the Bar in the face of gender barriers and other challenges and to examine the differences women lawyers have made for the legal profession, for other women, and for the greater society. For the first time, the complete history of women lawyers in Maryland is presented, from the colonial era to those who fought for suffrage, to acceptance of women into the legal profession and gaining a "seat at the table" in pursuit of social equality. The stories of these women are derived from the books in which they signed their names, marking their admission to the Bar, court records detailing their cases, the birth and death certificates and census records of their families, and newspapers reporting their professional and personal lives. For multiple generations, women have continually persevered in the face of obfuscation, with the support of family and each other. The story is of collaboration with each generation of women building on the progress of its ancestors at the Bar.

The creation of *Finding Justice* is itself a testament to the collaboration of a diverse group of women lawyers, including practicing attorneys, educators, and judges, each bringing her own unique perspective and appreciation of the efforts of others who forged a path. Above all, the story of each woman lawyer in this book is a lesson in hope that, with support and perseverance, challenges that appeared insurmountable may be overcome. In finding justice, a single individual may open doors, not just for herself, but for generations to come.

Andrea Leahy, Chair of the Finding Justice Project, September 27, 2013

This acknowledgment of the people who collaborated to establish the Finding Justice Project (the Project) and produce this book is a story that reflects the passion and determination of the women brought to life so eloquently on the ensuing pages. Our journey began in 2006 when Judge Lynne Battaglia recruited a small group of lawyers, judges, and scholars to explore the idea of publishing a literary work on the neglected history of women in the law in Maryland. Through a series of meetings that included Judge Battaglia, Kristen Brinster, Esq., Harriett Cooperman, Esq., Judge Deborah Eyler, Barbara Grzincic, Esq., Cynthia Leppert, Esq., Ava Lias-Booker, Esq., Michelle N. Lipkowitz, Esq., Professor Paula Monopoli, Julie Rubin, Esq., Sky Woodward, Esq., and myself, the fledgling project developed a work plan and a vision statement.

Because Maryland judges are prohibited from fundraising, we had to establish at least two separate working committees. Judge Battaglia formed an Editorial Committee by expanding the initial group to include Professor Meredith Render, Kathleen Shemer, Esq., Judge Audrey Carrion, Judge Diane Leasure, Kathleen McDonald, Esq., Elizabeth Kameen, Esq., Mary Murphy, Esq., Meredith Render, Esq., Michelle McDonald, Esq., Nancy Sloane, Patricia Smith, Esq., Robin Page West, Esq., Professor Taunya Banks, and Tracy Brown, Esq. In June 2008, the committee welcomed new members Maureen Dove, Esq., First Lady and Judge Catherine O'Malley, Wendy Karpel, Esq., and Professor Margaret Johnson.

The Development Committee was initially cochaired by Julie Rubin, Esq., and Ava Lias-Booker, Esq., followed by Anne Albright, Esq. (Since then Governor Martin O'Malley appointed Judge Anne Albright and Judge Julie Rubin to the Circuit Courts for Montgomery County and Baltimore City, respectively.) Over the last six years, members of the Development Committee have included Jim Astrachan, Esq., Alison Asti, Esq. (now Circuit Court Judge, Anne Arundel County), Kathleen Cahill, Esq., John Davey, Esq. (now Circuit Court Judge, Prince George's County), Maureen Dove, Esq., Marci Gordon, Esq., Warren Hamel, Esq., Elizabeth Hewlett, Esq., Susan Leviton, Esq., William Murphy, Esq., Kathleen Pontone, Esq., Ferrier Stillman, Esq., Wendy Schiff, Esq., Mayda Tsaknis, Esq., and Sky Woodward, Esq.

Even as these committees began developing work plans, a consequential effort was underway. Given the enormous research challenge presented by the meager recordings of women's accomplishments, Judge Battaglia recognized that, initially, the literary work required the identification of women who were admitted in the early period, from 1902 until 1974. Judge Deborah S. Eyler led the effort to create this list, which often immersed her and Kathleen McDonald in original, archival research. The primary source used to identify women admitted to the Bar in Maryland was the Test Book signed by all attorneys admitted in Maryland and maintained by the Clerk of the Maryland Court of Appeals (the Maryland State Archives maintains the first Test Book from 1851 to 1916). Under the direction of Dr. Edward Papenfuse, Emily Oland Squires, and Jennifer Hafner of the Maryland State Archives, interns Amber Robinson, Allison Smith, and Erin Troxell created and compiled scans of the original Test Book cards. The contents of the entire Test Book were copied onto a computer list, from which Judge Eyler was able to eliminate those lawyers who clearly were male and create a separate database of names that were clearly female. A number of names were not readily identifiable as only initials were used. The interns utilized the resources at the Archives as well as the ancestry.com database to determine the genders of members of the Bar whose names were ambiguous, and to locate information about the Bar members identified as female. The interns at the Archives also compiled background information for those women attorneys identified on the list. In 2012, Judge Battaglia led the completion of the full list of women attorneys, from 1902 to November 1, 2012. A list of names for whom the interns and law clerks were unable to determine gender was distributed to the Bar Library of Baltimore City and the Maryland State Bar Association. Several people, some members of the Bar, and some from the general public helped to identify women lawyers from 1902–1914. The result is a list of nearly 25,000 women admitted to the Maryland Bar, which is a testament to the progression of women in the legal profession in this state (see Appendix C).

Meanwhile, Jim Astrachan and Julie Rubin made the introduction to clients who generously donated their creative talents to design the Project's image. After the title "Finding Justice" was chosen, Sarah Eisner and her team at Eisner Communications suggested that it be more specific, so that a more complete title, "Finding Justice: A History of Women Lawyers in Maryland," was born. The publisher then added "since 1642" to the mix. Tracey Halvorsen and Amy Goldberg of Fastspot, L.L.C., assisted in the development of marketing materials.

Finding the right home for the Finding Justice Project was the more vexing issue. In order to raise money and obtain grant funding, we needed to work under the umbrella of a 501(c)(3) organization. Rather than create a new organization, we hoped to find an organization that shared our vision and was willing and able to serve as a repository for research and any royalties from the literary work. The Finding Justice Project eventually found an enthusiastic sponsor and home in the Maryland Women's Bar Association Foundation, originally founded by Wanda Caporaletti, Esq., and Elizabeth Loggia, Esq. The vision and purpose of the Foundation matched those of the Finding Justice Project. Moreover, the Foundation already had a scholarship program for law students in place—a perfect use for any future royalties.

At a Special Meeting of the Board of Directors held on September 11, 2007, the WBA Foundation officially established the Finding Justice Project Committee and voted unanimously to add Wendy Karpel, Cynthia Leppert, and myself as new directors of the Foundation. We later added Lade Anjorin, Esq., and Kristen Brinster. Kristen now serves as President of the Foundation. As Chair of the Project, I am forever grateful to these women for giving the Project a home and for their enthusiastic contributions and support in response to my constant requests for Board guidance and reviews. Kristen Brinster and Cynthia Leppert especially have expended much time and toil on the administration of the Project—from tax returns and charitable organization filings to daily correspondence and insurance agreements. I also thank my law partner, Steve DeSmet, Esq., who created and continues to maintain the Finding Justice Project Website and who laboriously assisted with mass mailings and in the drafting and development of agreements, consent forms, releases, and advertisements.

Once the Project's structure and marketing image were in place, the Development Committee, led by co-chair Julie Rubin, held its first fundraiser in January 2009. The event was hosted by Warren Hamel and the Venable, L.L.P., law firm at their new law offices in downtown Baltimore. Womble Carlyle Sandridge & Rice, P.L.L.C., and Calvert Fine Wine & Spirits also graciously sponsored this event. Concurrent with its first fundraiser the Finding Justice Project grew with the addition of an Honorary Committee.

Chaired by the former First Lady of Maryland, Frances Hughes-Glendening, the members of the Honorary Committee included former U.S. Secretary of State Dr. Madeleine K. Albright, Dr. Shaila R. Aery, Constance R. Beims, Eleanor M. Carey, Esq., Kathleen A. Costlow, Dr. Carol W. Eaton, former First Lady of Maryland Kendel S. Ehrlich, Esq., Dr. Janet E. Dudley-Eshbach, Nancy S. Forster, Esq., Dr. Nancy S. Grasmick, former Dean Phoebe A. Haddon, former Senator Barbara A. Hoffman, Nina R. Houghton, former Lieutenant Governor Kathleen Kennedy Townsend, Esq., Belkis Leong-Hong, Ava E. Lias-Booker, Esq., Lois K. Macht, Sayra W. Meyerhoff, Esq., Tucky P. Ramsey, Roberta R. Roper, Esq., former Dean Karen H. Rothenberg, Carmen M. Shepard, Esq., Felicita Sola-Carter, and Carolyn H. Thaler, Esq.

On the heels of a successful first fundraiser, the Project won a grant of $3,500 from the Maryland Bar Foundation. Much credit goes to Maureen Dove, who donated many hours researching grants and drafting grant applications. Continuing to gain momentum, the Development Committee, led by Anne Albright, planned its second fundraiser held in June 2009, which was graciously hosted by Susan S. Oldham, Esq., in her beautiful home in Potomac, Maryland. Despite severe weather and traffic gridlock—atypical even for the DC area—the June fundraiser was another great success.

Much credit goes to *The Maryland Daily Record* for its support of the Project's marketing efforts. Suzanne Fischer-Huettner and the staff at *The Daily Record* enthusiastically donated numerous in-kind advertisements for the Project's search for an author and to promote the Project's "Women Pioneers Concert."

In June 2009, following a nationwide search and months of advertising for and interviewing of candidates, the Project hired an author for the book. Within months, the Project suffered its most significant setback when the author withdrew from the Project. Rather than paralyze the Project, this event inspired Judge Battaglia to formulate a new approach. The book would be written by different women who would assimilate the history of Maryland's pioneering women in law. By harmonizing this research through their distinct voices, the authors would produce a superior literary work.

Another aspect of the literary work to unfold in the wake of the new approach was the endeavor to interview women in the legal profession and capture their efforts to become lawyers and their ensuing struggles and achievements. Kathleen McDonald, Esq., as well as members of the selection committee, Judge Deborah Eyler, Michelle McDonald, Esq., Mary Murphy, Esq., and Evelyn Lombardo, Esq., worked to identify women in the profession to interview, while Judge Battaglia sent letters soliciting nominees to the local bar associations and other community-based organizations. Forty-eight women, all of whom became members of the Maryland Bar between 1952 and 2010, contributed their personal histories through interviews with either Kathleen McDonald or Judge Battaglia or by a written questionnaire. Thanks to the generous resources donated by the Administrative Office of the Courts and the work of Diane E. Feuerherd, Jason Clark, and Ed Fanning, the interviews were videotaped at the Judiciary Education and Conference Center in

Annapolis, Maryland. Transcriptions of these interviews, portions of which appear in the pages of this book, were made possible by a generous donation of Kerr McDonald, L.L.P.

On November 12, 2011, the Project enjoyed its most significant fundraising event when Piotr Gajewski, Music Director and Conductor of the National Philharmonic Orchestra of Washington, DC, conducted a special tribute to women composers at the beautiful Strathmore Concert Hall in Rockville, Maryland. The concert was hosted by Dr. Madeleine K. Albright, and featured violinist Chee-Yun. The concert was greatly acclaimed. Patrick McCoy of the *DC Performing Arts Examiner* had this to say in his review published on November 16, 2011:

> Though there has been much progress in our society in the area of equal rights for women, most would agree that there is more to be done. On Saturday night, the Music Center at Strathmore was the setting of a program themed "Women Pioneers" which celebrated the accomplishments of women with female American composer Amy Beach's *Grand Mass in E-flat major* being the perfect vehicle for that purpose. Beach is considered by many to be the first female American composer of eminence and her mass was performed in Washington, D.C. perhaps for the first time in a major concert hall setting.
>
> Similarly, Florence Beatrice Price is considered the first African American female composer of stature. The 64th Secretary of State, Dr. Madeline K. Albright served as the guest host. Albright was by far the perfect choice, herself serving as our nation's first female Secretary of State from 1997–2001. The inception of the concert theme on women came into being as a result of the Finding Justice Project, founded in 2006 "to celebrate the often neglected achievements of our foremothers."

LexisNexis, through the efforts of Dianne McClintock Callahan, was the top sponsor of this event. Jim Astrachan and Julie Rubin are duly recognized for making this sponsorship possible. Many thanks to Jim, Julie, Anne Albright, Sayra Meyerhoff, and Carolyn Thayler for all of their assistance in planning the event.

Other sponsors included: Kerr McDonald L.L.P.; Vincent J. Leahy, Jr.; O'Malley, Miles, Nylen & Gilmore, P.A.; Sayra Wells Meyerhoff and Neil Meyerhoff; Carolyn and David Thaler; Nina Rodale Houghton; Anne and Warren Hamel; Sutherland & Brinster, P.A.; Dr. Shaila Arey and Pat Schiavonne; McGuire Woods, L.L.P.; and Susan Carol Elgin. Special thanks to *The Daily Record* and Maximilian Franz whose photographic prowess so beautifully captured the event. We are eternally grateful to Dr. Madeline Albright and the National Philharmonic, especially Todd Eskelsen, Chair, Piotr Gajewski, Music Director and Conductor, and others who worked so hard behind the scenes, including Ken Oldham, Deborah Birnbaum, Nancy Coleman, and Filbert Hong.

Numerous institutions have contributed research and resources over the years, including the Maryland State Archives, the Maryland Historical Society, Women of Achievement in Maryland History, Inc., and the Maryland Women's Heritage Center. Jill Moss Greenberg, the President of the Heritage Center, was even willing to spend a day in a freezing storage POD with me, sifting through heaps of books, files, and photos generously donated by Frances Ann Glendening on behalf of Women of Achievement.

Chief Judge Robert M. Bell, of the Maryland Court of Appeals, was an early and enthusiastic supporter of the Project, always providing insight and assistance at every turn. His leadership of the Administrative Office of the Courts, and the efforts of many of the wonderful people who work there, helped to facilitate many logistical conundra.

Of course, the University of Maryland School of Law and the University of Baltimore School of Law are recognized for their significant and constant support. Professor Paula Monopoli, Founding Director of the University of Maryland School of Law's Women,

Leadership & Equality Program, contributed substantial resources to the early research efforts by hosting meetings at the school and dedicating law school interns for research. One student, Maggie Lynch Selwood, researched and drafted short biographies on the first women admitted to practice law in Maryland for inclusion on the Project's Website and as part of Judge Battaglia's dynamic Finding Justice presentation.

Professor Jane Murphy and the University of Baltimore School of Law contributed greatly to the Project by hosting meetings, providing interns and law library resources for research, and through sponsoring events and publications. In the Fall of 2011, the *University of Baltimore Law Forum* published Judge Battaglia's article, "'Where is Justice?' An Exploration of Beginnings," as a forerunner to this book. The events sponsored by the law school included a forum on October 6, 2011, entitled "A Legacy in Law," showcasing UB alumnae and the Finding Justice Project with a keynote presentation by Judge Battaglia.

My heartfelt thanks go to all of our generous donors who are listed in Appendix D in the back of this book, especially the University of Baltimore Foundation, Inc., LexisNexis, and the Maryland Bar Foundation. Finally, I thank the founder of this Project, Judge Battaglia, the Board, the Committees, the authors, and all volunteers for their prodigious efforts and commitment to "finding justice" throughout the Project's setbacks and triumphs. It has been an honor to work with all of you on this labor of love.

CHAPTER ACKNOWLEDGMENTS

Chapter 1: *Against All Odds: Maryland's Earliest Women Attorneys*

Judge Battaglia wishes to thank Evelyn C. Lombardo, former law clerk, Diane E. Feuerherd, former law clerk, and Hannah Levin, current law clerk, for their assistance in research and drafting.

Marc A. Nardone, former law clerk, Bill Gangler, former law clerk, and David Nohe, Kristina Miller, George Dungan, Heather Jones, Pierce Murphy, Michael Silvestri, Mary B. Waugaman, Cynthia M. Wolf, Jennifer Erin Brown, and Carrie Bohrer, interns, for their research efforts.

Dr. Edward C. Papenfuse, Jennifer Hafner, and Maria Day, of the Maryland State Archives, for their archival research assistance.

Chapter 2: *Etta Maddox: An Eternal Advocate for Maryland 's Women, from Admission to the Bar to Access to the Ballot*

Michelle Mitchell wishes to thank Devon Holmes, for her research efforts on Etta Maddox.

Chapter 3: *The Role of Political and Social Movements on Women's Entry into the Legal Profession in Maryland, 1902–1920*

Professor Jane C. Murphy wishes to thank her research assistants, Hannah Dawson and Brittaney Fabiano, students at the University of Baltimore School of Law; and the excellent law librarians at the University of Baltimore School of Law and the Milton S. Eisenhower Library at the Johns Hopkins University.

Chapter 4: *Women Lawyers in Community, 1920–1940*

Judge Battaglia Michelle Mitchell wishes to thank Evelyn C. Lombardo, former law clerk, Diane E. Feuerherd, former law clerk, Alicia Shelton, former law clerk, and Hannah Levin, current law clerk, for their assistance in research and drafting.

Chapter 5: *African American Women Admitted to the Bar in Maryland, 1946–1974: Four Profiles in Public Calling*

Chancellor Phoebe Haddon wishes to thank University of Maryland Francis King Carey School of Law alumni and staff: Dean's Fellow Rachel W. W. Granfield, '11, J.D., M.F.A.; Research Fellow Maximilian Tondro, '10, Ph.D.; Ryan H. Easley Research Fellows Max Siegel, '12, and Sanjay De, '12, J.D.; and especially Jane Wilson, Director of Public Relations, who spent countless hours overseeing the chapter's research, production, and editing of drafts. She is especially grateful to Joan Sessoms Ford, '71, who was generous with her time and insights about her experience at the law school as an African American woman during the early 1970s.

Chapter 6: *The Impact of Mentoring and Other Influences on the Career Development of Women Lawyers*

Judge Diane O. Leasure (ret.) wishes to thank Ellen Cobb (graduate of the University of Baltimore School of Law and Member of the Law Review), who conducted the interviews, did research, and assisted with editing the chapter.

Chapter 7: *Oral Histories*

Thanks to Media Services Group, Office of Communications and Public Affairs, Maryland Judiciary, specifically Jason Clark; and Ed Fanning, for filming the forty interviews and the authors' roundtable; Kathleen M. McDonald, for conducting the interviews, in addition to Judge Battaglia; and Kathleen M. McDonald, Evelyn Lombardo, Brett Joann Jackson, and Denise Shaffer, for compiling the stories drawn from the many interviews into a single discussion.

Appendix C: *List of Women Attorneys*

Judge Battaglia and the Project wish to thank Alyssa LaBarre (Bedell) and Caroline Miller, former law clerks of Judge Deborah S. Eyler, Alicia Shelton, former law clerk, and Hayley Tamburello, intern, for their assistance in completing the list of women attorneys.

Finding Justice

Supreme Bench of Baltimore City with Judge Elsbeth Levy Bothe on the left and Judge Mary Arabian in the center.

Photographer and date unknown.
Courtesy of the Maryland State Archives.

INTRODUCTION

The Honorable Julie R. Rubin

Passion, perseverance, and pride: These are the hallmarks of each woman featured in this book. These women are the pioneers of the female presence in Maryland law. Their determination and refusal to bow to those who railed against the notion that women could or should be lawyers cleared the way for the rest of us. And we are the better for it—we, the State of Maryland; we, the citizens of Maryland; we, the women of Maryland; and we, the members of the Maryland Bar. The presence of women lawyers in Maryland is, itself, of historic significance, as the state of Maryland was among the last states to admit women to the practice of law (in 1902). This appears to have had no residual ill effect on the presence or advancement of Maryland women in law. Indeed, by all accounts, perhaps the opposite is true. It is no exaggeration to state that the changes in the substantive laws of the state brought about by the efforts and voice of Maryland's women in law, dating from the very start of our admittance to the Bar in 1902, are massive in every manner of speaking. And yet, the significance of Maryland's women lawyers as a body has, until now, gone unstudied.

Far more than a book of celebration, which it certainly is, this book also closely examines and discusses the complex and vital contributions of women lawyers in Maryland to substantive law and, therefore, to society, our everyday lives, and also to the lives and practices of other women in law through private mentoring and professional membership organizations. Also included in this book are the oral histories of more than forty women admitted to practice law in Maryland in more recent times. Not only do their stories illustrate the tremendous strides that Maryland's women in law have made in increasing access to careers in law, these stories also reveal that we continue to face obstacles tied to our traditional roles in and out of the home. In the present day, these obstacles most often relate to balancing family and professional responsibilities (a challenge not unique to the practice of law) rather than confronting perceptions that women are inherently ill-suited to the practice of law. The view that women should not practice law—because, for example, aggressive advocacy is unbecoming or contrary to our "natural" spirit, or that women's responsibilities should be limited to wife and mother—is firmly embedded in many cultures outside the U.S. and is still held by many within our country, although surely by considerably fewer than as recently as twenty years ago.

In setting out to answer the question, "Where is justice?" the members of the Finding Justice project wanted to know, in essence, how we as Maryland female lawyers got to this point.[1] But, as often happens in the process of research, what we discovered was far more complex than the individual stories of the fascinating women who came before us. In addition to the personal stories of our predecessors—stories which are punctuated by unexpected humor, searing disappointment, and stunning displays of courage—we discovered that the totality of women's contributions as lawyers, beginning from the moment women first asserted themselves as lawyers during the seventeenth century, so radically changed the content and trajectory of substantive law—and, therefore, the society on which it is imposed—that an equally important and interesting question revealed itself: "Where would we be without women lawyers in Maryland?"

Women's Suffrage Parade, 1914.

Photograph by Harris & Ewing.
Courtesy of the Library of Congress, Harris & Ewing Collection.

This book not only tells the stories of our predecessor sisters-in-arms in recognition of the significance of their struggles as they relate to the thousands of Maryland women in law who have since followed, but also examines the vital role these women played (and continue to play) in the fabric and evolution of Maryland's law and society. The monumental changes in law and society brought about by their presence in the field of law include not only areas commonly couched in terms of "women's issues," such as suffrage, gender equality in jury service, the right of women to hold and inherit property, and our right to be parties to contracts, but also areas of general consequence to humanity at large, including racial discrimination in public housing, miscegenation, racial integration in public education, juvenile justice, family law, and more.

Beginning with women—Margaret Brent the most famous among them—appearing frequently in Maryland courts as attorneys-in-fact during the seventeenth century and the early phases of the statutory "professionalization" of (and formal exclusion of women from) the practice of law during the eighteenth century, this book also traces the legislative evolution of the legal identity of Maryland women and their capacity in the eyes of the state to appear as attorneys in courts across the state. Throughout Maryland's history, the presence of women in the law has brought about not merely changes in the population of lawyers and the dynamic of the practice of law as it crossed gender lines; our presence has effected lasting and significant changes in law itself and, therefore, on society.

The early women of the legal profession defied myriad obstacles as they worked their way into the "good old boys club." These obstacles were not localized to popular notions of womanhood but, rather, were ordained by our nation's highest court as the law of a woman's place in the wider world. In 1872, three U.S. Supreme Court Justices, in a concurring opinion, harangued that it was against the "divine ordinance" for women to enter the legal profession and that, instead, the "paramount destiny and mission of woman" was to "fulfill the noble and benign offices of wife and mother."[2] Until the late nineteenth century, statutory regulations in Maryland restricted the practice of law to white males, and it wasn't until 1902 that women were permitted to practice law. Even long after 1902, women were largely rejected as colleagues of their brothers at the Bar (for example, by refusal to allow women to become judges, law school administrators, or even members of bar associations) and high-ranking professionals viewed the specter of a female lawyer as a severe threat to social order.

Josephine Beiderhasse and Inez Milholland Boissevain in Suffrage Parade, 1913.

Photograph attributed to the Bain News Service. Courtesy of the Library of Congress.

As examined more closely in the chapters that follow, our predecessors' refusal to accept these restrictions had lasting and magnificent effects far beyond gender equality in the Bar. I include here a handful of illustrative examples.

The suffrage movement in Maryland benefitted tremendously from the spirited passion of several of Maryland's women lawyers. In 1894, the Maryland Suffrage Association (MSA) was co-founded by Henrietta "Etta" Haynie Maddox, hailed as "Maryland's first woman lawyer" for her 1902 hard fought admission to the Bar, and her sister, Emma Jane Maddox Funck, a famous suffragette in her own right. Seven years later, in 1901, Maddox became the first female graduate of the Baltimore Law School.

The MSA lobbied for a bill to remove the word "male" from the Maryland Constitution in 1898. The bill apparently did not succeed. According to her case before the Court of Appeals, it was the use of male pronouns in the statute governing admission to the Maryland Bar that prevented Etta Maddox from sitting for the 1901 bar exam following her graduation from Baltimore Law School. It was not until Maddox, along with a group of women lawyers from across the nation, lobbied Maryland's Legislature in 1902 that the law was changed to allow women to be admitted to the Maryland Bar.

As Chapter 2 of this book suggests, it may have been Maddox's involvement with the suffrage movement that propelled her to seek a law degree. Regardless, there can be no doubt that her tenacity for the vote served her well in her fight for a seat at the Bar. Despite the fact that her 1901 graduation from law school was hard won and well earned, Maryland refused to allow her to sit for the Bar examination following her graduation. Following a now-famous and much-publicized battle with Maryland's high court and state legislature, Maddox won the right to take the bar examination in June 1902. Thereafter, she was the first woman to pass the Maryland Bar Examination.

All the while, the mission of the MSA did not suffer from Maddox's attention to the study of law. To the contrary, the MSA confronted social and legal inequities far beyond what its name suggests, including the abolition of child labor and equal pay for equal work. Eight years after Maddox passed the bar examination, she drafted the first bill to amend the Maryland State Constitution to give women the vote—a high profile venture that met a cold reception with Maryland's legislators. Several times over the following years, Maddox, flanked by her sister, Emma, and other Maryland suffragettes, lobbied for the right to vote under state law.

The wave of Portias who followed Etta continued

Social News—Clubwomen To Fight For Jury Service

10 Groups Going To Annapolis

Hearing On Bill Before Legislature To Be Held Wednesday Afternoon At State Capital

Special Car To Carry Delegates From City—Act Introduced By Four Women Legislators

"Clubwomen To Fight For Jury Service," February 17, 1935.
Courtesy of The Baltimore Sun.

All Women Jury for Baltimore.
Photograph attributed to William Klender, date unknown. Courtesy of the Maryland State Archives.

and Jeanette Rosner Wolman, both of whom marched in suffrage parades as children.[3] These women served as examples for the next generation of young women seeking admission into and equality in the legal profession. Zetzer started the first all-women law firm in Maryland and became the first woman to be admitted to the Maryland State Bar Association in 1946. Wolman became the first woman admitted to the Bar Association of Baltimore City in 1957. These women also had long-lasting and far-reaching impact through their roles as mentors of other women in law. Although neither Zetzer nor Wolman would take the bench, both women mentored women lawyers who became judges. For example, Wolman was a noted mentor of Judge Kathleen O'Ferrall Friedman and Judge Elsbeth Levy Bothe (both retired judges of the Circuit Court for Baltimore City).

Notwithstanding Maddox's and others' valiant and sustained efforts, Maryland was one of the few states that refused to ratify the Nineteenth Amendment to the Unites States Constitution in 1920; the Maryland Legislature never relented in its refusal to grant women the right to vote through the state legislative process. Although these women's efforts did not turn the tide in Maryland in favor of a woman's right to vote, their dedication and unrelenting passion for the right to vote raised and maintained state-wide interest in the subject over the course of more than two decades until the Nineteenth Amendment was passed.

Maryland's women lawyers brought about major change in a core component of our legal system: Jury duty. It comes as no surprise that women prevailing in their fight to be members of the Maryland Bar was closely tied in time to the movement for gender equality in jury duty in Maryland—a battle that lasted from 1921, when the first Maryland legislation on the subject was proposed (and met with resounding defeat), until 1947 when, following the Maryland State Bar Association's admission of women, Maryland's Legislature passed legislation mandating gender equality in jury duty.

Among the myriad of women lawyers who made the right to participate as a juror their cause, one noted leader in this fight for equality was Helen Sherry. Sherry was admitted to the University of Maryland School of Law in 1920, the first year it admitted women. Four years after her admission to the Maryland Bar in 1923, Sherry joined six other women lawyers to found the Women Lawyers' Association of Maryland, the predecessor to the Women's Bar Association of Maryland, in part in answer to their rejection by the then men-only Maryland State Bar Association and Bar Association of Baltimore City. Sherry's public crusade to incorporate women into mandatory jury duty began in approximately 1930 when, in her role as legislative chairwoman of the Federated Women's Club of Maryland, she began speaking to political groups on the subject. She would later testify before Maryland's House Judiciary Committee and other legislative committees in the Legislature. In 1947, the Maryland Legislature relented and passed legislation mandating gender equality in jury service.

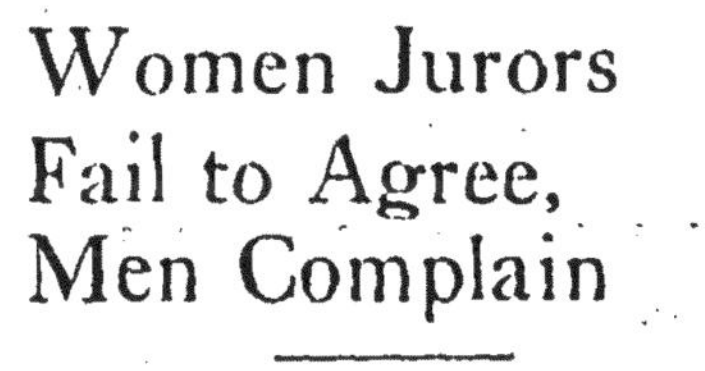
Women Jurors Fail to Agree, Men Complain

"Women Jurors Fail to Agree, Men Complain," September 29, 1939.
Courtesy of The Baltimore Sun.

Maryland's women lawyers also had much to say about Jim Crow and its progeny. Well before the mid-1940s, when Jane Marshall Lucas became the first African American woman to be admitted to the Maryland Bar, the voice for civil rights and social justice was populated by several female leaders who would later attend law school in Maryland. Although some did not pursue the practice of law, many continued or intensified their work for equality and social justice after leaving law school better armed for the social and legal battles that lay ahead. Elaine Carsley Davis and Juanita Jackson Mitchell stood out for their prominence in the fight for racial equality. Both women enrolled in the University of Maryland School of Law in 1946, and they became the first African American female graduates from law school in the state of Maryland in 1950. Harkening back to her pre-law life as a teacher, Davis devoted her law degree and experience (both professional and scholastic) to the effort to desegregate public schools. Throughout her law career and until her death in 1992, Mitchell was a leading voice in the crusade against state-sanctioned racial discrimination and the gross inequities that resulted from such discrimination—including, early in her law career, a 1951 lawsuit by the NAACP against the University of Maryland for failure to desegregate all of its professional schools. Her lifelong passion for civil rights spanned all manner of public injustice, police brutality, voter registration, and desegregation in education, theaters, municipal swimming pools, public beaches, and public housing.

While Maryland's women in law have been responsible for remarkable and profound changes in law and in our communities statewide, special attention is due to the history of Maryland's women lawyers helping other women. As demonstrated across all chapters of this book, Maryland's women in law have a rich history of standing up for other women, particularly those without a voice or in danger of falling victim to inequities in the law. The story of Joanne Colledge, convicted in 1669 of infanticide, demonstrates how a group of seven unmarried women, fortified by strength in numbers, petitioned the Provincial Court to prevent Colledge's execution—the sentence for her crime.[4]

During the Progressive Era (approximately 1890–1920), we see women lending their collective voice to suffrage associations such as the earlier-mentioned Maryland Suffrage Association, which also fought for women's equal pay rights and other like causes. Although the number of women at the Bar began to grow (slowly but surely) following 1902, exclusion from then-male-only bar associations isolated women lawyers and denied them the professional and personal value of camaraderie and networking.

For Batter or For Worse.
Courtesy of the Women's Law Center of Maryland.

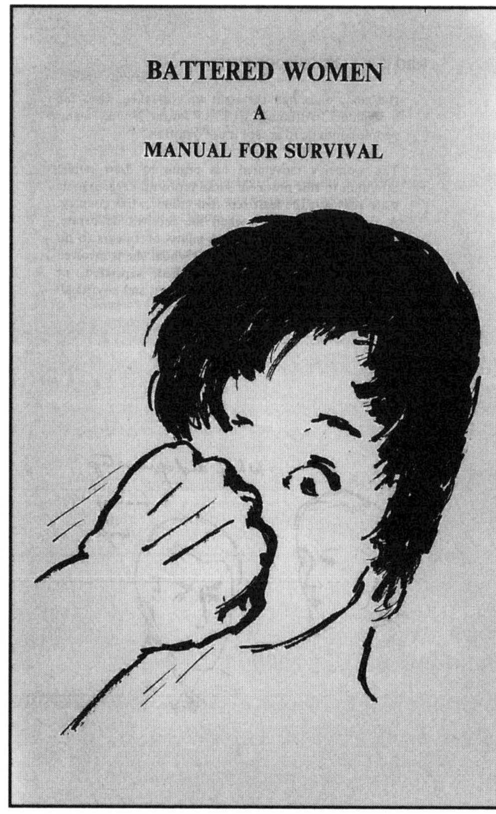

Battered Women: A Manual for Survival.
Courtesy of the Women's Law Center of Maryland.

Beginning in 1927, early predecessors to the Women's Bar Association of Maryland were formed in response to the refusal of the Maryland State Bar Association to admit women. While women lawyers mentoring and coaching one another has surely never been limited to the confines of a membership organization, the creation of a women's bar association provided a framework within which to network, support one another, and concentrate women's resolve to become part of the fabric of Maryland's legal profession and not to remain a distant annex.

In 1971, the Women's Law Center of Maryland was created through the efforts of several women lawyers, led chiefly by the Honorable Kathleen O'Ferrall Friedman, Ann Hoffman, and Susan Handwerger Tannenbaum. The Women's Law Center was formed to address myriad legal issues for un- and under-represented women and children, including representing victims of domestic violence, and fighting for the right of women to use their maiden names, a matter of keen importance to married women who could not obtain credit or housing in their own names.[5] In addition to answering critical and ongoing calls for the protection of women's and children's rights, the Women's Law Center provided, and continues to provide, rich opportunities for women lawyers, law clerks, and interns to work together for rights that are of personal as well as societal importance and magnitude.

This book answers two questions: (1) What is the history of female lawyers in Maryland? and (2) What substantive changes in law and society can be attributed to Maryland's women in law? The women mentioned in this introduction are selected examples from the scores of women who, together, form the history of Maryland's women in law. These stories are here developed and told through the eyes of several of today's women in law—the authors of the chapters that compose this historic book. The stories of these women are, of course, unique to each of their lives, but their passion and tireless work for change, humanity, and equality have been shared by many of Maryland's women in law. The stories collected by the Finding Justice Project reveal the genealogy of many of the privileges and protections women lawyers in Maryland, indeed all Marylanders, enjoy today. These women bettered the state of Maryland not only by opening doors once closed to women lawyers, but by improving the condition of life for all Marylanders by virtue of their lives in the law.

Women's Law Center Logo.

Courtesy of the Women's Law Center of Maryland.

A conjectural charcoal drawing of Margaret Brent by Edwin Tunis, ca. 1934.

Courtesy of the Maryland State Archives.

CHAPTER ONE:

Against All Odds: Maryland's Earliest Women Attorneys

The Honorable Lynne A. Battaglia

The story of women attorneys in Maryland originates with the founding of the colony itself, during the 1600s, when settlers from England began populating the shores of St. Mary's County. At that time, the practice of law had not yet become a profession, so that men and women frequently brought their own cases to court or appointed someone without specialized legal training to transact their business, rather than employing an attorney-at-law.[1] Colonial women regularly appeared in court as attorneys-in-fact, representing others' interests and, in some cases, presenting their own matters.[2]

The powers afforded to women attorneys-in-fact depended largely upon their marital status.[3] A married woman was known as a *feme couverte*, a vestige of feudal times, while a single or widowed woman was referred to legally as a *feme sole*. Each retained her own special status:

> The *fême couverte* (married woman) had no legal or civil entity. She could not own property, make a will, sue or be sued. Lord Coke, in 1600, defined the status of the married woman in the famous sentence: "Husband and wife are one before the law, and the husband is that one." When a *fême couverte* came into court, therefore, it was only as her husband's representative and with his permission.
>
> The *fême sole*, on the other hand, be she spinster or widow, could hold property:—land, buildings, ship, merchandise, personal belongings and so forth. If she had children, she was the head of her family and, to a large extent, her own mistress with rights approaching those of our contemporaries. In court, therefore, she spoke for herself and also, at times, in behalf of others.[4]

Margaret Brent was the most well-known woman attorney-in-fact in Maryland and, perhaps, in all of the American colonies. In the records of the Provincial Court of Maryland, her name appears 124 times between 1642 and 1650.[5] Brent was a *feme sole,* who had never married.[6] She arrived in Maryland during 1638, along with her sister, Mary, and several servants, with a grant of land.[7] They settled below Fort St. Mary's in St. Mary's City on a tract of land known as "Sisters Freehold."[8] As a businesswoman and member of the propertied class, Brent frequently made appearances in court to collect her debts and was also given a power of attorney by her brother Fulke "to transact business for him in his ffriday 21th Jan.

The ffreemen bownd to attend the Assembly appeared except m^{r} ffenwick, m^{r} Thorneborough, Mr Brookes & George Saphyer

Summons to George Saphyer to be att the Assembly forthwth vppon sight &c

was read certaine orders to be obserued in the howse during the Assembly

Came Mrs Margarett Brent and requested to have vote in the howse for her selfe and voyce allso for that att the last Court 3^{d} Jan: it was ordered that the said Mrs Brent was to be lookd uppon and received as his L^{ps} Attorney. The Gou^{r} denyed that the s^{d} Mrs Brent should have any uote in the howse. And the s^{d} Mrs Brent protested agst all proceedings in this p̃nt Assembly, unlesse shee may be p̃nt. and have vote as afores^{d}

Orders &c.

Published eod. 1 That noe one of the howse shall use any reuyling speeches or name any one by name but by another signification Viz. the Gent. that spoke last or the like.

Governor and Council (Proceedings) Transcription of Margaret Brent's Request for Voting Rights, Proceedings and Acts of the General Assembly January 1637/8-September 1664, Archives of Maryland, Vol. 1.

Courtesy of the Maryland State Archives.

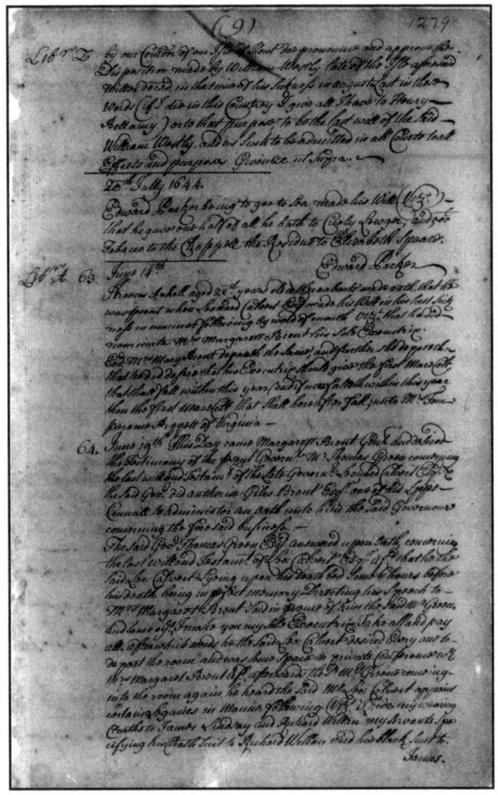

Deposition regarding Leonard Calvert's last wishes, naming Margaret Brent as his Executrix from Prerogative (Wills, Original Record).

Courtesy of Maryland State Archives.

absence."[9] So energetic and respected was Brent that Governor Leonard Calvert often consulted her on matters of political import.[10]

In 1647, when Governor Calvert died unexpectedly, Brent was named his executrix.[11] The Provincial Court granted her letters of administration, which authorized her to resolve claims filed against Governor Calvert's estate and also to collect debts owed the deceased governor.[12] Because Governor Calvert's death left no one to act on behalf of Lord Baltimore, the absentee Proprietor of Maryland, the Court determined that Margaret Brent, as the administrator of Leonard Calvert's estate, should be accepted as "his Lordship's attorney."[13]

In her position as Governor Calvert's administratrix and Lord Baltimore's attorney, Brent was called upon to act to avert a crisis in the colony's financial affairs. Governor Calvert had hired mercenaries from Virginia to quell a local rebellion, and, when the fighting was over, the soldiers filed suits against Lord Baltimore for payment. Brent discovered that the governor's estate was insufficient to pay the soldiers' wages. Initially, in order to raise monies to satisfy the debt, Brent demanded two votes in the General Assembly, one for herself as a landowner and one as Lord Baltimore's attorney.[14] She was refused, to which she purportedly declared, "Where is justice?"[15] As a last resort, Margaret decided to sell some of Lord Baltimore's many droves of cattle and some of his thousands of acres of land. When Lord Baltimore objected, the assemblymen who had denied Brent voting rights unanimously rose to her defense. They wrote to Lord Baltimore that "it was better for the Collonys safety at that time in her hands than in any mans else in the whole Province" and that "she rather deserved favour and thanks from your Honour for her so much Concurring to the publick safety....”[16] Three years later, in 1650, Brent moved to what is now Fairfax County, Virginia, where she built a home on a piece of land she named “Peace.”[17] That same year, she purportedly wrote to Governor Stone asserting she “would not intangle my Self in Maryland because of the Ld Baltemore’s disaffections to me.”[18]

Brent’s experience as a *feme sole* differed significantly from that of her married counterparts, although these women also appeared in court exercising significant powers, either express or implied, on behalf of their husbands. Wives conveyed land, recovered debts, signed leases, received rents, defended their husbands’ reputations, and sued and were sued on their husbands’ contracts—but only as a result of having gained permission from their husbands in a power of attorney.[19] For instance, Grace Barnes received a power of attorney from her husband John “over his premises” in 1676, as follows:

> Know all men by these prsents That I John Barnes Planter of Maryland in the County of St Maryes have Assigned Ordained & made & in my stead & place putt & Constituted my trusty & well-beloved wife Grace Barnes to be my true & lawfull Attorney for me & in my name & for my use to Also Sue Recover & Receive all & every such Sume of money tobacco Mrchandize due to me the said John Barnes Giveing & therefore Granting unto my said wife my whole power strength & Authority in & about the premises And to follow all & every such Act & Acts thing & things device & devices whatsoever in the Lawe for the Recovery of any such debts or Sumes as aforesaid for me & in my name to Sue Execute Receive & performe as fully largely & amplely in every respects to all intents construccons & purposes as I my selfe might or could doe if I was then my self e in my proper person prsent Ratifying & allowing & holding firme & stable all & whatsoever my said lawfull wife shall lawfully doe or cause to be done in or about the Execution of the prmisses by vertue of this I sett my hand & Seale this Twenty sixth day of July 1676[.][20]

Barnes served as John’s attorney-in-fact in business and property matters until he died in or after 1681.[21] Similarly, in 1680, Hester Cordea received a power of attorney from her husband Mark to be his “true full and Lawfull Attorney... within the province of Maryland aforesaid or Collony of Virginia.”[22] Anne Hammond also appeared in court representing her husband, John, while he was “out of the country” in an action to recover debts that he owed to a Walter Hall in 1659.[23] In 1655, Ann Danby (alternatively spelled “Dandy”) not only was a witness in her husband’s capital murder trial, but also may have served as his defense attorney.[24]

While transacting business on behalf of their husbands pursuant to a power of attorney, married women may also have “pushed the envelope” to gain greater autonomy. For instance, a Mrs. Pakes, when questioned regarding her ability to enter into a contract, asserted that “shee had a Lre of Attorney from her Husband to doe any busines whatsoever.”[25]

In a related vein, the first jury comprised entirely of women, married and unmarried, acted to acquit a

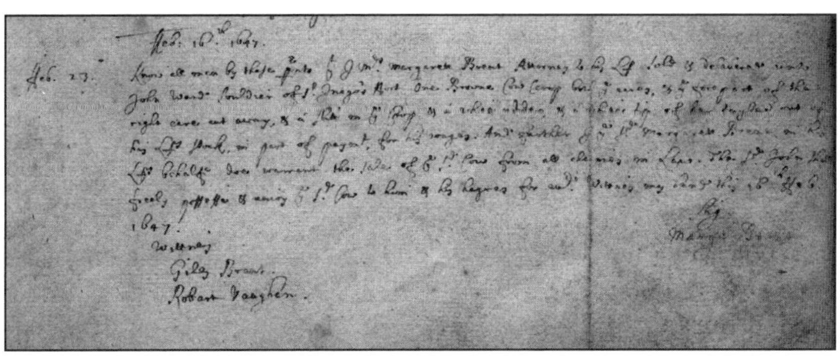

Governor and Council (Proceedings), St. Mary’s Provincial Court Proceedings, describing Margaret Brent’s sale of Lord Baltimore’s cattle.

Courtesy of the Maryland State Archives.

servant woman charged with committing abortion.[26] The jury was empanelled in 1656 to examine Judith Catchpole and determined that Judith "had not had any Child within the time Charged," and found that Ms. Catchpole's male accuser, who had since died, was not of "Sound Mind."[27]

In 1658, Governor Josias Fendall issued a gubernatorial proclamation prohibiting wives from being "admitted or allowed as attorneys for their husbands."[28] Although the historical record is unclear as to why he did it, one author theorized that the gubernatorial proclamation was a backlash against there having "been so much freedom in the matter of women appearing in court as 'attorneys in fact.'"[29] Governor Fendall was the half brother of Philip Calvert and was appointed governor at the height of the unrest between the Puritans and Catholics.[30] The proclamation was rendered null and void in 1660, however, after Fendall attempted to overthrow the Proprietary government, and, as a result, his acts and orders were decreed by the Provincial Court to be "torne from among the Records."[31]

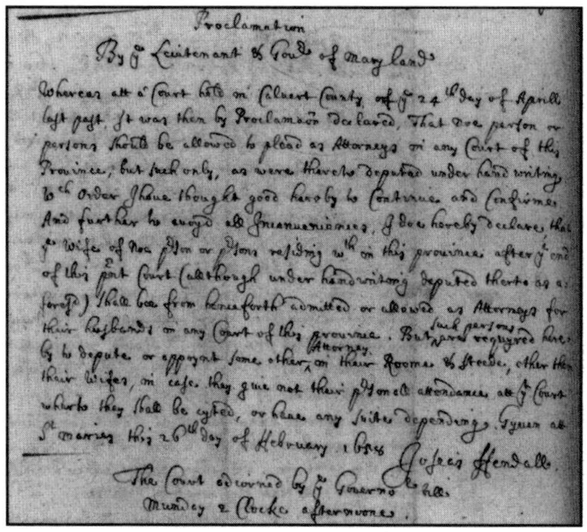
Proclamation

Provincial Court (Judgment Record), Governor Fendall's Proclamation, c. 1658.
Courtesy of the Maryland State Archives.

Once widowed, a married woman or *feme couverte* returned to the legal status of *feme sole*. Mary Vanderdunke, a physician and a widow at the time, brought two debt actions in 1661 against former Governor Fendall and Christopher Russell. In her case against Fendall, she produced in court a letter from him engaging her to heal his three servants. Vanderdunke "demanded a warrant against Mr. Fendall in an action of debt to the value of 1200 lbs. of Tobacco."[32] In her case against Christopher Russell, she sought collection of 1,600 pounds of tobacco as payment for her releasing Russell "of the Accoumpts that was betwixt them."[33] In that case, Hugh O'Neale testified on behalf of Vanderdunke.[34]

During the same period, Vanderdunke married Hugh O'Neale. She was no longer a *feme sole*; O'Neale was named as a defendant in an action against her for a debt that accrued prior to her marriage.[35] In addition, Vanderdunke appeared in court to defend her name in a defamation of character case, although O'Neale was noted as filing the Complaint on Vanderdunke's behalf.[36] In that case, William Heard had spread a rumor that Vanderdunke had poisoned Joane Parker. At the hearing before the Provincial Court, Heard apologized,

> owning his fault and declaring that hee neuer intended to defame or troble her…and hearby acknowledge himself very indiscreet…if that her Credit may bee thereby any ways stained hee both humbly desire her and her housband to forgiue him, hee being Contented to pay the Cost and Charge of suit….[37]

Heard promised to pay 400 pounds of tobacco as compensation.[38]

Gertrude James, one of Kent Island's earliest settlers and widow of the Reverend Cartwright James, brought suit in 1650 against Captain Evelin for seizing her cattle.[39] James was also issued a power of attorney by the pioneer William Claiborne regarding his share of stock that was held by a company in London.[40]

Upon the death of her husband, a married woman often ensured the financial security of her family by serving as executrix of her husband's estate. From 1649 to 1752, thirty women in St. Mary's County served as executrixes of their husbands' estates (see Table 1.1).

Table 1.1: List of Executrixes of Estates in St. Mary's County, Maryland, 1649–1752

Name of Executrix/Administatrix	*Description of Activities*
Katherine Hebden Marshall	Served as administratrix of the estate of her first husband, Thomas Hebden (1649).[1]
Ann Johnson Dorrington	Served as administratrix of the estate of her first husband, Peter Johnson (1655/6).[2]
Ann Danby (Dandy)	Served as executrix of the estate of her husband, John Dandy, following his execution (1657).[3]
Jane Smith Taylor Eltonhead	Served as administratrix of the estate of her husband, William Eltonhead (1657).[4]
Agatha Morris Langworth	Served as executrix of the estate of her husband, James Langworth (1661).[5]
Mary Lashley Bogue	Served as executrix of the estates of her two husbands, John Bogue (1667) and Thomas Trueman (1684).[6]
Martha Lewger	Served as executrix of the estate of her husband, John Lewger (1669/70).[7]
Sarah Cole Claw Younger Benton	Served as executrix of the estates of her first two husbands, William Cole (1669) and William Claw (1675).[8]
Mary (Marie) Lindsey Mackloughlin	Served as executrix of the estate of her first husband, James Lindsay (1671).[9]
Elizabeth Stockes Large Morgan	Served as executrix of the estate of her first husband, John Stockes (1672).[10]
Rose Gerrard	Served as executrix of the estate of her husband, Thomas Gerrard (1673).[11]
Hester (Ellen) Lecompt Cordea	Served as executrix of the estates of both of her husbands, Walter Hall (1673) and Mark Cordea (1685).[12]
Katherine Lewis Shore	Served as administratrix of the estate of her first husband, John Lewis (1677).[13]
Anne Evans	Served as executrix of the estate of her husband, Thomas Evans (1679).[14]
Rebecca Clocker Askins Dayley Sim-mons	Served as executrix of the estate of her husband, John Askins (1680).[15]
Mary Evans Lamb	Served as administratrix of the estate of her first husband, Anthony Lamb (1682).[16]
Julian Legitt Powell Whittor	Served as administratrix of the estates of her first two husbands, Thomas Legitt (1684) and John Powell (1698).[17]

Table continues on page 32

Table continues from page 31

Name of Executrix/Administatrix	*Description of Activities*
Audrey O'Daly Cocks Llewellin Taylard	Served as administratrix of the the estates of her first two husbands, William Cocks (1684) and John Llewellin (1698), and as executrix of the estate of her third husband, William Taylord (1711).[18]
Abigail Thomas Lewis	Served as executrix of the estate of her first husband, Robert Thomas (1685).[19]
Anne Bankes	Served as executrix of the estates of her two husbands, Thomas Bankes (1685) and Edmond Dennis (1687).[20]
Ann Abington	Served as executrix of the estates of two of her husbands, Andrew Abington (1691) and Samuel Watkins (1694).[21]
Katherine Bevin Cambell	Served as executrix of the estates of her two husbands, William Bevin (1694) and John Cambell (1695).[22]
Elizabeth Turner Carberry	Served as executrix of the estate of her husband Thomas Turner (1696).[23]
Mary Heard Tant Ford	Served as executrix of the estate of her first husband, James Tant (1717).[24]
Annastatia Langham (Langhorn)	Served as executrix of the estate of her husband, William Langham (1717).[25]
Moor Langley	Served as administratrix of the estate of her husband, John Langley (1717).[26]
Elizabeth Daft	Served as executrix of the estate of her husband, Charles Daft (1721).[27]
Dorothy Leigh	Served as executrix of the estate of her husband, John Leigh (1736).[28]
Elizabeth Herbert Daft	Served as executrix of the estates of her two husbands, Mark Herbert (1739) and Matthew Daft (1750).[29]
Mary Little Baley Fear	Served as executrix of the estate of her first husband, John Little (1729) and as administatrix of the estate of her second husband, Thomas Baley (1752).[30]

Notably, married and single women attorneys-in-fact advocated on behalf of one another in at least one instance. This is evidenced by a petition prepared and exhibited in 1669 by a number of women—including Elizabeth Rousby, Mary Keene, Ellinor Smith, Ann Dorrington, Mary Larkin, Grace Parker, and Mary Williams—to prevent the execution of Joanne Colledge after she had been found guilty by a jury of "bearing a live female bastard child and thereafter killing her."[41]

The experience of early women attorneys in Maryland suggests that colonial women entered the courtroom by necessity, whether to administer the estates of their husbands, to collect debts, or to transact business, as delineated in a power of attorney. Even Margaret Brent, the most prolific colonial woman attorney-in-fact, did not enjoy parity with her male counterparts, as evidenced by the refusal of the General Assembly to grant Brent a vote when she was acting as attorney on behalf of Lord Baltimore.[42] As the practice of law became professionalized during the eighteenth century, men seeking to earn a living through the practice of law mitigated the necessity for women to carry out the legal affairs of their families.

Litigation became more formalized and unyielding as the complexities of common law pleading were imported from England to the colonies.[43] In addition, improvements in transportation and shipping led to increased importation of English law books, and, by mid-century, wealthy lawyers in every colony had amassed "law libraries of considerable size and diversity."[44] In addition, the legal system responded to the expansion of commerce, and debt litigation became "formalistic and unforgiving," including the importance of commercial paper and bills of exchange.[45] This "marked a transformation from a legal system that allowed litigants to address their grievances in ways that were essentially communal to one that elevated predictability and uniformity of legal relations over responsiveness to individual communities."[46] The declining importance of the household economy in the wider world of business also coincided with the decline of women coming to court to pursue their debtors and transact business.[47] Finally, as life expectancies improved, women were less likely to be called upon to administer their husbands' estates:

> In the first years of settlement there were very few women, a fact that inflated their importance, and surviving sons were likely to be too young to act as executors of their late fathers' estates. In later years the sex ratio approached one to one, women lost much of their bargaining power, and sons were likely to live long enough to act as executors of the family estate.[48]

By the early 1700s, the Maryland General Assembly had enacted a statute addressing qualifications for bar membership, coinciding with the formalization of legal practice.[49] The 1715 statute provided that "no Attorney or other person whatsoever shall practice the Law in any of the Courts of this province without being Admitted thereto by the Justices of the Severall Courts."[50] Although "Attorney" and "person" were gender neutral terms, the statute makes clear that only men were eligible; just a few lines later, the masculine pronouns, "he," "him," and "himselfe" are employed.[51] By the 1730s, the formalization of legal practice worked to the exclusion of women, as women were not accepted as apprentices in law offices, nor could they become licensed to practice law.[52]

In the western "frontier" states, a dearth of untrained professionals enabled women to gain access to the professional bar far sooner than in their eastern counterparts.[53] The practice of law on the frontier was an amalgam of the military court-martial, Indian tribal justice, and the ad-hoc development of "squatters courts" that sprang up in response to an immediate need for the determination of disputes about boundaries.[54] This kind of "makeshift justice" also fostered loose standards for admission to the profession. In Iowa, for instance, "[t]he usual practice was to appoint a committee of three from the local bar to examine the candidate. It was sometimes said that one of the requisites for admission was the price of an oyster stew for the committee."[55] The harsh life of the frontier, moreover, required women to share in the labor of building homes, towns, and schools. As a result, "the need that new territories had for women settlers contributed to a more balanced view of women and their abilities than existed back East."[56]

Schools in the American West were coeducational from the outset, in part because men did not enroll in sufficient numbers to support them. As noted by one author, "when the impetus came for more and better law schools in the West and for higher standards for admission to the Bar," frontier women were uniquely situated to gain a stake in that process.[57] It is not surprising, then, that Iowa became the first state to admit a woman to the practice of law when Arabella Mansfield was admitted to the Bar in June 1869. The western states of Missouri (1870), Michigan (1871), Utah (1872), Ohio (1873), Indiana (1875), Wisconsin (1875), Minnesota (1877), California (1878), Kansas (1881), Nebraska (1881), Washington (1885), Oregon (1886), Montana (1890), Colorado (1891), Nevada (1893), South Dakota (1893), Idaho (1895), Oklahoma (1898), and Wyoming (1899) all admitted women to the professional bar before Maryland (1902) would formally admit the first Portia to practice.[58]

A married woman's property rights also drastically limited her ability to practice law, or any other profession. Under the common law, a married woman had no legal existence separate from her husband: "[b]y marriage, the husband and wife are one person in law: that is, the very being or legal existence of the woman is suspended during the marriage, or at least is incorporated and consolidated into that of the husband: under whose wing, protection, and cover, she performs everything."[59] In effect, a married woman could not contract or enter into a partnership independent from her husband, nor could she keep her earnings or hold property for herself, all capabilities which were reasonably necessary to the practice of law.[60]

A series of legislative enactments beginning during the 1840s, known as Married Women's Property Acts, gradually loosened common-law strictures on real and personal property ownership by married women. Although fostering parity between *feme couverte* and *feme sole* is often cited as a rationale underpinning the legislation, the early acts were derived from a desire to both shield women from the ignoble business of property ownership and to preserve familial wealth in the form of inheritance by the eldest son. The first iteration of the Married Women's Property Act in Maryland came in 1843. That provision is concerned more with the preservation of familial wealth than enabling married women to own property independent of their husbands.[61] In 1843, the General Assembly enacted Chapter 293, which aimed to protect a married woman's property from the creditors of her husband.[62] The legislation was a response, in part, to depressed economic conditions of the 1840s caused by excessive speculation culminating in the Panic of 1837.[63] Notably, the Maryland act was modeled on that of Mississippi, which was enacted in 1839 and designed to preserve "familial wealth in the form of large plantations and the contingents of slave labor necessary to make them profitable."[64] As noted by another author, "[t]he development of slavery, especially with the growth of the native-born slave population," during the early 1800s was the most crucial element in the functioning of the plantation economy. Marital property laws enacted at this time were geared toward the preservation of that system.[65]

Another provision, Section 8 of Chapter 293, however, provided that a married woman could keep for her "sole and separate use" $1,000 of money or other property that she acquired "by her skill, industry or personal labour," ostensibly enabling a married woman "to establish a small capital account and obtain credit."[66]

The practical import of the "sole and separate use" provision embodied in Section 8, however, was limited. In *Neale v. Hermanns*, 65 Md. 474, 5 A. 424 (1886), the Court of Appeals construed that section narrowly, adhering to the common law rule that a husband was entitled to any income or property of his wife under coverture, although the General Assembly had abrogated that rule, at least in part, more than forty years earlier. In that case, a husband and wife, the Hermanns, moved in with Mrs. Burger and claimed that the three agreed to exchange Mrs. Hermanns's care of Mrs. Burger for payment. Mrs. Hermanns performed, among other household duties, washing and ironing. Following Mrs. Burger's death, Mr. Hermanns sought enforcement of their agreement and claimed that the earnings belonged to Mrs. Hermanns. The Court of Appeals disagreed, however, reasoning that Mrs. Hermanns had not demonstrated that she worked independently from her husband:

> From their relation as husband and wife she is personally working for him and in his interest; though she has the privilege, if she wishes, to work for herself. Circumstances should show that she had so elected. Nothing in the evidence of Hermanns tends to show that his wife was to be paid for the service to be rendered in her own right. If he meant by "we" and "us" himself and his wife, as we suppose he did, then it was a joint service that was to be paid for, and the promise was to pay accordingly and the husband would be entitled and not the wife in her own and separate right.[67]

Thereafter, in *Baker v. Hedrich*, 85 Md. 645, 37 A. 363 (1897), the Court of Appeals awarded a widow, against her decedent husband's administratrix, money and other property resulting from her raising and selling poultry, eggs, butter, and other products from her husband's farm, because she had proven they agreed that any profits would belong to her. As a result, the attendant "sole and separate use" provision embodied in Section 8 did little in practice to change conditions to enable married women to enter the legal profession. That is, in order to "engage in labor for her own benefit" independent from her husband, a married woman was nevertheless required to seek permission from her husband, even after the enactment of Chapter 293 in 1843.[68]

In 1851, a constitutional provision was enacted to require the Legislature to "pass laws necessary to protect the property of the wife from the debts of the husband during her life, and for securing the same to her issue after her death," in the same vein as the earlier act geared toward the preservation of familial wealth. Creating a life estate for a married woman in the property of her husband shielded real property and slaves from the repayment of debts, preserving the instruments of what was a plantation economy.[69] This is so because property subject to a life estate may not, while the life tenant is alive, be used to satisfy debts of the remainderman because the life tenant is "the absolute owner of the income of the property during the life tenant's lifetime."[70]

Two years later, Chapter 245 of the Maryland Laws of 1853 provided that property "belonging to a woman at the time of her marriage" or acquired after marriage through "purchase, gift, grant, devise, bequest, descent or in a course of distribution shall be protected from the debts of the husband, and not in any way be liable for the payment thereof," with the proviso that she did not acquire the property from her husband in an effort to "prejudice" or defraud his existing creditors.[71] Similarly, the 1853 Act also abrogated the common law requirement of a trustee to manage a married woman's separate estate, providing that "It shall not be necessary for a married woman to have a trustee."[72]

Chapter 245 appears to have been enacted as another matter of debt protection, particularly to curb the possibility for greater debtor fraud by husbands, as opposed to benefitting married women.[73] In *Schindel v. Schindel*, 12 Md. 294 (1858), a wife left her husband and returned to live with her mother, claiming misconduct and cruelty by her husband as the causes of her separation from him. The wife sought the "rents, produce and profits" of her property, which she owned at the time of the marriage. The Court of Appeals, interpreting both the 1842 and 1853 laws, denied her request, and determined that the constitutional provision "does not operate to change the rights of property acquired by marriage so as to deprive the husband of all of his marital rights secured to him by common law."[74] Rather, "the act of 1853...protects the property of the wife from the debts of the husband, but does not, in any other respect, alter or impair the marital rights of the husband therein."[75]

In 1860, the General Assembly codified the married women's property act as Article 45, entitled the "Husband and Wife" provision. Section 2 enabled a married woman to have a "separate estate" for her separate use that she could transfer or devise "as if she were a *feme sole*, or...convey the same by a joint deed with her husband."[76] Maintenance of a separate estate enabled a married woman to "maintain a separate credit, and to be independent of the misfortunes and improvidence of the husband," although this enactment did not coincide with the entry of women in the legal profession.[77]

The next major change came in 1867, when the General Assembly once again amended the former Article 45 to permit married women to lease real property "as if she were a *feme sole*":

> That all deeds hereafter made to married women of real estate or chattles real, it shall be competent for the grantee or lessee to bind herself and her assigns, by any covenant running with or relating to said real estate or chattels real, the same as if she was a *feme sole*.[78]

In *Worthington v. Cooke*, 52 Md. 297 (1879), the Court of Appeals interpreted the provision as an exception to the common law rule that "a married woman cannot contract so as to make herself liable," and provided that a married woman, separate from her husband, could lease property and be sued for her failure to pay rent.[79] A married woman's independent property rights, however, could still be limited by the written instrument conveying the property interest to her.[80] The 1867 revision is significant, because, as a practical matter, it permitted married women to enter into a lease.

The most significant legislative change came in 1898, when the General Assembly enacted Chapter 457 of the Maryland Laws, enabling a *feme coverte*, just as a *feme sole*, to enter into contracts, with the attendant rights and responsibilities. As described by one commentator,

> The provisions of sec. 5 are abundantly simple; their clear intent and purpose, is to divest the wife of the clogs which marriage formerly thrust upon her; she has now the powers of a *feme sole* to contract, and may make any contract at law that she could have dum sola; she is under no disability to sue on any of her contracts, and this is so even where the contract was made by her prior to her marriage; she can now sue on her ante and post-nuptial contracts as a *feme sole*; and a married woman can now be a partner in Maryland, since the disabilities under which the Court of Appeals, in Bradstreet v. Baer, held that she labored, have been removed; moreover, under the statute, *she has the power to engage in any business, etc., and to contract as fully as if she was unmarried.*[81]

The 1898 Act attempted to place married and single women on the same legal footing.[82] The legislative history underpinning the 1898 law in Maryland is unavailable, although we can glean some insight into the social and cultural influences of the 1898 Act from similar legislation in neighboring states. New York's Married Women's Property Act was a model for similar legislation throughout the nation, including Maryland.[83] That act was derived from a petition drive that involved important figures in the early women's rights movement—including Ernestine Rose, Elizabeth Cady Stanton, and Paulina Wright Davis—and "represented one of the first times in American history that women had organized to further their own political interests."[84] In essence, suffragettes believed the economic parity in terms of property ownership could also foster political parity in the right to vote. Similarly, in Maryland, the Maryland Suffrage Association lobbied during 1898. For instance, on the same day that the 1898 Married Women's Property Act Bill was introduced in the State Senate, the Maryland Women's Suffrage Association also lobbied for a bill to remove the word "male" from the state constitution.[85] It may be, then, that the 1898 Act is linked, at least in part, to the movement for greater emancipation of women.

Baltimore from Federal Hill, 1831, by Henry J. Megarey.
Courtesy of the University of Baltimore, Langsdale Library, Special Collections.

Despite legislative efforts to equalize the legal status of *feme soles* and *feme covertes*, cultural perceptions of marriage and womanhood made the pursuit of the legal profession particularly daunting (not unlike the quest for women's suffrage). Women entering the medical profession apparently did not face the same limiting social norms. This is due, in part, to cultural perceptions of women as having a "'special' talent for nurturing," which "seemed to dictate a career in medicine."[86] At an address at the opening of the Women's Medical College of Baltimore in 1895, Dr. Charles O'Donovan opined that women were particularly suited to the medical profession: "Especially fitted is she to be a physician. Nowhere else can she use so well her own peculiar gifts; in this profession above all others are required the nicest tact, the most comforting gentleness, the readiest sympathy, the gentle touch and soft voice that woman is endowed with far beyond the lot of her sterner brothers."[87] Dr. O'Donovan encouraged the class entering in 1895 to pursue science while maintaining their "femininity":

> Show to the world that the pursuit of scientific research, while it must broaden, need not harden you; that the beautiful gentleness of femininity is as much at home by the troubled cot of the dying child as in the glittering radiance of the brilliant ball-room; that your soft eyes can as readily respond to the call of the sufferer for kindly sympathy as be used to inflame the passions of an ardent lover; that your soothing voice harmonizes perfectly with the dim surroundings of the room in which the battle between life and death is being keenly contested.[88]

In contrast, attorneys were viewed as aggressive, even combative, in tension with the prevailing notions of femininity: "[F]or a woman to play the law game as a man does violates sex role norms, a transgression that is negatively judged by others and that can create anxiety in the transgressor. To fit the stereotypical image of an advocate means being argumentative and aggressive, characteristics that are traditionally condemned in women."[89] Women were said to exist in a "separate sphere"; social convention built a boundary from the "male domain of public life."[90] In 1873, the Supreme Court of the U.S. upheld the denial of Mrs. Myra Bradwell's application to the Illinois Bar, based on her gender. The majority of the justices held that the Privileges and Immunities Clause of the Fourteenth Amendment did not extend to the right to practice law in state courts, the effect of which "was to turn the issue of women lawyers over to the state legislatures and state courts."[91] Justice Joseph P. Bradley, in his separate concurring opinion which was joined by two other justices, echoed the "separate spheres" theory:

> [T]he civil law, as well as nature herself, has always recognized a wide difference in the respective

spheres and destinies of man and woman. Man is, or should be, woman's protector and defender. The natural and proper timidity and delicacy which belongs to the female sex evidently unfits it for many of the occupations of civil life. The constitution of the family organization, which is founded in the divine ordinance, as well as in the nature of things, indicates the domestic sphere as that which properly belongs to the domain and functions of womanhood. The harmony, not to say identity, of interests and views which belong, or should belong, to the family institution is repugnant to the idea of a woman adopting a distinct and independent career from that of her husband.[92]

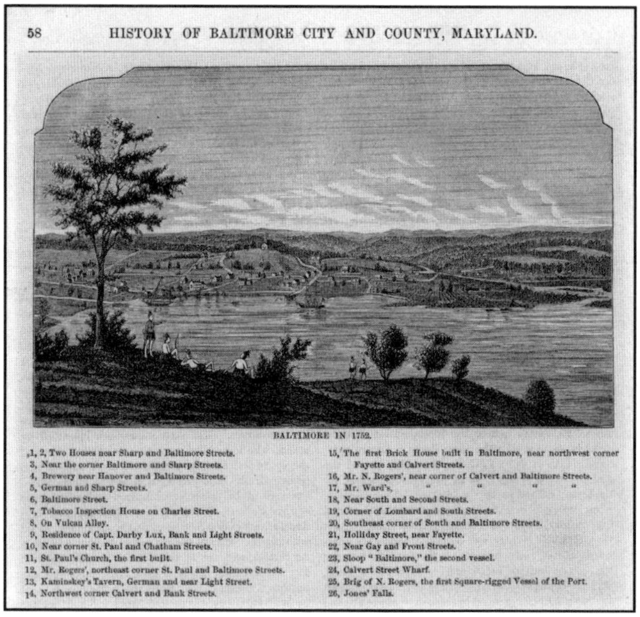

History of Baltimore City and County, Maryland, 1752.

Courtesy of the University of Baltimore, Langsdale Library, Special Collections.

Belva Lockwood, ca. 1880–1890.

Photographer unknown. Courtesy of the Library of Congress.

A half-century of legislative enactments in Maryland, then, did not erode the conception of a woman lawyer as antithetical to nature. There is no greater example than Belva Lockwood, one of Maryland's first woman lawyers, who was married and widowed several times throughout her lifetime. More than one judge cited Lockwood's marital status as a basis for denial of her admission to the Bar.[93] Lockwood, though, described herself as "undaunted by conventions," which enabled her to persevere in her pursuit of the legal profession.[94]

Lockwood was born Belva Bennett on October 24, 1830, in Niagara County, New York, where she was fascinated by *The Holy Bible* as a child and attempted to perform miracles through sheer willpower.[95] She finished school at fourteen and, in her words, immediately became "a teacher of those who so recently had been my associates."[96] She became engrossed in women's rights issues after realizing her pay was half that of her male counterparts.[97] She married Uriah H. McNall in 1848 and gave birth to a child before Uriah died in 1853, when she was only twenty-two.[98] Lockwood resumed her education after she was widowed, but she faced resistance due to her marital status: "I was reminded that 'married women were not supposed to attend school, even though widowed,'" she wrote, and she was asked, "'What did I expect to make of myself?' and other impudent questions."[99] Lockwood graduated with honors from the Genesee Wesleyan Seminary in 1857, where her interest in the law was sparked.[100] In 1866, after the Civil War had ended, Lockwood migrated south to the District of Columbia, where she accepted a teaching position and immersed herself in the politics of the city and the nation.[101] While teaching in Washington, she began to study Blackstone's *Commentaries* and also began attending law lectures at the Columbian College.[102] In 1868, Belva married Reverend Ezekial Lockwood, a Civil War veteran, Baptist minister, and practicing dentist.[103] In the same year, she attempted to enroll in law school at the Columbian College but received a letter of rejection from the school's president on October 7, 1869, which read:

> Madam,—The Faculty of Columbian College have considered your request to be admitted to the Law Department of this institution, and after due consultation, have considered that such admission would not be expedient, as it would be likely to distract the attention of the young men.[104]

The National University Law School opened the following year, and Lockwood enrolled along with more than a dozen other women.[105] Only she and one other female student, Lydia Hall, completed their studies, but the women were refused diplomas and prohibited from participating in commencement.[106] Apparently, "the faculty told the two women that because they had not studied long enough they were not going to receive diplomas, or be permitted on the stage with the men on graduation day."[107] Lockwood petitioned unsuccessfully to be admitted to the District of Columbia Bar, and then traveled while campaigning for Horace Greeley's losing presidential bid.[108] Upon returning from the campaign trail, Lockwood wrote to President Ulysses S. Grant, the "president *ex officio*" of the University, and, two weeks later, she received her diploma.[109] After obtaining her diploma, Lockwood was able to gain admission to practice in several courts in Washington, DC, including the Police Court, and she began a busy practice specializing in claims against the federal government, including pensions and bounties for military enlistment.[110] Belva Lockwood became the first woman admitted to the U.S. Supreme Court Bar on March 3, 1879, after enlisting the help of then Senator Joseph E. McDonald in her campaign.[111] According to one reporter, Lockwood

WOMEN LAWYERS.

MRS. LOCKWOOD IS DENIED ADMISSION TO THE MARYLAND BAR.

Correspondence of the Baltimore Sun.

UPPER MARLBORO, Md., Oct. 17, 1878.

The application of Mrs. Belva A. Lockwood, the female lawyer of Washington, for admission to the bar of the Circuit Court of Prince George's County, was decided adversely by Judge Magruder yesterday. In the course of his decision he said: "God has set a bound for woman. Man was created first and woman after and a part of him. Like the sun and the moon moving in their different orbits, the great seas have their bounds, and the eternal hills and rocks that are set above them cannot be removed." He spoke of Mrs. Lockwood and Mrs. Lavinia C. Dundore, also an attorney, who accompanied her, as two wandering women. He said he prayed God the time would never come when women would be admitted to the Bar of Maryland. Upon the conclusion of his decision Mrs. Lockwood rose to make a remark that the court had misunderstood the principal point in her brief, when Judge Magruder ordered her to take her seat, saying he would not hear her. Mrs. Lockwood was also told to "sit down" as she was about to ask the court to put the decision in writing. The court was then adjourned.

Mrs. Lockwood, as the Judge left the court-room, gave notice that she desired to address the members of the Bar and others present, to explain her position, and that she had obtained permission of the Commissioner of the County to use the room. She was afterward notified by a bailiff of the court that she would not be allowed to speak in the court-room, and, at the suggestion of one of the members of the Bar who, like others, desired to hear her explanation, she made a speech from an adjoining portico, in which she spoke of the court in a very severe but respectful manner, and criticised its decision. She was frequently applauded. Her audience numbered nearly 100 persons. Before she left Marlboro Mrs. Lockwood said she intended to get the case before the highest court of Maryland, either by a writ of mandamus or other proceeding, and that while at first she did not care to be admitted other than to plead the particular case for which she was employed, she had now made up her mind to follow the case to the end, and have the whole question settled by the Supreme Court of the State. She has a case at Port Tobacco to-morrow, in which she will file a similar application if she is not allowed to file the necessary pleadings in the case in which she is interested. She was recently permitted to file an important civil suit in the Federal Court of Baltimore County, involving some $50,000, in the case of Roynello against Atocha. She says the Judiciary Committee of the United States Senate has decided that there is no need of further legislation to admit her to the United States Supreme Court, and that she thinks she will be finally admitted to the courts of Maryland.

"Women Lawyers. Mrs. Lockwood is Denied Admission to the Maryland Bar." Correspondence of The Baltimore Sun *(October 17, 1878).*

Courtesy of The New York Times, *October 19, 1878.*

engaged in "an unconscionable deal of lobbying," and Lockwood agreed that "nothing was too daring for me to attempt."[112] A year later, in 1880, she became the first woman lawyer to argue before the nation's highest court in *Kaiser v. Stickney*, which involved the execution of a deed that bound Caroline Kaiser's property for the payment of a debt.[113] Lockwood ironically argued that Kaiser, as a married woman, could not legally be party to a contract that burdened her own property.[114]

Lockwood's practice also brought her to Maryland's courts, where she valiantly struggled to gain admission. In 1878, Lockwood sought admission to the Prince George's County Bar, seeking to make a motion in an estates case in which she represented the plaintiff.[115] Judge Daniel R. Magruder would not permit her to speak in court, but did allow one of the male members of the Bar to read her motion into the record.[116] When Lockwood persisted that she did not wish to "embarrass any of the male members of the bar anymore by having them read her pleadings or motions," she was asked by the court to submit a brief "setting forth her claims for admission," which she did.[117]

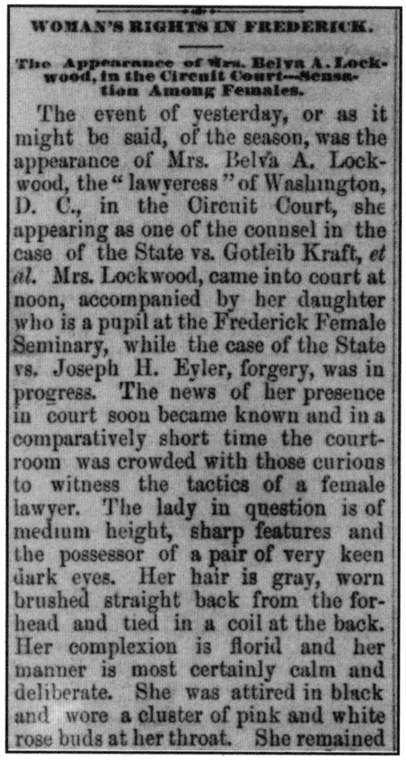

WOMAN'S RIGHTS IN FREDERICK.

The Appearance of Mrs. Belva A. Lockwood, in the Circuit Court—Sensation Among Females.

The event of yesterday, or as it might be said, of the season, was the appearance of Mrs. Belva A. Lockwood, the "lawyeress" of Washington, D. C., in the Circuit Court, she appearing as one of the counsel in the case of the State vs. Gotleib Kraft, *et al.* Mrs. Lockwood, came into court at noon, accompanied by her daughter who is a pupil at the Frederick Female Seminary, while the case of the State vs. Joseph H. Eyler, forgery, was in progress. The news of her presence in court soon became known and in a comparatively short time the courtroom was crowded with those curious to witness the tactics of a female lawyer. The lady in question is of medium height, sharp features and the possessor of a pair of very keen dark eyes. Her hair is gray, worn brushed straight back from the forehead and tied in a coil at the back. Her complexion is florid and her manner is most certainly calm and deliberate. She was attired in black and wore a cluster of pink and white rose buds at her throat. She remained

Article, "Woman's Rights in Frederick," Frederick Daily Times, *March 9, 1880.*

Courtesy of the Maryland State Archives.

In denying Lockwood's admission, Judge Magruder opined that "God has set a bound for woman. Man was created first and woman after and a part of him. Like the sun and the moon in their different orbits, the great seas have their bounds, and the eternal bills and rocks that are set above them cannot be removed.... I pray to God that the day will never come when the women of Maryland will be admitted to the bar."[118] At this time, Lockwood was widowed, her husband, Ezekial, having died in 1877. Although Lockwood had graduated from law school, received her diploma, and practiced in a number of courts, the "law of nature" was again invoked in 1881 by Judge William Hayden of the Circuit Court for Carroll County, in denying her application for admission to the Bar of that county:[119]

> The law of nature destines and qualifies the female sex for the bearing and nurture of the children of our race and for the custody of the homes of the world and their maintenance and honor. And all life-long callings of women, inconsistent with those radical and sacred duties of their sex, as is the profession of the law, are departures from the order

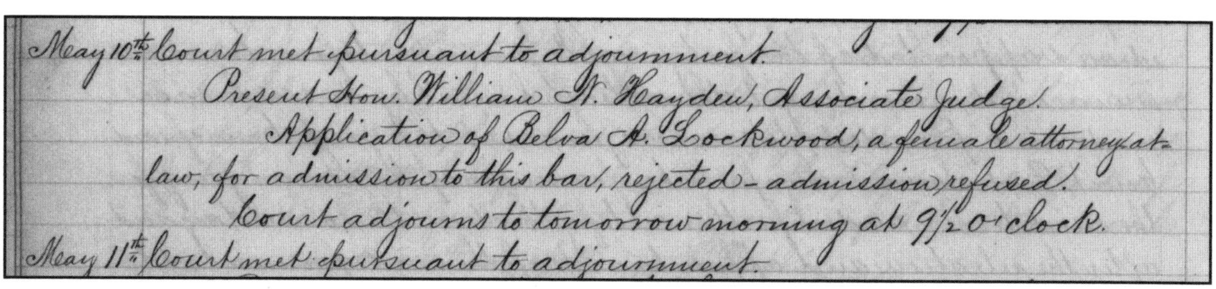

May 10th Court met pursuant to adjournment.
Present Hon. William N. Hayden, Associate Judge.
Application of Belva A. Lockwood, a female attorney-at-law, for admission to this bar, rejected - admission refused.
Court adjourns to tomorrow morning at 9½ o'clock.
May 11th Court met pursuant to adjournment.

Carroll County Circuit Court (Minutes) denial of bar admission for Belva A. Lockwood, May 9, 1881.

Courtesy of the Maryland State Archives.

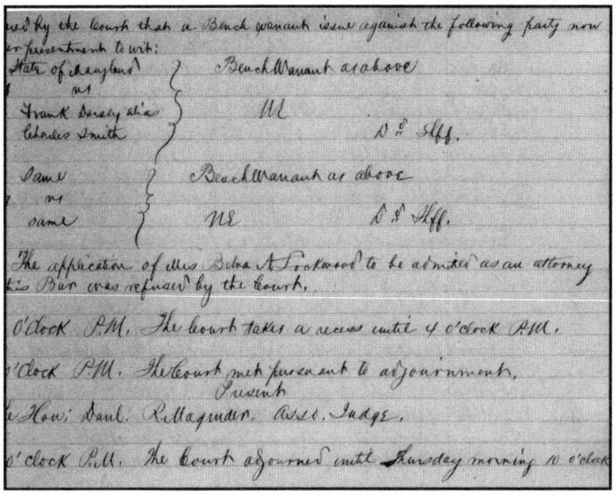
...ed by the Court that a Bench warrant issue against the following party now
...r presentment to wit:
State of Maryland } Bench Warrant as above
vs
Frank Dorsey alias
Charles Smith } NE D. S. Sff.
Same } Bench Warrant as above
vs
Same } NE D. S. Sff.
The application of Mrs Belva A Lockwood to be admitted as an attorney ... this Bar was refused by the Court.
... O'clock P.M. The Court takes a recess until 4 o'clock P.M.
...'clock P.M. The Court met pursuant to adjournment,
Present
...e Hon: Danl. R. Magruder, Assi. Judge.
...o'clock P.M. The Court adjourned until Thursday morning 10 o'clock

Prince George's County Circuit Court (Docket) Prince George's County Circuit Court Minutes, October 16, 1878, denial of application of Belva A. Lockwood.

Courtesy of the Maryland State Archives.

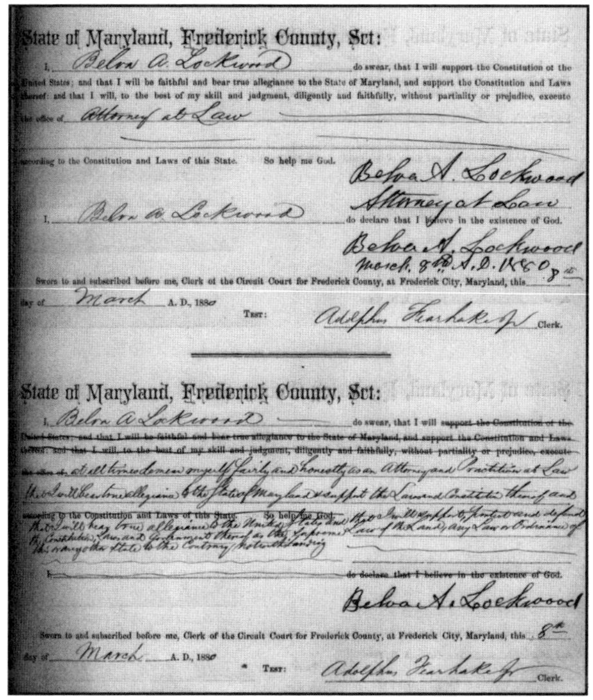
State of Maryland, Frederick County, Sct:
I, Belva A. Lockwood do swear, that I will support the Constitution of the United States; and that I will be faithful and bear true allegiance to the State of Maryland, and support the Constitution and Laws thereof: and that I will, to the best of my skill and judgment, diligently and faithfully, without partiality or prejudice, execute the office of Attorney at Law according to the Constitution and Laws of this State. So help me God.
Belva A. Lockwood
Attorney at Law
I, Belva A. Lockwood do declare that I believe in the existence of God.
Belva A. Lockwood
March 8th A.D. 1880
Sworn to and subscribed before me, Clerk of the Circuit Court for Frederick County, at Frederick City, Maryland, this 8th day of March A.D. 1880
Test: Adolphus Fearhake Jr Clerk.

State of Maryland, Frederick County, Sct:
I, Belva A Lockwood do swear, that I will ... shall at all times demean myself fairly and honestly as an Attorney and Practitioner at Law ... will bear true allegiance to the State of Maryland and support the Laws and Constitution thereof ... So help me God. ... that I will support, protect and defend the Constitution, Laws and Government thereof as the supreme Law of the Land, any Law or Ordinance of this or any other State to the Contrary Notwithstanding
Belva A. Lockwood
Sworn to and subscribed before me, Clerk of the Circuit Court for Frederick County, at Frederick City, Maryland, this 8th day of March A.D. 1880
Test: Adolphus Fearhake Jr Clerk.

Frederick County Circuit Court (Test Book) Copy of Testbook, Circuit Court for Frederick County, March 8, 1880.

Courtesy of the Maryland State Archives.

> of nature, and when voluntary, treason against it. The cruel changes of life sometimes baffle both sexes, and may leave women free from the peculiar duties of their sex. These may need employment, and should be welcome to any not derogatory to their sex and its properties, or inconsistent with the good order of society. But it is public policy to provide for the sex, not for its superfluous members; and not to tempt women from the proper duties of their sex by opening to them duties peculiar to ours. There are employments in life not unfit for female character. The profession of law is surely not one of these.[120]

Lockwood did succeed in gaining admission, first to the Bar of "the federal court, Baltimore."[121] In 1880, she was admitted to the Circuit Court for Frederick County.[122] More than a decade after her failed attempt in Prince George's County, Lockwood was granted admission to the Prince George's County Bar by Judge Brooke, Judge Magruder's successor, who indicated that he could not refuse her, as "her papers showed admission to the bar in Frederick County."[123] With her admission in Prince George's County, Lockwood was apparently able to "take up again the case she was compelled to drop eleven years" before.[124]

In 1898, the General Assembly revised the statutory scheme regulating attorneys in Maryland. Among the changes was the creation, for the first time, of the Board of Law Examiners.[125] The newly created Board, consisting of three members of the Bar of at least ten years' standing who were appointed by the Court of Appeals, was responsible for assessing the qualifications of bar applicants and empowered to assess fees to cover costs and expenses.[126] Whereas the previous system was more informal and decentralized, in which Belva Lockwood had gained admission on a piecemeal basis to the various county bars, the new bar admission regime created a single, centralized Board, directly answerable to and under the control of the Court of Appeals.[127] In 1902, after successful lobbying by Etta Maddox and her allies, the General Assembly

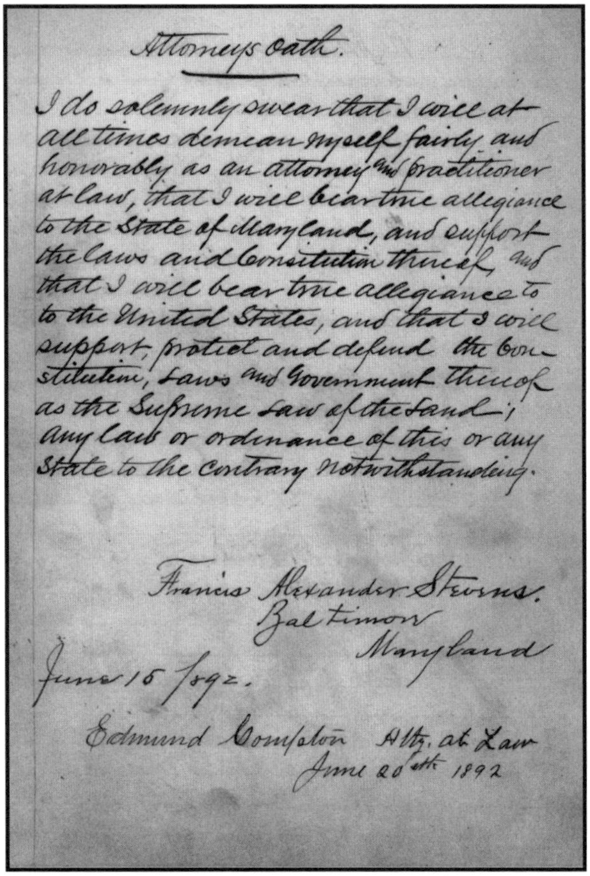
Attorneys oath.

I do solemnly swear that I will at all times demean myself fairly and honorably as an attorney and practitioner at law, that I will bear true allegiance to the State of Maryland, and support the laws and Consitution thereof, and that I will bear true allegiance to to the United States, and that I will support, protect and defend the Constitution, Laws and Government thereof as the Supreme Law of the Land; any Law or ordinance of this or any State to the contrary notwithstanding.

Francis Alexander Stevens.
Baltimore
Maryland
June 15 1892.

Edmund Compston Atty. at Law
June 20th 1892

Prince George's County Circuit Court (Test Book)
Oath of Belva A. Lockwood at Attorney at Law,
October 12, 1892, pp. 200–201.
Courtesy of the Maryland State Archives.

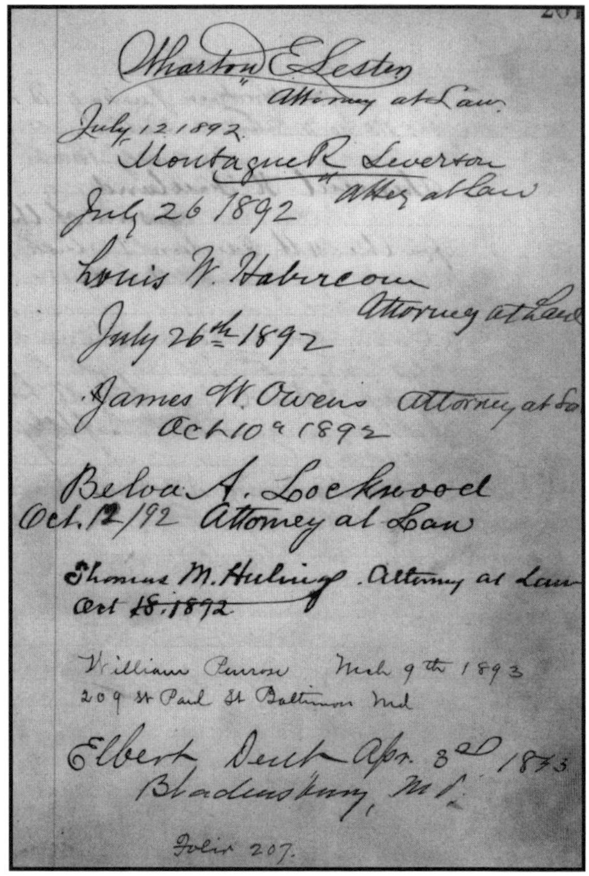
Wharton E. Lester
Attorney at Law
July 12 1892.
Montague R. Leverton
Atty at Law
July 26 1892
Louis W. Habercom
Attorney at Law
July 26th 1892
James W. Owens Attorney at Law
Oct 10th 1892
Belva A. Lockwood
Oct. 12/92 Attorney at Law
Thomas M. Hulings Attorney at Law
Oct 18, 1892
William Curran Mch 9th 1893
209 St Paul St Baltimore Md
Elbert Deck Apr. 3rd 1893
Bladensburg, Md.
Folio 207.

Prince George's County Circuit Court (Test Book)
Oath of Belva A. Lockwood at Attorney at Law,
October 12, 1892, pp. 200-201.
Courtesy of the Maryland State Archives.

amended the Bar Admission Statute to permit women to be admitted.[128]

Another woman, Catherine Hunckel, practiced law in the same region and during the same time period as Belva Lockwood, but their experiences were worlds apart. In 1893, Hunckel became the first woman to graduate from a law school in Maryland, the Baltimore University School of Law.[129] Hunckel graduated from law school with her husband, Otto, who was admitted to the Baltimore City Bar that same year.[130] It was not until Otto died in 1897 that she took over her husband's practice.[131]

Like Lockwood, Hunckel sought admission to the Bar by motion in 1902. Her motion was denied, however, because she had graduated from law school almost a decade earlier, outside of the time period set by the General Assembly for exemption from the examination requirement.[132] Hunckel neither sat for the bar exam nor reapplied for admission.[133] According to newspaper articles, however, she continued to practice law and was considered a "well-known woman lawyer" with offices on North Calvert Street in Baltimore City.[134] During that period, the General Assembly had enacted a "Practicing without Being Admitted

Belva Ann Bennett Lockwood with Senator Southerland, 1915.
Photographer unknown. Courtesy of the Library of Congress.

Belva Ann Bennett Lockwood, Lawyer, 1915.
Photographer unknown. Courtesy of the Library of Congress.

to the Bar" provision, which made the unauthorized practice of law "for any fee, gratuity, gift or reward" a misdemeanor offense, punishable by a $100 fine and thirty days in prison, although no records have been found of its enforcement against Hunckel.[135]

The first female attorneys in Maryland, such as Margaret Brent and Belva Lockwood, set the tone for women attorneys in the coming generations with their perseverance and willingness to challenge societal norms. In their time, social norms that manifested in the acceptance of women in the medical profession limited women from becoming the Portias of their day, because the sense of attorneys as combative and aggressive was in direct conflict with the perception of women as feminine. Becoming a female attorney was a challenge assumed by the most pugnacious and determined women, who would pave the way for female attorneys to come.

Photograph of Miss Etta Maddox in Margie H. Luckett,
Maryland Women, Vol. 2.
Courtesy of the Maryland State Archives.

CHAPTER TWO:

Etta Maddox: An Eternal Advocate for Maryland's Women, from Admission to the Bar to Access to the Ballot

Michelle R. Mitchell

Introduction

Historically touted as "Maryland's first woman lawyer," Henrietta "Etta" Haynie Maddox, was born in Baltimore on January 6, 1860.[1] The Maddox family had a rich heritage in Maryland, as her ancestors were some of the earliest settlers in Maryland and took an active interest in local political affairs.[2] Etta had a relatively privileged upbringing. Like many other first-woman lawyers, she grew up in a middle-class family in which women's education was encouraged.[3] Her father, John T. Maddox (known as Squire Maddox), was a magistrate, which was a position that carried with it significant prestige and at least modest wealth. Squire Maddox's position in the legal community undoubtedly provided Etta with firsthand exposure to the legal profession, one that she would enter during the early 1900s. Unfortunately, Squire Maddox died in 1892, nine years prior to Etta's graduation from law school.[4]

Etta's mother, Susanna (Moore) Maddox, lived until 1914. From newspaper records, it appears that Etta resided with her mother at least intermittently throughout her adult life.[5] Etta was the youngest of three girls born to Squire and Susanna Maddox. Margaret Ann (a school teacher) was the eldest, and Emma Jane (a lifelong woman's suffragist) was the middle daughter.[6]

The details of Etta Maddox's early life are largely unknown and may be unknowable. Despite her notable achievements for Maryland's women, a formal effort at a biography was not attempted until 1950, seventeen years after her death.[7] Etta herself never authored an autobiography, and no journals or diaries have been located. In fact, Etta refused to provide biographical information in her later years.[8] There are no immediate descendants from Etta or any of the three sisters.[9] Neither Etta nor her eldest sister ever married or had children.[10] Although Emma Jane did marry, she did not have children.[11] Thus, there are no direct descendants of Squire Maddox who may have retained memorabilia or other historical items relating to the accomplishments of his daughters, or who could pass along stories about dinner table conversations in the Maddox household—a household headed by a respected magistrate with three strong-willed and intelligent daughters.

Accordingly, much of what we know of Etta Maddox is derived from local newspapers that covered her efforts, the obstacles she faced, and her failures and accomplishments. Additionally, her own writings to the Court of Appeals and advocacy before the General Assembly provide insight into her staunch belief in women's rights. The writings and newspaper attention, however, did not begin until well into her adult years. As a result, some of the probing questions that we would hope to learn about her life may never be answered: At a time when women were rarely seen in the legal profession, why did she fight for admission to the Bar? What inspired her to fight harder than any other Maryland woman had, to acquire this privilege? Did her parents (in particular, her father) support her efforts? She was approximately forty years old when she entered law school; why did she undertake post-graduate education so late in life?[12] Adding to that peculiarity, Etta had a successful musical career; what drove her to want to practice law?[13] These are but some of the questions that can only be answered by inference or deductions from the writings that do exist and the knowledge we glean from her post-law school days.

Given that Maddox came from a family of means and given that she had already established herself in the musical community as a successful and respected vocalist, Etta's motivations were not likely financial in nature. The evidence suggests that her motivations were more selfless in seeking betterment for Maryland women. As will be demonstrated herein, there is no doubt that her primary passion in life was women's rights. Even prior to law school, Etta was active with the suffragist movement, and her political activity continued up until her death. Accordingly, her admission to the Bar was likely a step in the larger women's rights movement—and, in particular, a step toward the ballot.

In spite of the lack of autobiographies, journals, diaries, and other direct sources of information about Maddox, we are privileged to have a record of Etta's own words in the form of newspaper interviews, briefs to the Court of Appeals, and other political writings. Through these, we are able to characterize Maddox as tenacious, driven, ambitious, articulate, and intelligent. Through these, we are able to state, with confidence, that Etta's undying efforts were made for the women of Maryland.

Maddox's Path to the Law: From a Voice for Song to a Voice for Advocacy

Etta graduated from Eastern Female High School, one of the few female high schools in Baltimore, in 1873.[14] She was an accomplished musician who was well known for her beautiful mezzo-soprano voice. In fact, after graduating high school she pursued a musical education degree at the Peabody Institute in Baltimore for three years (from 1873–1875) and, afterward, continued with her musical education and training by studying for grand operas. Etta taught voice lessons and sang in many local light operas.[15] Additionally, she performed at many of the women's suffrage meetings, an organization (and cause) to which she devoted a substantial part of her life and talents, above and beyond her vocal prowess.[16] Etta received public accolades for her vocal performances, including a concert with the Marine band at the National Theater in Washington, DC, in 1882. *The Washington Post* reported that "each of Miss Maddox's numbers was encored, and she responded with 'Angels Ever Bright and Fair,' and 'Nearer My God to Thee.'"[17]

Her family was purportedly opposed to a career on the stage, which resulted in her vocal accomplishments being shared with the community, largely by her singing in the choirs of local churches.[18] In particular, she sang in the choirs of the First Presbyterian Church and Brown Memorial Church, and, a precursor to many "firsts" for Etta, she was Director of the Seventh Baptist Church Choir, a position rarely held by a woman.[19]

Maddox was in her late thirties or early forties when she applied to Baltimore Law School. In contemplating her inspiration for entering into a field almost entirely dominated by men, certain factors are particularly noteworthy, her relatively late age being one. Given her successes as a singer and musical director, it seems unlikely that Etta was looking for a career change due to her inability to thrive in the musical field. To the contrary, she was well known in the musical circles of Baltimore, Washington, and Richmond.[20] Certainly, Etta's vocal achievements, coupled with her family's relative wealth, would have made financial betterment an unlikely reason for her career shift at her age.

WOMEN AS LAWYERS.

Maryland Had the First One, but Does Not Admit Them Now, and Is Asked to Reconsider.

From The Baltimore Sun.

Miss Etta H. Maddox of Baltimore, who recently graduated at the Maryland University Law School and was refused admission to the bar on account of her sex, made a strong appeal to the Senate Judiciary Committee in Annapolis on Thursday afternoon. A bill making legal the admission of women to the bar has been introduced in the Senate and is now in the hands of the committee.

Accompanying Miss Maddox were Mrs. Ellen Foster of Iowa, a member of the bar; Miss Laura Clay of Kentucky, Miss Gail Laughlin of the New York bar, Mrs. M. B. Thomas of Maryland, and Mr. H. B. Blackwell of Massachusetts.

The hearing took place in the Senate Chamber. Most of the Senators were present, besides a great many other persons, and at its close Senator Bryan told the ladies that the committee had listened to them with pleasure and profit, that they would consider the bill with care, and, he hoped, decide upon it with wisdom.

Miss Maddox introduced each of the speakers with appropriate remarks, most happily expressed.

Mrs. J. Ellen Foster of Iowa was the first speaker. She told of her own admission to the bar in 1875. She studied law, she said, to keep her husband at home and practiced in partnership with him. While engaged in practice she cared for her children.

Dr. Cora Eaton of Minneapolis said that the test of genius is to know when to act, and Maryland has now an opportunity to enact a law which will be historical. She did not ask it as a matter of chivalry, though she had always heard of the chivalry of the South, but as a matter of right. It is not a revolution, but an evolution, and the admission of women to the Maryland bar will surely come.

Miss Laura Clay, President of the Equal Rights Society of Kentucky, was introduced as a genuine Southern woman. She said her maternal grandfather, Elijah Wenfield, was a Marylander, and that she is no stranger to the methods of Maryland thought. "Kentucky is indebted to Maryland," she said, "for much of its civilization, and Kentucky treats women most liberally. Civilization is measured by the advancement of the woman. We do not undervalue chivalry, and do not think the chivalry of American men, North and South can be beat, but I appeal, in the name of justice, for the right of women to earn their bread. It is a matter of strict justice. The State is injured when it makes it harder for any woman to make a living."

Miss Gail Laughlin, a practicing attorney of New York, was the next speaker. She was most simply and becomingly dressed in black with a lace collar and cuffs. She said she was asking for nothing new, but simply that Maryland should return to her ancient spirit of liberality; for the first woman to practice law in the United States was Mistress Margaret Brent of Maryland, 250 years ago. She gave her experience as a practicing attorney and said there is nothing in the way of it. In thirty-three States women are admitted and only in seven, including Maryland, are they excluded. In five the question has not arisen. Miss Laughlin reviewed the decisions upon the subject and made a legal argument of decided force and ability. She stated that in France, India, Canada, Japan, and other countries women are admitted as lawyers. There are many who prefer to be represented in the courts by women, and it is their right to have them. In the schools women have stood highest and have been declared to have the best legal ability of their classes. If the people don't want women lawyers they will get no practice. All the women are asking for is the opportunity to use the abilities they have to promote right and justice. From time immemorial the law has been typified by the figure of a woman. The speech was an earnest and most forceful one, and was heartily applauded.

Henry B. Blackwell of Massachusetts said: "This is not a question of woman suffrage. It is simply whether a woman, entirely qualified, will be permitted to practice in the courts. You should not put a slur on the women of Maryland by saying they are inferior to those of other States." He reviewed the history of the admission of women to the bars of various States, and declared that a Southern State, Missouri, has the honor of being the first to admit them.

In conclusion Miss Maddox thanked the committee for their courtesy and the Maryland men who were present for their attention to the speeches which had been made.

"Women as Lawyers: Maryland Had the First One, but Does Not Admit them Now, and Is Asked to Reconsider."

The New York Times *(February 23, 1902).*

The fact that higher education in Maryland was very limited for women prior to 1900 may seem like the most obvious reason that Maddox did not pursue a legal career earlier in her life. The vast majority of lawyers at that time, however, received their training through legal apprenticeships rather than formal education; thus, the gender restrictions in schooling doesn't entirely explain Etta's delay in entering the legal profession, particularly given that Etta's father was a practicing magistrate with a fair number of connections in the local legal community. Furthermore, as Judge Battaglia explored in the previous chapter, Baltimore Law School was not the first institution in Maryland to admit female law students; the law school at Baltimore University graduated Miss Catherine Hunckel in 1893, seven years before Etta elected to attend law school.[21] While there is no question that the limited access to law schools, generally, was certainly an obstacle to women's entry in the legal profession, this limitation alone does not exclusively explain the timing of Etta's own entry in the law.

As will be discussed further, below, Maddox was staunchly devoted to women's rights and, in particular, to the women's suffrage movement.[22] She was an active member of the Baltimore Woman's Suffrage Association since 1898, and she helped organize the Maryland Suffrage Association in 1904 and was an active member until she died (the word "active" being an understatement).[23] As a result, Etta's entry into law school and acceptance into the legal profession may have been stepping stones, albeit quite significant, for her larger quest for equality for women, rather than for merely personal or selfish ambitions. This conclusion is consistent with Etta's explanation to local media of her reasons for fighting for admission to the State Bar: "I am willing to make the effort, not only for myself, but for women who may wish to take up the same profession."[24]

Regardless of the motivations that spurred her entry into the legal field, Etta Maddox became the first woman to graduate from the Baltimore Law School on June 6, 1901.[25] The law school was a two-year program consisting of thirteen members in the graduating class—Etta being the only woman.[26] It was reported that while she would graduate, "she will not be admitted to the bar, as that privilege is accorded only to men in Maryland," despite the fact that thirty-seven other states allowed women to practice law at that time.[27] This was, of course, an obstacle that Etta aggressively aimed to defeat.

Naturally, Etta's colleagues in the suffragist organizations were aware of her law school attendance; immediately after her graduation, she was presented with a medal for her achievement by the Woman's Suffrage Association. Etta, as the Secretary of the Baltimore Woman's Suffrage Association, authored the very minutes of the meeting in which she received this medal for her accomplishment. Apparently, in an effort to surprise Etta, the cards announcing the June 12, 1901, meeting stated that its purpose was the consideration of a "fete" (party). Etta recorded that, "in so far as the furtherance of this subject was concerned, the meeting was a decided failure. It developed later that the meeting was called to give the Secretary of the Association 'a surprise.'"

The minutes also reflect that "Miss Maddox responded and acknowledged a great surprise had been given her. Refreshments were served and the association adjourned at a late hour."

The medal was emblazoned with the Maryland Coat of Arms on one side, and on the other it was inscribed, "June 6, 1901—Women's Suffrage Association to Miss Etta Haynie Maddox, First Woman Lawyer in Maryland."[28] Given that there were female attorneys-in-fact

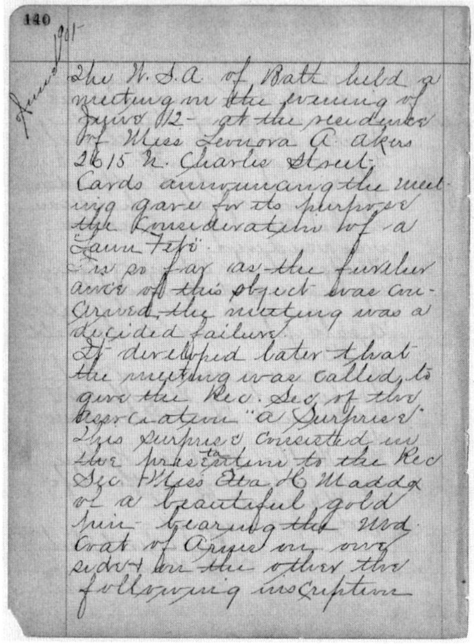
140
1901
June
The W.S.A. of Balt. held a meeting on the evening of June 12 - at the residence of Miss Lenora A. Akers 2615 N. Charles Street. Cards announcing the meeting gave for its purpose the consideration of a Lawn Fete. In so far as the furtherance of this object was concerned the meeting was a decided failure. It developed later that the meeting was called to give the Rec. Sec. of the Association "a Surprise". This surprise consisted in the presentation to the Rec Sec. Miss Etta H. Maddox of a beautiful gold pin bearing the Md. Coat of Arms on one side & on the other the following inscription

Baltimore Women's Suffrage Association's meeting minutes, June 12, 1901.
Courtesy of the Enoch Pratt Library.

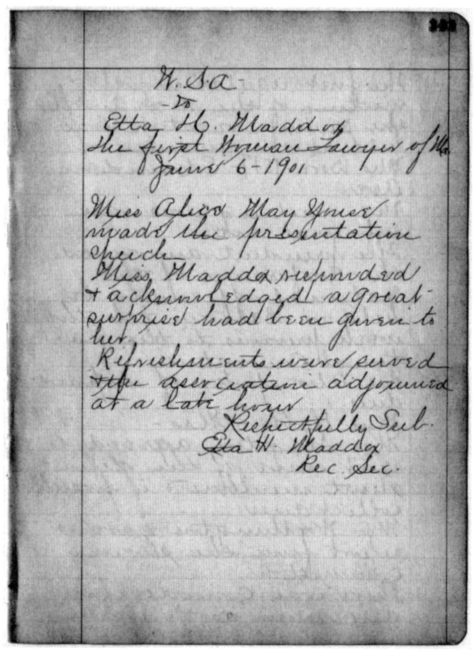
W.S.A.
to
Etta H. Maddox
the first Woman Lawyer of Md.
June 6-1901
Miss Alice May [illegible] made the presentation speech.
Miss Maddox responded & acknowledged a great surprise had been given to her.
Refreshments were served the association adjourned at a late hour.
Respectfully Sub.
Etta H. Maddox
Rec. Sec.

Baltimore Women's Suffrage Association's meeting minutes, June 12, 1901.
Courtesy of the Enoch Pratt Library.

"HIM" INCLUDES "HER"

Major Venable Thinks Women May Practice Law.

THE RULE OF INTERPRETATION

Only Exception Is Where Such A Construction Would Be Absurd Or Unreasonable.

"'Him' Includes 'Her', Major Venable Thinks Women May Practice Law," June 26, 1901

Courtesy of The Baltimore Sun.

Court of Appeals of Maryland, Annapolis, 1905.

Photograph by the Detroit Publishing Company. Courtesy of the Library of Congress.

in Maryland prior to Etta, the fact that the Women's Suffrage Association dubbed her the "First Woman Lawyer" before she was admitted to the Bar may be evidence that Etta's acceptance to the Bar was on the suffragists' larger agenda.

The press closely followed Etta's graduation and interviewed her about her intentions to challenge the state's preclusion of women in the practice of law so that, as one reporter characterized it, "women may get a chance to exercise their persuasive influences over the jury."[29] Utilizing sexual innuendo to characterize a woman's desire to be a litigator, as well as to rationalize fears about woman litigators, was commonplace around this time. A 1907 article from *The Baltimore Sun* described "women who have a burning desire to become lawyers and make love to juries...."[30] The perception of a woman lawyer as a "seductress" troubled some male attorneys, given that traditional Victorian etiquette of the time rendered it difficult for a "proper gentleman" to engage in a legal attack on a female lawyer in court.[31] Some male lawyers touted the danger of female attorneys being that "a handsome and seductive advocate would have it all her own way with a susceptible jury."[32] Others lamented that male attorneys were "defenseless against the feminine ammunition [of] beauty, charm, sensuality and feigned helplessness."[33] Suffice it to say, fears and doubts rooted in sexism were prevalent in the years surrounding Maddox venture into the legal profession.

Nevertheless, the perseverance and determination with which Maddox approached all endeavors relating to women's rights is indicated by her statement:

> I am willing to make the effort, not only for myself, but for women who may wish to take up the same profession. I hope to get what I want without encountering any serious opposition, but I am prepared for discouragements. If I am refused the privilege of taking the examination for admission to the bar, I will keep on asking until I get permission to take it. If the next Legislature refuses to strike out the word 'male', well, I'll petition again, that's all.[34]

Mrs. Edward Addison Greeley, a well-known female attorney from New York who championed women's acceptance into law schools and the legal profession, was interviewed in the aftermath of Etta's graduation.[35] Mrs. Greely pointed out the unusual aspect of

Maddox's position vis-à-vis the State's prohibition: the duel facts that the State permits her access to obtain a law degree but denies her admission to practice law.[36] Greely expressed her hope that "the very spirit of conservatism which distinguishes the State of Maryland would shield Miss Maddox" from this seeming injustice.[37] Other locals similarly expressed support for Miss Maddox's admission. Major Richard M. Venable, founding partner of Venable, Baejter & Howard, now Venable L.L.P., was a proponent of women's admission to the Bar.[38] His opinions on Miss Maddox's application were sought, and he expressed his belief that the Act of 1898, Chapter 139, which removed the word "male" and replaced it with "applicant" when referring to admission to the Bar, was a demonstration that the intention of the Legislature was to open the field to both genders.[39] Maddox would later expand upon this very argument in her brief to the Court of Appeals in Annapolis. Despite the many voices of support, Etta was correct that she would be met with discouragements before success.

Etta Maddox's Application for the State Bar Is Denied by the Court of Appeals

Due to an illness shortly after her graduation, Maddox did not request to sit for the bar examination in June 1901; rather, she advised of her intention to do so in the fall.[40] True to her word, on October 28, 1901, Etta petitioned the Court of Appeals of Maryland for permission to take the State Bar Examination.[41]

The Court of Appeals granted Etta's request to file a brief in support of her position, with a filing deadline

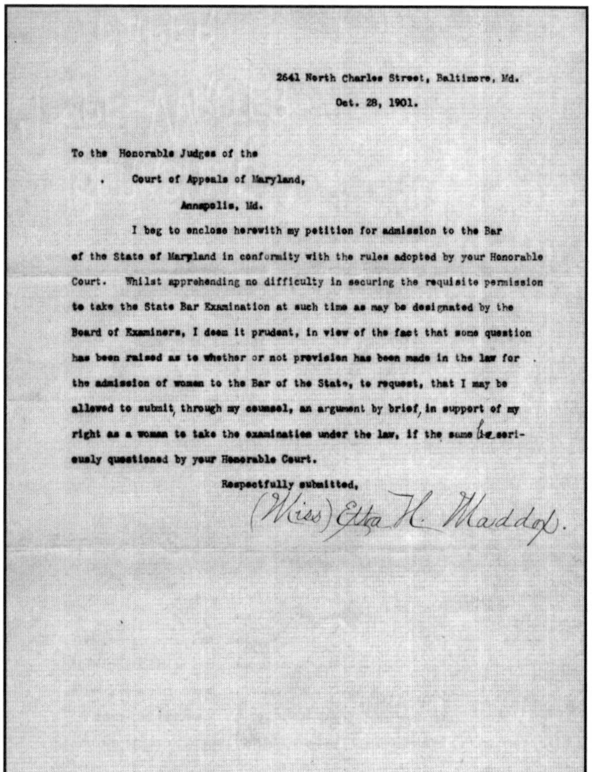

2641 North Charles Street, Baltimore, Md.
Oct. 28, 1901.

To the Honorable Judges of the
Court of Appeals of Maryland,
Annapolis, Md.

I beg to enclose herewith my petition for admission to the Bar of the State of Maryland in conformity with the rules adopted by your Honorable Court. Whilst apprehending no difficulty in securing the requisite permission to take the State Bar Examination at such time as may be designated by the Board of Examiners, I deem it prudent, in view of the fact that some question has been raised as to whether or not provision has been made in the law for the admission of women to the Bar of the State, to request, that I may be allowed to submit, through my counsel, an argument by brief, in support of my right as a woman to take the examination under the law, if the same be seriously questioned by your Honorable Court.

Respectfully submitted,
(Miss) Etta H. Maddox.

Court of Appeals (Bar Applications) Etta H. Maddox, April Term 1902.

Courtesy of the Maryland State Archives.

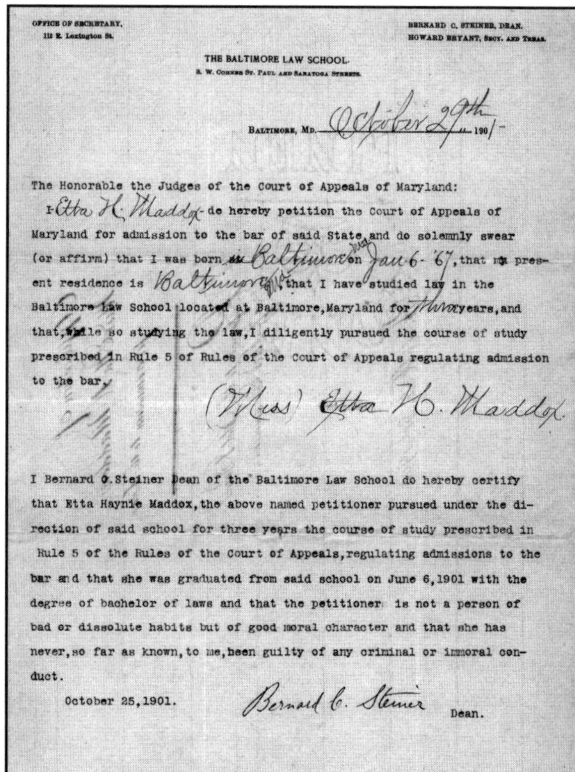

OFFICE OF SECRETARY,
112 E. Lexington St.

BERNARD C. STEINER, DEAN.
HOWARD BRYANT, SECY. AND TREAS.

THE BALTIMORE LAW SCHOOL.
S. W. CORNER ST. PAUL AND SARATOGA STREETS.

BALTIMORE, MD. October 29th 1901

The Honorable the Judges of the Court of Appeals of Maryland:

I Etta H. Maddox do hereby petition the Court of Appeals of Maryland for admission to the bar of said State, and do solemnly swear (or affirm) that I was born in Baltimore Md on Jan 6 '67, that my present residence is Baltimore Md, that I have studied law in the Baltimore Law School located at Baltimore, Maryland for three years, and that, while so studying the law, I diligently pursued the course of study prescribed in Rule 5 of Rules of the Court of Appeals regulating admission to the bar.

(Miss) Etta H. Maddox.

I Bernard C. Steiner Dean of the Baltimore Law School do hereby certify that Etta Haynie Maddox, the above named petitioner pursued under the direction of said school for three years the course of study prescribed in Rule 5 of the Rules of the Court of Appeals, regulating admissions to the bar and that she was graduated from said school on June 6, 1901 with the degree of bachelor of laws and that the petitioner is not a person of bad or dissolute habits but of good moral character and that she has never, so far as known, to me, been guilty of any criminal or immoral conduct.

October 25, 1901. Bernard C. Steiner Dean.

Court of Appeals (Bar Applications) Etta H. Maddox, April Term 1902.

Courtesy of the Maryland State Archives.

of November 11, 1901.[42] With the assistance of Howard Bryant, her attorney and former law school instructor, Etta filed a brief with the Court of Appeals, expounding upon her right to take the State Bar Examination.[43] It is noteworthy that Mr. Bryant readily provided Etta with credit for her work on the brief and included a handwritten note in its appendix advising that "[t]his brief was prepared by Miss Maddox herself and whatever there is of merit in it is due to her Efforts."[44]

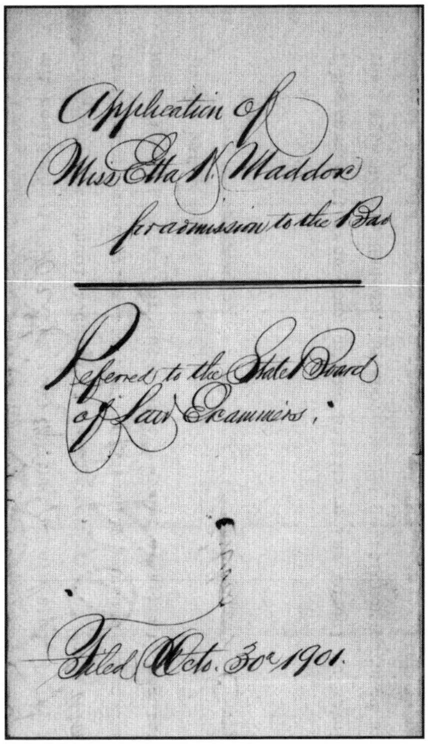
Application of
Miss Etta H. Maddox
for admission to the Bar

Referred to the State Board
of Law Examiners.

Filed Octo. 30th 1901.

Court of Appeals (Bar Applications), Etta H. Maddox, April Term 1902.

Courtesy of the Maryland State Archives.

In support of her position that women should be held eligible for Bar admission in Maryland, Maddox maintained that the practice of law was "a natural right" that all persons inherently possess and is "dependent in no way upon legislative authorization."[45] Etta's brief was well-researched, and she cited to multiple jurisdictions which had admitted women to the Bar *without* the passage of special statutes expressly authorizing their admission. Those jurisdictions included Colorado, Connecticut, the District of Columbia, Indiana, Iowa, Kansas, Maine, Michigan, Missouri, Montana, Nebraska, New Hampshire, North Carolina, Ohio, Pennsylvania, Utah, and Washington.[46] This extra-jurisdictional precedent was significant to Etta's argument, as she fully anticipated the judiciary's inclination to defer this controversial decision to the Legislature.

Etta employed statutory construction and interpretation of the Bar Admission Statute to support her claim. Chapter 139 of the Act of 1898 amended the provision to remove language that previously utilized "any male citizen of Maryland" as the precursor to describing those eligible for bar admission. The new provision omitted reference to male and instead utilized "all applications for admission to the bar."[47] Etta argued that this change established that there was "nothing tending to disqualify an applicant for admission to the Bar in consequence of her sex."[48] She cited a decision from Indiana, which held "all restrictions of human liberty, all claim for special privilege, are to be regarded as having the presumption of law against them, and as standing upon their defence, and can be sustained, if at all by valid legislation, only by the clear expression or clear implication of the law."[49] The Maryland Act of 1898, Etta argued, did not exclude women by either express words or necessary implication.[50] Anticipating the Court of Appeal's reliance upon "his," "he," and "him" in other portions of the Bar Admissions Statute, Etta argued that the Maryland Code utilized masculine pronouns in multiple areas, including penal laws, which necessarily apply to all genders, not only from logical necessity, but vis-à-vis the Sixth Rule of Interpretation in the Maryland Code, which provided "that the masculine includes all genders except where such instruction would be absurd or unreasonable."[51]

Finally, Etta relied upon a constitutional "privileges and immunities" argument, given the Act of 1898's provision that members of the Bar in any other state may be admitted to the Bar in Maryland without examination.[52] That provision had no exclusion or limitation regarding women. Thus, if a woman could be admitted under this provision vis-à-vis her membership in a Bar of another state, then it clearly was not the intention of the

Legislature that female lawyers originating in Maryland should be excluded.[53]

After skillfully arguing statutory construction, statutory interpretation, and constitutional privileges, Etta addressed the policy implications of the Court of Appeal's decision. These arguments, in particular, evidence her passion on the equality of women not only in the legal profession, but in every aspect of social, political, and economic matters. This portion of the brief, included here in its entirety, provides invaluable insight into the beliefs that likely inspired Etta to continue with her quest:

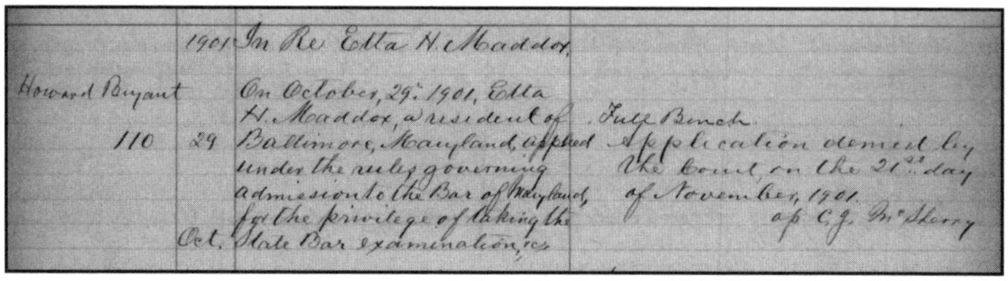
1901 In Re: Etta H. Maddox
Howard Bryant
110 29 Oct.
On October, 29: 1901, Etta H. Maddox, a resident of Baltimore, Maryland, applied under the rules governing admission to the Bar of Maryland, for the privilege of taking the State Bar examination, &c.
Full Bench.
Application denied by the Court on the 21st day of November, 1901.
op C.J. McSherry

Court of Appeals (Docket) In Re: Etta H. Maddox.

Courtesy of the Maryland State Archives.

> All progress is recent. These statutes and decisions, except in the case of Margaret Brent, have all come in the last generation, during the last thirty years, when the public mind has become more accustomed to the idea of woman being a thinking, accountable, responsible individual.
>
> An ancient synod happily decided that women have souls. Our modern Courts and Legislatures are being convinced that women have minds. In an address before the American Bar Association, August 1901, the Honorable William P. Rogers, of Indiana, upon the subject, "Is Law a Field for Woman's Work, said: 'The story of woman's admission to the Bar in the United States is one of contest and struggle. We, their brethren, being already within the gates with legal power to keep those out who were of the opposite sex, have not extended a very hearty welcome to our sisters in law[.] If the road has been open for them to enter, it has been only because with their own hands, they have torn down the obstacles, and cleared the rubbish.
>
> The Revolution is over. Its results exist to-day and all around us....The tendency of the age is to throw open and not to close up the so-called learned professions.... Public sentiment has emancipated woman from the restraints which formerly circumscribed her life and fettered the freedom of her actions.
>
> Positive legislation has everywhere broken down the barriers within which woman was formerly confined....Will Maryland take notice of these changes, and the rights which have grown out of them?
>
> The other learned professions of this State are open alike to the sexes.
>
> If nature has endowed women with minds, if our colleges have given her education, if her energy and diligence have led her to knowledge of the law, and if her ambition directs her to adopt the profession of the law, shall it be said to her, at the dawn of the Twentieth Century, that she shall not be permitted to pursue the vocation to which her tastes lead her, and for which her studies have qualified her—and that the profession of law is of all the professions and vocations in Maryland, the only one from which she shall be excluded,—that there is a sex limit to justice and equity. It has been said, that when Courts cannot solve such questions by reference to books or cases, they must decide by that common sense of justice which is natural to men, by that "right reason comfortable to nature" of which Cicero speaks.[54]

Despite Maddox's well-articulated and convincing arguments that women should be admitted under the current law, on November 21, 1901, the Court of Appeals rejected Etta's position.[55] The Court of Appeals further held that the right to practice law was not a natural inherent right to every citizen; but was dependent upon and regulated by statute.[56] The Court of Appeal's opinion was consistent with the U.S. Supreme Courts's decision in *Bradwell v. Illinois*, 83 U.S. 130 (1872), in which the Court held that the privileges belonging to the nation's citizens did not include the right to practice law; thus, states could restrict licensures as they saw fit.[57] In further support of its holding, the Court of Appeals relied upon its own holding in *In re Taylor*, a case involving the request of an African American male for admission to the Bar. While the applicable statute at that point in time included the provision "for any white male citizen," the same arguments regarding the violations of the Privileges and Immunities Clause of the Fourteenth Amendment were made.[58] The Court of Appeals found "conclusively settling" its holding in *In re Taylor*—that the "privilege of admission to the office of an attorney cannot be said to be a right or immunity belonging to the citizen, but is governed and regulated by the Legislature, who may prescribe the qualifications required, and designate the class of persons who may be admitted."[59]

The Court of Appeals interpreted the statute that regulated bar admissions, Chapter 139 of the Maryland Laws of 1898, as meaning that only males were eligible for bar admission; further it could not (or would not) broaden the law to include a class of persons not so intended by the Legislature. The Legislature's substitution of "applicant" for "male" was not intended to broaden the class of those eligible for admission, according to the Court of Appeals.[60] To the contrary, the only purpose for amending the Bar Admission Statute was "to change the method of admitting applicants."[61] Furthermore, the Court of Appeals found ample pronouns in the new statute that characterized the term "applicant" as "his," "him," and "himself."[62] As a result, any attempt to interpret the statute in a gender-neutral manner would attribute to the Legislature an intention that never existed.[63]

Along those lines, the Court of Appeals emphasized that its holding should not be misinterpreted "as disparaging the laudable ambition of females to become lawyers," rather, the Court believed it would overstep its judicial powers to pronounce which persons shall be eligible for admission to the State Bar:

> It is for the General Assembly to declare what class of persons shall be admitted to the bar. We have no power to enact legislature. The Courts can only interpret what the Legislature adopts. If we should say that females are entitled to be admitted to the bar, when the Legislature has not said so, we would exceed our authority and usurp the functions of a different and independent department of the State Government.[64]

In closing, the Court of Appeals stated that, if the Legislature believes "that females ought to be admitted to the bar, it can so declare."[65] Until the Legislature so acted, the Court of Appeals had "no power to admit the applicant and her request to be allowed to stand for examination must be denied."[66]

Though surprised by this decision, Maddox's determination did not waver. In an interview after the Court of Appeals issued its opinion, she was quoted as saying:

> I am surprised but not disappointed.... I fail to see how the Court could arrive as such a conclusion.... As the State law now stands, any attorney who has been practicing in another state for five years can come here and be admitted to the Bar without examination... Yet the Court refuses me—a native of thc State and a taxpayer—the privilege of taking the examination.[67]

Regarding the Court's reliance upon the masculine pronouns in the statute as precluding her admission to the Bar, Maddox retorted, "If a woman may come under the designation of 'he' in a statute defining a felony and fixing its punishment, it is hard to conceive that she cannot, under the same designation, be brought within the terms of a statute defining civil rights. If a statute require[s] that the owner of a city lot should remove the snow from 'his' sidewalk, it will be held to extend to men, women and children."[68]

Etta Maddox's Plea to the Legislature Is Met with Success

Nevertheless, undaunted by her rejection by the judiciary, Maddox presented her case to the Legislature, requesting that a bill be introduced which would permit women to be admitted to the Maryland Bar. Etta's eloquence equaled her persistence, and, in January 1902, her request came to life in a bill introduced by Senator Jacob Moses.[69] The bill amended the law to provide, "Women shall be permitted to practice law in the State upon the same terms, conditions, and requirements, and to the same extent as provided in this Article with reference to men."[70]

In February 1902, Maddox appeared before the Senate Judiciary Committee, accompanied by women lawyers from other states, to testify at a hearing on this matter.[71] It was noted that "[m]ost of the Senators were present, besides a great many other persons."[72] It is noteworthy that the legislators' apparent willingness to embrace Etta's cause for bar admission and participate in the hearing on the subject was in stark contrast to the indifference (at best) to Etta's subsequent pursuits of suffrage bills where the Senate could barely convene the committee's members to sit for hearings. This disparity will be discussed in further detail below.

The local papers of the time almost uniformly described warm receptions and favorable reactions to Maddox's delegation for bar admission. In fact, the delegation of supporters that Etta convened was described as "so formidable that it is expected to overawe the [Senate Judiciary] committee."[73] Most of the women who accompanied Etta were admittees to the Bars in other states, describing their path to admission proudly, and characterizing the advancement of women as a measure of civilization.[74] Maryland was certainly in a minority, as it was emphasized that women were permitted to be admitted to the Bar in at least thirty-three states, and only seven states (including Maryland) precluded women from the Bar.[75] Miss Gail Laughlin, a practicing attorney in New York, reviewed these jurisdictions and noted that in five of the remaining seven states, the question of woman's admission to the Bar had not yet arisen.[76] It was shrewdly pointed out that, "[f]rom time immemorial, the law has been typified by the figure of a woman" and, thus, to close its doors to women seeking to practice law was the height of irony.[77] Emphasizing another irony, Etta stated:

> Maryland was the first of the colonies to admit women to the bar. Margaret Brent on January 3rd, 1648, was by order of the Court admitted to the bar as the Attorney of Lord Baltimore. I hope Maryland will not be the last of the States to give women the right to practice law in her courts.[78]

After the hearing, Senator Bryan told the ladies that the committee had "listened to them with pleasure and profit, that they would consider the bill with care, and, he hoped, decide upon it with wisdom."[79]

Interestingly, *The Baltimore Sun* dismissed any perceived opposition by members of the Senate Judiciary Committee as being attributable to the fact that its members "are lawyers and do not want to try cases against a pretty girl lawyer."[80] In fact, overall support for Maddox's bill seemed widespread; an editorial published ten days later in the *Sun* touted the bill as "a measure which appeals strongly to the general sense of fair play.... Women have the same right as men to make a living, and it is unjust to shut them out from any legitimate field of effort."[81]

The bill was passed by the Senate on March 4, 1902, by a vote of fourteen to two and was sent to the House of Delegates where it passed on March 31, 1902, by a vote of fifty-four to nine.[82] While the final vote on the bill was overwhelmingly supportive, Maddox's tenacity may be responsible for the degree of success. It was reported that she spent the last night of the session in the Senate fighting any opponents of the bill who were trying to kill it by adding unfavorable amendments.[83] On April 8, 1902, Governor John W. Smith signed the bill into law, finally and formally opening the legal profession to women. The adopted provision provided in full: "Women shall be permitted to practice law in this State upon the same terms, conditions and requirements and to the same extent as provided in this Article with reference to men. No discrimination shall be made on account of race, creed, complexion or previous condition of servitude."[84] Accordingly, Maryland's bar admissions were stripped of all gender barriers.

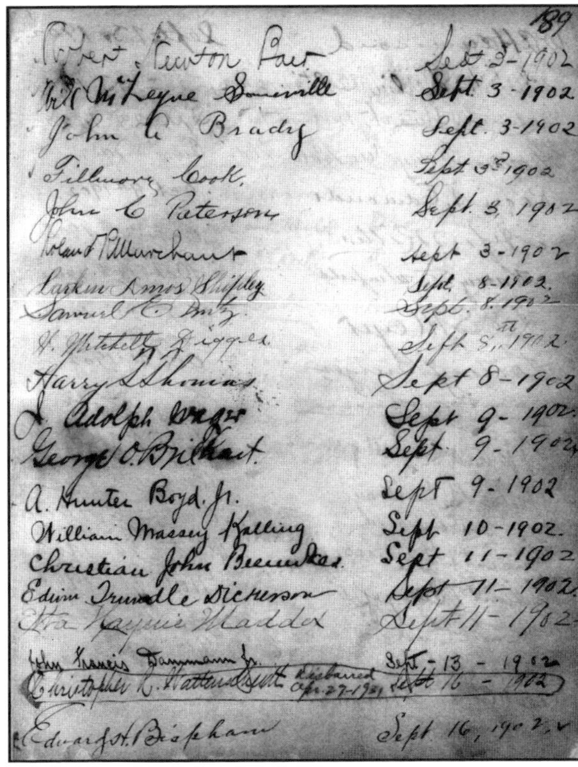

Testbook signature of Etta Maddox, Court of Appeals (Test Book), Etta Haynie Maddox, September 11, 1902.

Courtesy of the Maryland State Archives.

Etta Haynie Maddox Becomes Maryland's First Female Lawyer

Maddox promptly took the bar examination in June 1902 and passed, "very creditably," becoming the first woman to pass in the State of Maryland.[85] Naturally, Maddox's status as the first woman to pass the bar examination was well publicized. Even prior to being formally sworn in, her appearance in the courthouse in Towson generated what was characterized as a "mild sensation."[86]

> Woman Lawyer Creates Mild Sensation at Towson
>
> There was quite a stir yesterday in the Court House in Towson when Miss Etta H. Maddox, the only woman lawyer in Maryland, made her appearance there.... Miss Maddox had visited the court house before but was not recognized.... But yesterday she was formally introduced as the only woman who has applied for admission to the bar, and who passed the examination, and the news ran about the court house like wildfire.
>
> The employees in the office of the Court Clerk, the Record Office, and other departments left their desks to get a look at the caller and to watch her going to and from about the building. Miss Maddox was all business and seemed unaware of the attention she was attracting....[Miss Maddox] said, ...'I am not here on legal business as I have not been sworn in....I am simply here on some administrative matters.'

Maddox's accomplishments were well-publicized, and her ultimate admission was met with anticipation by the local populous. On September 11, 1902, her undeterred tenacity and proficient advocacy resulted in her being sworn in as a member of the State Bar, becoming the first woman lawyer in Maryland.[87] A few weeks later, Etta's former professor and advocate, Howard Bryant, moved for her admission before the Supreme Bench of

Baltimore.[88] Maddox also went on to be admitted to U.S. District Court in Maryland in 1911.[89]

While women were able to be admitted to the State Bar in Maryland, the Baltimore City Bar Association remained closed to Maddox and other women until 1931.[90] Because the Maryland Bar Association and American Bar Association required membership at the local level as a condition for membership at the state and national level, this exclusion also precluded Etta's membership to both of these associations, although there is no evidence that she ever made an effort to become a member of these associations.[91] Perhaps Etta did not believe it to be a pivotal step for women's rights or, perhaps, she chose her battles carefully, striving for those things with more far-reaching benefits to women. This limitation must not have significantly impacted her career or further ambitions regarding the ballot; if it had, the outspoken Maddox certainly would have addressed it.

Etta Maddox's Legal Career

According to directory listings, Maddox maintained a private law office in Baltimore City from 1903 to 1915, after which her office was listed as her home address.[92] The crux of Etta's legal career involved handling the legal and real estate work for her parents' estates.[93] Etta also maintained a general civil and administrative practice, such as representing local property owners in an effort to have a telephone pole removed.[94] However, it appears that Etta devoted a significant portion of her professional time to divorce cases and familial disputes. The first matter on which Etta was listed as the attorney of record in the Circuit Court for Baltimore City occurred in July 1903. Etta represented Mrs. Margaret Leslie, a married woman who sought to sell property that she jointly owned with her husband, Henry C. Leslie. In a Petition for a Writ de Lunatico Inquirendo, Etta wrote that Mr. Leslie "has been for more than two and one half years of unsound mind, and a lunatic without lucid intervals, and that he is not capable of the government of himself."[95] Mr. Leslie was subsequently declared to be of "unsound mind," and the Circuit Court appointed Etta to be Mr. Leslie's Committee and to be "authorized to join Margaret A. Leslie in all deeds and papers necessary to pass the title and interest" of the Leslies' property.

Maddox successfully tried her first case in 1904 before Judge Sharp in Baltimore Circuit Court.[96] Etta's client, Gertrude Campbell, was a sixteen-year-old girl who had filed for divorce on grounds of abandonment and petitioned for alimony. The court awarded \$3.50 per week in alimony and \$15.00 in attorney's fees.[97] Regarding Etta's conduct during her first trial, it was reported that she "showed no trepidation in opening the case."[98]

Consistent with their familial interests, Etta and her sister, Emma, were named by Maryland Legislators to be members of the Board of Directors of the United Patriotic Home for Protestant Orphan Children of Maryland, which was incorporated by the General Assembly in 1906 as a home designated for children committed to it by the state courts or by their parents.[99] There is surprisingly little other historic information on this Home for Orphans, and it is unclear how long the home was in existence, how many children it supported over the years, and the extent of Etta's role at the home over and above being a board member. Needless to say, her appointment to the board is yet another example of Etta's proclivity for both public service as well as her interest in helping the underrepresented and less fortunate.

In 1912, in an effort to ensure fair disposition for women in domestic disputes, Etta advocated the creation of a Court of Domestic Relations for divorce cases, in which female juries would be used for divorce cases in which the woman was the complainant.[100] She not only supported a specialized and independent court to adjudicate domestic problems, but also for ensuring that domestic matters be aired in an open forum.[101] In discussing the existing requirement of taking testimony by an examiner, Maddox stated:

[t]he present system of secrecy regarding divorces is to be condemned. Collusion and connivance between the two parties seeking divorce is too easily possible as things now exist. A great many cases in which divorces are now granted would never come into the divorce court at all if a hearing of the family difficulties in public was the price to be paid.[102]

Maddox advocated for the enactment of uniform divorce laws and more stringent limitations on a divorced persons' ability to remarry.[103] In so doing, she demonstrated that her underlying beliefs and principles surpassed her financial motivations; naturally, had her changes been implemented and divorces were harder to obtain, Etta's client-base would also have diminished. Regardless, it is clear that, after actively practicing domestic law for more than a decade, she remained fervent in her belief that the public airing of divorces (coupled with the threat of all-female juries) would do more to encourage (or humiliate) men into appropriate marital behavior. Her support of women and children in private practice dovetailed nicely with her larger and far more publicized efforts: that of woman's suffrage.

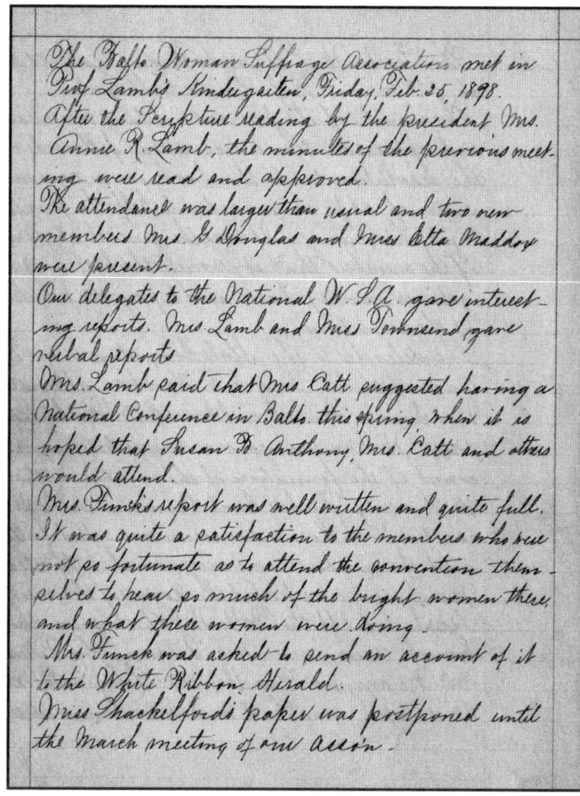

The Balto Woman Suffrage Association met in Prof Lamb's Kindergarten, Friday, Feb. 25, 1898.
After the Scripture reading by the president Mrs. Annie R. Lamb, the minutes of the previous meeting were read and approved.
The attendance was larger than usual and two new members Mrs. G. Douglas and Miss Etta Maddox were present.
Our delegates to the National W.S.A. gave interesting reports. Mrs. Lamb and Miss Townsend gave verbal reports
Mrs. Lamb said that Mrs Catt suggested having a National Conference in Balto. this spring when it is hoped that Susan B. Anthony, Mrs. Catt and others would attend.
Mrs. Funck's report was well written and quite full. It was quite a satisfaction to the members who were not so fortunate as to attend the convention themselves to hear so much of the bright women there, and what these women were doing.
Mrs. Funck was asked to send an account of it to the White Ribbon Herald.
Miss Shackelford's paper was postponed until the March meeting of our assn.

Baltimore Woman's Suffrage Association meeting minutes, February 25, 1898.

Courtesy of the Enoch Pratt Library.

Sisters for Suffragists: Etta and Emma Fight for the Ballot

Maddox's efforts to gain women's acceptance to the Bar were likely a stepping-stone to a larger goal: women's right to vote. The suffrage movement had begun to capture Etta's attention well before she ventured into the legal profession.[104] In fact, her extensive involvement with the suffragists (well prior to law school) may have been what propelled her into the legal field, harboring an intent to strike down one of the formidable barriers which precluded women from achieving equality. The fight for equality within the legal profession was a precursor to her fight for equality in the eyes of the law.

As mentioned, prior to her legal career, Etta and Emma Jane Maddox Funck were members of the Baltimore Woman's Suffrage Association. The minutes of the BWSA reflect that Etta first became a member on February 25, 1898. "The attendance was larger than usual and two new members, Mrs. G. Douglas and Miss Etta Maddox were present." Within two months, Etta Maddox had been elected to the Lecture Committee of the BWSA, along with her brother-in-law, Dr. J. William Funck, and her sister, Emma, was elected President.

In 1904, Etta and Emma helped found the Maryland Suffrage Association and remained deeply committed to the women's suffrage movement throughout their lives. The association's purpose went beyond obtaining the right to vote; it included efforts to obtain equal pay for equal service, the abolition of child labor, and the abolition of capital punishment, among other things.[105]

In fact, after enfranchisement in 1920, the Maryland Suffrage Association continued its pursuit of its other outstanding goals under the newly formed Women's Democratic Club of Baltimore.[106]

To forward the interests of women's suffrage, Maddox began to attend every session of the General Assembly in 1904.[107] Her persistence in this regard was unmistakable, as she vowed to attend every session in the future "until women are given what they believe to be their due in the matter of suffrage."[108] Etta's efforts were not limited to Maryland, however; she was also part of a delegation of women who pressured national lawmakers in Washington, DC, for passage of a law granting woman the right to vote.[109]

In 1910, Maddox drafted the first bill ever presented to the Maryland Legislature, which would have amended the State Constitution to give women the right to vote.[110] Etta's bill was drafted with the assistance and support of the Woman's Suffrage Association, and its success (or failure) was being followed by national organizations around the nation.[111] Etta presided at a hearing held by the Committee on Constitutional Amendments on February 14, 1910. With more than 400 women in attendance, the speakers that she convened included Dr. Anna Howard Shaw, President of the National Suffrage Association; Rev. Olympia Brown, of Wisconsin; Miss Bell Kearney, of Mississippi; and local leaders: John Grill, Esq.; Etta's sister, Emma (Maddox) Funck; her brother-in-law, Dr. J. William Funck; Rev. John Straton, Rev. Peter Aioslie, Dr. Flora Pollack, Mrs. Mary Haslup, Mrs. Mary Holton, and Mrs. Melva Coswell.[112] Each member of the delegation wore a button with the slogan, "Equal Rights for All."[113]

In stark contrast to the warm receptions that Maddox and her colleagues received when advocating the women's Bar Admission Bill, the Maryland Legislators showed little enthusiasm for the bill which would grant women the right to vote. It was reported that members of the Legislature Committee "seemed rather shy of appearing" and, in fact, only one of the members was seated when the meeting was called to order—and that member was Mr. Pairo, the delegate who assisted Etta in organizing the meeting and formally introduced the bill.[114] Having spotted another member in the Hall, Mr. Pairo called Mr. Benson to his seat, and ultimately two other men "mustered up the courage to join him."[115] Perhaps the sheer number of suffragist supporters (between 400 and 500) converging on the state capitol intimidated the State delegates; perhaps the national attention that this particular hearing had received caused the elected legislators to shy away from the limelight; or perhaps it was purely disinterest and/or opposition to the suffragist movement which resulted in a lackluster response by the Maryland Legislature to this historic hearing. Regardless of the reason, the suffragists' pleas were not widely or warmly received by the Maryland Legislators.

In spite of the lack of a wide or warm reception, the speakers organized by Maddox reportedly made very compelling and eloquent arguments. The proponents of women's right to vote took several different stances in an effort to achieve their end. Rev. Straton noted that there were 7,000,000 women wage-earners in the U.S. and, thus, in order to protect their rights, "they should be given equal political rights with male wage-earners."[116] In short, the argument was akin to the claim of "taxation without representation." Rev. Straton also maintained that women's ability to vote would "elevate our politics" due to her "splendid and pure influence."[117] Dr. Flora Polluck, of the Johns Hopkins University in Baltimore, argued that women should be permitted the right to vote so that the children of Maryland's citizenry had a voice. She stated that, under the current system, "the mother is powerless to protect her children, and the law does not."[118] Contrary to the usual tact of blurring distinctions between men and women to forward the equality argument, the advocates were highlighting the differences between men and women to forward the argument that a female voice is necessary in the political system.

Etta's sister, Emma Funck, said that women of all classes would either desire or benefit from the

Print of the State House, Annapolis.
Artist and date unknown. Courtesy of the Library of Congress.

Old Senate Chambers, Annapolis State House.
Photographer and date unknown. Courtesy of the Library of Congress.

responsibility borne upon them with the right to vote: "wealthy unemployed women need the ballot to give them responsibility, as well as women in active life, who should have it for their protection."[119] Even women who claim they did not want the right to vote "should be aroused to a sense of responsibility."[120] Thus, Mrs. Funck took the position that the right to the ballot, in and of itself, would make women better citizens. Rev. Peter Ainelle, a longtime supporter of the suffrage movement, also touted the ability of women to elevate politics through their participation: "in the States where woman suffrage now prevails, humane legislation has greatly increased and has lifted those States far above those in which male suffrage alone prevails."[121] Rev. Anna Shaw reiterated that women's entrance in the workforce demanded admission to the ballot and noted that "the old poetic chivalric ideas about the sex" no longer applied in twentieth-century Maryland.[122] Unfortunately, despite the eloquent speeches and multi-faceted arguments, the response of the General Assembly's Committee on Constitutional Amendments was to table the matter, in a sixty-one to eighteen vote.[123]

Two years later, in 1912, the various state suffrage associations joined in requesting a constitutional amendment, which would permit women the right to vote. Similar to the efforts of 1910, hearings were held, and, similar to the 1910 result, the suffragists lacked the votes.[124]

In 1916, Etta and her sister, Emma, lobbied again for a state constitutional amendment for full suffrage for women, and again, the bill failed to pass.[125] An interesting insight into Etta's strong-willed personality or, perhaps, her frustration with the lack of progress during this time period is revealed in a confrontation she had with Samuel Brown, as reported by *The Baltimore Sun* on January 22, 1916.[126] The altercation involved Etta and other suffragists purportedly calling the Legislators "a lot of mossbacks." Etta denied referring to the Legislators, generally, as mossbacks, but instead specifically "asked Delegate Brown if he preferred to be regarded as a mossback or an intelligent man, and left the decision of that matter entirely to him."[127]

The dialogue between the two was recited in *The Baltimore Sun* and purportedly went as follows:

> "We came here expecting to find a body of intelligent men,...but I must say you are a bunch of mossbacks. Now, Mr. Brown, are you a mossback or an intelligent man?" asked Etta.

"I'm a legislator, madam, and I'm down here representing the people in my county," replied Delegate Brown.

"How about the women: Are you representing them?" asked Etta.

"I certainly am," answered Mr. Brown, "but the women in my county have something else to do besides run around the State like some women I know."

Etta became indignant, "I would have you know, Mr. Brown, that we are the busiest women in the State of Maryland."

Delegate Brown retorted, "Heaven knows that's true...and Heaven help the men you've got! And don't think, madam, that you can come down here and bullyrag us into suffrage. That isn't the way to do it."

To which Etta responded, turning to her colleague, "Come along, Ella, there's another mossback in the House."[128]

In the article covering this altercation, Maddox was never identified by name; rather, she was described as "an elderly suffragist dressed in black."[129] While Etta did not object to being described as "elderly," she did take issue with being described as the "woman in black."[130] Etta noted that her name was fairly well-known, and, therefore, she preferred that her name be used when referring to her actions.[131] She believed that the "woman in black" reference was both discourteous and disrespectful, to her and to her cause. She explained:

> We who believe that women are entitled to the right of suffrage...and who are trying to convince the members of the Legislature that they ought to give it to us are in Annapolis on serious business. We are serious and earnest women, working for a cause we believe to be right and just. We do not like being made objects of ridicule. Many men do not agree with us and we find no fault with them for that, if their objection to woman suffrage is based on thought and honest consideration of the subject. But we do object to any legislator refusing to consider the subject, which is being seriously considered by most of the civilized nations of the world.
>
> Those men at Annapolis represent us as they represent others in their counties and districts, and we feel that we have a right to expect them to think of and to consider honestly the measures we submit to them. That is all we ask. We try to convince them that we are asking only those things that are right and to which we are entitled, but we find no fault with them if, after honestly thinking over the matter, they cannot accept our point of view. Men like Delegate Brown, who seems to have closed his mind entirely upon the subject, who will not even think about it, we do not hope to convince and we let them alone. Had I known the manner of man he was I should not have wasted his time or mine in discussing the manner with him. But, at least, I expected from him what I and others who are working with me have received from other members of the Legislature—courtesy and a respectful hearing for an important matter, presented in a perfectly courteous and respectful manner.[132]

As discussed further, below, women ultimately won the right to vote in Maryland not through their own representatives in the Legislature but rather through the ratification of the Nineteenth Amendment on a national level by other, more progressive states. The Nineteenth Amendment to the U.S. Constitution was ratified in 1920 by thirty-six states, but, notably, Maryland was not one of them.[133] This fact reflects both the significant obstinacy that Etta faced in the Maryland Legislature on the issue of suffrage and the remarkable persistence she exhibited in continuing to pursue equality despite repeated rejection.

Sisters for Suffrage: The Influence of Emma Jane

Before venturing from the suffragist movement, a brief examination of the person who was likely one of the greatest (if not the greatest) influences on Maddox is warranted. Familial influence, as a whole, undoubtedly impacted Etta's quest to be recognized formally by and accepted into the legal profession. Squire Maddox's role as a magistrate not only provided Etta with a firsthand look into the legal profession, but also provided Etta's family with the means to educate the three daughters at good schools and provide them the opportunity to be independent (two of the three never married) as well as the time to commit to political causes. Etta's sister, Emma Jane Funck, however, clearly had the greatest impact on Etta's direction in life and, in particular, her political activism.

As mentioned above, Etta was the youngest of three sisters. Margaret Ann, a school teacher, was the eldest, but Etta was particularly close with, and influenced by, Emma Jane Funck.[134] Like Etta, Emma graduated from Eastern High School in Baltimore and attended the Peabody Conservatory of Music. She, too, was an accomplished vocalist but did not make this her career.[135] Emma married Dr. J. William Funck who, like his wife, became an active campaigner for the women's suffrage movement.[136] Emma Jane worked tirelessly for the suffrage movement in Maryland for most of her life. She was President of the Baltimore Suffrage Club and Maryland Suffrage Association for more than thirty years.[137] In fact, Emma's tenacity and dedication are often credited for keeping the women's suffrage movement alive during periods of waning interest and increasing despondency.[138]

Even in the aftermath of achieving the right to vote, there was no respite for Emma Maddox: her next mission became to encourage women to utilize the right for which she and others so diligently fought.[139] After enfranchisement, Emma organized the Maryland Federation of Republican Women in 1921 and continued her efforts to improve women's rights and opportunities within the state.[140] Emma rose in the ranks of the Republican Party, becoming President of the Baltimore Republican Club. She ran for public office twice but was never elected.[141] She died in March 1940, seven years after the death of her sister, Etta.

Meanwhile, after ratification, Etta Maddox became a founding member of the Women's Democratic Club of Baltimore, rising to the chairman of the advisory board by the time of her death in 1933.[142] While ultimately associating themselves with different political parties, the sisters remained very close, sharing and thriving in political activism with the ultimate goal—equality for women on all fronts—being the centerpiece to both their missions.

It would be unfair to state that Etta Maddox followed in her sister's footsteps, as Etta was clearly a woman to be reckoned with in her own right; and, together these two remarkable sisters made significant and historical achievements which positively impacted women in Maryland. Etta and Emma likely influenced and inspired each other to continue with their lifelong fight for women's equality. Thus, it is more accurate to state that they walked side-by-side during these campaigns and were consummate sources of support for one another.

Etta Maddox: Honored in Life and after Death

Etta Maddox died on February 19, 1933, in the home of her sister, Emma.[143] Etta's health was reportedly failing over the previous five years, but, seven weeks prior to her passing, she was stricken with a serious illness.[144] Despite being a lawyer responsible for handling her family's legal and real estate affairs, Etta died intestate, with no direct descendants.[145] Much of her property was held jointly with Emma, who was both the sole heir and administrator of her estate.[146] Many people, representing the various facets of Etta's life and accomplishments, attended her funeral to pay their respects to the brilliant musician, dedicated suffragist, political activist, and Maryland's first female lawyer. Newspapers of the day summarized her life's achievements as follows: instrumental in having Maryland law changed to permit women to practice law, the first woman lawyer in Maryland, consistently working for woman's rights, co-founder of the first suffrage body in the state, and author of the first suffrage bill in the state, among others.[147]

In the annual memorial proceedings to honor deceased members of the Bar, the president of the Bar Association of Baltimore City (of which Etta was never a member) moved for the Supreme Bench of Baltimore City to accept a number of biographies, including that of Etta Maddox, written by Francis L. Mooney.[148] Mr. Mooney summarized Etta's notable achievements and concluded by noting that, "with her death, Maryland's women suffered the loss of a great leader."[149]

Etta is buried in Greenmount Cemetery in Baltimore. Her tombstone features the scales of justice and the following inscription:

> Maryland's First Woman Lawyer
> Etta Haynie Maddox
> Died February 19, 1933
> Graduated in Law in 1900
> Admitted to Practice Law in the
> State of Maryland in 1902
> And the District Courts of the
> United States in 1911[150]

The Women's Bar Association of Maryland posthumously honored Etta Maddox's accomplishments, in 1950, by presenting her portrait to the Women's Bar.[151] The Association deemed Etta the patron saint of women lawyers in Maryland and described her as the "most militant of suffragists," "pioneering" and "indomitable," all of which befit Etta's character and accomplishments.[152] Finally, in 2003, 101 years after her admission to the Maryland Bar, Etta Maddox was inducted into the Maryland Women's Hall of Fame.[153]

Maddox's accomplishments were significant not only for Maryland's women lawyers, but for all of Maryland's women. With this in mind, I turn to some of the historical underpinnings that will place her achievements in a historical context.

Historical Context: Maryland—A State of Firsts or Lasts?

As Etta Maddox herself astutely noted, while Maryland can boast that it provided the U.S. with its first female attorney in Margaret Brent, it was one of the last of the states to admit women formally to the Bar. The natural questions are: "Why? And to what can Maryland's lag be attributed?" Many plausible theories come to mind: perhaps this delay can be explained by the state's eastern location, which rested in Old-World Victorian principles of the feminine gender's role, contrary to the more liberal (or liberating) views of the Western states; perhaps the delay can be explained by the lack of formal education open to women wanting to enter the legal profession in Maryland; perhaps the reign of the traditional Old Guard Democrats (former Confederates) in Maryland stifled progressive thought about women's rights; perhaps the perceived ties between the suffrage movement and bar admission resulted in less support for the latter, due to fear of the former; perhaps the socio-political environment in Maryland created obstacles for the advancement of women; or perhaps Maryland simply needed someone with the perseverance, determination, and tenacity of Etta Maddox to open the doors of the legal profession to women. More likely than not, each of the above factors coalesced to preclude women from formally entering the legal profession until Etta overcame the barriers and took her place in history.

The aforementioned factors will be discussed further, but, not unexpectedly, no one explanation will be agreed upon by all. Many authors have explored the timing of women's formal admission to the legal profession, both in the U.S. and abroad. As Mary Jane Mossman concluded in her comparative study on women lawyers, "the history of the first woman lawyers seems to require attention not only to the intersection of gender and the legal professionalism but also to the circumstances of their individual lives."[154] Mossman herself engaged in a detailed analysis of the timing of women's admission into the legal profession throughout Europe but, ultimately and albeit reluctantly, concluded that "individual circumstances and aspirations of the women themselves" provided the best explanation for that particular woman's achievement at that particular time.[155] Thus, while the socio-political ideals of the time may help provide the context in which Maddox's achievements were accomplished, the circumstances and personal goals of the individual woman account for much of the achievement.

A Belgian barrister, Louis Frank, who was assisting a woman, Jeanne Chauvin, with her application to admission to the Paris Bar, requested information about women lawyers in the U.S. to use as precedent to support Chauvin's admission.[156] Attorney Mary Greene summarized the American women's experience in 1896 as follows:

> While prejudice still prevails, especially in the States bordering upon the Atlantic, it grows less, as women continue to prove their ability to perform the work, and to master the difficulties incident to the comprehension of legal principles and their application to actual practice. The gentlemen of the bench and bar have been almost uniformly courteous and helpful. In the 15 States of the Union that do not yet admit women, their absence from the bar is simply due to the fact that no women have ever yet applied for admission there...[157]

Accordingly, the prevailing thought appeared to be that women who attempted to achieve bar admission would ultimately acquire it. Six years before Etta's admission, *Leslie's Illustrated Weekly* stated: "The prejudice and opposition which so long obstructed [women's] progress are rapidly disappearing. Women are now being received and recognized by their brother member of the profession...."[158]

Etta Maddox expressed a similar opinion about Maryland's position on women in the Bar. After graduating from law school and discussing her desires to practice law with a local newspaper, she was quoted as stating the following: "A great many of the men here do not realize that women have been admitted to the Bar in so many States. When I told a lawyer in town the other day that women were allowed to practice law in New York, in Pennsylvania and in many of the other Eastern States, he said 'Why, I thought they were only allowed to do it out on the prairies.'"[159] Etta's working assumption, therefore, was that the Maryland Legislature did not wish to exclude women from practicing law; rather, it merely "had not given any thought to opening the field to women."[160] Perhaps Etta's supposition was correct, and Marylanders simply didn't seriously entertain the notion that non-prairie woman may also desire to practice law. Nevertheless, in the eternal debate as to whether history makes the man or a man makes the history—or, in this case, history makes the woman or a woman makes the history—we cannot ignore the influence of socio-political surroundings.

Location and Law School: Hindrances for Women in Maryland?

At the time Etta Maddox graduated from law school, there were thirty-seven states in which women could be admitted to the Bar.[161] Some of those states had admitted woman to the Bar without the passage of additional special statutes; notably, some of those states had statutes which utilized the male pronoun—"he," "his," and "him,"—which formed one of the major grounds upon which the Court of Appeals of Maryland relied in rejecting Etta's plea for admission.[162]

Other states required the passage of special statutes, like the one ultimately passed in Maryland, to admit women to the Bar.[163] The states that languished behind Maryland in admitting women to the Bar were North Dakota (1905), Alabama (1907), Tennessee (1907), Texas (1910), Mississippi (1914), Vermont (1914), Georgia (1916), South Carolina (1918), Rhode Island (1920), Delaware (1923), and Alaska (1950).[164] It is noteworthy that, of the eleven states that followed Maryland's first admission of women to the Bar, all but three were Eastern states.

As discussed in the preceding chapter, while one might instinctively believe that women raised in the more developed and industrialized Eastern cities would have greater professional opportunities than those of the less-developed territories in the trans-Mississippi West, the opposite proved to be true. In reality, the shortage of resources in the Western frontier necessitated that women step into the roles that may have been traditionally dominated by men. As a result, this "contributed to a more balanced view of women and their abilities than existed back East.... the myth that [women] were faint-hearted and in need of special protection could not be perpetuated on the frontier."[165]

Whether due to a broader perception of equality or to limited financial resources, the academic systems in the West differed from the East in a pivotal manner: they were, at the outset, largely coeducational.[166] Accordingly, women had far better opportunities to enter the legal profession in the West.[167] Interestingly, in some Western states, as prosperity grew, the tolerance for women's participation in traditionally male professions diminished.[168] One explanation is that, with prosperity and urbanization, came a more rigid class system which, in turn, limited a woman's opportunities. Ironically, neither the lower working class nor the extreme upper class would typically cultivate aspiring female attorneys. Working-class women were restrained by economic demands and the consummate need to work, and upper-class women were restrained by the imposition of "Victorian notions of femininity."[169] Given that "Victorian notions of femininity" were far more prevalent in Eastern states, these states, not surprisingly, were more likely to lag behind Western states with respect to opening the legal profession to women. In short, the most industrialized areas created a more inherently rigid class system, which appears to have limited women's opportunities and stifled their motivations.

During the 1870s, around the time Etta Maddox was completing her high school education and musical training at the Peabody Conservatory, thirteen jurisdictions had admitted women to practice law, six by statute and seven by court approval. Notably, all of these jurisdictions were Midwestern and Western states, with the exception of the District of Columbia and North Carolina.[170] The availability of free public school education, coupled with industrialization during the 1880s and 1890s, however, resulted in a palpable shift in thought and opportunity for those women seeking education in the legal profession.[171]

When discussing the availability of law school education, it is important to recognize that, until the late nineteenth century, the majority of lawyers were informally trained through apprenticeships with local active attorneys.[172] Apprenticeships remained the primary method of entering the legal profession until "law schools began to emerge as the more rigorous, formal and prestigious path into the profession" in the late 1800s.[173] Thus, it is difficult to attribute the timing of women's bar admissions entirely to the acceptance of women in law school, given that law school was not the primary means by which any citizen became a lawyer. Many aspiring women lawyers with family connections to the legal profession apprenticed in an effort to qualify for admission to the Bar. In 1890, more than half of married women lawyers were married to lawyers, and many single women came from families with members who were lawyers.[174]

While logic would dictate that a state willing to admit women into law school should be equally willing to admit women to the Bar, this equation did not apply globally. For example, South Carolina admitted its first woman into law school in 1890 but did not admit women to the Bar until twenty-eight years later, in 1918.[175] By contrast, its sister state, North Carolina, admitted the first woman, Tabitha Ann Holton, to its Bar in 1878.[176] Mrs. Holton did not attend a law school; rather, she studied law on her own and under the tutelage of her father and was admitted to practice by motion.[177] Thus, while law schools' decision to open doors to women removed one hurdle, the fight to be permitted to practice law in each state was a separate obstacle.

Opportunities for women in legal education expanded during the early twentieth century, and, certainly with the advent of World War I—coeducation accelerated as male enrollments declined.[178] Etta Maddox's enrollment in law school occurred at a time when acceptance of women was still novel: only 1,010 women in the nation were lawyers, according to the 1900 (Twelfth) Census.[179] It wasn't until 1920 that most law schools were open to women, which was the primary factor in the rapid increase of women lawyers in subsequent years.[180]

As discussed in the preceding chapter, women lawyers were met with far more societal resistance than were women doctors. In fact, the number of women doctors rose from 2,423 in 1880 to more than 7,000 by 1900, approximately seven times the number of women lawyers.[181] Societal stereotypes may have made the transition for women into the health-care profession easier. Women doctors were seen as a natural extension of women's nurturing roles as mother and caregiver; additionally, their necessity could be justified as protecting feminine modesty by treating women patients.[182] In contrast, the legal profession was perceived as one "that demanded not only cold objectivity and the mastery of facts, but also cunning, toughness, and the ability to deal with a sordid world."[183] Femininity and the legal profession simply did not merge as easily as femininity and the health-care profession.[184]

The Link between Bar Admission and the Ballot

Women's participation in a wider range of professions, particularly in the Western states, permitted women to substantiate their need and ability to participate in government and political office, specifically with reference to the right to vote. Women's efforts to gain acceptance in the legal profession, in particular, appears to have preceded or, at a minimum, coincided with women's fight to obtain the right to vote. In fact, the widespread recognition of this association propelled the initial trepidation about bar admission by male decision-makers of the time; that is, men feared that permitting women to practice law would lead to their right to the ballot.

The link between female lawyers and suffragists is seen as far back as the nation's first female attorney, Margaret Brent, who is discussed in detail in the preceding chapter. In fact, Brent is touted as being one of the first women's suffragists, striving to acquire the right to vote in 1648 before the Maryland General Assembly.[185] Like Brent, Etta Maddox was an enduring suffragist who persistently fought to obtain the right to vote for women and was a pivotal figure in the ultimate realization of that goal for Maryland's women. These early Portias used their status and experience as attorneys to further assert their right to vote. Given that women's efforts to obtain admission to the Bar were closely tied to the women's suffragist movement and given that Etta Maddox's lifelong passion was to obtain the right to vote for Maryland women, appreciating this connection is important.

Perhaps women who believed in equality and wanted to fight for equality in the political arena believed that their voice would be strengthened with a law degree, or perhaps one's study of the law breeds the understanding and significance of equality under the law. Regardless of which begets which, the suggested link between Etta's passion for the suffragist movement and her quest to obtain the right to practice law is not singular to her. Many historians agree that the admission of women to the Bar was inextricably linked to the struggle to achieve the woman's right to vote.[186] In fact, the perceived association between bar admission and the ballot drove legislators and judges alike to be wary of women who wanted to practice law for fear that one would result in the other. The inverse of this was also true: some judges, who were opposed to admitting females to the Bar, utilized the women's inability to vote, hold public office, and sit as jurors as a basis for their opposition, the theory being that lawyers were officers of the court; accordingly, women, who could not vote or participate in politics, were unfit to be officers of the court.[187]

Cognizant of this pervasive viewpoint or fear within the legal field, the attorney who represented Myra Bradwell in the U.S. Supreme Court, Matthew Carpenter, was questioned about the relationship between the right to practice law and the right to vote. In an effort to downplay any perceived link between the two, "to allay fears of the justices," Mr. Carpenter took the position that the right to vote was not a privilege or immunity (as was the practice of law); rather, it was a political right.[188] In the aftermath of *Bradwell*, state court judges began to rely upon the inability of women to participate in politics as a basis to support their holdings that women were unable to practice law.[189] Thus, women's exclusion from political and judicial office was seen as tied to their preclusion from being deemed officers of the court.

In fact, some have argued that the aspiring women lawyers who attempted to diminish any connection between bar admission and the ballot—as was done in *Bradwell*—"constrained broader reform efforts to achieve the franchise for all women."[190] By keeping singularly focused on acquiring bar admission and casting aside (even for arguments sake) any link between the practice of law and the right to vote, women's suffrage may have been impeded. It would be inaccurate, however, to hold culpable the women lawyers who successfully obtained bar admission for delaying the right to vote. While both issues fell within the broad umbrella of women's equality under the law—and, thus, were often dual missions of women's activists groups during the late-nineteenth and early-twentieth centuries—the right to vote and the right to engage in a particular occupation were distinct matters requiring distinct legal considerations. That a woman underscored the distinction in her quest to gain admission was unlikely to have set back the suffragist movement, as some intimate.[191] To the contrary, by obtaining admission into a male-dominated field, women began to tear down the barriers created by years of (mis)perceptions of the limitations on women's ability to understand, analyze, and even practice law, which, in turn, forwarded the suffragists' interests in gaining equality under the law. To proffer that women would have obtained the ballot sooner, if only aspiring women lawyers had argued that the right to bar admission and the right to the ballot were indistinguishable, supposes that the judiciary and legislators of the time would be more accepting of blanket equality for women than a piecemeal acquisition of equality.

Certainly, with respect to Maryland, it is highly unlikely that the ballot would have been achieved any sooner than it was: Maryland was one of the last states to ratify the Nineteenth Amendment. Meanwhile, Maddox's struggle to obtain admission to the Bar was met with far less resistance than her struggle to obtain the ballot. As discussed above, Etta's appearance before the Legislature in 1902 was met with a warm reception and an overwhelming vote in favor of women's acceptance to the Bar. Conversely, Etta's appearances before the Legislature on the issue of the ballot were neither warmly received nor widely accepted, and Etta faced defeat each and every time the ballot issue came to a vote. In reality, if Etta had taken the position that the two were co-existing inseparable rights, then women's bar admission may have taken even longer to obtain.

There is no question that the movement to achieve formal acceptance to practice law was inextricably tied to the women's rights movement overall; women, however, universally waged these battles on an independent basis. In fact, although not centrally organized, lawsuits were filed in at least seventeen states between 1869 and 1901 by women in an effort to be admitted to their respective state bar.[192] Meanwhile, several national organizations, dating as far back as the early 1800s, advocated for local, state, and national laws that would permit women the right to vote.[193] These activists concentrated on the single issue of suffrage and went directly to the lawmakers to educate and persuade them to support the goal of suffrage. Thus, while the principles of equality saturated both, the suffrage movement and quest for bar admission were unique and independent battles.[194]

Others have theorized that women lawyers, after obtaining bar admission and practicing law, were more apt to define themselves as professionals and less likely to relate to nonprofessional women, thereby driving a wedge in the suffragist movement, which often had overwhelming support among nonprofessionals.[195] Again, the notion that the admission of women lawyers resulted in negative sequelae for the suffrage movement seems unfounded. There were, admittedly, many women lawyers who wanted to enter the profession for one singular purpose: to be lawyers. Their goals and ambitions never went beyond their desire to practice law.[196] While many women lawyers may not have actively engaged in the suffragist movement, they were nevertheless advancing the women's movement generally. By engaging in a successful legal practice, they were helping forward women's efforts to obtain equality, even as they demonstrated that women's abilities went beyond the delicacy and gentle graces of her sex and that a woman could be as successful as a man in the field of law. While not vocal activists, as was Etta, these women quietly broke down barriers in their day-to-day practice of law. Thus, status as a woman lawyer rendered them an exceptional (but quiet) force for change at that time.[197]

Without question, the interplay between suffrage and bar admission was a recognized concept—and reared itself largely when naysayers to the bar admission wanted a basis for their denial of the same. The interplay was certainly relevant to Etta Maddox's mission: she clearly believed that the structural barriers to the *practice* of law needed to be demolished before the ideological barriers pertaining to *equal treatment* of women under the law could be met.

Maryland Also Lags in Granting Women the Right to Vote

Maddox's fight to obtain bar admission in Maryland, while historic, lasted only a year. Her fight to obtain the vote, however, lasted her lifetime (and beyond). In spite of Etta's (and others') persistent and dedicated efforts over several decades, the suffragists were unsuccessful in convincing the Maryland Legislature to pass a constitutional amendment to secure the right to vote. Even when forced to vote on the issue on a national level, Maryland was in the minority of states that rejected the constitutional amendment.[198] In fact, while the Nineteenth Amendment was ratified nationally with the requisite thirty-six states, Etta did not live to see Maryland ratify the Nineteenth Amendment. Maryland was one of twelve states that opposed ratification, which is remarkably similar to its status as being one of the last thirteen states to admit women to the Bar.[199]

Maryland lagged in establishing equal access to both the legal profession and the ballot for women. That similarity aside, there were likely very different reasons for the delay in opening the legal profession to women versus the downright refusal to grant women the right to vote. With respect to the former, the General Assembly demonstrated a willingness to open the doors to women in the legal profession when first approached with such a bill by Etta and her colleagues in 1902. By all media accounts and by calculation of the vote itself, bar admission did not appear to be an extraordinarily controversial issue in the Maryland Legislature, which in no way diminishes Etta's role in achieving the same. While Maryland certainly lagged behind other states in admitting women to the Bar, when first presented the legislative option to do so, the bills passed quite easily.

By contrast, there was uniform resistance in Maryland against a women's right to vote for several decades after Etta's conquest of the bar admission.

In the following chapter, Jane Murphy explores in greater detail the Progressive Era within which Maryland's socio-political and economic circumstances may have contributed to the obstructionist attitude fostered by many of the General Assembly toward women's suffrage. Two factors stand out in relation to Maddox's success on the bar admission front and disappointing failure on the ballot front: First, when Etta happened to present her Bar Admission Bill to the General Assembly in 1902, it was comprised of very progressive-minded delegates. In fact, after the 1896 elections there was a Republican majority in the General Assembly, which led to the passing of a myriad of progressive legislation during that session.[200] Even when the Democrats regained control during the early 1900s, it was only by a slim margin, and the Democrats who were elected to office were more reform-minded.[201] Delegate Moses, who introduced Etta's bill on bar admission and chaired the hearing on the bill, was elected in 1899 and was just such a reformist Democrat.[202] Thus, the Reformers made several advances in 1902 session, including but not limited to granting women the right to practice law.[203]

To place Maryland's politics in context, unlike many of the states to its south, Maryland was not a one-party state in the wake of the Civil War. Maryland was largely comprised of Democrats, known as "Old Guard Democrats," who were supported by Marylanders who favored the South during the Civil War, as well as urban workers, owners of utilities, and other businesses that relied heavily on government contracts.[204] In fact, the head of Maryland's Democratic organization, Senator Arthur Gorman, and Baltimore City's "boss," Isaac F. Rasin, the head of the largest urban organization, worked closely together to assure their continued power and often used illegal means to do so.[205] It was the discovery of abuses that gave Maryland's Republican Party the opportunity to gain control. Maryland's Republican Party included those who had favored the Union during the Civil War, businessmen, and most blacks who voted with the party of Lincoln.[206] The Republicans were the most strongly associated with reform movement at that time, although some "reform Democrats" also supported what later developed into the Progressive movement.[207] In 1895, the Reform Republicans swept elections across the state, including the gubernatorial election won by Republican Lloyd Lowndes.[208]

It was during this time, when the Reformers occupied leadership roles in the state government, that the bill permitting women's admission to the Bar was considered and passed. Notably, when the Democrats regained the majority in 1903, progressive reforms temporarily ceased.[209] To a certain degree, therefore, the timing of Maddox's approach to bar admission was beneficial.

There was likely a more rudimentary force at play, however, wherein the General Assembly demonstrated an acceptance of women in the legal profession but steadfast resistance to women's suffrage: power. Permitting women the ability to practice law did not impact the control that white men had over the state of affairs in Maryland on political, social, and economic fronts. The Democrats in control of the General Assembly during the bulk of Etta's most aggressive suffragist efforts were "old South" Democrats whose opposition to women's suffrage was not only rooted in sexism, but also in racism. Notably, just as Maryland rejected the Nineteenth Amendment, Maryland had also been one of the few states to fail to ratify the Fifteenth Amendment, which gave African Americans the right to vote, fifty years earlier in 1870. Many theorize that the opposition to women obtaining the ballot was rooted in the fear of more than doubling the black-Republican vote (given that most blacks at that time voted Republican).[210] Granting all women the right to vote would substantially shift the power in state politics to the progressive Republicans, an idea loathed by the Democrats.[211]

Maddox's successful pursuit of bar admission—while a pivotal step in the women's rights movement—did not threaten those in power, Republican or Democrat alike. As one of Etta's speakers explained at the Senate hearing on bar admission: "if the people don't want women lawyers, they will get no practice. All women are asking for is the opportunity to use the abilities they have to promote right and justice."[212] Granting women the ability to practice law did not, by itself, guarantee their success at the practice of law and, more significantly, permitting women to practice law did not disturb the balance of power for elected officials as the right to ballot would threaten to do. Accordingly, the fear of relinquishing power (by those in power) may be one of the primary distinguishing factors between Maddox's triumphant quest to open the state's courtroom doors to women attorneys and her unsuccessful lifelong struggle for women's suffrage.

Conclusion

Etta Maddox was a fighter; she demonstrated this quality not only in her fight for admission to the Bar, which was successful, but especially in the decades of battles she initiated and led on behalf of women and their right to vote. Perseverance that is met with success is rewarding, and Etta's quest to obtain admission to the Bar was certainly remarkable. Perseverance in the face of repeated defeat, however, is the definition of tenacity, and Etta's resolve that all women should be treated equally never wavered in spite of lifelong defeats on the suffrage front. Women of Maryland, lawyers and nonlawyers alike, benefitted from her unwavering determination to make life better for women. Etta challenged prevailing thought, she challenged standing law, and she fought for both equality of opportunity in the practice of law and for equality of women in the eyes of the law.

Etta Maddox unabashedly defied the sentiment reflected in a concurring opinion by Justice Bradley, of the U.S. Supreme Court, that "the natural and proper timidity and delicacy which belongs to the female sex evidently unfits it for many of the occupations of civil life.... The paramount destiny and mission of woman are to fulfill the noble and benign offices of wife and mother."[213] She was neither timid nor delicate in her struggles to achieve equality for women. And, certainly, we are eternally grateful that Etta's paramount destiny or mission was to pursue and obtain equality for women in Maryland. Her willingness to act on behalf of all women is clear in her actions and succinctly summarized by her statement, "I am willing to make the effort, not only for myself, but for women who may wish to take up the same profession."[214]

CHAPTER THREE:

The Role of Political and Social Movements on Women's Entry into the Legal Profession in Maryland, 1902–1920

Jane C. Murphy

Introduction

The rise of women in the legal profession in Maryland was shaped by a wide range of factors, including national, state, and local political and social movements. As one scholar has noted, "[W]omen's lives are complex and... region, period, personality, and circumstance crucially influence what a subject is able to make of herself."[1] In this chapter, I explore how those circumstances—personal and political—influenced the first group of eight women admitted to the Maryland Bar between 1902 and 1920. These women—Etta Maddox, Anna Grace Kennedy, Emilie Doetsch, Marie Elizabeth Kirk Coles, Mary Virginia Meushaw, Helen F. Hill, Emily Dashiell, and Grace Gerber—constituted the "first wave" of women admittees (see Appendix A).[2] They were admitted in a period that spanned the turn of the twentieth century through the end of World War I and corresponded with the reform movements of the Progressive Era in the United States.

The stories of these women are linked with the broader story of these movements, which brought together a coalition of business leaders, philanthropists, social workers, and lawyers who sought to reform government and change and broaden its role. The story of Etta Maddox, told in the previous chapter, demonstrates that the circumstances leading to a woman's decision to become a lawyer during this era and the struggles that followed are complex and, in many ways, unique. But each of these women's stories have common elements, and all were shaped by the Progressive Era in Maryland.

The Progressive Era began as a response to the social dislocation that occurred in Baltimore and urban areas around the nation, as people moved from rural to urban areas and new waves of immigrants settled in America's cities at the end of the nineteenth century. Along with the larger population, Baltimore experienced increased crime, poverty, and family dysfunction. Progressives believed that the government, if honest and efficient, could be a force for positive social change to respond to these problems. They formed coalitions to improve the fairness of elections and expose political corruption. Wanting to participate in elections and in a government no longer limited by massive corruption, many of the first women, particularly Etta Maddox, and Emilie Doetsch, worked to obtain women's right to vote.[3] Emily Dashiell became involved in government and the political process by working to change laws to provide greater protection for women and children.[4] Others, such as Anna Grace Kennedy and Helen Hill, moved from the private to public sphere by engaging in philanthropy to improve health care or education.[5]

After briefly summarizing the national context for the Progressive Era, I examine how this period unfolded in Maryland and the ways in which these and related movements influenced this first group of eight women admitted to the Maryland Bar during this period. What role did the Progressive Era movements and the women who were involved in them play in encouraging this group to seek admission to the Bar? How did the social and political environment affect post-admission career choices for these pioneers?

By exploring the conditions that gave rise to Maryland's first women lawyers, this chapter will also continue the discussion from Chapter Two about why Maryland was among the later states to admit women to the Bar. The jurisprudence and changing statutory landscape tell part of the story, but the legal reforms did not occur in a vacuum. The broader social and political context provides a greater understanding about why Maryland lagged behind other states in both the removal of barriers and the numbers of women admitted following that removal.

A number of social historians have lamented the lack of scholarship examining the social conditions that provided the context for the entry of women into the professions.[6] Others have encouraged scholars to challenge the traditional approach of analyzing legal doctrines to chart the course of women's rise in the legal profession and instead examine "the omitted stories of ordinary people, and in particular, the experiences of women, to make sense of the meanings of social and legal patterns in the lives of people affected by them and, in turn, creating or resisting them."[7] In this chapter, I seek to fill that gap and meet that challenge for one group of women lawyers in Maryland.

The Rise of the Progressive Era in the U.S. and Maryland

The National Movement

At the end of the Civil War in 1865, the U.S. population was still largely rural and the economy largely agricultural. By the 1890s, the nation was profoundly altered. Although the present geographic boundaries of the country were established by purchases made by the mid-nineteenth century, the population doubled between 1860 and 1890.[8] The growth was particularly rapid in urban areas such as Baltimore. While only twenty-one cities had populations of more than 50,000 in 1870, that number had increased to forty-four cities by 1890, with the ten most populous American cities containing 250,000 to 1,000,000 people.[9] Baltimore, in 1890, ranked seventh with 434,439 people, ahead of San Francisco at eighth and behind Boston at sixth. This population growth, particularly in the cities, was fueled by a new wave of immigrants coming to the U.S. from southern and eastern Europe, particularly Italians, Poles, and Russians. Beginning about 1910, the so-called "Great Migration" of African Americans from the rural South

"Lunch counter, signs in different languages. Immigrants at Locust Point."

Photographer and date unknown. Courtesy of the Maryland Historical Society.

"A street full of Baltimore immigrants lined up and ready to start for the country to the berry farms. Wolfe Street, near Canton Avenue, Baltimore, Maryland."

Photograph attributed to Lewis Wickes Hine, 1910. Courtesy of the Library of Congress and the Maryland Child Labor Committee.

Detail of "Delegation of Maryland Women at Capitol on Prohibition Hearing, 1926."

Photograph attributed to the National Photo Company. Courtesy of the Library of Congress.

to the Northern cities added to the growth and diversity of American cities during this period.[10]

This move to the cities was prompted, in large part, by the changing economy.[11] One historian described the American economic growth between 1860 and 1890 as "rapid, dramatic, and unprecedented," making the U.S. an "industrial giant."[12] With this transformation came a wide array of social problems. While the growing economy had raised the standard of living for many Americans, the gap between the rich and the poor became greater and more visible during this period. Journalists and others began to expose the dismal living conditions of poor, unskilled factory workers, and their families in urban areas.[13] Poor housing in urban tenements, high infant mortality and disease, and bad working conditions were straining the limited public and private services of that time. State and local governments, largely controlled by party bosses who ran political machines, were unable to effectively respond. The Progressive Movement brought together a range of people from the spheres of business, politics, and social welfare who shared a common interest in reforming government so that it could address these social problems.

Women played a central role in many of the Progressive Era's movements. The public leadership roles many women assumed were considered by many to be a departure from the more private role of women throughout the nineteenth century, when the roles of men and women were sharply divided. As noted in Chapter One, the ideology of "separate spheres" was reflected in both legal and social norms.[14] It emphasized the separation of work and home and assigned clearly differentiated roles to women and men; men occupied the public realm of work and politics, while women were the central actors in the private domain of home and family.[15] But women's extensive volunteer work during the nineteenth century began their transition from private actors to public leaders in service to their families and the less fortunate in their communities. As two historians described it, "[t]he history of American philanthropy is largely the story of networks of women volunteers who were the mainstay of urban reform and charity as early as 1850."[16]

The Progressive Era triggered a new energy and focus to this charitable work. Women's clubs and local organizations joined together, and many began to focus on causes such as child labor, health care, education, creating courts for children, curbing the consumption of alcohol, improving race relations, and securing the right to vote for women. White middle-class women joined with working women to form national organizations focused on these causes, including the General Federation of Women's Clubs, the Women's Christian Temperance Movement, the National Consumers League, and the National American Women's Suffrage Association.[17] African American women, who had separate women's clubs during this time, joined together in 1896 to form the National Association of Colored Women's Clubs, under the leadership of Mary Church Terrell.[18] Other African American Progressive-Era organizations founded by women include the National Council of Negro Women and National League for the Protection of Colored Women. White and African American women worked together to help form other national organizations during the Progressive Era, including the National Association for the Advancement of Colored People (NAACP) in 1909.[19] All of these opportunities to promote important causes as part of these largely female clubs and organizations laid the groundwork for women's increasing role in the public sphere.

Prominent "first-wave" feminists such as Jane Addams in Chicago and Lillian Wald in New York City joined with other women and men to form organizations designed primarily to serve poor communities rather than advance political causes. These organizations, called Settlement Houses, were housed in large buildings located in the crowded immigrant neighborhoods of industrial cities. They provided the community's residents with services such as classes in English and other subjects for women and children, day care, libraries, and other resources intended to mitigate the impact of poverty on families. The Settlement Houses, in which more than seventy-five percent of the workers were women, also functioned as sites for research and advocacy. Workers documented the problems of the poor they served and used the data they collected to advocate for social change, with "residence, research, and reform... the 3R's of the Movement."[20]

"Women at Lexington Market, Baltimore, 1850-1910."

Courtesy of the Library of Congress.

The Progressive Reform agenda, then, included a number of initiatives led by women and aimed at improving the lives of children, women, and families. The women who joined the movements from the charitable organizations were primarily middle- and upper-middle-class women, many of whom had attended college.[21] While most were white, some African American women were also influential in the movement, despite the intense racism of the time.[22] Most of these women were homemakers or philanthropists, but some were engaged in paid work. While most of these women held unskilled jobs, some were teachers or nurses, and, later, librarians and social workers—professions which began almost exclusively with women in the mid- to late-nineteenth century.[23] The opportunities for women in the male-dominated professions—the practice of medicine, engineering, and, particularly, law—were limited, but advances were made in the period leading up to the Progressive Era.

As a result of all of these circumstances as well as the efforts of numerous nineteenth-century women who pushed the issue through courts and legislatures, women began to gain formal entry to the Bar in the late 1860s.[24] By 1895, thirty-five of the forty-eight states, in addition to the District of Columbia and the territory of Hawaii, were admitting women to the Bar.[25] By 1897, there were 300 women lawyers in the U.S., causing one British commentator to remark, "the lady lawyer [in the U.S.] meets us here, there and everywhere."[26]

Even as the late-nineteenth century brought with it the political and social conditions needed to lift the formal barriers to women's entry into the legal profession in many jurisdictions, it was not until the two decades of the Progressive Era that women were admitted to the Bar in significant numbers.[27] This occurred when both the political events of the time and the "professionalization" of law changed and expanded the practice of law. Pressure to raise and improve the standards for entry into the professions, including law, stemmed from the same concerns that fueled much of the reform of the era—corruption and inefficiencies in government, particularly in judges and others interpreting the law throughout the nation. In addition, the complexity of the new industrialized economy and its attendant social problems created the need for more formal and comprehensive legal education. As a result, training for the practice of law moved from apprenticeships in law offices to colleges and universities.[28]

While many universities and law schools did not admit women, those that did gave women an entrée into the profession that did not rely on their having a father or husband willing to apprentice them. Lawyers and judges also formed professional organizations to regulate the profession through ethical rules and continuing education.[29] This "cleaning up" of the profession may have also enhanced its attractiveness to women put off by the cronyism and frequent ethical breaches of the old system.[30] At the same time, the potential for the law and courts to improve the lives of families was expanded through the Progressive Era's movements. These movements—including the Settlement House Movement, Juvenile Court Movement, Temperance Movement, and Women's Suffrage Movement—often involved the same activists and had goals that reinforced one another. Many of the priorities and successes of the movement—child labor laws, clean water, compulsory public education, and public support for single heads of households—also reflected the concerns of women and families. A number of scholars have commented on the way in which women's volunteer work in these organizations and earlier charitable organizations laid the foundation for a more public role for women in the legal profession. Contrasting the actual experiences of nineteenth-century women with the narrow conception of women found in Justice Bradley's concurrence in *Bradwell v. Illinois*, Martha Minow makes a broader point about the connections of women's role as family members, their involvement in volunteer work, and their movement into the legal profession:[31]

> [V]olunteer activities by women in benevolent and reform associations during the 19th century built upon conceptions of women's domestic roles as women claimed expertise in public virtue and exported a conception of family norms to the public realm. These volunteer activities also drew women into positions of political influence beyond their traditional sphere, and from those positions, women challenged historical limits on their rights while also preserving aspects of their traditional roles. In leaving their traditional sphere women did not abandon their family roles, nor did they adopt autonomous individualism. Instead, women in effect created a shadow government of social services animated by norms of caretaking. Some women also sought to redefine the role of law to encompass collective responsibility for vulnerable members of the community.[32]

The range of groups that worked together during the Progressive Era approached the task of government reform with a variety of political goals.[33] But many women were drawn to the cause because of the importance of these issues to the well-being of families and because they believed "an investment in [children's] human capital [is] a legitimate and important function of government."[34] Law, in the form of new legislation and new models for courts, had become an important vehicle for social change to improve family life and respond to increasingly important social issues like conditions for women and children in the nation's growing industrial base. Women were drawn to this new vision of the law as a "helping profession."[35] As one late-nineteenth-century female law student at the University of Michigan declared, "There is something besides law to be studied. It is human justice."[36]

The Progressive Era in Maryland

While the entire nation experienced a period of dislocation and trauma at the end of the Civil War, Maryland's position as a border state made the effort to rebuild more difficult and complex. As one historian described it, "Marylanders both championed liberty and relied on slavery. They welcomed opportunity yet clung to tradition. In weighing the benefits of individual liberty and local liberty against those of moral experiment and the power of central government, citizens of this oldest border state have divided more than once."[37] In post-war Maryland, former slaves and other African Americans experienced better conditions than those in living the South. But many Marylanders resisted efforts to promote public education, access to the professions and trades, and granting the right to vote for African American males.[38]

The passage of the Fifteenth Amendment to the U.S. Constitution by two-thirds of the states in 1870 guaranteed, in theory, the right to vote for African American males in Maryland. But Maryland was among the states that failed to ratify the Fifteenth Amendment, a fact which reflected the state's lingering resistance to granting full equality to African Americans, including the right to vote.[39] Other conditions contributed to the troubled social and political environment in late-nineteenth-century Maryland. Divisions between the poor and the rich became deeper as economic conditions worsened in Maryland during the 1870s and 1880s; these divisions were manifested in labor disputes throughout the state, particularly in the mining and railroad industries.[40] Women, children, freed slaves, and, later, the European immigrants changed the composition of the working class, as businesses replaced skilled labor with low-wage, unskilled workers.[41] Both urban and rural areas lacked underground sewer systems or sewage treatment facilities. Diseases such as typhoid fever, diphtheria, and small pox resulted from unhealthy drinking water and spread quickly in the overcrowded living and working conditions of the urban poor.[42] Deaths from these diseases were common throughout the state, particularly in areas with the larger populations such as Cumberland, Frederick, and Baltimore. Ineffective municipal services also led to major fires in densely built areas like Baltimore.[43] From the miners in western Maryland to the watermen on the Eastern Shore, to the factory workers in Baltimore, poor living and working conditions and low wages added to the general atmosphere of unrest.

Thus, as the twentieth century dawned in Maryland, the problem that spurred national reform efforts—namely, corrupt governments unable to respond to the growing needs of their citizens—existed throughout the state. But as the state's population moved from rural to urban areas, Baltimore became the financial, political, and social center of the state. Like other major American cities at that time, it had experienced a dramatic increase in population during the last decades leading to the new century. From 1870 to 1900, Baltimore's population increased from 250,000 to 500,000 people.[44] This population growth was fueled by immigrants from, among other places, Central, Eastern, and Southern Europe, and also by African

Jones Falls from Federal Hil, 1903.
Photographer unknown.
Courtesy of the Maryland State Archives.

Covered Bridge over Jones Falls.
Photographer and date unknown.
Courtesy of the Maryland State Archives.

American freed slaves from other parts of Maryland and the South. By 1900, almost half the state's population lived in Baltimore, and the city's citizens provided more than half the state's tax revenue.[45]

Baltimore was also center of both the problems and the reform efforts that followed. Along with population growth, Baltimore, like many other American cities, was experiencing rapid industrialization. For example, picnic grounds at Sparrows Point were transformed by the construction of "four blast furnaces, a rail mill, and other assorted plants, piers and rail yards."[46] As the economy shifted from farming to manufacturing, the new workers needed housing, health care, schools, and other public services. While life was quite pleasant for those with financial resources, new social problems emerged for the working class. These included long work hours, dangerous conditions in the workplace, children working instead of attending school, and rampant discrimination based on national origin, race, and religion. One reporter's description of a neighborhood in East Baltimore, during the 1880s and 1890s, reflects both the poor living conditions immigrants experienced and the negative assumptions made about them in the community:

> A crowded place of tenement houses, saloons, filthy shops, foul odors, hideous noises.... Trees, flowers, lawns...gardens were sorely lacking.... They crowd into tenement houses, eat unwholesome food, breathe impure air, shun water and despise soap. Their children are covered with several layers of dirt. The women go unkempt, the men unwashed.[47]

The so-called Gorman-Rasin political "machine" ran Baltimore during this time. Isaac Freeman Rasin, officially the clerk of the Court of Common Pleas, became the "boss" of the state's Democratic organization during the 1870s and 1880s and ruled Baltimore. The Democratic party of post-Civil War Maryland was largely made up of conservatives who had favored the South during the Civil War.[48] Rasin joined forces with Arthur Gorman, a U.S. Senator from Maryland, in 1870. Gorman controlled the Maryland General Assembly, which meant the two men "established themselves as the foremost political powers in Maryland."[49] The governments created by this political structure were not prepared to address the new needs of the city's population. As one historian described it:

> Police and fire protection, good roads, adequate schools, and pure water could not keep pace with the expanding population. New services were needed but not provided. The lack of a sanitary sewage system was a prime example. Housing was another. The poor migrant to the city…frequently could not afford even the cheapest of row houses and had to settle for renting a few rooms in the crowded, dirty tenements of the slums.[50]

Courts were among the institutions diminished by inefficiency and corruption. Judicial elections were often controlled by the "machine," resulting in the selection of "tainted" judges.[51] Court staff, with political boss Isaac Rasin at the center, used their positions to extend both favors and punishment.[52] One lawyer described the Baltimore Criminal Court of the late 1870s as "a sink of iniquity into which no honest man enters without a shudder and from which no scoundrel emerges without a triumph."[53] The lawyers who practiced in these courts, trained largely before law schools were established and during a time when they were not subject to ethical codes or regulation, were also subject to criticism about both their competence and their conduct. Chief Judge James McSherry of the Court of Appeals, Maryland's highest court, described the Maryland Bar at the end of the nineteenth century as overcrowded with "utterly incompetent and unworthy practitioners."[54] Interestingly, just five years later, this same judge would author the opinion, as discussed in Chapter Two, which denied Etta Maddox admission to the Bar.

This political corruption and the ineffective governmental response to the social problems from population growth and industrialization triggered calls for both private action to address the problems and political reform to make government more effective. These calls came from a variety of groups in Maryland, but women played a central role from the start.[55] As one commentator on this era in Maryland noted, "Never before had Maryland women played such an active and effective public role."[56] Women benefitted from the opportunities for higher education in Maryland provided by the colleges established for women during the nineteenth century (including Rev. John F. Goucher Woman's College, the College of Notre Dame, as well as early co-educational universities such as Johns Hopkins) and expanded their domestic roles to include political and social reform.[57] During the 1890s and the early-twentieth century, women played leading roles in groups such as the Baltimore Charity Organization Society, the Arundell Good Government Club, and Maryland Federation of Women's Clubs (MFWC)—that were advocating for changes in the law which would improve the lives of poor women and families.[58] For example, the MFWC "built a network of women whose concerns ranged from the slop of oyster-packing houses to the dangers children faced in George's Creek coal mines."[59] Led by women such as Mary Richmond, a pioneer in the field of social work, the Baltimore Charity Organization was among the organizations that successfully advocated for juvenile courts and compulsory education in Baltimore.[60] During this time, women also founded the Baltimore chapters of two other organizations that advanced the causes of protecting family health and well-being: the Children's Playground Association and the National Consumers League.[61]

Working with local churches and synagogues, women were also active in the aforementioned Settlement House Movement, where classes and legal clinics were organized to help communities improve and prosper.[62] One of these women, Henrietta Szold, the daughter of a Hungarian immigrant rabbi, established evening classes so immigrants could learn English and other skills, thus becoming a "pioneer in establishing a self-help program that was later adopted by cities throughout the country."[63] As was true of other women throughout America, this volunteer work "drew [Maryland] women into positions of political influence beyond their traditional sphere."[64]

Finally, many of the leading women activists of the Progressive Era in Maryland were members of organizations fighting for two causes: the fight for Prohibition and the fight for women's right to vote. These movements, both nationally and in Maryland, often drew on the same women to lead their organizations.[65] Nationally, Elizabeth Cady Stanton and Susan B. Anthony were early leaders of both temperance and women's suffrage groups.[66] In Maryland, many of the women who fought for the right to vote were also members of the Maryland chapter of the Women's Christian Temperance Movement (WCTU).[67]

The Temperance Movement brought together those urging abstention from liquor with a wide range of religious, social, and political motivations. Before the Civil War, temperance groups had promoted voluntary abstinence but the societal changes brought by industrialization, immigration, and the rapid expansion of cities with all its attendant ills spurred a call for legal prohibition. While the WCTU was "loosely hinged on abstention from alcohol, [it] raised a variety of concerns, including domestic violence, social reform, and political empowerment."[68] Seeing alcohol use as a major contributor to poverty, family violence, and sexual assault, particularly in the growing cities of the early-twentieth century, many women saw prohibition as a way to strengthen the family.[69]

Many women in the WCTU viewed acquiring the vote as a means to garner support for Prohibition as well as other Progressive Era causes such as child labor, compulsory school laws, and broader opportunities in higher and professional education for women.[70] Both movements attracted a wide range of women, including many wealthy, socially prominent women and professional women from medicine, academia, and, later, the law. While groups such as the Equal Suffrage League, the Maryland chapter of the Women's Suffrage Association, and the Maryland WCTU clashed over goals and tactics, these organizations and these causes were particularly important in moving Maryland women into public leadership positions and linking them with like-minded women around the nation.[71]

The Pioneers: The First Women Admitted to the Maryland Bar

The Barriers to Admission before 1902

At the beginning of the Progressive Era, around 1890, Maryland was among the fifteen states or U.S. territories that still did not admit women to the Bar.[72] In order to appreciate fully the challenges and accomplishments of this first group of women, it is important to analyze both why Maryland lagged behind most of the rest of America in lifting the barriers to law practice and the changes that finally led to the admission of the first woman, Etta Maddox, in 1902.

Many factors contributed to Maryland's delay in admitting women to the Bar.[73] At the turn of the twentieth century, most states in the South still prevented women from practicing law.[74] Rigid gender roles, which placed women in the private domestic sphere, were particularly strong in the post-Civil War South.[75] Maryland's position as a border state increased the cultural and political similarities with its neighbors to the South. Many of Maryland's politicians and judges embraced this traditional view of women and believed that women were best served when they were kept "out of the often-dirty business of politics" and related fields.[76] This view of women is reflected in the fact that, despite the consistent work of women in several organizations over almost two decades, Maryland never passed its own women's suffrage bill and failed to ratify the Nineteenth Amendment until 1941.

Perhaps more significantly, many Marylanders, particularly those in Baltimore's Democratic Party and those in the rural areas on the Eastern Shore and southern Maryland where the African American population was among the highest in the state, feared the dominance of the black (male) vote. Indeed, Maryland was among the few states which had not ratified the Fifteenth Amendment when it became law in 1870.[77] Despite the ultimate defeat of the political machine and the old Democratic Party, the machine worked hard to limit the power of the black vote, and discrimination against blacks remained strong in Maryland through the late-nineteenth and early-twentieth centuries. When the Progressives began to win elections and seriously challenge the existing political order during the 1890s, the Rasin-Gorman machine stepped up its efforts to enact legislation aimed at disenfranchising African Americans.[78] These efforts culminated in a proposed constitutional amendment in 1901 that would "require all voters except those whose grandfathers had voted to pass a test on the U.S. Constitution," a requirement that would exempt all white voters and prevent most blacks from voting.[79] Although the so-called Poe amendment was defeated by Maryland's voters each of the three times it appeared on the ballot, the successful campaign to defeat this and other similar tactics involved a substantial effort over a number of years.[80]

This fear of the black vote worked against the advancement of women's legal rights in several ways. Those who saw the newly enfranchised black men as a political threat predicted that giving women the vote would only lead to more voting against their special interests. As a result, they fought women's suffrage and other gender equality efforts.[81] In addition, those who might have joined the fight for women's equality were preoccupied with protecting the right of African American males to vote.[82]

Another factor undermining the political power of those favoring women's equality was Baltimore's limited power in Maryland's legislature at the turn of the twentieth century. Baltimore, the center of the fight for women's rights and other reform initiatives, was severely underrepresented in the General Assembly. Despite having almost half the state's population and producing more than half the state's tax revenue, Baltimore had only eighteen of the state's ninety-one delegates and only three of the state's twenty-six senators.[83] As a result, the reform initiatives that usually came from Baltimore often suffered defeat in the Legislature. Indeed, Maryland failed to ratify the Constitutional amendments that embodied two of the major causes of the Progressive Era reform—Prohibition and women's right to vote. Historians have concluded that, even at the height of the Progressive Era, Maryland never had the coalition to fully enact the social and political reforms of the Progressive Era.[84]

Finally, there was a correlation between the jurisdictions that provided opportunities for legal education for women and the bar admission rates for women that helps explain why Maryland was late in admitting women. Jurisdictions with law schools that admitted women generally broke down barriers to female admission before those where legal education opportunities were more limited or non-existent for women.[85] For example, the District of Columbia, although clearly influenced by the culture and social norms of the South that re-enforced women's traditional roles, was among the first jurisdictions to admit women, admitting its first woman, Charlotte Ray, in 1872.[86] By 1920, only California, Illinois, and New York had more women practicing law in their states than did the District of Columbia.[87] Although Howard University's Law School in the District educated Charlotte Ray, it was the presence of the Washington College of Law, founded in 1898 and the first law school founded for women, that facilitated both the early admission of women and the relatively high numbers of women admitted to the Bar in the District.[88] Not only was Washington College focused on supporting its female students, but it was among the few law schools where the administrators and faculty were primarily female. In the other jurisdictions that were among the first to admit women and did so in relatively high numbers, legal education was also open to women.[89]

By contrast, the University of Maryland School of Law did not admit women until 1920. A second law school in Maryland, the Baltimore Law School, admitted women, but only for a short time from 1900 to 1907. A third law school, Baltimore University Law School, founded in 1890, admitted one woman, Catherine Hunckel. She became the first woman to graduate from a Maryland law school but was never admitted to practice. She attended law school with her husband, Otto, and never applied to take the Maryland Bar. The Baltimore University Law School was later merged into the Baltimore Law School, which, in turn, was merged into the University of Maryland.[90] Notably, only five of the first eight admittees were able to attend law school in Maryland.[91]

Despite these obstacles, the legal profession opened to women in Maryland in 1902, when Etta Maddox succeeded in persuading the General Assembly to amend the statute governing admission to the Bar.[92] Her admission was followed by the admission of seven other women over the next two decades (see Appendix A). A brief look at the lives of these women provides insights into what might have motivated this "first wave" of female lawyers and what sustained them through the isolation and discrimination they endured. These eight women had a number of circumstances in common. Some of these circumstances reflect the limitations on women's opportunities during the early twentieth century, while others reflect the improved environment for women's leadership and emerging public role that also existed at that time.

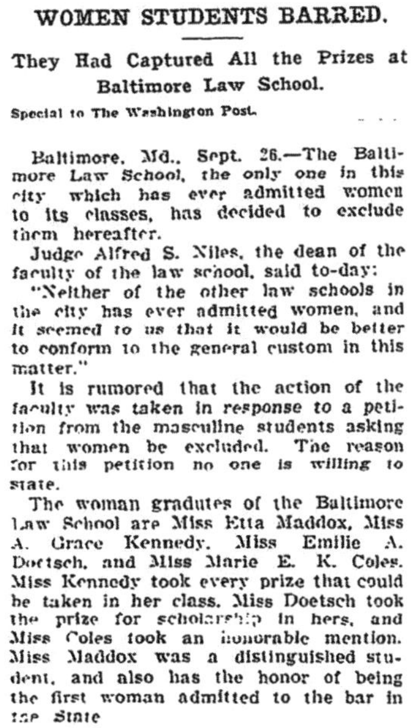
WOMEN STUDENTS BARRED.

They Had Captured All the Prizes at Baltimore Law School.

Special to The Washington Post.

Baltimore, Md., Sept. 26.—The Baltimore Law School, the only one in this city which has ever admitted women to its classes, has decided to exclude them hereafter.

Judge Alfred S. Niles, the dean of the faculty of the law school, said to-day:

"Neither of the other law schools in the city has ever admitted women, and it seemed to us that it would be better to conform to the general custom in this matter."

It is rumored that the action of the faculty was taken in response to a petition from the masculine students asking that women be excluded. The reason for this petition no one is willing to state.

The woman gradutes of the Baltimore Law School are Miss Etta Maddox, Miss A. Grace Kennedy, Miss Emilie A. Doetsch, and Miss Marie E. K. Coles. Miss Kennedy took every prize that could be taken in her class. Miss Doetsch took the prize for scholarship in hers, and Miss Coles took an honorable mention. Miss Maddox was a distinguished student, and also has the honor of being the first woman admitted to the bar in the State

"Women Students Barred. They Had Captured All the Prizes at Baltimore Law School."

The Washington Post, *September 27, 1907.*

The First Wave: Common Ground

Socio-Economic Status

As was true of most women with access to higher education during the early twentieth century, most of the first eight female admittees came from well-to-do families.[93] Etta Maddox's family has been described as "middle to upper class."[94] While little is known of her mother, both of Etta's parents were believed to be descended from American colonists.[95] Her father's position as a Baltimore City Magistrate has been described as one "that likely would have provided the family with significant wealth and prestige; the family lived in areas of Baltimore that were considered 'extremely fashionable.'"[96] Her fellow legal pioneer, Emilie Doetsch, was also from Baltimore, one of five children born to Louis J. Doetsch and Johanna Pohl Doetsch.[97] She attended a private German church-affiliated school, the Zion School.[98] Louis Doetsch was a lithographer with a successful business and was able to send all five of his children to college, a significant and unusual achievement in the early twentieth century. Correspondence from Emilie to college friends, when she was in her thirties and after her father's death, describes trips to Europe that she, her mother, or her sisters enjoyed, suggesting that the family enjoyed a comfortable financial position.[99]

While nothing is known about Helen Hill's parents, her brother was also educated as a lawyer and was admitted to practice.[100] She also attended a private law school, enrolling at the age of seventeen, an age at which she was unlikely to have funded her education on her own.[101] Grace Gerber and her younger brother, Samuel Gerber, also had the opportunity to attend professional school. In fact, following his graduation and successful political and medical career as the coroner for Cleveland, Ohio, Samuel Gerber went to law school and was admitted to the Bar.[102] Census records reveal that these ambitious siblings came from a family with eight children. Their parents, Julius and Bessie Gerber, were Russian immigrants who were clearly in a position to encourage their children to leave the state and go "west" for, in Grace's case, educational opportunities unavailable to her in Maryland.[103]

Emily Dashiell was born to a large family of five girls and was identified in her obituary as a "descendant of a French Huguenot who settled in Somerset County in the 1660."[104] While her family was originally from Somerset County, her parents, Charles and Elizabeth Dashiell, moved the family to Baltimore, where Charles Dashiell was a long-time city editor of *The Baltimore Sun*.[105] Although her father died when she was in her teen years, the family is likely to have had resources to educate Emily.[106] While not wealthy, the extended Dashiell family appears to have been a prominent Maryland family, owning property in Princess Anne County and other areas on the Eastern Shore.[107]

There is little known about the economic circumstances of Mary Meushaw or Marie Kirk Coles. Census records show that Marie Coles lived in Baltimore City with a group of women that included her mother, her sister, her mother's sister, and another woman unrelated to them. Her mother was an immigrant from England. Her father is not listed in the census information, suggesting that he was not a part of their household.[108] Anna Grace Kennedy's parents were Irish immigrants who originally settled in West Virginia. With her father employed as a carpenter and her mother as a homemaker, it is unlikely the family was wealthy or even solidly middle class.[109] These circumstances make her achievement in graduating from law school and becoming the second woman admitted to the Maryland Bar even more remarkable.

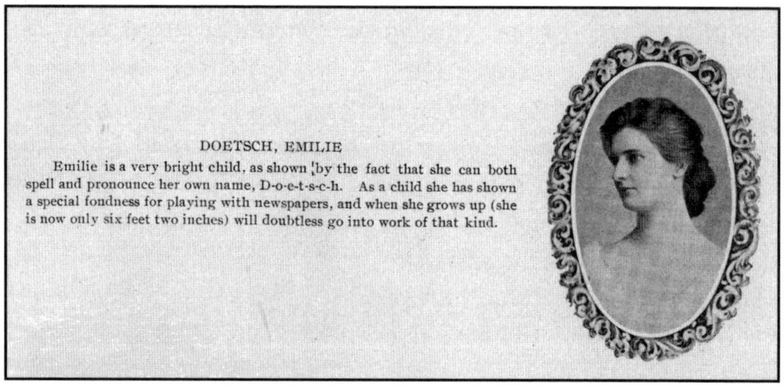
DOETSCH, EMILIE

Emilie is a very bright child, as shown by the fact that she can both spell and pronounce her own name, D-o-e-t-s-c-h. As a child she has shown a special fondness for playing with newspapers, and when she grows up (she is now only six feet two inches) will doubtless go into work of that kind.

Donnybrook Fair, 1904, Emilie Doetsch.

Courtesy of Goucher College.

Academic Success

Another common thread among the "first wave" is that they all had distinguished academic careers. Five of the eight first admittees were the only woman in their classes.[110] At best, they experienced law school without the support many women derive from other female students and faculty; at worst, they had to endure some hostility and resentment from their male colleagues and faculty.[111] Despite this difficult environment, they all distinguished themselves in law school with prizes and/or high grades. Five of the women—Anna Kennedy, Marie Coles, Helen Hill, Mary Meushaw, and Grace Gerber—were recognized at their undergraduate or law school graduations with valedictory or other prizes. Anna Kennedy not only won prizes for "thesis and scholarship" at her law school graduation, but *The Baltimore Sun* reported that she also received the highest score on the State Bar Examination that year.[112] Marie Coles was also recognized for her thesis when she graduated from Baltimore Law School.[113] Ranked highly among her male colleagues, Mary Meushaw was given second prize at graduation for her "excellent work" and academic achievements.[114]

Helen Hill, upon her graduation from American University Washington College of Law, 1900.
Courtesy of American University, Washington College of Law.

Decisions About Marriage and Children

The family lives of these women suggest that the "we can have it all" philosophy, which is much debated among twenty-first-century feminists, had not yet taken hold in early–twentieth-century Maryland. Seven of these eight women never married and never had children.[115] Grace Gerber did marry and had one child, but the marriage ended in divorce. She married Simon Nobel Silverberg, who was also an attorney, in June 1930.[116] Underscoring the unusual circumstance of two attorneys marrying in 1930, *The Washington Post* reported the marriage in an article entitled "Pair's Romance Goes From Courts to Altar" and described Grace as "Hagerstown's first and only woman lawyer."[117] The couple had one child, a son named Seth Samuel Silverberg, who was born in 1931 or 1932.[118] There is little record of the circumstances surrounding the parties' married lives and divorce. According to census records, by 1940 Grace had resumed the use of "Gerber," no longer used the name "Silverberg," and was living with her parents without Simon in Washington County, at a time when her son was eight years old.[119] Newspaper accounts of Simon Silberberg confirm that he married at least three other times, twice before his marriage to Grace and at least once after their divorce: An article announcing his marriage, in 1921, to his childhood sweetheart, Rose Caplan, describes him as having divorced six months prior to the marriage to Rose.[120] He then divorced Rose with some public acrimony in 1924.[121] Genevieve J. Silverberg is listed as Simon's surviving spouse at his death in 1965.[122]

Grace and Simon's son, Seth, went on to become a lawyer himself, being admitted to the Bar in Maryland from the Third Judicial Circuit (Baltimore County and Harford County) in October 1959.[123] There is little information available about his career other than his membership in the American Bar Association's Section of Insurance, Negligence and Compensation Law, listing his office address in Baltimore and, later, in Miami, Florida.[124] There are no other records describing Seth's professional or personal circumstances.

While some of the early pioneering women lawyers in other states were able to combine families and careers, only one of Maryland's early admitees married or had children.[125] There is nothing in the biographical information available about these Maryland women that provides insight into their choices in this area. A national history of women lawyers, however, does provide some clues. While noting the lack of unanimity of views on whether or how to balance marriage and a career, Virginia G. Drachman suggests that many early women lawyers were unmarried by choice. They believed that "marriage imposed too many domestic obligations on women and was incompatible with a serious career."[126] For others, the fact that they were single may have necessitated the need to support themselves, which, in turn, led them to the law.[127] Still others believed that a decision to pursue a legal career was a decision to forgo marriage and a family, because many women of the time believed men did not want to marry women "with set ways, independent character, who are able to care for themselves."[128]

Finally, although the legal barriers to women's practice of law were rapidly disappearing throughout America, there was little evidence of the corresponding social and political changes needed to support women's efforts to balance family life and legal careers, particularly in Southern and border states like Maryland. As a result, there were few options for child care and other support for combining motherhood and a career throughout much of the twentieth century.[129] Although the availability of safe and affordable child care continues to be a challenging issue well into the twenty-first century in America, it was not until the reforms of the Progressive Era that child care outside the home began to be seen as a necessary support for many parents, even where they were fit and able to care for their children when not working.[130]

Participation in Progressive-Era Causes

Probably the most important shared experience that prepared and sustained Maryland's first admittees to be pioneers in the legal profession was their common involvement—both before and after their admission to the Bar—in the social and political organizations that flourished during the Progressive Era.[131] Etta Maddox, Emilie Doetsch, and Marie Kirk Coles were all active in the Women's Suffrage Movement before they attended law school. Etta Maddox, perhaps the most visible and active political leader of the first group of admittees, was an active member of the Maryland Suffrage Association (MSA), which she helped found with her sister, Emma Maddox Funck, in 1894.[132] While primarily focused on gaining the right to vote for women, the MSA was also focused on a variety of women and children's causes including fair labor laws, equal pay for women, compulsory education, and the appointment of women to important governmental and political bodies. This work honed Maddox's leadership skills and brought her into contact with women leaders from around the nation. One of Maddox's biographers suggests that "it seems likely that Etta's fellow suffragists encouraged her to attend law school from the very beginning, and may have been a significant factor in her decision to do so."[133] The support of the MSA for Maddox's decision to attend law school is evidenced by their awarding her a medal upon graduation, commemorating her status as "The First Woman Lawyer in Maryland."[134]

After she secured the right to be admitted for herself and all other women in Maryland, she continued to work on causes related to the advancement of women, particularly the right to vote. She was also a regular speaker before the Women's Christian Temperance Movement, supporting the issues common to the two groups, including suffrage.[135] After the right to vote was secured, the Maryland Suffrage Association became the Women's Democratic Club of Baltimore, and Maddox continued to be an active member, working to affect social change on issues such as the effort to improve schools and abolish capital punishment and child labor.[136] She was also a leading voice for family law reform and an early voice for the establishment of a separate family court, a movement that grew out of the Progressive Era's Juvenile Court effort.[137] She also worked with other early female admittees to reform Maryland's marriage and divorce laws.[138]

Emilie Doestch contributed to the Women's Suffrage Movement, describing herself as an "ardent suffragist."[139] Filing daily stories for *The Baltimore News*, she participated in the women's suffrage march from New York City to Washington in February 1913.[140] As she described it:

"Suffragette Parade—Washington Street, Easton, Md."
Photographer and date unknown.
Courtesy of the Talbot County Historical Society.

"Suffragette Parade—Washington Street, Easton, Md."
Photographer and date unknown.
Courtesy of the Talbot County Historical Society.

Suffragist March on DC.
Photographer and date unknown. Courtesy of the Maryland State Archives

> [I] was one of Rosalie Jones "martyrs" who marched from New York to Washington in the dead of Winter to bring about the conversion of President-elect Wilson. Officially, I was a "war correspondent," but The News didn't ask me to walk every step of the way. I did that because I wanted to.[141]

Later, she served as the managing editor of *Equal Rights,* the newspaper for the National Woman's Party.[142] Doetsch appears to have been drawn into the law and public life by other movements of the Progressive Era. Once women achieved the vote in 1920, she was the first woman to run for the Baltimore City Council in 1923, a year that was described by *The Baltimore Sun* as "the high water mark in Baltimore women's interest in politics...turning out in masses unprecedented in any election since the passage of the equal suffrage amendment."[143] She ran on a platform that called for an expanded role of women in government, enlargement of the Child's Welfare Bureau, and other efforts aimed at improving the lives of women and children. Although Doetsch lost the election, she received the most votes of any candidate in her party, the Citizens Independent League.[144] In her correspondence to fellow Goucher College alumnae, she describes the mixed reaction of voters to a female candidate as she campaigned door to door and thanks her "sisters" and friends whose "cooperation and support" made it possible.[145] She concludes that, despite the loss, the campaign was worth it and notes the importance of women getting involved in politics and government:

> I emerged from the combat as the 'first Baltimore woman who ran for the City Council', instead, as I had fondly hoped, being the first to 'sit' in it. Still, someone had to make the break and, even if you fail, it serves notice on the political powers-that-be that women are emerging from their old indifference and that they mean to have their share in the running of the government....

> I hope, if any of the rest of you have a chance to run for public office, that you won't be scared, but will jump right in. Women are needed in politics, and college women in that respect have bigger responsibilities than others. And whatever the outcome, the experience is worth-while.[146]

In 1934, Doetsch applied for a seat on the new court that many view as the crowning achievement of the Progressive Era—the Juvenile Court.[147] Although she was endorsed by many local and national figures who wrote letters of support to then-Governor Harry Nice, she was not appointed.[148] She continued to advocate for women's issues throughout her life, including working for the inclusion of women on juries and the admission of girls to the city's elite high school.[149]

While there is no record of Emily Dashiell's political activity prior to her admission to the Bar in 1918, her work on women's and family issues while a lawyer was consistent with that of her early admittee colleagues.[150] She chaired a committee to create a Maryland Chapter of a Progressive-Era organization, the National Federation of Business and Professional Women. An article describing her role in this organization describes the goals of the federation as "the furtherance and protection of the interests of women in the business, professional and civic world."[151] She also served as Chair of Maryland's Young Women's Christian Association (YWCA), an organization started in 1876 Chicago, the center of Progressive-Era political activity, "to promote the religious, moral, and intellectual welfare of young self-supporting women."[152] Although the YWCA was initially an organization that engaged in religious and racial discrimination, by the 1890s it was focused on providing shelter and training to poor women and, later, men. Dashiell was also very active in the Maryland Chapter of the League of Women Voters, a national organization formed during the last meeting of the National American Woman Suffrage Association approximately six months before the Nineteenth Amendment was ratified, giving women the right to vote. The League's history describes it as a "mighty political experiment" aimed at helping newly enfranchised women exercise their responsibilities as voters.[153] One newspaper reported Emily Dashiell's activities on the League's Committee on the Legal Status of Women, focusing on her work advancing the Maryland Chapter's legislative program on marriage and divorce laws.[154] The League's legislative agenda in family law focused on strengthening the family by criminalizing abuse against women and children, creating stronger regulation on entry into marriage, and expanding fault grounds for divorce. She was also Maryland's delegate to the League's National Committee on Uniform Laws Concerning Women, which made broad recommendations on women's rights on a range of issues, including property and family law.[155]

Prior to entering law school, Grace Gerber was an active member of a number of the philanthropic and charitable organizations in Maryland that provided leadership during the Progressive Era. These included membership in her local chapter of the Women's Club, Civic League, and Meridian Club.[156] She also held leadership positions in the Maryland branch of the League of Women Voters, attending the National Convention as a Maryland delegate in 1921.[157]

While there is no evidence that their efforts reached the same levels of leadership as Maddox, Doestch, and Dashiell, Mary Meushaw and Marie Kirk Coles were also involved in the suffrage movement in Maryland.[158] There is also evidence that Helen Hill was involved in the movements on both a state and national level, joining with her fellow Washington College of Law alumni and other women lawyers, under the direction of Dean Ellen Spencer Mussey of Washington College of Law, in a well-publicized suffrage parade in New York City a year after her graduation from law school.[159]

Other evidence that the political and social climate of early-twentieth-century Maryland encouraged more public and leadership roles for this group of women are found in their philanthropic work. Anna Grace Kennedy served as the captain of a team to raise money for Mercy Hospital in Baltimore.[160] Helen Hill was a tireless fundraiser for her alma mater, the Washington College of Law.[161] When she was elected President of the Alumni Association of Washington College of Law, one local paper declared, "There doesn't seem to be any restriction on 'woman's sphere' in the District of Columbia."[162] Hill also used her leadership position as a Washington College alumna to organize events focusing on the Progressive-Era causes important to women such as providing welfare programs to assist dependent mothers.[163] She also used her position to inspire and welcome "the young women graduates" of the Washington College of Law who followed her.[164] Similarly, Emilie Doetsch was on the Board of Directors of the Alumni Association of Goucher College and used the position to urge, among other goals, the appointment of "Goucher Women" to important state commissions and boards as part of an overall strategy in which "women must stand behind women."[165]

Finally, that these women supported and socialized with one another and other women in Maryland's Progressive reform movement lends support to the idea that they shared common political and social interests and drew support from the associations made in their progressive causes. For example, Emilie Doetsch and Anna Grace Kennedy were reported as attending a law school graduation party celebrating Marie Elizabeth Kirk Coles that was held by Coles's sister.[166] On a more practical level, Doetsch also found support from leading Progressives such as Anna Corkran and Mrs. Donald Hooker, who supported Doetsch, respectively, in her efforts to become the first woman elected to the Baltimore City Council and to become appointed to the Juvenile Court bench.[167] Emily Dashiell and Grace Gerber also worked together with the Committee on Uniformity of Laws Concerning Women to promote and solve such issues as fairness in divorce laws and pensions for working mothers.[168]

This review of the activities of these women in both the traditional philanthropic and charitable clubs of the nineteenth-century and the more political organizations of the Progressive Era reveals two important insights about the timing and the motivation of this first group of Maryland women lawyers. First, this organizational work helped groom some of these women for leadership. It also exposed them to women from around the nation who were pursuing careers, including the law. While only one of the first eight of Maryland's women lawyers was married, most of them were from traditional middle- or upper-class families. Thus, but for the exposure to both the issues and the other women in these organizations, these Maryland pioneers might have settled into more sheltered lives, living with family members and assuming household and caretaking duties. Instead, they extended these caretaking values into the world through their political and charitable work.

In addition, as the ideas of the Progressive Era began to take hold—that government and law could be forces for positive social change, particularly in the lives of women and children—the law became more attractive as a profession to women like Maddox, Doetsch, and Dashiell. The role that law and lawyers could play in achieving the goals of the Maryland Suffrage Association and the other groups these women were involved in became apparent, and these women were motivated, despite numerous obstacles, to complete a legal education and gain admission to the Bar. Like the many women before them who had fought to gain bar admission in other states, "the volunteer activities also drew [these Maryland women] into positions of political influence beyond their traditional sphere, and from those positions, [these] women challenged historical limits on their rights and sought to redefine the role of law to encompass collective responsibility for vulnerable members of the community."[169]

Opportunities after Admission to the Bar: Discrimination and Determination

After overcoming hurdles to attend law school and pass the Maryland Bar Examination, the early female admittees shared the common experience of facing discrimination and struggling to establish a legal career. Despite their impressive and, in some cases, extraordinary academic achievements, none of the women reached great levels of achievement in the legal world, at least by traditional standards. There were no judges, law faculty, or members of large firms in the group. Indeed, there is no evidence that three of the early admittees—Anna Grace Kennedy (admitted 1906), Marie Elizabeth Kirk Coles (admitted 1907), and Mary Virginia Meushaw (admitted 1909)—ever practiced law. The remaining five did struggle to pursue legal careers either by creating their own firms or by working in governmental or law-related jobs that did not involve the practice of law.[170] Etta Maddox's own struggle began, of course, when she was denied admission to the Bar after graduating from law school in 1901. She then challenged the denial of admission, first in the courts and then, successfully, in the General Assembly. Following her admission to the Bar in 1902, she established her own law practice. Much of her practice was consumed with trust and estates matters related to her family's personal and business interests and family law cases for low income women, "perhaps because it was the one area where poor women—the type of client least likely to be able to afford a male lawyer—often needed a lawyer."[171]

Emilie Doetsch, who was admitted in 1907 but was initially unable to find a legal job, pursued her passion for progressive and women's causes as a journalist, working, among other places, as a reporter for *The Baltimore News*.[172] She ultimately broke barriers when she was the first woman to run for the Baltimore City Council (unsuccessfully) and the first woman to serve as an Assistant City Solicitor. Doetsch, a Republican, resisted the effort to remove her from the position when a Democratic administration assumed power three years after her appointment. She was ultimately forced out and began a private law practice "but found the going rough during the 1930's because of the continuing prejudice against women."[173] In her correspondence, she describes the difficulties in establishing a law practice during the years leading up to the Great Depression and references the continuing difficulties women faced in the practice of law:

> [I] opened an office with Marie Presstman, lawyer and member of the Maryland State Board of Motion Picture censors. It was a hard uphill fight, inasmuch as the depression was just setting in, and even lawyers of established reputation were feeling the pinch. I shall never cease to be amused at the irony implicit in a letter that was sent to all the women members of the bar as well as to the men by the Baltimore Bar Association asking them to contribute to a fund to aid needy lawyers, in the face of the fact that the Bar Association had never admitted women to its membership.[174]

Emilie ultimately gave up the practice, choosing to become the librarian for *The Washington Times-Herald* at a time when she needed the steady income to help her sister-in-law support four children after Emilie's brother's sudden death.[175]

Helen Hill began her career as a title examiner for the District Title Insurance Company, a position that did not require a law degree.[176] She also worked in government—an area that would become a common practice setting for many women over the years—first in the U.S. Court of Claims and then in the Claims Section of the Income Tax Division of the Bureau of Internal Revenue.[177] Emily Dashiell also worked in government and in a variety of settings which did not involve the traditional practice of law or representing individual clients. During World War I, she worked for the Edgewood Arsenal, "handl[ing] important contracts for Government supplies."[178] She also worked as a law librarian for both an insurance company and a law firm. Finally, she developed the curriculum and trained those entering the surety business at Fidelity and Deposit Company.[179] This last position garnered some press attention, in which the reporter describes her in the classroom as "the very essence of femininity, Miss Dashiell sits efficiently in the one corner of a big room and directs her class of six men. There is just a suspicion of shyness in her manner."[180]

Grace Gerber, the last of this pioneering group to be admitted, also caught the attention of her fellow classmates in a similar way. According to a story in *The Baltimore Sun*, as the youngest of three women in her class, she was the one who took much of the brunt of her male colleagues' criticism.[181] The night before the "weeding out" committee, twenty male students showed up at her boarding house and apologized for their personal attacks upon her and asked if she would help them to prepare for their quiz.[182] By the time that she graduated, her seemingly-adverse male colleagues were the ones who threw her the most graduation parties.[183] This story suggests why she may have gained so much support in her race as a Republican for the House of Delegates.[184]

In addition to her work in politics, Grace Gerber also appears to have been the most successful of the group in the traditional practice of law. Admitted in 1920, she established her own practice in her hometown of Hagerstown, a city in west-central Maryland in which she had grown up and her parents still lived. Although little is known about the nature of her practice, it was described in *The Tercentenary History of Maryland* as "pleasant and lucrative."[185] That same history acknowledges her struggles in reaching this modest level of success:

> Exceptional ability alone was not enough to win success for this ambitious young woman She was forced to use every atom of her determination, indomitable courage, and the strength of her forceful personality to secure even a hearing in a profession controlled by and filled with men.... That she has secured a hearing and broken down the walls of prejudice means not only her personal triumph, but the entire cause of professional women.[186]

Although all of these women shared Grace Gerber's range of talents in their academic and professional pursuits, this brief history reveals their difficulty in obtaining legal employment. The limited opportunities and the fairly public struggles of these women may have discouraged most other women from pursuing the law during the two decades following Etta Maddox's admission in 1902. Any women who followed the newspaper accounts of Etta Maddox's efforts to gain admission to the Bar in the courts and through the Legislature—or Emily Doetsch's unsuccessful efforts to keep her job as Assistant City Solicitor, be appointed to the Juvenile Court Bench, or win an election to City Council—may have been deterred from joining the struggle. Fortunately for the many women who ultimately followed, these unusual eight pioneers endured and led the way.

Conclusion

By 1920, when the last of the "first female wave" was admitted to the Bar in Maryland, every state Bar in the nation was admitting women, women were admitted to almost all law schools, and the number of female lawyers across the country "soared."[187] This exploration of the political and social conditions in Maryland that lead to the first group of women being admitted to the Maryland Bar provides some clues about both the barriers that delayed their admission in Maryland and the conditions that supported this first group. After the Civil War, Maryland, like many other states, struggled to adapt to a new economy, new demographic patterns, and a new political structure. But Maryland's position as a border state made its efforts to incorporate women and newly freed African Americans as full and equal citizens

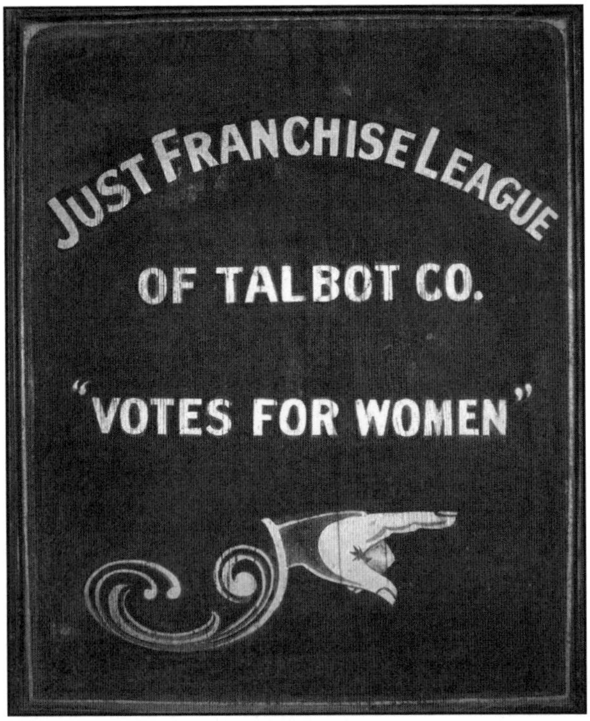

"Just Franchise League of Talbot Co. 'Votes For Women.'"
Date unknown.
Courtesy of the Talbot County Historical Society.

particularly challenging. A substantial segment of the political power structure in Maryland reflected the values of its neighboring states to the south. This resulted in both a very traditional view of women's roles, which limited women to the domestic sphere, and a resistance to fully implementing the rights of equal citizenship for black males. These circumstances undermined the struggle for women's rights, including the right to vote and practice law. In addition, Baltimore, where most of the progressive politicians were concentrated, was underrepresented in the General Assembly during this period. Finally, women had very limited access to legal education in Maryland until 1920.

Despite these barriers, the dawning of the Progressive Era in Maryland created conditions that finally facilitated the entry of women to the Bar. Most of the early admittees and other women who were active in Progressive-Era reforms came from families with the means to provide, first, for their education and, later, for the leisure time to allow the pursuit of volunteer work. When the Progressive Era's energy and its women-led causes spread to Maryland, most of these early admittees answered the call. They led organizations, like the Maryland suffrage movement, designed to advance the status of women and improve the lives of families and children. These experiences gave them a taste for the world of public service and ideas, and the Progressive Era's focus on law as the engine of change encouraged a focus on legal careers. With Etta Maddox achieving the initial victory of bar admission, she and most of her fellow female early admittees continued their work on behalf of women and families during their legal careers. Creating opportunities to practice law in Maryland during the early twentieth century was a struggle for these women, making their efforts and achievements all the more remarkable. Even those who gained admission but did not practice contributed as trailblazers and examples.

All of Maryland's women lawyers who followed these women, from those described in subsequent chapters of this book to those who will attend law school in future years, owe a significant debt to Maryland's "first wave." Their strong desire to serve the greater good, in addition to their intelligence, courage, and tenacity in the face of legal, social, and political obstacles, made possible the many achievements of the generations of women lawyers who followed them.

CHAPTER FOUR:

Women Lawyers in Community, 1920–1940

The Honorable Lynne A. Battaglia

Between 1920 and 1940, in the period following the Progressive Era, ninety-one women were admitted to the Maryland Bar, which was more than ten times the number of women who had been admitted since Etta Maddox paved the way in 1902.[1] Notably, many of the women who were admitted to the Maryland Bar between 1920 and 1940—including Helen Sherry, Marie White Presstman, Jeanette Rosner Wolman, Sarah Rosenberg Burke, Rose Zetzer, Henrietta Stonestreet, Helen E. Brown, Ida Kloze, Sophie Nordenholz, Anna Carton, and Nellie Marie Marshall—would play instrumental roles in advancing women's rights by overcoming legal obstacles and social inequities to establish their own careers, engendering the acceptance of women in the practice of law.[2]

This "explosion" in the number of women being admitted to the Bar was likely due, at least in part, to the existence of a local law school admitting women once again.[3] After Baltimore Law School closed its doors to women in 1907, a limited number of Maryland women, such as Helen Hill and Emily Dashiell, attended law schools in other states and then gained admission to the Maryland Bar.[4] Others, like Sarah Rosenberg Burke, applied for admittance to the University of Maryland School of Law; in 1917, her application was denied based on her gender. The University of Maryland asserted that women were not permitted to attend because there was a lack of toilet facilities in the law building for women, an excuse commonly used by "those bent on excluding outsiders from white male preserves."[5] Women continued to apply to the University of Maryland until 1920 when, having secured alternative bathrooms for the women across the street at University Hospital, the law school finally admitted women into its incoming class.[6] These initial University of Maryland law students included Sarah Rosenberg Burke, Adelaide Lindenberg, Helen Sherry, B. Olive Cole, Marie White Presstman, Fannie Kurland Kerpelman, and Ida Claire Lutzky—all of whom were admitted to the Bar in 1923 or 1924.[7] Thereafter, in 1925, the Mount Vernon School of Law, the predecessor to the University of Baltimore School of Law, also began admitting women.[8]

Many of the women entering law school during the 1920s, 1930s, and 1940s were raised in families that either placed emphasis on higher education or were involved in the legal community, which likely contributed to their desire to pursue a legal education.

State's Attorney's Office, Baltimore City Court House, c. 1900 (Clarence M. Mitchell, Jr. Courthouse).

Photographer unknown. Courtesy of the Maryland State Archives.

Helen E. Brown's inspiration to pursue a legal career was her grandfather, a circuit riding judge in Indiana.[9] Like Etta Maddox, Jeanette Rosner Wolman had a father, Adolph Rosner, who was active in the legal community, and she credited his encouragement with her decision to become a lawyer.[10] Mr. Rosner, a father of eight, worked as a buyer for Gimbels department store.[11] Despite his limited formal education, Mr. Rosner was named as a substitute magistrate by several governors, and, although he served only occasionally, he regularly attended court to observe criminal trials.[12] At the courthouse, Mr. Rosner was known for his generosity—offering cigars to the elevator operators, bringing baked goods for the secretaries in the State's Attorney's Office, offering financial assistance to indigent defendants, and frequently taking judges out for lunch.[13] Mr. Rosner was considered to be "very advanced for the time," as he was a supporter of women's suffrage and, in 1914, when Jeanette was twelve years old, he hoisted her on the family pony to ride in suffragist parades.[14]

When Jeanette was a junior in high school, she wrote the Dean of Columbia Law School seeking admission. The response was short: "Columbia does not admit women to its law school. If you're interested in going to college, apply at Barnard."[15] Despite the rejection from Columbia, Jeanette refused to relinquish her goal of attending law school. In 1921, as a sophomore studying social science at Goucher College in Baltimore, she told her father that she wanted to be a lawyer.[16] Her father accompanied her to the University of Maryland School of Law, where she was accepted immediately, and he paid her tuition for the first semester.[17]

As part of the first class to include women, sisters Helen Sherry and Fannie Kurland Kerpelman attended the University of Maryland School of Law together in 1920, shortly after Helen and her husband, Louis, had their first child.[18] Helen and Fannie were raised in a family of ten children, out of which five became lawyers and two became doctors, which suggests that the family valued higher education.[19] Katherine Kurland and Rhona Kurland Melnicove, Helen and Fannie's younger sisters, were likely inspired by their older sisters' success in law school and followed in their footsteps to obtain their legal degrees as well.[20]

Once admitted to the University of Maryland School of Law, female students were limited to attending night classes. This policy was unfortunate, but it did have some positive effects because it allowed working women like Jeanette Rosner Wolman, a social worker for the Jewish Children's Bureau, and Ida Claire Lutzky, a reporter at *The Baltimore Post*, to maintain jobs during the day while attending law school at night.[21] Additionally, students who were married women could, should they wish, address their household responsibilities during the day.

For the first time, a significant number of the women admitted to law school and the Bar during the 1920s, 1930s, and 1940s were married and raising families.[22] This was a sharp contrast to the Progressive Era, when most women remained single during their legal studies and law careers.[23] Anna Carton attended night classes at the University of Baltimore School of Law while her husband, Nathan Carton, cared for their son, who was

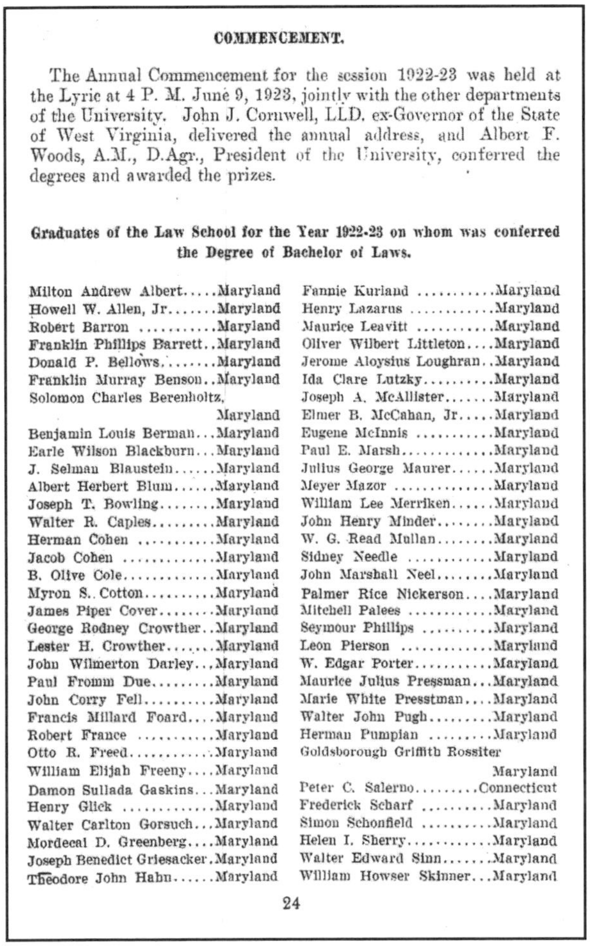

COMMENCEMENT.

The Annual Commencement for the session 1922-23 was held at the Lyric at 4 P. M. June 9, 1923, jointly with the other departments of the University. John J. Cornwell, LLD, ex-Governor of the State of West Virginia, delivered the annual address, and Albert F. Woods, A.M., D.Agr., President of the University, conferred the degrees and awarded the prizes.

Graduates of the Law School for the Year 1922-23 on whom was conferred the Degree of Bachelor of Laws.

Milton Andrew Albert.....Maryland
Howell W. Allen, Jr.......Maryland
Robert Barron ....Maryland
Franklin Phillips Barrett..Maryland
Donald P. Bellows........Maryland
Franklin Murray Benson..Maryland
Solomon Charles Berenholtz, Maryland
Benjamin Louis Berman...Maryland
Earle Wilson Blackburn...Maryland
J. Selman Blaustein......Maryland
Albert Herbert Blum......Maryland
Joseph T. Bowling........Maryland
Walter R. Caples.........Maryland
Herman Cohen ....Maryland
Jacob Cohen ....Maryland
B. Olive Cole.............Maryland
Myron S. Cotton..........Maryland
James Piper Cover........Maryland
George Rodney Crowther..Maryland
Lester H. Crowther.......Maryland
John Wilmerton Darley...Maryland
Paul Fromm Due.........Maryland
John Corry Fell..........Maryland
Francis Millard Foard....Maryland
Robert France ....Maryland
Otto R. Freed............Maryland
William Elijah Freeny....Maryland
Damon Sullada Gaskins...Maryland
Henry Glick ....Maryland
Walter Carlton Gorsuch...Maryland
Mordecai D. Greenberg....Maryland
Joseph Benedict Griesacker.Maryland
Theodore John Hahn......Maryland
Fannie Kurland ....Maryland
Henry Lazarus ....Maryland
Maurice Leavitt ....Maryland
Oliver Wilbert Littleton....Maryland
Jerome Aloysius Loughran..Maryland
Ida Clare Lutzky..........Maryland
Joseph A. McAllister.......Maryland
Elmer B. McCahan, Jr.....Maryland
Eugene McInnis ....Maryland
Paul E. Marsh............Maryland
Julius George Maurer......Maryland
Meyer Mazor ....Maryland
William Lee Merriken......Maryland
John Henry Minder........Maryland
W. G. Read Mullan........Maryland
Sidney Needle ....Maryland
John Marshall Neel........Maryland
Palmer Rice Nickerson....Maryland
Mitchell Palees ....Maryland
Seymour Phillips ....Maryland
Leon Pierson ....Maryland
W. Edgar Porter..........Maryland
Maurice Julius Pressman...Maryland
Marie White Presstman....Maryland
Walter John Pugh.........Maryland
Herman Pumpian ....Maryland
Goldsborough Griffith Rossiter Maryland
Peter C. Salerno.........Connecticut
Frederick Scharf ....Maryland
Simon Schonfield ....Maryland
Helen I. Sherry...........Maryland
Walter Edward Sinn.......Maryland
William Howser Skinner...Maryland

24

"Graduates of the Law School for the Year 1922–23."
Courtesy of the University of Maryland.

ANNA W. CARTON

Heuisler Honor Society; Member of Board of Directors, Vice-Pres., University of Balto. Branch Natl. Women's Bar Asso.; Secretary to Staff of Yearbook.

This gifted young woman successfully combines the roles of wife, mother and student.

By her quick grasp of difficult legal problems and by her capacity for detail and hard work she has won the esteem and admiration of her fellow students; and by her kindliness, good nature and unfailing generosity she has won their friendship. Not a few of the members of the class of 1933 would have abandond the study of law had it not been for her encouragement and her willingness to act as coach.

She is a member of the Heuisler Honor Society, being the only woman to enjoy that distinction.

Yearbook photograph of Anna W. Carton, 1933.
Courtesy of the University of Baltimore, Langsdale Library.

then only two years old. The Cartons came to Maryland from North Dakota so that Nathan could join his brothers in a merchandising business which purchased goods to sell to several stores throughout Baltimore.[24] Married as teenagers, the Cartons had one son, Marvin, but Anna Carton was unsatisfied with a purely domestic life: "I was very bored with the occupation of a housewife, which was sitting around with other housewives and talking about babies."[25] In 1933, Anna Carton became the first married woman and mother to graduate from law school in Maryland, and she was in the top ten percent of her class.[26]

Nellie Marie Marshall similarly married as a teenager and raised three sons before considering a career in law. In 1935, at thirty years old, Nellie completed her high school education and enrolled in the Mount Vernon School of Law, graduating with top honors in 1939.[27]

The path to practicing law after graduation presented substantial challenges, as the social and political climate of the time cast women in a "second-class role" and male-dominated law firms were hesitant to accept women into their ranks, refusing to hire or even interview women for lawyer positions.[28] Jeanette Rosner Wolman recounted challenges that her University of Maryland School of Law female classmates faced:

> Ten or twelve women started law school in my class, but among the 103 students who graduated in 1924, only two women, in addition to me, received law degrees. One was the late Ruth Schapiro Newman, who became a sole practitioner. The other was Matlida Williams, who served as the office manager of a prominent Baltimore law firm during law school. After graduation, she asked to work at the firm as a lawyer but was turned down because she was a woman. Williams never practiced law; she later married a classmate, the late Fulton F. Bramble, and their son now is the managing partner of Niles, Barton & Wilmer.[29]

Seeking to practice after being admitted to the bar, Rose Zetzer found "there was no law firm that wanted to take you in," and she was given offers to take dictation instead.[30]

In the post-Progressive Era, women lawyers were still so rare in court that, when they appeared, audiences would gather to "see how the lady would do."[31] Many women lawyers embarking on careers as solo practitioners had difficulty securing clients as they did not have the connections and contacts of their male counterparts, largely due to their exclusion from city and state bar associations. Nor could women lawyers rely on the support of middle-class women to obtain clients, because, in middle-class families, the husband typically selected the lawyer to handle the family's business and legal matters.[32] In limited instances, judges would appoint women lawyers to certain cases, and, as a result, most female trial lawyers represented primarily other women or indigent clients.[33]

For some, such as Sophie Nordenholz, maintaining a solo practice was facilitated by working in tandem with male attorneys in matters such as criminal defense and by representing her husband's organization, Deutsches Haus, in appealing the denial of the organization's liquor license.[34] Similarly, Helen E. Brown started her legal career working with R. Palmer Ingram, who had a law practice defending individuals charged with prohibition violations.[35]

Other women lawyers found greater access to the legal field upon graduation by practicing in firms with their husbands. After being admitted to the Bar in 1924, Sarah Rosenberg Burke married Joseph Burke, also a recent law school graduate, and the couple began their legal careers practicing together.[36] Ida Claire Lutzky, who graduated from law school with Sarah Rosenberg Burke, married their classmate, Bernard U. Proser, and the couple opened a Highlandtown law office together in general practice.[37] It is likely that, for some women, the joint practice of law also represented a way to balance family and career by forming "personal and professional union[s]."[38] Jeanette Rosner Wolman practiced law with her husband, Paul C. Wolman, from the time she was admitted to the Bar until his death fifty-three years later, which she felt allowed her to pursue her passion for the law while being "a homemaker, a wife, a mother" to her two sons, Paul and Ben, who became lawyers as well.[39]

Helen Sherry began her legal career in practice with her husband but continued to practice independently after the couple separated in 1929.[40] Among the women lawyers of her time, Sherry appears to have had one of the most active solo practices; she frequently made headlines as she represented clients in personal inju-

Helen E. Brown profile.

Photographer and date unknown.
Courtesy of the Maryland State Archives.

ry, breach of contract, and criminal defense cases.[41] Sherry was the first Maryland woman to argue a case in front of the Court of Appeals of Maryland in 1929, a case which she won.[42] One of her highest profile cases was as defense counsel for William Niemoth, a reputed Chicago gangster, for which she served as local counsel along with W. W. O'Brien, Niemoth's Chicago attorney, throughout the lengthy three-year case that ended when Niemoth's conviction was upheld on appeal in 1931.[43]

Helen Sherry also worked on various cases as co-counsel alongside other women lawyers such as Ida Kloze, which suited the desire of many women lawyers, themselves striving to make headway in the legal profession, to band together.[44] Emilie Doetsch opened a law office with Marie Presstman in 1932, and together they faced the challenge of securing clients without the established reputations of more seasoned male lawyers.[45] Three years later, Doetsch represented the Women's City Club, securing a $9,000 reduction in real-estate tax assessment for the organization.[46]

In 1940, Rose Zetzer, Anna Carton, Lottie Friedler, and LaRue Parke found mutual support in one another when they formed the first all-female law firm in Maryland.[47] The firm had a general practice with a focus on domestic relations, but the women encountered resistance, even from their clients.[48] For instance, Zetzer recounted that she was first paid for her legal services with panty hose and candy, as some clients did not feel the need to pay women for the legal services they provided.[49] Another client described the lack of female accoutrements in the office housing Zetzer and three other female lawyers: "[H]er office in the Munsey Building is as stiff and formal as that of any United States Supreme Court justice. There is not a flower in sight and the whole group of rooms, which she shares with three other women lawyers, is dominated by heavy, calf-bound legal volumes."[50]

During the twenty-four years that the firm was active, it allowed the women to combine resources for clients and also facilitated the development of mentoring relationships.[51] Rose Zetzer was described by her colleagues as "feisty," a "little pushy," and a "hard-working trailblazer" who would help provide funding for women involved in lawsuits whom Zetzer believed to be victims of sex discrimination.[52] Zetzer mentored her young partners, LaRue Parke and Lottie Friedler, who noted that she was "totally for the young women lawyers so they could get a break in life."[53]

Unsurprisingly, new women attorneys benefitted from the experience of their more-seasoned counterparts, even in terms of manner of dress and presentation. By way of example, many new women lawyers were uncertain of whether or not they should wear hats in court. LaRue Parke, who was admitted in 1942, described seeking guidance from "older women lawyers" on whether hats were acceptable in court: "I was not expected to wear a hat, but none told me there was a law against it."[54] Uncertainty arose, because male lawyers were expected to remove their hats when entering a courtroom, but women spectators and witnesses were not required to remove their hats in court.[55] In commenting on the subject, one Baltimore City judge remarked, "If [a woman lawyer] appeared in my court wearing a hat I might form certain mental reservations regarding her good judgment," while another judge stated, "If a woman happens to be appearing before a jury, it would be up to her to decide whether she is more attractive with a hat or without it."[56] The debate over whether women lawyers could have worn hats was indicative of the type of mixed reaction women lawyers received. Women lawyers were faced with the dilemma of whether they should follow the examples of male lawyers or forge a new identity for the "woman lawyer."[57]

National Association of Women Lawyers, 1930.

Photograph by Harris & Ewing. Courtesy of the Library of Congress, Harris & Ewing Collection.

The support women lawyers found in practicing together, combined with their exclusion from male-dominated bar associations and an increase in numbers of women lawyers, lead to the development of formal organizations for female lawyers, such as the Women's Bar Association and its precursor groups. The first organizations in Maryland comprised solely of women lawyers included the Inez Milholland Club and the Women's Lawyers Association, both formed in 1927.[58] The Inez Milholland Club, "named for the New York Portia and suffragist," was formed, in March 1927, by a group of University of Maryland School of Law graduates to "encourage growth in the number of women lawyers."[59] Helen E. Brown was the organization's first president, and, by 1935, it had successfully merged with the women's legal sorority, Phi Delta Delta.[60]

During the spring of 1927, a group of women lawyers (including Henrietta Stonestreet, Adelaide Lindenberg, Goldie Miller, Helen Sherry, Sarah Burke, Marie Presstman, B. Olive Cole, and Jeanette Wolman) gathered at the home of Ida Kloze and founded the Women's Lawyers Association of Maryland.[61] They drafted a tentative constitution, elected officers, and began communications with the National Association of Women Lawyers.[62] The stated purpose of the organization was to promote "fraternalism and an interchange of ideas."[63] According to Wolman, the dozen or so members "started getting together to talk over our problems."[64] The organization facilitated the monthly gathering of women lawyers to hear how other professional women such as Dean Grace Hayes Riley, of the Washington College of Law, were able to obtain positions of distinction in their careers.[65] Stonestreet remarked that the women were inspired and encouraged to see the success achieved by other women.[66]

In 1929, four members of the Women's Lawyers Association—Henrietta Stonestreet, Emilie Doetsch, Helen Sherry, and Marie Presstman—formed the Women's Bar Association of Baltimore City, with the goal of gaining admission to the Baltimore City Bar Association.[67] These first female applicants were characterized by the press as the "feminist invasion."[68] Despite the fact that each application was endorsed by a judge of the Supreme Bench of Baltimore City and by prominent members of the local bar, the Baltimore City Bar Association denied women admission by a vote of sixty-eight to fifty-six on the basis of their gender.[69] The all-male organization members claimed that allowing women to join would open the doors for African Americans as well and argued that, if women were present at the meetings, the men would not have the same freedom to tell stories or partake in certain "refreshments."[70]

In recounting to the National Women Lawyers' Journal the resistance the women faced from the Baltimore City Bar Association, Stonestreet declared:

> We sympathize, but are not impressed. They didn't want women in offices, but women came. They didn't want women in the professions, but women came. They didn't want women in colleges, but women came. They didn't want women in the barber shops, but look at them.
>
> The Baltimore Bar Association may think it is strong enough to stand against the stream, but we rather think it over-estimates itself. In fact, we are so sure it over-estimates itself that we venture a prophecy. In a few months, or perhaps a few weeks, the four ladies turned down yesterday will crash the gates and lead in a regiment of their sisters. It isn't pleasant to contemplate, but there's no use being blind to the facts.[71]

While Stonestreet's prophecy that the women would secure admittance to the local bar association would not come true for two decades, the women vigilantly pursued admission to the State and Baltimore City Bar Associations to gain equal access with their male counterparts. The Women's Bar Association of Baltimore City eventually merged with the Women's Lawyers Association to form the Women's Bar Association and, as Jeanette Wolman explained, "[M]ore and more women came in... [b]ut we always continued to apply for membership in the Baltimore Bar Association so we could feel equal. They just kept turning us down."[72]

After twenty consecutive years of application and denial, Rose Zetzer was the first woman admitted to the Maryland State Bar Association in 1946.[73] Her application that year was supported by two judges of the Supreme Bench of Baltimore City, Judge Joseph Sherbow and Judge E. Paul Mason, which precipitated an amendment to the Maryland State Bar Association's constitution to formally admit women.[74] "I never thought I'd live to see the day," she said, reasoning that the members' objection to including women in the all-male organization "centers in their fondness for sitting around with their feet up and telling stories...."[75] Her admission solidified Maryland as the first original American colony to have a woman attorney, Margaret Brent, but the last state to admit women to a state bar association.

The Baltimore City Bar Association's informal policy of excluding women as well as minorities took a significantly longer time to overcome.[76] Thirty years after her initial application, Jeanette Wolman became the first woman admitted to the Baltimore City Bar Association when the members voted to "discontinue the practice" of excluding members based on color or sex.[77]

Women's right to participate on juries was also a central concern for the women lawyers of the 1920s, 1930s, and 1940s. For a woman charged with a crime, having other women on the jury was essential to being judged by her peers, and, for a woman serving on a jury, her service meant recognition of her right to participate in the judicial system. Much like the women lawyers of the Progressive Era who had advocated in support of suffrage, many of the women lawyers of the 1920s found that legal pursuits and social activism went hand in hand. Their legal educations made them uniquely qualified advocates for the legal and political rights of women and also acutely aware of the correlation between the social perception of women and the perception of women's abilities as lawyers. "Frequently frustrated by the limits they found in the law, a number of the early women attorneys took to soapboxes, the lecture circuit, campaign platforms and the streets to bring about social change."[78]

Bar Group To Admit Women;
Upsets 50-Year Precedent

June 30, 1946.
Courtesy of The Baltimore Sun.

Throughout the nation, many people felt that the right to jury service was implied with the passage of the

Nineteenth Amendment, yet several states, including Maryland, continued to deny women this right.[79] The challenge to the state's denial of women's right to jury service was raised during 1921 in Maryland's courts before the judges of the Supreme Bench.[80] At first, women lawyers were not always aligned in their viewpoints on what the role of women in relation to juries should be. Henrietta Stonestreet argued to the bench: "While I do not think it a bad thing for women to serve on juries, I am opposed to calling Maryland women to jury service at this time. I do not think that women of this State, in which the majority of women were opposed to suffrage, have had sufficient training in public life to have fitted them for jury service."[81]

WOMEN MAKE PLEA FOR JURY SERVICE

Delegation Of 200 Appears Before House Committee Favoring Farrington Bill

SING AS THEY MARCH

Call On Governor But He Declines To Commit Himself For Or Against Measure

Women Make Plea for Jury Service: Delegation of 200 Appears Before House Committee Favoring Farrington Bill," February 26, 1943.

Courtesy of The Baltimore Sun.

In 1931, Helen Sherry not only drafted a bill on behalf of the Federation of Women's Clubs, introduced by Delegate Farrington of Montgomery County, which provided for women to serve on juries, but also testified in support of the bill when it was presented to the General Assembly.[82] Sherry faced resistance, just as Etta Maddox had when she authored a bill in support of women's suffrage and advocated in support of the bill to the Maryland Legislature two decades before.[83] Sherry urged women to support jury service as a duty of citizenship and "the only way to get a really representative jury."[84] When the bill establishing women's right to jury service was presented before the House Judiciary Committee, 200 women appeared in support.[85] Sherry testified that women were prepared for the "burden as well as the benefits of citizenship."[86]

Helen E. Brown, inspired by Emma Maddox Funck and the women who led the suffrage movement in Maryland, was an ardent advocate for women's right to jury service and testified in support of the bill to the Legislature in 1931.[87] Brown contended that the presence of women on juries was necessary to put a woman defendant or witness at ease, knowing that "there was someone in the jury box who could grasp the woman's point of view."[88] Two weeks later, a group of nearly 100 women attended a hearing before the House Judiciary Committee, arguing that there were "inescapable differences of sex" and that the majority of women did not want to serve on juries.[89] Henrietta Stonestreet expressed strong opposition to the jury service bill, and opponents were supported by the only female member of the legislature, Mary Risteau of the House of Delegates, who had earlier characterized proponents as "a small group of women who claim that they speak for the women of this state and are demanding that women be forced into service."[90] The bill did not pass, but a new measure was introduced nearly every year thereafter.[91]

In 1939, the issue was again raised to the General Assembly, and Helen Sherry, Anna Carton, and Rose Zetzer testified in support of the jury service bill, arguing that women jurors would provide an alternative viewpoint that would enhance the integrity of the judicial process. Carton testified: "We do not seek to usurp any of the privileges or prerogatives of the male sex... [w]e only ask to be allowed to share an important civic duty with them."[92] Legislators had a "misguided sense of chivalry" in contending that sex offenses would offend the sensibilities of women, and Zetzer and others responded by asserting that a woman's view in such cases would "give a better cross-section of opinion."[93] Despite persistent lobbying by proponents, the Legislature continued to strike down the bills offered to establish the right to jury service. The Legislature responded that, regardless of an organized minority in support, in general women in the state did not want to serve on juries.[94]

Three Women Register for Jury Duty in New York City, 1937.

Photograph by a staff photographer at The World Telegram. Courtesy of the Library of Congress.

The turning point came in 1946, when the Women's Bar Association and other women's organizations collectively formed the Maryland Committee for Women's Jury Service.[95] With amplified support, less resistance, and three women serving in the House of Delegates who were all in support of the jury service bill, the Maryland Committee for Women's Jury Service focused on the role of women as lawyers and other professionals, to counter the opposition's argument that jury service did not comport with women's role in the home.[96] The Committee also presented a survey showing that eighty-five percent of women favored jury service in Maryland.[97] When the bill next came before the Senate Judiciary Committee, women supporters turned out in droves, taking over the Senate chamber to demand the right to jury service:

> They overflowed the Senate seats, peered down upon the heads of members of the Senate Judiciary Committee from the crowded gallery, jammed the doorways and lined the walls in their pressure on behalf of Senate Bill 99.... More than 300 women in furs and feathered hats took the seats of the senators on the main floor. Extra chairs were required just to seat them. The hearing was marked by cheers, hisses, applause and the pleas of more than 30 women speakers, but there was but one opponent to the bill.[98]

Representatives from the Maryland Committee for Jury Service for Women and the Maryland Federation of Women's Clubs spoke on behalf of the attendees, and Helen E. Brown testified that, as a trial lawyer, she felt "verdicts given by grand and petit juries would be improved by the presence of women on such juries."[99] The Senate Judicial Proceedings Committee provided a favorable report, and the jury bill finally passed in March of 1947.[100] In June of that year, approximately 3,200 women were interviewed for jury service, and another 2,800 would be interviewed three months later.[101] Courthouses were renovated to be equipped with women's facilities, and, in September, eleven women served together on a jury in Baltimore City Court.[102] At the end of their service, the women wrote a letter of thanks to the judge, telling him that it had been an honor to serve and that jury duty was an educational experience.[103]

Just as women lawyers were involved in the struggle for women's right to jury service, they sought to become involved in social change by obtaining positions of authority in government. The Women's Bar Association and its members offered support for the women seeking appointment to various legal positions and advocated on their behalf.[104] Emilie Doetsch, in her campaign as the first woman to run for a position on the Baltimore City Council in 1923, stated, "[w]omen stepping into the legislative chambers of the municipal government will result in greater efficiency."[105] In a letter to her former classmates at Goucher College, Doetsch asserted, "[s]till, someone had to make the break and, even if you fail, it serves notice on the political powers-that-be that women are emerging from their old indifference and that they mean to have their share in the running of the government."[106] Doetsch was later appointed Assistant City Solicitor in 1928, the first woman to hold that office.[107]

Helen E. Brown was one of six women who ran for a seat in the House of Delegates in 1930, and, while she was unsuccessful, three other women won seats that year.[108] Brown received two successful appointments as Assistant City Solicitor and Magistrate on the Bench of the Housing Court, a position that had never been held by a woman. In advocating for her appointment to the bench, the Women's Bar Association called on Governor-elect Harry W. Nice to make good on his campaign plank for "women's equality."[109] As Magistrate, Brown adjudicated violations of landlord and tenant housing codes issued by health inspectors. She was compared to her male predecessor and received criticism from the press that "[p]erhaps in a moderate Portia this quality of mercy is becoming," but her decisions from the bench—granting sentencing postponements, allowing the opportunity to come into compliance with laws, and giving credit for rectified violations—would lead to violators disregarding health notices, opting instead to take their chances in court.[110] Brown was not deterred by her critics and continued in public service, later teaching domestic relations at the University of Baltimore School of Law and earning an appointment to be the chairman of the Workman's Compensation Department of the Maryland Roads Commission.[111]

Helen E. Brown on her horse at home, 1952.

Photograph attributed to James O. Colliflower. Courtesy of the Maryland State Archives.

The Women's Bar Association supported Anna Carton in her campaign, albeit unsuccessful, for a seat in the House of Delegates under the campaign slogan, "It takes a woman to clean out the House."[112] In 1942, another founding member of the Women's Bar Association, Rose Zetzer, became the first woman elected to the Board of Directors of the Legal Aid Bureau, and, in 1943, the Women's Bar Association nominated Zetzer and Helen E. Brown for seats on the Supreme Bench of Baltimore City.[113]

In 1951, Zetzer sought to become the first female prosecutor in the State's Attorney's Office of Baltimore City and asked Judge Burnita Shelton Matthews, of the U.S. District Court for the District of Columbia, for support. Judge Matthews suggested exerting pressure on the newly elected State's Attorney to follow through on his campaign promises to hire a woman attorney by reaching out to an influential female Democrat: "I am going to ask India Edwards to try to get the Baltimore job done through Democratic channels. She is genuinely interested in women getting ahead."[114] Zetzer was ultimately denied the position, apparently because of her religion, although her letters to Judge Matthews evidence the nascent development of a network of women attorneys coalescing to gain a more prominent stake in the legal profession.[115]

In 1954, Nellie Marie Marshall became the first woman and first grandmother in Baltimore City to win a city-wide election when she was elected judge of the Baltimore City Orphan's Court.[116] Subsequently, with the backing of the Women's Bar Association, Marshall was the first woman to run for election for a position on the Supreme Bench of Baltimore City and also the first woman to file for the Democratic nomination for U.S. Senate.[117] For Marshall, her interest in legislation paralleled her desire to practice law, as she continued her legal practice in family and probate work until shortly before she became ill with cancer.[118] Many women lawyers combined legal and public service careers, and, in 1965, Jeanette Rosner Wolman was appointed by Governor Tawes as the first chairperson of the Maryland Commission on the Status of Women, which recommended minimum wage to all employees, regardless of sex.[119]

In 1962, Zetzer and Brown established the Marjorie Cook Foundation (the Foundation) to provide aid to "women who are 'discriminated against or have suffered in their occupations or received injury to self or property because of unequal laws.'"[120] Zetzer and Brown were named trustees of the estate of Marjorie Cook, the daughter of a prominent Baltimore attorney, who was devoted to the cause of women's rights and left nearly $500,000 of her will to "further the cause of equality for women."[121] The Foundation provided Zetzer and Brown the opportunity to mentor women from across the nation who were experiencing discrimination based on their gender, encouraging them to "'Keep fighting. Get after members of the Legislature and your Congressmen. It is up to those two votes to help [women] put laws that will help [them].'"[122] The Foundation also supported Kathy Kusner's fight to obtain a jockey license from the Maryland Racing Commission in 1968.[123]

In 1972, Nellie Marie Marshall accompanied Mary Emily Stuart, a twenty-two-year-old woman, to the Circuit Court for Howard County. Stuart, who was represented by Mary Ellen Brooke, the president of the Women's Bar Association, challenged the Howard County Election Board's decision to remove Stuart from the registration rolls, "because she would not be identified by her husband's surname on the registration lists." She had recently married Samuel Austell, Jr., but asked the Circuit Court to reinstate her birth-given name, Stuart, on the list of registered voters.[124]

Marshall's support and presence was important, specifically because she, too, had refused to change her name when she married Charles Tyszko. Although the Baltimore City Board of Elections threatened to bar Judge Marshall from voting, because of her refusal to use the surname Tyszko, it never made a decision, and she continued to use the surname Marshall.[125] Stuart's attorneys used Marshall as an example to support the notion that a woman changes her name upon marriage based on custom, not law.[126] The Circuit Court Judge, T. Hunt Mayfield, disagreed and ruled that the common law of Maryland requires a woman, upon marriage, to change her surname and, thereby, her legal identity to that of her husband.[127] The Court of Appeals of Maryland, in a landmark decision, reversed.[128] Although Stuart's and Marshall's cases focused on voter registration, the resulting conclusion, which acknowledged the independent legal status of married women, would have greater impact on married women, enabling them to enter into contracts and obtain credit cards independent of their husbands.

First Mother, Then Lawyer, Now High-Court Candidate

"First Mother, Then Lawyer, Now High Court Candidate," April 14, 1956.

Courtesy of The Baltimore Sun.

Like the women lawyers before them, the women lawyers of the 1920s, 1930s, and 1940s made important strides in women's political rights, persisting in the face of rejection and exclusion from the legal profession, to establish a place for women in the practice of law in order to benefit society. Their perseverance, coupled with familial and collegial support as well as an increase in the number of women entering the legal profession, allowed them to gain admittance in state and local bar associations, to secure women's right to jury service, and to establish a community of support for the women lawyers to come. Seventy years after being admitted to the Maryland Bar, Jeanette Rosner Wolman reflected on her contribution to this period in women's legal history and remarked:

Jeanette Rosner Wolman.

Photographer and date unknown.
Courtesy of the Maryland State Courts, Office of Communications and Public Affairs.

> I think women take more of an interest in politics because they can participate. Just like in law when I became a lawyer. Little by little, we fought for the right for women to belong to the bar, to become partners in law firms, to become judges, and eventually it became accepted. I guess that doesn't make for a big story, but I was there and I worked for it and I still do.[129]

Ninety years after the first class of University of Maryland School of Law graduates that included women, the Court of Appeals of Maryland had its first female majority, with the appointment of the first woman Chief Judge, Mary Ellen Barbera, and the first female African American, Shirley M. Watts, to the state's highest court.[130] The campaign for equality continues, but the status of women lawyers in Maryland was forever changed by the endurance and perseverance of the women of the 1920s, 1930s, and 1940s.

CHAPTER 5:

African American Women Admitted to the Bar in Maryland, 1946–1974: Four Profiles of Public Calling

Phoebe A. Haddon

Introduction

In 1946, President Harry Truman appointed Sadie Tanner Mossell Alexander, a highly successful African American lawyer in Philadelphia, to the President's Committee on Civil Rights. Alexander, who by then had been practicing law for almost twenty years, would eventually found a civil rights law firm and acquire a long list of distinguished public service appointments, all as part of a legal career spanning more than six decades.[1]

That same year, the first African American woman was admitted to the Maryland Bar, Jane Cleo Marshall Lucas of the University of Michigan School of Law, and the first two African American women to earn law degrees in Maryland, Elaine Carsley Davis and Juanita Jackson Mitchell, enrolled at the University of Maryland School of Law.[2]

In this chapter, I chronicle the barriers that prevented women of color in Maryland from entering the legal profession until the mid-1940s. I first give a brief historical account of blacks in Maryland and then consider how barriers such as the legacy of Jim Crow laws shaped the professional experience of four African American women who made an impact after graduating from law school.

Jane M. Lucas, LL.B.
Date unknown. Courtesy of Howard University.

Detail of Jane Marshall Lucas and fellow members of the law faculty of Howard University. Photographer and date unknown. Courtesy of Howard University.

Although geographically close to Pennsylvania, where Sadie Alexander had made a name for herself as a female African American lawyer, Maryland lagged behind other states in terms of the opportunities it offered women to pursue a legal career.[3] Opportunities were especially scarce for women of color, who were forced to overcome the double hurdles of gender and race. While records are incomplete and often ambiguous, a preliminary analysis of law school registration data in Maryland suggests that race was a more potent barrier to participation in the legal profession than gender. The University of Maryland School of Law, for instance, admitted its first white female students in 1920; the later-founded University of Baltimore School of Law, meanwhile, included white female students among its first graduates in 1928.[4] But it took *Pearson v. Murray*, a 1936 decision from the state's highest court, before the University of Maryland School of Law opened its doors to African Americans, and it was another six years before Emily Orchard enrolled, becoming the first woman of color to do so.[5]

Orchard's tenure was brief, and she did not graduate.[6] Because enrollment records are incomplete and often ambiguous regarding a student's race or ethnic heritage, the data that follow are estimates at best. It appears that, from 1942 to 1969, approximately 211 women enrolled at the University of Maryland School of Law, but only eighteen—or approximately eight and a half percent—were women of color.[7] Enrollment patterns were much the same at the University of Baltimore School of Law, which, during the same period, enrolled 208 women, of whom only four—or approximately two percent—were unambiguously women of color.[8]

Charm and Brains Combined

MISS EMILY V. ORCHARD,
daughter of Mr. and Mrs. James F. Orchard, 422 N. Arlington Avenue, Baltimore, who received her master's degree in sociology from the University of Pennsylvania on June 10. She is a 1930 graduate of Douglass High School and was graduated from Morgan College in 1934.

"Charm and Brains Combined," June 20, 1936.
Courtesy of The Afro-American.

The overwhelming majority of these women of color were African American. The University of Baltimore School of Law, for instance, graduated only a single Asian American woman in 1961 and may have enrolled two Hispanic women in 1930 and 1931 who did not graduate. Similarly, only two Asian American women graduated from the University of Maryland School of Law during this period, in 1967 and 1971 respectively, and possibly one Latina woman in 1969.[9]

Scope

Due to the lack of information about many of these women and this book's focus, I provide profiles of four exceptionally talented and committed female lawyers of color who studied law in the state of Maryland, passed the bar examination, and were admitted to the Bar.[10] The story begins in 1942, when Emily V. Orchard, a social worker, became the first such student enrolled at the University of Maryland School of Law, and ends in 1974, when law school enrollments of women of all races and ethnicities began to increase significantly in the state.[11]

Some of these women built distinguished careers in multiple disciplines, despite the significant obstacles facing any lawyer who was not part of the traditional white-male elite.[12] Lena King Lee, for example, taught for thirty-three years in the Baltimore City public school system before turning to full-time private practice in 1964 and then launching a vibrant political career two years later in the Maryland House of Delegates. Others used their legal training as an enhancement to other careers. Elaine Carsley Davis, for instance, used her J.D. to integrate and shape the state's emerging system of public higher education. With or without traditional practice experience, many of the women of color who pursued legal education in Maryland prior to 1974 did so because they shared the conviction that the law was a powerful tool for achieving social justice.

An inclusive scope is also appropriate when one recalls that these women came of age in an era when the education and professional ambitions of all women, regardless of race, conflicted with social pressure to make marriage and motherhood the primary focus of their lives. As Mari Matsuda notes, "In becoming lawyers—the most public of professionals—[such women] were obviously defying separate-sphere ideology" that restricted women's work to the privacy of the home.[13]

Additionally, restricting the focus only to those who went into private practice, as many legal historians have done, would limit this study to those women of color embodying "the ideologies of elite lawyers and the structure of the profession"—a rare commodity when most women of color were "doubly marginalized by the intersection of race and gender prejudices," as Professor Kenneth Mack notes.[14] Professor Mack proposes an alternate approach—one that looks at the social history of the legal profession as it was practiced "from below" by lawyers typically excluded from the white male elite, such as immigrants, people of color, and women. This allows one to capture the experience of more women of color and, in so doing, to gain new insights and a richer perspective on the impact of legal education in Maryland for nontraditional students and practitioners. In other words, looking "from below" can expand one's understanding of the legal profession's history.[15]

Matsuda reminds us that "Gerda Lerner, a preeminent feminist historian, has long urged the writing of women's biography."[16] I share her conviction that stories of historically underrepresented people can help us understand struggles for equality, and she offers a scholarly model in *Called from Within: Early Women Lawyers of Hawai'i* (1992), which recounts the lives of seventeen pioneering women lawyers in Hawaii. As she observes:

> By writing about outstanding female historical figures, we remind ourselves that powerful, inventive, and history-shaping women have always existed. We provide role models for women in the process of inventing themselves, and we dispel myths about the limitations of women's abilities. Most written history is men's history, creating the false picture that only men have been, and should be, responsible for important public tasks.[17]

Historical Context

When Emily Orchard enrolled at the University of Maryland School of Law in 1942, women and people of color in Maryland had faced barriers to the legal profession for almost three centuries.[18] Maryland had been a slave state, but, as many of the other chapters in this book document, women of every race and economic status were barred for centuries from representing any but their own interests in court.

Circumstances for women of color were less restrictive in some other states. For example, in 1796, Luce Terry, a free black woman, gained national recognition by arguing a series of lawsuits to preserve her husband's title to land in Vermont that had been deeded to him during the 1760s. Although Terry had two lawyers, she argued the case herself in front of Justice Samuel Chase, of the U.S. Supreme Court, who was riding the New England circuit. Justice Chase, a native of Maryland, was reported to have said that Terry "made better argument than he had heard from any lawyer at the Vermont bar."[19]

Over time, both women and African American men in Maryland and other states started to challenge their exclusion from the profession. Black males were the first to succeed in gaining access to law schools and state bars; they were then followed by white women.[20] Women of color lagged behind for decades.

Sharp Street Memorial M. E. Church

REV. WILLIAM H. DEAN

CORNER DOLPHIN AND ETTING STREETS

10 a. m. Adult Bible Class. 11 a. m. SERMON REV. J. W. HAYWOOD D. D. of Morgan College. 2.30 p. m. Sunday-school. 3.30 p. m. ANNUAL SERVICES JUVENILES COURT CALANTHE K. of P., Mrs. Rosa Richardson. Mgr. 3.30 p. m. HUGH WATSON CLUB in GYM. .BENEFIT AGED HOME. Music MR. and MRS. CHRISTY. 5 p. m. SERMON by PASTOR TO BALTIMORE CITY LODGE G. U. O. O. F. Monday 8.30 p. m. MUSICALE and MAY POLE WRAP by Miss Cornelia Brooks and 50 children. Admission 10 cents. Wednesday May 30 Decoration Day at Mt. Auburn. Lunches and refreshments on sale, benefit $7.000 Drive.

Friday June 1st., address Mrs. Hazel Mountain Walker. The first colored woman Lawyer to be admitted to the Bar in the State of Ohio and Sister of Miss Elsie May Mountain Executive Secretary of Community House. Auspices of choir. Admission 25 Cents.

"Sharp Street Memorial M.E. Church," May 25, 1923.

Courtesy of The Afro-American.

Though legally barred from many aspects of public life, blacks in Maryland created a long tradition of activism and self-advocacy, due, at least in part, to the state's large and well-established free black community, the like of which was not found in any other slave state.[21] At the outset of the Civil War in 1861, the numbers of free blacks and slaves in Maryland was nearly equal; in Baltimore, free blacks comprised more than ninety percent of the black population—the largest such concentration in the U.S.—and outnumbered slaves nearly twelve to one.[22] Women comprised a majority of the free black population, though the degree by which they outnumbered men varied by region.[23] By 1850, some black families in the state could trace their freedom back three generations or more.[24]

Though freedom did not guarantee financial prosperity (many free blacks lived in worse conditions than slaves), the social and psychological benefits of freedom cannot be discounted.[25] The large number of free blacks, as well as high literacy rates and cohesive social organizations, provided a foundation for political activism in the African American community that began during the nineteenth century and continued throughout the twentieth. Many African Americans in Baltimore were active in the abolitionist movement, and many participated in the Underground Railroad.[26] During the Civil War, six regiments of Maryland blacks, comprising 8,718 men, fought on the Union side.[27] And after the war, in 1892, a newspaper, *The Afro-American*, was founded in Baltimore by a minister to ignite political activism in the black community, a function the newspaper continued to perform for more than a century, through the struggle for civil rights, and into the present day.[28]

In Baltimore especially, churches were the focal point of the free black community. They became launching points for black social organizations, education, activism, and community leaders and also provided less tangible but equally vital qualities: black consciousness, self-respect, and pride.[29] As early as 1802, a group of blacks constructed the first building to house Sharp Street Memorial United Methodist Church, which became one of the foremost institutions of Baltimore's black community for the next two hundred years.[30]

From its earliest days, the scope of activities at Sharp Street was impressive. It took over a Quaker school for black children, hosted speakers and discussions, raised funds to help escaped slaves, and housed the Bible Institute that eventually became Morgan State University.[31] Later, other black churches would undertake a similar scope of activity, either through the church itself or affiliated fraternal and welfare organizations that helped impoverished members, offered discussions of current events, and sometimes pursued political activities, such as working for the right to collective bargaining.[32] The churches and their affiliated groups thrived. By the time of the New Deal, there were more than 400 social clubs and 200 churches in Baltimore's black community alone; both venues had emerged as important proving grounds for future political leaders.[33]

Women's roles in churches and the social organizations were mixed. Although women comprised the majority in black churches and were active and vocal participants, they were not treated as men's equals and were restricted to performing significant but unofficial and less prestigious functions.[34] The affiliated fraternal organizations and social groups seem to have been largely gender-segregated, but women were just as active as men, if not more so: during the late 1830s, nine of the fifteen associations in Baltimore were women's organizations.[35] Their work continued well into the twentieth century; for example, the Organization of Colored Democratic Women played a major role in Theodore McKeldin's election as Mayor of Baltimore and, later, as Governor of Maryland.[36]

African American involvement in politics occurred just as the first blacks tried to join Maryland's legal profession. Charles S. Taylor, a Massachusetts-licensed lawyer who sought to practice in Maryland, gained admittance to the federal courts in Maryland but was rejected by the Supreme Bench of Baltimore City, whose decision was upheld by the Court of Appeals in 1877.[37] Eight years later, Charles Wilson, another Massachusetts lawyer in Maryland but one who was not interested in practicing, agreed to serve as plaintiff in a second attempt to gain admission to the Baltimore Bar.[38] This time the effort was successful. Although Wilson was never actually licensed, his victory paved the way for Everett J. Waring to become, in 1889, the first African American to be admitted to practice in Maryland.[39]

Efforts to close this small window of equality ensued. In 1891, two years after Waring was admitted to practice in Maryland, students at the University of Maryland School of Law, with the support of Dean John Prentiss Poe, signed a petition urging the exclusion of blacks from the school.[40] As requested, the School of Law refused to admit blacks and expelled the two black students who were already there.[41] This ban on African American students of any gender continued; in 1933, Harold Arthur Seaborne, the first black applicant in forty-two years, was summarily rejected because of his race.[42]

Two years later, Charles Hamilton Houston, Thurgood Marshall, and William Gosnell brought the case of Donald Gaines Murray to the Baltimore City Circuit Court.[43] They had found a perfect plaintiff in this Amherst graduate and former member of the City-Wide Young People's Forum; they went on to find the perfect judge in Eugene O'Dunne, a judge about whom even H. L. Mencken could find no fault.[44] After a trial, O'Dunne ordered that Murray be admitted, and he refused a stay until the state's appeal was heard.[45] The Court of Appeals upheld O'Dunne's decision, and the University of Maryland School of Law was officially desegregated.[46]

Legal desegregation, however, did not end attempts to keep blacks out of the school. Sometime later, the president of the university offered to pay William H. Murphy, Sr.'s tuition and travel expenses if he would attend Harvard Law School instead of the University of Maryland.[47] Murphy refused, and he became the third black student at the University of Maryland School of Law and, later, a judge.[48]

Civil rights organizations began to formalize during the early twentieth century with the inception of the Niagara Movement in 1905, which merged five years later into the NAACP (National Association for the Advancement of Colored People).[49] A Baltimore chapter was chartered in 1912 but soon collapsed until twenty years later, when Lillie Mae Carroll Jackson, the mother of Juanita Jackson Mitchell, breathed new life into it.[50]

Profiles of Selected African American Women Admitted to the Maryland Bar, 1942–1974

I have chosen to profile only four of the women who were among the first African American graduates of the University of Maryland School of Law to be admitted to the Maryland Bar, including Juanita Jackson Mitchell and Lena Lee, who are well known. The characteristics and themes that unify their stories, however, are also found among those other women who were not as well-known but are profiled in this chapter.

As noted, African American women faced discrimination, struggling against the twin barriers of race and gender. Given that double burden, they did not consider law school enrollment, much less bar admission, in significant numbers until more than twenty years after the first white female students were admitted to the University of Maryland School of Law and more than forty years after Etta Maddox passed the bar examination and became the first woman at the Bar in Maryland.[51]

Racial discrimination also affected the educational opportunities of most African Americans in the state. Both male and female African American students at the University of Maryland School of Law were likely to have had elementary and secondary educations that were inferior in resources to those of their white counterparts, a consequence of Jim Crow laws and informal racial barriers across the nation. Although black communities throughout the state demonstrated an early and ongoing commitment to literacy and espoused educational equality, Maryland's black schools were, by the turn of the twentieth century, clearly and substantially inferior to those for whites.[52] The poor educational foundation for many African Americans made college and graduate school comparatively challenging, and, for many students, the environment was not welcoming.[53]

Given these challenging circumstances for most women of color, it is not surprising that the small number who surmounted them to complete law school and earn admission to the Bar were atypical and extraordinary; all four women profiled here were academic achievers who came to the University of Maryland School of Law with other advanced degrees, sometimes from prestigious institutions. Juanita Jackson Mitchell and Emily Orchard held master's degrees from the University of Pennsylvania. Elaine Carsley Davis was awarded a Ph.D. from the Johns Hopkins University.[54] Davis also had two bachelor's degrees, one from Coppin Teachers College (now Coppin State University) and one from Morgan State College (now University).[55] Lena King Lee earned a master's degree from New York University.[56]

These women, like most African American women, needed to earn a living. Three of the four women profiled here were older students who came to law school with existing careers and studied law to further them. They continued to work full-time while in law school and, in the case of Juanita Jackson Mitchell, to raise children as well.[57]

This combination of factors—educational inequality, scarce economic resources, and, in some cases, law school enrollment while advancing another career—were consequences of unequal opportunities and expectations; what activist Pauli Murray called Jane Crow.[58] These were powerful barriers that prevented all but the most tenacious, intellectually talented and fortunate women of color from even attaining legal education, much less achieving bar examination passage and admission to the Bar.

In addition to tenacity and talent, the women who succeeded in overcoming these barriers enjoyed the staunch support of their families and spouses. Elaine Carsley Davis's husband, Robert Clark Davis, attended law school with her for at least a year.[59] Joan Sessoms's mother gave her the idea to go to law school, and Sessoms credits her father with the fact that she stayed in law school; Lena King Lee and Juanita Jackson Mitchell received tremendous encouragement from their husbands. Mitchell also counted her mother as a great influence as well as a source of emotional and financial support.[60]

The women profiled here all pursued some form of commitment to working for the public good. Elaine Carsley Davis, though she never practiced law, worked for the integration of public schools and public higher education.[61] Joan Sessoms, who had a long legal career in the federal government, headed the Office of Federal Contract Compliance Programs in the U.S. Department of Education.[62] After retiring from the Baltimore City public school system, Lena King Lee practiced law and became a skilled politician, serving on several politically appointed commissions and councils and in the Maryland House of Delegates, to which she was elected at the age of sixty.[63] Juanita Jackson Mitchell went on to become one of the foremost civil rights leaders of her time.[64]

Despite the racial, gender, social, and economic barriers they faced—or, perhaps, because of them—the professional lives of these women are illustrious examples of what I term a "public calling" to the law. The public calling of the law includes an obligation to bring equality to the justice system.[65] It invokes not only a lawyer's skills, but also her values: equality, fairness, and justice. It also means working to open the legal field and legal education to those who have traditionally been denied a place among its practitioners.

Many individuals with such a calling have personally suffered discrimination, an experience that inspires in them a vision of service grounded in a commitment to equal access and fairness—justice for all. Such individuals often carry that vision and commitment forward into their communities, touching thousands of lives as lawyers, certainly, but also as teachers, mentors, business leaders, activists, or elected officials; they are public servants, in the broadest sense of that term. They bring a moral compass to their work and we, as a society, are all enriched by their presence. In short, a public calling drove these women to overcome the barriers they faced and to work to ensure that the experiences of others who followed were enriched.

Juanita Jackson Mitchell (1913–1992)

In the autumn of 1946, the University of Maryland School of Law opened its doors to an "unprecedented number of 20 [black] students," heralded the Baltimore newspaper, *The Afro-American*.[66] These students included three African American women: Elaine Carsley Davis, Virginia Jones, and Juanita Jackson Mitchell.[67] All three women viewed law school as a means of enhancing their pre-law careers; they enrolled as evening students while maintaining their existing jobs.[68] One of those women, Juanita Jackson Mitchell, was to achieve remarkable influence and recognition not only in Maryland, but nationally through her work for the NAACP. Although our discussion of her work is longer than that of the other women profiled here, the length is justified, given the richness of Mitchell's legal career, abundance of historical material about it, and national stature of her achievements.

Juanita Jackson Mitchell was the daughter of Lillie Mae Carroll Jackson, a dedicated activist for black equality and a fervently religious member of Sharp Street Memorial United Methodist Church.[69] Lillie and her husband, Keiffer "Jack" Jackson, had been traveling church entertainers, but she and their daughters returned to Baltimore when the girls reached school age.[70] A son of sharecroppers, Keiffer Jackson wanted his children to be well educated.[71] Lillie came from an educated family; her father had been a school supervisor, and her mother was a teacher, as she was.[72]

After returning to Baltimore, Lillie Mae Jackson successfully invested in real estate and does not seem to have been particularly interested in politics until two events changed the direction of her life.[73] In 1918, her face was severely disfigured by an operation for mastoiditis, which had been performed in a doctor's office after a white hospital refused to admit her for surgery.[74] A decade later, because of their race, her daughters, Juanita and Virginia, were refused admission, respectively, to the University of Maryland at College Park and the Maryland Institute College of Art in Baltimore.[75] In response, the Jacksons moved their daughters to Philadelphia, where they lived with an aunt. Juanita enrolled at the University of Pennsylvania (Penn) and Virginia at the Philadelphia Museum and School of Art.[76] Lillie Mae sent them off with a charge to return to Baltimore and "give back so our people can be free."[77]

Philadelphia was a revelation for Mitchell. A far less racially restrictive city than Baltimore—which she once described as "living hell" for blacks—it invited her to imagine an integrated world. And it inspired her to realize the vision of her parents, who had "reared [her and her siblings] with a sense of destiny, a mission" to "help the masses of [our] people."[78] While at Penn, Mitchell quickly became involved in groups to promote interracial friendships and tolerance, joined the black sorority, Alpha Kappa Alpha, and led a successful movement to end the racial segregation of Penn's dormitories. Her education helped her acquire confidence and informed her vision of an integrated society offering equal opportunities to all.[79]

Mitchell completed her B.S. in education from Penn, graduating with honors at age eighteen.[80] Before she was twenty-five, her success as a civil rights activist had made her a national figure; the NAACP announced her appointment as youth coordinator by putting her portrait on the cover of its magazine, *Crisis*, and, in 1936, *The Atlanta Daily World* celebrated "[t]he gifted young woman [who] organized the now *nationally* known City-Wide . . . Forum in Baltimore."[81] Confident of her mission to end discrimination, Mitchell created an alternate vision of a black woman as an engaged political activist—a sharp contrast to the previous canonic image of a genteel lady, also shown on the cover of *Crisis*.[82] Mitchell did not retreat

Juanita Jackson and Lillie Mae Jackson, 1928.
Photographer unknown. Reprinted with the permission of Baltimore *magazine, May 1999.*

into the shadows but insisted on holding the system accountable for its hypocrisy. "We do not beg for civil rights as crumbs from the table of democracy. We insist on our right to sit at the table," she said.[83]

Mitchell's career began in 1931, when, after graduating from Penn, she, her sister Virginia, and, it appears, her future husband, Clarence Mitchell, Jr., organized the City-Wide Young People's Forum, with Lillie Mae as an advisor.[84] Each week the Forum drew approximately 500 African American youths, from ages sixteen to twenty-four, of all social classes. It became a vibrant community organization, in sharp contrast to Baltimore's moribund NAACP branch and more staid Urban League chapter.[85] During its ten-year existence, the Forum attracted some 330,000 attendees to its events and provided a pipeline to the

NAACP as well as education and training in civil rights activism.[86]

Under the leadership of the Juanita Jackson, the Forum engaged in cultural, educational, social, and political activities. It hosted a weekly lecture series featuring prominent figures such as W. E. B. DuBois, Mary McLeod Bethune, Charles Hamilton Houston, Thurgood Marshall, and James Weldon Johnson. It organized a political campaign against lynching, sponsored annual intercollegiate debates and musical competitions among black institutions, and conducted a black voter registration drive in response to the 1932 redistricting of the Baltimore City Council, which had resulted in the first all-white City Council since Reconstruction.

Juanita and Lillie Mae also led the Forum in organizing boycotts to increase the hiring of African American staff by city institutions and by stores that sold to the black community, including a highly successful one that forced the A&P supermarket chain to end its ban on hiring black employees.[87] Mitchell's leadership in the boycott created the most "unified response to blatant discrimination" seen in Baltimore, and it caused such concern among the white shop owners on Pennsylvania Avenue, one of black Baltimore's major retail areas, that they sued to enjoin further picketing.[88] When the court granted a permanent injunction barring future picketing, Mitchell launched fundraisers to pay for the appeal. Though the injunction was upheld, she gained valuable experience in organizing mass protests.[89]

In 1932, Mitchell also worked with the NAACP's national secretary, Walter White, to revive the Baltimore NAACP branch by creating a youth wing called the "NAACP Boosters." The next year, when she was just twenty-two, Mitchell relinquished the presidency of the Forum and joined the NAACP as national youth coordinator and White's special assistant.[90] She wrote a constitution for the youth branch, raised funds, and traveled throughout the country to revive or found local youth chapters. She then joined Mary McLeod Bethune, one of the wise elders of the civil rights movement, to found the National Council of Negro Women.[91] At the same time, Mitchell returned to the University of Pennsylvania, where, in 1935, she earned an M.A. in sociology.[92]

That same year, Lillie Mae Jackson, Mitchell's mother, accepted the challenge of reinvigorating the Baltimore branch of the NAACP.[93] More importantly, the NAACP prevailed in *Pearson v. Murray*, which found that the University of Maryland School of Law's admission barriers for black students violated the

Juanita Jackson Mitchell speaking at a rally for a NAACP membership drive, 1935.
Courtesy of Larry Gibson, Professor of Law at the University of Maryland Francis King Carey School of Law.

Equal Protection Clause of the Fourteenth Amendment of the U.S. Constitution.[94] The decision inspired Mitchell and others who sought major change through legal institutions. "We liked the NAACP as a channel," Mitchell later wrote, "[because of its] approach for working within the system, working within the law."[95]

By 1935, Mitchell was clearly immersed in a highly successful career. However, when her long-time friend and Forum colleague Clarence Mitchell, Jr. proposed, she accepted. After waiting for him to assume his position as the head of the Urban League's chapter in St. Paul, Minnesota, she resigned her own position at the NAACP so as not to overshadow his.[96] Nevertheless, soon after arriving in St. Paul, she sought to revive the local NAACP branch (displeasing some Urban League leaders), continued to fundraise for the organization and, just before the birth of her first child in 1939, represented it and the youth of "the race," at President Roosevelt's Conference on Children in a Democracy.[97]

By the next autumn, she had accepted White's invitation to return to the NAACP to lead the Baltimore membership drive as a contract worker, not a volunteer—an affirmation of her value at a time when women often served civil rights organizations for minimal compensation and recognition.[98] While Juanita moved back to Baltimore, with their first son and another child on the way, Clarence remained in Minnesota for half a year to finish his work, and then accepted a new job in Washington, DC.[99] Mitchell described an "almost total commitment to the struggle for freedom" that she shared with her husband:

> Charlie Houston had helped give us that sense that a whole lot of these things we were tolerating happened only because Negroes themselves were not asserting their constitutional rights. Clarence and I had this commitment of urgency, and of giving our all to the struggle.[100]

During the next several years, Mitchell organized a city-wide voter registration drive and a march of 2,000 protesters in Annapolis who objected to the killing of a black soldier by a white officer from the Baltimore police force—a force whose head was appointed by the governor, not the mayor.[101]

By 1945, Mitchell was convinced that she needed a law degree to pursue her mission to end discrimination. She enrolled in the University of Maryland School of Law, attending class at night while also raising two children and bearing her third child during her first year of law school; she took only two weeks off after the birth before returning for her final exams.[102] Clarence, who commuted to work in Washington, supported her decision and helped with the care of the children (he later earned his own degree from the University of Maryland School of Law).[103]

For the black women profiled here, the support of family and friends, male and female alike, was crucial. Mitchell's colleagues at the NAACP, particularly Charles Houston, encouraged her to become a lawyer. Houston planned to enlist Mitchell as the "Baltimore arm" of the NAACP legal initiative; she would initiate the team's lawsuits, while he took them over as they proceeded through the appeal process.[104] Mitchell clearly shared Houston's conviction that "there is an unlimited field in the law for young Negroes who are willing to make the fight. The lawyer is going to be the leader of the next step in racial advancement."[105]

Mitchell excelled in law school, becoming the only woman and one of two blacks on the eighteen-member editorial board of *The Maryland Law Review*.[106] "There is no segregation at all, and relations are completely good," she told *The Evening Sun*.[107] She remained committed to fighting racial discrimination, choosing to write a case-note article on a civil rights subject, two recent Maryland decisions barring the enforcement of racial covenants.[108] This was not an abstract issue for her, as her later description of the campaign leading to this victory shows: "The NAACP's successful restrictive covenant cases in 1948 before the Supreme Court cost over $200,000, 23 years of litigation and the life of Charles Houston, from overwork."[109]

After graduating with her LL.B. in 1950, Mitchell did confront racially based restrictions on her legal career. The bar review courses refused to admit blacks, and office landlords refused to lease to them. Mitchell overcame the first challenge by studying independently and passing the Maryland Bar Exam on her first attempt; her mother resolved the second challenge by buying a downtown office for Mitchell's solo law practice.[110]

Mitchell immediately took up Houston's charge to "sue Jim Crow out of Maryland with the Fourteenth Amendment."[111] Within a month after taking the bar exam, she joined a group of two adults and several children to integrate Baltimore County's Fort Smallwood Park. Although stone-throwing hoodlums blocked access to the beach, Mitchell returned later to integrate public beaches as part of an NAACP campaign.[112]

The NAACP remained the primary channel for Mitchell's civil rights work.[113] She was involved in its lawsuits against the University of Maryland, parts of which remained segregated for sixteen years after *Murray*.[114] Even after the university relented and admitted blacks in 1951, it refused to admit those from out-of-state, prompting Mitchell and the NAACP to threaten more legal action.[115] Mitchell also joined Donald Murray in filing a 1951 lawsuit to integrate the commercial facilities at Friendship Airport (now BWI Thurgood Marshall Airport), a suit backed, but not directed, by the Baltimore NAACP.[116] Mitchell joined her mother, other NAACP representatives, and publisher Carl Murphy, the chairman of the organization's new legal redress committee, for a meeting with Governor Theodore McKeldin to protest the widespread brutality of the Baltimore City police department against African Americans and to seek the dismissal of the police commissioner, a gubernatorial appointee.[117] Soon after this, Mitchell became the secretary of the NAACP legal redress committee, for whom she filed charges of racial discrimination in employment by the Coast Guard's Curtis Bay shipping yard. She also filed suits to integrate Fort Smallwood's municipal beach and Baltimore's public swimming pools and to enjoin the operation of segregated parallel beaches at Sandy Point State Park (Mitchell was a plaintiff in this last case).[118]

Mitchell's commitment to ending segregation and her vision of a less racially-restricted world that was first inspired by her sojourn in Philadelphia were strengthened by her month-long trip to Europe with her mother in the summer of 1951. They traveled to celebrate her graduation from law school and to visit her sister, who was studying music in Italy.[119] She wrote a series of columns for *The Afro-American* describing the relaxed racial attitudes of Europeans and urging Baltimore's mayor and state's attorney to visit their Italian relatives to address their own racial prejudice:

> It is wonderful to be free from the fear of humiliation because of one's race... Baltimore's ridiculous racial restrictions will be very much harder to take after this European experience.... Here in this faraway country, I, a foreigner, am being treated with the courtesy and respect and dignity to which decent human beings are entitled, of which I have been robbed far too long in my own hometown, in my own country which my race helped build and make and which our tax dollars help support.... And may God give us the strength to open our closed mouths in social protest that will reverberate in the ears of our city officials until every vestige of those unchristian, barbaric practices which stain our community are removed. Baltimore's jim-crow may not lynch our bodies, but it does something far more terrible. It lynches our souls.... [I]t is worth the financial sacrifice to make a trip to Europe, to know and feel how it is to be treated as a human being and begin to realize how far back in the Dark Ages Baltimore is in its racial practices.[120]

Mitchell found Baltimore's racial barriers as strong as ever upon her return. She successfully vanquished a gender barrier when, in 1952, she and Lena Lee were the first women admitted to the Monumental City Bar Association. The Monumental City Bar Association, a black lawyers' organization, was founded in

1935 by Thurgood Marshall and other black lawyers who were barred from the white Bar Association of Baltimore City.[121]

Mitchell embarked on one of her most significant battles in 1953 when, in the run up to *Brown v. Board of Education*, she and the Baltimore NAACP took up the cause of four black students who had been denied admission to the historically all-white Mergenthaler School of Printing, Baltimore's only technical school.[122] After rejecting the school board's proposal to offer a similar course of study at a yet-to-be-built black vocational school, Mitchell and other NAACP lawyers filed suit on behalf of their carefully selected plaintiffs to integrate Mergenthaler. That School's new facilities made it "one of America's most modern vocational education centers."[123] A month later, Mitchell filed another suit against the school board, seeking to integrate the all-white and all-female Western High School.[124] These two cases—the first in state court and the second in federal court—made Baltimore the first Jim Crow city to desegregate after *Brown*. The Baltimore City School Board quickly dropped its segregation policy in June 1954, despite the State Board of Education's unanimous refusal to consider integration until the Supreme Court issued its follow-up *Brown* remedy decision that was scheduled for the next year.[125]

Mitchell and the Baltimore NAACP legal redress committee immediately filed motions to integrate beaches and Baltimore's public swimming pools, asserting that *Brown* applied to public accommodations as well as schools.[126] After the NAACP won an injunction barring segregated beaches as unequal, the state refused to accede, claiming, at first, that proposed future "improvements" to the black beach justified lifting the injunction. When that failed, the state chose to keep the beaches closed while it filed an appeal to avoid integration.[127]

After two years of legal battles rising all the way to the U.S. Supreme Court, Mitchell and the Baltimore NAACP won a decisive victory in 1955, when the Court affirmed the lower courts' application of *Brown* to beaches, the first application of *Brown* outside of education. The legal victory for Mitchell and the Baltimore NAACP pushed Baltimore and Maryland to the forefront of the civil rights struggle.[128] Although the decision led Baltimore officially to desegregate its municipal swimming pools the following summer, *de facto* segregation remained the norm throughout the 1960s.[129] The state's recalcitrance toward integration forced Mitchell's legal redress committee to choose its suits carefully, as she candidly acknowledged soon after *Brown* in explaining the NAACP decision to "battle for the beaches" while postponing the struggle to integrate public education in Maryland outside of Baltimore.[130]

Once Mitchell prevailed in expanding *Brown*'s application of the Fourteenth Amendment to all state activities, she returned to the challenge of forcing the Maryland Board of Education and individual counties to integrate their public schools, partnering in a series of cases over the next decade with the national NAACP's Legal Defense Fund, then led by Thurgood Marshall.[131] Following the *Brown* remedy decision, in which the Supreme Court gave a softened directive to implement integration "with all deliberate speed," Marshall convened a conference of national NAACP leaders, including Mitchell, in July 1955. The group developed the following plan as described and acted upon, by Mitchell:

> We will set our own deadline, September 1955. If no start toward desegregation has been made by that date, we will take the school boards to court, county by county. The Supreme Court has given us the legal ammunition.[132]

As these cases moved their way through the courts, Mitchell filed other suits to expand the reach of the Fourteenth Amendment.[133]

She also remained active as a community organizer, adding more than 50,000 new voters to the Baltimore City rolls through successful registration drives in 1957–1958 and in 1960.[134] Also, in 1960, she led an

Program, memorial service, Juanita Jackson Mitchell, July 11, 1992, The Beginning of a Brilliant Legal Career, 1950, page 12.
Courtesy of the Maryland State Archives.

Program, memorial service, Juanita Jackson Mitchell, July 7, 1992. Juanita Jackson Mitchell in Action, page 8.
Courtesy of the Maryland State Archives.

investigation which found that the U.S. Veterans Administration had discriminated against blacks when selling homes in Baltimore, and she used those results to pressure the agency's headquarters in Washington, DC, to launch an internal probe.[135]

In 1963, she assumed the presidency of the Maryland conference of the NAACP, succeeding her mother, who remained head of the Baltimore branch.[136] That same year, Governor J. Millard Tawes led the passage of a bill banning segregation in public accommodations, the first such law passed by a state below the Mason-Dixon line.[137]

Also, in 1963, President Kennedy invited Mitchell to participate in the White House Conference on Women and Civil Rights; three years later, President Johnson invited her to his White House Conference, "To Fulfill These Rights," which focused on steps to improve the education, justice, and economic security of black communities after the 1964 Civil Rights Act.[138] Her participation in the latter, as well as her record as an activist, likely led to her appointment as chair of the Education Committee of Baltimore's Model Cities program, which was part of President Johnson's War on Poverty that sought to revitalize economically deprived city neighborhoods.[139] Mitchell also played an important role in Maryland's response to the U.S. Supreme Court's "one man, one vote" decision, successfully challenging the General Assembly's proposed redistricting solution for maintaining the congressional district imbalance that favored the sparsely populated Eastern Shore over Baltimore.[140]

She also continued to address another major complaint of the black community in Baltimore: the arbitrary disrespect and brutality of the Baltimore Police Department. In 1966, she won a major victory when the Fourth Circuit declared illegal a massive search of 300 houses in an African American neighborhood without warrants based on an anonymous tip and ordered the department to cease this practice.[141] At the same time, Mitchell sought to build connections with the police and city government. As part of her effort to reduce police brutality, she spoke to the Police Wives Association about the importance of introducing police training and co-chaired the Mayor's Task Force on Police-Community Relations from 1965 to 1967.[142] In 1970, she formed Freedom House to "build a bridge of cooperation between the police department and the city in our neighborhood" and increase the police force's hiring and promotion of blacks to make it more reflective of the city's population.[143] Mitchell also demonstrated her conviction that the ranks of government officials must reflect the constituents served in order to be effective by her legal challenge to Charles County's paucity of black teachers.[144] Although she lost the case, she pursued it all the way to the U.S. Supreme Court, determined to promote change by effective use of the law and community involvement.

Throughout Mitchell's life, she continued her involvement in the community, spearheading efforts such as the Stop the Killing Campaign in the 1980s and speaking out on social justice issues.[145] In 1981, she was named a Dean's Visiting Fellow at the University of Pennsylvania's Faculty of Arts and Sciences.[146] In 1984, her husband, Clarence Mitchell, Jr., died, and shortly afterward she became ill, but even this did not stop her activism.[147]

Her influence as a civil rights pioneer extended to future generations of her family and continues today. Her grandson, Keiffer Jackson Mitchell, Jr., served for several years on the Baltimore City Council and is now a Maryland state legislator.[148]

Elaine Carsley Davis (1921–2013)

Elaine Carsley Davis was the only child of parents who were "not schooled, but educated," as she put it. Her mother was a self-taught dressmaker, her father a chauffeur who taught himself auto mechanics and opened his own business. Both parents encouraged their daughter, who excelled in school, to pursue her education.[149]

Davis's commitment to education began with the attainment of two bachelor's degrees, one from the historically black Coppin Teachers College (now Coppin State University) in 1942 and one from Morgan State College (now Morgan State University) in 1943.[150] After winning a summer scholarship from Morgan State to study mathematics at the University of Pennsylvania in 1945, she completed the requirements to teach junior high and received a bonus with the approval of the Board of Education.[151] That same summer, she married Robert Clarke Davis, a returning World War II veteran, and together the pair entered the University of Maryland School of Law's evening program in the fall of 1946.[152]

Robert Clarke Davis planned to use law as a tool for pursuing a related field: he hoped to start a real estate business, an interest linked to his existing career managing public housing projects for Baltimore City.[153] Davis left his legal studies in his third year. He went on to serve on the committee of the new zoning commission that created a new zoning code for Baltimore City in 1957, and, in 1960, became the director of Harlem Park's urban renewal area.[154] Like Clarence Mitchell, Jr., Clarke Davis was interested in the law and supported his wife's ambitions. As with the other women profiled in this chapter, the strong support of their husband and families—providing financial, social, and emotional support as well as professional connections—was vital to Elaine Carsley Davis.[155]

Elaine Carsley Davis was a high school mathematics teacher in a Baltimore City public school with no plans to practice law when she enrolled in law school.[156] Her motives for pursuing a legal education were straightforward: when her husband complained about the evenings she spent away from home taking business classes, she enrolled with him in law school, so they could spend more time together.[157] Davis's first-year grades were high enough that she, like Mitchell, was invited to apply for a place on the Maryland Law Review.[158]

Although Elaine Davis did not immediately use her legal skills or law license to challenge the discrimination she had experienced, she did, like Juanita Mitchell, devote her life to public education and to Baltimore City public schools, in particular, during the long struggle for desegregation. In 1953, she began work on a master's degree in education at the Johns Hopkins University, where she may have been the first African American female graduate student.[159]

Immediately after earning her M.Ed. two years later, she began her doctoral work in education, also at Hopkins, winning three national fellowships as well as being initiated into Phi Beta Kappa, a prestigious honor society, upon completion of her Ph.D. In 1958, she received what was almost certainly the first Ph.D. that Hopkins awarded to an African American woman.[160] In the midst of her studies, she had two children—the first in 1952, after graduating from law school, and the second in 1958, while finishing her Ph.D. During all but two of these years, she continued to work in the Baltimore City public schools.[161]

Not surprisingly, Davis's doctoral dissertation focused on education law, specifically judicial rulings on assertions of governmental immunity by school districts, an issue directly related to the ongoing struggle to desegregate public schools.[162] While these questions drew on her legal background, they were also directly relevant to her personal experiences fighting racial discrimination within the Baltimore City public schools. She received, for example, one of six "unprecedented" appointments of black staff to supervisory positions—appointments regarded as "token steps" towards desegregation by one of the two black members of the school board.[163]

In 1963, Davis exchanged her responsibilities as a principal for those of Baltimore City Public School System's "supervisor of special projects" and then, three years later, as Director of Curriculum Development. She also represented the city's school system in the 1968 Model Cities Program.[164] By 1973, Davis had become a top aide to Roland Patterson, Baltimore's first black school superintendent, and became intimately involved in the sweeping decentralization and rationalization promoted by Patterson.[165] His reforms, intended to effect desegregation, created a political furor that led to his ouster in 1975 by white members of the school board who opposed his integration plans of 1974 and 1975.[166] Frustrated at the opposition to Patterson and his reorganization of the school system in which she had been "deeply involved" as the "senior educational officer to the superintendent," Davis retired in 1974, becoming Associate Professor of Education at the Johns Hopkins University and Associate Director of the Education Division of its evening and summer programs.[167]

While on the front lines of the desegregation struggle in the Baltimore City public schools, Davis simultaneously participated in the related struggles to integrate and reorganize public higher education in Maryland, initiatives launched by Governor J. Millard Tawes in 1963. The reorganization created a tripartite division of public higher education institutions: the University of Maryland, under its Board of Regents; the former teachers colleges, to be transformed into liberal arts institutions, under their Board of Trustees of State Colleges; and the community colleges, remaining under their local and the state Boards of Education. The Maryland Advisory Council for Higher Education would provide overall guidance for the reorganization.[168] In 1966, Davis was named one of the original members of the Special Committee on Community Viewpoint, a body created both to advise the council on its annual reports about the reorganization's master plan and to serve as an information conduit between professional educators and the broader community.[169] Davis represented the Baltimore City Public School System on this committee for the three years before the Council was reshaped in 1968.[170]

Governor Tawes also appointed Davis in 1965 to the Board of Trustees of her alma mater, Morgan State College. Morgan State had fought the initial reorganization proposal that grouped it with the five teachers colleges, under a single board of trustees, arguing successfully that, as an existing liberal arts college, it would be placed at a disadvantage if forced to compete with the teachers colleges for state funds.[171] The final law instead allowed Morgan State to retain its autonomy until three of the five teachers colleges earned accreditation as liberal arts institutions, at which point Morgan State would be joined under the Board of Trustees of State Colleges.[172] The newly appointed State Colleges Board of Trustees almost immediately sought authority over Morgan State by claiming that the teachers colleges had made sufficient progress toward accreditation.[173]

Morgan State's role in the newly reorganized state system was a political flashpoint, since it had been the only public liberal arts college open to African Americans until the University of Maryland finally admitted its first black undergraduate in 1951. Morgan State and its legislative backers sought to ensure it would retain a competitive role with the University of Maryland; they were successful in obtaining approval for Morgan State to offer graduate studies but failed to stop the creation of an undergraduate branch of the University of Maryland in Baltimore County (UMBC), which they regarded as a rival that was launched to reduce Morgan State's status in the Baltimore region.[174] Davis joined the Morgan State board as it confronted these and other controversies in the changed world of higher education, including a vigorous debate about whether Morgan State should recruit white students—a contentious question that saw two other women lawyers of color, Juanita Jackson Mitchell and Lena King Lee, take opposing positions.[175]

Two years after Davis joined Morgan State's board, the Trustees of the State Colleges declared that all five of the former teachers colleges had achieved accreditation and demanded that Morgan State merge with these new liberal arts colleges under the State Colleges Trustees.[176] After a rancorous debate and an unsuccessful lawsuit by Morgan State alumni, Morgan State lost its board. Davis, however, played a crucial role in smoothing the transition, when, five weeks later, Governor Spiro T. Agnew appointed her to the State Colleges Board.[177] Morgan State's president praised not only Davis's appointment as a former Morgan State trustee but also how it doubled the black trustees on the Board.[178] Davis joined Judge Robert Watts, one of the original members and also a person of color.[179] She, along with Mrs. Thomas W. H. White, Jr. followed Elizabeth Cole, a distinguished woman lawyer, strong integrationist, and general counsel for the Commission on Civil Rights' Public Education Section, as the first female trustees.[180] Davis shared Cole's background in law and educational administration as well as her experience with desegregation.[181]

Davis became the first non-white woman on the State Colleges Board, bringing her particular viewpoint based on her experiences—as a graduate of two of the colleges under the board's jurisdiction as well as her unique perspectives as both a lawyer *and* a professional educator—to a board composed of both attorneys and educators. As a trustee, Davis was not afraid to express views out of favor with the public or the rest of the board. She was the lone dissenting vote against the board's 1969 approval of Coppin State remaining independent, predominantly black, and focused on education. Davis believed Coppin State needed to be integrated immediately and become a true liberal arts college; although she lost that vote, the next year she was appointed chair of the board's committee that selected Coppin State's new president and was also one of four trustees who chose the new president of Morgan State.[182] She was the trustee most critical of the slow pace of integration at the colleges, challenging the institutions to go beyond words to produce meaningful change.[183]

Despite her willingness to disagree, she earned the respect of the other trustees, becoming the chairwoman of the Board's Finance and Budget Committee in 1968. There, she questioned the validity of the complaints of inadequate facilities at Bowie State in 1969, pointing out to striking students, who were seeking more funds, that the school received more per pupil than had been projected.[184] This was a sensitive situation, since Governor Agnew's decision to arrest several hundred students the year before, during a demonstration on the same issue, was indelibly linked with the riots that broke out the next day after news of the assassination of Martin Luther King, Jr.[185] Davis's tough diplomacy and identity as an accomplished black woman enabled her to deal successfully with the wrenching change to these institutions, historically segregated by race and gender, in the midst of nationwide upheaval. In recognition of her leadership, she was chosen to be the Vice-Chair of the State Colleges Board of Trustees in 1970; three years later, she became the Chair, one of the first black women to attain such a prominent role in higher education and a position that garnered national attention.[186] She received wide-spread recognition of her leadership skills locally as well. Davis was appointed by Mayor William Donald Schaefer to the Baltimore Jail Board and she was also appointed by the president of Goucher College to its Board of Trustees in 1972.[187] She later joined the board of the Rouse Company just as its ambitious remaking of Baltimore's Inner Harbor was reaching fruition.[188]

Lena King Lee (1906–2006)

Lena King Lee was born July 14, 1906, in Sumter, Alabama, the daughter of Samella and Lula King.[189] As her father searched for work, the family moved to Illinois and then to Pennsylvania, where he became a coal miner and an activist for worker's rights. He earned enough to send Lee and her two siblings to private boarding schools. Lee graduated third in her high school class of seventy, in which she had been the only African American student. She accepted a scholarship at Cheyney Training School (now Cheyney University, near Philadelphia), earning a teaching certificate there in 1927. She moved to Maryland to teach, first in Annapolis and then, in 1931, in Baltimore.[190] There, she taught sixth grade, married Baltimore businessman Robert R. Lee in 1937, and, two years later, earned a bachelor's degree in education from Morgan State College.[191] Lee, like other African Americans, was prevented from enrolling in graduate studies at the University of Maryland College Park, which remained segregated until 1951. As a result, she earned a master's degree from New York University in 1947, traveling to and from New York City every weekend for years.[192]

Lena King Lee, 1975.
Photograph attributed to Kenneth M. Brooks Studios, Inc. Courtesy of the Maryland State Archives.

In 1947, Lee was also promoted to principal at the Henry H. Garnet Elementary School. She appreciated the promotion, but her frustration with what she saw as the Baltimore City School Board's long delay in awarding it prompted her to enter the University of Maryland School of Law that autumn.[193] Lee, like her classmates Juanita Jackson Mitchell and Elaine Carsley Davis, continued to work while in law school and enjoyed the strong support of her husband.[194] By her third year, she was the only African American woman enrolled; her classmate Verda Welcome had withdrawn without a degree, and Elaine Carsley Davis and Juanita Jackson Mitchell had graduated.[195] Lee herself graduated in 1951 and was granted admission to the Maryland and Baltimore Bars a year later, becoming the first black woman to be admitted to the Bar Association of Baltimore City.[196] She remained in education, however, joining the American Federation of Teachers as its first black member and continuing her work in the Baltimore City Public School System until her retirement in 1964.[197]

Lee assumed civic responsibilities in 1955, when Mayor Thomas D'Alesandro appointed her to the seven-member Baltimore Redevelopment Commission (BRC) and then to the Baltimore Urban Renewal

VOTE FOR

LENA K. LEE

DEMOCRAT FOR

HOUSE OF DELEGATES

FOURTH DISTRICT

EDUCATOR - BUSINESS WOMAN
CIVIC WORKER - LAWYER

You need a LAWYER as a law-maker in the House of Delegates

Lena K. Lee Is Endorsed By
AFL-CIO Labor Union, A.D.A., Afro-American Newspapers, The Sun Newspapers, Democratic Ladies Guild, City-County, Democratic Organization, Maryland League of Women's Clubs, United Christians.

VOTE FOR LENA K. LEE

Pull Lever 13D

Vote the D Line FIRST

Authority Lorraine L. Thomas, Treasurer

Vote for Lena K. Lee, Democrat for House of Delegates, Fourth District.

From the Lena Lee Collection, Thurgood Marshall Law Library, University of Maryland Francis King Carey School of Law.

VOTE FOR

Lena K. LEE

FOR

HOUSE OF DELEGATES

Lever 13D

She is dedicated, she is tough and independent. She has long and varied experience, ability and courage to work for her state and community.

Lena K. LEE has served on many commissions. She has been a school principal, is a practicing lawyer. She is listed in two editions of "Who's Who Of American Women".

VOTE THE ENTIRE 4th DISTRICT DEMOCRATIC TICKET

FOR SENATE

Clarence MITCHELL, III 5D
Verda F. WELCOME 6D

FOR HOUSE OF DELEGATES

Murray ABRAMSON 7D
Victorine Q. ADAMS 8D
Troy BRAILEY 9D
Isaiah (Ike) DIXON, Jr. 10D
Calvin D. DOUGLASS 11D
Harvey H. EPSTEIN 12D
LENA K. LEE 13D

Hit the "D" Line FIRST!

Vote twice on Councilmanic Questions A - B On "A" Pull lever down over AGAINST; then also on "B" Pull lever down over FOR.

You Must Pull Both Levers

General Election — November 8, 1966

Vote for Lena K. Lee, Democrat for House of Delegates, Fourth District.

From the Lena Lee Collection, Thurgood Marshall Law Library, University of Maryland Francis King Carey School of Law.

and Housing Agency.[198] Eight years later, when Governor J. Millard Tawes launched the reorganization of higher education in the state, he appointed Lee to the new Maryland Advisory Council on Higher Education, the body that proposed a new governance structure for the University of Maryland and former state teachers colleges.[199]

After her retirement from the Baltimore City Public School System, Lee practiced full-time with Nicholas & Gosnell, and her work as a lawyer extended into state politics.[200] She immediately supported Joseph Tydings's successful bid for the U.S. Senate in 1964. Two years later, she won the Democratic primary for a seat in the Maryland House of Delegates as part of a slate with Clarence

Mitchell, III, the son of her law school classmate Juanita Jackson Mitchell. Lee found her political base among teachers and women, who saw her "as one of us." She won the racially charged election that November, which pitted Democrat George Mahoney against Republican Baltimore County executive Spiro Agnew, whom Lee and Mitchell endorsed. Lee was sixty years old at the time of her election.[201] During her legislative career, she made the interests of women and children her key priorities, supporting such innovations as mandatory kindergartens, day nurseries for low-income working mothers, educational television, tougher penalties for child abuse, and improved school facilities. She also founded the Maryland Legislative Black Caucus and became known for her efforts to defeat misguided bills.[202]

Lee retired from the legislature in 1982, because of health concerns, but continued a full-time law practice in the areas of family, contract, and criminal law.[203] Until her death in 2006, at age 100, Lee remained a member of Sharp Street United Methodist Church, the bedrock of civil rights activism and the church of the Jackson-Mitchell families.

Joan Sessoms Ford, also known as Joan Elsie Sessoms (b. 1946)

In the mid-1960s, as an undergraduate at the University of Maryland in College Park, Joan Sessoms felt so confused about her future that, one night, she asked her mother what she should do with her life. "Go to law school," her mother replied. "And now, go to bed."[204]

More than forty years later, at her retirement in 2009, Sessoms could look back at a successful, productive career in the federal government that began after her graduation from law school in 1971. Throughout her career, she remained focused on civil rights, as she moved from her first job in the general counsel's office of what was then the U.S. Department of Health, Education, and Welfare (DHEW) to her final position as Regional Director of the U.S. Labor Department's Office of Federal Contract Compliance Programs, Southwest and Rocky Mountain Region, where she addressed discrimination in employment by federal contractors on the bases of race, sex, national origin, color, disability, and veteran status. Her professional commitment to civil rights was deliberate, she says, and the result of her personal experiences of racism and discrimination, which, as she put it, "prescribed my career."[205]

Both of Sessoms's parents played small but pivotal roles in her legal career. Her mother not only sparked the young student's initial interest in the law, but later suggested she call the University of Maryland School of Law for guidance on undergraduate courses to prepare her for a legal education. The call was fortuitous; it began a long, mentoring relationship between Sessoms and then-Assistant Dean William G. Hall, Jr. Like many of the early African American female students at the University of Maryland School of Law, Sessoms was a Baltimore native, a graduate of Frederick Douglass High School, and a member of an educated, middle-class family. Her mother was a high school counselor who held a bachelor's degree from Morgan State College and a master's equivalency in guidance and counseling from McCoy College of the Johns Hopkins University. Her father was a small businessman who attended Howard University and came from a long line of blacks who operated successful small businesses in the African American communities in the South.

Assistant Dean Hall guided Sessoms both before and during her law school career and ultimately helped her obtain her first position at DHEW. There was little guidance provided at the University of Maryland for aspiring law students. Sessoms would telephone Assistant Dean Hall every semester. She discussed with him the courses she planned to take and sought his advice and counsel on whether her course selections would be helpful in attending law school. Assistant Dean Hall was extremely helpful and kind. During one of Sessoms's last calls to him, after her application had been made to the University of Maryland

School of Law, Assistant Dean Hall informed her that she had been accepted as a member of the first-year class. It was a joyous moment for both of them. The joy of being accepted, however, was short-lived.

Once enrolled, the isolation and hostility the young female student experienced as both a woman and an African American during her first year was so overwhelming that she wanted to withdraw. Her father was sympathetic but emphatic: "When we start something, we don't quit," he told her. Without him, "I wouldn't be a lawyer today," Sessoms said.

The intensely competitive academic environment during Sessoms's first year, common in legal education at the time, exacerbated an already difficult situation.[206] During orientation the first-year students were told the now familiar admonition to look to the left, look to the right; one of the people on either side of them would not be back the following year. Sessoms did return for her second year and enjoyed the "sweet revenge" of shocking many of her white male classmates, whose hostility abated somewhat once the first year of intense academic competition was over.[207] But Sessoms was also aware that the loss of so many classmates depressed morale for those who remained. "There was a pall over the entire second year," she said.[208] Nevertheless, Sessoms made friends. Her best friend was a white female student from southern Maryland whom she never saw again after graduation. She also was friends with many Jewish students, who had to cope with anti-Semitism at the law school, and with many of the recently returned Vietnam veterans in her class.

Most of the few other black law students were alumni of Morgan State who had participated in a summer pre-law program at Boston University. Although the group increased the number of African Americans at the University of Maryland School of Law, Sessoms believed that the concept of the pre-law program was racist, since it laid the groundwork for judging the potential performance of all African Americans at the law school and potential black applicants and enrollees by the performance of that small group. "Everybody was supposed to sink or swim" based on the showing of the Morgan State group, she said. The administration "could not connect with judging Black people as individuals."[209] The quotas of approximately ten black students and ten women students were well-intentioned but perverse attempts at affirmative action. The professors at the University of Maryland School of Law conducted extra course-tutorial sessions for the black students and provided practice examination experiences. Sessoms did not participate in this extra assistance program. It seemed destined to demonstrate that blacks were incapable of being lawyers based on a small sampling of students. Sessoms's mother had begun her career as a Latin scholar and a teacher of English and history. She had taught Sessoms English composition, correct grammatical usage, and analytical thinking, with an emphasis on building one's vocabulary. These skills proved necessary and invaluable in law school.

Some of the Morgan State College alumni did not graduate, because, in Sessoms's opinion, they were less prepared for law school; moreover, the attrition of the group was not an anomaly. During the 1960s, there were several instances of African American students being dismissed for poor academic performance. One of the great champions of black students at the University of Maryland School of Law was, unsurprisingly, Juanita Jackson Mitchell, herself a University of Maryland School of Law graduate who would go to the law school and lobby for those who had sought to be readmitted or removed from academic probation. Her mother, NAACP icon Lillie Mae Carroll Jackson, was also involved in these efforts; Jackson and Mitchell, according to Sessoms, "wanted Black people to prove they should have a chance to go to the University of Maryland School of Law."[210]

Sessoms viewed the expulsions and probations as stemming from societal racism and, concomitantly, the students' poor preparation. She observed that one of the student's exams, which he had asked her to review, might have been "written by somebody who was in the tenth grade"—an opinion she did not share with the African American male classmate who had written it because of concern he would be totally discouraged. She began to believe that the problem was larger than the lack of preparation of any one small group of law students: "I said to myself, 'This is systemic. The whole system has not prepared Black students.'" A pre-law course at Boston University could not compensate for a lifetime of unequal educational opportunity. Sessoms believed that language arts, writing, and analytical skills were vital. The students were certainly very intelligent, but the educational system had not taught them the appropriate language arts skills that would enable them to communicate their knowledge in a written form as required in law school. Sessoms saw herself as part of the University of Maryland School of Law's exploration into the admission of more black students, believing that she, too, was being judged as a symbol of her whole race. "I not only had to graduate for myself," she said, but for every other African American student as well. As one of her white classmates loudly pronounced, he was going to win the University of Maryland School of Law's first year moot court competition because his opponents were a "nigg--- and a girl." Although the white student was not referring to her, Sessoms and her Jewish partner were recognized for winning the First Round Moot Court Competition. She graduated in 1971 and immediately passed the Maryland Bar. She was admitted to the Maryland Bar in January 1972.[211]

After graduating and passing the bar exam, Sessoms secured a position with the general counsel of DHEW, with the help of Assistant Dean Hall. Once again, she felt like a representative for all African Americans and was told outright that the department was trying out the black lawyers and, if the newly hired lawyers succeeded, more would be hired. Sessoms remembers wondering at the time how her ability and performance had any connection with the performance of other students who had different backgrounds and levels of ability and had attended different law schools. It was "a heavy burden to carry," she recalled, like being forced to speak for an entire race.[212]

As Attorney Advisor at DHEW, Sessoms was assigned to the Higher Education Branch of the General Counsel's Civil Rights Division. She became counsel in actions by DHEW against Maryland, North Carolina, and Texas, based on systemic discrimination in higher education against students, particularly black students attending historically black colleges and universities (HBCUs). DHEW had found that vestiges of past discrimination remained at these colleges and universities, adversely affecting the students in attendance. This work helped to address Sessoms's concerns, which had arisen during law school, that the higher education systems retained remnants of past discrimination at HBCUs, which disadvantaged black students in competing in professional and graduate schools. She also handled many cases involving the desegregation of elementary and secondary education systems.

Sessoms later moved to Texas, where she continued working for DHEW. Subsequently, as Chief Regional Civil Rights Attorney for the Department of Education's Office for Civil Rights in Dallas, she focused on desegregation in that state's higher education programs. She was instrumental in the preparation of the Texas Higher Education Desegregation Plan, which addressed many of the deficiencies at the state's historically black institutions. The thrust was to ensure that no student of any race would be dissuaded from attending historically black institutions because of the quality of education and opportunity they afforded. She also addressed complaints of discrimination on the basis of sex under Title IX of the Education Amendment of 1972, complaints of discrimination on the basis of disability under Section 504 of the Rehabilitation Act of 1973, as well as complaints of discrimination on the bases of race, color, and/or national origin under Title VI of the Civil Rights Act of 1964.

Later, when she became Regional Director of the U.S. Department of Labor's Office of Federal Contract Compliance Programs (OFCCP), of the Southwest and Rocky Mountain Region, she worked to prevent or sanction employment discrimination based on race, color, sex, national origin, veteran status, and disability in a twelve-state region. At the time of her retirement, she was fighting discrimination against Latino employees and the use of employment tests to discriminate in hiring. The work was engaging for Joan Sessoms Ford: "The more I did, the more I was drawn into the work because there was so much going on."[213]

Like the other University of Maryland School of Law alumnae profiled in this chapter, Sessoms believes her decision to dedicate her career to civil rights was a direct result of her own experiences: "All the things that had happened to me in my early life impacted my psyche," she said. Looking back over her legal career, Sessoms can see the consequences of her work. "Very few people, except for those I worked with, know of my contributions," Sessoms stated, but, nonetheless, she is tremendously gratified by her career as a civil rights attorney. "My role," she said, "was to work day to day on small cases and complaints of discrimination and to help individuals or classes of individuals one case at a time." The DHEW had promised her the opportunity to be "an attorney working for people," and that concept informed her entire thirty-eight year career. "I am so grateful," she said, "that I had the opportunity to do work, prescribed by my law school experience, that helped people whose civil rights had been violated."[214]

Conclusion

African American women had to fight double barriers of race and gender in order to enter the legal profession. Despite the unequal opportunities they faced, for many having an education that led to the practice of law became a tool for fighting discrimination and creating social change. These women of color, with their tenacity reinforced by the encouragement of spouses, parents, extended family, and the professional colleagues who supported them, led to significant breakthroughs not only for them, but also for society.

CHAPTER 6:

The Impact of Mentoring and Other Influences on the Career Development of Women Lawyers

The Honorable Diane O. Leasure (Retired)

In the post-World War II era through 1974, formal mentoring programs for female lawyers were virtually nonexistent. The influence and encouragement of family members and friends within and outside the legal profession, along with sheer determination, were powerful forces in propelling these early women lawyers to pursue their dreams and achieve the reality of a career in the law.

Historically, mentorship in the legal profession has had profound significance. In fact, prior to the late 1800s, an aspiring lawyer received training while serving as an apprentice for an experienced lawyer.[1] Law schools have since replaced the system of legal apprenticeships, and finding a mentor within or outside of this academic setting can often determine the prospective lawyer's level of career success.[2]

Women who became lawyers prior to 1974 were a tremendous source of encouragement and support for those who followed them in the profession. While there have likely been innumerable women who have been positive mentors for other female lawyers, some stand out for their grace and strength in the face of adversity and for their seemingly endless support of young women lawyers.

One name that is synonymous with mentoring is Jeanette Rosner Wolman, who was admitted to the Maryland Bar in 1924. She and six other women—Sarah Burke, Henrietta Stonestreet, Ida Kloze, Adelaide Lindenburg, Goldie Miller, and Helen Sherry—formed what would become the Women's Bar Association of Maryland (WBA).[3] They joined together in 1927, after the exclusively male Maryland State Bar Association (MSBA) refused admittance to four of the seven founding members, and created the Women's Lawyers Association for the purpose of "promoting fraternalism and an interchange of ideas."[4] The Women's Bar Association was formed in 1929 "to promote women's eligibility for membership in state and national bar associations and to promote the appointment of women lawyers to various legal positions."[5] By 1936, the two groups had merged into one organization known as the Women's Bar Association of Baltimore City.[6] The MSBA remained the last state bar association excluding women until 1946, when Rose Zetzer, a WBA member, was finally admitted.[7] The WBA has flourished in the many decades since its modest beginnings, and one essential part of the WBA's mission statement is to "promote and advance the interest of women engaged in the practice of law and advance the status of women in society."[8]

Through the Women's Bar Association—and on many other levels—Jeanette Wolman became a mentor to many. The Honorable Kathleen O'Ferrall Friedman (admitted in 1967) said of her: "She's been a soldier in the fight for women's rights, a pioneer in the legal profession, and a role model for women lawyers. She's an accessible person who was always willing to talk with young lawyers and share her experiences with them."[9]

In addition to Judge O'Ferrall Friedman, Constance K. Putzel (admitted in 1945) and retired Baltimore City Circuit Court Judge Elsbeth Levy Bothe (admitted in 1952) are a few of the women attorneys from this era who consider Jeanette Wolman a mentor.[10] Judge O'Ferrall Friedman, who has become a highly regarded role model and mentor in her own right, notes that Jeanette Wolman was "part of the first wave of woman lawyers" and was responsible for women being admitted to the Baltimore City Bar Association (BCBA).[11] Indeed, the WBA pressed for women to be included in the male-dominated professional associations that served as gateways to the legal profession.[12] Jeanette Wolman broke through one of the more stubborn barriers when she was admitted to the BCBA in 1957, more than a decade after the MSBA began including women.[13] She was a leader who encouraged other women to network with one another and to get involved in bar association work with an eye to achieving leadership roles.

Jeanette Wolman's positive impact on women lawyers was acknowledged in 1991 when she was named one of the first recipients of the American Bar Association's prestigious Margaret Brent Women Lawyers of Achievement Award. The Margaret Brent Award is given to women who have not only achieved professional excellence in their field, but also "influenced other women to pursue legal careers, opened doors for women lawyers in a variety of job settings that historically were closed to them, and/or advanced opportunities for women within a practice area or segment of the profession."[14] In other words, the Margaret Brent Award honors women who are mentors. Indeed, the Oxford English Dictionary defines mentor as "a person who acts as a guide and advisor to another person, especially one who is younger and less experienced" and, more generally, "a person who offers support and guidance to another; an experienced and trusted counselor or friend."[15] In 2007, the honor of receiving this award was also bestowed on the Honorable Irma S. Raker, a retired Court of Appeals judge who was admitted to the Maryland Bar in 1973.[16]

Another frequently recognized mentor to younger women lawyers is the Honorable Mary Arabian, who was admitted to the Bar in 1945. As a young lawyer, she, in turn, found a friend and mentor in William Donald Schaefer, who later became Mayor of Baltimore City, then Governor of Maryland, and finally Comptroller of Maryland.[17] They became partners in the firm Schaefer, Waltjen & Arabian in 1951 and remained close friends until her death in 2002.[18] In 1961, Judge Arabian became the first woman to serve on the Municipal Court of Baltimore City, the precursor to the District Court of Maryland, and, in 1974, she was appointed to the Supreme Bench, which later became the Circuit Court for Baltimore City.[19] She was also President of the Women's Bar Association from 1954 to 1956.[20] Even after her retirement in 1991, Judge Arabian returned to the circuit court as a recalled judge and "to mentor her former law clerks and other young lawyers."[21] Indeed, she mentored many young women lawyers, including Mary Ann Saar, who became a member of the Maryland Bar in 1966 and served as Secretary of Public Safety and Correctional Services from February 26, 2003, to January 17, 2007.[22] Saar later wrote an article on the importance of mentoring, in which she described the impact Judge Arabian had on her career:

> She always encouraged me to reach beyond what I thought my capabilities to be. When I became a deputy state's attorney, she encouraged me by saying: "You can do anything at all in this world if you want to do it. If you fail, you fail. You will never be 100 percent successful in everything you do."[23]

The Honorable Ellen L. Hollander of the U.S. District Court for the District of Maryland (admitted in 1974) considers Judge Arabian to have been one of her most staunch supporters in her successful quests for her two state court judicial appointments.

Another example is the Honorable Rita C. Davidson, who was admitted to the District of Columbia Bar in 1952 and to the Maryland Bar in 1963. She was the first woman to serve on the Court of Appeals, Maryland's highest court.[24] She also was the first woman to serve on the Court of Special Appeals, Maryland's intermediate appellate court. Judge Davidson was a role model for many women, as she exhibited the competence and success to which so many young women lawyers aspired. When she died at age fifty-six from cancer, she was honored by the Court of Appeals as "not only a person of large intellect, but one of great compassion."[25] Indeed, she once brought a law clerk and her husband into her home for several weeks when they suffered a fire in their apartment.[26] The Women's Bar Association of Maryland established the Rita C. Davidson Award in 1985, the year of her death, "to honor individuals who have contributed to the integrity of the legal profession, advanced the interests of women engaged in the practice of law, promoted legal education, aided in the administration of justice, and advanced the status of women in society and the legal profession."[27]

In the truest sense of "giving back," many of the women admitted to practice law during this era were committed to becoming mentors to others. They became the giants upon whose shoulders others would later stand. For instance, retired Court of Special Appeals Judge Rosalyn B. Bell, a 1965 admittee to the Bar, initiated a conference in 1987 for training women lawyers in the judicial selection process, a conference that has been repeated by the Women's Bar Association of Maryland numerous times due to its resounding success.[28]

In addition to collecting anecdotal historical data for this chapter, in-depth interviews were conducted with eight women who were admitted to the Maryland Bar during the late 1960s and early 1970s. These interviews highlight the enduring positive influence that women admitted to the Bar prior to 1974 had upon those who followed them into the profession. The women interviewed also related stories about the encouragement and support they received from their family members and male colleagues at the Bar. Interviews were conducted with retired Baltimore City Circuit Court Judge Kathleen O'Ferrall Friedman; U.S. Court of Appeals for the Fourth Circuit Judge Diana G. Motz; Chief Judge of the U.S. District Court for the District of Maryland Deborah K. Chasanow, U.S. District Court Judge Ellen L. Hollander; retired Montgomery County Circuit Court Judge Ann S. Harrington; and attorneys M. Natalie McSherry, Eleanor M. Carey, and Ann M. Turnbull. Judges O'Ferrall Friedman, Motz, Chasanow, Hollander, and Harrington were all recipients of the Rita C. Davidson Award. Other parallels can be drawn between these women, despite the fact that they came to the profession from different backgrounds and with diverse life experiences. Although there were no formal mentoring programs available to any of them, all eight of the women interviewed for this chapter expressed their view that personal relationships were the key to their career advancement.

The Influence of Family

Many of the earliest women lawyers appear to have been influenced by forward-thinking family members. Etta Maddox, Maryland's first female lawyer, was likely inspired by her father, Justice John T. Maddox, and supported by her older sister, Emma Jane Funck, who was President of the Maryland Suffrage Association.[29] Her brother-in-law, Dr. J. William Funck, was also an advocate of women's suffrage.[30] Later, Jeanette Wolman was encouraged to pursue law by her father, businessman Adolph Rosner, who helped her enroll in the University of Maryland School of Law (now known as the University of Maryland Francis King Carey School of Law) in the second year women were admitted to the law school.[31] Lena King Lee, one of the first African American graduates of the University of Maryland School of Law, describes her coal-miner father as a major influence, because he held her to "very high standards."[32] Familial and cultural heritage also influenced many early women lawyers, as a number were either Jewish immigrants or the daughters of Jewish immigrants.[33] This includes Rose Zetzer, who, with Anna Carton and Lottie Friedler (admitted in 1933 and 1940, respectively), formed Maryland's first all-female law firm.[34]

Though many early women lawyers remained single, some were encouraged by supportive husbands. Anna Carton, the first mother to graduate from University of Baltimore Law School, attended classes at night, while her husband cared for their two-year old son.[35] Many early women lawyers went into practice with their husbands such as Helen Sherry, admitted in 1923, Jeanette Wolman and Sarah Rosenburg Burke, admitted in 1924, Constance Putzel and Lee Miller Fuller, admitted in 1946, and Doris Peterson Scott, admitted in 1949.[36] Such family law firms facilitated the practice of law by women lawyers who were otherwise often offered jobs as secretaries, despite their completion of a formal legal education program.[37]

Ann Turnbull, 2003.

Photograph attributed to Olan Mills. Courtesy of Hon. Diane O. Leasure.

Like many of these early female lawyers, many of the women interviewed for this chapter identified male attorney relatives as being influential and supportive of their decision to pursue a legal career.

The Honorable Diana G. Motz, admitted to the Maryland Bar in 1968 and the first woman from Maryland to serve as a member of the U.S. Court of Appeals for the Fourth Circuit, was not planning to follow her father's footsteps into the practice of law.[38] Her father was a renowned trial lawyer in Washington, DC.[39] She planned, instead, to pursue a career in advertising upon her graduation from college.[40] When she learned that the advertising firm J. Walter Thompson required a drawing for the application, she knew she would never be in advertising, and she enrolled in the University of Virginia School of Law, where she was one of only two women in her class.[41] Judge Motz recounts that her father was not particularly enthusiastic about her going to law school, because he thought it would be "a hard road for a woman to hoe."[42] Despite her father's initial reservations, once she made her decision, both her father and her mother were very encouraging and supportive of her endeavor.[43]

Ann Turnbull was admitted to the Maryland Bar in 1971 and comes from a long line of lawyers.[44] Both of her grandfathers, her father, and four of her uncles were lawyers. Although there were no female lawyers in her family, she was surrounded by male relatives who were lawyers. When she graduated from college and was contemplating her next step, she decided to do what others in her family had done and enroll in law school.[45] Thus, she was both inspired and encouraged by the lawyers in her family.

Although she, too, came from a long line of lawyers, this was not the reason M. Natalie McSherry decided to become a lawyer.[46] Natalie, a partner at Kramon & Graham, P.A., was admitted to the Maryland Bar in 1974. Her great-grandfather was Chief Judge James McSherry, who she describes as being "a product of his times." Coincidentally, he was the Chief Judge of the Court of Appeals of Maryland when Etta Maddox's 1901 application for admission to the Maryland Bar was denied, in part because the statute governing bar admissions used the word "he," rather than being gender-neutral. Despite the fact that the Court of Appeals denied her petition, Chief Judge McSherry encouraged Maddox to take the matter to the Legislature and ask it to change the language of the statute. Indeed, in the opinion he authored denying her admission, he wrote: "We are not to be understood as disparaging the laudable ambition of females to become lawyers. It is for the general assembly to declare what class of persons shall be admitted to the bar."[47] She did go to the Legislature, the law was changed, and Etta Maddox was admitted to the Bar in 1902. Today, Chief Judge McSherry's legacy includes not just one but three great-granddaughters who are lawyers in Maryland.[48]

There have been many generations of lawyers in Natalie McSherry's family, including her father who practiced out of the family home in Frederick, Maryland. He was a major inspiration to her and had this to say when his daughter was sworn into the Maryland Bar: "If you could learn to overcome your innate female emotionalism, you could become a pretty good lawyer." Then, over the years, he enjoyed it when people ceased saying, "I hear you have a daughter who is a lawyer," and instead asked, "Are you Natalie McSherry's father?" Although she initially resisted the idea of following in her male family members' footsteps and planned to become a teacher or mathematician, Natalie developed an awareness of social justice while attending college in the 1960s, and enrolled at the University of Maryland School of Law.[49]

Like Ann Turnbull and Natalie McSherry, Judge O'Ferrall Friedman comes from a family of lawyers.[50] She recalls that, as a child, she was very "talkative" and that people would tell her that she should be a lawyer.[51] The idea stuck with her because her father, grandfather, and uncle were all lawyers. Her father was successful and enjoyed his work, which gave her the sense that "people who were fulfilled were lawyers." As a result, being a lawyer was always a goal of hers. When she shared her plans with her father, however, he asked her why she did not want to be a teacher "like other women." But Judge O'Ferrall Friedman was determined and pursued her dream of becoming a lawyer. Her parents were unable to share her later legal accomplishments with her, as her father died when she was a sophomore in college and her mother died during her last year of law school. Despite being deprived of her parents' support due to their untimely deaths, Judge O'Ferrall Friedman received familial

Rededication of the restored portrait of Chief Judge James McSherry, October 19, 1995. Photograph attributed to James Schingler.

Courtesy of the Maryland State Archives.

support from her older brother who is also a lawyer. Although he is not a lawyer himself, Judge O'Ferrall Friedman views her husband as her number-one supporter and believes that her career benefitted greatly from his support and encouragement over the years.[52]

Judge Hollander's father, Harold L. Lipton, was an enormously influential role model for her who, unfortunately, passed away while she was in high school.[53] She knew she wanted to be a lawyer as early as her elementary school years, because she wanted to emulate everything about her father. Judge Hollander concedes that, although she might not have known at that age what a lawyer did, she knew that, if her father was one, that was what she wanted to be. She recognized the pride her father had in his chosen profession. He often told her that he felt that lawyers had a role in making society a better place, and he stressed the importance of defending unpopular causes in order to protect the rights all citizens enjoy. Judge Hollander credits her father with imparting to her the value of hard work as the principal ingredient of success, the value of public service rather than personal recognition, and the value of having an unwavering commitment to excellence.[54]

Another woman who credits her lawyer father as being the inspiration for her desire to become a lawyer herself is Eleanor "Ellie" Carey, who was admitted to the Bar in 1973.[55] She recalls that, when living in Rhode Island at the age of six or seven, she thought being a lawyer was "walking down the street and having everybody say 'hello' to you, talking to everybody, and being concerned about everybody." As Ellie grew older, she would often discuss cases with her father, and his love of being a lawyer is what inspired her. That said, when she was thirteen or fourteen, he told her that she might not like being a lawyer. This caution was not meant to discourage her but to tell her that most women lawyers would spend their time in the library because they were not welcome in Rhode Island's courts. Ellie nevertheless pursued her dream of being a lawyer, and her father was a great source of support for her.[56]

Another family supporter of Ellie Carey's was her husband, Anthony M. Carey, who was a practicing lawyer when they met. Although she had reservations about attending law school after being out of college for seven years, he expressed confidence in her abilities to succeed in law school. It was his encouragement that prompted Ellie to apply to law school. When she graduated from law school, however, she encountered some hiring resistance from large law firms. In one or two cases, large law firms in Baltimore would not hire her, because her husband was an attorney at a competing firm. At another large firm, the head of the maritime department said, "We don't hire women here," reasoning that he did not think she could take over a ship with an armed federal Marshal. Ellie Carey was later hired at Frank, Bernstein, Conaway & Goldman (hereafter referred to as Frank, Bernstein).[57]

The Honorable Deborah K. Chasanow, admitted to the Maryland Bar in 1974, credits her husband, retired Maryland Court of Appeals Judge Howard S. Chasanow, with providing support of her desire to become a jurist.[58] They met while she was working for the Attorney General's Office and he was a Circuit Court Judge in Prince George's County, Maryland. In her words, "I would not be here, where I am today, were it not for his absolute confidence in me and his support and encouragement." Judge Howard Chasanow encouraged her to apply for her first federal job as a Magistrate Judge in the mid-1980s, and then urged her to put her name in the mix for a District Court vacancy in the early 1990s.[59]

The Honorable Sherrie L. Krauser, who was admitted to the Maryland Bar in 1973, credits her mother with paving the way for her legal career by making it seem normal for a woman to work and be a mother at the same time. Judge Krauser's mother is the Honorable Bess B. Lavine, who was admitted to the Maryland Bar in 1959 and is now retired from the District Court of Maryland. Judge Krauser was appointed to her mother's seat on the District Court bench when her mother retired. In Judge Krauser's words, "[m]y mother inspired me to believe that I could achieve professional success without sacrificing the personal fulfillment of marriage and children."[60]

The Support of Male Colleagues

As important as familial support for attending law school and becoming a lawyer was, the support that early female lawyers received from their male counterparts was also invaluable, particularly in an era in which women lawyers were heavily in the minority. Indeed, for many young women lawyers of that time—in the words of the Honorable Diana G. Motz—"there were no women role models."[61]

Judge Motz was the first female lawyer to join Piper & Marbury (now known as DLA Piper), a large Baltimore firm, when she was hired in 1968. In her view, the firm was ready to hire a woman, particularly since the New York firms had been hiring women for the last three or four years. She says that her male colleagues were "very pleasant, very professional, and nobody asked when I was going to have babies."[62] Her positive career experience at this firm, and, in particular, the support she obtained from her male colleagues, propelled her in her career.

Similarly, when Ann Turnbull graduated from University of Maryland School of Law in 1971 and was interviewing for jobs, it was hard to find a female lawyer in any of the large Baltimore law firms.[63] The women who were in private practice at that time were either solo practitioners or members of smaller firms. Ann feels that her timing for entering the legal job market was serendipitously good. She graduated late, after taking time off to marry and have a baby. When she was ready to begin practicing law, many of the big firms were just beginning to think they should hire women. Had she gone straight through law school and graduated in 1967, the large firms may not have been to the point of seriously considering hiring female lawyers. Ann had interviews with many of the larger firms and ultimately accepted an offer to become the first female lawyer at Frank, Bernstein.[64]

Ann Turnbull describes many of the lawyers and partners at Frank, Bernstein as role models. While there was no formal mentoring program, in her words, "they were always there to answer questions and help you with things. You could ask them questions and get advice. You could get a lot of guidance on how to do things.... I guess you would call them mentors." Ann's male colleagues were very important to the development of her career, because they taught her how to be a lawyer. Naturally, because there were no women there before her, she did not have a female mentor at the firm.[65]

While an undergraduate student at the University of Maryland, the Honorable Ann S. Harrington planned to attend graduate school until a male friend, who was attending law school, suggested that she enroll in law school instead.[66] Since there were no lawyers in her family, his encouragement and support were very important to her and facilitated her decision to pursue a legal career.[67]

After her graduation from law school, Judge Harrington was employed as a judicial law clerk for the Honorable John McAuliffe, who at that time was a Circuit Court Judge in Montgomery County. Judge Harrington describes him as instrumental in launching her legal career. He was a mentor as well as a teacher. She relates: "[H]e would sit and talk about every case, every motion, and bring me along academically on issues in the cases I had not yet seen. It was like an apprenticeship that benefitted me as much as him." That clerkship helped her to secure her next job as an assistant state's attorney in the Montgomery County State's Attorney's Office. The Honorable Andrew Sonner, retired from the Court of Special Appeals, was the State's Attorney at that time and the one who hired her. Judge Harrington describes him as very progressive since he was one of the first state's attorneys in Maryland to hire women—she was the third female prosecutor in his office. She remained in the State's Attorney's Office until her appointment to the District Court Bench. Judge Harrington, who retired from the Circuit Court for Montgomery County in 2009, credits both Judge McAuliffe and Judge Sonner with providing valuable assistance in her pursuit of her judicial appointments.[68]

Natalie McSherry clerked at Garbis & Schwait, a small Baltimore tax firm, while attending University of Maryland School of Law.[69] She credits this experience with opening many doors to the legal profession. The name partners were two young lawyers—Marvin J. Garbis, of the U.S. District Court for the District of Maryland, and Allen L. Schwait, who later served as a judge on the Circuit Court for Baltimore City—who hired University of Maryland law students as law clerks. The three law clerks they hired that year were all women, and Natalie describes herself and her two fellow law clerks as the first "old-girls network." She is grateful to both men for providing the opportunities to learn and being supportive of her career development.[70]

Realizing that she did not want to work in a tax firm after her graduation from law school, Natalie joined Whiteford, Taylor, Preston, Trimble & Johnson (now known as Whiteford, Taylor & Preston, L.L.P.) as its nineteenth attorney. She identifies some of her male colleagues at the firm as being mentors who, by their example, taught her the mechanics and subtleties of being a good lawyer. In her view, formal mentoring programs are helpful but "do not hold a candle to a natural relationship." She describes herself as having been "quietly persistent"; she developed mentoring relationships with more senior lawyers by approaching them, asking questions, and inviting them to lunch as a way of developing and continuing the relationships. Her quiet persistence paid off in another way. When she joined the firm, she wanted to be a trial attorney while the male associate hired at the same time did not. He was assigned to the Litigation Department (which, at the time, was all male) and she was assigned to the Corporate Department. It seemed that many of the male partners believed a woman would not perform well as a litigator. Nevertheless, eager for courtroom time, Natalie picked up some district court cases by offering to help colleagues with smaller cases. After two or three years of working with pensions and quietly litigating on the side, she had a conversation with one of the partners in the Litigation Department. He initially resisted moving her because the insurance adjusters "were a pretty tough crowd" and probably would not want to work with a woman. She replied, "[t]he ones I've worked with so far haven't had a problem," and his jaw dropped. About a year later, the opportunity to switch to litigation full time arose, and Natalie took it immediately. Natalie ultimately became the first female partner at the firm.[71]

The Honorable Ellen L. Hollander started as a judicial law clerk for U.S. District Court Judge James R. Miller, Jr.[72] Judge Miller had a profound effect on her budding legal career. She views him as being the model of the consummate trial judge who "combined an incredible work ethic with keen intelligence and common decency." She entered private practice upon completion of her judicial clerkship.[73]

Hon. Ellen L. Hollander, 2009.

Photographer unknown.
Courtesy of the Maryland State Archives.

Judge Hollander is reputed to be the first part-time female partner at a large law firm in Baltimore, although she is quick to point out that "part-time" really meant being paid less to not have to work on weekends. She received the support of her male colleagues at Frank, Bernstein when she requested permission to work part-time and still achieved partnership status with the firm during that time. The arrangement she negotiated for herself undoubtedly opened doors for other female lawyers who wanted to strike a similar balance between career and family.[74]

Like Ann Turnbull, who preceded her at the firm, Judge Hollander views her male colleagues as having been more role models than mentors. In her words, they taught by showing "how smart they were, how knowledgeable they were about the law, how much pride they took in their profession, and how attentive they were to the needs of their clients." They were totally supportive of women attorneys and regarded them as valuable contributors to the strength of the law firm.[75]

After her graduation from Stanford Law School in 1974, Judge Chasanow clerked for the Honorable David L. Cahoon of the Circuit Court for Montgomery County.[76] To this day, she considers him to be a wonderful friend and mentor whose example and temperament she admired. Both he and her parents steered her in directions they thought were good for her, without explicitly discussing them. Her career was also influenced by Stephen H. Sachs, who was the Attorney General

M. Peter Moser, accomplished attorney and fly fisherman in Popham Beach, Maine, August 2007.

Courtesy of Eleanor M. Carey.

Ellie Carey and Steve Sachs at the home of Liz Moser, March 9, 2013.

Courtesy of Eleanor M. Carey.

Congresswoman Barbara Mikulski, Ellie Carey, and Steve Sachs celebrating Steve's victory in the Democratic Primary of the 1978 Attorney General election.

Courtesy of Eleanor M. Carey.

for Maryland during her tenure with that office. She recalls that he took pride in developing the skills of the attorneys who worked in the Attorney General's Office. She became Chief of the Criminal Appeals Division and considers herself quite fortunate to have worked on several cases with him, including cases argued before the U.S. Supreme Court. Judge Chasanow was appointed as U.S. Magistrate Judge for the District of Maryland in 1987, and remained there until President Clinton nominated her to U.S. District Court for the District Court of Maryland in 1993.[77] In 2010, Judge Chasanow was elevated to Chief Judge of the U.S. District Court for the District of Maryland; she is the first woman to hold this position.[78]

Ellie Carey took a different approach to developing relationships with her male colleagues at the Bar. She ran with them—literally.[79] She used to run with Baltimore City Circuit Court Judge Marshall A. Levin, Baltimore City Circuit Court Judge David Ross, Harry Kaufman, Peter Moser, and others at Gilman School in Baltimore. Judge Levin, an avid newspaper reader, would share his knowledge as they ran.[80] Ellie recalls soaking in his wisdom: "He would talk and run, and all I had to do was listen."[81] The running talks were more than mere lectures however; the whole group would share in the conversation, discussing current events and legal developments. Harry Kaufman, a lawyer and physical-fitness advocate known for popularizing running in Baltimore, was the leader of the pack, urging everyone in the group to get out and run.[82] He was out there every day at six o'clock in the morning, and when it rained he declared it was "like taking a shower with your clothes on."[83]Of them all, she particularly considers Peter Moser, a well-known Baltimore attorney and advocate of legal ethics, a mentor.[84] It was he who made it possible for her to interview at Frank, Bernstein, where she became the firm's second female lawyer (Ann Turnbull was the first).[85]

Like Judge Chasanow, Ellie Carey considers Stephen H. Sachs, who was a litigation attorney at Frank, Bernstein at the time, a mentor and role model. Ellie worked for him at the firm and believes he was extraordinarily influential in the turning of her career. Moreover, Sachs had a different sort of running in mind than her previous mentors. When he pursued his interest in running for Attorney General, she was thrilled at the idea and eager to work for him, subsequently becoming his campaign manager. After he was elected, he appointed her as Associate Deputy and, later, as Deputy Attorney General. After serving as Deputy Attorney General, Carey entered the political arena herself as a candidate for Attorney General. She ran for this position twice—first in 1986 and again in 1994. Only one other woman had run for that position, and that had been many years prior to Ellie's campaign.[86]

Along with Judge Chasanow and Ellie Carey, the Honorable Diana G. Motz identifies Stephen H. Sachs as one of the male lawyers who most impacted her career.[87] After taking a year off from Piper & Marbury for the birth of her daughter, she joined the Attorney General's Office and was assigned to what is now called the Department of Human Resources. Judge Motz recalls that he treated women equally and that she learned a lot from him during her tenure with the Attorney General's Office. Coincidentally, Rita C. Davidson was Secretary of the Department of Human Resources at the time and, in that role, the first woman in Maryland's history to hold a Cabinet position. Judge Motz remembers occasions when she had the privilege of arguing cases before Judge Davidson on the Court of Appeals and recalls times when they were the only two women in the gallery of the courtroom.[88]

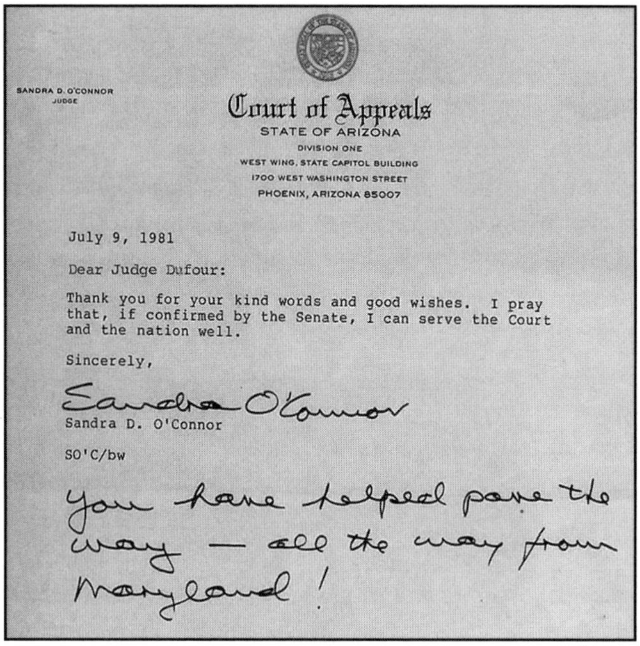

SANDRA D. O'CONNOR
JUDGE

Court of Appeals
STATE OF ARIZONA
DIVISION ONE
WEST WING, STATE CAPITOL BUILDING
1700 WEST WASHINGTON STREET
PHOENIX, ARIZONA 85007

July 9, 1981

Dear Judge Dufour:

Thank you for your kind words and good wishes. I pray that, if confirmed by the Senate, I can serve the Court and the nation well.

Sincerely,

Sandra O'Connor
Sandra D. O'Connor

SO'C/bw

You have helped pave the way — all the way from Maryland!

Letter from Justice Sandra Day O'Connor to the Hon. Kathryn DuFour.

Courtesy of The Catholic University of America, DuFour Law Library, Washington, DC.

Women Mentoring Other Women

The connection between early women lawyers in Maryland and the U.S. Supreme Court is a reciprocal relationship. The Honorable Kathryn DuFour was admitted to the District of Columbia Bar in 1936 and to the Maryland Bar in 1942. She became the first female circuit court judge in Maryland when she was appointed to the Maryland Sixth Judicial Circuit Court in 1955, and, in the following year, she won an election to remain on the bench for a fifteen-year term.[89] Justice Sandra Day O'Connor was an important role model to many female lawyers, as she was the first woman to be appointed to the U.S. Supreme Court. "When President Ronald Reagan appointed Sandra Day O'Connor to the Supreme Court in 1981, Judge DuFour sent her a congratulatory telegram. Justice O'Connor replied, reminding DuFour that she had 'paved the way, all the way from Maryland.'"[90] Judge Chasanow also considers Justice O'Connor an inspirational figure. She vividly recalls the first time she met the Supreme Court justice, when she spoke at a Women's Bar Association dinner shortly after joining the bench, and the impact Justice O'Connor had on her as a young lawyer.[91] Judge Chasanow also recalls the moment she walked into the Supreme Court and saw Justice O'Connor on the bench for the one case she argued before the high court. In fact, Justice O'Connor wrote the opinion in *Macon v. Maryland*, in which the Supreme Court ruled in Judge Chasanow's favor by a margin of seven to two.[92] Judge Chasanow has seen her on other occasions since that time and considers her to be a mentor, role model, and continuing source of inspiration.[93]

The influence of female educators as mentors cannot be overlooked. The Honorable Kathleen O'Ferrall

Friedman describes her educational experience at the College of Notre Dame of Maryland (now Notre Dame of Maryland University) as having been a driving force in her pursuit of a law degree.[94] Although she was out of college before the feminist movement really took hold, she recalls with great fondness and appreciation the many women professors, some of whom were nuns, who were tremendous role models. She considers all of them to be very accomplished and tremendous examples of women of achievement who successfully ran a big business and taught college-level classes. Judge O'Ferrall Friedman was profoundly affected by one professor in particular, historian Dorothy Brown, a "wonderful mentor," who was studying for her doctorate at Georgetown University at the time and later became the chair of the Department of History and then Provost at Georgetown. Another, economics professor Elizabeth Morrissy, was an advisor to presidents Franklin Roosevelt and Harry Truman.[95]

Judge Shirley B. Jones, with Judge Joseph H. H. Kaplan, Judge Soloman Baylor, Judge Milton B. Allen, Judge Edgar P. Silver of the Supreme Bench of Baltimore City, and James R. White, 1978.

Photographer unknown. Courtesy of the Maryland State Archives.

Judge O'Ferrall Friedman is convinced that being in an all-female college environment, free from competition with men, enabled the students to speak freely and express their opinions. With the college's emphasis on public service, she left Notre Dame with a sense of civic mindedness and a sincere desire to contribute to her community and to the world. Judge O'Ferrall Friedman describes her entire educational experience at Notre Dame as a "mentoring environment" and one in which she was encouraged to pursue her career dreams. In fact, it was encouragement by the college's Academic Dean, Sister Bridget Marie Engelmeyer, which tipped the scale in favor of her applying to law school. The decision was a bold one, for it was the early 1960s, a time when few women entered law school, and her father had already questioned the wisdom of such a move.[96]

The Honorable Irma S. Raker, retired from the Court of Appeals, is another oft-mentioned mentor. "She mentored talented lawyers, usually young women lawyers, setting a standard as the first female assistant state's attorney in Montgomery County, Maryland (1973–1979), as Associate Judge on the District Court of Maryland (1980–1982), as the third woman judge ever on the Montgomery County Circuit Court (1982–1994) and as the second woman to be sworn in, in 1994, as Judge on the Maryland Court of Appeals, the state's highest court."[97]

Other women appointed to the judiciary have been role models to women lawyers who also wish to attain that professional goal. Judge O'Ferrall Friedman was the fourth woman appointed to the Circuit Court for Baltimore City.[98] She and other female lawyers looked up to the two female judges who were already members of that bench—Judge Mary Arabian and Judge Shirley Jones. In Judge O'Ferrall Friedman's words, "their mere presence, their being there, said to us that we could do this, too." These female predecessors were highly regarded jurists, who were taken seriously and achieved many professional successes. The examples they set meant a great deal to those, like Judge O'Ferrall Friedman, who followed them. Judge Jones later left the Circuit Court for Baltimore City, when she became the first woman appointed to the U.S. District Court for the District of Maryland in 1979.[99]

Judge Hollander also considers Judge Mary Arabian enormously influential and keeps a photograph of herself and Judge Arabian in her chambers, directly behind her desk in a glass case of her most cherished possessions.[100] Judge Hollander met Judge Arabian "through the kind introduction of the late Judge Norman Ramsey." When Judge Hollander expressed her interest in becoming a judge, U.S. District Court Judge Ramsey suggested she speak with Judge Arabian. Notably, Judge Arabian was also mentored by Judge Ramsey, who was responsible for her getting her first job while she was still in school.[101] Judge Hollander followed his advice and made an appointment to speak with her, and she and Judge Arabian became good friends.[102]

Judge Hollander describes her friendship with Judge Arabian in the following manner: "It was such good fortune to meet someone like Judge Arabian, who was a role model to so many women, and have her take a liking to me. We just hit it off. She was very warm and generous to me and extremely supportive. She believed in me, and I was the lucky beneficiary of her wisdom and kindness." Judge Hollander remembers Judge Arabian as being a quiet but persuasive advocate in her willingness to recommend her to Judge Arabian's good friend and mentor, Gov. William Donald Schaefer, for two state court judicial positions—the Circuit Court for Baltimore City and, later, the Court of Special Appeals of Maryland.[103]

Judge Hollander recalls that there were few women in the profession when she was admitted to the Maryland Bar. As more women were admitted, they created "support systems" with each other. She speaks of the tremendous influence of the Honorable Diana G. Motz in providing support and encouragement to her. She first met Judge Motz at the Attorney General's Office and spent more time with her when they both worked at Frank, Bernstein. Judge Hollander describes Judge Motz as one of her advocates who always endeavored to open doors for her. Indeed, Judge Hollander succeeded Judge Motz on the Court of Special Appeals. Years later, Judge Motz encouraged Judge Hollander to apply for a vacancy on the U.S. District Court for the District of Maryland. She applied, received the nomination, and was appointed to the Federal Court bench in 2011.[104]

Women Lawyers Carrying on the Tradition of Mentoring

Taking a page out of their predecessors' book, the women interviewed for this chapter are all tireless in their support of others who have followed them in the profession. While at the Attorney General's Office, Ellie Carey was instrumental in establishing a job-sharing arrangement for one of the female lawyers.[105] This effort resulted in young mothers being able to share a job and work part-time. In her role of hiring people for the office, she also worked closely with others to reach out to African American lawyers as potential hires. One important mentoring relationship grew out of her campaign for Attorney General. She mentored her Deputy Campaign Manager, Colleen Martin-Lauer, who went on to become one of the most significant political and fundraising consultants in Maryland.[106]

Judge O'Ferrall Friedman was influential in establishing the Women's Law Center of Maryland, Inc., in 1971, along with Ann Hoffman, and Susan Handwerger Tannenbaum, both of whom were admitted to the Maryland Bar in 1972.[107] Finding that there was a tremendous amount of inequity of treatment under the law, The Women's Law Center, Inc., a non-profit organization, was formed to advocate "for an equal playing field for women and children."[108] The organization provides

Frances Hughes Glendening, Bess B. Lavine, and Sherrie L. Krauser.

Photographer and date unknown. Courtesy of the Maryland Women's Heritage Center.

valuable volunteer opportunities for law students and others interested in working to protect and preserve the rights of women and children. Moreover, Judge O'Ferrall Friedman's law clerks and interns benefited greatly from their time working with her. One former intern, Judith Moran, describes her not only as a mentor, but also as a role model and champion.[109] Her former law clerk, Lila Shapiro-Cyr, now a partner at Ballard Spahr, L.L.P., describes her as an "excellent role model of a woman in the profession."[110]

In addition to Judge O'Ferrall Friedman, Judges Harrington, Motz, Chasanow, and Hollander have worked to establish mentoring relationships with their judicial law clerks, many of whom have been female. Judge Harrington expressed that she tried to have the same relationship with her law clerks as she had with Judge McAuliffe—creating a working and teaching environment during their clerkships and reaching out in the legal community to assist them in launching their own careers.[111] Judge Motz also assists her law clerks in getting their desired job placements and becoming established in their careers.[112]

Network 2000, Inc., a non-profit organization, was established in 1993 with the mission of promoting the advancement of women in professional and executive positions. Ellie Carey, Natalie McSherry, and Mary Ann Saar, a founding member, have all participated in its programs.[113] Mentoring has been a key component in Network 2000's outreach to prepare women to rise up in the leadership of the institutions in their chosen fields.[114] These women have served as mentors for this program, which was formalized as *Effective Impact* in 2008 and which fostered mentor-mentee relationships for the purpose of developing women leaders.[115]

Ann Turnbull mentored a young law student, Mary Sanders, when she was a lawyer at Frank, Bernstein.[116] Mary Sanders is now one of her law partners at Turnbull, Nicholson & Sanders, P.A., a law firm they established in 1998.[117]

Similarly, Natalie McSherry has been a mentor to many younger lawyers. One such example is her mentoring of Harry S. Johnson, who was the first African American lawyer at Whiteford, Taylor & Preston L.L.P., where he is now a partner. She encouraged him to become active in the bar association; it was excellent advice, and Mr. Johnson became the first African American president of the Maryland State Bar Association. There are many others she has mentored over the years, including her own family members. Her son is a recent graduate of the University of Maryland Francis King Carey School of Law and is the fifth generation of the McSherry family to receive his law degree from that institution.[118]

Conclusion

There are a myriad of success stories that can be attributed to the support that these early women lawyers received from their families, their male colleagues at the Bar, the public advocacy groups they formed and participated in, and the encouragement they received from the women who preceded them in the practice of law. Although there were certainly obstacles along the way, their persistence and determination in achieving their goals resulted in their individual and collective successes.

As reflected in this chapter, there is a long history of women lawyers attributing their success to the relationships they developed. Some of these women actively recruited their chosen mentors, while others took advantage of bar association and other networking opportunities to find their mentors and to build their support systems. Mentoring relationships develop in many ways and present themselves in a variety of forms, and informal mentoring opportunities are no less effective or valuable than the formal mentoring programs available through the various bar associations and organizations such as Network 2000. There is no question that, for the new lawyer, the vitality of a legal career is tied to the relationships developed, cultivated, and maintained throughout one's career.

The efforts of all of the early women lawyers referenced in this chapter and their commitment to excellence and mentoring have paved the way for those who have followed them in the profession and will continue to do so for many years to come. For the experienced practitioner, the importance of "giving back" cannot be overstated. Becoming a "second- and third-generation" mentor is important to the continued movement towards equality in the legal profession.

CHAPTER SEVEN:

In Their Own Words: Oral Histories of Maryland's Women Lawyers

Compiled by Evelyn C. Lombardo, Brett Joann Jackson, Kathleen M. McDonald, and Denise Shaffer

Each woman who has pursued the practice of law in the state of Maryland had her own unique experience, and yet all shared four commonalities that are the focal points for this chapter: a perseverant attitude and altruistic desire pervaded their careers; the decision to pursue a career in law was influenced by the encouragement of their families; all overcame challenges to become a lawyer; and collegial support, as well as mentoring and networking, played significant roles in their career development.

What follows are oral histories of various women lawyers who share their stories in their own words.[1] Forty-eight women were self-nominated or nominated by members of the state, local, and specialty bar associations for inclusion in this oral history chapter, and all answered uniform questions, conducted during 2012–2013 by way of an in-person interview or through a questionnaire, about the value of one's own perseverance, tenacity, and motivation; the impact of familial support on their decision to become a lawyer; the overcoming of obstacles in law school and the first years of practice; and the importance of mentoring and networking by others.[2] Individually and collectively, they represent a unique personal experience of which pioneering lawyers Margaret Brent and Etta Maddox would be proud.

Perseverance and Altruism: Motivations Contributing to Women Becoming Lawyers

A strong belief in herself and the desire to help others were evident in every woman interviewed. The practice of law undoubtedly brought on challenges that, historically, directed some women away from the practice of law. The women interviewed, however, credited self-reliance, confidence, and a "bound and determined" to succeed attitude with providing the necessary motivation to forge ahead in the face of adversity.

Judge Kathleen O'Ferrall Friedman (admitted in 1967, Circuit Court for Baltimore City, 1985–2002): You know, when I went to law school, I was bound and determined that I was going to graduate.... I was feisty, I was ready to take on [anything]. So whether it was in law school or whether it was at Legal Aid or whether it was in private practice, I wasn't going to sit back, I was going to take on. I was going to be not aggressive but assertive, which is a good word. And I had in my mind that I was going to succeed, that nobody was going to be a barrier to my success. And I guess, in a way, I was talking to myself, because, when I think back on it, I think back to having some trepidation and to being concerned—was I going to be able to do this? But I was bound and determined. And so I think I presented a sort of bound and determined kind of personality.

Tiffany Franc (admitted in 2010): I just really liked the challenge. And, I think, throughout my life I have found [that] even if no one is saying to me, "You can't do it," I think that, on some level, that's what I'm perceiving. And, growing up, I was lucky to be in the same foster home, so my first foster family is my adopted family. But we used to have six to seven kids in the house at any time, and that was my mom's full-time job—fostering children.

One of my biggest sort of mottos in life is that, no matter how hard you have it, somebody always has it worse, and that's really what drove home with me growing up in that environment. And so some people hear my story, and they think, "Wow, you're amazing." And I don't really see it that way, because I see that I had every opportunity to be nothing but exceptional, whereas other people don't have, aren't given, aren't afforded those opportunities.

And so, I think, just going through life saying, "Well, I was a foster child, and I was abused as a child, so I shouldn't be able to go to law school, but I'm going to do it anyway." Well, now I'm in law school, so maybe I shouldn't have a job, too, but I'm going to do it anyway. And you know what? I'm ready to have a family, and it's going to be tough, but I'm going to do it anyway, because that's what I want. And, I think, I just have never held myself back from doing what I want and making it work for me.

Mary Ann Day (admitted in 1976): I was the first woman who litigated in Washington County, and it was sink or swim. And there were some moments of really struggling with court, especially in Washington County. One of the judges insisted—I was married to a gentleman by the name of Michael Day at that point, and my opinions came all addressed to Mrs. Michael Day. And I just couldn't convince the judge that this really wasn't who or what I was. I had a judge physically stop me in the hall, swing me around to face him, and ask me if I had a bra on.

There were things that were unpleasant... [but] you don't grow and learn from the wonderful, nice things that happen. But they are also the things that make you figure out who you are and where you stand and whether you can take the heat that comes with it. I don't want to say I was abused. I mean, I think I got a far easier ride in Washington County than I would have gotten in the big city. I dressed the way I chose, which was not the dress-for-success mode. And I didn't get hit by a glass ceiling, I got supported by the people around me. But there were interesting moments of dealing with male lawyers that made it interesting.

Judge M. Brooke Murdock (admitted in 1978, Circuit Court for Baltimore City since 1997): My passion has carried me through the day. I have loved my professional life enormously. It's been very, very rewarding.

The desire to help others, which developed from a personal interaction with the judicial system or experiences of social or societal injustice, was a powerful motivator to pursue a career in law.

Tiffany Franc: My exposure to lawyers occurred very young—when I was very young, when I was put in foster care at three. I had lawyers and social workers. And so every time I go to the Baltimore County Circuit Court, it's kind of like coming home, because I remember spending a lot of my childhood there, because my adoption wasn't actually final until I was twelve.

Judge Catherine C. Blake (admitted in 1977, Magistrate Judge for U.S. District Court for the District of Maryland, 1987–1995, U.S. District Court for the District of Maryland, since 1995): At college in junior year, I signed up for something called [the] Kennedy Institute of Politics. It was at Harvard. And they had a court watching project where students went to observe a judge in the lower court. I forget if it was called district court, but the sort of first court that one went to in Massachusetts, which at that time was not a court of record. And this particular judge that we were assigned to go and watch and take notes on was famous for saying that the [U.S.] Constitution did not apply in his courtroom. And he sometimes got away with it, because, again, it was not a court of record. You could have a de novo appeal, and if people felt too aggrieved, they would just go to the next level. [I was] part of [a] seminar that was being taught by a lawyer from a lawyer's committee for [a] civil rights kind-of-place in Boston. And that all led me to think that there were some interesting things to do in law school. And I actually did my senior thesis for the government department on a public defender's office. Went and watched and volunteered and did one of these organizational models. [For example], how does the public defender's office work from a political science, organizational point of view?

Judge Yvette Bryant (admitted in 1986, Circuit Court for Baltimore City, since 2006): I recall the 1968 riots. Each night, as we were driving home, we were stopped by the National Guard. The same guard stopped us each night. I can recall feeling powerless in the face of the firearm in his possession. It was hurtful and humiliating to watch my father have to submit to the inquiry night after night. That memory is etched in my mind. I had a clear understanding of the importance of having the law for protection, because of the manner in which the law was used against us. I was six at the time.

Ann Rhind Sparrough (admitted in 1972): I grew up in Southeast Washington. I went through the DC public schools in Southeast Washington. I graduated from Anacostia High School. My class was seventy-four percent African American. And not only that, if I remember correctly, only twenty-five people in my class, which again was about, I think, 150 people, went to college straight out of high school. It was [expected] you went out and you got a job or you had children, got married, or whatever, but you didn't necessarily go to college.

Estelle Fishbein (admitted in 1968): I decided to become a lawyer, because I felt strongly about civil rights, racial and religious discrimination in our society, and [the] problems of the poor. I was very idealistic and thought that, as a lawyer, I could best contribute to bring about a more just society. I think that, for me, it indeed was a calling, inspired in great part by my following current events and reading, always reading. I also was completely ignorant about how difficult it would be for me as a woman to find a job as a lawyer.

Julie Landau (admitted in 1980): I think my desire to go to law school was based on some altruistic ideas. I wanted to help people—I'm a child of the sixties—[to] protect the Constitution. And I think that's what drove me.

Master JoAnn Asparagus (admitted in 1980, Domestic Relations Master, Circuit Court for Kent County): When the whole issue of women's rights came up, I was right there with them. And, you know, we had all kinds of arguments, depending upon which segment of this argument you represented, as to whether or not black women should be involved in women's liberation and this whole issue of genocide, which I never ever was able to grasp. But, you know, it was a continual thing of one issue right after another.

Judith Catterton (admitted in 1973): I was interested in social causes. One of the reasons we went to Europe was we were pretty frustrated with the Vietnam

War, and one of the reasons we left the country was that. So coming back and thinking about what to do, there were thoughts in my mind about environmental law. I interviewed with Ralph Nader; in fact, when I graduated from law school, I was offered a job with Ralph Nader—[I] was going to be a Nader's raider. So I think that was part of it. But it wasn't any more specific than that.

Elizabeth (Liz) Loggia (admitted in 1979): There was another influence. This was during the Vietnam War. I graduated from high school in 1961, and I lived in Plainfield at that time, we had moved to Plainfield, New Jersey. And the draft board in Plainfield—there was a draft then—had five men on it, and four of them were lawyers. So anybody who went to law school was deferred. So, a lot of my friends from high school would go to college. Many went to Rutgers; it was a state university. And they didn't have to worry about getting drafted, so they'd go to law school. I had friends from high school also who were going to law school. So that was kind of an influence, too.

The Familial Influences that Led Women to Become Lawyers

The career success and satisfaction enjoyed by the women interviewed were largely attributable to their hard work and dedication. Almost all of them readily acknowledged, however, that their decision to enter law school was significantly influenced by family or friends. A parent who was a lawyer or who attended law school, obviously, exposed children to the practice of law at a young age.

Elizabeth (Liz) Loggia: My father was a lawyer, and my mother actually went to law school for a semester with her sister. And I'm sure times were very different then; it was in the 1920s, but she did drop out. But my father completed law school and practiced in New Jersey up until the time he died. And so that had a great influence on my life, because we were brought up in a household where his reasoning basically was legal reasoning. Not that he held forth or anything, but that was just the way he thought.

Mary Ann Day: My mother and father went to law school during World War II, and, as my mother said, they admitted women and the lame, the halt, and the blind, because that's the only people that were left in the country. So, as I understand it, there were a whole group of women who came out of law school during the war years, and then the law schools shut back down in terms of women. My mother raised two lovely children, but she did not practice law. But what I got as a true benefit out of it was dinner-table discussion—my father practiced, he was also a CPA. So we got not only the intellectual discussion, but it was discussed from the mindset of two lawyers. And I think that lawyers think very differently than people in general do.

Judge Barbara Kerr Howe (admitted in 1969, Circuit Court for Baltimore County, 1988–2001): My dad, my father, Nelson Reed Kerr, was a lawyer, and he worked for the New Amsterdam Casualty Company when I was little and then had his own private practice on the side from our house. And so we always had a room in our home that was his office, and there was a waiting room where clients wind up, because those were the evening hours. And then, after that, he left New Amsterdam Casualty Company, where he was a bond counsel, and had his own practice in Towson, first in the Duncan Building and then at 116 West Susquehanna, which was a home which he converted to offices. The county took it by condemnation, so then he purchased 210 West Pennsylvania Avenue, and that's where he was when I became a lawyer. So, when I explained to him that I was going to go to law school, he told me that I was completely nuts. I was married and had two small children. He said, "You'll never be able to do this." And I said, "Oh, just wait, because I know I'm going to do it."

Barbara Loveless Holtz (admitted in 1970, on the influence of her father, Judge Ernest Loveless): As my mother said, we started talking about cases when I was three, but, certainly during my formative years, law and politics were always very interesting to me. My father ran for the House of Delegates and was elected for two terms in 1954 and 1958, and I can remember going down into the House chamber and sitting on his lap or on Carlton Sickles's lap, who was another member of the Prince George's delegation, watching the swearing in, looking up at the galleries, and just thinking, "This was it; this was really something that I wanted to be part of."

For others without familial ties to lawyers, their parents' values of hard work and education influenced their decisions to go to law school and, later, their success in practice.

Judge Diane O. Leasure (admitted in 1982, Circuit Court for Howard County, 1995–2011): I very much credit my parents. My parents were both first-generation Americans, and, although my mother did not work outside of the home, my father did a very traditional upbringing. But just [a] tremendous work ethic. And they were, as parents, just so supportive of all of us and, still to this day, they're just real champions for us achieving whatever goal we've set for ourselves. But [we] also learned from them that, if something is worth doing, it's not going to be easy, and it shouldn't be easy, you know; you have to do certain things in order to achieve those goals.

Master Rita Rosenkrantz (admitted in 1967, the first female domestic-relations master in Montgomery County, Maryland): I grew up in a small town in West Virginia, and my father had a grocery store. My mother had been a bookkeeper for a Packard agency in Scranton, Pennsylvania, where she was born and grew up. And it was always assumed, I don't know that we even talked about it, but I was always going to go to college. Education was very important. My mother had left school after eighth grade to go to a business college, and that's where she got her bookkeeping and accounting training. My father came to this country by himself when he was sixteen years old and worked in various retail businesses and ultimately opened a grocery store. He was really, for the time and his background, incredibly successful. He became [the] president of the state retail grocers' association. But, more to the point, he was, in his spare time because he was very good at languages, the interpreter in the county courthouse.

Barbara Maher (admitted in 1969): My father was illiterate, actually. His family came from Italy, and they lived on a farm, and they wanted him to work on the farm. They did not appreciate education, [the] old Italian immigrants. So my mother said my grandparents would bribe the police chief with vegetables, so that he wouldn't make my father go to school. So my father was uneducated, but he was a very smart man. He had his own business, he learned the farming business and, as a young man, he used to drive his horse and buggy into Boston [Massachusetts] as a teenager and sell vegetables from the farm. And that's what he did most of—that I can remember. He wholesaled fruit and vegetables, because, back then, there were the small grocery stores; there were not supermarkets then. But when I say illiterate, he could write for his business "celery," "carrots"; you know, everyone could read that and understand that. But he couldn't really pick up a newspaper or a book and read it. He could write his name, and I don't think he could write much else.

Mayda Colon Tsaknis (admitted in 1977): [In Puerto Rico, where I grew up], my mom opened a business; her father-in-law gave her money, I believe it was $700, but it was 1929 or something like that, and she went ahead and opened a business. She had a ninth-grade education, but she was very, very smart. She said that a ninth-grade education back then was the same thing as a college degree. And my mother spoke and read English; you know, that was her second language, and she had her business. She always worked, as far as I knew.

Some women that observed their parents, namely their mothers, had to work unexpectedly to support their families or express regret that they had not pursued a career themselves.

Judge Rosalyn B. Bell (admitted in 1965, Circuit Court for Montgomery County, 1980–1983, Court of Special Appeals, 1983–1993): I got into [law] in an entirely different way, I think, because my father left my mother. I was about six or seven. And my mother had to make a living. It was [the] Depression then. And she did a marvelous job. She had been educated as a teacher, but, at one point, she told me she didn't want to go back to teaching, because she left teaching during World War I, because she could make more money working in a guy's job at the railroad. And so she wasn't going to go back to teaching; she couldn't afford it, because it was always understood by her and by me that I would go to college. I mean, I don't ever remember her not saying that's what I was going to be doing at some point. And my mother eventually made basically a very good living doing a job that—most of the jobs she did were men's jobs. She took over the running of my father's landscaping firm and his flower shop and ultimately had the most active and busiest flower shop in Trenton [New Jersey], where I was growing up. So it never occurred to me that I couldn't do anything that I really wanted to do.

Nancy Forster (admitted in 1985): There were five of us in my family, and my mother did not work at the time, and my father, when he passed away when I was six, suddenly, my mother had to go out and find a job. That was also influential, had an influence on me, because I saw her strength, too. Because, at the time, a lot of people in our extended family wanted to split the kids up. One aunt, in particular, wanted to take me, and my mother just refused. She said, "Absolutely not. These are my children. We're staying together." And she managed. And I think that that was sort of always my thinking: that, you know, I'll manage, I'll get it done.

Christyne Neff (admitted in 1990): My mom is a strong woman who, I think, felt she didn't get the things that she wished she'd have access to. And so she didn't necessarily call herself a feminist, but I think I got a lot of sort of feminist feedback, [in] which she was very clear: I needed to have a career, I needed to take care of myself, I needed to be strong. And so I got a lot of that from her, I think, her belief that I needed to be on my own two feet and that, you know, she didn't have those opportunities.

Judge Kathleen O'Ferrall Friedman: My mother was a homemaker. She was involved in volunteer work. She was very involved in the civil league. But there is something that's interesting that I think influenced me with my life and the decisions in my life. My mother came from a German Victorian-type of family, male dominated, and she always wanted to be an actress. And she, as a young woman, was in amateur acting in the Baltimore area, but she was absolutely forbidden to seek a career. She really wanted to go to New York and study acting, but she was not allowed. And so she subsequently married and had four children and, as I say, was involved in volunteer work. But I grew up with a sense that my mother was dissatisfied with the opportunities that she had in her life.

Mayda Colon Tsaknis: I remember, when I was eight or nine years old, there were four siblings, two girls and two boys. I'm the youngest of them. And my father—we would sit down to have dinner, and my father always said, as far as I can remember, I was like nine years old, "If I have money to send only two of you to school, it will be the girls." My father was very advanced. He said, "Because the boys can always go and dig ditches. Secondly, because I don't want my daughters to ever depend on a man for their livelihood." If you have a wonderful husband, fantastic; but if you do not, you don't have to stay with a man just because you have to depend on that man.

Barbara Maher: My mother [whose parents were from Italy], amazingly fought very hard [with her parents] to get to high school. Back then, she had two sisters who were not allowed to go to high school, but my mother just pushed and pushed, and I guess drove her parents crazy until she graduated from high school. She always told me [she received] twenty pieces of gold, because she was the best student in Spanish. And she was—my mother was very proud of this job—she was the private secretary of Mr. Kenworthy of Kenworthy Brothers, a factory, I think a shoe factory in Stoughton [Massachusetts]. And she was very proud of that.

The impact of parents' and siblings' investment in the achievements of their daughters or sisters cannot be overstated. Because their relatives impressed upon them that they "could do anything," these women grew up having the impression that traditional gender barriers were surmountable.

Judge Audrey Carrion (admitted in 1985, Circuit Court for Baltimore City, since 1999): One of my biggest mentors is my mother. And my mother never graduated from college. She only went through high school, but she always instilled in us the fact that you could do anything. In fact, when I was about thirteen or fourteen, she gave me this placard that I still have in my chambers that says, "Don't ask whether your daughter should be a lawyer—or marry a lawyer or a dentist—just ask her to be one." And it never even crossed my mind, given the fact that she always said education is number one and you could do anything that you want to. So I never thought that I couldn't do this. Her motto was, "You come into a room, and you come into a room like you belong." And I've always done that. And so I'd never had that sense that I can't accomplish this, or even that it's going to be harder. Of course, when you grow older, you learn that there are certain obstacles that you have to deal with, but, as a child, as a young teenager, I never thought that at all.

Judge Theresa Nolan (admitted in 1976, Circuit Court for Prince George's County, 1997–2000): So phenomenal in my background is my mother—the quietest, most wonderful woman in the world, nothing like me. She used to always tell me, "You can be anything you want to be, you know." And even when I was having all those babies [Judge Nolan had nine children when she began attending law school], she'd say "Oh, you're going to hit the heights, oh, my goodness," you know, this kind of thing. I was just home having babies. So she knew—she knew something was going to happen to me.

Master Jo Ann Asparagus: I've got to say that my father, who may not have been the most expansive person in the world, somehow conveyed to me that I could do whatever I wanted to do. So I can't truthfully say that I felt like I couldn't do it. I did not think about a lot of things, and that may have been because of where I was born or what-have-you.

Carol Garfiel Freeman (admitted in 1977): I was originally pre-med. My parents always encouraged me to be a professional. I originally wanted to be a doctor, because there was a program on the radio during the war called "Hop Harrigan, Ace of the Airways," and he had a nurse named Gail Nolan. I've checked it out on the Internet; my recollection is correct. My father said, "Don't be a nurse; they take orders from doctors. Be a doctor."

Kathi Hill (admitted in 1984): [My parents] taught me I have a responsibility to something bigger than me and myself, and so I remember J. Glenn Beall's lever number was 5A when we had levers for voting. I remembered George Mahoney's jingle on his way to Washington [DC]. My dad was a precinct chair for Congressman Long. So I was doing political microphoning in my dad's truck when I was seven. My parents never told me to go to college, but they never dissuaded me when they figured out I was going, probably about third grade, when I probably broke it to them. But I always felt supported by them in a quiet way. They and my grandparents supported me in whatever I did, and, you know, we worked through college and law school. And my grandparents lent me money for my first suit. I went down [to] their house, and I asked for money, and then I paid them back. And then, when it came time for my second suit, I borrowed money again and then paid them back, because I was cleaning houses and bartending at the time to get through law school.

Reena Shah (admitted in 2007): I was the only child; I was a girl. In India at that time, when my parents were raising me, I think it was very common that, if you had one girl, then there's an expectation, "Well, when's the boy going to come?" And, for my parents, this was it, and so they put everything into me. And there's a very strong ethic about education, so, you know, there's just the feeling and knowledge that, if you are well educated, then that will open up the pathway to life for you. And so my parents always believed that, and they invested everything in my education. And, in fact, I think a big reason for their emigrating to this country was probably for my development and opportunity.

Nancy Forster: My oldest brother [was] eleven years older than me. He's since passed away, but he and I were extremely close. There were five in my family, and I was the fifth of five, and he was the first of five. He was always very success oriented, and he became quite successful himself [but] not in law. And he sort of took me under his wing, because my father had passed away when I was six, and my mother had to go out and get a job, because she didn't work before that. I wouldn't say [he was] like my father, obviously, but we were very close. And he sort of prodded me in certain directions. He's the one who prodded me to go to college, because my siblings in between did not, and he did. And I think that it was his influence, more than anything, that I needed to be a professional, something professional that I could, you know, really make a good living. That was always his concern, too, but that I could be productive is the way I said. I really eschew saying I can make a difference. It was, "Be productive, have a meaningful life and career," and he's the one who got me started in that direction.

Evelyn Cavanaugh (admitted in 1989): My great aunt, and that's the lady who raised me, would always encourage me. She said, "I want you to go to school. I want you to have an education. I want you to have a good job, make something [of yourself]." And, from a very young age, I always wanted to be a lawyer.

Spouses, already in law school, also played a significant role. Humorously, spouses were not always overtly encouraging; some of these women wanted to go to law school to ensure their spouses paid attention or did not fall asleep on the drive home.

Barbara Maher: I went to Boston College, and I was an elementary education major at my mother's insistence, because there were more jobs for elementary school teachers. And I taught for ten years before I went to law school. And I was teaching in Washington, DC, I was teaching [a] special class, and I really loved that job. And my husband started law school, and our best friend that my husband had worked with at Naval Intelligence was going to the University of Baltimore. And my husband was going, and I was teaching, and they used to say to me, "Why don't you come to law school?" And I'd say, "I can't go to law school. I'm an elementary education major."

So this might be disappointing to people, but it hadn't even occurred to me to go to law school. But my husband was driving all by himself from Washington to Baltimore on the Baltimore-Washington Parkway, and he went to night school, and I was afraid he'd fall asleep. And so I decided maybe it would be a good thing if I tried to go to law school, so I could be with him and he wouldn't fall asleep on the Baltimore-Washington Parkway. So there was a woman who was a registrar. She was a wonderful person at the University of Baltimore; her name was Mrs. Joyce. And I called Mrs. Joyce—and at that time, you only needed two years of college to get into law school in Maryland—and I said, "Mrs. Joyce, I have a bachelor's degree from Boston College, and my husband's in the law school, and I'd really like to come." And she said to me, "Come along, dear," and that's how I got into law school.

Judge Rosalyn B. Bell: I went to college, graduated, got married, and I married the most wonderful guy who ever came down the pike. He had supported every single thing I ever wanted to do. And I decided after a couple of years of marriage that I wanted to go back to school. And I had gotten a job in a lawyer's office, and I decided, "Well, I think I'll go and be a lawyer."

Judge Barbara Kerr Howe: The thing that motivated me the very most, although I had thought from a very young age someday I'd like to be a lawyer, was that my then-husband, who's the father of my two beautiful children, was in law school, and he was not a particularly good student. He didn't attend too many classes. And so it got time for the first semester's examinations. He had no notes; he had not particularly been well-prepared for any classes, even those he attended. And so there was a gentleman named Mike Meredith who was his classmate, and Mike said, "Well, Sheldon, you have Barb call me, and I'll read her my notes, and I take to speed writing." So Michael and I were on the phone for several hours then; for example, [on] personal property, he read me his notes, and I took them down, and I spent the rest of that night reading them back to my then-husband. And the next night after he came home from his examination, I said, "Tell me what the questions were," and he did, and I thought I could have passed that exam. As a matter of fact, I think I could do better than he probably just did.

Strong female role models—some lawyers, some not—influenced many women to in their choice to attend law school. Exposure to well-educated women in positions of power and leadership strongly influenced their sense that a woman could aspire to a professional career that had traditionally been dominated by men.

Evelyn Cavanaugh: There were no lawyers in my family and [none] as close friends. When I was about eight years old or so, there was one lawyer in this little small Southern town. And she was a woman of color. Her name was T. Ione Diggs. And I never knew what the "T" was for until many years later. But she was a very statuesque woman, and she had this booming voice. So she was at our elementary school one day for some type of program, I don't know which, and she spoke, and I was awed by her, her presence, her appearance, her diction, her distinction. She just seemed to know everything, as far as I was concerned as a young child. I had the occasion to meet her, and, you know, I'm a little kid and probably shaking in my knees. I told her how I thought about her, and I told her I wanted to go to law school, and she encouraged me. As a matter of fact, we had a very small community, and it was a segregated community, but almost all of the children there knew other children's parents, and they all seemed to sing in unison, finish school, you know, go to college, and this is what we heard. The teachers in school were very encouraging.

Elizabeth (Liz) Loggia: When I was a teenager, I [had] a friend—we're still friends. Her mother was a lawyer, and she was a very determined sort of person, and she had gone to undergraduate and law school, at night and so forth. And I remember her telling me how she had her own practice; it was a part-time practice, and she had an office in Poughkeepsie [New York], and she had a secretary. And I thought, "You know, this is great; you can have a practice, you can have children," because she had two children, and she really was a role model to me for a long time, and she was active in the Poughkeepsie Bar. I don't know, she died with her boots on. But she was involved for years and years, and both her children became lawyers, too. And she was important to me.

Nancy Forster: I interned with Senator [then-Congresswoman] Barbara Mikulski. I did anything she wanted me to do. I was a runner—I got lunch, got coffee, and did whatever she needed. At the time, her chief-of-staff was Ann Lewis, and I'm sure she doesn't even know it, [but she] had the biggest influence on me probably at that time in my life than anybody. She was strong, she was confident, she scared me, she terrified me, but, at the same time, I was drawn to her. I was like, "Wow, this lady really gets things done," and she sure did. And she was just nonstop always. And I would just marvel at her and how intelligent she was and still is and how she just commanded the room all the time, even when Barbara Mikulski was there. I was just fascinated with her. And then I became very interested in politics at that time.

Master Joanne Suder (admitted in 1977, Master Examiner, Circuit Court for Baltimore City): I think there were two influences for me. One, my best friend's father was a lawyer, and he just loved what he did, and I adored him, you know, and so he was an influence. And our high school, which is Notre Dame Academy, was an interesting place. It was a girls' school, but a lot of the nuns were there because they were semi-retiring, so the nun to student ratio was like nine to one. There [were] a lot of them. And one of the nun's sisters was an attorney, and, you know, I got to know her a little bit, and she was way beyond our time. And I thought that was very interesting.

Ellen Callegary (admitted in 1978): The Mercy [High School] nuns are particularly [influential]. I had Notre Dame nuns from kindergarten through eighth grade, and the Mercy nuns were organized, and they were picketing against nuclear power, you know. I mean, they were just really involved. I also think the particular culture of the Mercy nuns was, at that time, supportive of my sort of social-justice inclinations. And then, when my mother died, I was a junior going into my senior year, and they were just so supportive of helping me through that.

Judge Audrey Carrion: [My high school] was a Catholic school taught mostly by women. It was all in English, except for Spanish, of course, and they were all nuns, female nuns, including the school administration, [in which a nun] was a principal. I think it's really important to expose young girls to that kind of environment, where they can understand that they can do anything they want to, because they see role models that are doing it.

Mary Roby Sanders (admitted in 1990): I went to a Catholic high school, and although now there [are] no nuns, back then there were, and they were very empowering. Although their role was viewed as not being very empowered, they are very empowering, I feel, to high school girls.

For many of these women who chose to go to law school after they had children, becoming a lawyer was a means to be independent and support themselves and their families and/or to engage in a career beyond their home.

Nell Strachan (admitted in 1974): I had two small children. I was bored to tears as a housewife. I wanted something that would be more challenging and engaging. I'd been an English major. It was as difficult then to take an English major degree and transform it into a lucrative job as it is today. And I had just moved to Baltimore.

Judge Theresa Nolan: I was home for ten years with nine babies, and we had to have a car. So I tried to get a job, [but] nobody would hire me, because of all the children. So my brother was a great friend of a lawyer in Upper Marlboro, Oscar Dooley, and he needed a secretary. So that's how I fell into it. And then, some years later after I had two more babies, I just happened to tell my bosses, who were two young guys by that time, that I'd love to be a lawyer, because I was like a paralegal. They gave me everything, when I think about it.... I didn't know what I was doing, but I just learned. And I was fascinated. I thought that would be so wonderful. And my idea at the time was just to help my lawyers, not to do anything else.

Master Rita Rosenkrantz: I moved to Pittsburgh [Pennsylvania], and I was working in a business school teaching accounting, and I met my husband. I left the business school and was working in a CPA office again, having passed the CPA exam and become a CPA. And we were married and had two kids, two girls, and moved a lot. My husband's [work] was in computers, and, in those years, they said the initials IBM stood for "I've been moved." But we lived in nine houses in the first ten years we were married. So I was doing the volunteer things you're supposed to do for the organizations [and] never got beyond stuffing envelopes. Because every year at the end of the year [I was told] I did such a great job, they asked me to be [the] chairman of the committee. I'm chairman of the committee for three days, we move. So by the time we got to Montgomery County, I was really tired of moving. But what was so hard was pulling up roots, finding new doctors, new friends, and new organizations. And I was pretty depressed. In fact, I think I was probably clinically depressed. I don't know. But my younger brother was just finishing undergraduate school and going to law school, and he said, "You know, you ought to take the LSATs. You like taking tests. You'll do well. It will be fun." So I did.

The Challenges, Personal or Common to All Women, in Becoming a Lawyer

The admission of women to the Maryland Bar in 1902 did not translate into immediate acceptance of women into the legal community. Women were singled out, beginning in law school where some classmates, law professors, and even bathroom facilities did not willingly adjust to a female presence in the legal profession.

Judge Theresa Nolan: I can remember being—sitting down in the lobby studying—and this man saying to me, "You have no right to be here. You're taking a seat away from a man who has to raise a family."

Judge Kathleen O'Ferrall Friedman: Well, let me say this: I only had one very—what I would call—discrete experience, an incident, but it was only one person, and it was a student, and it was the first night that I arrived at law school. And this young man came up to me and said, "What are you doing here?" And I said, "Excuse me?" And he said, "Why are you here? Don't you know you're taking up the seat for a man?" And I said, "You know, I don't know what you're talking about, and you're just going to have to get over it," and I brushed him off. And he never bothered me again, but I thought it was laughable, and I didn't take it very seriously. But I do remember that some of the other women, we talked about it. And so there was a network of women who were—whether it was day school or night school—who kind of kept in touch with each other, and the women were very supportive of one another. But I have to tell you that my night-school class was very supportive of me. I never felt, except for that one person, anybody in night school who resented my being there or, you know, thought that I was a threat to him in any way. A lot of these men were married men who had families and were going to law school, if not to practice law, to enhance their backgrounds, yes. They worked for insurance companies or whatever. Now, a lot of them actually did go into the practice of law, but I never had any problem with that.

Judge M. Brooke Murdock: I remember the first day of law school, the man who sat next to me said to me, "Why are you here? You're taking up a man's seat." And I was struck by that, although I didn't pursue the conversation. But what it resulted in was that I bonded very strongly with the women who were in my class, I mean, because you did have this sense—this is 1973–1974—that things were changing, but they were not changed yet.

Mary Ann Day: And the articulated concern was that we were all going to take the place of some man who was going to go earn a living, and we were going to go be mothers and not use our law degrees and that it was a waste of resources. Is that what I really think was going on? I don't know. I mean, I think sometimes just having women in an environment that had been stag was disconcerting.

Nancy Forster: One of the things I did notice is there weren't very many female professors. In fact, in my entire three years, I only had two, Barbara Mello—you know, I adored her and that was constitutional law—and the other was Ann Pecora. And I did notice that, as a student, I thought it was odd. But the one thing that really does stand out in my mind: there was a professor, who shall go nameless, that taught, and he was a clear, clear misogynist. I mean, he just did not like female students, and you got the real sense that he did not think we belonged in law school, and he treated us like that. And that was my first year. And so a group of us classmates—women and a man, too, one of my good friends—would always talk about it afterwards—you know, what is wrong with this man? It's 1981, for God's sake. But that was just the way he dealt with us.... I mean, you could just see it—he enjoyed belittling a woman when she got the answer wrong, but he never did that to the males, never. I mean, he would help them along in answering the questions, but the women never got that help. And it was just really blatant. And we all knew it.

Judge Elsbeth Levy Bothe (admitted 1952, Circuit Court for Baltimore City, 1978–1996): I actually liked being one of only three women out of the 100+ men in my class, about a dozen women in the entire school. In my time, there was no female faculty in any law school anywhere. Most of the male teachers treated the women students indiscriminately—or favorably, because they assumed (untrue in my case) that, being exceptional, we were "smarter," more ambitious, and deserving than our male counterparts. There were, however, a couple of professors who couldn't accept the notion of women aiming to compete in the profession. They would occasionally vent their disdain by calling on a woman to answer compromising questions such as, "What legal recourse has a prostitute who receives a rubber check?" I would respond straight, as though I didn't get the joke, and the professor would look confused and turn elsewhere.

Master Rita Rosenkrantz: We had a criminal law professor who picked on the quietest, most reserved woman in our class—actually, there were close to fifteen or twenty women in that section—to recite about a rape case. And it wasn't so freely talked of in those years. And everybody, all the women, were up in arms because they thought it was terrible that he had picked on her.

Cheryl Hepfer (admitted in 1972): The first day I had three classes, and, coincidentally, I was called on in the first class. Then, coincidentally, I was called on in the second class, and then, shockingly, I was called on in the third class. So it was a setup. And the third class, of course, it was criminal law. I was asked how much penetration was necessary to prove the crime of rape. I mean, they wanted me to quit or give up or hightail it out of there or whatever it might be. But, in fact, it bonded me to the other guys. They had a lot of respect for me, because I stood up to them and slammed right back at the professors.

Estelle Fishbein: Generally, I did not feel that I was treated differently because I was a woman. Most professors were fair. However, I recall one instance when, in a small seminar given by a visiting professor, we were required to prepare a paper and give an oral presentation. I chose to prepare a paper arguing for the use of public authorities to finance public works such as bridges, tunnels, etc. Since I was pregnant, I was anxious to complete my paper and present it as soon as possible. Therefore, I was the first student to volunteer to present my paper and defend it. At the conclusion of my presentation, the professor congratulated me and made the remake that it was "the best paper he had ever received from a woman." When I received my grades, I was pretty disappointed to see that he gave me a "B."

Judge Rosalyn B. Bell: Because I came [to law school] with [my husband], I think [I] would have said I was accepted, and I didn't have the same problem. But we had only one bathroom per floor, and there were four years of night school. So we had four floors, but the women only had one of the floor's bathrooms. When there was a break and they would have to go to the bathroom, there was an elevator, but it was a very poor elevator, so we would have to go running down the stairs to get it.

Jo B. Fogel (admitted in 1970): In the law school, they didn't want women. The women were assigned to the old men's locker room on the second floor as our ladies room. And I would say most of the male students were more accepting; others weren't at all. And most of the professors weren't at all, were angry that we [women] were there, angry that we were taking up space of a man who needed a job or who would do much better and who they could make raucous jokes with.

The practice of law presented its own set of challenges. "Lady Lawyers" or "lawyerettes," as some were called, encountered skepticism and exclusion from managing partners, male colleagues, and judges who, in some instances, required convincing that women belonged in the courtroom. With ambition and a thick skin, they moved from otherness to acceptance.

Judge Diane O. Leasure: Because a lot of the clients were longstanding clients of the firm, the two founding partners who were male had traditionally done their litigation work. And I remember distinctly one case, where one of the founding partners asked me to handle their case. He was an elderly gentleman who was not used to dealing with a female and who was very polite. There wasn't a problem that way, but I had asked him to get some more information for me that I needed. And I remember him calling the next day. [He] couldn't remember my name, was talking to the receptionist saying, "I need to speak to that lawyerette." So that became sort of a joke in the firm, that I was the lawyerette. The case went well, and then, after that, he called me directly, which, of course, made me feel good that he at least had confidence in me for future matters after that point.

Judge Deborah S. Eyler (admitted in 1982, Court of Special Appeals of Maryland, since 1997): I had a judge in Baltimore County, I was appearing in front of him. This was in the days when the same judge who was going to be the presiding judge in a jury trial was holding a settlement conference on the morning of trial. That doesn't happen now. But I was in front of this judge for quite some time. We were trying to settle the case, and it wasn't settling, and we all took a break, and we were standing outside of his chambers in the hallway. There were a lot of lawyers. The judge came out to go someplace and was walking along, and he stopped and looked at me and he said, "How come a nice girl like you isn't a nurse?" And he actually didn't mean that in a bad way, but it was just so out of touch.... that was probably in 1982 or 1983, probably '83. There were other judges that were sort of condescending, you know, [would] pat you on the head, not physically, but that kind of attitude. But, as time went by, that changed. It changed, I think, partly because more women became judges, but also because women proved themselves as lawyers, and it became serious.

Naima Said (admitted in 1991): I was going through documents [at the corner of the courtroom], and I was just kind of reading, and I felt someone touch my hair in the back. I turned around, and it was one of the male judges. He goes, "Oh, it's very admirable that you wear it long," and I was like, okay, [that's] a little awkward. He goes, "Oh, because women, you know, a lot of women attorneys cut their hair." Like, yeah, yeah, judge, and it was a little embarrassing. So I felt that it was a little sexist, because I don't think he would have walked up and ruffled one of the guy's hair.

Ann Turnbull (admitted in 1971): When I was first practicing at Frank, Bernstein, when I called another lawyer on the phone, I would always say, "This is Ann Turnbull, and I'm an attorney who represents so and so," because, otherwise, they would assume you were the secretary. If I just called and said, "I'm Ann Turnbull on behalf of so and so," they would say, "Well, let me talk to the boss." You had to get past some of those things. I also remember the first time I was in court where the other lawyer, my opponent, was also a woman. Nowadays, you see that all the time. You can walk into any courthouse and there's a female public defender and a female prosecutor. It was a little startling, because this was the first time, this would have been in the seventies [1970s]. I think the other woman was Elsbeth Bothe, who later became a judge. She's a retired judge from Baltimore City. So Elsbeth is over there on one side, I'm over here on the other side, and the judge comes out and, of course, he's a man. And he looks at us, and he goes, "Oh my God! Am I a lucky man or what? Two lady lawyers!" You'd never say a thing like that today. But those kinds of remarks were commonplace. But you present your case and go on.

Those kinds of reactions from people—it's so hard to equate with today's world, because people don't say or even think those things anymore. They're used to women lawyers. They're used to women everything. That was a challenge, but I thought it was really fun to be the only woman at my big law firm for a while. We used to have partner meetings, and Robbie Goldman would come in—he was our senior partner—and he would always go, "Alright gentlemen and Ann." Everybody in the firm was good to me, and I had a lot of great experiences.

I don't tell these stories with any kind of resentment. It wasn't like that; that's just how it was. In order to get past all that—[to] just succeed, be a lawyer, and have a career—you had to let those things roll off. If you got into a conversation with somebody who said, "What do you do, research in the library?" you wouldn't confront them and say, "Why are you making a sexist comment?" You would just say, "No, I do whatever I am doing."

Julie Landau: So the hard, the most difficult circumstances that women litigators, who were I think strong-willed women, faced when they were in court with male judges and possibly female judges is being perceived that they're coming on too strong, when the same behavior from a man would not be harshly criticized. So a woman is called a bitch. It's like, whoa, you know. And I can remember one occasion a judge telling me I had my claws out.

Judge Kathleen O'Ferrall Friedman: But, yes, one of the things that [was said]—it didn't happen a lot, I'm not suggesting that it happened a lot, but it happened frequently enough that it was tiring, but at any rate—was, "Well, you don't have to be emotional." But, of course, I wouldn't take it, you know, [and]... I would say, "On the contrary, what I'm being is firm and consistent, and you're the one that's being emotional." And that would usually shut them up. But, you know, it was irritating, and it would stir me up inside. And so that's why the women's organizations were so important, because the Women's Law Center and the Women's Bar Association, organizations like that [were] where we could go to dinner meetings, we could have programs, and we could talk about what we were experiencing, we would support and reinforce one another.

Judge Barbara Kerr Howe: I recall, after having been sworn in, I was so excited to be on this bench, because I had been on the district court for a number of years, and, you know, this was a really big deal for me.... In any event, I marched down the hall in the circuit court building, and I had my little gold key for the judge's elevator, and I was going to use this key to get in this private elevator to go up to the fifth floor, which is where my chambers were. And here came [a more senior male judge] walking down the hall, and he put his arm around my shoulder, and he patted me on the shoulder, and he said, "Don't worry, honey, we're not going to give you anything hard to do." So that was one of my first introductions to the Circuit Court for Baltimore County.... I was livid. I said absolutely nothing to him. I went up to my chambers, and I called Joyce Grimm, who was the assignment commissioner, and I said, "Joyce, do you have any murder cases down there that are ready for trial?" She said yes. And, in those days, we didn't have very many murder cases; they were few and far between. She said, "Yeah, we have one." I said, "Assign it to me, please, I want to try that case." And so she did, and I did.

Cheryl Hepfer: I had a male client, and I appeared before a master, and I stood up at counsel table and said, "Good morning, Your Honor. My name is Cheryl Hepfer. I'm here representing my client," and the master looked at me over his glasses and said, "Are you a lawyer admitted to the bar of Maryland?" And I was shocked and embarrassed, because this was in front of my client. He hadn't even asked me to approach the bench. And I said, "Yes, Your Honor, I am," and thought, "Well, my client must wonder." And then, the next week, I had the misfortune of appearing before the same master, who looked at me over his glasses and said, "Are you a lawyer admitted to the bar of the State of Maryland?" And I turned to the other attorney, who was a man, and said, "May we approach the bench?" He said yes. And I said to him, "That's the second time in two weeks that you've asked me that question, and I'd like to know how many men you've inquired." And he started hemming and hawing, and I said to him, "If you ask me that again, I will assume that you have a problem with your memory, and I'll report you to the Judicial Disabilities Committee." And it never happened again.

Anne C. Ogletree (admitted 1974): As I look back, most of the difficulties I had in the profession were with one judge in particular, who is now deceased and shall remain nameless, who persisted in calling me "Miss Anne" in front of a jury. He meant no harm, but calling me "Miss Anne" at the same time he was referring to my male opponent as Mr. Smith, or Mr. Jones, or whatever was demeaning. Every time he did so I would ask to approach, put my objection on the record, and then we would continue. I am not sure he ever understood my objection.

Ann Rhind Sparrough: It was my supervising attorney who had an office in Hyattsville [Maryland], which meant that we would meet in Hyattsville and then he'd drive me to Upper Marlboro [Maryland] for whatever we were going to do and then back. So we had a lot of time to talk on the beltway. And he insisted that I would be, in five years, practicing law out of my kitchen. And I said, "No, I don't think so."

Deena Hausner (admitted in 2002): I think the old-boys network is still alive and kicking.... You know, just like you go into a judge's chambers for a settlement conference and the opposing counsel is a slightly older man, and they spend five minutes shooting the breeze about who they played golf with and—not that it's offensive necessarily, but you just know that they're having a connection—I'm just sort of sitting there listening to them talk about what golf clubs they like. So I think there's that aspect to it.

As women began becoming lawyers in greater numbers, they challenged social and cultural norms that traditionally envisioned them as caretakers and nurturers rather than as advocates. The notion that the legal profession was no place for a woman was, perhaps, most engrained in the criminal law arena.

Sandra A. O'Connor (admitted 1967): I had my very first murder [trial], and you had your very first murder probably four months after you started on a trial team in Baltimore City.... And my very first murder was a rape murder of a three-year-old. So this wasn't like [I] started with the barroom murders. And Mr. Harold Rose was the homicide detective. So I get the murder, and he discovers that I have the murder. So Mr. Harold Rose marches down to Charlie Moylan and says, "No broad is trying my murder case." And so Charlie said, "Oh, yes, she is." And I learned about it, and we ended up marrying, and we've been going at it ever since. Won the case. Won the case. So I guess he decided I was all right.

Judge Ann S. Harrington (admitted 1974, Circuit Court for Montgomery County, 1992–2009): As a young lawyer newly hired in the State's Attorney's Office as a prosecutor, I think it was harder for me to develop rapport with police officers testifying in the cases I was handling, such that they trusted my judgment. I think some officers expected me to be intimidated or defer to their wishes in deciding what cases to try. Over time, that concern evaporated.

Judge M. Brooke Murdock: Certainly [there was pushback] in the State's Attorney's Office. I was hired to be a law clerk to the homicide division, and I was told by the division chief that I couldn't go to police headquarters, because I might be offended by the foul language, which really put me at a serious disadvantage in not being able to properly prepare—[to] help the lawyers prepare cases—because I couldn't go down to homicide to look at the files. And I think that the division—the head of the division—really thought he was protecting me from things to which ladies did not expose themselves. But, fortunately for me, there was a lawyer, the head of the trial division, who had a homicide case and he asked if he could borrow me, again, because he felt that women should be allowed. And so he took a risk, stood up to his colleagues, and said, "Well, let Brooke come and help me with my homicide case." And then he sent me down to the homicide division, and, of course, the detectives were uncomfortable, perhaps initially because there had never been a woman, although there certainly were women prosecutors at that time, and they tried felony cases. So maybe it was a question of a combination of my youth and the fact that I was a girl.

Master Joanne Suder: One of our duties at the public defender's office was to attend lineups twice a year when your schedule came up. And Mr. Murrell would not let me do it because it was at night, and I said, "Listen, everyone else is doing it. I'm doing it." He said, "You're not doing it." I said, "I am doing it...." Finally, it was a compromise. He had the police pick me up to go to the lineup, and the police delivered me back to my car.

Women attorneys who chose to become mothers fulfilled, and continue to perform, dual roles of advocate and caretaker. Many of these women attorneys weighed the impact of that choice on their professional lives.

Judge Diane O. Leasure: There were a number of things that our firm expected us to do at that time, like not be pregnant at the same time, which had a benefit. It was sort of suggested that it would be really nice if we weren't pregnant at the same time, but it had the added benefit of us being the same size. We had one maternity wardrobe that we could share, because business maternity suits were a little pricey for associates at the time. So that had a benefit.

Judge Deborah S. Eyler: I was a summer clerk at Whiteford Taylor in 1980, and I knew that I wanted to have a baby—and that it was possible that I would be pregnant during my third year [of law school]. And no one at the firm asked me any questions like that whatsoever, but my assigned mentor, Jim Chason, who's a great guy, at that time, on my last day, I went in and said to Jim, "You know, I think I need to tell you that I may be becoming pregnant and—so that you can take that into consideration," which was, of course, a completely ridiculous thing for me to say. And we joke about that now as the day that I came in and told him that I wanted to have his baby. I knew that I wanted to have [a baby, and it] at least crossed my mind that I would not be a lawyer. It crossed my mind that it would be difficult juggling it all, but I sort of planned it out that way.

Major Rose Forrest (admitted in 2007, Major, Maryland Army National Guard, JAG Corps.): Simultaneously with my military career [and] my legal career, I've also been a mother. My son was actually born immediately after my bar exam—my water broke during the bar exam in 2007. So I went back to work full-time as an attorney, after he was born, with a small firm in Glen Burnie. And then when my daughter was born, I was looking to get a little bit of a break. I'd missed my son's first steps, I'd missed a lot of things, so I worked part-time. I brought her into the office with me. And then when she was three months old, that's when I became a JAG officer, and I took both of my children with me to about four months of training in Virginia.

I have the luxury of all the women who've paved the way before me. I think what's been different in my experience from my male peers isn't so much that I'm a woman but that I'm a mother and those challenges that I've experienced. I remember my daughter was three days old, and I had a trial, and I had to say to the judge, "I've got to pump every couple of hours" and she was great about it, and she let me use her office.

Evelyn Cavanaugh: They would say, "Mom, if you have to study, we'll be very quiet." I said, "Thank you," you know, and that kind of thing. "Mom, when will you finish?" "Mom, when are you coming back?" So it was a dash to law school, you know, staying up when they're asleep and studying during the course of the night and trying to be available to them as well as doing what you have to do.

Monica Haley-Pierson (admitted 1989): I had one of those big, huge [classes with] 400 people in a classroom, and, since I had a baby—he was about three then, or four maybe—I didn't want him to disrupt the class. We walked hand-in-hand up all those steps to sit at the very top row, so I wouldn't, hopefully, cause any disturbance. And he was great. I brought toys and stuff. And so I just took my notes from the top row and—so, I mean you have to figure it out on your own. There's nobody to tell you what to do.

The particular challenges and competing demands of motherhood and family life required a deliberate attention that was often difficult. Many struggled to find a way to "have it all." Their responses made clear that balancing a fulfilling personal life with a legal career required a staunch commitment to creating the life they wanted. In the end, they found that skills gained as a working mother, such as time management and mediation of family disputes, are advantageous in a legal career.

Mary Ann Day: I think the real juggling act that women have to come to terms is with how you raise a family and be a lawyer.

Judith Catterton: I don't think I balanced well the demands of the job, wifery, and parenthood—and, you know, some of this is generational. I think I came up feeling, knowing, realizing, thinking that I had to work harder and that I had to be out there, I had to be really pressing to make my way through and in the male-dominated world of law. And because I saw it that way, whether that was illusion or not, I think I had made some sacrifices that were ill-advised. I think that I put career first.

Kristin Herber (admitted in 2001): This whole work-life balance—you know, the Holy Grail, I think of it as—this tidbit of advice that I'm hoping someone can give me. And I've attended the Women in the Law for DRI [Defense Research Institute], and I've attended countless seminars where women, we're going to talk about this work-life balance, and I would sit there and go, "Okay, they're going to tell me the answer. I know it, they're going to tell me exactly how to do it." And, you know, there isn't one and it took me a couple—ten years—to realize that there isn't an answer, that there isn't the balance, there isn't an answer, there isn't a having it all, you know. I think it's just being flexible and really being able to realize that there are going to be times when you're failing at something.

Major Rose Forrest: To be honest, sometimes it's just survival. You want to give your children all your attention, you want to give your clients all your attention, and it's very, very difficult to do. You always feel like you're letting someone down. It's very important to have rules. When I'm home, my cell phone is off, my email is off. I have this time set aside for my children, and then, also, when I'm with my clients, when I'm working, to have somebody that I trust to take care of my children, so that I can give my clients my, you know, my undivided attention.

Judge Deborah S. Eyler: I was a single mother, sharing custody, but the primary custodian. So that took a lot of juggling around. What I found, though, was I was always completely up front with people. I had heard through the grapevine something that I'd completely disagreed with, which is: if you're a woman lawyer, you shouldn't have pictures of your children in your office. And, you know, you're just going to have to accommodate and never ask for any favor based upon childcare or anything like that.

I took the completely opposite tack. I made it clear to people that there were only certain days that I could do a deposition, for example. And that, if I did a deposition on a certain date, it was going to have to end at a certain time. And I can tell you that it was hard to juggle, but I think being straightforward about it never—I never had a negative reaction to that. And, you know, I don't know if it was because, for the most part, I was dealing with men, and they understood women and children because they had tended to come more from the generation where the woman was at home taking care of the children, but I never had a problem with that. And, I think, [it was a benefit] being honest about my situation. I mean, I was the second—I believe—female partner, litigation partner at Whiteford Taylor, and I eventually became the head of the litigation department. But everybody knew my situation, that I was a single mother, that I had responsibilities, but I could be counted on whenever necessary to get the work done.

I did not view my job as being a part-time job, because I was a single mother. I had to respond to clients and their needs, and I did move heaven and earth to make sure that I could do everything at one time. And I've got to point out, again, my group of quote "girlfriends" from law school and sort of extended from there. If I had a situation where I had to work late and I needed somebody to pick up Andrew, that's who I called, and they always came to my rescue. So, yes, it wasn't easy, but I knew what my goal was.

Linda Woolf (admitted in 1985): Work-life balance has always been the biggest challenge throughout my career. My husband and I overcame this by making the decision that he would stay home with our child. That freed me to work the type of hours that were demanded of a young lawyer. My time at home and with my child was always quality time.

Sally B. Gold (admitted in 1976): My practice is a family law practice. Issues develop on evenings and weekends. Courts and clients have no interest in accommodating a lawyer's personal life. I have found, however, that everything I do in my personal life informs and improves my professional competence. By way of example, my daughter works in the theater, and we attend lots of theatrical productions. I often use the lyrics of Broadway songs in my opening or closing to tell the story of the marriage. The people I meet in my personal life—by service on boards, for example—have become clients or have been a referral source. The fuller a life one has, in addition to one's practice, the better a lawyer one is.

Judge Theresa Nolan: Well, you know, people laugh about it, but having a big family, you learn a lot about organization, and you learn about time management, and you learn to do eighty things at one time. Like I say, not one spare minute in that house did I not have the tape-recorder hooked up. The kids would say, "Mom's wired for sound," you know, that kind of thing, but nobody wants to do anything when you're scrubbing the toilet, do you know what I mean? There [are] a lot of things that you have to do in the house—ironing, putting groceries away, and all that.

Judge Diane O. Leasure: I've certainly had experiences that I would say were less than pleasant as a result of being a female, particularly being a female trial lawyer at the time when I started to practice, but, over the years, I found it to be certainly more gender neutral, which is a very good thing. And I find being not only a woman, but a mother as being great training for the job, especially for being on the bench, because sometimes you feel like you're presiding over these disputes, you're trying to be the peacemaker, you're trying to help people find solutions to problems, which is something I think we naturally do as women.

The Roles of Support, Mentoring, and Networking in Career Development

Women lawyers often have considered both formal and informal networks as crucial to their development in the profession. One of the most cherished sources of support came from their own community of family, close friends, and babysitters, who all played essential roles in supporting women lawyers while they went to law school, studied for the Bar, and ventured into the practice of law.

Judge Theresa Nolan: Nobody makes it by themselves. The first encouragers I have, of course, are the children. I mean, they were really very cooperative and all that.

Judge Kathleen O'Ferrall Friedman: Well, I was very fortunate, because I married a man who was very supportive. And we really were a team.

Dorcas R. Gilmore (admitted in 2007): Throughout law school, my husband, parents, and sister were my greatest support. Their unwavering encouragement and excitement about my journey were important throughout the law school and bar-study process. In particular, my husband, Chad E. Harris, was a phenomenal support and study partner. Because we decided to attend law school together, he was able to be a steady source of support who actually understood the law-school experience, and he was the best bar-study partner I could have hoped for during a challenging experience.

Naima Said: I was just surrounded by incredible people at that time in my life. And honestly—I don't know—it was like angels were sent to take care of me. My secretary turned out to be this amazing woman when I started out. When my son was three and four, she would come to my house, because if I had a case in Virginia at the asylum office at 8:00 in the morning, she'd be at my house at 6:00, brushing my son's teeth, combing his hair, getting him dressed, and getting him to school. It was just amazing. And I had no family. I was the only person. I came as an immigrant. I was the only person, you know. And then, suddenly, I was the only person in my house with three kids. But I was just so lucky. I had amazing support. Didn't know this woman from, you know, Adam. She just showed up. She was a client and had gone off for many, many years, and one day her husband called complaining that she either got laid off or quit her job. He [asks], "Will [you] give her a job?" and I said, "Sure, tell her to come and see me."

Barbara Maher: I almost didn't take the bar exam, though, because of a sick child. I had not taken a bar review, but I was signed up to take the bar exam, and my friend, who is a nurse, took care of my seven-month-old Susan every day. Jim would take her over there, and I'd straighten up the house, and Susan would go to my friend Nancy's house. And the day before the bar exam, Susan got a terrible, terrible cold, and I called Nancy, and I said, "Nancy, I can't take the bar exam because Susan is really sick." And she said to me, "What can you do for that child that I can't?" And, because of her, I took the bar exam. I probably never would have taken it again, because I had two children then, and how do you study for a bar exam with two children?

Barbara Loveless Holtz: I was blessed, blessed with an incredible grandmother surrogate babysitter for ten years. And, after that, I had nannies in the house when my younger children got to middle school. But throughout the first ten years of schooling for my oldest child, my next child was born when she was seven and then when she was eight, so I had two younger and one going into middle school and high school. But so blessed with this sitter, who was like a grandmother, made my children excited when I was on my way home to get them, took care of them, talked about the practice, what mommy and daddy did for work. Although one of my children told her third-grade class that her mother took paper from one side of her desk and put it on the other side.

Judge Barbara Kerr Howe: I found this wonderful woman named Leona Hummel, and she became my housekeeper. And she would come, and I would leave, having prepared dinner in advance for her and the children, and she was just fabulous. And I would get home around eleven o'clock, as with Sheldon, and one of us would take her back to her house, and she came three or four nights a week.

Women also received support from their employers, many of whom were men, who encouraged them to go to school to further their career.

Judge Theresa Nolan: Bob Law and Ron Sinclair were my bosses, and they're the ones that started me in college and the ones that made me think I had a brain, you know. It was so exciting to go to work and discover that you have a brain to do things.

Judge Deborah S. Eyler: I started working as a paralegal in 1977, and Pam White was a new associate at that time, and Nancy Frame Gregor was also a new associate. And, I think, they were, maybe with one other exception, they may have been the only women at the firm. Very, very encouraging. Both of them, [but] especially Pam. I mean, she went out of her way—when I talked about [whether I] should apply to law school—to talk to me about it, even though I didn't work very closely with her. I mean, to this day, whenever I see her, I say you were the lawyer that was really nice to me when I was a paralegal. So, yeah, she definitely influenced me. And I could see that she and the men, too, were—I could see the work they were doing, and it was at that point that I really had gained the confidence to think I could do this, and this is an area that I love.

Barbara Loveless Holtz: Judge Audrey Melbourne was on the bench with my father. And I have to say that she was probably the first woman lawyer who I ever became very closely associated with. She became a mentor for me, in the sense of being a woman. I was already well on my way to the career and committed to the career, but she helped me in that regard and helped me get my first job after law school.

Some of the most reliable and valuable support came from colleagues. Experienced attorneys, both men and women, provided important insight into the challenges and rewards of practicing law.

Judge Diane O. Leasure: I think there was tremendous mentoring in my firm, both from the two founding partners as well as the other associates who were there, particularly Nancy Slepicka from the female standpoint. She was there before me, definitely helped to pave the way. There were a number of things that our firm expected us to do at that time, like not be pregnant at the same time, which had a benefit. Obviously, we added more female lawyers after I came as well as male lawyers. So our whole culture of our firm was very supportive from a mentoring standpoint.

I remember when Justice Sandra Day O'Connor was appointed. It was, I think, right before I passed the bar, but, anyway, she was at an event in Prince George's County, [a] Women's Bar Association event. There were five attorneys in the firm at that time; two of us were female. And I remember Jack Fossett, one of our founding partners, you know, gathering us and going up to [Justice O'Connor] and saying, "I just want you to know that two-fifths of my firm are women." And he was so proud of that and understandably so. It was really nice. So there was a lot of mentoring there.

Judge Deborah S. Eyler: I would say that the female models were more influential. And I'll especially point to when I was a summer associate at Whiteford, Taylor & Preston, where I ended up practicing. Natalie McSherry was a very big model for me, because she was the first woman to work there, she was the first woman who made partner. And she was very encouraging and herself had, you know, a fascinating story of wanting to do litigation and not being allowed to do litigation at first but working her way into doing that sort of work.

Judge Catherine Blake: Certainly, at the firm it was a combination of there were partners that I liked working with and took an interest in my career and what I was doing. There was also the support of the other folks my age coming in. Again, it was not a lot of women, even though they did have the partners, but there was one other woman that came in with the group of associates. There were about six of us, and it was the support—again, it's sort of getting back to what I was saying about law school, having the colleague, the co-worker that also was female and was looking at some of the same issues that was very helpful—to me as well.

Outside of their employment in law firms, women attorneys also found female mentors throughout the legal profession, including judges, who shared resources, information, and a "place to hang your hat."

Master Rita Rosenkrantz: I remember when Judge [Rosalyn] Bell went to the circuit court and one of the things that happened, because there were, I don't know, maybe twenty-five or thirty or forty women in the county practicing then, but she said, "When you're in trial, you can always leave your coats in my office." Because the women lawyers had to carry their coats to trial, and the men never did. And it made such a difference. It's such a little tiny thing made such a difference.

Judge Diane O. Leasure: There were obviously other lawyers that I considered to be great mentors. Theresa Nolan, who just was appointed to the district court bench shortly after I came to the practice, you know, was a role model from the standpoint that she was an example of what could be accomplished. It was not an easy road for her, but she persevered, and, to me, that just said if you want something badly enough, you just keep trying and doing the best you can to achieve that goal. So she was a tremendous mentor.

Master Rita Rosenkrantz: Had a lot of male friends in the profession, and many of them were extremely helpful, but the real help came from other women. There were not a whole lot of women before me, but those that were, particularly those I knew from the legal sorority I belonged to in law school, were extremely supportive. A couple in Prince George's County, and I don't know if you would have known Rose Mattingly—I think she was before your time—but she used to send me clients all the time. And then one of my friends from law school, who also went to law school late [and] lived in Virginia, and we used to refer clients back and forth to each other when there was something in the other state. But women were very helpful in that regard.

Women of color, who faced an additional barrier to entry, forged relationships with one another to overcome prejudice and create a more inclusive legal community both in law school and in practice.

Mayda Colon Tsaknis: The interesting thing is that, when I went to law school to apply, the dean discouraged me. The dean said to me, "If we have people that have been born and raised in the U.S. and have not been able to make it," he says, "I don't think that you're going to be able to make it." I was Hispanic, my English still was, you know, not very good. I had the accent, which I still have; it's the same accent. And so there were some Mexican Americans in the university, and I guess that—I don't know how well they were doing, you know what I'm saying—he discouraged me. I wanted to start right away and take a summer class, and he didn't let me. He says, "No. If you are still interested, I will let you in, because you have the grades and you have the necessary points to get in..." To be frank with you, I have learned or I thought for many, many years that there were more discriminating here in the [United] States against women than in Puerto Rico. That's how I saw it.

Judge Audrey Carrion: There were no other Latinos that I knew about [in law school] nor were there any Latino professors. And so I wound up probably socializing a lot with the African American students and doing a lot of programs and community involvement with minorities, other minority students.

Judge Yvette M. Bryant: Overall, I enjoyed my law-school experience. I entered law school in 1983, when the University [of Maryland] was deeply engaged in attempting to achieve diversity. I believe that, out of the 250 or so first-year students in our class, roughly one-fifth were African American. The university had a two-week program designed to acclimate African American students to the rigor of law school. Judge Evelyn Cannon served as our instructor. The class had the intended effect—made me feel welcomed in the school environment.

After several years, I went to work for a large firm. I still had the benefit of receiving good work and was able to build some of my own clients. However, I had an incident where a partner referred to my type as "N" lawyers—in my presence. After the incident, the administrative partner tried to make me understand that he was just "kidding" and did not really mean what he said and was just "joking." I told the administrative partner that, when the good ole boys went looking for someone to lynch, they found it entertaining but that the man on the tree did not find it funny. But I promised to give my departure a second thought. Following my conversation with the administrative partner, the offending partner came to my office and told me that he dreamed my father was a white, middle-aged, and rugged outdoorsman. Then, a few days later, he came in and told me the following "joke." He said that three black people were competing on Jeopardy and that, instead of saying "the question is," they kept saying, "the question be."

I left the firm, although I was ensured that I would be made partner a few months down the road. I did not want to leave the firm, but, after the comment and joke, I moved up my departure date.

Many of the women interviewed credited the camaraderie embodied in professional women organizations, especially the Women's Bar Association and the Women's Law Center, with playing a central role in encouraging them.

Master Rita Rosenkrantz: When I was first admitted, one of the things you do is apply for membership in the county bar association. They couldn't find applications. They were very reluctant to have women lawyers in the association back in the beginning, because they were men, because they were in control. And, in fact, they really, I think, couldn't distinguish us from their wives. Women are supposed to be men's property.

Judge [Rosalyn] Bell was really instrumental, if not alone, in starting the Women's Bar Association in Montgomery County. I was sharing space with a woman who had graduated a year and a half before I did, and she called us one day and said, "Get all the women in Montgomery County together; we should have some kind of group. Because the men have them, we ought to have it, too."

Judge Rosalyn B. Bell: And Elsa [Kaufman] did that. She had sort of a little cocktail party, and she invited all these women and all. And I then got up and told them what I saw was wrong with the world in saying that the trouble is you've only got one woman judge in Montgomery County; you had another one who was an appellate judge, but she did not participate at all in the Montgomery County Bar Association, but I did. And when I said my goal is to have more women judges in this state, I said, "The only way we do it is one way: that's organize, organize, organize." And I did get them organized. I did it with a group of women. I took all the women's little local bar associations that they had and brought them into one roof and went around and got to all and got them to have their own organization of saying whether the woman was a good candidate or not. I wasn't just out to get women candidates, I wanted the best women to get it. And they didn't even know how to do it.

I had been going to the National Association of Women Judges's meetings and discovered a great many things that they did. And one of the things that they did was, one of them had a day called "So You Want to be a Judge." And I got a friend of ours who's also on the bench, Louise Scrivener—she was head of the Women's Bar then—and I said, "Okay, we've got the women's commission," which I also had gotten to have a special commission to deal with domestic violence.

Sally B. Gold: I have had a relationship with the Women's Law Center since I was a law student, serving as its president for a period of time. Its mission is to improve laws as they affect women and children. A secondary goal has been to increase the number of women on the bench and to increase the awareness of issues affecting women and children among members of the judiciary. My friendships with other like minded people and the feeling of accomplishment for having contributed to changes in the law and the judiciary have been very meaningful. Although I have been a member of several other boards, no other organization has the same combination of a wonderful cause and smart interesting people like the Women's Law Center.

Judge M. Brooke Murdock: Well, I definitely had people in my life who facilitated the next move or suggested the next move. And, early in my career, these were mostly men.... Then, there were many more women lawyers and, then, I started networking with the women lawyers and became very active in the Women's Law Center, which was a group of women lawyers who had political agendas with regard to all kinds of issues, which were totally fascinating. And I was in the Women's Law Center all the way, really, for years and years and years, was eventually their president, and then, when I became a judge, could no longer participate in the Women's Law Center.

And while the issues were very interesting, the camaraderie of the women was so supportive and so helpful. And they would be the people who would say to me, you know, "Why don't you try this?" or "Why don't you try that?" or some woman would do something. Like I met some women who were assistant U.S. attorneys, and I thought, you know, a federal exposure would probably be a good idea and, perhaps, the fact that I'm a prosecutor, I need to be on the other side to sort of have a more balanced view of the kinds of criminal cases that I'm dealing with.

So those kinds of women were just critical to my whole development. We were contemporaries. It wasn't until really I got to the bench that I found older—older in terms of service, not necessarily in terms of age—women who really were helpful in mentoring me. Early on, we were all sort of in it together, and that was very helpful to just talk about ideas and what about this. And, of course, the Women's Law Center attracted women from all kinds of practices.

Jo B. Fogel: Both Judge McCullough and the lawyer that I worked with said, "If you're going to do something, do what you like, but go do it." You know, you have to be active. And so I joined the Montgomery County Bar, and I was active in the Bar. And the Women's Bar—the Women's Bar in terms of Montgomery and Prince George's County—was a Baltimore entity, and there weren't enough of us, really, in either county. But Judge Bess Lavine wanted to become a district—people's court, district court judge. And she really understood politics. And so she organized the Prince George's Women Lawyers' Caucus, and there must have been, on a slow day, seven of us; on a big day, there were fifteen of us. We would meet at the Fireside Restaurant on Greenbelt Road. And Judge Melbourne came for a while. You know, it was just the women who were out in private practice. And we just talked about lawyers to watch out for, what to do here or there. It was a great self-help group and, again, networking kind of thing. And we formed the coalition. I'm trying to think, the judge was the first chair. Judge Lavine and then Donna—I can't remember her name. [She] was a lawyer in Hyattsville that worked for Hervey Machen. [She] was the second, and then I was the third chair. And it was really great. And then, when the Women's Bar got enough of a critical mass, I guess in the early [1980s], then we became a chapter of the Women's Bar.

Bar associations allowed women to network with their colleagues, both male and female, and demonstrate that they had the same "leadership traits and skills."

Judge Diane O. Leasure: I think when I first started practicing, obviously, one of the first things I did was join the Women's Bar Association, state bar association, Prince George's Bar Association. But although it wasn't easy at times, I really made the effort to become involved in the mainstream bar association, because I thought it was important for our male colleagues to not so much get used to having female colleagues but to see that we can also develop leadership traits and skills and be involved in organizations from a leadership standpoint. That's something I've always enjoyed doing, and I just knew that, in order to achieve that, particularly with the Prince George's Bar where I was fortunate enough to have served as [the] president of that association, it was very, very important to be involved. Plus, it just fulfills you from a professional standpoint.

Many of the women interviewed, in realizing the value of networking and mentorship in their own careers, perform the role of mentor to this day.

Judge Diane O. Leasure: There is that desire, to give back to mentor attorneys who come after you. Networking, I think, is just as critical. I find it to be also very satisfying. I still do it to this day, because I think it is that important. And just to help pave the way for others. It's a fabulous profession, and you just want everybody who enters it to feel as lucky and fulfilled I know as I have felt having been involved in the profession.

Kristin Herber: No, I don't think it's past that point [of needing mentors]. And there's a couple of women, young women in my firm, who are midway through their career. We don't have too many new associates who are women; they tend to be men for whatever reason, and I don't think that's anything other than that's just who we have. But we do have some women who, you know, have young children, who, I think, do need cheerleaders. They need someone to keep them motivated and make them—to have a sounding board for when they have a bad day and someone to talk to. I mean, I think the problem is that there aren't many women to look to say, "Oh, okay, this is where I want to be" or "[this is] what I want to have." And so, not that I try to make myself look like what they want to have, but I do try to make them realize that it is possible.

Christyne Neff: I think that's where mentoring and coaching does come into play... you know, we all have to put in those points and [be] given the chance to fumble and then learn from it and do it again. And I think too often a lot of women get that chance, and then they go, "Oh, well, that didn't work," and they get pulled out and they don't get the next chance.

Judge Kathleen O'Ferrall Friedman: Now, I do want to say one more thing about that, and that is this idea of being careful not wanting to mimic a man in how you function. And I think that's been one of the benefits of networking and organization, that we've helped each other to learn that we can be assertive, be firm, but still be courteous and respectful to everybody that's involved in the case and prevail. And you don't have to be rude, you don't have to be ugly, you don't have to be overly aggressive. You can be yourself and do this.

Advice to the Next Generation of Women and Lawyers

In spite of the challenges of the legal profession, these women maintained that becoming a lawyer opens doors, for women and men.

Christyne Neff: I think being a lawyer is an opening to so many things. I just see it as such a skill-building thing in terms of how you advance an idea, advocate an idea, win an idea, and that can be used in so many ways. So I think I would, if I thought that's what she wanted. You know, I wouldn't push her there because I think you can also be miserable in law school.

Reena Shah: Yeah. I would say, "Do it." I would say, "Do it, because, once you become a lawyer, you understand so many conversations that you thought you understood before, but you understand them at a deeper level." If you listen to the radio—I mean, I listen to NPR, that's where I get my news; and I commute an hour, so that's sort of my only source [of news] and my [alone] time, but if you listen, you see all of these conversations that people are having, these great debates, you know, and people talk about court opinions and talk about this. Law is sort of all around us.

And, you know, I had no [early] interaction with the law, and I think most people don't have interaction with the law unless they choose to. The population I deal with, the poor people, have a lot of interaction with the law, a lot of interaction with the court. That is just not my experience. Maybe [for] a speeding ticket I have to go to court or something like that but nothing else. But it's all around us, all the decisions, and you just have a greater understanding.

So, for women who are seeking this [career], I would say, "Do it, because you understand things better, you can make sharper points," especially women who have a certain goal. If they're [saying to themselves], "I want to empower this particular population," or "I want to do this work to make the environment better," I think you need a law degree. I think you can be certainly great as an organizer, you can be great as a policy person, but there's something that the law degree lends in your ability to interact and your ability to, I think, effectuate change. So I would encourage it.

Dorcas R. Gilmore: For a young woman or young man considering a career as a lawyer, I would emphasize the importance of having a clear vision of one's career goals and reasons for pursuing a legal career. I often discuss the value of the law as a tool for social justice, as well as understanding and navigating the American economic, political, and social structure, and I then advise that there are multiple ways to create change and to make sure the law is the best option for that particular person.

Mayda Colon Tsaknis: I would love to see women continue to go into the profession. I think it's a beautiful profession, and you have so many avenues in which you can express yourself. But what I think is important is for women to also have mentors. And I encourage them, I say, "Go to law school, but then try to get a clerkship with a judge, try to work for the public defender for a few years, work with a state attorney's office for a few years and then decide what it is that you want to do, but try to get a mentor."

Judge Rosalyn B. Bell: I also think that one of the things they're going to have to do is more of them are going to have to go out on their own, and, if they do, they're going to have to watch what they do in some ways; that is, they're not going to have some of the same advice that they would have gotten if they had gone to a larger firm. But if they go to the larger firm, they can sometimes get stuck in a job or in a field that they really don't want to be in.

Judge S. Ann Brobst (admitted in 1978, Circuit Court for Baltimore County, 2009–2012): I would tell a young woman that she should become a lawyer. The number of things you can do with the license are unlimited. A woman also needs to have something to fall back on if times get tough, whether it's a license to practice law, a teaching certificate, or a scuba diving masters. I tell young men the first part, not the second.

To the next generation of lawyers, these women emphasized the need to be yourself, to work hard, and to be passionate about helping others.

Judge Diane O. Leasure: And I've always been, I think, very goal-oriented or directed or at least tried to envision. I might not have known what I wanted to do when I went to college or for several years after that, but I can say that, once I entered the legal profession, I've never looked back, never regretted the decision. It's been extremely fulfilling to me and continues to be. And I think you just decide what you want the course of your life to be, and you just figure out how to get there.

Judge Deborah S. Eyler: I truly believe that merit does trump everything, and that it's difficult and discouraging to work with people who might look down on you because of your gender or background or whatever, some totally irrelevant thing. But if you work hard and do a good job, people will accept you.

One thing I found is that, when I was applying for a judgeship, several lawyers who had been my opponents in cases, in cases where we'd fought really hard, were so happy to write letters for me. Now, maybe they wanted to get rid of me, I don't know, but [it was] extremely complimentary. And I would say [to] deal with people fairly, deal with people honestly, know that what comes around goes around, but do your very best for your client while being completely honest. And if you do that and you do it in a meritorious way, you will be accepted. And I would say that for the males and females.

Mary Ann Day: If you want to be a litigator, be prepared to be tested. Find a lawyer who you like and respect, who's been in the trenches a while and ask them for support and guidance. Don't look for discrimination under cabbage leaves, and work hard, know what you're doing, go to court prepared. Be the things that make you a good lawyer and be yourself.

I think women lawyers today view discrimination differently than I see it. If somebody hadn't whacked me over the head with it, I don't see it and I think sometimes women get confused. They want someone to open a door for them and let them off the elevator first and give them the perks of being female, but they want to be equal everyplace else. And it doesn't happen. You get A or you get B, but you don't get A and B.

Barbara Maher: I would say—well, probably my own experiences—don't look to be discriminated against, because if you do, you probably will be. Treat everybody as though they're going to treat you the same way, and I think that that probably is the best thing. I think women who really say, "Oh, this is a terrible thing, it's such a disadvantage," I think those women don't get along well with men, you know. And, I mean, I went to Boston College the second year that it was coed, so it was primarily men. And very often in my practice, I would be the only woman in the room, and so I think you have to be comfortable with the opposite sex. And I was not raised with a brother or even [had] a close relationship with my father, but I think you have to develop a rapport with men. And if you have that rapport as well as with women, if you have that rapport with both sexes, and I can't tell you how to do it, but you just have to, then I think you're going to do fine, you're going to do fine.

Dorcas Gilmore: For a young woman, I also emphasize that a legal career will require being rather adept at juggling multiple demands, and it is important to be clear about her plan for taking care of herself as she pursues a legal career. I would tell her to always be herself. I would reiterate what a mentor told me, "Do not feel that you have to change to fit into the law school culture. The legal profession will be better, because you are who you are."

Linda Woolf: My advice to a young woman would not really differ from a young man. I would tell the young person that a successful career in the law requires a great deal of time and dedication. I would encourage them to try as many different legal areas as possible while in law school, internships, etc., and to seek guidance from older practitioners, most of whom are happy to share their experiences.

Anne C. Ogletree: If I were talking today to a young woman who wished to make a career in the law, I would have to tell her three things: (1) make time for yourself and your family, no matter how hard it may be; (2) remember that you enter the profession to help people, not just to make money—the most satisfaction comes from knowing you've made a difference in someone's life; (3) if there comes a time when you no longer enjoy what you do, think about another career. One has to love the law to stay whole. I think my advice to a young male lawyer would be the same.

Kathi Hill: You know, I feel fortunate. I was in a small community where my boss understood that he looked better when his people looked better, and he believed in that, and that's something I believe in, too. It's something I tell women all the time, young women attorneys: when we empower each other, we all get lifted, we all are better as a profession. Don't think of it as competitive. Too many people today think that it's the competition and the anger and the loudness that makes us adversarial. And no, you know, we can do our adversity in the courtroom. Nobody is going to win an argument outside the courtroom. Nobody wins an argument in the middle of an argument. Nobody [can] be more macho and more confrontational and more aggressive, and it doesn't wear well, it doesn't work for them, it doesn't work for anybody.

Master Rita Rosenkrantz: I'd tell them [newly admitted lawyers] that they have to do their best all the time, and if their best isn't good enough, to get better, that you can't count on being mediocre and being a lawyer, not really. And you have to care about your clients. I think that's something that's very hard to do these days with the large firms. It was very easy when we had our solo practices, because it was a personal relationship. I think it's much harder now. But you have to care about your clients. You have to always do your best and strive to do better. And if somebody dumps on you, just keep going, because it doesn't help to fight that person.

Estelle Fishbein: I have mentored many young women and men in the course of my career and have noted repeated concerns about [the] quality of life in law firms demanding incredible amounts of billable hours. Fortunately for me, I have never been employed under such circumstances. Yes, frequently the needs of the university clients I served intruded on the time I could spend with my family, but I felt that I was serving a higher cause than accumulating billable hours. My advice to both young men and women has been the same: look for a career in the law that matches your motivation for being a lawyer.

Judge Kathleen O'Ferrall Friedman: And maybe it's come out in what I've said here. But I think, first and foremost, you have to be yourself. I think you have to work hard, and I think that you have to persevere, you have to have perseverance. That's a really important piece. And I think the other thing you have to do is read fiction. I think you have to read a lot of fiction, because fiction helps you learn about who you are and who other people are and gives us a sense of common humanity. And regardless of what we're doing—whether we're in the legal profession or the medical profession or the educational profession or the business profession, whatever it is—having a sense of common humanity is—and politics, throw a little of that in our politics—that's like a core. And you get that from reading good fiction. All fiction's fun for the summertime. Good fiction. Good literature.

Judge Theresa Nolan: And the thing is that I always say, "You've got to bloom where you're planted." I mean, this is what I tell my children and grandchildren. You're in a job, you do the best you can. But always have your antenna up, always be looking around for what you really want to do. Do a good job at what you're doing, because I don't care if you're just filing, you've got to do a good job. And that everything that you do now is going to help you in the future no matter where you are. So, I mean, be proud you're a lawyer. I still pinch myself I'm a lawyer, and, you know, I got it the hard way, that's why. Maybe some of these students may not have gotten it the hard way. Just be yourself and treat everybody with respect, treat everybody like they're just walking into your living room.

Appendix A: Biographical Information on the First Eight Women Admitted to the Maryland Bar, 1902–1920

Table 1: Biographical Details of the First Eight Women Admitted to the Maryland Bar

Name	*Marital Status*	*Undergraduate School*	*Law School*	*Date of Admission to the Bar of Maryland*
Etta Maddox DOB: January 6, 1860 DOD: February 19, 1933	No evidence that she married	The Peabody Institute	Baltimore Law School	September 11, 1902[1]
Anna Grace Kennedy DOB: 1877	No evidence that she married		Baltimore Law School	March 30, 1906
Emilie Doetsch DOB: June 30, 1882 DOD: June 8, 1969	Single[2]	Goucher College	Baltimore Law School	January 29, 1907
Marie Elizabeth Kirk Coles	No evidence that she married		Baltimore Law School	December 9, 1907
Mary Virginia Meushaw	No evidence that she married		Baltimore Law School	March 12, 1909
Helen F. Hill DOB: September 27, 1879 DOD: March 14, 1966	Single[3]	American University	Washington College of Law	April 24, 1912
Emily Dashiell DOB: January 19, 1886 DOD: February 3, 1983l	Single[4]	Johns Hopkins University	George Washington College of Law	February 21, 1918
Grace Rebekah Gerber	Married[5]	Western Maryland College (McDaniel)	Valparaiso University School of Law	November 19, 1920

Table 2: Work Experience and Organizational Involvement of the First Eight Women Admitted to the Maryland Bar

Name	*Work Experience Pre Bar Admission*	*Work Experience Post Bar Admission*	*Other Organizational Involvement*	*Progressive Era Organizational Involvement*
Etta Maddox	• Traveled the country as a vocalist	• Practiced law for a number of years		• Active Member of Maryland Suffrage Association, which she helped her sister found in 1894
Anna Grace Kennedy	• Public School Teacher (Taught law, bookkeeping, typewriting and stenog-raphy).	• Never practiced law		• Raised funds for Mercy Hospital

Emilie Doetsch		• Reporter for the Baltimore News • Managing Editor of Equal Rights • Librarian for Times Herald • Private Practice during the 1930's	• First woman to run for Baltimore City Council in the 5th district). • Assistant City Solicitor to A. Walter Kraus.	• Domestic Relations Committee Chairman for National Women's party • Participated in a march for women's rights from New York to Washington, DC • Endorsed for Juvenile Court judgeship • Secretary of Goucher's Alumnae Quarterly • Avid Suffragist • Advocated for admission of girls into Baltimore Polytechnic Institute • Advocated for women jurors
Marie Elizabeth Kirk Coles				• Active in the Women's Suffrage Movement
Mary Virginia Meushaw				
Helen F. Hill		• Worked for thirty years in the claims section of the income tax division of US the Bureau of Internal Revenue Service • Early in her career she worked in the U.S. Court of Claims • Title Examiner for District Title Insurance Co. for sixteen years • Admitted to practice before DC Supreme Court in 1901 • Admitted before the U.S. Supreme Court		• Active alumnus of Washington College of Law-
Emily Dashiell		• Conducted the training school established by George T. Radcliff for the Fidelity and Deposit Company • Insurance Company Law Librarian • Worked for a Baltimore Law Firm • Librarian at the library of Congress	• Appointed to the committee for marriage and divorce laws for the legislative convention • During WWI handled contracts for government supplies	• Chair of the Maryland Chapter of the Young Women's Christian Association • On a committee that made "wife and child abandonment" a criminal offense • Chair of the Maryland Chapter of the National Federation of Business and Professional Women
Grace Rebekah Gerber		• Private Practice in Hagerstown, MD.	• Fall 1921 candidate for MD House of Delegates	• Interested in community welfare and civic life • Member, the Women's Club, Civic League and the Meridian Club • Committee member for League for Uniformity of Laws Concerning Women

Appendix B:
Historic Photographs of Courthouses in Maryland

Baltimore City Courthouse, 1903.

Photographer unknown.
Courtesy of the Library of Congress.

Baltimore County Courthouse, 1809.

Photographer unknown.
Courtesy of the Maryland State Archives.

Frederick County Courthouse, ca. 1865–1875.

Photograph attributed to J. Davis Byerly.
Courtesy of the Maryland State Archives.

Caroline County Courthouse, 1951.

Photographer unknown.
Courtesy of the Maryland State Archives.

Prince George's County Courthouse.

Photographer and date unknown.
Courtesy of the Maryland State Archives.

Carroll County Courthouse, 1897.

Photographer unknown.
Courtesy of the Maryland State Archives.

Garrett County Courthouse.

Photographer and date unknown.
Courtesy of the Maryland State Archives.

Montgomery County Courthouse, 1950.

Photographer unknown.
Courtesy of the Maryland State Archives.

Queen Anne's County Courthouse, 1953.

Photographer unknown.
Courtesy of the Maryland State Archives.

Howard County Courthouse, 1936.

Photograph attributed to E. H. Pickering.
Courtesy of the Library of Congress.

Montgomery County Court Room, 1931.

Photograph attributed to Jack E. Boucher.
Courtesy of the Library of Congress.

Washington County Courthouse, 1917.

Photograph attributed to J. D. Trovinger.
Courtesy of the Washington County Historical Society.

Charles County Courthouse, ca. 1946–1956.

Photographer unknown.
Courtesy of the Maryland State Archives.

Talbot County Courthouse, 1953.

Photographer unknown.
Courtesy of the Maryland State Archives.

ANNA A. TULLY

THE Daughter of the Regiment. Has promised to be a sister to each and every one of us, and has been accepted by everybody except Kaylus, who doesn't believe in big families. None of us were particularly keen about having women classmates, but Miss Anna has won all hearts and now we don't know what we would have done without her. Her presence in the class has been a wonderfully refining influence. Quiet and deep like a placid pool—never ruffled—always the same. We are all all for her.

Yearbook photograph of Anna A. Tully, 1928.
Courtesy of the University of Baltimore, Langsdale Library.

Hildagardeis Boswell, 1971.
Photograph by Stu Whelan.
Courtesy of the Maryland State Archives.

Appendix C:
List of Women Admitted to the Maryland Bar, 1902–2014

The following is a list of the 24,927 women admitted to the Bar of the Court of Appeals of Maryland as of December 31, 2014. For those admitted before 1975, only the year of admission is known; for those admitted after 1975 the full date is listed. Names of those who have been disbarred, as of December 31, 2014, have been removed. A further list at the end consists of fifty-three individuals admitted to the Bar in Maryland whose gender could not be determined. For full details on how this list was created, please see the *Preface and Acknowledgments* on pages 9 and 10.

1902

Maddox, Etta Haynie

1906

Kennedy, Anna Grace

1907

Doetsch, Emilie A.

1908

Coles, Marie E. K.

1909

Meushaw, Mary Virginia

1912

Hill, Helen F.

1918

Dashiell, Emily

1920

Gerber, Grace R.

1921

Deckelman, Jennie Plotkin

1922

Woods, Florence M.

1923

Cole, B. Olive
Kurland Kerpelman, Fannie
Lindenberg, Adelaide
Lutzky Proser, Ida Claire
Prestman-Presstman, Marie White
Sherry, Helen

1924

Burke (Berkowitz), Sara R.
Cohen, Hilda
DiMarco Tumminello, Anna E.
Rosner Wolman, Jeanette
Schapiro, Ruth
Williams Bramble, Matilda Dare

1925

DeLashmutt Moore, Emilie F.
Miller Freed, Goldie Rose
Vorsteg, Ethel R.
Zetzer, Rose S.

1926

Brown, Helen E.
Kaufman Quigley, Ora V.
Kloze, Ida Iris
Selenkow, Annette
Stonestreet, Henrietta Dunlop

1927

Hall Wolf, Dorothy M.
Johannsen, Mildred E.
Zimmerman, Mary Helen Campion

1928

Gersow, Lillian
Greenberg, Rosalind
Gueydan, Lucie Marie
Rosenberg, Jennie
Siegel, Jeanette R.
Simpson, Vivian V.

1929

Laynor Wheatley, Florence M.
Sinnott, Katherine
Tully, Anna A.

1930

Coplan, Fannie A.
Goldring, Mavis Althea

1931

Poster Hurwitz, Tillie

1932

Kefauver, Gladys Austin
Kurland, Katherine
Lockwood Coblentz, Bona Rosina
Nordenholz Thau, Sophie K.
Wheatley Hassencamp, Catherine A.
Wyniger, Evelyn Marie
Zaccaro, Irene Marie

1933

Carton, Anna W.
Kone, Mary Galloway

1934

Grabau, Mary Christina
Green, M. (Mary),
McCubbin (or Maccubbin), Clare
Musgrave, Anne S.
Pugh, Edna Catherine
Rowe, Charlotte Catherine
Truitt, May Hatton

1935

Gomborov, Estelle Williams
Kravetz, Dorothy M.
Snure, Anne

1936

Cahn, Doris
Chestnut, Elizabeth Maxwell Carroll
Doub, Elizabeth Boys
Goodwin, Frances
Hyman-Picking, Ida Maud
Pierce, A. Margaret
Wood, Susanna Marie

1937

Laukaitis, Agnes H.
Leikind, Ida S.
Pelton, Clarise Burkholder
Snyder, Lena

1938

Hoffman, Grace
Miller, Regina
Udell Samet, Beatrice

1939

Evert, Margaret Louise
Heyman, Anne R.
MacNab, Marian Wilcox
Massing, Tillie
Mooney, Margaret Elaine
Wilber, Dorothy Elizabeth
Wright, Margaret Stockley

1940

Floyd, Pauline Margaret
Friedler, Lottie
Marshall, Nellis Marie
Melhikof, Rebekah
Robertson, Emma Sadtler
Scherer, Anne M.
Shaivitz, Phyllis D.
Waldrop, Emmal Ballard

1941

Ayres, Mary Dale
Brockman, E. Louise
Lauer, Magdalene
Loveless, Helena Louise
Luken, Catherine E.
Rutkow, Vera Constantine
Williams, Evelyn

1942

Awerbuch, Bertha
Harris Frances Neff
Kendall, Rosa V.
Lawlor, Kathryn J.
Parke, H. LaRue
Rulien, Thelma Masinia
Russell, Margaret M.
Toner, Adeline Meyer

1943

Bensel, Pearl Irene
Bloedorn, Helen May
Green, June Lazenby
Harrington, Mary E.
Holden, Dorothy Eileen
Kurek, Jean Wand
LaNeve, Evelyn Marnay
Stack, Laura May
Whaley, Mary Howard

1944

Brown, Sarah Abbott
Bruster, Arabella G.
Coonan, Margaret E.
Decker, Virginia Doyle
Huntt, Bernadine C.
Schammel, Katherine M.
Sleeth, Annarose C.
Temple, Margorie L.

1945

Arabian, Mary
Bates, Dorothy Nicholson
DeBusk, Edith
Goodbee, Kathryn Ann Dodge
Hall, Eunice M.
Hansen, Marjorie D.
Hboza, Jean Burrows
Leiman, Jane Inez Mehner
Peck, Charlotte Anne
Plantholt, Maria E.
Putzel, Constance Kellner
Sheilds, Ina W.
Yonkers, Genevieve Asenath

1946

Burrows, Anne E.
Clemson, Mary Gray
Fichter, Rosanne H.
Jackson, Dorothy Theresa
Lucas, Jane Marshall
Meislahn, Charlotte Krug
Miller, Lee C.
Pine, Charlotte Weikinger
Russell, Ruth Startzman
Sachs, Jeannette M.
Schwartz, Jane

1947

Baker, Julia Clayton
Brannock, Shirley Ruth
Eisner, Lllian Keilsohn
Sellers, Ruth Dexter
Simpson, Jane L.

1948

Axelman, Hannah R.
Garrett, Sarah A.W.
Garvey, Lucy Ann
Goldstein, Hazel Horton
Hahn, Lillie G.
Hardy, Idella
Karzon, Allaire Urban
Knopf, Frances
Main, Charlotte W.
Roe, Caroline N.

1949

Bishop, Ruth Howard
Cohen, Naomi Biron
duBois, Rose Yvonne
Main, Mabel Sarah
McIntyre, Katherine Araminta

1950

Davis, Elaine Carsley
Dingee, Dorothy C.
Frederick, E. Marie Burnham
Hendershott, Susan Jane
Mitchell, Juanita Jackson

1951

Bright, Betty Jane
Brown, Augustana Hanlon
Dushane, Doris A.
Koone, Alice
Pecora, Margaret J.
Pine, Gypsie Lee
Remey, Paulina W.
Wahl, Blanche G.

1952

Blair, Madeleine Raring
Green, Mae W.
Hodel, Florence
Lee, Lena S. King
Levy, Elsbeth
Mehegan, Constance M.
Miazga, Matilda M.
Pearson, Beverly S.

1953

Allen, Elizabeth Houston
Beers, Dorothy L.
Hammer, Ruthellen
Howard, Georgia E.
Kaltenbach, Mary J.
Mattingley, Rose M.
McKnew, Della Karpelles
Powell, Dorothy Jean
Sherwood, Suzanne Ruth

1954

Angelos, Fannie
Bagley, Mariana D.
Christ, Margaret Louise
Clarke, Frances M.
Farley, Alice V.R.
Rand, Alice Marion
Scheeler, Mary Katherine
Stesch, Helen Dempsey
Taylor, Ernestine E.
Thomas, Marilyn Charlotte

1955

Alcarese, Andrea M.
Canter, Margaret Ann
Costello, Hilary W.
Ditman, Helen C.
Dooley, Claire L.
Harris, Marie Zuras
Knight, Mildred M.
Oppenheim, Catherine Faith
Servary, Nellie Adams
Siskind, Ronni C.
Sweeney, Mina Katheryn
Walsh, M. Rita

1956

Abramson, Anna A.
del Russo, Alessandra Luini
Eckhardt, Elizabeth Mae
Gill, Mary Regina
Macht, Lois Kleiman
McMillen, Ruth E.
Reid, Rheta Thomas Hennessy
Weiner, June L.
Williams, Priscilla E.

1957

Doehler, Clare M.
Hutchinson, Eileen M.
Kerr, Elaine Worley
Lynch, Wilma S.
Morrison, Joan Notre Dame

1958

Collison, Hilda M.
Crawford, Eleanor Allred
Kennedy, Irene
McCurdy, Mary Jacqueline
McKenzie, Ann L.
Rosemary, Ruth M.
Tennis, Nancy P.

1959

Armanas, Elena
Bagnell, Colleen N.
Davis, Beverly Anne
Lavine, Bess B.
Levy, Gloria Fraidin
Quinn, Esther Cady
Sanford, Mary Jane
Sliwka, Helen A.
Wheltle, Margaret Maie

1960

Breslaver, Ruth Cooper
Burton, Joan Hubbel
Day, Barbara Price
Dougherty, Janet C.
Forman, Ruth Disnmore
Gridley, Lily Hutcheon
Jacobs, Marjorie Leona
Moser, Elsa L.
Murphy, Charlotte P.
Pearre, Sarah Warfield
Rosenblatt, Iris Pearl Kahn
Roylance, Elizabeth Senger

1961

Binkowski, Jane Mary
Cawood, Katherine Kelly
Clagett, Lucile
Cohen, Harriette
Diggs, Kathryn E.
Fiedler, Virginia Bay
Gallagher, Nadine Lane Chapman
Goldberg, Barbara
Janney, Clara Dale McKeel
Josephson, Rhea Chapman
Schwartz, Marion E.

1962

Alexander, Nancy Milan
Baker, Helen Estes
Docter, Marcia Kaplan
Ellison, Sylvia Seymour
Hancock, Betty Jean
Holt, Marjorie Sewell
Melbourne, Audrey Earnshaw

1963

Adamska, Elzbieta Klementyna
Babcock, Barbara Allen
Davidson, Rita Charmatz
Fenn, Janet Rockwell
Ginsburg, Harriet Ann
Gofreed, Margorie Slaiman
Lambird, Mona Salyer
Martin, Jeanne A.
Mitz, Virginia Rattin
Samols, Selma Wolfsohn
Schliefer, Clarice Mary
Tennery, Elizabeth

1964

Guhring, Elizabeth
Hackett, Patricia Janet
Kaufman, Rose Schiffer
Kramer, Anne Kay
Terzian, Louise Anderson
Zimmerman, Natalie R.

1965

Bell, Rosalyn Blake
David, Marlene
Epstein, Marsha Nan
Sachs, Sheila Kleinman
Sharp, Sherry Boyd
Spicer, Barbara Ann
Swartzendruber, Roberta Lamb
Tidler, Carmen Delia
Walker, Mary M.
Yaffe, Barbara S.

1966

Brooke, Mary Ellen
Coleman, Nancy Ann
Cowen, Beatrice Mosner
Finn, Jane Adams
Gresser, Sharon Ann
Kaufmann, Elsa Raichelson
Levitsky, Carol Leigh
Lutz, Elizabeth May
Millman, Sondra Renee Linden
Rubin, Sheila Sherman
Saar, Mary Ann Tuur Willen
Shadoan, Arlene T.
Walch, Mary J. Woods

1967

Bernstein, Arlene Roberta
Campbell, Cleopatra
Cole, Diane Phyllis Clive
Dyson, B. Patricia Parish
Erlich, Phyllis Joy
Furtick, Sandra Ann
Hirsch, Gladys Elkin
Lipsitz, Eleanor Jean
O'Ferrall, Kathleen M.
Pfeifer, Susan Elizabeth
Pfeiffer, Hesna Johnston
Richardson, Mary Alice Christmas
Rosenkrantz, Rita Reitman
Storm, Mary Elizabeth
Suchy, Cecily McDonald
Verplanck, Sara Ann

1968

Aldridge, Donna Carolyn
Beaman, Dorothy May
Clark, Elizabeth Taylor
Fishbein, Estelle Ackerman
Hogenaur, Julie K.
Kapral, Jean Hansen
Levedahl, Kathryn B.
Love, Nancy Ruth McCortney
Mahoney, Margaret Proctor
McGrath, Dorothy
Pintos, Eugenia S.
Pitkin, Beatrice C.
Rinehardt, Mary Ellen Travers
Trivers, Patricia Anne
Warner, Geraldine Baker

1969

Beling, Dorothy Mandel
Bendit, Devy Judith
Bray, Karen E.S.
Daly, Barbara Gibson
Gentile, Beth-Anne Fischer
Gosnell, Erica Laufer
Howe, Barbara Kerr
Johnson, Mary W.
Lehane, Joanna Sabalauskas
Maher, Barbara Ann
Motz, Diana J. Gribbon
Nilson, Elizabeth Logan
Poage, Cyntha Jean Resare
Raphael, Jo Ann Strom
Ross, Joanne Elizabeth
Samborsky, Mercedes Casado
Sugar, Carol Stark
Sykes, Judith Konowitz
Thomas, Patricia Ann
Torek, Lorraine English

1970

Bednarek, Irene
Birkholz, Gertrud Maria
Creed, Barbara Bywater
Dailey, Lillian Virginia
Diamond, Alison D.K.
Espy, Carolyn Ann
Fogel, Jo Benson
Galloway, Judith Taylor
Goldberg, Pamela Procuniar
Hemelt, Mary Dolores
Holtz, Barbara Loveless
Jordan, Jerry Deneise
Klooz, Marie Stuart
Kornbau, Anne Miller
Luff, Ellen Martina
Paige, Nancy Ellen
Palumbo, Elaine Frost
Rody, Emily Miller
Russell, Susan Whittington
Schulte, Diane Gail
Spotts, Jean Stratakis
Stark, Judith Pulliam

1971

Criste, Virginia Spiegel
Duvall, Geraldine Veronica
Harlem, Marilyn Ruth Yoseloe
Noble, Doris Ann
Turnbull, Ann McKendrick

Jorgensen, Mary Beth
Julian, Elizabeth Lena
Kane, Patricia Lisehora
Kanterman, Frances Ellen
Karker-Jennings, Katherine
Kaufmann, Marlene Montague
Keating, Joanne Patricia
Kellner, Evelyn M.
Keriakos, Mary Jane
King, Nancy M. P.
Koby, Elizabeth Burns
Kohan, Virginia Casey
Lake, Shirlie Norris
Landau, Julie Ellen
Lewis, Elizabeth Hathaway
Lewis, Leah H.
Needham, Juliana Vermelle
Norton, Judith E.
Paizs, Cecilia Baldwin
Rogers, Antoinette C.
Weinberger, Robin Janick

11-20-1980

Belt, Norma Jean Kraus
Brown, Ellyn Louise
Denick, Robin Williams
Dowling, Martha Catherine
Hahn, Cynthia Meyers
Hellauer, Marianne Schmitt
Jensen, Karen A. Murphy
Johnson, Cassandra Tsintolas
Kandel, Paula Marie
Lees, Gail Rahn
Long, Margaret Harrington
Mayo, Rachel Richardson
McDermott, Ellen Jaye
McDonald, Kathleen Morris
Mero, Judith Corbett
Mullendore, Susan Elizabeth
Murray, Ethel Drennan
Musgrave, Dawn Oxley
Nickerson, Ethel Drennan Murray
Novak, Nancy Jean
Oetgen, Phyllis Mary
Paul, Ellen Ivy
Phelan, Jeanne Marie
Reider, Helen Linda Dallas
Ridgley, Roberta Sacks
Ries, Leslie Sarubin
Ripley, Shirley Marie
Robertson, Joann Chalfont
Robinson, Deborah Lynn
Romine, Leslie Moore
Rosenthal, Joanne Miller
Ross, Cynthia Ann
Ross, Donna Lee
Rubin, Denise Debra
Ryan, Priscilla Marbury
Schmitt, Marianne Jeannette
Schuett, Linda M.
Schultheis, Lisa Nicole
Schulze, Jillyn Kaberle
Sherman, Charlotte Ann
Shultz, Catherine McCullough
Siegel, Sharon Rosenthal
Sieverding, Pauline Ann
Sills, Donna Marie
Singleton, Judith Schroeder
Smith, Andrea Lynn
Smith, Kathleen Conley
Steiner, Christine
Stiney, Catharine Ann Borysiewicz
Stoffer, Ellen
Stransky, Renee Laniado
Taber, Nancy Carroll
Taub, Kathy Sperling
Temin, Hilda Rosenberg
Toolan, Kathleen M.
Vuynovich, Lydia
Wible, Connie Lee
Wood, Judith Ann
Young, Barbara Ann
Zweig, Wendy Jan

12-2-1980

Joffe, Carol Ann

12-29-1980

Berlin, Patricia Ann

5-21-1981

Allan, Jane Langan
Andersen, Pamela Davis
Babbitt, Barbara Ann
Bernard, Marielsa A.
Billman, Leslie Gail
Bottum, Mary Peacock
Brandt, Linda Anne
Brown, Pamila Junette
Burgess, Gail Veroneca
Byrd-Tillman, Jacqueline Pearl
Cimino, Audrey Soutiere
Cohn, Robin Blum
Cooper, Caroline Schaefer
Cote, Johanna G.
Craig, Carol Sooby
Crockett, Catherine Grayson
Dasburg, Mary Lou Diaz
Davis, Julie Welch
Deering, Anne Lawrence
Dunn, Ellen Miller
Dykes, Cynthia Ann
Finegan, Joanne Marie
Flanagan, Ann Lappen
Foley, Elizabeth M.
Garcia, Patricia Davis
Garofalo, Annette Beatrice
Gavin, Carol Ann
Glasser, Sherrie B.
Goldberg, Patricia Mitchell
Gordon, Cornelia Bright
Greene, Barbara Bakal
Greil, Harriet Cohen
Hall, Monica Nugent
Herman, Judith F.
Holmes, Barbara Esther
Houseal, Dona Elizabeth
Johnson, Jill Emily
Jones, Sharon E.
Katz, Marcia Minka
Kincaid, Linda Anton
Kohler, Sharon Teresa
Lindner, Irene Mae
Loje, Louise Whallen
Ludington, Gay Lucile
Mathias, Susan Joy
May, Sharon Angela Harper
McCall, Elizabeth Cecil
McComas, Susan K. Cosgriff
McElroy, Carolyn Jean
McEvoy, Patricia Margaret
Meltzer, D. Leah
Silva, Marion Turnbull
Wootton, Eugenia Cooper

5-22-1981

Bond, Sue Ellen
Cummins, Theresa E.
Dubin, Susan Beth
Langrill, Mary Elena
Morris, Cynthia Jones
Nauman, Mary Kathleen
Oler, Carren Susan
Panlilio, Linda Lee
Parsons, Patty Leigh
Passo, Janice Marlene
Petruzzelli, Nanette
Pinkney, Crystal Eulalia
Pivec, Mary Elizabeth
Pontone, Kathleen
Pownall, Dixie Lee
Reed, Judith Ellen
Rhodes, Mary Frances
Rice, Kathleen Spear
Ross, Joan Carol
Schneeberg, Sara
Settle, Susan Anne
Showalter, Judith Anne
Sitterding, Martha Ann
Smith, Patricia Anne
Smith, Valerie Johnston
Spencer, Sondra Lynn
Strandberg, Rebecca Lindsey Newman
Sullivan, H. Margauret
Sullivan, Jeanne Mary English
Thomason, Evelyn Kay Betts
Waxman, Barbara Baer
Widman, Christine Marie
Widmann, Wendy
Woodson, Jo Ann Cornelia
Zavos, Michele Ann
Zawitoski, JoAnne

6-2-1981

Feldman, Ruth Tenzer
Haspel, Linda
Quigley, Laura Anne
Ringler, Susan Moss
Rinker, Martha Lillian
White, Beverly Jane

11-3-1981

Fink, Varda Naomi
Manning, Margaret Mary
Miller, Ann Fox
Nesse, Madeline
Rayndon, Darra Lynn
Russell, Susan H.

11-10-1981

Wilson, Anne Byrd
Jacobs, Donna Leah

12-1-1981

Badgerow, Dana Buell
Norman, Jane Carol

12-10-1981

Adler, Maxine
Allen, Mary Donohue
Allison, Kaye Arleen
Andrews, Denise Ader
Ashley-Farrand, Margalo
Askin, Karen Gallant
Auerbach, Maren Kathleen
Baron, Jean Szekeres
Bastress, Susan Belle
Bayly, Susan Leonard
Berlin, Sherry Breuer
Bernstein, Robin Andrea
Biener, Kunnigunda Mariah Rachel
Bigley, Shirley Lou
Blue, Elizabeth Pindell
Bond, Trudy Beth
Bosma, Sabine Elizabeth D.
Bowen, M. Elizabeth
Braver, Cleo Patrice
Breuer, Sherry Lynne
Brunton, Judith Rae
Bull, Amanda Ellen
Butkovitz, Myrna Ann
Butler, Theresa Marie
Butrum, Lisa Anne
Callahan, Cynthia
Campbell, Susan Dancy
Clark, Lillian Porchetta
Cloutier, Valerie Valenti
Cole, Maryland Hartge
Comer, Vivian Adelia
Coulahan, Kathleen Ann
Dancy, Bonita Joyce
Davis, Terri Anne
Dee, Lynda Marie
Doman, Allisyn Marie
Doyle, Julia Ann
Duffee, Georgia Carol Habicht
Durbin, Lynne Marie
Ellinghaus-Jones, JoAnn
Ellmore, Karen Lee
Eno, Mary Irene
Ersek, Donna Jane Nicholson
Framm, Rhonda Ilene
Friedman, Ellen Sudranski
George, Bebe Violet
Glaser, Paula Jean
Greenblatt, Debra Dunitz
Grissom, Sally Cromwell
Hall-Eckroade, Sandra
Hennessey, Michele Bernadette
Hicks, Cassandra Pauline
Hierholzer, Virginia Arlene
Hoffman, Denise Meryl
Hopkins, Leigh Hastings
Howe, Joyce A.
Ike, Alice Denise
Illsley, Gladys E.
Jacobs, Molly Bruce
Kaludis, Karen Maria
Kantruss, MacKenzie A.
Kaplan, Sarah Rachel
Kennell, Laura Elaine
Kerr, Nancy Holland
Kilpatrick, Jean Elise
Kisiel, Yvonne Marie
Klein, Stephanie Hollis
Klein, Susan Elizabeth
Kohler, Alison D.
La Fayette, Renee Jeanne
Langdon, Jeanne Louise
Lee, Deidre White
Lennon, LaRue Gassman
Lentz, Sally Ann
Lunsford, Vicki Lee
Masciarelli, Lisa Dixon
O'Connor, Patricia M.
Oppenheimer, Nanette L.
Partridge, Kay Blythe
Posner, Susan Flax
Rosthal, Meg Lynn

Sfekas, Lauren Ann
Stahl, Sherri M.
Thall, Linda B.
Trosch, Janet Cohen

12-11-1981
Canter, Virginia Rafalko
Corwin, Marjorie Ann
Crucetti, Maureen Collins
Dean, Patricia Ann
Hughes, Elizabeth Roe
Jamison, Susan S.
Kotvis, Jill Alison
Madavo, Kathleen Dorothea
Mathers, Carolyn Palley
Maumenee, Anne Elizabeth
McGough, Eileen Teresa
McHugh, Janet Ellen
Meengs, Karen Lorraine
Mensi, Carolyn Ann
Merkle, Paula Kathleen Krahn
Moriarty, Erin Frances
Mullan, Geraldine Marie
Murphy, Linda Lucille
Neilson, Barbara Louise
Newell, Lisa Marion
Newman, Monica Louise
Nykiel, Christine A.
O'Hara, Norine Rendulich
O'Meara, Mary Laurette Theresa
Ostovitz, Linda Sorg
Papillo, Jeanette Phylis
Pearlstone, Esther Siegel
Pinkerton, Barbara Pecora
Plante, Jeanette Anne
Poole, Diane Marie
Rasin, Martha Frisby
Reed, Cheryl Ann
Rosenbluth, Robin Ann
Rost, Rynthia Manning
Ryan, Aline Clare
Sassin, Lynn Bonnie
Schwartz, Rachael Ellen
Schwartzstein, Linda Ann
Selby, Terri Taylor
Shaffer, Theresa M.
Shannon, Mary Ann
Sharp, Cynthia
Sheehy, Kathleen
Shubin, Susan Dishler
Soifer, Naira Bat-zion
Solomon, Wendy Kay
Somerville, Martha Henry
Souder, Susan
Stanfield, Sally Fite
Sundt, Ann Newman
Swain, Barbara Giffen
Teitelbaum, Judith Zerivitz
Testa, Adena Wright
Thomas, Faith Elise
Thompson, Mary Melinda
Thurlow, Katharine
Ticer, Ileen Marsha
Tillman, Mary Hencke
Watson, Gail Thuman
Weber, Joan Arlene
Whittaker, Kristina Bisset
Williams, Alexandra Nichols
Woodland, Beth Hope

1-5-1982
O'Neill, Kathleen Ann

2-2-1982
Rhodes, Sherry Leigh

3-2-1982
Arbuckle, Pamela Jo
Heimlich, Judith Dale

3-30-1982
Becker, Nancy Anne
Brown, Lane Roberta
Gottlich, Vicki
Schiffman, Mary Beth

5-4-1982
Alston, Carolyn
Davis, Joyce Patricia
Kaplan, Peggy Crespi
Smith-Hill, Gloria F.
Spooner, Linda Greer

5-22-1982
West, Nancy Carolyn

5-25-1982
Aelion, Jeanne Katherine
Ambrose, Janice S. Rodnick
Arnowitt, Kim
Artimovich, Patricia Marie
Aviles, Candace Ann
Ayers, Adeline
Bailey, Myriam Marquez
Barish, Ellen Gail
Benett, Susan Lynn
Berg, Elayne Janet Plimack
Birkel, Joyce Augusta
Bluefeld, Judith Lee
Bobo, M. Elizabeth
Bollero, Barbara L.
Bradley, Christine Porter
Bradley-Brown, Christine P.
Brown, Penelope Johnson
Bullard, Louisa Jenkins
Carr, Maureen Johnson
Carrigan, Araceli G.
Cashour, Mary Catherine
Cohen, Cindi Ellen
Cohen, Sandra Jane
Colby, Deborah Schloss
Cole, Jeanette Lockhart
Cole, Patricia Ann
Colson, Deborah Anne
Colton, Carolyn
Coltri, Laurie Ann Schalit
Comenetz, Sandra R.
Connelly, Patricia Ellen
Conrad, Marcia R.
Craig, Mary Drickey
Crow, Alexis Irene
Cutler, Hollie Shawn
Davis, Laura Ellen
De Araujo, Roberta Lia
Despeaux, Lois Sandra
Eason, Lecia Michele
England, Katherine Ann
Ermer, Marilyn Sandra
Eyler, Deborah Sweet
Finley, Janice Alaine
Flanigan, Susan Strout
Flax, Sherry Hamburg
Gavigan, Marie Manuele
Goetze, Susan Laurie
Gorman, Mary Corrigan
Hamburg, Susan Hayes
Hamilton, Linda Marie
Hawvermale, Nancy Lori
Hoffman, E. Lynn
Howard, Marguerite Eleanor
Hrehorovich, Anne Marie
James, Nancy Eva
James, O'Melia Vanessa
Junghans, Constance Ann
Katz, Judith
Keller, Susan Tina
Kelley, Alice Anne
Knepper, Christine Virginia
Koerner, Barbara Irene
Launer, Susan Lynn
Lederer, Christine Lotte
Lev-Tov, Sheila Chidakel
Lewis, Patrice E.
Long, Nancy Louise
Malone, Lynne B.
Masser, Barbara Nagengast
McDowell, Donna Schultz
McKennan, Marian
McNamar, Mary Ann Lyons
Metz, Sandra J.
Myers, Jill Joline Hyman
Nathan, Susan Gail Sugar
O'Brien, Eileen Dalaplaine Day
Ogden, Cassandra Sneed
Olsen, Pauline Belle
Parlow, Dianne Cynthia
Pelletier, Renee Martha
Podell, Lynn Beth
Popow, Nikia Marie
Prevost, Nicolette Theresa Hunter
Puentes, Linda Castillo
Rawlings, Illona Sheffey
Razulis, Marie Helen
Regan, Maureen Teresa
Richmond, Bonnie Lee
Riley, Cynthia Ann
Robbins, Jennifer L.
Rodriguez, Maria de Loreto
Samosuk, Teresa Marie
Sanger, Donna Carol
Scher, Ann Batten
Schwab, Priscilla Anne
Sears, Cathy Cobbs
Seaton, Leah Jane
Setren, Janice Morrison
Seyferth, Mary Bernice
Shankman, Ellen Beth
Shaw, Melanie Marva
Sheeskin-Hershey, Debra
Shinevar, Karen Kay
St. Clair, Amber Denise
Starkey, Franzella Hayward
Suh, Ann Sungmie
Taylor, Bernice Harriette
Teasley, Mary Ann
Thaler, Carolyn H.
Thornton, Mary Boulware
Thornton, Patricia Maureen
Tsacoumis, Stephanie
Wagar, Barbara Jane
Walker, Doris Guinevere Green
Webb, Vicki Eileen
Weisse, Robin Lee
Welch, Suzanne Kirby
Wenck, Patricia Kelly
West, Patti Diane Gilman
Williams, Romaine Norma
Witte, Kathleen Elizabeth
Woodruff, Debra Gough
Zimmerman, Patti Diane Gilman

6-2-1982
Arnold, Susan Ann
Bird, Charles Coleman
Brown, Monroe Davis
Copaken, Sylvia
Doyle, Christine M.
Henry, Marie Rana
Kunen, Jessica Robison
Lombardo, Amelia Gwyneth
Murphy, Pamela Jeanne
Snowden, Beryl Denise
Stone, Laura Elena
Zapor, Mary Lee Stout

9-9-1982
DiPasquale, Maria Teresa
O'Brien, Kathleen Ann

10-5-1982
Tonat, Valerie
Trestman, Marlene

11-3-1982
Sjoerdsma, Ann Gretchen

11-30-1982
Eastman, Hope

12-1-1982
Huber, Linda Claire
Karpinski, Irena Izabella
Luxenberg, Deborah Y.
Sellers, Dorothy

12-2-1982
Macklin, Laura Winifred Susan
Morrow, Merle Helen

12-3-1982
Gipson, Tracy Ann
Silber, Susan Clare

12-9-1982
Alexander, Lauren Gordon
Alkon, Mitchell Ira
Anderson, Mary Jeanne
Atkinson, Janice Lynn
Bailey, Sharon Darlene
Balcerzak, Ann Moylan
Barker, Mary Theresa
Baumgartner, Deborah Ann
Becker, Joyce Kuhn
Blick, Wincy Harriet
Bookstein, Julie
Boyd, Karen Barry
Boynton, Lynn Caudle
Brasier, Marilyn June
Braverman, Sharon Lee
Brogan, Susanne
Buechner, Elizabeth Jacobs
Bullington, Sandra Rose
Bunja, Anne Elizabeth
Burke, Delia Anne
Cahill, Kathleen Mary
Carter, Jeanne Gerber
Carter, Linda Cheryl
Chaly, Ingeborg G.
Cherry, Susan Maria
Clarke, Mary Florence Willis
Clarke, Veronica Marie
Coffay, Mary Wintz
Cohen, Nancy Ann
Cohon, Maureen Bunny
Collins, Cynthia J.
Corey, Elizabeth Holton

Cox, Patricia Ann
Crain, Sondra Harrison
Crouse, Jeanne M.
Cutler, Miriam Juliette
Dart, Penelope Sue
Davis-Loomis, Nancy L.
Demedis, Margaret Louise
Dimka, Teresa Rees
Donahue, Diana Dawn
Donohue, Joanne Dekker
Downs, Mary Alane B.
Duzor, Rosemary Harlinski
Eddy, Meryl Lea Kahle
Eisner, Lori Joy
Evans, Kathleen Anne
Fillmore, Lisa Ann
Footer, Sheila
Friedman, Susan Meyers
Frucci, Eleanor Leila Miller
Gardner, Jeanne Brown
Gelber, Nancy Rabin
Gerbes, Jane Jensen
Golden, Barbara Gail
Golden, Linda Arlene
Goldman, Judith Rose
Goldner, Gail Ilene
Goldsmith, Idie Regina
Gottlieb, Sharon Engleberg
Hamilton, Sandra Elaine
Hanchett, Karen Marie
Hankin, Ann Dunlap
Harrison, Ellen
Hawes, Nina Rivers
Hernandez, Carmen Dorotea
Hess, Lois Ann Katz
Hoggan, Judith Anne
Holmes, Linda Ann
Holtz, Rebecca Jean
Honeywell, Elizabeth Carroll
Horrom, Nancy Jane
Hurwitz, Susan Claire
Janofsky, Julie Chapin
Jenkins, Catherine Smink
Jenkins, Jane
Job, Barbara Cottman
Johns, Madalyn Elizabeth
Kahn, Ilene A.
Kaplan, Sheila
Klein, Susan Joy
Koenig, Karen Sue
Konovitz, Lori Susan
Kralec, Judith Ann
Kramer, Mary Morton
Kroupa, Sharon Ann
Krug, Mary Maddox
Lages, Janet Rossum
LaMar, Margery Sullivan
Lambert, Patricia McHugh
Langan, Elena Betty
MacNeille, Ann
McBride, Lois A. Fenner
Russell, Kathleen Flynn
Staton, Donna Hill

12-10-1982

Beery, JoAnne Samborsky
Daniels, Lani L.
Ficaretta, Teresa G.
Grant, Catherine Wenzing
Heinssen, Ruth Sterling
Hermann, Deborah M.
Hoffman, Joan Soellner
Holcomb, Toni S.L.
Hutchins, Sarah Snyder
Karp, Lois Rudo
Leasure, Diane Orlick
Leppert, Cynthia Louise
Loftin, Valerie Watkins
Lustig, Susanne Sable
Magnant, Renee Janet
Maistrellis, Judy Kepner
Mallas, Pamela
McCabe, Carroll Louise
McCaffrey, Eileen Ann
McCauley, Patricia Anne
McDonough, Mary Theresa
Mehl, Karen Ann
Miller, Barbara Louise
Miller, Linda McGill
Miller, Marleen Bleich
Mitchell, Shelby Felice
Monaco, Stephanie Melnicove
Moore, Deborah Black
Moore, Melissa Maynard
NaPier, Patricia Mathias
Neal, Julia Christian
Norton, Lynne Loomis
O'Neil, Nancy Doerr
Parker, Lauren Michele
Perez, Una Maria
Perlman, Linda Susan
Peyton, Jerri Ann
Phillips, Lynette Michelle
Pisaro, Theresa Lynn Osterman
Platt, Susan Jean
Poling, Susan Ann
Powers, Eileen Elizabeth
Raley-King, Jackwelyn
Reichel, Randi Faythe
Rhodes, Sharon Lynn
Rice, Mary Thompson
Riley, Mary S.
Riordan, Marie Therese
Robertson, Amy Bernstein
Rothstein, Saundra C.
Rupp, Mary Foote
Salins, Mary Josephine
Salomy-Algazi, Ruth
Sameth, Patricia A.
Samuel, Sally
Schabes, Sarah Ruth Vitsick
Schwartz, Patricia Anne
Segel, Lisa Stearman
Sensue, Elizabeth A.
Shearer, Donna Patricia
Shearin, Kathryn Kay
Shortridge, Deborah Green
Siegel, Marilyn Caplan
Slavin, Denise Margaret Noonan
Sloane, Maxine Isa
Smearman, Claire Ann
Smith, Judith Ritchey
Smith, Sharon Deniese
Sobel, Alice Ann
Soldo, Linda J.
Spritz, Nancy S.
Starks, Carolyn
Stemley, Betty Ann
Stevens, Catherine Ann
Storch, Patricia DuVall
Straight, Audrey Kuh
Talley, Debra J.
Traub, Lois M.
Turi, Dorothy June Gottfredsen
Tyson, Kathy S.
VanMechelen, Jacklin Bruner
Veazey, Katherine Anne
Vorachek, Darlene Ann
Warren, Rebecca Jackson
Weiskittel, Lynn Miller
Weiss, Mindy Roberta
Weiss, Shirley Harriet
Whitman, Susan Rochelle
Wild, Susan Ellis
Wolman, Rachel M.
Wright, Joyce L.
Wright, Martha Jayne
Wyatt, Sharon Paulette
Zelkind, Rachel Enid
Zerolnick, Barbara S.
Zoll, Robin Taylor
Meier, Michelle Susan

1-4-1983

Gintling, Karen Janette
Hinrichs, Liane K.
O'Shea, Suzanne Matt
Reich, Ellen Judith

1-17-1983

Jeffers, Anna Dolores

3-1-1983

Massey, Carolyn Mai

4-5-1983

Savrin, Janet Alane

5-3-1983

Pierson, Sara Clark

6-1-1983

Fettmann, Patricia Virginie
Johnson, D'Ana Edwina
Owens, Christine Lou

6-2-1983

Jones, Linda Heiserman
McCartney, Kathleen Susan Maley
Moore, Linda Gayle

6-3-1983

Pancost, Karen Beth Segal
Phillipps, Marion B.
Wilbon, Joan Marie

6-6-1983

Allen, Ann Rose
Barnhart, Gloria Anne
Belton, Tonia Yvetta
Betts, Zita Yolanda Johnson
Blair, Julie Hunt
Bonanni, Deborah A.
Bouchard, Catherine
Burchuk, Hillary Beth
Bush, Barbara Lynne
Cheung, Virginia Lee
Clark, Courtney Wray
Coleman, Heidi Lewis
Concolino, Jean Ellen
Cross, Judith Ann
Dalton, Mary Colleen
Dornbrand, Faith Diane
Dowling, Nancy Frances
Dunlap, Karin Roberts
Fine, Bobbie
Freed, Sharon Valerie Laskin
Freimark, Linda Hope
Gallick, Rosemary
Gardner, Ashley Joel
Gilmore, Maureen Kelleher
Goldenberg, Judy-Lynn
Goodman, Peggy Hirsch
Gordon, Rochelle Louise
Grasso, Kathi Lucille
Greenberg, Emily Ruth
Griisser, Susan Ann
Hamlin, Carole Bonnett
Harkleroad, Teresa Lynn
Head, Dora Louise Williams
Head, Joan Gunhild
Heard, Wanda Keyes
Henson, Jacqueline Ann
Holtzman, Terry Ellen
Hotchkiss, Mary Adams
Hutton, Suzanne Adair
Jacobs, Ilene Janet
Jenkins, Wendy Meredith
Jones, Diane Rachael
Jutras, Allise Kathryn
Kasputys, Patricia Jeanne
Kent, Deborah Ann
Killeavy, Kathleen McEvoy
Kimmich, Elaine Ruth
Kopec, Ruth Mary
Koppel, Grace Anne Dorney
Lawry, Elizabeth Clara
Lithotomos, Valerie Joanne
Mandell, Gail Ellen
Mathias, Lynn Goldman
Mattern, Cathy Lynn
McClendon, Donna Lisa P.
McNabb, LuAnn Maciulla
Miller, Karen Sue Joy
Moore, Dana Petersen
Nesse, Janet Marsha
North, Pamela Lee
Obermeyer, Sarai Kahn
Perkins, Martha Jane
Perron, Margaret Irene
Pinson, Tracey Lee
Racine, Barbara Eby
Raines, Lisa Joy
Reese, Laurel Paretta
Rhea, Melissa
Ringler, Phyllis Jane
Ripley, Jeanne Marie
Sarch, Susan Holly
Schamest, Joanne
Schild, Rena Karen
Schwartz, Jill S.
Shandell, Andrea T.
Stam, Heidi
Stanley, Valerie Joan
Stephenson, Kay Eileen
Swan, Carol Lynn
Thompson, Maureen Anne
Tibolla, Susan
Tillerson-Adams, Sheila R.
Towey, Mary Lucia
van der Ham, Ellen Ora
Vasco, Joanne
Wallace, Cheryl Yvonne
Watts, Lisa Mark
Welch, Patricia Ann Davidson
Willoughby, Maureen
Wilpone, Seri Ann
Wolf, Cyd Beth
Wolff, Margaret Anne Miller

6-22-1983

Bowman, Rebecca Gene

Farber, Beth Mina
Floreen, Nancy Marie
Glasco, Jo Mertred Franklin
Goodman, Carol Jean
Jenkins, Sandra Laureen
Raisher, Deborah Woolf

9-12-1983
Baenen, Deborah Merrick

9-21-1983
Tucker, Andrea Shelley

9-27-1983
Anderson, Rosalind Diane

10-4-1983
Keener, Mary Lou

11-1-1983
Howard, Deborah Singer

12-20-1983
Abramson, Jo Ann
Agard, Judith Andrews
Akerley, Mary Sweeny
Ammon, Bernice Charlotte
Anchors, Marcia Jean
Armentrout, Katharine Jacobs
Arthur, Sara Helen
Atallah, Laila Kathleen
Bacot, Janet Diane
Baker, Susan Dixon
Ball, Catherine Ann
Barish, Rhoda Stephanie
Barnhart, Virginia Wood
Basaman, Eileen Theresa
Bender, Leslie Carol
Benderson, Judith Kunzman
Benjamin, Nadine Walker
Berman, Pamela Leaderman
Besel, Sharon Gertrude
Blank, Karen Nancy
Bolling, Anne Dale
Boyle, Virginia Cecilia
Brennan, Mary Daly
Brill, Julia Mercedes-Marrero
Burger, Kirsten Anne
Burka, Diane Peri
Cauley, Betty Kay
Center, Judith Ann
Chance, Carol Eleanor
Chiet, Richelle Merril
Clark, Alice Gail Pollard
Clarke, Martha Vestal
Claxton, Joan Shank
Clemente, Coleen Ann Smith
Clopton, Karen Valentia
Conger, Suzanne Xonophane
Copeland, Barbara Barton
Cortezzo, Mary Rose
Crosswhite, Kristine Ann
Dietrich, Margaret Ann
Donnell, Sandra Joyce
Dunn, Elizabeth Monroe
Duyer, Katherine Sacco
Edwards, Christine Annette
Ehrlich, Karen Lynn
Eidelberg, Lisa Dopkin
Farinholt, Kathryn Spencer
Feldman, Debra Greenbaum
Finkelstein, Rona S.
Fox, Mary Anne Mullen
Freedman, Roberta
Garner, Jean Ann
Giller, Susan Gail
Gillette-Meadows, Merri Jo
Glasser, Margaret Donaldson
Goebert, Mary Elizabeth
Goldsborough, Judith Lee
Gordon, Hedy Helen
Gordon, Millicent Edwards
Grabowski, Joan Bernice
Granat, Zelle Debra
Green, Susan Ruth
Grey, Billie Jay
Gwinn, Laura J.
Hamilton, Mari Anne Therese
Holland, Marcella Amelia
Hollandsworth, Marla Jean
Hollis, Debra Lynne
Hornbeck, Rebecca M.
Howanski, Kristine Anne
Hystad, Cheryl Lynne
Iannone, Linda Marie
James, Carol Lynn
Jenkins, Nancy Gale
Johnson, Pamela Randi
Jones, Jean Marie
Jurrius, Cynthia Marrah
Kameen, Elizabeth Mary
Kendrick, Suzanne Chalfant
Kent, Cynthia Hitt
Kinikin, Sherry Ann
Kirkland, Bonnie Anne
Kirwan, Susan Myra Geller
Koplow, Ellen Lori Saltzman
Kountz, Barbara Curnin
Landskroener, Cristina Harding
Linder, Rita A.
Loewenthal, Michele
Lusby, Ruth Atkinson
Robinson, Margaret Dearden
Skolnik, Carolyn Waters
Stephens, Virginia Kelly
Strachan, Laura Hawkins
Talbott, Stacy B.
Taub, Robin Bernstein
Vice, LaVonna Lee

12-21-1983
Airey, Jo Ann Rbyczynski
Baumgartner, Nancy Helen
Becker, Joan Marie
Boone, Susan V.
Carrier, Susan Martielli
Chazen, Candace Sandler
Crawford, Mary Catherine
D'Aiutolo, Diane Virginia
Delisle, Jacqueline A. Moore
Friedman, Neile Sue
Gruber, Ellen R.
Hassman, Sara Penn
Hill, Marie Elise
Hollen, Cynthia L.
Hornig, Karen Stakem
Irving, Beth Hollie
Kelly, Erica Thyberg
Kreinar, Barbara Matthews
Kreiner, Jo-Anne Tillman
Kunzer, Kathleen Estelle
Kupferberg, Marcia Susan
Lane, Patricia Rohrmayer
Lassen, Elizabeth
Levine, Marta Schoepfle
Levy, Donna Marie
Lewis, Laurie Diane
Lock, Louise Ann
Lodge, Laura Power
Loya, Pamela Kirkbride
Madigan, Elizabeth Rishton Carswell
Malakoff, Eve Helen
McCafferty, Sarah
McCally, Cheryl Ann
McCarthy, Roberta Bole
McMillan, Donna Marie
McMullen, Carolyn Virginia
Miller, Wendy Joy
Minna, Myrna Lynn
Minot, Deborah Farmer
Miraglia, Cynthia Stegman
Monsees, Cathy Ventrell
Montgomery, Julie Ann
Moseley, Sarah Alison
Neal, Anne Carter
Negron, Sheryl Jane Pinkey
Nichols, Roann
Nyiri, Mary Patricia
O'Brien, Eileen
O'Connor, Margaret Mary
O'Neill, Noreen Ellen
Oshinsky, Carol Ann
Oshoway, Rebecca
Palmer, Anne-Steuart Vaughan
Palmer, Barbara Eisenberg
Palumbo, Katherine
Pavlos, Sharon Cox
Peitersen, Mary Elizabeth
Peterson, Mary Beth
Platt, Hilary Gerald
Polis, Susan Amy
Pomerantz, Jane R.
Potter, Katharine Ann
Powell, Ann Maria Reinsel
Preis, Mary Langdon
Pugh, Rosalyn Elaine
Regan, Janet Noel
Reggin, Alda Pauline
Reilly, Erin Rosalie
Ritterhoff, Clare Julia
Robinson, Sandra Hawkins
Rosenberg, Debra
Rosenzweig, Roni Beth
Rowe, Kathryn Michele
Ryon, Joan Elizabeth
Santomas, Ann Margaret
Schiff, Janis Boyarsky
Schoeck, Kristen Isabel
Schwartz, Madeline Beth
Shepard, Judith Tidd
Shepherd, Bridget Ann Duffy
Shuman, Lisa Jane
Skalla, Barbara Suzanne
Snyder, Lisa Raschal
Sobieski, Karen Ann
Sockwell, Diane Stokes
Solt, Julie Stevenson
Souzon, Jane Ann Cosson
Symonds, Wendy Robins
Tabackman, Regina Marilyn Sharp
Tarantola, Leslie Ellen
Tavss, Mona Binder
Taylor, Margaret Lee
Thomas-Wolock, Wendy
Tilghman, Barbara Mary
Tilghman, Susan Seidel
Ward, Roberta Mae
Watkins, Susan Cary
Weiser, Meryl Cecile
Wells, Carlotta Porter
Whalen, Teresa
White, Penny Jo
White, Suzette Schofield
Whitman, Patricia Mary Egan
Wickham-Smith, Delma
Wilkins, Susan Michael
Wirsching, Paulette Patrice Tudor
Woodside, Carolyn C.
Yee, Deborah Zeiler
Yurkow, Maryellen Adams
Zeller, Evelyn May
Zimkus, Valerie Agatha
Zuckerman, Carol Ann

1-10-1984
Benzil, Sharon Beth
Bove, Marcia Elizabeth
Brushart, Sandra Thornhill
Cummings, Jill
La Rocca, Michele
Sablosky, Ann Hope
Schindler, Ethel

1-11-1984
Jordan, Mary Donn Rossi
Karu, Anita Elaine
Kramer, Elaine Frances

1-12-1984
Moses, Debra Gail
Peterson, Charlotte Romelle
Porter, Allison Rae
Ravdin, Linda Jane
Saue, Jacqueline Marie
Stetina, Penelope Jane

1-18-1984
Todes, Judith Claire

1-31-1984
Nathan, Jane Frances
Stern, Hillary Adrienne
Stocklin, Valerie

2-10-1984
Glosser, Jill Paige

3-6-1984
George, Joan Meris

4-3-1984
Fisher, Marilyn Hope

6-4-1984
Horowitz, Lisa Abbey

6-5-1984
Abromson, Ellen Jane
Brown, Patricia Lamdin
Don, Beth Loewenstein
Feldman, Susan Boochever
Gartrell, Bernadette A.

6-6-1984
Haberle, Therese Marian
Hiatt, Susan Eisner
Johnson, Melissa Catherine
Joiner, Rande K.
Kelly, Kathryn Ann
King, Florence Rowena
Notarius, Joyce Milner
Sinclair, Susan Anne
Smith, Diane M.

6-7-1984
Powell, Louise Charlotte
Terrell, Kate

6-21-1984
Ackerman, Shelley Marcia
Adler, Lesley Collie
Ahearn, Marie Penny
Allen, Nancy Sue
Alsop, Robin Diane
Applefeld, Laurie Sue
Aronson, Roberta B.
Atkinson, Rena Vaughn
Ayers, Jayme Lynn
Beattie, Lynn Frances
Beattie, Mary Beth
Bell, Cheryl Maria
Berenson, Sandra Zela
Besche, Deborah K.
Best, Alegra J. S.
Biro, Susan Lori
Brehm, Tobey Glee Patno
Brown, Mary Denise
Burdette, Cathy Jo Veatch
Burrell, Sharon Veronica
Burt, Marianna Inga
Calore, Lynda Jacqlyn Lapinski
Cannon, Winifred Elaine
Carter, Beverly Barrett
Cassilly, Sarah Ann Hollister Davis
Chidakel, Susan Shirley
Clesner, Lisa Pia
Cohn, Gail Rudie
Cole, Rebecca Scrivner
Corey, Marian Faye
Corry, Jennifer Ann
Cramer, Rachel Deborah
Curtiss, Gayle Libby
D'Ambra, Mollie Roemer
Dane, Michele Anne
Dankos, Helen Agnes
Davis, Mary Elizabeth
Dempsey, Michele Andrea
DeVigne, Renee Yvonne
Doucette, Sharon Samson
Drummond, Patricia Anne Nimmerrichter
Eisenhauer, Rachel L.
Ely, Susan Marie
Eveland, Janet Carol Lansberry
Fanego, Ana Maria
Feldt, Patricia Norton
Field, Randi Sue
Finn, Maureen Michelle
Freeze, Janet Gayle
Garrett, Margaret Mary Robins
Gattuso, Christina Marie
Glaser, Patricia Jeanne
Gorecki, Stephanie Gayle
Gray, Patricia H.
Gurevich, Linda Schiller
Haines, Betty Meads
Hambrick-Stowe, Elizabeth Anne
Harvey, Patricia Ann Bambakos
Helwig, Nina Macfadden
Hightower, Judith Lynne
Hill, Kathi
Hoffman, Claire Shapiro
Horton, Ellen Vivien
Hull, Stephanie Jean Armstrong
Ikram, Shirin
Inuzuka, June K.
Karp, Judith Sturtz
Karpay, Jeannette Maddox
Kemper, Ellen Rhona
Kilchenstein, Grace Badolato
King, Nancy Margaret
Kirstaetter, Elaine McCoy
Klein, Lisa Ellen
Kleinberg, Deborah Rebecca
Koehler, Christine T.
Koehler, Debra Bocim
Kuhns, Joyce Ann
Latin, Shelley Patricia
Lee, Cynthia Ann
Lewis, Katherine Dumas
Lewitan, Dinah Halpern
Lopez-Thompson, Magda
Lucanik, JoAnn
MacKay, Donna Beth
Maggio, Patricia Leslie
Marder, Sue Ellen
Mason, Lillian Linz
Massey, Jill Anne
Mattei, Andrea Marie
Mayer, Susan S. J.
Milkis, Janice Marie
Minor, Laura Cecelia
Monroe, Sharman Javette
Montgomery, Joan F.
Mullally, Laura Francis
Murawski, Roberta Lee
Noone, Anita Maria
Northern, Christina Ann
O'Connor, Jan
O'Donnell, Patricia
Orlando, Terasa M.
Osterman, Elizabeth G.
Pence, Mary Shelton
Perry-Harris, Deborah
Polovoy, Amy Lynne
Poux, Jacqueline Kathleen O'Shea
Radcliff, Barbara Mae
Raney, Carla Hope
Riley, Eileen Carr
Rossowski, Jane
Sadowsky, Shelley
Schwan, Joy McElroy
Sheinkman, Katherine Ruben
Silver, Gambi Lee
Silverman, Marjorie Adele
Smith, Donna Marie
Smith, Tonya Monique
Spatz, Sherrill Robin
Spence, Susan Lee
Sullivan, Susan Riley
Swanson, Lucia DiSalvo
Talty, Kathleen Anne
Tierstein, Joanne
Titus, Marlene Kruppa
Tong, Elizabeth Bagby
Totaro, Denise Elaine
Truhe, Janet Marie
Ventrell, Karen
Walzl, Lois Joann
Watts, Shirley Marie
Watts, Vicki Ballou
Weisz, Lucy Ann
Wilkinson, Elizabeth Fisher
Williams, Sallie Elizabeth
Wylie, Bonnie
Younger, Patricia Ann
Zigel, Ana Claudia Langbort

7-9-1984
Bosley, Deidre A.
Fiscella, Caryn Frances
McCullough, Dorothy B.
McHale, Margaret Geraldine
Sartwell, Rachael Karen
Swan, Alva Allen

9-11-1984
Bakonyi, Linda Barbara
Entwisle, Elizabeth Bradbury
Harrington, Helen Ina
Lempert, Lauren Kass

10-2-1984
Pepper, Beth
Schulze, Nancy Elizabeth Lark

12-4-1984
Berschler, Barbara Ileen
Cohen, Nancy Lynn
Feldman, Clarice Rochelle
Forbes, Pamela Borland
Gehring, Barbara Glose
Mauro, Fay Ramsey
Murphy, Jane Caroline

12-5-1984
Eagle, Judith Graybeal
Freeston, Margaret Ann
Kravetz, Katharine K.

12-6-1984
Nelson, Sharon T.
Roudiez, Cecelia Travers
Weller, Pamela Lynne

1-7-1985
Taylor, Leslie Ann

1-12-1985
Milligan, Susan Marie

1-15-1985
Wray, Susan Hardy Duncan

1-17-1985
Adams, Elizabeth Spencer
Albright, Karen Melody
Aldrich, Janet Gray
Allen, Stacy L.
Ancel, Marci
Anderson, Marilyn Ellen
Annis, Terri Lynn
Anson, Melanie Deidra
Antalek, Melinda B.
Armstrong, Kimberly Susan
Austin, Susan Belle
Azrael, Miriam Lapp
Baer, Deborah Carol
Baldoni, Barbara Lucille
Barbera, Mary Ellen
Barnes, Sandra Irene
Belle, Aeronita Christine
Berman, Cynthia A.
Betz, Jean Louise
Bilodeau, Jean Sheftic
Boland, Lois Elaine
Bowyer, Louise Margaret
Boyer, Helen Stacey
Boykin, Jacquelyn Starks
Brain, Deborah Diane
Brennan, Anne Talbot
Brentley, Joyce Ann
Brockmeyer, Cathleen Cawley
Brooks, Diana Andrea
Brown, Janet Klein
Bryant, Jan Maureen
Bryce, Teresa A.
Buckner, Kathleen Carole
Budoff, Sheila Kraft
Bunty, Jacqueline Marie
Buonanno, Mary Beth
Burka, Sharon Lisa
Burton-Graham, Laura Anne
Calcagnini, Regina Anne
Carpenter, Rosemary Gladue
Carter, Susan Warfield
Carter, Toi Yvette
Chase, Judy Bednarz
Cinquegrani, Gayle C.
Clark, Catherine Bethune
Clark, Elizabeth Louise
Clovis, Debora Lee
Cody, Dolores Lorraine
Cohen, Laura Eve
Colborn, Carol
Connelly, Paula Jane
Cooper, Susan Marie
Cox, Linda Theresa
Craighead, Kathryn Coffey
Cukor, Martha Scholz
DeFrancesco, Susan Ellen
Dicker, Sharan Sue Fluhr
Dickerson, Shelby A.
Dorman, Ellice Schiller
Drucker, Alison Ruth
Drummond, Keven
Duncan, Alison MacDonald
Durkan, Catherine
Eden, Donna Zink
Emenheiser, Pauline Garber
Epstein, Carol Benjamin
Etting, Paula Sutton
Ewing, Patricia Ann
Falanga, Ingrid Doris
Falk, Theresa Fenelon
Fenner, Mary Ann
Fitch, Joyce Nan
Forrest, Leslie B.
Forster, Nancy Susanne
Fox, Diane A.
Gainen, Susan Rose
Gallagher-Duff, Kathleen T.
Garber, Linnette McClure
Gary, Alice Wainwright
Gay, Dorothy P.
Geldon, Anne Wolman
Gelpi, Yolanda Rivas
Gilhooly, Kathleen Ann
Glass, Verna Houghton
Gold, Robin Kofsky
Goldman, Daniela L.
Greenberg, Lauren Adler
Gregory, Amy Coley
Grillon, Jacquelyn Elizabeth
Guerney, Janis Elizabeth
Hajost, Theresa Wirtz
Hannigan, Barbara Bulger
Hannigan, Susan Marzec
Hart, Janet Marie
Heller, Donna Rae Holdeman
Henderson, Aline J.
Henry, Karen Louise Federman
Herrick, Susan Elizabeth
Herrity-Faust, Anne Marie
Hershey, Cheryl Leiter
Herzing, Theresa M. O'Malley

Hirsch, Marla Durben
Hoban, Gerry Ellen
Holjes, Crystal S.
Hollister, Anne Marie
Holton, Wendy Lee
Horton, Deirdre Reidy
Hurry, Linda Nelson
Jarrell, Ann O.
Jarrell, Elizabeth Merle
Jennison, Beverly Ann Petersen
Jessamy, Patricia Coats
Jones-Smith, Jacqueline
Jorgenson, Barbara A.
Kandell, Ellen Fran
Kardon, Robin D.
Kehoe, Susan Elizabeth
Kennedy, Elena
Kestenbaum, Barbara Ann
Kimball, Katharine White
Knapp, Nancy Illona
Koenig, Karen H.
Kotz, Kathryn L.
Kraft, Sheila Ann
Legg, Frances Agnes
Lewis, Fraeda J.
Lopiano, Anne Debelius
Lynch, Noreen Anne
Lynn, Shelah F.
Majev, Janet Brandt
McManus, Mary Patricia
Pais, Mara Devine
Purpura, Nancy Maggitti
Schmitt, Diane Festino
Shea, Theresa Burian
Smith, Melanie Karsh
Strong, Barbara T.
Tobin, Diane Adkins
Trader, Barbara R.
Vanderhoof, Martha Gower
Vannier, Ariel
Viens, Gail Borjeson
Young, Orsia Foudos

1-18-1985

Ayars, Jean Louise
Bailey, Sherrie Robinson
Bar, Cynthia M.
Burgoyne, Madeleine Scott
Casey, Patricia Pritt
Coconis, Tasha
Curry, Nina Smeltzer
Daniels, Denise Ann
Davies, Darlene Thomas
Davis, Julia Paschal
Day, Althea R.
Fallon, Mary Kathleen
Gebler, Hillary Sloane
Gibson, Glynis
Gisriel, Brenda Schadt
Hoover, Lesa Noblitt
Kurtze, Therese M.
Lacy, Elaine Marzetta
Lamb, Su Zann
Landman, Jessica Catherine
Lane, Susan Elizabeth
Langston, Joann Hawkes
Lankford, Sara Elaine
Laufer, Janet Ann
Lavan, Maryanne R.
Lawson, Deborah Ann
Levi-Goerlich, Susan Rae
Levin, Toby Milgrom
Levine, Phyllis Beth
Levy, Joanne Marie
Lewis, Audrey Joan
Lieberman, Cynthia Milan
Lisman, Carol Kaufmann
Lonergan, Kimberly Ann
Long, Annette Kathryn
Lopez, Ivette
Lord, Susan Moses
Magnuson, Laura Tise
Mahan, Norma Dee
Maloney, Diane Marilyn
Marinelli, Debra McMahon
Massof, Darcy Rood
May, Frances Patricia Finnernan
Mays, Paula Benita
McKee, Margaret Moran
McKenna, Judith Ann
McLaren, Mary Ellen
McMinn, Tamzin MacDonald
McNally, Patricia Anne
McQuade, Martha Jane Peeler
McWeeney, Laura C.
Mead, Lauren Grossman
Mehlert, Ann M. McGowan
Messerschmidt, Carole Jean Wagner
Metlin, Elaine
Milton, Priscilla Wilson
Monk, Lynn Alison
Montague, Serena Colonna
Moore, Mary-Jean Secoolish
Morgan, Kaye Lynn
Morris, Susan Reid
Morrison, Valerie Perrin
Muller, Elizabeth Russell
Myers, Gloria Jean
Nathanson, Sheila Gay
Nelson, Hedy L.
Nieber, Laura A. N.
Nowak, Michele Ann
O'Brien, Julia Louise
O'Donnell, Katy Colleen
O'Keefe, Vicki Elizabeth
Ojala, Elizabeth Miriam
Omberg, Cynthia Shaw
Paavola, Angela Dey
Pailet, Janet L.
Palmer, Barbara Johnson
Parris, Kay Louise
Perry, Beverly Lee
Peskin, Sandra Gay Reich
Pettus, Carla Gertrude
Podell, Bari Sue
Pollack, Nancy Beth
Poole, Lisa Shank
Potthast, Catherine A.
Pyles, Cynthia Jessen
Qualiana, Mary Katherine
Raffel, Doris Ruth
Ragland, Elizabeth Ann
Raposo, Cynthia Ann
Recio, Francisca Marco
Reed, Martine Billet
Reed, Rhea Ruth
Reznick, Seema
Rhodes, Elizabeth Ann
Robertson, Melissa Ann
Robinson, Susan A.
Robinson, Victoria Regina
Rodgers, Janice M.
Roese, Elizabeth Susan
Rose, Norma L.
Rosenfeld, Dana Beth
Rubelmann, Donna Ann
Saks, Lisa Jane
Sargent, Joan Taranto
Saulsbury, Frances
Schmalzl, Mary Wood
Schonberger, Anita Beth
Schulman, Ronnie Esther
Schultz, Juanita L.
Sharpe, Maxine Gail
Shemer, Kathleen Fantom
Shirley, Madeleine Ruth
Siegel, Valerie Lee
Silver, Robin
Silverberg, Margaret Rose
Silverman, Lisa R.
Sinclair, Mary Grace
Skerpon, Lynn Loughlin
Skinner, Tracey E.
Smith, Catherine Ann
Sommers, Evalyn Lindahl
Sparks, Karen
Spiess, Susan Elizabeth
Stein-Samaras, Harrie Renee
Stephenson, Marcia Avis
Stroup, Janis Irene
Stultz, Cheryl Andrea
Sullivan, Rose Ann
Sultan, Shaheda
Sussman, Karen Laurel
Sweeney, Mary Rosewin
Taylor, Cheri Price
Taylor, Nancy M.
Tiger, Ruth Gail
Townsend, Kathleen Kennedy
Turner, Leslie Elaine Smith
Vance, Jennifer Wysong
Vidmar, Sheila Mosmiller
Voelkel-Hanssen, Mary Martha
Vogel, Cynthia Lynn
Vollstedt, Maryruth
von Euler, Barbara
Wager, Adrian
Warner, Anne Homer
Warner, Deborah Pearson
Webb, Beth Louise
Weiner, Eileen J.
Weiss, Wendy Lisa
Welch, Adelina Maria
Wells, Jacqueline Erika
Wheatley, Elizabeth Regina
White, Angela Rene
Williams, Janice Lee
Williams, Serena M.
Wind, Karen Kay
Wolffe, Bernadette
Wright, Jane Marie Peloquin
Young, Nancy Ge Wong
Young, Roni Broden
Zajic, Elisabeth Crow
Zeide, Janet Sharon
Ziglar, Suzanne Gay

2-5-1985

Anderson, Jennifer Mary
Baldwin, Janice Briscoe
Briscoe, Janice Lynn
Carwell, Louise Margaret
Cunningham, Leonore Smith
Kaufman, Bonni Fine
Rapaport, Marnie Joy
Resnikoff, Jill Berkowitz
Schreiber, Jessica Joan
Sullivan, Lucine Marie
Wassel, Cheryl Rae

3-4-1985

Gorman, Joan Mary

5-10-1985

Herrmann, Margaret Ellen

6-4-1985

Braeman, Kathryn M.
Conlin, Marcia Lee
Costilo, Leslie Barry
Culver, Anna Mary
Eldredge, Jane MacDougal
Feinberg, Judy Lynn
Gonzalez, Maria Elena
Sweet, Linda Beth

6-5-1985

Harding, Vicki Ruth
Kafker, Arlene
Van Susteren, Greta Conway

6-6-1985

Gorfkle, Judith Louise
Quinn, Rosemary
Rasenberger, Ann Louise
Ruscitella, Maria M.
Stein, Kathie Ann
Surace, Cathy S.
Vanderryn, Margrit Wolfes

6-26-1985

Alexander, Jeanne Marie
Anderson, Jeanne Albrecht
Astrove, Lyda Larkins
Barry, Margaret Martin
Bavender, Ann
Bayer, Janet Carol
Bennett, Laurie
Berlin, Mary Ann L.
Beverley, Cassandra Renee
Blechman, Margaret Jill
Blimline, Marilyn Elaine
Boswell, Nancy G.
Carrion, Audrey J. Sylvia
Clemons-Sacks, Donna
Cline, Michal Brenda
Cohen, Susan
Colladay, Coralyn Frances
Colton, Clare Ivey
Conaway, Teresa Louise
Coon, Lois Reynolds
Darcy, Bonnie Jean
Day, Camilla Ann
Deger, Anita Candy
Dobbins, Madeliene Humphrey
Einaudi, Carol Peacock
Engel, Diana R.
Engelhard, Sharon Kay
Evans, Cynthia Heckathorn
Fajer-Smith, Debora
Ferguson, Jeannine Claire
Flournoy, Hartina
Fuchsluger, Donna Jean
Garrand, Agnes Cahill
George, Carole Shelbourn
Goldman, Donna Bradford
Goldring, Esther Hannah
Goodwin, Julie Diantha
Gordy, Emily Patterson
Gouse, Abbe Monica
Grindrod, Sharyn Fenster

Gross, Teri-Ann Faye
Henry, Kim Meris
Hester, Catherine Chen
Hewlett, Elizabeth Marie
Hillas, Barbara Anne Dillon
Hilson, Anita Eley
Hotten, Michele Dudley
Hwang, Marian C.
Imhoff, Donna B.
Infante, Gwen Pohl
Jenkins, Harriett G.
Jones, Peggy Coppala
Keating, Mary Theresa
Killea, Carolyn Ann
King, Carole Wayne
Kirwin, Kathleen Denise
Kordek, Kathleen A.
Kraskin, Sara Gale Dunham
Lamb, Jennifer Spivak
Landsman, Gail Renee
Lawson, Carol Jeanne
Layton, Linda Thater
Leichman, Sherry L.
Lescher, Marirose Kathleen
Levy, Deborah Peyton
Loeber, Patricia Ann
Lytle, Nancy M.
Malis, Michelle Chyatte
Markoya, Judith Darrylyn
Marvin, Mary Jean
Mason, Rosanna Marie
Matlin, Linda Sharon
McAleer, Kathryn Susan
McMurtry, Vanda Bruce
McShea, Sandra Wharton
Mech, Ann Baldwin
Meloy, Dorianne Avery
Meriwether, Rebecca Callcott
Milbourn, Elizabeth Jean
Mitchell, Pamela Diane
Moran, Frances Cabrini
Morningstar, Mary Patricia
Mulitz, Barbara Cheryl
Naser, Cristeena Gilbert
Nelson, Maureen
Nicks, Judy
O'Brien, Karen Marra
O'Reilly, Laurie Pyne
Orvis, Mary Ellen
Owens, Chris A.
Parker, Judy Ann
Pesyna, Janice Lynn
Rechsteiner, Vera Ann
Ropshaw, Carolyn Crouch
Rost, Catherine Haley
Ruffin, Victoria Geraldine
Sachs, Margaret R.
Sampedro, Ruth Mercedes
Sapper, Debra Kolodny
Schmidt, Helen D'Artois
Segal, Cynthia Ellen
Seibert, Nancy Bernice
Shadd, Audrey Mae
Shapiro, Amy Ellen
Sheehan, Sharon M.
Shuch, Terry Maxine
Silverman, Jane Gayle Glickman
Sklorman, Sheryl L.
Smith, Karen Ann Urbaitis
Spector, Natalie Helen
Steinborn, Carla Anne
Tayman, Laura Pellatiro
Tovar, Myread Marie
Triplin, Thelma J.
Tucker, Linda Beth
Webb, Sarah Eckert
Weiner, Shirley J.
White, Carolyn
White, Pauline Kelly
Ziadie, Lola Maria Susanne
Henley, Susanne Koster

7-1-1985
Bees, Margaret M.

8-30-1985
Natter, Elizabeth Ungar

9-10-1985
Bank, Rita Mae
Botluk, Diana
Bradford, Martina Lewis
Bradley, Elizabeth Ann Glennie
Everett, Nancy Elizabeth
Fellenzer, Joy Anne
Frumkin, Nancy Lee
Gardner, Debra Lynn

9-12-1985
Villa, Ellen G.

11-5-1985
Robertson, Cindy
Samuels, Barbara Ann

12-9-1985
McDonough, Eileen T.
Ricks, Jo Lynn Littman

12-10-1985
Alper, Nancy Lynn
Cooper, Ellen Schiff
DeGraff, Martha Hager
Di Benedetto, Dawn Valerie
Dobmeyer, Ann Marie
Donnelly, Marguerite Anne
Galbraith, Carol Jean
Glynn, Rosemary Kohler

12-11-1985
Crane, Robyn Lillibridge
Jackson, Margo Ericka
Kreitzberg, Ellen
Lasater, Nancy Elizabeth
Marlette, Cynthia Ann

12-12-1985
Dingle, Julie A.
Rosenberg, Ellen Phyliss
Wolf, Susan Ellen
Woodard, Beverly Jean

12-17-1985
Johnston, Barbara Lee

12-19-1985
Abad, Jessie Margaret
Ackerman, Debra Lee
Anderson, Nancy Lynne Smith
Apostolakos, Mary Jean
Arnsbarger, Linda Ann
Bannat, Betty Cockrill
Bawnik, Tammy Sue
Beavan, Bonnie Jo
Beckman, Marlene Doris
Bellassai, Cara Courtney
Bentley, Elaine S.
Blair, Lori Lynn
Blizzard, Diane C.
Bortnick, Janet Edelstein
Boucher, Kathleen Mary
Boyce, Susan Bernadette
Bradley, Janet Arlene
Brennan, Patricia C.
Breslaw, April Anne
Broache, Pamela Thomas
Brown, Georgia Faye
Brueger, Kathleen Suzanne
Byrne, Olivia Sherrill
Canan, Ellen Patricia
Cannon, Cheri Lynn
Cashman, Marie
Chagnon, Kathleen Ann
Chambers, Andrea Jane
Chappell, Patricia Louise
Chassy, Reina Lee
Chesser, Karen Christy Holt
Cihan, Beverly Jeanne
Cleary, Lauri Eff
Cohn, Robin Frucht
Cooney, Mary-Jo
Cooper, Gail Gallatin
Corken, Cathleen Mary
Corley, Judith Lee
Crabb, Jennifer Hope
Cuffee, Diane Virginia
Curtin, Debra Lynn
Dalton, Jane Gilliland
Daniel, Tami Patrice
Darrah, Paula Jean
Daugherty, Marie Baumeister
Davis, Rachel Olivia
De Cervens, Jeanne
DeMartino, Gaelynn Teresa
DeMouy, Rosemary Lynn
Deserio, Kim Marie
Dicus, Joanne M.
Dietz, Phyllis Podolsky
Dittmann, JoAnn Smith
Dobbs, Kathryn Ann
Dubin, Andrea Sue
Ebersberger, Katherine Marie
Ellis, Joyce Lynn
Emerson, Caroline Elizabeth
English, Barbara J.
English, Catherine Ames
Epstein, Louise K.
Evans, Beth Louise
Farley, Patricia O'Conor Barrett
Fenwick-Baker, Theresa Diane
Fischmann, Elizabeth Jean
Fisher, Erica Jay
Fisher, Miriam Louise
Flury, Carolyn D.
Fordis, Jean Burke
Forney, Karen Bragg
Fried, Leslie Blair
Fruchter, Susan Carol
Gallagher, Julie C.
Garinther, Carol Khachian
Garten, Ilene Stephanie
Gebhard, Cathy
George, Mary Jo
Gerken, Karen Marie
Gerstung, Elizabeth Christina
Gilleran, Alexa J.
Glatter, Amy Susan
Gordon, Judith Ellen
Grantland, Brenda Gail
Greenberg, Jill Merle
Greenberg, Linn Turner
Greenfeld, Beth
Guth, Cheryl Lee O'Donnell
Haddad, Michele Lynn
Hagan, Ellen Boland
Halkousis, Sylvia Barbara
Hanfling, Phyllis
Hanrahan, Catherine Anne
Harford, Nancy Ann
Harris, Brenda Valentine
Hawthorne, Margaret Deirdre
Haycox, Sue Ellen
Haynes, Elizabeth McAlister
Heinrich, Amy B.
Heyman, Amy Rebecca
Hill, Barbara Jean
Hock, Diane Bridget
Hogue, Louise Anne
Hoskins, Kathryn Kelley
Hotchkiss, Phyllis Ann
Hudson, Barbara Jean
Jackson, Jone Lemos
Jacobs, Carolyn
Janulis, Diane Marie
Johnson, Katherine Anne
Jones, Katherine Jean
Kahan, Linda S.
Kaiser, Sheryl Leigh
Kates, Anna Tuerk
Katz, Elaine Cweiber
Keane, Mary Carolyn
Kearney, Wendy Sue
Keir, Nancy E.
Kendrick, Martha Mary
Kerr, Karen Ivy Federgreen
Klassen, Kathryn Helen
Kraus, Heather Holt
Lanzon, Christine E.
Laws, Rebecca Ann
Leder, Miriam Michal
Lee, Ellen
Leone, Carmela
Levinson, Beth Lynn
Lieberman, Elizabeth Rae
Liebschutz, Elizabeth H.
Longson, Sarah Elizabeth
Low, Mary Alice
Lowy, Nomi Irene
Moran, Deborah L.
Mullady, Melissa Johnson
Nell, Christine Barilla
Park, April Oh
Plantamura, Mary Lawless
Pott, Claudia A.
Preston, Judith Curchin
Schaeffer, Donna McCabe
Schellie, Anne DeRenzo
Stockhamer, Jordana Enig
Taylor, Laurell E.
Underberger, Lori Lobel
Weitzel, Nomiki Bouloubassis
Weymouth, Lucy Chapman
Wolcott, Roberta Dunlap

12-20-1985
Alden, Phyllis
Andrus, Meredyth Smith
Cadoux, Cathleen White
Callahan, Ellen Ann
Coates, Cathi Van de Meulebroecke
Concannon, M. Linda
Cook, Joan Nugent
Davis, Darlene Rae

Fili, Denise Marie
Fleisher, Renee L.
Gilbert, Kimberly Aileen
Groover, Jacqueline Schmitt
Hudson, Mabeth Wilson
Jack, Connie Williams
Lynch, Gabrielle Marie
Lynch, Mary Elizabeth
Macht, Jane
Magner, Anne Cushing
Malone, Elizabeth Sahlin
Marcil, Loreen Marie
Margolis, Leslie Seid
Marzetta, Susan Marie
Mason, Deborah Miller
Mastrovito, Marie-Anne
Matthews, Ann Kimberly
Mazure, Kathleen Louise
McClure, Helen Pendleton
McFarland, Mary Margaret
McGarey, Barbara Marticelli
McGowan, Krista Ann
McLaughlin, Christine Dolores
Merrick, Doris Marie
Miller, Sheira
Moeller, Linda Dunn
Molloy, Elizabeth Margaret
Morrell, Mindy A.
Mott, Patricia Davison
Munkel, Diane Marie
Munter, Jennifer Lannon
Musslewhite, Kathleen Haw
Myckowiak, Vicki Sherman
Nelson, Marilyn E.
O'Brien, Andrea Marie
O'Brien, Lisa Stello
O'Day, Jodi Rae
Oldewurtel, Mary D.
Olson, Kathryn Elizabeth
Oram, Kathleen
Oster, Catharine Reeves
Park, Silvia Mihae
Partlow, Jeanette Glose
Percy, Linda Eve
Perkins, Jennifer Sheila
Phillips, Angela Marie
Pierre, Jeffri Thomas
Porter, Mary Lacy
Powell, Darlene Wright
Prestigiacomo, Patricia
Ranard, Ellen Scheinberg
Randel, Ellen French
Regelin, Nancy Patricia Boyle
Rice, Gail Simone Elliott
Rogers, Barbara Ann
Rosselot, Anne Patricia
Roth, Karen Berntzen
Rubin, Carol Louise
Rubin, Carol Snyder
Ruffner, Malissa
Russell-Forrester, Nancy Hill
Russo, Becky A.
Saffran-Brinks, Carol
Sakamoto-Wengel, Joy Reiko
Saunders-Brooks, Joanne Sandra
Schaeffer, Ruth Ellen
Schechter, Susan Ellen
Schreiner, Sara Baker
Seeger, Arline Michelle
Seiger, Randi Studley
Shields, Natalie Ann
Shiff, Wendy Lozinsky
Shuham, Caryl Sandler
Siegal, Melissa Cynthia
Silverman, Pamela Steele
Smith, Celine Marie
Smith-Jones, Teri Christine
Speer, Denise Lynn
Spell, Cynthia Louise
Stanley, Marian R.
Stein, Gail Ellen
Stikas, Tina Marie
Strickler, Elizabeth Ann
Sylvester, Patricia Rynn
Tandy, Marlene Karen
Targan, Halette Hart
Taylor, Gwendolyn Dunham
Townsend, Pegeen Anne
Troch, Kathryn Lee Grund
Unkle, Barbara Simmons
Veilleux, Jean Wright
Wanger, Beth R.
Ward, Anne Friederici
Wash, Vickie Lynn
Weinberg, Nancy Ann
Weinman, Deborah Kramer
Welch, Lisa Thayer
Wildemann, Mary Elizabeth
Williams, Margaret Lynn
Wilson, Julia Anne Taylor
Wise, Kathleen Marie
Wood, Cynthia Ruth
Wood, Stephannie Anne
Woolf, Linda Semesky
Worthington, Katherine Ann
Wozny, Irene Bernadette
Zawitoski, Gina Monath
Zeller, Elizabeth Ann
Zimelman, Robin Laura
Zrake, Virginia Ann

12-21-1985
Schweitzer, Margaret Marie

1-3-1986
Bittner, Eileen Meren
Blake, Anne McChristian
Bryant, Susan Kay
Butler, Ellyn Sporn
Carnes, Kelly Hawkins
Dexter, Vicki L.
Fagan, Madeleine Weiss
Floyd, Sheryl Lynn
Lee, Anne Cunningham
Lipkin, Rhonda Beth
Meister, Karen Goldstein
Morris, Lee Willis
O'Lear, Janice
Sabrin, Amy Roxanne
Skillman, Deborah Lacey
Smith, Anna Teresa
Terres, Nora Todd
Tetro, Valerie Lisabeth
Utrecht, Carolyn
Weiss, Joan M.
Wise, Joan Alexandra Sylvester
Zale, Karen Bruton
Zanar, Louise P.

1-28-1986
Brown, Kristen Wilkins
Durrell, Piper Lee
Kusske, Kathryn Ann
Orlich, Rebecca Sue
Pennington, Kathleen M.
Powers, Ann
Sullivan, Joanne Monica
Wolfer, Judith A.
Woodward, Nancy J.

3-4-1986
Lindsay, Mary Clare
Mitlak, Stefany L.
Rand, Kristen Maria

4-29-1986
Watson, Leila Hirayama

6-3-1986
Lincicome, Francine Teresa
Stellmann, Elizabeth Springer

6-4-1986
Beck, Ronna Lee
Butler, Bonnie Jo
Condos, Barbara Moir
Flanagan, Fern Leslie Renee

6-5-1986
Carson, Ellen Godbey
Goodgal, Paula Ann
Goodman, Carolyn Greta
Habbert, Rebecca Jane
Hansen, Susan Taylor
Hill, Andrea
Knox, Joyce Anne Hanks
Lobo, Cynthia Marcia Wimer
Mell, Paula Irene
Mentkowski, Sheila Conlon
Mickey, Anne Ellison
Miller, Barbara Rose

6-6-1986
Arnett-Kremia, Meri
Outlaw, Phyllis J.
Patrick, Marlys Elaine
Perilstein, Linda Joy
Porter, Mary T.
Seras, Barbara J.
Shanks, Margaret McCloskey
Soponis, Gaylin Gramse
Stewart, Margaret Ann
Stovall, Brenda Joyce
Woodall, Barbara Susanne
Yanni, Palma Ruth

6-25-1986
Aluisi, Kim DiGiovanni
Anderson, Alda Almira
Anderson, Elizabeth
Anderson, Kelly Copeland
Andrias, Katherine Ann
Awalt, Deborah A.
Baden, Naomi Joy
Bailar, Susan Lee Zuckerman
Barrett, Deborah Ann
Basha, Leigh-Alexandra
Bauer, Susan Marie
Beffa, Margaret Catherine
Bell, Mary Maureen
Bender, Susan Walker
Benedetti, Janet Lynn
Bernstein, Donna Beth
Bisco, Deborah Jean
Bowlus, Helen Elizabeth
Brace, Michele Jill
Branzelle, Judith Alpern
Brenner, Alana S. Culver
Brown, Alicia Marie
Callahan, Cheryl L.
Cassel, Jennifer Kathryn
Cooke, Marie Fischer
Corning, Diane Hutcheson
Costley, Cassandra LaVerne
Cummins, Ruth Wagonheim
Davis, Jo Ann M.
Della Noce, Dorothy J.
Devine, Erin R.
DiPietro, Elena R.
Dolan, Elizabeth Scullin
Dowling, Melissa Hamilton
Drescher, Tammy Cohen
Duff, Lydia Belknap
Egan, Christine Louise
Epps, Melea Rose-Cherie
Escobar, Karen Ann
Essex, Maureen Frances
Faure, Dianne Maria
Fenerty, Margaret Mary
Fischer, Susan H.
Fisher, Bonnie Helfgott
Fleeman, Mary Grace
Fox, Elizabeth Elliott
Frame, Ilene Sharon
Fries, Annette Rooney
Gagner, Sue Frix
Gefen, Lisa Jane
Gelber, Judith Lee
Gibbs, Meredith Ellen
Gilbert, Phyllis Beverly
Goldberg, Susan Gayle
Goldsmith, Sharon Eden
Goldstein, Diane Carol
Good, Christina L.
Gorbaty, Dena Gutman
Gottesman, Marcia Ellen
Hammond, Jennifer Lynn
Hankin, Janet Selenkow
Harris, Joan Irene
Harrod, Katie Nichols
Haynie, Sharon Earlene
Heller, Susan J.
Hens-Greco, Kathryn Mary
Horowitz, Lisa D.
Hudson, Cathleen Quigg
Hurwitz, Roseanne Apfeldorf
Jakabcin, Ann Gray
Jeffrey, Deborah Judith
Johnson, Diana Ethelyn
Johnson, Gail Kimberly
Jorgensen, Lanese Esther
Josey, Leronia Arnetta
Kaden, Nancy Fox
Kaplan, Leslie Ann
Kent, Mary Margaret
Kerbel, Susan Getz
Kleederman, Eva Susan
Kleinke, Christine D.
Knight, LeDora
Koetter, Cornelia Maria
Krask, Karen Jean
Lanchester, Michelle
Lax, Michele
Lieberman, Mindy Ann
Lowe, Sally Adams
Lyga, Patricia Martin
Maitland, Nancy Marie
Mangold, Donna Simonek
Marchetta, Joanne Susan
Markwitz, Debra Joan
McCarthy, Patricia Ann
McKenney, Patrice M.
Mikva, Laurie I.

Miller, Susan Ann
Murdock, Patricia Lynne Collins
Murphy, Mary Barbara
Myles, Monica Anastasia
Nichols, Diane Spencer
O'Brian, Valerie R.
O'Keeffe, Lois Hope
Oaks, Robin Linda
Oh, Rachel Mihwan
Oldham, Susan Sheehan
Olshaker, Carolyn Clemente
Orlowski, Sandra DeLong
Osterman, Elizabeth Gilbert
Phelps, Susan G.
Piche, Diane Marie
Press, Cheryl Ellen
Quattrocki, Carolyn Annette
Quinn, Julene Marian
Raffaele, Donna Marie
Richards, Lori Ann
Ritchie, Alice Saulnier
Rivera, Severina B.
Rosenblum, Susan Landis
Rothenberg, Charlotte Faye
Royal, Laurice DeAnne McDonald
Saladoff, Susan Vogel
Salzman, Janice I. Greenberg
Samuels, Marsha Krawitz
Sattari, Caroline Anita
Scherr, Kandace L.
Schroeder, Mary Jane Theresa
Shean, Michele Siobhan
Siers, Rhea Donna
Smith, Cinda Kay
Spangler, Kathleen Ann
Stefan, Susan Frances
Streimer, Laura Ann
Thrane, Karen Kunen
Towson, Michele Sandy
Treanor, Claire Marie
Tucci, Gail Atwell
Tucker, Laura M.
Turner, Merle Kasten
Turner, Terri Lynn
Vanni, Elizabeth Anne
Wagner, Anne Marie
Waldron, Mary Grace
Walker, Linda Ann
Wang, Catherine
Weinberg, Lynn F.
Westbrook, Kathryn Vivian
Whitaker, Tracey Leigh
Whiteford, Susan Penny Mears
Williams, Babette Deanna
Winer, Lisa Beth
Zane, Daria Jean
Zimmer, Kyle Jacqueline
Zupan, Katheryn Daymee

7-8-1986

Gardner, Lissa Joy

7-17-1986

Paterson, Amy Blaymore

9-8-1986

Davidovski, Mira
Holmes, Margaret Fry
Peltz, Paulette Beatrice
Phillips, Joy LaNelle
Sapir, Judith S.
Scott, Sean Megan
Townsend, Marilyn
Wall, Joanne Foster

9-30-1986

Vass, Deborah Sue
Welcome, Mary

12-29-1986

Adams, Theresa Mary
Ahmed, Farhat Tasneem
Aldouby, Sharon Lynn
Arthur, Megan Mary
Aviles, Kimberly Corbin
Barnes, JoAnna Judith
Barthel, Carol Ann
Benecke, Eileen Rose
Bernstein, Tobie Ellen
Binstein, Nina Mostoff
Birnbaum, Karen Rhea
Birrane, Kathleen A.
Blomquist, Claire Prin
Bollinger, Judith Ann
Bowe, Karolyn Loretta Northrop
Bowman, Nancy R.
Brideau, Carol Ann
Briggs, Virginia Lee
Brodeur, Paula Elizabeth
Brown, Alison Jeanette
Bryant, Yvette Michelle
Bunker, Mary Garrett
Cahill, Elizabeth Ann
Calder, Kathleen Anne
Case, Elizabeth Jane
Casey, Regina Ann
Chamblee, Andrea E.
Chase, Geri Lyons
Chavis, Kathy
Chi, Loretta Elizabeth
Christie, Sharon Ann
Clark, Avery Thenear
Clark, Cynthia Lee
Clarke, Toni Evon
Cleaveland, Patricia Ann
Clements, Roxanne S.
Cobun, Susan D.
Cohen, Sheila A.
Collins, Patricia Ryan
Cook, Deborah Susan
Corsini, Patricia Elizabeth
Cowan, Joyce Aileen
Crupiti, Niti
Cytryn, Suzanne I.
Danz, Erin Margaret
Davis, Laura Helen
DeBernard, Carolyn H.
Defensor, Lisa Snawder
Delaplaine, Lindsay Bruce
Detrick, Kimberly Beth
Devlin, Mary Elizabeth
Diamond, Yvette Nancy
Doberman, Amy Rose
Domike, Julie Ronder
Drake, Julie Ann
Durham, Eleanor
Eby, Marianne Patricia
Edwards, Kerry Lynn
Eisenberg, Linda Marlene
Ellis, Kathleen Anne
Fjermestad, Colette Randi
Fleming, Linda P.
Fronden, Constance M.
Frulla, Gail Debra
Fusting, Diana Quigley
Gately, Blaise Marie
Gavin, Kathleen O'Connell
Gibbon, Elizabeth Johanna
Goldfarb, Elissa Eidelman
Goldman, Donna Smith
Goslee, Jannai Charlana
Gould, Nancy Katherine Deshler
Graeff, Kathryn Grill
Grattan, Susan Amy Arbucho
Greenberg, Wendy Jo
Guarino, Karen Shedd
Hackett, Susan Jane
Hall, Theresa M.
Halpern, Ellice Andrea
Handy, Althea Marie
Haslinger, Nancy Lee
Hast, Mary Elizabeth
Hayutin, Robin Gale
Heaton, Sharon B.
Hemeter, Elizabeth Pollard
Hickes, Susan Healey
Hochman, Nancy Ellen
Hoogstraten, Anne E. Kelleher
Hoover, Susan Leslie
Hornstein, Ellen Ruth
Horvath, Diane Ellen
Hull, Edith
Iannotti, Gail Knetzer
Jacobs, Elizabeth Ann Gross
James, Mary-Dulany
Jameson, Ann Harwood
Jeffers, Margaret O'Shea
Johnson, Elizabeth Anne
Jones, June Marie
Joselson, Tracy Jennifer
Kalish, Cecilia C.
Karmiol, Grace Celia
Karwasinski, Joan Loring
Keane, Christine Elizabeth
Keegan, Judith M.
Kelley, Elizabeth Claire
Kenyon, Judith Diane
Kenyon, Mary Kathleen
Kershner, Lisa Ann
Kiernan, Leslie Berger
King, Sarah Christine
Klamp, Carolyn Ann
Klein, Lori Diane
Knight, JoAnn Kathryn
Knight, Katharine Mary
Kramer, Susan Frances
Laguarda, Wendy R.
Lankenau, Patricia Agliano
Larkin, Donna Bartenfelder
Lent, Susan Heck
Maley, Susan C.
Mankofsky, Lisa Sara
McEneney, Victoria A.
Nathans, Caroline Frieder
Poulos, Anthi Helleni
Schakel, Linda Beth
Selle, Kathryn Hess
Siskind, Roberta G.
Thompson, Victoria Cawood

12-30-1986

Athey, SueLyn Smith
Bragunier, Amy J.
Brinkhoff, Robbin E.
Brokaw, Laura Ilene
Bryant, Carol Suzanne
Bumgardner, Eunice Lin
Carr, Lettie Moses
Cohen, Aileen Miller
Converse, Jane Spilman
Cross, Colleen R.
Cunningham, Linda T.
Donohue, Dorothy M.
Edwards, Jehanne McIntyre
Epstein, Jayme Rizzolo
Gaughan, Barbara Ann
Hunter, Helen-Louise Simpson
Keller, Diane Elizabeth
Kleger, Elizabeth Adkins
Kulish, Carol
Ladd, Christine Robitscher
Lally, Rosemarie
Lebo, Diane
Lee, Carley Denlinger
Leiner, Jill R.
Lewis, JoEllen Dardick
Lias-Booker, Ava
Liss, Esther Hannah
Lubin, Melanie Senter
Lubitz, Lynn Ann
Lucasse, Mary Louise
Lunga, Eileen Marie
Lynch, Ann Frances
Mabry, Catherine Bryan
Machen, Judith Amanda
Mainor, Jo Margaret
Mangan, Nancy Felix
Mangel, Claudia Pap
Marinelli, Jayne
Markowitz, Deborah Levitin
Marks, Pamela Diane
McChesney, Kathleen Marie
McClelland, Michelle Olivia
McDermott, Kathleen
McIntosh, Robbyn Renee
McLeod, Cheryl Annette
McNeal, Mary Helen
McPherson, Mary Tracy
Miller, E. Suzan
Mitchell, Kristine Anne
Modlin, Stephanie Paula
Morton, Mary Catherine
Mulrenin, Colleen Ann
Munday, Mary Angela
Nadeau, Linda Ann
Naiman, Eleanor Cynthia
Nayo, Lydia Anne
Neelon, Gail Elizabeth
Nicolle, Lori Anne
Noto, Anne Doris
Novak, Nancy Diane
O'Reilly, Kathleen
Orcino, Rose Marie
Oshman, Michele Theresa
Owen, Amy Sanborn
Owens, Wendy J.
Paxton, Sally Patricia
Phillips, Rosemary Leeds
Pierson, Rachel Adelman
Pollack-Matz, Fran Marcy
Porter, Nicole Elizabeth
Pouring, Marie Dorothy
Powell, Leslie Allison
Psoras, Cynthia Leslie
Reed, Dana Anne
Reicher, Terri Lee
Richardson, Linda Louise
Rigby, Suzanne

Rind, Alison Wendy
Rogers, Helen Frances
Rogers, Kathleen Elizabeth
Rohde, Bridget Michael
Rotbert, Suzanne L.
Ruley, Nancy Lee Selig
Salomon, Sheila Mary Faulkner
Sanders, Lisa Smith
Santoni, Jane Patricia
Savage, Katherine Dowd
Schiller, Sally R.
Sengstacke, Diane Leonard
Serrette, Cathy Hollenberg
Sette, Sarah Margaret
Shaffer, Stacy Proctor
Shaffert, Robin Laurette
Shapero, Loretta Ellen
Shein, Caren Silver
Shweky, Cindy Rae
Siegel, Stacy Enid LeBow
Smith, Anastasia Watson
Smith, Jennifer Alisa
Sneed, Maree Frances
Snow-Freling, Stacey Jane
Snyder, Cheryl Darlene
Spivey, Karen Drabik
Stanton, Sharon Reynolds
Stegemann, Traci J.
Steinberg, Julie Ann
Steinberg, Stephanie Shuster
Steinkoenig, Kristine Marie Luise
Stern, Lisa A.
Stinner, Sally Ann
Stoner, Nancy Kaye
Strollo, Lauren Mary
Strothman, Doreen Ann
Sullivan, Kathryn Ellen
Swisher, Laura A.
Taylor, Katherine Lee
Taylor, Vanita Michelle
Teleky, Cathy Briskie
Temchine, Judy Lynne Wolfson
Thompson, Leah Denise Embry
Thompson, Trisa Jean
Thornton, Amelia Louise
Tonkonow, Sherry Rippel
Townsend, Lynn H.
Trivas, Jill Robyn
Ullman, Robin Hirsh
Vaughn, Melanie Ann
Veltrop, Virginia Cheatham
Voelkel, Joanne DeSalle Finnegan
Waddell, Tina Marie
Walker, Dorothy Elizabeth
Watkins, Andrea R.S.
Wax, Marjorie Helen
Wei, Helen Colleen
Whelihan, Deborah Murrell
Whitehall, Beatrix Deborah Maria
Wilkens, Susan Mann
Wilkinson, Sandra Lee
Williams, Pamela McKenzie
Wilson, Brenda Jo
Wiss, Catherine Jean
Wood, J. Lynne
Yodice, Kathleen Ann Barbara
Young, Donna Marie
Zamora, Irene Patricia
Zembas, Kimberly A.

1-5-1987
Bostwick, Carolyn Leslie
Bosworth, Ellen Cohen
Boughton, Nancy Lynn
DeLano, Mary
Garber, Abigail B.
Glass, Elizabeth Ann
Isensee, Lynne Crofton
Koch, Elizabeth C.
Lewis, Laurie Ann
Martorana, Carmen Joseph
Miller, Susan Stevens
Naclerio, Jacqueline Morrison
Parker, Mary Ann Baird
Rachal, Janelle Marie
Tolmach, Elisabeth Joy
Ullman, Rachel Sobin
Young, Charlotte Diehl

1-6-1987
Baurley, Marion E.
Bergmeister, Debra S.
Friedman, Myrna E.
Groner, Arlene Pianko
Hamann, Elizabeth Ann
Murray, Dana Hendricks
Savit, Diana Majorie

1-7-1987
Eleff, Susan Lynn
Fidler, Genine Macks
Griffith, Beverly Peyton
Hayes, Charlotte Anne
Labella, Janet E.
Landau, Gail Bissell
McNamara, Mary Beth
Millman, Laura Diana
Norcross, Mary Kathryn Ryan
Potter, Linda Lane
Slous, Joan
Solomon, Elaine Deborah

1-8-1987
Logan, Ann Hyatt
Ribnick, Catherine Adelaide
Rosenberg, Ruth Helen Borsuk
Sheffield, Pamela
Shepard, Carmen Mercedes
Stevens, Dinah
Wagner, Brenda C.
Wickouski, Mary Stephanie
Wideman, Suellen

2-2-1987
Carpenter, Eleanor A.
Ferber, Rosamond Susan
Francus, Andrea Joy
Jensen, Julie Jean

2-26-1987
Berson, Sherry Melissa
Carr, Alexandra Allen
Miller, Lynn Ilene
Schwartz, Stefanie Lisa

3-30-1987
Hagen, Andrea Danice
Turkett, Angela

6-1-1987
Trivers, Patricia Anne

6-5-1987
McMahon, Elizabeth Lorion

6-17-1987
Adelman, Faith Robin
Albright, Elizabeth L.
Alexander, Jan Marshall
Alfonsi, Christina Marie
Almazan-Altobelli, Selene Ann
Ames, Joanne
Ardery, Joan
Bachenheimer, Cara Conway
Banks, Lisa Anne
Barnett, Lena Sue
Bay, Kathleen Anne
Benziger, Monica Stoffel
Berg, Margery Ellen
Berkovsky, Terrell Marie Fisher
Billie, Marie Harmon
Birch, Susan Jane Campbell
Blank, Kathleen Marie
Bleecker, Rebecca Ellen Ryder
Blough, Delores Ann
Bodley, Mary Gately
Bolz, Annette Marie
Boscolo, Shari Cohen
Brennen, Marisa Basilico
Briceland-Betts, Deborah
Broner, Annette L.
Brown, Patricia Mary Clare
Brown, Virginia Louise
Brozena, Sarah Harrison
Buckleitner, Anne Louise C.
Buckley, Jackie Alean
Bullman, Barbara Ellen
Burgess, Victoria Marie
Burkhart, Lori Ann
Burr, Justyna Beckwith
Burton, Constance Dowd
Calcote, Donna Yvonne
Campanella, Carolyn J.
Canter, Jane Ann
Capute, Courtney Goodridge
Church, Cathy Christine
Clark, Xonna Maria
Clarke, Catherine Therese
Cobb, Dawna Marie
Coffin, Robin Sue
Cole, Judith Kathleen
Coleman, Dorothy Burke
Collins, Christina Agas
Cook, Karen Lee
Cooke, Teresa A.
Coyle, Marcia Ann
Craig, Amelia Audrey
Creighton, Audrey Ann
Darrah, Diane Carol
Davidowitz, Cheryl Kiel
Dawkins, Angela Marie
Douglas, Patricia Byrne
Drake, Mary Linda Currie
Dryden, Cathy Ann
Duclos, Suzanne Loranger
Dumais, Kathleen Marie
Dunn, Charlene Margaret
Ehrlich, Wendy Ida
Emery, Dorothy Anne
Essrick, Carol Barbara
Evans, Suzanne Althen
Evelyn, Aubrey DeLisle
Fairbanks, Wendy Wisdom
Farmer, Janet Mary
Felix, Nadine G.
Fleischmann, Darlene Amy
Florence, Faye Ann
Franceschi, Kristin Helena Ranum
Franklin, Ellen Greenwell
Freeman, Honora Morrissey
Gallagher, Constance Irene
Gamber, Anne Carroll
Garland, M. Teresa
Gerling, Nancy Lynn
Gildea, Lorie Ann Skjerven
Goldman, Celia
Gooden, Karen L. Williams
Greenberg, Erica
Greenzaid, Nadine Rachelle
Grinde, Ingrid Elisabeth
Groce, Ramona Fraiter
Groedel, Caryn Markowitz
Gurowitz, Leah Harriet
Haas, Nancy
Hackley, Mary Keiling
Hall, Lyssa Eileen
Hamm, Sherrai Victoria
Herbert, Amelia Ann
Hileman, Elizabeth Lee
Hodge, Dorothy Gardner
Hoffman, Carole Fleming
Hostage, Barbara Ann
Hudson, Laura Claydon
Infante, Marie Catherine
Ireland, Elizabeth Leonard
Jacks, Margaret Stevens
Kane, Laura E.
Kassell, Susan
Keating, Nancy L.
Keelty, Lana Marie
Keough, Teresa Ann
Kidd, Mary Dolores
Kiefer, Karen La Verne
Klair, Mary Seeley
Koenig, Claudia Ivonne
Krapf, Maria Giovanna
Kuhn, Mary Anne Frazier
Lambros, Cristin Carnell
Larrabee, Pamela G.
Lash, Kathleen Davis
Leader, Leslie M.
Lenz, Eileen Mai
Leonard, Susan Leigh
Lesniak, Mary Ann
Lewis, Judith Ann
Lindeman, Holly Nan
Melehy, Karen Ann
Mittelstaedt, Crystal Dixon
Pullano, Wendy D.
Roberts, Donna Maria
Rosen, Lynne Susan Blume
Savage, Lenore M.
Terlep, Susan H.

6-18-1987
Berger, Suzanne Tidler
Brown, Claudette McDonald
Caplan, Nancy S.
Duden, Nancy McCutchan
Fortuna, Victoria Rettberg
Gilbertson, Kristina
Loving, Jane G.
Major, Linda Dodd
Marr, Margaret Helen
Martin, Dawn Eileen
Matthews, Jolie Helene
McDonald, Patricia Lynn Pearce
McKee, Dana Whitehead
McKinnon, Laurie
Minkin, Susan Carole

Moran, Joan Frances
Morelli, Denise Marie
Murray, Milissa Ann
Nethercott, Michele Maxine
Novak, Sheila Hogan
Page, Jennifer Hettler
Perrone, June Marie
Pietrafesa, Sharon Eleanor
Reich, Mary Winifred
Richards, Valerie Ann
Ringle, Judith Ann
Robinson, Deborah Lea
Rodney, Ruth Anne
Saccarelli, Gale
Salus, Therese Irene
Schafer, Judy D'Amico
Schiller, Anne Mari
Schindel, Caren Z.
Schnitzer, Susan Fern
Schutrum, Susan Margaret
Shaw, Pamela Louise
Sheain, Carole Sue
Shimek, Michele Marie
Short, Jo Ann Marie
Silberstein, Myra R.
Simonsen, Carolyn McDaniel
Simpson, Lori Schultz
Smith, Carol Ann Speed
Smith, M.L.
Solomon, Barbara Kaplan
Solomon, Maria Teresa
St. Jean, Deborah
Stallone, Phyllis Urciolo
Stear, Deborah Kay
Subotnik, Claire Dinah
Sullivan, Mary Elizabeth
Taylor, Michelle Briere
Tervala, Debra June
Thoma, Corinth L.
Townshend, Rodica Juliana
Tullius, Jean K.
Ullmann, Deborah Anne Marie
Vassallo, Carol L.
Vona, Barbara Kulacki
Wagonheim, Sylvia Stoler
Walla, Sharon Clayton
Warren, Cynthia Green
White, Susan Greenwood
Wilcox, Ann Christine
Williams, Belinda Lee
Wolff, Paula Fitzgerald
Yashar, Susan Amy
Yee, Janet Smith
Yost, Kimberly Miser
Zannoni, Lisa Wink

6-25-1987

Ayres, Barbara Lee
Clark, Leslie Ann
Dellon, Leslie Karen
Heffernan, Joan Ann
Kester, Deborah Susan
Liddell, Gloria Washington
Liken, Becky Joy
Mason, Gail Diane
Minerbi, Laurie Burg
Purdue, Ann Roberts
Schlosberg, Claudia Ellen
Shaw, Helen Lessin

7-7-1987

Jacobson, Judy Ann

7-27-1987

Chester, Beatrice G.
Distenfeld, Yvonne Schlafstein
Edmisten, Jane Moretz
Kumin, Laura Anne
Linn, Deborah Ann
Malfa, Katherine Anne
Marcoux, Marie Celeste
Murphy, Mona M.
Tomola, Natalie Tesny
Volz, Elizabeth Beebe
Weimer, Deborah Jean

9-9-1987

Argent, Margaret Lee
Arnell, Wendy Patrice
Fax, Nancy Gruenberg
Finucane, Alexandra Kortschmaryk
Hecht, Ayala Rachel
Hill, Denise Pamela Adams
Kearney, Mary M.
Langer, Elizabeth
Oglethorpe, Jean West
Sherry, Marcy Nan

11-2-1987

Boskey, Jill Ann
Winston, Rhonda Reid

12-3-1987

Kamens, Toby Jill
Locklear, Arlinda Faye
Storm, Anne-Marie

12-4-1987

Daniel, Miriam Wally
Diehl, Deborah Hilda
Fehst, Geraldine R.
Geiersbach, Rachel Elon
Golden, Vicki Greene
Henneman, Carolyn Hughes
Williams, Christine Ann

12-7-1987

Fein, Leslie Grabin
Henn, Elizabeth Stein
Ince, Mary Ann Rapp
McWhite, Melinda Falgout

12-8-1987

Hammond, Denise Cafaro
Mayrer, Jane Goodhue
Poster, Nancy Diane
Powers, Erica Levine
Steel, Candida Staempfli
Stovall, Lois Helena Grace
Walter, Judith Lynn

12-22-1987

Acevedo, Elaine Beverly
Adams, Eleanor Jean Kaplan
Adams, Laurie Elizabeth
Adams, Melissa Lee Moyer
Albright, Anne Korbel
Allen, Julia Christina
Almy, Monique Desiree
Amato, Maria-Claudia Theresa
Andrews, Mary Sigrid
Aquino, Mary Edna McDonald
Armani, Bernadette V.
Ashby, Pamela Lewis
Bacigalupo, Tracy Ann
Barbera, Denise Marie
Baron, Susan Howe
Bauer, Stacy Lyn
Baylin, Victoria Allyson
Beckstead, Kathleen Leonard
Bell, Mary Catherine
Bell, Ramona Marie
Bertler, Lisa Lynn
Bibbins, Odessa Bradley
Billet, Deborah Beth
Blake, Barbara Cecilia
Bobroff, Rochelle
Bonner, Loretta Marie
Boudreau, Cheryl Rowland
Boyd, Sandra Jean
Brackett, Jacqueline Ann
Braymer, Nancy Anne
Brown, June Blanchard
Burch, Jana Marie Corn
Burgin, Meryl Davis
Burgos, Linda F.
Burke, Kathleen Glen
Burrell, Robin Denise
Caldwell, Janice
Campbell, Clara Eva
Campion, Renee
Canning, Annabelle Brainard
Carey, Jeanne Barr
Chambers, Sharon Michele
Chissell, Crystal Robbie
Chumley, Loren Lee
Clark, Melissa Hammersley
Clay, Carol Ann
Cohen, Joan Grayson
Colarusso, Jeanine Beaubien
Coleman, Janet Ketterling
Colfelt, Frieda Schlemeyer
Cook, Holly O'Grady
Corley, Deborah Lynn
Cornett, Sherry Lynn
Coursey, Carole Joann
Cowley, Stacey Diane
Credit, Sharon Donkervoet
Cronin, Catherine Agnes
Daniel, Bobbie J.
Dart, Patricia A.
Datesman, Susan Kay
Davis, Patricia Hardy
Davis, Roxanne Liane
Dawson, Diann
DeBoissiere, Janette Earl
Decker, Lisa Marie
Dennis, Mary Joan Margaret
Desmond, Cecilia Marie
Devine, Susan Joan
Diana, Natalie Hulen
Dixon, Wanda Jean
Dominik, Cynthia Ann
Donovan, Patricia Anne
Dubbs, Mary Ann
Duhig, Diane
Dunn, Patricia Dawn Laird
Duvall, Donna Morris
Duvall, Elizabeth Jane
Dwyer, Mary Paula
Eckstein, Suzy Lynn
Ellis, Susan Diane
Engelhardt, Mary Jane
Entzeroth, Lyn Suzanne
Evans, Joanne Gaines
Farace, Suzanne K.
Fender, Carolyn Tweed
Ferguson, Margaret Ziegler
Fields, Jane Ellen
Finnerman, Doris Susan
Fivehouse, Michele B.
Fleming, Carolyn Hariton
Flynn, Janice Mary
Foley, Lisa Anne
Forrester, Althea Marie
Fowler, Rochelle Block
Frey, Elizabeth Jesukiewicz
Gamble, Sharon Rose
Gaul, Vickie Lynn
Glenn, Carol Elise
Golding, Debra Michele
Goldman, Kathryn Miller
Goldsmith, Leslie Demaree
Goodman, Elizabeth Ann
Grace, Patricia Ann
Gray, Susan Baker
Graybill, Nina Margaret
Greene, Debra Coggins
Griffin, Caroline A.
Griffin, Mary Teresa
Griffith, Anne Elizabeth
Grosfeld, Sharon Marcia
Gusman, Nancy Linda
Hazlett, Susan Hower
Healy, Margaret Lillian
Holec, Filippa Lynn
Hopkins, Monica Vernetta
Hosford, Elizabeth Marie
Howard, Anne Kelley
Hunter, Janice Kay Johnson
Hutchins, Miriam Elizabeth
Iliff, Sarah Harris MacDonald
James, Annie Deloris
Jansak, Kathryn Anne
Jefferson, Regina Therese
Jivens-McRae, Grace H.
Jones, Charlma Ovette
Jung, Debra Ann
Katz, Shoshana
Kehinde, Ann Karn
Kelly, Sandra Lynn
Kent, Mary Jane Briody
Kerxton, Jill K.
Kessler, Frances Elizabeth
King, Patricia Lorraine
Klauber, Geraldine Ann
Kraus, Virginia Anne
Krevor-Weisbaum, Sharon
Krizman, Lisa Kopf
Kunst, Susan Ann
Kurtz, Carolyn Eve
Lafferty, Tammy Lynne
Lamdin, Ann Louise
Land, April Isabel
Land, Margaret Ann
Landis, Mary Jennifer
Lanier, Margaret Leah
Lank, Diane Margaret
Lansey, Sheryl Anita
Lawrence, Deborah Anne
Laynor, Anne Kelly
Leaman, Kimberly A.
Lennig, Dorothy Janet
Lewis, Regina Hollins
Lipsetts, Patricia S. Gainer
Lipton, Cheryl Kay
Littrell, Rebecca Linthicum
Mancini, Cynthia H.
Mason, Andrea Dobbs
McGillivary, Tracy B.
McVicker, Shelley Jane
Mezzanotte, Mary Love
Muenter, Kimberly Kahoe

O'Day, Carol A.
Prete, Lorraine Marie
Pupkin, Randi Alper
Russo, Leslie Hayes
Sachitano, Nancy Antoinette
Sarbanes, Dina E.
Schulman, Leslie Cohen
Shealer, Valerie Irvine
Shere, Helene O'Neil
Smith, Susan Beth
Sullivan, Donna LaPlaca
Taub, Debra K.
Vaillancourt, Amy Heit
Ward, Margaret Fonshell
Wilford, Elaine Ruth
Yost, Sally
Zuckerman, Janet A.

12-23-1987

Barry, Mary Snyder
Beall, Sharon J. Ritter
Black, Nancy G.
Blair, Courtney Ann
Brady, Georgia S.
Bruner, Patricia Taylor
Camard, Sandra Lynn
Caravaggio, Jill Diane
Cross, Cynthia Rebecca
Deraska, Tricia Fung Kam
Edelman, Doreen M.
Ehrlich, Kendel Sibiski
Fish, Elizabeth A.
Fleshman, Sheila Faye
Franzen, Lisa Sullivan
Kinsey, Kathy M.
Leahy, Debra Wynne
Lord, Elizabeth Osenton
Lorenz, Dorothy Whitlock
Lucas, Shelley Virginia
Mack, Deborah Ellen
Magdeburger, Natalie Carmean
Mandel-Trupp, Lisa
Mara, Dorothy
Marble, Susan Joy
Marindin, Jennifer Ritchie
Markush, Robin
Masterton, Kathleen Joan Colleen
Matovcik, Lana Shay Ward
Maupin, Margaret Ann
McAfee, Carol Joan
McGowan, Carol Murray
McKenzie, Patricia Ann
McMillan, Susan
McMillen, Sandra Sue
McMullen, Patricia Cathleen
Michael, Debra Ann
Mikalonis, Lisa Rycus
Miller, Jane Chace
Miller, Michelle Marie
Mitchell, Janet Heather
Mitchell, Molly Ruth
Mitz, Lisolette Elaine
Modell, Karen Lynne
Montgomery, Laura Denise
Morris, Mary Frances
Morton, Cynthia Dod
Munaker, Judith Jane
Murray, Jane Elizabeth Cairns
Murray, Patricia Carmen
Myles, JoAnn Patricia
Nachman, Susan Andrea
Nagelhout, Mary Jane
Needle, Barbara Wachter
Neill, Rachael Valentine
Neuder, Lori Susan
Nicholson, Robin Miller
Nickols, Saundra Ann
Nicolaides, Christine Marie
Nord, Jill C.
O'Connell, Anne Wright
O'Conor, Marian McHale
O'Day, Sharon Patricia
O'Neill, Patricia Diane
Olafson, Vicki Renee
Oliver, Aileen Elizabeth
Ostendorf, Marika McVey
Papagjika, Mary Antoinette
Patterson, Judy Layne
Payne, Karen Sherwood
Pennington, Brenda Karen
Pereira, Melanie Cecelia
Pettit, Joan Beaumont Cobb
Philbin, Jeanne
Pia, Audrey Lucretia
Pladna, Leslie Ann
Price, Donna Bates
Rader, Lindsey Ann
Raffaldini, Barbara Catherine
Ramsey, Deborah M.
Redman, Kathy Anne
Rhodes, Laura Kelsey
Rickman, Tamara Schiebel
Rinn, Christine Clements
Rivkin, Deborah Lynne
Rockwell, Janice Bole
Rollinson, Marjorie Anne
Rosenfeld, Michele McDaniel
Rubin, Elisabeth Siegenthaler
Ruff, Karen Plumer
Sachar, Eliana Steimatzky
Samley, Deborah Stachniewicz
Sapp, Conwell Fader
Savino, Janet Ann
Schaller, Temma Lora
Scheinfeld, Judith Susan
Schoenfeld, Julia Lynne
Schubert, Debra Gae
Schultze, Carol Elizabeth
Senecal, Kathleen O'Shea
Sengstack, Jane Elizabeth
Sexton, Brenda Alverta
Shaughnessy, Cynthia Zee
Sheehan, Mary Agnes
Shelton, Angela Denise
Sherman, Judy Joffe
Shoff, Mary Graham Smith
Shore, Nina Abby
Sideris, Nicole Jean
Sidle, Sandra J.
Simpson, Louise McBride
Smith, Nancy W.
Smith, Susan Lynn
Smolarek, Mary Alice
Snyder, Sharon Ann
Somerville, Susan Crawford Murray
Spencer, Shelley Lynn
Stanley, Barbara McClellan
Stein, Eileen Barbara
Steinberg, Susan Renee
Stevens, Melanie Lee
Stillman, Ferrier Rose
Swain, Margaret Ellen
Tabb, Rebecca
Teasley, Gloria Robinson
Terry, Alicia Arleen
Thornton, Sherri Lorine
Townsend, Angela Marie
Tranchida, Brenda Joyce
Trippett, Lillian McBee
Triscoli, Donna Friedlander
Vaughn, Jacqueline Rowland
vom Eigen, Ann Hadley
Vural, Cheryl Purtee
Wallace, Diana June
Weaver, Jane Diedrich
Weinstein, Mindy Ellen
Wiggin, Pamela Gwyneth
Willard, Madelon Henehan
Wilson, Jane Allen
Wolf, Deborah Anne
Wolfe, Frani Cohen
Yellen, Susan Gail
Yinger, Emily Moskowitz
Zissman, Sharon Debra

1-5-1988

Anderson, Merry Chavez
Bennett, Jeanne Marie
Conway, Janice Eileen
Cook, Leila Holmes
Donovan, Susan Mason
Girard, Victoria Walker
Jones, Deborah Ballman
Mattera, Renate Staley
Munshell, Shauna Brennan
Niles, Mary Ellen
Orleman, Mary Catherine
Quinn, Maureen Elizabeth
Raffel, Mimi Ann
Rankin, Catherine Amanda
Robbins, Kristen Elizabeth Konrad
Sagawa, Shirley Sachi
Spencer, Nancy Jane
Wilson, Elizabeth Davis
Wilson, Shari Taylor
Zolet, Theresa Irene

1-17-1988

Kelly, Andrea Forrester

2-4-1988

Agus, Deborah B.
Brenneman, Diane Marie
Hastings, Karis Alison
Kossow, Amy Elizabeth
Kurss, Cheryl Amy
Marsh, Jo Bennett
Parker, Janice Shelton
Thomas, Sheila Yvette

3-3-1988

Catanese, Joanne F.
Rose, Laura Lynn

4-29-1988

Harrigan, Clare

6-2-1988

Babb, Barbara Ann
Bocskor, Catherine E.
Crosby, Dianne Irene
Fickes, Karen N.

6-3-1988

Hafner, M. Gayle
Harkless, Catherine Ebert
Jackson, Kathleen A.
Marshall, Katherine Marie
McArthur, Virginia A.
Newhouse, Marilyn Cheryl
Young, Lauren

6-6-1988

Anderson, Pamela H.
Macbeth, JoAnn Engelke
Pfotenhauer, Jeanette
Sandza, Elizabeth Barry
Sarjeant, Karen Jones
Sigmond, Carol Ann
Smith, Leslie K.
Straszheim, Janelle Sherfy
Taylor, Frances H.
Tramontano, Karen A.

6-14-1988

Abraham, Margaret Johnston
Adler, Debra Bucalo
Ain, Linda Katz
Baldwin, Dana Suzanne
Banjavic, Denise J.
Barlow, Wendy Smith
Barone, Mary Ann
Barton, Joyce Ann
Beckert, Karin Moore
BelClaire, Julie L.
Bender, Kathryn Christian
Besok, Karen Ann
Bias, Tamla Lynn
Biondo, Vitina Amy
Blakemore, Mary Eleanore
Blumberg, Marjorie
Blume, Susanne C.
Board, Natalie Lynn
Borinsky, Elizabeth Marzo
Bower, Jessica E.
Bright, Deborah Sue
Britton, Kathy Marie
Browder, Mary E. M.
Brown, Videtta Arthyne
Bry, Alexandra Rachell
Buck, Keri Ann
Butler, Diane Reilly
Carey, Crystal L.
Cartier, Linda Claire
Chaharbaghi, Stephanie Lynn
Chalawsky, Mary Cina
Cherner, Norma Rae
Ciccone-Fiorentino, Maria D.
CitaraManis, Tammy Jean
Cohen, Janet Ann
Comella, Patricia A. Egan
Conklyn, Elizabeth Allison
Derivan, Sharon Katherine
Doane, Margaret Mary
Donohue, Deborah Anne
Donohue, Sara Marie
Dorzdoski, Joanne C.
Douglas, Barbara Jean
Ducassou, Kathy L.
Dulin, Carol J.
Dwyer, Debra Lynn
Edwards, Regina B.
Ellington, Arnell Tonya
Emmanuelli-Perez, Edda
Ewachiw, Mary C.
Fassett, Mary Jean
Fealey, Anne Marie
Fernandez, Marilys Delfina
Flack, Jill Diane
Gelfarb, Daryl Waldman

Goldfarb, Amy Beth
Gray, Melissa Donnelle
Greenblum, Erika
Grubbs, Cynthia Musta
Guggenheim, Jana Kay
Hammel, Robyn Ennis
Henkel, Mary Denise
Hitchcock, Teresa Kislowski
Hoffman, Lisa Kristine
Huang, Pamela D.
Hubbard, Christine W.
Hugoson-Burnett, Britta Agnes Mariana
Jackson, Leslie Dolores
Jackson, Monet Theresa
Jordan, Susan Lynch
Kamenentz, Doris Low
Karangelen, Dana Kent
Katz-Haley, Laura
Kiese, Karen
Kinds, Beverly Rene
Kitchings, Valerie E.
Koban, Linda Abram
Koch, Mary McNamara
Krebs, Catherine Kaiser
Krivda, Mary Kathleen
Lamson, Bernadette Fowler
Lebbin, Deborah Hildebrand
Lebowitz, Linda Susan
Levin, Joann Early
Levin-Tavares, Jennifer
Lo, Josephine Suk-Yin
Lum, Virginia
Malek, Margaret Arenas
Marshall, Kimberly Diane
McAuliffe, Karyn Brewer
McCurdy, Janet Irwin
McLlarky, Kathleen Ann
Meyer, Kristine L.
Minardi, Ann Segura
Moewes, Denice Elizabeth
Morrison, Jane Hylinski
Nelson, Sharon Denise
New, Cheryl M.
Norman, Diane Eleanor
Novak, Barbara
O'Brien, Bernadette Christine
O'Connor, Janis Marie
Palmieri, Denise Lenore
Plotkin, Teresa Cavalier
Porter, Tania May
Purnell, Donna Lynne Comegys
Regenhardt, Linda Dianne
Remington, Cluadia Marie
Riggs, Lisa Rene
Riva, Martha Collier
Robinson, Patricia Ann
Rosen, Corinne Gisele
Salowe, Lori Ellen
Schroeder, Jane M.
Schwartz, Jill Susanne
Shapiro, Elizabeth J.
Silverman, Deborah Ann
Simpson, Delphia Theresa
Simpson, Tina L.
Small, Pamela Beth
Smith, Jennifer Lynn
Sneider, Terri Lynn Juana
Sober, Debra Greenstein
Sproat, Carolyn Hovey
Stainbrook, Judith S.
Stewart, Nancy Keller
Sullivan, Diane Cross
Taylor, Anne Therese
Taylor, Barbara Grisdale
Tenen, Elise Ann
Thatcher, Linda Hitt
Tilley, Wanda Elizabeth
Traub, Maxine Hope
Trujillo, Sara Denise
Trust, Milena Yulia
Turner, Tammy Lorraine
Uehling, Kathleen Kay
Vroom, Marilyn Ann
Watson, Regina Maria
Webb, Maurene Epps
Weller, Nancy Leibowitz
York, Jeanette Saker
Jordan, Lynn Rankin

7-27-1988

Giampetro, Andrea
Richardson, Ann Heilemann-Bishop
Shaw, Ann
Starr, Helen Pollock
Williams, Carolyn H.

9-8-1988

Caron, Susan S.
Hatchette, Joy Yvette
Pritzlaff, Sarah Page

12-1-1988

Ollila, Betty

12-15-1988

Abrams, Mary Jones
Adams, Deborah A.
Aitken, Melissa E.
Angel, Lindell Kay
Appelbaum, Karen Ann
Applewhite, Francine Laura
Argentieri, Judith Diane
Attanasio, Margaret Ada
Austin, Kathryn Sabrina
Badder, Marianne
Bailes, Zandra Y.
Baker, Warrenetta C.
Balenson, Jeri Lynn
Balhoff, Frances Nugent
Bamberger, Joanne Cronrath
Barber, Claudia Adeline
Barlow, Kathleen Thorne
Barnett, Janice E.
Barr, Karen L.
Benner, Susan C.
Berliner, Marie Christine
Bielinski, Mary Bridget
Black, Laura Bernkrant
Blackwell, Edith Ruth
Bloom, Anne Wilson
Bloomfield, Susan Berry
Bobbish, Laury Ellen
Bogle, Darlynda Key
Bolling, Jocelyn G.
Bowerman, Amy Shannon
Brault, Joan Frances
Braye, Linda Marie
Breggin, Linda Karen
Brennan, Donna Suzanne
Bridgham, Bethany Joy
Brinley, Deborah Ann
Brooks, Linda Leona
Brophy, Faith M.
Brown, Susan Claire
Buie, Deborah Denise Harcum
Burgan, Susan Ellen
Campbell, Catherine Marie
Carreno, Lisa Gale
Chase, Laura Louise
Chesson-Wureh, Yvette Nmuna
Chytla, Anna Y.
Cochran, Deborah Paula Donick
Colender, Andrea Elizabeth
Collins, Deborah Ashare
Collins, Wynter Reneaux
Connelly, Christine Ella
Cook, Mary Rose Elizabeth
Crandall, Susan H.
Crowley, Margaret Ann
Cruttenden, Danielle Medas
Cybulski, Louise
Czarski, Theresa V.
Darby, Sandra Howard
Davis, Otelia Lynch
De Shields, Tarra R.
De Torres, Roseanne Shawn
Deakin, Barbara J.
Dedianko, Patricia A.
Di Giannantonio, Patricia Eileen
Diamond, Cindy Renee
Dixon, Ann Holcomb
Donnelly, Lynn Marie
Donohoe, Teresa R.
Downes, Elizabeth
Doyle, Sylvia Y.
Dwyer, Deborah Elaine
Eagle, Sara Bonnie
Edmunds, Julie Ann
Ehrenberg, Robin
Elliott, Ramona Dee
Elmendorf, Caroline Gosse
Elmore, Kathleen Marie
Ensor, Judith Claibourne
Fargo, Mary Elizabeth
Farrell, Kimberly Ann
Fawcett, Kari Holm
Feldman, Ellen Berkow
Fentress, Lisa Denise
Ferguson, Mary Ann
Fishman, Laura E.
Fisk, Robin J.
Fitzgerald, Colleen M.
Fitzpatrick, Anne Elizabeth
Flynn, Mary Ellen J.
Frye, Jocelyn Cecilia
Furnari, Theresa Ann
Galvin, Corrie Scherrer
Gasnier, Philippa Therese
Gedanken, Lynne Edda
Gede, Ellen Frank
Geraci, Linda A.
Gilmore, Angela Denise
Glancy, Maureen
Glazer, Marci D.
Golden, Susan M.
Goldgeier, Eileen S.
Good, Kathryn A.
Grant, Patti Lillian
Gray, Jan D.
Greene, Ava Danelle
Greig, Denise Ann
Grigg, Carolyn Hill
Hall, Patricia S.
Hall, Tina Ann
Handler, Roanne
Hankin, Susan J.
Harris, Patricia Ann
Harris, Phyllis K.
Hartke, Victoria Riess
Hastings, Cary Leigh
Haugh, Susan Marie
Hayes, Lisa Helene Rice
Hazman, Laurie Renee
Henderson, Bessie C.
Henderson, Stephanie R.
Hennessey, Stacy Leigh
Henry, Mary Ellen
Herman, Nancy Jo
Hickey, Eileen Guilfoyle
Hildreth, Phyllis Drennon King
Hirsch, Cathy Brice
Hirshkowitz, Debra J.
Hogan, Joanne Marie
Hood, Suzanne Lechthaler
Howie, Teresa Ann
Huffman, Elizabeth Marie
Hurley, Karen McGee
Hynes, Mary Gwen
Iodice, Pamela M.
Jackson, Stacey Evelyn Young
Jennings, Teresa Lynn
Johnson, Janet Thomas
Jones, Patricia G.
Kalin, Mary Ann Kanis
Katkish, Cynthia
Katz, Mindy Herman
Kelley, Jenifer Fasano
Kelley, Lori L.
Kelly, Deborah Persis
Kettering, Sharon K.
Khan, Karen Ann
Kidd, Susan Mary
Kinstler, Sloane Fried
Kirsch, Helen Gordon
Lacaze, Stephanie D.
Leitess, Anne Colt
McErlean, Cathy A.
McGinley, Anne Marie
Mergele, Anna Hay
Miller, Patricia Maurine
Milne, Susan E.
Moen, Mary Ann D.
Mulerin, Kim Mary Czubaruk
Phillips, Michelle Henderson
Poole, Kathryn Brewer
Portner, Valerie Floyd
Rothell, Bonnie Hochman
Ryland, Barbara Helen
Schmidt, Jo Anna
Schneider, Bonnie Gullatt
Schwartz, Carmen G.
Schwartz, Marni Beth
Simpson, Karen Johnson
Sinsky, Joanne Harris
Stillman, Mary Danforth
Terry, Leisa G.
Upshaw, Inga Oesterle
Wagner, Jan Marie
Warren, Melissa Allison
Wilkowsky, Karen R.

12-16-1988

Aboyan, Nancy McKeown
Agate, Kathryn McCarl
Buckley, Carrie Holly
Carter, Jennifer Williams
Cecere, Leah Thompson
Cummins, Jill Reid

David, Maureen Walsh
Dunn, Elizabeth Ann
Dwyer, Nancy E.
Elliott, Karen J.
Forero, Janet A.
Furman, Suzanne Fechter
Halstad, Leigh Swann
Hofer, Susan Lee
Johnson, Julia Elizabeth
Kline, Amy Kushner
Kostun, Kera Ivana
Kovelant, Barbara Hunter
Kronmiller, Wendy Ann
Kropp, Edith Mary
Laboy, Paula Titus
Lawrence, Allison Kay
Lebowitz, Dore J.
Lee, Arlene Frances
Lee, Shu Fan
Leiser, Sharon Lynne
Lesnick, Patricia Marie
Lettman, Dawn Sharon
Levan, Elissa D.
Levin, Diane Swint
Levy, Harlee Beth
Lisic, Annabelle L.
Long, Sylvia Vanderford
Lovill, Kathryn Webb
Luckey, Jane Rutherford
Lynch, Josephine A.
Lyons, Elisabeth Jill
Mackler, Lorraine Newman
Macksey, Brigit M.
Maes, Joan Ruth
Mahasa, Zakia
Maier, Jody
Makris-Gouvas, Maria
Mangel, Linda Ellen
Marcolin, Carla Maria
Margulies, Laura Jacobs
Marley, Robyn Harmon
Marquez, Awilda R.
Martin, Susan Marie
Massey, Shirley Sause
Mathews, Gisele Marie
May, Kathryn Turner
McCray, Lora Ann
McLaughlin, Sheila Jean
McTighe, Susan Browne
Mejia-Dietche, Ana Isabel
Mellow, Juliet
Melvin, Vera Britt
Michael, Helen Katherine
Michaels, Anastasia
Milburn, Kimla Thompson
Miles, Mary Virginia
Milton, Jeral A.
Mitchell, Gail M.
Mitchell, Kathy Lynn
Moncada, Kirsten Jane
Moran, Sharon Margaret
Morris, Karen Leslie
Morrow, Jill Stacy
Moses, Carolyn Jane
Muffolett, Hoehn-Saric
Murakami, Kimi N.
Nash-Goetz, Karen
Neil, Janice J.
Neil, Rhonda L.
O'Brien, Anne J.
Ockey, Celia Hobson
Olmert, Amy Mitola
Ozur, Miriam Dee
Panagakos, Lynn Elaine
Patton, Patricia Ann
Peregoff, Donna Lynn
Petty-Todd, Juanita
Phelan, Christine Virginia
Phillips, Victoria Fisher
Polcen, Jane Frances
Pomares, Carmen Rosario
Poole, Lisa Lee
Pratt, Stephanie Marie
Prietz, Eve Estelle
Prince, Mary White
Purcell, Anita Tedesco
Quinlan, Cecile Celeste
Rappaport, Isabel Libby Crystal
Rath, Margaret Elizabeth
Raymond, Sharon Leigh
Reff, Alisa Helene
Reid, Catherine M.
Richard, Diana Gale
Robinson, Gayle Lisa
Rofel, Marjorie J. Moritz
Rohart, Leanne
Rolinski, Sylvia Jiva
Rose, Cheryl Eslin
Rubel, Ellen Amdur
Rubin, Sharon Sirota
Rudow, Gillian Nancy
Ryan, Mary Ann
Rye, Patricia A.
Salzberg, Claudia Gesa
Sanchez, Vilma Luisa
Sanders, Ruth Armfield
Sandy, Jeanne
Saunders, Christy McFaul
Schaefer, Donna Mae
Schafer, M. Kathryn
Schechter, Mara E.
Schmidt, Rosemarie
Schoenthaler, Lisa Winer
Schoshinski, Mary Claire
Schulze, Margaret Anne
Scott, Wendy Murrill
Segal, Nancy E.
Seide, Melissa Anne
Seifert, Amy Joann
Senft, Louise Phipps
Shein, Pamela Beth
Shreaves, Cynthia A.
Silva, Cristina Rose
Snyder, Donna Leigh
Stafford, Mary Joanne
Stanton, Jo Anne Renee
Stavely, Catherine Elizabeth
Stokes, E. Francine
Storch, Gloria Beverly
Suh, Song
Sullivan, Sarah R.
Sullivan, Sheila Jane
Swanstrom, Deborah Ann
Sweeney, Julie Theresa
Tarver, Kimberly Nickelson
Terrell, Thalia B.
Thomas, Jennifer Harris
Thompson, Aetna M.
Thomson, Christine Markman
Thornton, Courtney Sheppe
Tvrdy, Linda A.
Ulstrup, Julia Somerville
Van Bergen, Ellen
Waldman, Ellen Anne
Warfield, Amy Joann
Watts, Genelle Roberta
Webb, Lorraine Jenkins
Weese, Tracy
Weiner, Jeanne Gerstley
Wertz, Vicki Lynn
Wesker, Natasha
Westerbaan-Klein, Anne Marie
Wexler, Robin Lenkin
White, Barbara Jayne
Wiley, Jane Baker
Williams, Adrienne Susan Weitzner
Williamson, Carolyn Chappell
Withum, Mary Frances
Wohl, Rachel A.
Woodall, Judy Lynn
Worden, Jeanine M.
Wright, Carolyn Deanna
Wright, Kimela Burnedette
Yoder, Carol Redgrave
Zorzi, Mary Elizabeth

1-5-1989

Bliss, Mary Ellen
Brownell, Bonnie J.
Cornelius, Linda S.
Cornick-Dandridge, Karen A.
Costigan, Maureen
Doty, Margaret Elizabeth

1-6-1989

Hedlund, Carel Theilgard
Jowdy, Joy Renee
Markowitz, Petrina M.
McDonald, Joyce Kallam
McKee, Pamela
Messick, Sandra E.
Meyer, Katherine Anne

1-9-1989

Cochran, Martha Lou
Dolan, Sandra Lee
Mugane, Bridget R.
Orlidge, Kimber Leigh
Palmer, Nancy
Ross, Susan Elizabeth
Schneiderman, Lenore
Schukoske, Jane Ellen
Smith, Nancy Jane
Spradley, Lynn Suzanne
Strebel, Sandra Jeanne
Vinitsky, C. Elyse

1-10-1989

Breckenridge, Jeniphr A.E.
Lambros, Demetra Daniel
Poland, Suellen S.
Sammet, Priscilla A.
Warshawsky, Laura Beth Margolis
Weller, Helen Elizabeth
White, Susan Smith

2-2-1989

Hardwick, Karen Michele
Ittig, Judith Bacorn
Johnson, Deborah A.
McBrayer, Martha Martin

3-2-1989

Powe, Cindy Wofford

4-27-1989

Alexander, Annie Rose Brimbield
Ying, Evelyn Soon-soon

6-1-1989

Cates-Harman, Stephanie
Steel, Laura Nachowitz

6-2-1989

Abramowitz, Ava J.
Bellucci, Janice Madelyn
Ferber, Betty Naomi
Forsyth, Jan Dague
Greenfield, Marsha Rae
Harrison, Elizabeth
Kahn, Penny
Lamont, Colleen A.
Luken, Bonnie Louise
McDonald, Sheila C.
Robbins, Elaine

6-5-1989

Barton, Ellen Louise
Baumerich, Carol Andrea
Miko, Kathleen M.
Monroe, Arianne Hale
Nolan, Margaret Ann
Ogle, Karen Ellen
Rossen, Leslie Ellen
Sandler, Kaylene Wright
Schultz, Nancy S.
Teisberg, Janice Chaleen
Wharton, Ellan Kathryn
White, Anne Walker
Woody, Kathleen Joanna

6-14-1989

Aist, Jennifer Buran
Barnes, Michelle
Beckett, Candace Helene
Berman, Frances R.
Bernard, Michelle D.
Bernardo, Andrea Quinn
Berriman, Ann Elizabeth
Brown, Laura Breyman
Burdick, Leona Lee
Cavanaugh, Evelyn Welch-Bridges
Chartier, Susan Therese
Childs, Mary Jo
Clarke, Deborah Jeanne
Clinton, Julie Ann
Coleman, Caroline Jill Morrel
Cooper, Holly Cohen
Coravos, Pamela
Coyne, Carol J.
Crawford, Jessie Lyons
Demos, Bessie Sotirakos
DeVuono, Linda M.
DiBacco, Deborah Z.
Donohoe, Mary Anna
Dove, Lori
Dwyer, Linda Marie
Eldredge-Pace, Wendy Appler
Epstein, Fern R.
Fisher, Alene
Fitzpatrick, Tracey Davis
Ford, Susan Turner
Frederick, Donna S.
Frisina, Shellie Ann
Garfinkle, Gail Roberta
Giller, Ruth Watson
Glennon, Theresa
Gordon, Carol Marie
Gottlieb, M. Gail
Graham, Barbara Rae
Grimes, Debra Sue

Harris, Deborah L.
Hawk, Wynee Elizabeth
Hawkins, Daretia M.
Haynes, Farnese Naomi
Higgins, Carole Ann
Holmes, Katherine Anne
Horn, Elizabeth C.
Hougland, Amy Conner
Hughes, Elizabeth
Jacobson, Joanne Gumprich
James, Teresa McGrane
Jones, Karen Leslie
Keim, Alison Mary
Kim, Heesun Grace
King, Ann Marie A.
Kruger, Karen J.
Lawyer, Vivian Moore
Leahy-Fucheck, Andrea M.
Leighton, Julia L.
Lett, Lisa A.
LeVons, Sheila Lovenia
Lifson, Randi Sue
Lomax, Mary Claire
Maher, Susan Schuppner
Marcial, Sharon Ann
Martin, Amanda Jean Howard
Martin, Laura Leigh
Marvel, Connie Godfrey
McCulla, Margaret Cleopha
McDonough, Helen Anne
McFarling, Serita Frost
McInerney, Maura Irene
McKenna, Deirdre Anne
McLeod, Christine Ellen
McLeod, Gwendolen Catherine Lesh
Montgomery, Janice Arlene
Morales, Shirley Odaliz
Mullin, Karen Elizabeth
Mund, Shelley Beth
Murphy, Donna Mae
Nicolette, Carol Lynn
Olson, Barbara K.
Owens, Jane Susan
Parker, Lynn Perry
Parkinson, Nancy Beth
Potthast, Ann M.
Powell, Elana Jane
Powers, Catherine Gleason
Pyott, Mardi Frances
Ramos-Neitz, Yvonne L.
Reichle, Linda Kimberly
Ridgell, Dolores Owens
Rollin, Miriam A.
Rovner, Janice Leslie
Rowland, Maureen L.
Rudek, Elizabeth Ann
Ruggieri, Margaret Christine
Russell, Jacqueline S.
Russo, Elizabeth Murray
Schuyler, Anne Ross
Scott, Cheryl Ann
Shell, Robin Barnes
Shellow-Lavine, Jill R.
Shrader, Patricia Brown
Skupien, Deborah Howland Young
Smith, Kathleen Ann
Solomon, Nancy Brave
Stabach, Carolyn M.
Strauss, Francine Rachelle
Truesdell, Stacey L.
Van Deusen, Marie
Van Scoy, Donna Elizabeth
Vitek, Marsha Chircus
Voorhis, Lisa Lett
Wagner, Kimberly Lee
Walker, Brenda K.
Ward, Margaret Mascelli
Washington, Gina Studdard
Waxman, Randi Mazer
Weidman, Susan Pittard
White, Elizabeth A.
Wilson, Jerrolyn Patricia
Wilson, Katherine Estelle

6-15-1989

Cho, Kyung Hee

9-7-1989

Benarieh, Ziva
Goodman, Sharon McNeilly
Malkin, Rachel Esther
Mills, Marcia J.
Sasso, Kelly Joann
Vanston, Kathleen Mary
Vinci, Maria Gabriella

10-5-1989

Beninger, Elizabeth Smith
Randolph, Helen

12-18-1989

Abrams, Michelle Jan
Akerley, Kathleen Winters
Alibrando, Karen Joyce
Amoroso, Kathleen Marie
Angelos, Frances Melissanos
Archie, Jennifer C.
Arnold, Elizabeth Howell
Austin, Bonnie J.
Aviles, Karen Jean
Badger, Janet F.
Bagoly, Shelley Lynne
Baker, Marilyn L.
Baker, Sandra Elease
Barrett, Denise Charlotte
Bath, Sydney Baird
Becker, Donna C.
Behan, Kathleen Anne
Benjamin, Denise M.
Bergamini, Carolyn Hodges
Berman, Joanne Helene
Berney, Jean M.
Bertram, Catherine Drissel
Bird, Susie Kim
Blair, Deborah Feustle
Blaner, Kathleen L.
Blasingame, Lynn G.
Bohanan, Melody Jo
Bormel, Frances Gail
Bowen, Karen Bayley
Bowling, Cynthia Jane
Boykin, Roberta Maccoun
Broussard, Mary Jo
Brown, Andrea Marie
Brown, Gloria Virginia
Brown, Linda Markey
Bruner, Paula Rene
Burkholder, Rebecca Rose
Burr, Barbara A.
Burrowes, Margaret Worster
Busky, Ann Failing
Buss, Emily
Butler, Midge Fae
Canavan, Sheila Cash
Cannon, Tracy Anne
Carter, Shawne Marie
Caruso, Maria Kristina
Chakrabarti, Chandrima
Chasen, Arlene Joy
Choi, Helen Frances
Clark, Barbara L.
Clingan, Lauren
Cohen, Sharon Renee
Collins, Catherine C.
Conkling, Carolyn Weber
Connery-Aujla, Charlotte M.
Cooke, Delores Couser
Crabtree, Karen Montgomery
Crawford, Mary Elizabeth
Crawford, Pamela D.
Critzman, Francina Jo
Croft, Julia Elizabeth
Dagenais, Sophie
Dawson, Tracey Brown
Delibera, Judith A.
DiMaio, Mary Malloy
Dolan, Kathleen Anne
Dowling, Maria-Kate
Duane, Jennifer Anne
Duessel, Nancy F.
Dufficy, Ellen Flinn
Durkan, Barbara
Duvall, Deborah Street
Earle, Lynda Elizabeth
Edwards, Mary Baker
Englehart, Mary B.
Erisman, Jane Meadowcroft
Fang, Vickie Inge
Farren, Nancy Bradley
Femiano, Jane D'Arcy
Ferraris, Patricia Ann
Feurer, Deborah Ann
Fields, Melanie Elaine
Flannery, Sharon Marie
Fleming, Kimberly Beryl
Forbes, Karen
Forgotson, Elizabeth Nell
Forrence, Jennifer L.
Frank, Julie Anne Grassman
Furman-Brown, Angela
Garvin, Karin A.
Geckos, Marietta Irene
Genua, Kimberly Ann
Gertner, Nancy B.
Gilmore, Tracy Anne
Goedert, Jo Ann Grozuczak
Goulet, Mary Elizabeth
Grady, Janessa Lynne
Gray, Theresa Mary
Greisman, Mary Sue
Grindle, Rita Kaufman
Haley-Pierson, Monica Marie
Halladay, Angela Kathryn
Harrison, Marcia Linn
Harting, Marta Denise
Hazlitt, Kristin Elisabeth
Helf, Sheila O'Connell
Hennessey, Mary C.
Hergenroeder, Barbara Leah
Hertz, Louise S.
Heyman-Magaziner, Rebecca L.
Hollmann, Janice L.
Holweck, Karen Denise
Hom, Frances M.
Hopkins, Carol Lynn
Hopkins, Catherine Quince
Hosain, Tulasi
Howell, Maria Francesca
Howze, Karen Aileen
Hunt, Sara Blackwell
Hyers, Ellen Walker
Jackson, Jolie Ann
Jackson, Kim Carla
Jacobson, Joyce Nouel
Jauregui, Gabriela
Johnson, Joy Anita
Johnson, Mary Ellen Quinn
Jones, Lauren Denise
Kamantauskas-Holder, Katrina Claudia
Kane, Francesca Robin
Kantorski, Nicole N.
Kenny, Leigh A.
Kerr, Karen Ann
King, Elizabeth Aldridge
King, Hope Renee
Klain, Eva Josephine
Klasky, Mindy Lynn
Knivila, Kelly
Knutson, Martha Ann
Kolakowski-Hollen, Donna Lynn
Kollman, Theresa Anne
Kopf, Randi
Krivak, Carla Magda
Krus, Cynthia Marie
Lipnick, Dale Keats
Louisy, Relinda
Miller, Kara M.
Padden, Jean Marie
Pliskin, Lisa Fair
Ponsonby, Patricia Ingram
Pronesti, Jennifer B.
Ring, Nancy Horwitz
Schuler, Lynda
Semo, Alina Miriam
Sledge, Margaret Mary
Smith, Kathleen DeSales Gast
Sykes, Barbara Ann
Turchan, Catherine Colbert
Vance, Karren Dickson
Victor, Jennifer R.
Ward, Denitta D.
Yeager, Beth Jackson

12-19-1989

Allen, Gail Diane
Angotti, Lynn Rutherford
Berk, Julia O'Hara
Boling, Andrea W.
Caporaletti, Wanda Gale
Cropper, Kathleen Smith
Deros, Patricia Mead
Feitel, Lorin Monroe
Frohman, EricaLynn
Gallo, Katherine R.
Grayer, Natalie Y.
Gushue, Tracy Mays
Hansen, Anjali Karina
Hathaway, Noreen Nelligan
Hoffman, Abigail Schussheim
Hudson, Barbara Shapiro
Johnson, Pamela McDade
Kasoff, Donna L.
King, Margaret Willis
Kornick, Susan Liu
Lambros, Zoe
Lavi, Terri Jane
Lazarus, Sarah Rifka
Ledner, Sherri Lee

Leons, Natalia Ruth
Lerer, Tracey Lynn
Levine, Deborah Malia
Levitt, Melinda Faye
Lewis, Martha Jean
Lexa, Margery J.
Lichtenstein, Susan
Lim, Ann Aeran-You
Linton, M. Desales
Livingston, Mary Jo
Lobelson, Jeanne N.
Lunden, Mary O'Malley
Lustig, Amy Wolf
Lynch, Michele Denise
Maguire, Maureen Ann
Mahler, Linda Lorraine
Mandelbaum, Randi Sue
Manogue, Megan McDonald
March, Sandra Bowling
Margolis, Vicki Ann
Marinelli, Stephanie Babb
Martz, Lauren Adele Statum
McCann, Phyllis Ann
McCloskey, Maureen Anne
McCoog, Arlene B.
McCormick, Judith A.
McGrath, Mary Elizabeth
McInerney, Eileen
Meckler, Janine Lynn
Melonas, Jacqueline Mellott
Minton, Sandra B.
Mintz, Mindy S.
Moore, Edna M.
Morgan, Sherri Lynn
Mourra, Mary Helen
Murphy, Mary Virginia
Murthy, Sheela
Nangle, Dana Sarah Jackson
Nathanson, Martha Dale
Neary, Constance J.
Ninassi, Susanne Bruno
Nolan, Janet S.
O'Callaghan, Cliona Regina
O'Connor, Kathleen M.
Ogorzalek, Lisa Lattal
Ortega, Beverly Ann
Orzach, Keren Hannah
Oulds-Dunbar, Valarie K.
Paterson, Andrea Suzanne
Peters, Christina Marie
Peterson, Patricia L.
Pfautz, Leanne
Powell, Agnes Cowan
Powell, Laurie Anne
Press, Carolyn Billett
Pressman, Jennifer Suzanne
Procopiow, Julie
Radner, Cathi L.
Raghavan, Latha
Randall, Emily Blythe
Rankin, Fern
Rath, Sieglinde Katharine
Recinos, Helen Hiser
Redd, Stephanye Ann
Reese, Mary Cecilia
Reiff, Laura Foote
Reilly, Eileen Anne
Rekenthaler, Karen Salditt
Remer, Jodi Caryn
Ridgway, Leslie Karas
Robeson, Lynn Alice
Robinson, Gail French
Rogers, Mary Agnes
Rollins, Anne-Herbert
Rose, Mariclair Burke
Rothmann, Dorene Marie
Ryan, Christine Marion
Ryan, Mary Elizabeth
Sampson, Ingrid Elizabeth McDonald
Schlossberg, Judith Lynn
Schwartz, Julie Crystal
Sharpe, Lori Reinhold
Shaver, Elizabeth Ann
Sheehan, Kathleen Kelly
Shelley, Staci Anastasia Rhodes
Shomaker, Elizabeth Norwood
Shueh, Sheila Onlin
Shycoff, Barbara Lynne
Siegel, Malinda S.
Siegel, Paula Joy Olevsky
Silva, Frances Cecile
Simons, Claudia Adrienne
Singer, Karen Miller
Stackhouse, Kathryn Adah
Statland, Sherryl Gayle
Staudenmaier, Ann Marie
Steele, Andrea White
Stewart, Lynn Kellene
Stob, Barbara J.
Stone, Margo Annette
Strauss, Connie L.
Talbot, Jill Suzanne
Taylor, Sharon L.
Thomas, Alexandra Kim
Thomas, Jeane A.
Timmerman, Jerianne
Tomcala, Karen Alane
Trimble, Sandra Ellingson
Tripoli, Lori Nicole
Tucker, Constance Annette
Turian, Samantha Renee
Turner, Lisa Moffett
Turner, Tracey Gann
Twardzik, Barbara Schmidt
Tweedy, Juli Martin
Vitale, Cathleen Marie
Vitale, Patricia Marie
Vojik, Linda Ann
Weidner, Mary Gould
Weinstein, Halee F.
Weiss, Erica Hope
Weixel, Alane Carol
Wells, Ellen Maureen
Wexler, Pamela Beth
Whitman, Elisa J.
Wollman, Stacie Joy
Wood, Mary Kathryn
Young, Lauren Raquel
Zemel, Avital G.
Zerwitz, Wendy Anne

1-4-1990

Crawford, Judith Kessen
Croft, Janice Gaston
Dailey, Margaret Susan
Edwards, Amy L.
Efros, Ellen A.
Engel-Cook, Carla
Ferguson-Southard, Denise Rochelle
Gallagher, Elizabeth

1-5-1990

Hudson, Michelle Mohamed
Kominers, Ellen Dickstein
Levick, Sandra K.
McNicholas, Cynthia A.
Whalen, Donna Hylarides

1-8-1990

McCaig, Nancy J. White
Rubin, Susan J.
Squires, Susan B.
Tiger, Abbe Robin
Uttal, Susan Lynn
Vogel, Karen Anne
Wilkof, Sandra Goldstein

1-18-1990

Richards, Kathleen Reilly

2-5-1990

Ballato, Josie Angela
Damplo, Susan M.
Flanagan, Catherine Maura
Haney, Dorene M.
Lasworth, Juliana
O'Lone, Mary Margaret
Simmons, Margaret Lee
Simon, Marcia Libes
Stewart, Barbara Lynn
Taylor, Jane Ryan
Weinberg, Linda M.

3-5-1990

Alu, Sheryl Jones
Lassalle, Annette Mary

4-5-1990

Anderson, Julie M.
Little, Joan Friedrun
O'Connor, Nancy Morrison
Pacheco, Debra A.

5-31-1990

Boyle, Elizabeth Margaret
Crawford, Carrie
Duvall, Suzanne Galane
Eaglin, Carolyn Currie
Fierst, Edith Udell
Fowler, Theda Braddock
Garron, Rachel S.
Hancock, M. Elizabeth
Lynch, Maura Louise

6-1-1990

Hoshall, Carol Lynn
Kate, Patricia Ann
Keane, Mary Elizabeth
Krejsa, Diane
Lawrence, Debra Michele
LeBel, Antoinette Patterson
Meister, Anne M.
Mitchel, Peggy Halpern
Shettle, Renee Wellford
Upton, Marianne Clifford

6-4-1990

Barker, Barbara B.
Epstein, Carol Paskin
Medaglia, Mary-Elizabeth
Riley, Susan L.
Robinson, Sara Moore
Rosen, Lisa Alpert
Solomon, Barbara Davis
Strassler, Heidi Weintraub
Straube, Michele
Strom, Kathy Silberthau
Wagner, Marilyn G.
Zusman, Lynne Kaplan

6-28-1990

Adams-Knight, Carol Chrispina
Andre', Michelle Antionette
Arnold, Josephine
Arthur, Ellen Hennessey
Babest, Andrea Christine
Barfield, Sheila Gail
Barron, Carol Ann
Beg, Sabina
Berado, Diane Marie
Bledsoe, Janice L.
Block, Debra Ellen Scurnick
Block, Elizabeth Cooper
Book, Joan E.
Boswell, Donna A.
Bray, Kimberly Ann
Brower, Cheryl Martineau
Buschman, Pamela S.
Cardwell, Lucy A.
Carr, Traci R.
Cartwright, Wendy Alise
Choudhary, Lena Thea
Christian, Dionne Elene
Cohen, Deborah
Cook, Mona Lisa
Cope, Jami G.
Cortez, Anne Elizabeth
Couch, Jamir R.
Cuccia, Justine Gayle
Delarue, Eileen Anne
Dodd, Maureen Moore
Doherty, Laurie Ann
Dorsey, Robin Howard
DuFour, Christine Braider
Edin, Barbara Lynn
Edmonds, Phyllis Pelote
Edney, Marsha Stelson
Eisner, Susan G.
Ellis, Lisa Petti
Evans, Nadine Sharnice
Fisher, Pamela Stowe
Foxx, Renee Cassandra
Fraser, Joan Catherine
Frasher, Elizabeth Ellen
Fugett, Sharon Maria
Gafford, Linda Ellen
Gardner, Cheryl E.
Gearity, Patricia Eileen
Gephardt, Mary Ella
Goldstein, Lois Ellen
Grant, Priscilla Ross
Hagen, Lillian S.
Haines, Sigrid C.
Hall, Jennifer Lea
Halleck, Heidi L.
Hansberry, Denise Yvonne
Hanss, Mary Beth
Heinze, Megan Marie
Ho, Helen Kwok Wai
Holmes, Sandra
Householder, Gina Marie
Huber-Scott, Kathleen
Jay, Barbara Leon
Jeon, Deborah Ariadne
Kaplan, Lucille Rosen
Kennedy, Gwen Elizabeth
Kessler, Gail Denise
Kiessling, Laura Sue
Klema, Johanna Marie
Kohutanycz, Margaret Mary
Kozero, Kathryn T.

Kupchyk, Areta Lidia
Kurtz, Pamela L.
Light, Barbara Ann
Longley, Susan Honeycutt
Louis, Dianna Marie
Lowery, Terri Ann
Maloney, Julia Ann
Matricciani, Roseanne Mary
McFerren, Daphene Rose
McGee, Suzanne
McGlone, Marie Helen
McGolrick, Susan Jane
McGuffey, Catherine P.
McKenna, Patricia Falco
McKnew, Louise Bouscaren
Mead, Margaret Callander
Michels, Mary Elizabeth
Morowitz, Nancy Harriet
Morphew, Wendy Sue
Norris, Gloria Jean
Nunzio, Kathryn Kraus
O'Hanlon, Loraine E.
O'Reilly, Juliana T. Schulte
Padams-Lavigne, Allison Katherine
Pantos, Monica Lillian
Parker, Holly Lynn
Parker, Lori E.
Parks, Elizabeth Koplar
Pflug, Victoria H.
Phillips, Virginia Simmons
Powers, Carolyn Zelda
Ragins, Darlene Denise
Rapaport, Susan Rachel
Ridgway, Constance Joan
Rothstein, Rachel Joy
Royster, Stephanie Lynette
Saff, Ruth E.
Saint-Preux, Josselin
Sanders, Mary Roby
Sazama, Kathleen
Schneider, Edythe Chasen
Schultz, Victoria H.
Shapiro, Lori Rae
Silver, Ellen Alice
Smith, Constance Fletcher
Smylie, Judy Grier
Sorel, Christiane E.
Suchinsky, Mindy Garoom
Tahernia, Susan
Tassi, Julie Amelia
Tetlow, Joanne Elizabeth
Wakefield, Darlene Alexander
Weinberg, Jolie Beth
Weinbrom, Sally Beth
Wilson, Dorothy Jean
Zimic, Deborah Lee

7-9-1990

Katz, Karen L.

9-4-1990

Miller, Peggy A.
Petree, Beth Ratliff
Tolmach, Madeleine Joan
Vitale, Deborah A.

10-4-1990

Stein, Lynn Ernest

11-1-1990

Costello, Stacy Elaine
Rowe, Kelly

12-18-1990

Adamo, Sonya Alison
Adams, Betty Smith
Adler, Beth Goldman
Aguggia, Amy L.
Albizo, Lynn Hano
Alexander, Carolann Ascolillo
Altemus, Christine Tryphena
Amith, Adina Naomi
Amos, Karen Dorothy
Anthony, Lisa Battalia
Applefeld, Cathy A.
Arichea, Miriam Ruth
Avanzato, Lynda Smith
Avery, Barbara Marie
Bass, Linda Phyllis
Bauer, Susan Affleck
Bechamps, Anne-Therese Janet
Beltrami, Charlotte Harris
Benzer, Sandra Harlen
Berthot, Kathryn Susan
Blandford, Marilyn
Block, Cristobel
Blum, Christine H.
Boia, Diane Deros
Bonanno, Nona Jean
Botek, Linda Jeanne
Boynton, Magdalena Albornoz
Brancato, Cynthia Clayton
Breen, Carole Margaret
Brennan, Amy Elizabeth
Brickner, Laurianne
Brinster, Sharon Marie
Broser, Lori Ellen
Brown, Bari Gail
Brown, Dianna Lynn
Brown, Jill Cannon
Buchanan, Melanie Marie
Buckel, Linda Walker
Burch, Barbara F.
Bustraan, Kathleen
Butler, Elise Abell
Butta, Rene Jeanenne
Byers, Rebecca Jane
Callan, Kathleen Mary
Campbell, Julia Bell
Carnicelli, Elaine M.
Carpenter, Karla L.
Carroll, Doritt L.
Casden, Caryl L.
Casenas, Jacquelline Winstanley
Celtnieks, Jeanne Trimble
Cirincion, Regina Mary
Clark, Margaret
Cochran, Eileen K.
Cohen, Michele Levy
Cohen, Shannon
Cohen, Sharon R.
Cohen, Susan Debra
Cohn, Halli Dee
Colbeth, Carol A.
Comeau, Mary Elizabeth
Copes, Helen Diane Hollenshead
Corcoran, Joan Marie
Costella, Margaret Frances
Costello, M. Elaine
Crawford, A. Lindsey
Crawford, Cynthia Cheryl
Creedon, Melanie A.
Crosby, Kathy Frances
Culbertson, Robin Duncan
Cutler, Julie Klein
D'Alessio, Donna M.
D'Avella, Denise M.
Davis, Anna Louise
Davis, Celia Anderson
Davis, Christine Frances
Davis, Melissa Robin
Dieter, Rebecca Lynn
Doniger, Melissa Jo
Donley, Elizabeth Sue
Downing, Tracy Octavia
Drake, Toni Denise
Draper, Ellen G.
Dufresne, Regina Marie
Durbin, Susan Chapman
Duval, Denise Marie
Ebersole, Mary Frances Theresa
Edgar, Mary Murphy
Edmondson, Catherine Elizabeth
Edwards, Elizabeth Mihalisin
Estrin, Laura Diane
Evans, Julia Kingsley
Evans, Mary Edna
Fahmy, Randa
Fahrenkopf, Allison Marie
Fales, Lisa Jose
Fanaroff, Rachel Sharon
Federici, Lisa Ann
Fee, Denise Ann
Feinroth, Maureen Donohue
Feldenzer, Adair Clarke
Ferguson, Carolyn Hope
Ferraro, Denise Marie
Ferrera, Teresita J.
Ferris-Hansen, Michele A.
Fletcher, Cassandra Michelle
Fontan, Nadine Louise
Forsman, Cheryl Lynn
Friedman, Lorraine Lee
Friendly, Deborah
Gado, Yasmine M.
Gaegler, Patricia A.
Gaffney, Donna Lynn
Galicich, Jeanne Marie
Garufi, Laura A.
Gaver, Mary Catherine Collins
Gering, Anne-Marie
Giachino, Renee Louise
Gilbride, Ann DeBaets
Gochoel, Karey Rose
Gold-Rand, Anne Susan
Goldman, Leslie Ayn
Gordon, Melissa Reynolds
Gordon, Susan Berman
Goren, Nancy Beth
Gray, Aisling Whitfield
Greezicki, Frances Geneva
Grisez, Karen Theresa
Grodin, Nancy Sharon
Gulick, Grace Kirchner
Gutierrez, Margaret Mary
Hale, Kimberly Anne
Hale, Shadonna Elena
Hamelburg, Jamie Kent
Hamilton, Renee Lizabeth Anne
Hankin, Joan Ellen
Hannan, Marylee
Hargest, Laura Anne
Hatton, Julia S.
Hazard, Katherine W.
Hebert, Jenny Lynn
Heller, Diane Beth
Heller, Laura Rebeccah
Herbert, Toni-Junell
Higdon, Anne Elizabeth
Hill, Eva Helena
Hill, Jean Sanford
Honick, Eve Michele
Hopkins, Barbara Leigh
Horvitz, Alissa Aaronson
Houseman, Lisa
Howie, Margaret-Ann Frances
Huebner, Janine
Huntington, Mary Ann Kirlin
Hurlock, Ann Foxwell
Hurwitz, Mindy Gayle Pittell
Huttar, Elizabeth J.
Iannicelli, Rebecca K.
Israel, Deborah Jean
Jacobs, Lauren E.
Jaeger, Lisa Marie
Jenifer, Laura Courtenay
Jimenez, Celine Marie
Johnson, Anne L.
Johnson, Patricia Coyle
Jones, Althea R. Stewart
Kaiden, Mindy Avonne
Kalil, Susan Mary
Katz, Jeri Beth
Katz, Michelle Stephanie
Knox, Kathryn E. D.
Kowarski, Ruth
Lamm, Linda Carol
Landow, Dana Banner
Macdonald, Amy Hurite
Malinowski, Carloyn S.
Malone, D. Kay
Morabito, Leah Bury
Murphy, Vanessa Ann
Pearlman, Eva Marie
Pera, Lonnie Anne
Poling, Jane Bennett
Pollack, Jane Laura
Rauber, Diane Boyd
Roytblat, Nadezhda
Russell, Mary Ellen
Schoenfeld, Stacey Ilene Hirsch
Tildon, Maria Harris
Vaughn, Lori Lane
Weiss, Deirdre Butler
Young, Amy Felices
Zamer, MaryBeth

12-19-1990

Bowman, Denise Marie
Brown, Katherine Elizabeth Leffler
Buffington, Joanne Tetreault
Burrow, Lisa Saveikis
Campbell, Celeste Aurelia
DeGross, Kimberly Rice
Diemer, Mary Seminara
Eaves, Angela
Ebersole, Jodi Kay
Ector, Aretha J.
Faerber, Yolanda Eleni Stefanou
Glasgow, Elizabeth B.
Gonzalez, Chellis Neal
Gwin, Doreen Stephanie Lader
Hamilton, Kimberly Urweider
Jennings, Stephanie Christine
Jessen, Ellen Rattigan
Johnson, Molly Treadway
Kim, Anna Lee

Kleine, Lisa Anne
Koeppel, Claudia B.
Kolodner, Jill Ann
Kopp, Pamela L.
Kratovil, Connie Lee
Kratz, Cynthia Masucci
Kyle, Bridget Louise
Lane, Alison Velez
Lattimore, Vera Robin
Laughlin, Diane Murphy
Lavalleye, Marie A.
Lavrin, Cecilia Inez
Lee, Patricia Yeun-Han
Lengyel, Melissa Ann
Lester, Jennifer Marceline
Levin, Laurie R.
Lewis, Anne Gref
Lewis, Sue Ann
Liebowitz, Ellen C.
Lienesch, Wendy Lux
Lisa, Toni-Jean
Lloyd, Ann Burke
Lloyd, Anna Ruth
Locraft, Linda Poppleton
Lolley, Marina M.
Lord, Nancy Theresa
Lord, Rebecca Ann
Louis, Jill Bernadette
Luzzi, Margherita Anne
Lynch, Lauren Ann
Lynn, Giannina
Lyons, Margaret M.
Magnus, Vicki Lynne
Magovern, Sara Ann
Maisano, Nancy Helene
Malanga, Christine Ann
Mann, Jennifer Karen
Markham-Itteilag, Nadine
Markley, Mary Jane Sheppard
Marx, Kathleen Elizabeth
Massuda, Cindy Ann
Matanoski, Mary Katherine
McAllister, Kathleen Flemming
McBride, Donna Ellen
McCallum, Deborah Kay
McDowell, Heather Leigh
McNamara, Mary Alice
Meltzer, Suzanne Cohn
Miano, Andrea Smith
Mikkelson, Katherine Zittel
Miller, Karen Bosley
Miller, Kelly Ann Walfred
Mills, Cheryl D.
Minggia, Angela R.
Minner, Julia Ann
Missal, Deborah Stashower
Mitnick, Janice S.
Montroll, Kim Ingrid
Moreland, Sarah Louise
Myers, Judith Rochambeau
Neff, Christyne Lynn Nagorski
Neumann, Gallo
Nichols-Thompson, Devethia
Nuta, Virginia Rhodes
Oken, Ilene J.
Olivieri, Mary Elizabeth Ann
Oner, Oya S.
Orr, Catherine Meghan
Osborne, Heather Aimee
Ovitz, Anne Downs
Papa, Rose Mary
Patrick, Angela Tamar
Pedas, Joanna M.
Peddicord, Julie L.
Pedersen, Nadean Barrie
Peppe, Melissa Lynn
Perry, Gail Ann
Pezzner, Ashley I.
Phillips, Kimberley Ann
Pies, Staci Layne
Pitt, Roberta Susan
Potter, Deborah Lynne
Powell, Tonia Jones
Prosser, Colleen Mary
Rager, Susan Noel Godman
Ramey, Mary Ann
Reamer, Jill B.
Reusing, Grace Elizabeth
Ridgell-Boltz, Laura
Rigaux, Stephanie Ann
Riley, Ruth Foley
Robinson, Jill Richards
Robinson, Joy Patricia
Robinson, Kimberly Bowen
Rochkind, Deborah Marilyn
Ryan, Mary Grace
Salmon, Beverly Breneman
Samuel, Miriam Sharon
Schejbal, Julie Ann
Schenken, Kathleen Marie
Schuster, Catherine L.
Schwartz, Wendy Helene
Seidman, Jill Reynolds
Shea, Donna Marie
Shelton, Gloria Wilson
Sherman, Susan E.
Siegfried, Mary Kay
Sim, Tai S.
Sloan, Deborah Savarese
Smith, Gina Monique
Soltys, Darlene Michele
Speed-Bost, Regina Y.
Spencer, Ellen Gale
Springer, Caroline Thompson
Squire, Julie Ellen
Stackpole, Kerin Elizabeth
Stanley, Denise Ramsburg
Steigleman, Amy Jean
Stevens, Eleanor H.
Stoker, Kimberly Manchester
Stoner, Tamara Alexander
Stosur, Elizabeth Komarek
Stright, Victoria A.
Sullivan, Leslie Anne Roberts
Supanick, Pamela Jill
Sutherland, Kathleen
Swyers, Joan Stentiford
Thew, Brenda Diane
Thornal, Donna Marie
Thornton, Monica Delphine
Toth, Michele Marie
Trainer, Corina Marie
Upton, Lois Ilaine Vignes
Victor, Stephanie Gail
Vozzella, Carmen
Wach, Kathleen Therese
Walker, Laura Marie
Walker, Lisa Louise
Ward, Cathleen Frances
Wassem, Leigh Anne
Watson, Julie Adoff
Weinstein, Kathleen Mary
Weinstein, Susan Dembo
Weinstein, Wendi Leigh
Wendell, Marcie Beth
Wennes, Marilyn Ann
Whelan, Barbara L.
White, Karen L.
Whittle, Elizabeth Ward
Wilson, Dori Aliza
Wittig, Sarah Grace
Wittik-Bravmann, Ann
Yao, Vivian Pei-Win
Zarin, Emily B.

1-3-1991

Boisvert, Elena Sallitto
Bruno, Marian R.
Campbell, Nancy Ellen
Cruz, Debra B.
Geise, Elizabeth Runyan

1-4-1991

Halpern, Linda Ann
Harvey, Tanya Ann
Kraft, Barbara J.
Ledig, Kathryn A.
Lowe, Virginia Cronan
McClanahan, Elizabeth A.

1-7-1991

Maisel, Tami Zay
Oliver, Michele Marie
Robins, Lucy B.
Wheeler, Anne Marie

1-8-1991

Coleman, Gail Susan
Dobak, Carol Lee
Hamel, Evelyn Anne
Lescure, Paige
Norris, Laurie J.
Pridgen, Kirsten Ann
Singer, Elizabeth Anne

2-4-1991

Bezdek, Barbara L.
Greenberg, Leslie Ellen
Hagen, Marie Louise
Kennedy, Elizabeth Ann
Letica, Terri Glubin
Luzietti-Myers, Debra L.
McDonald, Karen Elizabeth
Peltier, Virginia Fazo
Romine, Terry J.
Warner, Elizabeth
White, Beverly Jeanne

2-28-1991

Barker, Rosina Bateson
Brunn, Elizabeth Keller
Sigler, Ruth Ellen

3-1-1991

McCammon, Julienne

4-4-1991

Houghton, Vivian A.
Hughes, Sandra Lee
Spicer, Tracy Hudson

4-29-1991

Weiner, Merle H.

5-2-1991

Wilhelm, Cheryl Lynne

5-29-1991

Bennett, Susannah Marie

5-30-1991

Crisman, Virginia F.
Marcus, Stephanie Robin

5-31-1991

Ayres-Fountain, Caroline Patricia
Edgecombe, Karen H.
Lindskold, Barbara DiSalle

6-3-1991

Boothby, Orva Lee
Grebasch, Virginia Susan
Kleinman, Joan Diane
Levine, Sharron Patricia Ann
Lovell, Virginia F.
Martin, Elveta Michele
McKnight, Cynthia Garrett
Miller, Binny
Nace, Eleanor
Questal, Nina Hope

6-4-1991

Fokas, Kathy A.
Lyman, Jennifer Page
Ostrander, Michelle M.
Pannell-Findley, Pamela D.
Paulhus, Lorraine Robert
Quagliano, Julie A.
Sanders, Susan Lee
Swisher, Patricia Riley
Weiss, Francine Karen
Yu, Corrine M.

6-18-1991

Wain, Lita

6-20-1991

Aminelahi, Yeganeh
Angeletti, Sara Elizabeth
Anselmo, Pamela J.
Arrington, Aretha Jones
Baker, Jean Harvey
Beltran, Ana Teresa
Benaroya, E. Anne
Bessenyey, Ilona Maria
Bigham, Ellen F.
Bowen, Julia Anne
Brown, Joan Sue Miliman
Callis, Janet L.
Carnett, Carol L.
Carp, Tenley Anne
Chang, Diane Kim
Clingman, Sarah Linley
Coffey, Diane Marie
Cole, Carolyn M.
Coleman, Donna Maria
Collins, Natalie Thryphenia
Comentale, Andrea Grinbergs
Cooper, Lesley Beth
Corso, Louise
Crook, Anne Michele Knight
Curry, Marie Bernadette
Dean, Sandra W.
DeClark, Lisa M.
DeLong, Karen Lee
Demme, Nancy Carolyn
DePue, Cynthia Lee
Dickerson, Heather L.
Dilks, Laurie E.
Dillon, Denyse Sophia
Douglas, Katherine Cole
Downer, Edwina Vaughan
Dupre, Anne Proffitt
Epstein, Roni F.
Fisher, Mary Margaret
Fitzsimmons, Erin Marie

Fleig, Susan Findling
Forsythe, Joni Louise
Fountain, Sharon F.
Gold, Deborah Lynn
Goldberg, Terri L.
Goldsmith, Esten Hardee
Groves, Tracy McCabe
Hansen, Elizabeth
Hauck, Mary Bowman
Hertzler, Patricia A.
Hewitt-Jones, Kathryn
Hinden, Susan Wilson
Hiscock, Kathryn Ann
Hobbs, Ann Snow
Holland, Eva Marietta
Holliday, Lisa Katherine
Ipolito, Dorothy Ann
Jackson, Charlotte Agnes
Jacobson, Gail Einbender
Jenkins, Ronell
Karateew, Suzanne
Kasten, Katherine Elaine Clark
Katsoulomitis, Georgia Demetrios
Kaye, June Hoke
Kelly, Teresa Marie
Kennedy, Helen M.
Kennedy, Jayne Frances
Kindermann, Anna Laura
Korn, Monique Diane
Kuhn, Teresa Bolet
LaMarca, Susan F.
Lattimer, Susan Johnston
Leishman, Judy Dean
Lewis, Donna Ann
Linton, Terri L.
Littell, Melinda Skinner
Littlepage, Elizabeth Diane Martin
Longwell, Frances Roehrich
Lowe, Alison Anne
Lowery, Angela Marie
Luchsinger, Lise Louise
Madsen, Kay A.
Maloney, Millicent Benay
Marchibroda, Lonni Susan
Marken, Cheryl Susan
Massie, Dena Maria
McAndrew, Sara
McCall, Candace Louise Smith
McClanahan, Sheila Ann
McCready, Donna Jeanne
McDermott, Rosemary Agnes
McGarey, Jennifer Campbell
McGinley, Rita Elizabeth
McGough, Jane Elizabeth
Middleton, Lynn Knight
Miller, Elisabeth Anne
Murphy, Mary Colleen
Needham, Judith
Nippard, E. Josephine
Nolan, Bethanne Goodwin
Norden, Laura Klainer
Nunzio, Colleen Ann
Patrick, Tammy LaShawn
Peck, Karen Lee
Pelzel, Janet Louise
Pessin, Sharon Marburg
Philipsen, Nayna D.
Pierce, Kathleen Anne
Plave, Karen
Ram, Marion Heyna
Reilly-Brew, Cathleen
Ritter, Stephanie M.
Rubinovitz, Susan M.
Scales, Cinda Lynn Fink
Severson, Sarah Brooke
Shapiro, Suzanne Carol
Shaw, Lauren Grace
Shea, Catherine Anne
Shoobe, Joanne Gail
Silbaugh, Kathleen
Silver, Susan Ellen
Sinha, Neena Kumari
Slaff, Sara
Smerko, Beth Ann
Speetjens, Amy Lavin
Stotler, Leah R.
Sugar, Andrea K.
Swilley, Julianne L.
Teitelbaum, Kathi Weiss
Terborg, Susan Crandall
Thomas, Linda Marotta
Thompson, Patricia Sue
Townsend, Yolanda M.
Trayner, Colleen Marie
Treacy, Colleen Marie
Tromley, Gwen Burrows
Van Dee, Joyce Rogers
van Noppen, Emorie Pepper
Van Schaik, Carolyn A.
Venture, Veronica Ann
Wales, Linda Gayle
Warnken, Bonnie Lee
Watkins, Kay Bryson
Watnik, Robbi-Lynn
Witherspoon, Heather M.

9-5-1991

Anchors, Laurel Nesson
Doggett, Suzanne Wightman
Hatton, Kathleen Grosso
Lazar, Ellen West
LeFlore, Christine Dennis
Nestorides, Angelike M.
Stone, Ellen C.
Wiley, La'Vern D.

10-31-1991

Bollinger, Beth M.

12-5-1991

Ball, Jean Galloway
Blumenthal, Susan Gail
Brier, Wilma A.
Brown, Sarah E.
Bunting, Karen Camille
Cannon, Maureen Teresa
Chao, Margaret Tze-Ping
Chyun, Mary Schneider
Davis, Adrienne Jean
Feffer, Audrey Faye
Feldman, Lona Lee
Gastilo, Jane Carmen
Hack, Frances M.
St. James, Kim Marie

12-6-1991

Alarcon-Cigarroa, Graciela
Berger, Stacey R.
Blakely, Caroline E.
Helm, Sallie Harper
Hepworth, Joanne Roney
Hoffman, Victoria June
Kaslick, Mary Elizabeth
Kaufman, Beth Shapiro
Kramer, Mary Kay
Lucan, Alice Neff
Masurovsky, Laura P.
Rodwell, Donna M. Nutter
Russell, Deborah Moreland

12-17-1991

Abrutyn, Stephanie S.
Adams, Jamilah A.
Adler, Julienne I.
Albero, Christine Fatzinger
Alexion, Jennifer Ewing
Aliquo, Nancy A.
Almand, Andrea Tomko
Alpert, Esther Ann
Amano, Lesley Rose
Andrew, Louise C.B.
Appel, Nancy Susan
Arrasmith, Lisa Lynn
Austin, Amy Elizabeth Carter
Bangert, Sharon Johnson
Barkin, Pamela Lee
Baruch, Valerie Michele
Bauer, Allison F.
Beach, Danielle Colette
Becker, Donna Ellen
Beers, Rayanne Theresa
Begun, Tamar
Belanger, Jeanne Marie
Bennett, Jacqueline E.
Beresin, Marta Ilene
Beresovski, Catherine Marie
Berman, Nancy
Berndt, Dorcey M.
Berry, Michelle Geddes
Berzon-Goldstein, Marcia Karen Sherry
Block, Sharon I.
Blomstrom, Jennifer
Blunt, Jennifer Mari
Bonanno, Gale Carney
Bouscaren, Winslow F.
Boyd, Tammie Lynn
Boyle, Mary Teresa
Bozinko, Susan Marie
Brinster, Kristen Atkins
Brooks, Renee Battle
Brown, Venel D.
Bryant, Edith Bourne
Buckingham, Susan LaPadula
Buppert, Carolyn Knight
Byers-Goldman, Brooke Alison
Byington, Lisa Michele
Byrd, Adrienne Patrice
Calvit, Maribeth Ann
Carroll, Kathryn Genevieve
Cerlenko, Ariane E.
Charlton, Suzan Frances
Chase, Elizabeth Price
Chester, Gail Donovan
Christman, Anne Clark
Clark, Katherine Candis
Coe, Linda Beth
Colclough, Jacqueline Therese Caron
Cole, Janice Lynn
Connolly, Jacqueline O'Brien
Cousins, Patricia Gillis
Cowie, Evelyn Diane
Craft, Carla Draluck
Cramer, Carla DiPasquale
Crane, Margaret Mikita
Crook, Alice Marie
Curtis, Amber Dahlgreen
Daghir, Roberta Lee Kienast
Damie, Denise Ann
Davis, Denise
De Stefano, Gina Maria
Dehncke, Susan M.
Dever, Lisa Fox
Dillenburg, Margaret Anne
Drummond, Christine Cornett
Dyer, Beverly Gay
Eaton, Holly R.
Edens, Geraldine
Eisenberg, Elisa Ann
Emmons, Susan Rachel
Ernst, Beth Anne
Ettlinger, Lisa Diane
Fager, Mary Kathleen
Fain, Deidre Susan
Falconer, Gina Margaret
Farley, Michelle F.
Farrar, Tracey Lynne
Farrell, Anne Marie
Feinson, Clare
Fex, Cecilia Carina
Fiorino, Christina Marie
Florack, Michele Marie
Flynn, Catherine
Fogler, Carol Lee
Forfa, Tracey Hancock
Forgrieve, Grace Helen
Forman, Samantha Helene
Foster, Megan Lucille
Fouse, Stephanie Holmes
Fox, Cheryl Ann
Fox, Jacqueline R.
Fraser, Mary Ellen
Fried, Michelle D.
Friedlander, Tracey Kline
Garcia, Susan Jenks
Gavigan, Patricia Joan
Gazda, Deanna Lynne
Gell, Jane Jensen
Ghiladi, Khatereh S.
Gillespie, Veronica Murray
Gilliam-Collier, Vanessa D.
Gilpin, Ernestine Baker
Giove, Melissa Christine
Gladden, Lisa Adrienne
Glasheen, Megan
Glasser, Jill Andrea
Glessner, Elisabeth Joy
Goldberg, Donna Falck
Golomb, Cynthia L.
Goodman, Sheilah A.
Gordon, Kimberly Brown
Hopkins, Nancy C.
Jackson, Maria Carey
Kendrick, Cynthia L.
Kolesar, Patricia Evelyn
Kroll, Lori Ann
Luther, Cara Jeanne
Moran, Janet Fitzpatrick
Munsat, Susan Chertkof
Needleman, Christie Pierce
Nieuwenhuis, Ingrid A.A.M. Brinkman
Rasevic, Kimberly Dopkin
Richman, Ina L.
Salovaara, Julia Buchanan
Seidl, Sarah Curtis
Simmons, Andrea M. Dorsey
Stavrou, Pauline E.

Tayloe, Laura C.
Thomas, Jennifer Ammon
Titus, Marlana Kathryn
Uhl, Diane M.
Walters, Laura Campbell

12-18-1991

Bolog, Debra Helfand
Brown, Melissa Heitmann
Carreiro, Christine J.H.
Dyer, Liza Hamerman
Fedder, Janet Lanocha
Ferlise, Willis Gunther
Gordon, Lisa Beth
Gosnell, Marion L.
Goss, Margaret Eleanore
Green, Marie Andree
Greenfield, Rita Ann
Grunden, Ellen Barry
Hallas, Maria E.
Halpern, Cynthia Gould
Hammel, Mary Ann
Hanson, Shannon Thee
Harasti, Gina M.
Hardy, Helen Ann Welsh
Haris, Kim Noelle Dority
Harrison, Paige Elizabeth
Hart, Paula Lee
Hartka, Margaret
Haselman, Alexandria
Hayden, Caroline Bell
Heavner, Lisa L.
Heitkamp, Colleen Kay
Herzog, Judith Ann
Hickey, Constance Toohey
Hileman, Kristin Marie
Himelfarb, Phyllis-Jo
Hirsch, Charlene Ryan
Holmes, Sunanda Kumari
Hosmer, Alicia Watts
Houppert, Elizabeth Anne
Howard, Nancy Hall
Hughes, Susan Bakke
Hulit, Felicia M.
Inman, Lynne Charisse
Jackson, Maija Burns
Jason, Meredith Lee
Jennings, Alice S.
Johnson, Peri Lynne
Jones, Christine Anne
Jones, Jeanne
Kadir, Safia S.
Kampen, Cheryl Anna
Kane, Deborah Elizabeth Sanders
Karmarkar, Radhika Vasant
Kassouf, Jean Elizabeth
Kater, Karmen Marie
Kehoe, Rebecca Lynn
Kenealy, Timi Nickerson
Key, Jennifer L.
Kimmel, Angela Mary
Kirschner, Anne Michele
Knodell, Joyce Elaine
Kobrinetz, Alisa Beth
Koenigsberg, Ilene Carol
Konecke, Patricia L.
Konstant, Kallia
Kopman, Nancy J.
Kramer, Jacquelyn Millard
Kravitz, Deborah
Kretschmann, Keri Frances
Krohn, Carolyn Gilden
Kuhlke, Karen S.
Kuhlmann, Kristina
Kuray, Marilyn Joann
Lang, Elizabeth Marie
Lang, Michele Ann
Lange, Lori Ann Teresa
Lapides, Diane E.
Lasko, Jennifer Cathryn
Lawrence, Lisa Gale
Lenartowicz, Linda Diane
Lennon, Susan Marie
Leonard, Margaret M.
Leonnig, Dorothea R.
Levine, Victoria Anne
Levitan, Amy Mara
Ligos, Gioia Marie
Lock, Sarah Elsa Lenz
Locke, Vanessa D.
Lubman, Debra Ilene
Lucas, Patricia Jean
Lykos, Angela
Lyon, Jill Mace
Mack, Deborah Anne
MacMullan, Donna Marie
Madden, Anne Therese
Malanoski, Martinia Tekla
Manasevit, Patricia Allison
Marino, Cynthia D.
Mark, Diana A.
Marshall, Joanne Buck
Martin, Barbara Grusch
Martin, Cathryn M.
Mataban, Amy Korll
Mathias, Susan Maureen
Matthews, Kimberly Cheronn
Mayhew, Sharon Lynn
Mazumder, Nandita
McAfee, Laura K.
McBride, Anne Leslie
McCarty, Anna Nichols
McClelland, Jill Kleppe
McCurdy, Jesselyn Burnett
McLean, Christine Liane
McNeal, Sherae Monique
McQuade, Carolyn
McSherry, Christine Kilty
Meiburger, Mary Alexis
Meller, Lana Lynne
Mendelsohn, Jocelyn Stricker
Mericle, Linda S.
Messina, Bonnie Lynn
Michaelson, Melanie F.
Miclay, Jane L.
Miller, Tracy
Monahan, Mary Elizabeth
Morin, Elizabeth Clark
Morton, Padraic McSherry
Mosley, Ferne Louise
Mott, Joanne C.
Mount, DaNeeka LaVarner
Moyse, Elizabeth A.
Murdoch, Miranda Kemp
Murphy, Mary J.
Nardella, Kathleen Anne
Newman, Lynn Green
Niemeyer, Michelle Melin
Nightingale, Marjorie Ann
Novosel, Sarah Gowen
O'Donnell, Sherri Evans
O'Malley, Catherine Curran
O'Sullivan, Lorraine Nancy
Ogilvie, Kay A.
Paulsen, Margaret Ellen Miniter
Scanlon, Alice Kelley
Schoenfeld, Susan Elizabeth
Shane, Gail Suzanne
Stein, Carolyn Israel
Taylor, Jodi Lyn
Tucker, Jodi Ann
Utterback, Mary Margaret

12-19-1991

Alves, Krystal Quinn
Band, Erin Patricia
Barranco, Kimberly Smalkin
Bozentka, Lynn Marie
Brown, Stephanie D. Pullen
Bryant, Susan Michelle
Byun, Rhonda P.
Cate, Beth Ellen
Cottrell, Sheryl A.
Curran, Michele W.
Fink, Sandra Saltzman
Gossart, Elizabeth Anne
Greenberg, Deborah Rockman
Griffin, Michele Tucker
Hayward, Michelle Lee
Hendershott, Christine Robin
James, Deirdre A.
Kohen, Lynn Ann
Leetzow, Karen B.
Maguffee, Sarah R.
Mehring, Melissa Alexandra
Mugavero, Patricia S.
Nelson, Tina Smith
Orwick, Karen S.
Oshrine, Eugenia Reed
Pagan, Maria Luisa
Palko, Monica Jane
Papiewski, Suzanne Marie
Pare-Johnson, Alice Ann
Park, Susanna S.
Parker, Diane Michelle
Parker, Pamela K.
Patton, Nancy Anne
Peters, Louisa H.C.P.
Peterson, Michelle Marie
Pickens, Lynn Ellen
Pinkerton, Brooke A.
Plott, Margaret Mary
Podeszwa, Laura Lee
Polzin, Heather H.
Pontzer, Kathryn M.
Preston, Donna Burke
Price, Heather Lynne
Pritchard, Laurie I.
Quick, Helen Elisabeth
Raker, Stefanie L.
Rath, Lora M.
Rathbun, Colleen Annette
Raymond, Karen Maria
Reamer, Jodi Beth
Reaves, Helen Frances
Renne, Jennifer Lee
Reno, Sandra Lynn
Rockefeller, Kathryn Boyer
Rodgers, Peggy A.
Rodriguez, Dawn Marie
Rosenberg, Diane Sally
Ruderman, Marchelle Ann
Russell, Devy Patterson
Rypkema, Pamela Jo
Said, Naima M.
Satin, Wendy L.
Scanlan, Melissa Anne
Scheetz, Mary Alice
Schmell, Myriam Judith
Schmitt, Kathleen Dunivin
Segal, Julie Ann
Seiden, Stacy Beth
Seltzer, Diane Allison
Selvaggi, Annelise L.
Serra, Gina M.
Shea, Claire Small
Sheehey, Diane M.
Sherfy, Elizabeth Jean
Sheridan, Ann Marie
Shupert, Holly Denise
Siff, Jodi Lynn
Soltis, Debra Lynn
Sorge, Christine Marie
Spector, Deborah Gail
Staudenmaier, Therese L.
Stauffer, Susan J.
Steele, Patricia Marion
Steiner, Catherine Whitehurst
Stofberg, Cynthia Ann
Stone, Renee
Sweeney, Mary F.
Szczesny, Vasiliki P.
Tanenhaus, Marta Iris
Tanner, Yolanda Alicia
Tasher, Patricia Osores
Thomas, Joiava
Thomas, Linda Mitchell
Thyberg, Regina Wallace
Toomey, Mary Kate Appleby
Trainer, Theresa M.
Tso, Caroline
Tyler, Julia Jennings
Tyler, Millicent Esther
Valente, Roberta L.
Vallario, Angela Marie
van Brackel, Heather L. Stimson
Vieta, Jean
Wagner, Felice Cernobori
Walker, Kathleen Strahorn
Wallenius, Amy Roberts
Walters, Cynthia B.
Ward, Kimberly Smith
Warnick, Julie Ann
Wase, Randy Sue
Waterfield, JoAnn
Watson, Bridnetta Delores
Watson, Rosemary
Wazenski, Jennifer Lynn
Weaver, Patricia M.
Welsh, Robin Christine
Whipple, Lori Ann
White, Lisa Jennifer
Wiggins, Elizabeth Corinne
Wilhelmi, Angel Batlas
Williams, Louise Dean
Wolfe, Michelle Ann
Woodward, LoriJan Bazzano
Woolworth, Jocelyn Frank
Yang, Cindy
Yates, Elinor K.
Zunt, Monica Catherine

12-31-1991

Baynes, Abbie Gaillard

1-2-1992

Alquist, Nancy Virginia
Amiri, Noosheen
Antoniades, Vicki Basil
Golenzer, Vera Lea

Greer, Sue A.
Maples, Andrea Hansen
Paoli, Elena I.
Randle, Patricia Armstrong
Reidy, Arlene A.
Rogers, Melissa
Rus, D. Kathleen
Russo, Paula Ann
Sampsell, Catherine M.

2-6-1992
Barr, June Hatton
Heyman, Sherri Renee
Pierre, Marylin
Shek, Sherry

3-5-1992
Frank, Michelle Erin
Sciocchetti, Tina Elena

3-7-1992
Mollick, Georgina Marie

4-2-1992
Robinson, Carla Donata

5-7-1992
Jackson, Caryn Allison
Larkin, Mary Ellen

6-5-1992
Bradley, Stephanie Yvonne
Brooke-Davidson, Jennifer
Brusca, Sandra E.
Carey, Kathleen A.
Counts, Anne Bradley
Evans, Rachel C.
Ramsey, Ann Lockridge
Woodward, C. Victoria

6-8-1992
Fiscella, Lynne Julia
Maher, Patricia Marie
McClure, Rebecca S.

6-9-1992
Mullins, Laureen J.
Prioleau, Gwendolyn Delora
Slattery, Mary Frances
Suchman, Bonnie A.
Sullivan, Jan Elizabeth
Wertheim, Shauna Miller

6-17-1992
Ackman, Kay Leslie
Allen, Deborah Lynn
Allen, LaSonya DeLois
Asensio, Cheryl Ann O'Rourke
Balcar, Lynn Galambossy
Bandes, Amy Gabrielle
Barfield, Susie Jackson
Baronian, Jacqueline Manoushag
Beach, Judith Elaine
Beauchamp, Kay Lyn
Bender, Kristen A.
Benko, Meryl Ann
Berman, Jodi Denise
Birmingham, Joan Ann
Bloch, Rachel Leslie
Blumer, Stacey Michelle
Bormel, Ivy Lurie
Brady, Kathaleen Ruth
Brewer, Sandra Susan
Bruce-Watson, Abigale M.
Buck, Karen Ann
Bukas, Nancy Boggs
Burdick, Joy Ann
Burke, Dawn Marie
Butera, Laura A.
Buxo, Zoraida
Clifford, Samantha Ann
Cohill, Ellen Zelinski
Compton, Loraine Shadel Nyack
Costello, Kathleen Balthrop
Davis, Anne Brizzolara
Doyle, Ann E. Bands
Driggins, Twila Charlyse
Dubnow, Stacie F.
Duckham, Sarah M.M.
Eshmont, Joyce A.
Fabregas, Ana Isabel
Farr, Andrea Fraser-Reid
Fenske, Mary Gillen
Fitzwater, Kimberly Ann
Foresman, Pamela S.
Franceschini, Maria Michele
Freedman, Beth Anne
Frost, Elsie
Fusting, Amy
Gaary, Pamela Cecile
Garger, Melanie Marie
Gasiorowski, Beth Anne
Gates, Mary Eugenia
Gausvik, Cynthia Louise
Gilpin, Adele M.K.
Giral, Teresa Maria
Goldman, Nadia
Goldstein, Sheryl B.
Goodson, Antionice D.
Gray, Eunice
Griffin, Christi Diane
Gustafson, Sharon Fast
Guyker, Ellen Ulasek
Hachem, Rochelle Roca
Hall, Amy M.
Hardwick, Sherrie Scott Pauline
Henthorne, Heather Rose
Hirsch, Barbara Ellen
Hogarty, Jill A.
Howe-Barksdale, Sydney Terese
Hunt, Erica Rosemary Simone
Janoske, Catherine Virginia
Kanfer, Ilene Gordon
Keller, Cecelia Ann
Kelly, Patricia Ann
Kelly, Victoria Eve
Kimmich, Joan M.
Kincheloe, Pamela Barrow
King, Shelby Ann Tucker
Kinney, Deborah Jenkins
Kissler, Tracy Sanders
Klein, Susan Berg
Lacewell, Tonya Marie
Lambert, Melissa Lazarich
Lavigne, Carrie L.
Lee, Robin Linda
Lee-Bryant, Danita C.
Lolcama, Joan T.
Lundy, Sheila Edwards
MacKay, Elizabeth Denise
Maguire, Mairi Patricia
Manspeizer, Margo Evans
Mason, Terri Denise
McArthur, E. Pamela
McCann, Kathryn Denise
McClendon, Theresa Anne
McCullom, Michele Daniele
McElroy, Colleen M.
McFarland, Tina Renee
McIntosh, Gillian Louren
Merino, Dawn
Michels, Dina Luise
Miller, Amy Teresa
Mitchell McWilliams, Tammy Ann
Mocek, Joyce M.
Morganroth, Candi Lyn
Nadelman, Andrea Koyner
Nielson, Christine Saverda
Nyack Compton, Loraine Shadel
O'Neill, Sharon Patricia
Opsahl, Lisa S.
Osakwe, Lucy Vera
Oxman, Janna L.
Parks, Susan Engle
Parson, Cassia Weiner
Pate, Tracey Nicoll
Peek, Leslie Florestano
Pestaina, Kaye L.
Pharaoh, Marie Lott
Piermattei, Kim Anne
Pipitone, Mary Rosanne
Prats, Francisca Chandler
Prether, Amy
Pullen-Mossman, Cynthia
Rainis, Lynn Bromley
Reed, Belinda P.
Reinstein, Elizabeth Hillary
Revesman, Cynthia Kaplan
Rhett, Michelle Darlene
Richards, Nadia Allison
Riggs, Amanda Myers
Ringo, Michelle Anne
Riordan, Eileen B.
Robbins, Karen
Robertson, Yvette
Rodriguez, Joan Stiefel
Rowe, Angelia Taletta
Schneier, Leslye Morgan
Schoenhaar, Teresa Noelle
Schuetz, Elizabeth Frances
Sedgewick, Michelle Louise
Shaffer, Denise Oakes
Sheehan, Lisa D.
Sheetz, Shelly L.
Sheffer, Tracy Marie
Sinrod, Susan Adele
Sloane, Amy T.
Steadman, Marquita B.
Stern, Alissa Joy
Straus, Susan Koplovitz
Swartz, Emily K.
Taggart, Clare Kelly
Tate, Lisa J.
Terry, Lisa Victoria
Thomas, Jennifer Kathleen
Tillman, Elva Elizabeth
Tirone, Elizabeth Rose
Townsend, Faith Anne
Trainor, Elizabeth Ann
Unger, Suzanne Leonette
Walls, Molly B.F.
Walsh, Jacquelyn M.
Ward, Joyce Ann
Weinberger, Eleanor
Wells-Green, Lori J.
White, Vera Lynne
Wills, Marissa Dwor
Winters, Beth L.
Yuill, Barbara Ann

9-10-1992
Breault, Pamela Marks
Fitz, Rhonda Lynn
Fleck, Barbara
Friedman, Miriam Anne
Goering, Susan
Jividen, Patricia
Striegel, Alexis Marina

9-22-1992
Wing, Susan

9-25-1992
Riordon, Judith Gibbons

10-1-1992
Reinhardt, Heather Daniels

12-3-1992
Nifosi, Dana Christine
Quigley, Joan Ellen

12-15-1992
Abrams-Myers, Amy Susan
Adkins, Elizabeth Rosalee
Albert, Dawn Michelle
Albert, Edith Rodes
Alexander, Christine Tracy
Ambrose, Cynthia Lynn
Anderberg, Karen L.
Andrews, Mary Ellen
Arluk, Pamela Suzanne
Arthur, Jean Christine
Ashbrook, Alexandra Maria
Atkins, Pamela Ilene
Atkinson, Paula Gail
Avery, Shannon Elizabeth
Bailey, Catherine Zamaroni
Bailey, Linda A.
Barlow, Kristi
Becker, Robin Ann
Beegle, Cheryl Ann
Benavides, Nancy Lynn
Benet, Elizabeth Worthington
Blackwell, Suzette Wynn
Blecker, Jodi Harilyn
Bledsoe, Catherine Anne
Bloom, Sara Lynne
Bollinger, Maura Cantrill
Bonner, Anissa Jai
Boon, Kristy Davis
Borges, Elissa F.
Borin, Jill Melissa
Briley, Yvonne Mechelle
Brinkley, Sallie M.
Brodsky, Heidi Hookman
Browne, Maureen Frances
Bruce, Marie Celeste
Bryce, Beverly Gaustad
Bunning, Karen E.
Butler, Lori Ayn
Cain, Lauren Hooper
Calomiris, Carol Lynn
Candreva, Karen Friedel
Canning, Kathleen Holiday
Cantrill, Maura E.
Carnell, Teresa Burt
Carpentier, Deborah Ann
Carroll-Fischer, Catherine E.
Carson, Maria Cecilia
Carter, Jessica Veree

Cavanaugh, Colleen Ann
Cepko, Roberta Lynn
Cerniglia-Lowensen, Joan
Chang, Linda Stockton
Chappell, Amy Beth
Cherian, Limo T.
Christensen, Jeanne-Marie Bates
Chu, Sharon Chi-Hwei
Ciesla, Felicia A.
Clark, Denise Atkinson
Coffey, Justine Kate
Cohea, Maryann Shaughnessy
Condon, Maura J.
Cook, Cynthia Ruth
Costello, Karen L.
Costello, Kathleen Frances
Covington, Karen Kay
Crabill, Elizabeth Faecher
Crabtree, Elizabeth Anne
Crawford, Carol Anne
Curtin, Jennifer Kathleen
Davis, Hillary Galloway
Davis, Lesley A.
Davison, Diane Leigh
Dawes, Deborah Lynn
Day, Julia Ann
de La Viez, Barbara J.
Delaney, Maureen Ann
Dement, Pamela Rhea
Di Francesco, Christina E.
Di Franco, Tina
Dickinson, Leslie K.
Dolan, Kathleen Conlan
Donath, Nicole Beth
Dorion, Lisanne Cape
Dorsey, Melanie Graham
Drigotas, Elizabeth Eggleston
Drucker, Deborah Jane
Dubey, Sharon Connolly
Duby, Jacqueline Lee
Dukes, Charlene D.
Dunn, Tracey A.
Dymowski, Julianne Erin
Eisemann, Lisa Marie Lattwanzi
Ellis, Joan
Endress, Ellen Chapin
Engelmaier, Christine Raymond
Esposito, Denise
Estill, Alice Paige
Evans, Carolyn Wilson
Faass, Christina Bissell
Fairbairn, Vivian Carcamo
Fannon, Christine A.
Felten-Green, Daphne Serena
Fenlon, Karen Kozora
Fierberg, Janine Elise
Filippi, Laurie Anne
Finn, Stacy Ellen
Finnican, Lisa Anne
Flores, Cristina Isabel
Foran, Jeannine Marie
Fowler, Rhonda Gaile
Franzblau, Sandra
Friedman, Beth
Gastley, Diann Marie
Gemski, Carolann
Gillen, Cathleen M.
Glenn, Bambi C.B.
Gomez, Anna Marie
Henderson, Jocelyn Burns
Henneberry, Lisa G.
Holt, Carolyn M.
Jordan, Natalia H.
Kandel, Robin Frazier
Link, Kimberly Bilicic
Lovell, Gail
Lurie, Debra G.
Maddrey, Nicole M.
Mann, Jennifer Marie Corey
McClennan, Jennifer P.
McKinney, Margaret Jane
McNamara, Brenda Dunton
Miller, Pamela Dubret
Morris, Elise Davison
Neuman, Rhonda Cook
Palacios, Caitlin Shirer
Pechacek, JoAnne Breslin
Rindner, Karen C.
de Schwartz, Graciela Vazquez
Spelman, Kimberly Dunn
Waldman, Merle Yvette
Warren, Christine Joyce
Willard, Gail Gonya
Wrage, Alexandra Addison

12-16-1992

Anderson, Amanda Lannon
Bean, Teresa Rivera
Bellinger, Catherine Head
Blue, Kathy Murphy
Bogart, Lauren Liss
Brown, Anastasia D.
Cummins, Alisa Gross
Dachille, Kathleen Hoke
Fielding, Gabrielle M.
Gold, Jean McCambridge
Goodman, Ellen
Goolsby, Terry Pisano
Gordon, Julia R.
Graber-Lipperman, Elysa Lynn
Greenlees, Lisa Taeko
Grems, Kelly Compton
Griffith, Leza M.
Grimes, Nanette Gay
Gross, Anita Pellman
Grossenbacher, Karla
Grubber, Karen Lynn
Guben, Sue Walzer
Habermeier, Mollie Norwitch
Haislip, Kathleen Ann
Hamm, Nanci O'Brien
Hanna, Cheryl Ann
Hannan, Sonya Kazazian
Hargrove, Kim L.
Harzinski, Maureen Theresa
Hausmann, Wendy A.
Hearn, Katherine A.
Helinski, Laura Michelle
Helmlinger, Colleen Ferg
Helweg, M. Diana
Henninger, Laura Limongelli
Hewlett, Joycelyn Janice
Hiilivirta, Leena I.
Hills, Mary Ronan
Himmelhoch, Sarah D.
Hoffmann, Nancy Schiavetta
Hollinger-Quick, Marcy Ann
Holt, Diane Ruth
Huckaby, Michelle Lynn
Hughes, Kathleen Marie
Hurly, Kathleen Mary
Hurwitz, Rhonda Ann
Iancu, Carol A.
Iverson, Kelly Hughes
Jabloner, Amy B.
Jablonover, Lisa L.
Janis, Leslie Raker
Janis, Lynn Sandra
Jeffein Olin, Nancy Lynn
Jennings, Linda Joy
Jensen-Ney, Melanie Ann
Johns, Leah Chole
Johnson, Cynthia Kinney
Johnson, Joanne Elizabeth
Johnson, Lynne Ellen
Jones, Kathleen Corinne
Jones, Margaret Frances
Juda, Nancy Meredith
Judd, Jacqueline Jean
Kaplan, Stephanie Kalfon
Karpati-Lynch, Elizabeth Frances
Karpel, Wendy Beth
Katz, Marilyn B.
Kaye, Janice Ann
Kemp, Natonne Elaine
Kentz, Ellen Miskovsky
Kerxton, Amy Lynn
Keys, Erica Lynn
Kifer, Ruth E.
Kitt, Cheryl Fridkin
Kreckel, Jennifer Frey
Krohn, Deborah Anne
Kronz, Diane L.
Kunz, Kirsten Johanna
Kwak, Amy Clara
Labert, Jill S.
Land, Susan Julie
Lane, Laura K.
Larson, Amy Wright
Lauerhass, Theresa
Lee, Elizabeth Ann
LeFevre, Kristen R.
Leftwich, Norma B.
Levan, Naomi Joy
Levister, Michelle Nicol
Levy, Karen W.
Lezin, Katya Ursula
Licwinko, Mary Lou
Little-Fletcher, Sheryl Lynn
Lord, Karen Sue
Lotfi, Kathryn J.
Lowry, Heather A.
Luria, Joan Mary
Lyte, Laurie Ann
Mahoney, Kristen Marie
Mahony, Erin Adele
Malone, Patricia Ann
Manley, May-Lis Anne
Manocchio, Sandra Ann
Martin, Georgia A.
Martin, Maureen Elizabeth
Marts, Lisa Hyle
Marvin, Katharine Alexandra
Mathews, Susan Aeryll
Mazan, Kathleen Duffy
McCreary, Erin Lynn
McDonald, Michele Joan
McLaughlin, Kathleen Mary
McLoughlin, Mary Elizabeth
Melia, Laura Ann
Mendoza, Maria Cristina
Meyer, Cindy Lee
Milanes, Ginette Louise
Miller, Margaret Ruth
Miller, Melissa Ann
Miller, Patricia A.
Minikon, Patricia B.
Mitchell, Janet Ewing
Moylan, Dana Lynne
Mucha, Donna Lee
Myers, Kimberly Lillian
Naddaf, Mina
Nebens, Renee Ripp
Neufville, Nadine M.
Newsom, Elizabeth Wells
Nickerson, Anne Hamilton
Nightingale, Elizabeth Sara
Nitkin, Rebecca Anne
Nordenberg, Tamar S.
Novinsky, Sylvia K.
Nunn, Rachel Kathleen
O'Neil, Stacy Lynn
Odynski, Jeanette A.
Olin, Nancy Lynn Jeffein
Orjala, Ellen Jane
Ortiz, Pamela Cardullo
Pannier, Jane B.
Pauley, Susan H.
Peters, Andrea Janice
Phillips, Charon Harris
Reers, Carolyn Faith
Saiontz, Gabrielle Hopkins
Scheele, Margaret Jacobsen
Shehan, Deborah Miller
Shoop, Darcy A.
Watson, Rita Katherine
Webster, Mary S.
Whiteway, Andrea Macintosh
Zambri, Mary A.
Zimmermann, Terri Raye

12-17-1992

Bainbridge, Katherine D.
Bender, Honora Wohlgemuth
Edwards, Teresa Sommerfield
Fato, Kelly D.
Garvin, JoAnn F.
Gloor, Dana S.
Gurdak, Dianne Schaefer
Hanifen, Anne Walton
Hovermill, Virginia S.
Howell, Sherrie T.
Johnson, Cindy Lurene
Levin, Katherine Ann
McGuire, Debra Ann
Packard, Elise Barry
Parker, Alexis Anne
Parmet, Suzanne Hillary
Pasternack, Dianne
Pedersen, Lisa Denise
Peltzman, Cynthia G.
Penny-Ardinger, Cynthia D.
Pfaender, Kathleen Elizabeth
Phelps, Lori A.
Pierre, Lori J.
Plant, Katherine Warwick
Plaster, Amy Sandgren
Posin, Debra Ellen
Posner, Stephanie Gordon
Prasad, Sangeeta
Price, Paula A.
Profili, AnnMarie Helen
Prysant, Sharon Tasman
Pujari, Davina
Radford, Dana Christine
Rahal, Linda Ann
Rakatansky, Carol Rose
Ramirez, Linda Ann
Raubaugh, Christine T.

Reck, Deann Renee
Recker, Nancy Lynne
Refolo, Ann Stille
Reitkopp, Elizabeth Anne
Rennert, Jamie Palter
Rice, Janine Louise
Rice, Lynda Vincienne
Rice, Stacie Lynn
Ritter, Allison Marie
Ritter, Barbara Rosenthal
Robichaud, Sarah A.
Robin, Ellen Poris
Robinson, Farida Moreau
Robinson, Lydia S.
Robinson, Myrtle Cynthia
Rochlin, Andrea Leigh
Rochvarg, Ria Piesner
Rodgers-Waire, Cynthia E.
Rodney, Donna Marie
Rohaly, Kathleen Ann
Roll, Sharon Metro
Rosenzweig, Janice Popick
Rossmark, Claire Elaine
Rubin, Dawn L.
Rucker, Susan Sharer
Russell, Marsha Lynette
Ryan, Carolyn Elizabeth
Sansone, Lisa J.
Sapirstein, Lisbeth
Saunders-Owings, Monzella C.
Sawyer, Lisa M.
Schadt, Delia Turano
Schneider, Janice M.
Schwam, Lois
Schwartz, Maria Elizabeth
Scott-Thomas, Deborah
Seidel, Catherine Weller
Seunarine, Indra Cowsillan
Sharp, Michelle
Sheafor, Catherine M.
Short, Larri Alexis
Simoneau, Lynne Teresa
Singer, Jill
Sinozich, Paula A.
Slowinski, Ann Michelle
Smilan, Lisa E.
Smith, Judith Anne
Smith, Karen Lynn Grimes
Smith, Robin Rowell
Snyder, Frances Elizabeth
Sokolow, Karen E.
Som de Cerff, Johanna L.
Stafford, Graceanne
Steinfeld, Lauren Barnett
Stekler, Beth A.
Stephenson, Sheryl Naul
Stevens, Mary Elizabeth Glasheen
Stone, Georgia Sharon
Superko, Colleen
Tank, Margo H. K.
Tapscott, Barbara Musfeldt
Taylor, Lorri Ann
Teahan, Margaret Alice
Terwilliger, Lane Marlise
Tobin, Stacie Eileen
Torphy-Donzella, Elizabeth Ilene
Townsend, Darlene Elizabeth
Trageser, Stacie Diane
Turner, Deborah D.
Turner, Randi S.
Tyrrell, Judy Mathews
Tzou, Rebecca Landon
Ulgen, Carla Brigid
Vaias, Emily Jennifer
Valentine, Karen Marie
Valentino-Smith, Geraldine
Varner, Kim L.
Vazquez-Marty, Maria Jose
Warrenfeltz, Susan Marie
Washington, Eunice Harris
Weeks, Wendy Ann
Weikal, Wendy K.
Weiner, Lauri Ann
Weldon, Valerie Pettigrew
Welty, Pamela A.
Werner, Kathleen Marie
Wetsman, Lori B.
Wheeler, Glenda Mechelle
White, Deborah Rosen
Wilber, Kathryn Margaret
Wilhelm, Barbara Anne
Williams-Jones, Janice Lee
Williamson, Lisa Noel
Windham, Roberta Jean
Wobber, Kathleen Mary
Wolfe, Haleh Tavakol
Wonders, Kathryn Sue
Woods, Barbara Craig
Woodward, Tara Sky
Wrigley, Jill Lynne
Yourshaw, Cynthia Marie
Yu, Christina San
Ziegler, Marcie Robin
Zmuda, Jane McCarthy
Zuhowski, Susan
Zukerman, Margalete

12-18-1992
Casser, Karen Leslie
McLaurin, Claire Webber
Pilzer, Penny Ann

12-21-1992
DeBakey, Claire K.
Fields, Lynn C.
Mullane, Frances Hirschmann

12-29-1992
Farrar, Melissa Joan

12-30-1992
Johnson, Paula Camille
Stuart, Pamela Bruce
Young, Delores Ann

1-4-1993
Dodrill, Kimberly Carr
Friedman, Susan Balk
Harvey, Donna L.

1-7-1993
Bleyman, Anne
Conover, Carla
Freret, Carole A.
Huber, Victoria Marie
McCree, Heidi Bogardus
Roth, Claire Theresa
Sobel, Stacey Lee
Weiss, Jacquelyn
Winter, Ellen Sobel
Young, Dana Michelle

1-8-1993
Baach, Elise T.
Green, Denise Diane
Wessel, Jill Schlessinger

1-12-1993
Campoamor, Michele Lee

1-27-1993
O'Connell, Maureen Colette

2-4-1993
Allshouse, Cathy Cecile
Greenfeld, Helaine Ann
Macadam, Kimberly Anne
O'Brien, Tama
Paulson, Lele K.
Terry, Sharon Lee

2-9-1993
Hirschfield, Martha

2-18-1993
Ball, Pao Lin

3-1-1993
Bronte, Sharon

3-4-1993
French, Valerie C.
Lesperance, Jeannine Renee
Zimmerman, Dona Hope

3-8-1993
Wampler, Sherry K.

3-15-1993
Friedman, Debra Sue

4-5-1993
Grossman, Jessica L.

5-6-1993
Akers, Cynthia S.

6-3-1993
Wierman, Kathryn L.

6-14-1993
Green, CeLillianne
Horvitz, Laurie B.

6-15-1993
Goodman, Susan G.

6-17-1993
Henderson, Donna Jean
Sperduto, Kim Hoyt

6-18-1993
Nevius, Mary C.

6-21-1993
Curran, Diane J.
Robinson, Anita Earp
Sheehan, Angela Donovan
Shockley, Tamara A.

6-22-1993
Fisher, Marilyn M.

6-23-1993
Alden, Kristin Downs
Anielski, Tracy Louise
Atkins, Lesley Brand
Barranco, Lindsay Miller
Baumgarner, Marsha M.
Baxter, Jill McBride
Bell, Julie A.
Bell, Karen E.
Bennett, Kimberly Lacewell
Beraducci, Debra Anne
Bereston, Clara Melissa Martone
Bernstein Gaeta, Judith
Bjork, Sandra Smith
Bonardi, Sharonne Robinson
Bourke, Miriam Krell
Brabec, Elizabeth Anna
Bradley, Katherine Ann
Braunstein, Karen Lynn
Brissette-Minus, Kathy
Brown, Anna Lisa
Bullard, Karen Marie Froid
Burgett, Karen L.
Burgin, Gina M.
Byrley, Carolee Ireland
Carter, Jill Priscilla
Chabrow, Carolyn Debra
Chapman, Ruth Belville
Chernoff, Nancy Barnes
Cho, Jeannie Eun Kyung
Christello, Anna-Marie Teresa
Cogan, Ann Baer
Cohen, Jill Feingold
Cohn, Andrea Robin
Crary, Donna Louise
Cuffie, Frances Houston
Curtin, Yolanda Lauranzon
Cusick, Theresa Ann
Dale, Suzanne McGrath
Daly, Lisa Margaret
Danberg, Barbara Snapp
Davis, Margaret Roberts
DeMatteis, Cynthia Mary
Dennis, Alanna Wilkinson
Desverreaux, Jacquelyn N.
DiBacco, Christine Louise
Dobrov, Regina Victoria
Dominguez, Marie Therese
Donahue, Stephanie Foy
Doynov, Julia Bricker
Dubelier, Kristin Toini Landis
Dudley, Joan Charlene Bradley
Dudley, Sharon King
Eckert, Ann Marie
Ekweani, Ijeamaka N.
Encomienda, Maria Theresa C.
Engle, Jodee Lynn
Esfahani, Shari L.F.K.
Esmond, Brendy Bishop
Ettinger, Stacy Joy
Finlow, Leslie H.
Fiorentino, Kim Viti
Fitzpatrick, Kellyanne Elizabeth
Fleming, Lisa
Follansbee, Barbara Lynn
Ford, Delorice Price
Fraser, Lynn M.
Fritz, Tina Lynn
Gaeta, Judith Bernstein
Gaines, Martha Brune
Gallaher, Caroline D.
Ganiban, Elizabeth Rizzo
Gawthrop, Anne Elizabeth
Gil-Montero, Alexandra M.
Gill, Dahlia Ann
Grayson-Kelsey, ShaRon Marie
Greer, Bridgette Ann
Guthrie, Carolyn Nolde
Hackbarth, Margaret Ann
Haeckel, Dawn Kristine
Hanley, Jane Marie
Hanlon, Harriet Brown
Hardin, Jean Borkenhagen
Harleston, Bernice Anna Elizabeth
Harrison, Debra A.
Heneghan, Rena White

Hess, Geraldine Welikson
Hodges, Lisa Rene
Hogan, Marian L.
Hong, Jeannie J.
Hovatter, Debra Lee
Hughes, Beverly F.
Jackson, Jennifer Conron
Jacobo, Maria Patricia Castro
Jenefsky, Anna Elizabeth
Johnson, Denise Renette
Johnson, Renee L.
Jorgensen, Suzanne
Kamins, Rachel Marblestone
Kasten, Jenifer Nan
Kelly, Rose Marie
Kidner, Rebecca B.
King, Helena Ann
Kumar, Anjali
Lanois, Jill Ramirez
Latou, Bernice Lynne
Levin, Sharon G.
Levin, Toby Renee
Lewis, Susan Reid
Liddick, Kathy Jo
Lubin, Sandy
Lutz, Elizabeth M.
Lynch, Connie Robin
Mackert, Margaret Hartwell
Mandel, Pauline Ann
Marcus, Phyllis Hurwitz
Margolis, Judith Ellen
Maristch, Rita M.
Marsh-Armstrong, Kara
McFarland, Elizabeth A.
McGrath Dale, Suzanne
McIntyre, Stephanie Lyn
McLaughlin, Lisa Cresci
Miller, Juliane Corroon
Miller, Traci Kristine
Monaco, Elisabeth
Morrison, Mairi N.
Mulligan, Mary Jane
Munzell, Laura Kathleen
Murphy, Maureen Therese
Neustadt, Laurie Beth
Norman, Kathryn Murphy
Oh, Jessica Soonmi
Olsen, Elizabeth Yatco
Onyemaechi, Pauline Chinenye
Ottaviano, Deanne Marie
Patterson, Crystal Maria
Paul, Saswati
Pepper, Victoria Henry
Phinn, Melissa Marie
Pizzo, Mary J.
Porat, Liza Rachel
Power, Maureen J.
Pryor, Clara Dale
Quam, Laura Lee
Quirion, Jane Elaine
Rapp, Kathryn Mary
Reed, Kimberly Dawn
Reid, Deborah A.
Rennie, Kimberly Sue
Reznik, Carolyn Haya
Ritenour, Allison Ann
Roberson, Joi Lenore
Rogers, Margot M.
Romett, Joan Llewellyn
Ryan, Karin Marie
Schrein, Patricia L.
Scott, Fredrica Isabelle
Sherman, Bryn H.
Shipley, Twilah Stepter
Shotwell, Lynn Frendt
Silberbusch, Susan Milek
Silverman, Leslie D.
Silverstein, Susan Michele
Simpson, Suzanne Benvenuto
Snyder, Jill Robin
Snyder, Katherine A.
Spahn, Gay Ann
Spirt, Cynthia Dietz
Starrett, Sarah J.
Stipano, Claudine Noelle
Strama, Kimberly Lynn
Strom, Maria Kristina
Tanenberg, Ellyn Brandriss
Tanner, Julia K.
Theis, Kimberly A.
Vescio, Vanessa Catherine
Vitale, Clolita Maria
Wachen, Kimberly Anne
Wallace, Beverly Amy
Walter, Joan A. Gruner
Watson, Leticia Maria
Wescott, Carolyn Brennan
Williams, Andrea D.
Williams, Melzetta I. Knotts
Wirt, Laurie Blossom
Wood, Cassandra Leona
Yang, Yun Jung
Zent, Alice Marguerite
Zuercher, JoAnn Leigh

6-24-1993
Downey, Jane Lind

6-25-1993
Katz, Martha Lessman

6-28-1993
Hulbert, Victoria
Lecocq, Amy Michelle

7-1-1993
O'Donnell, Mary Park

7-6-1993
Sisson, Pamela Jeanne

7-16-1993
Pfarr, Kathryn

7-19-1993
Einstein, Laura F.

7-21-1993
Ross, Denise A.

8-10-1993
Garbis, Kendall Rose

9-2-1993
Winter, Margaret

9-8-1993
Etheridge, Jennifer K.

9-9-1993
Franklin, Susan L.
Katchka, Elizabeth Helen
Powers, Michelle Susan
Young, Martha Rose

9-30-1993
Hammer, Diann

12-2-1993
Albin, Mary Ellen
Begley, Margaret Curtin
Gould, Jill
McCullough, Harriet Gardenia

12-14-1993
Adeyeye, Valerie Vance
Akers, Margaret N.
Akins, Monica
Amato, Elita Ceta
Amrose, Sharon J.
Anderson, Paige Suzonne
Ardizzone, Kristen Kay
Ashbury, Heather Lee
Attias, Elizabeth Ellen
Audette, Rose Marie L.
Auer, Tanja Annette
Autieri, Nicole Felicia
Baccene, Karla Gayle
Bachkosky, Mary Michelle
Bailey, Suzin Carol
Ball, Scharon Lavear
Band, Kim-Haylee Loewenstein
Baroni, Tracy Lorraine
Barth, M. Krista
Bartley, Mary Victoria Esker
Bartos, Mila Finkelstein
Baylor-Thompson, Joyce Maezeppa
Beall, Rebecca Stewart
Behre, Nikki Snell
Bellanca, Amy Marie
Bellew, Sandra C.
Bender, Lisa Joy
Bennett, Kara C.
Berlin, Amy
Berlowe, Andrea L.
Bernstein, Susan
Bertola, Marta
Beyers, Carol J.
Binder, Andrea Berlowe
Blom, Brenda Bratton
Bookoff, Leslie I.
Borneman-Eckels, Janice
Bourbonnais, Christine J.
Brenneman, Lynn Edwards
Brizan, Glena Thelma
Brown, Amelia Logan
Brown, Barbara Ann Stewart
Bryant, Amy Davidson
Buckley, Kathleen Carlson
Busen, Janice Faith
Byrns, Melinda J.
Calkins, Lynn Estes
Callahan, Melissa Lee
Campolito, Becki Anne
Caramanica, Janice Faith
Carletta, Susan H.
Carmody, Carolyn Pauline
Cartwright, Kara Kinney
Case, Vera Lynne
Cavanaugh, Jodi Anneliese
Champlain, Laura Michele
Chesshire, Mary Claire
Chirolas, Christine Diane
Christensen, Jo Yolanda Maria Ippolito
Churchill, Diann Joy
Claypoole, N. Catherine
Clayton, Valerie Elizabeth
Conway, Corrie Fischel
Conway-Hatcher, Amy J.
Coover, Elizabeth A.
Corcoran, Christine Marie
Costas, Jennifer Anne
Coughlan, Traci Elizabeth
Crockett, Bonnie J.
Cross, Kim R.
Cudahy, Theresa Ellen
Cunningham, Yvonne Alphia
Daniel, Debra Yerg
Davis, Joanne L.
Desgalier, Kari Mason
Detling, Karen J.
Dewey, Elizabeth Renee
Dodge, Suzanne Elizabeth
Dohrer, Suzanne Marie
Drummond, Catherine Ann
Dubey, Susmita
Duclaux, Danielle M.
Dwyer, Adrienne Katherine
Edwards, Elizabeth Alice
Eichenmuller, Jennifer L. Johnson
Elkin, Molly Ann
Engram, Deborah Marie
Ervin, Inga Marie
Evelius, Karen Gessert
Everett, Felicia Williams
Faint, Mary Catherine
Farah, Hania E.
Farmer, Eileen Alice
Farrell, Alicia Anne
Fears, Shelly Jean
Feldmann, Linda Danielle
Ferris, Kimberly Ann
Finkler, Kira
Fisher, Jocelyn Marie
Fitzgerald, Patricia Barker
Flannery, Irene Marie
Fleishman, Tamar Alexia
Flood, Mary Anne
Force, Rae Ann
Forester, Georgina Yasue
Foster, Jody M.
Foughty-Deavers, Tracey S.
Fouts, Paulette Renee
Fowler, Margo S.
Fowler, Mary Katharine Antonia
Fraser, Lorraine Ebert
Freedman, Sharri Beth
Freeman, Judith
Fried-Rubin, Deborah
Frost, Jill Leslie
Galliani, Anastasia H.
Garey, Laurie Ann
Gbenjo, Anne Joyin Arinola
George, Allison Carr
George, Tracey E.
Germaise, Susan Lynn
Gerson, Susan Beth
Gilden, Violet Maret
Gill, Laura Leigh
Gill, Patricia Deon
Gilman, Michele Estrin
Gislason, Kristen Lee
Gitter, Rebecca Lynn
Giza, Laura Marie
Glinsmann, Maria Fuster
Goelman, Deborah M.
Goldmeier, Karen Elaine
Goolie, Jenifer Susan
Gottron, Denise Jaqueline
Gracia, Maria del Pilar
Grant, Paula Beth
Grau, Angela B.

Greenebaum, Susan Sann
Grena, Mary Ann
Griggsby, Lydia Kay
Grossman, Marla
Grotch, Gayle Rebecca
Halasz, Elizabeth Collins
Harris, Robin Janet
Horrigan, Lisa Carol
Howell, Sandra Foy
Hurley, Mary L.
McClure, Alexia Kent
Meoni, Susan Fitzgerald
Mouton, Sammie Lee
Murphy, Susanna Blake
Myers, Rebecca Dietz
Reed, Mary Lynn
Riley, Carrie Blackburn
Smyth, Colleen A.
Tancredi, Lisa Bittle
Terrenzi, Marisa Christine
Thomas, Laurie Breslin
Tow, Debra Ellen
Walcoff, Sheila Dearybury
Waxter, Ruth Allison
Weinberg, Paula Maria

12-15-1993

Billian, Dina
Bright, Loraine Lambert
Brisbin, Andrea Heffernan
Bruton, Kelly Ann
Budlow, Lisa Kahn
Chiesa, Abigail Mellin
Ciraolo, Caroline D.
Conover, Pamela Merlis
de Morgan, Dennise Noemi Longo
Dempsey, Cynthia Johnson
Duncan, Janell Mayo
Feigen, Georgina L. O.
Finegar, Natalie Ann McKeown
Frank, Jennifer Lee
Gabriel, Leanne
Gaskill, Valerie Lee Jackson
Gudsnuk, Sarah
Haller, Mary Beth
Hanson, Kathy
Head, Marla R.
Healy, Ava L.
Heller, Stacey Ilene
Heller-Ogden, Barbara
Henderson, Marigold K.
Herbert Lange, Desiree Michele
Herman, Miriam Florence
Hickey, Cynthia Armistead
Higashi, Kelly Ann
Hlavin, Jacqueline Ann
Hockensmith, Melissa Ottey
Hogan Vasquez, Mary Teresa
Hoke, Anne Elizabeth
Holadia, Manolita Akiko
Holden, Lisa A.
Hong, Patricia E.
Howell, Mary Elizabeth
Howells, Kelley Ann
Hurst, Melissa Ann
Ingersoll, Suzanne L.
Jackson, Bethany
Jackson, Lisa Lorraine
Jackson, Mary Beth Louise
Jackson Gaskill, Valerie Lee
Jacob, Nancy Susan
Jaudes, Phyllis Anne
Jenkins, Ellen Duffy
Jenkins, Terria P.
Jennis, Lisa Ellen
Joaquin, Pamela Schmidt
Johnson, Nancy Julius
Johnson, Sonja Jean
Jones, Andrea M.
Jones, Terri Ann
Jordan, Lisae Christine
Joseph, Martha E.
Judd, Kim Germaine
Kallins, Lauren Beth
Kane, Mary Lynne
Kayser, Susan M.
Keith, Melissa Ann
Kelly, Colleen A.
Khatri, Sheila H.
Kim, Cecilia Estelle
Kim, Sun Min
King, Susan Michals
Kingsley, Elizabeth Jane
Klink, Heather Anne
Knight, Mary Kathryn
Koch, Sherri Debra
Kocher, Heidi A.
Koeppel, Gabrielle
Koh, Patricia
Kordziel, Linda Liu
Kovac, Amy E.
Kowach, Kerrin McCormick
Krchnak, Karin Maria
Kressel, Marilyn F.
Krhounek, Kimberly Constance
Kroopnick, Emily C.
Kunin, Christy Cornell
Kursban, Mindy S.
Kwei, Mary Moody
Lander, Linette A.
Landmeier, Lisa M.
Lange, Desiree Michele Herbert
LaRosa, Mary Beth
Lassen, Wendy Anne
Leatherwood, Leslie Ann
Lee, Jennifer M.
Leete, Jennifer Sue
Leonhard, Sarah A.
Leslie, Kathleen Dick
Levine, Mia M.
Levitan, Lynn Rene
Libin, Nancy Crawford
Lindsey, Shirley A.
Long, Pamela Ann
Long, Tricia Johenning
Longanecker, Stacey Jean
Lowe, Diane Carol
Lucker, Leslie Anne
Lunis, Mary Guy
Lynch, Susan Carney
MacVittie, Lisa Anne
Maher, Karen Colleen
Mahoney, Kathleen Kibler
Majette, Gwendolyn Roberts
Mandel, Lauren Nicole
Mandis, Anita
Manning, Meredith
Marathe, Anupama V.
Marks, Stephanie Donna
Marquez, Melissa Marie
Marth, Ellen Ann
Martin, Julie Glass
Martinez, Wanda
Mathers, Carla Mae
Mathewson, Laurie McCutcheon
McCoy, Kimberly Anne
McGruder, Shawn Shyrlena
McGuckian, Rachel Theora
McInerny, Julia Wernett
McKinney, Rebecca Sue
McLean, Hae Kyung
McMorrow, Janice Lee
Medvetz, Thea M.
Mezick, Brenda A.
Michaels, Regina Victoria
Mitchell, Shauna Garlington
Mobley, Diane Kathleen
Montgomery, Sharen Morya
Moon, Mary Margaret
Moonan, Melisa Mara Cusolito
Moore, Cynthia Bonithia
Moscow, Karen Elizabeth
Moseley, Eileen Elizabeth
Mosley, Danielle Marie
Mosley, Monica
Moynihan, Kathleen Ryan
Murphy, Kathleen A.
Murphy, Maureen Ellen
Murphy, Michele Harrington
Muskus, Stephenie Suzanne
Nair, Katharine Gale
Neeb, Kimberly Ann
Neighbors, Cora Lee
Neiss, Dahlia Ida
Neun, Kristin Maria
Nimatallah, Leila
Nostrame, Catherine Anne
O'Brien, Kelly Leigh
O'Doherty, Maureen
O'Herlihy, Hilary Thomas Callaghan
O'Kane, Mona
O'Leary, Maureen
O'Neill, Evan Anne
Oliver, Nancy K.
Oliveri, Leslie D.
Ommaya, Shana Elizabeth
Orleans, Renee Sharon
Rafferty, Maria O'Sullivan
Rice, Mary Catherine
Roe, Karen Itkin
Saunders, Andrea Dawn
Schwab, Amy Hay
Siegel, Carla Markim
Smedley, Joan Kelso
Syms, Maria Mazzeo
Thomas, Donna M.D.
Vasquez, Mary Teresa Hogan
Vassallo, Barbara Ann Haas
Walsh, Annamaria M.
Walsh, Julie Christine Haanstad
Wiseman, Jennifer Holmes
Wright, Diane Elisabeth Kmak
Zane, Debra Gail

12-16-1993

Amiot, Susan Q.
Aylward, Jean Marie
Baechli, Maria Perugini
Brennan, Lisa Marie Shaw
Cammarata, Kimberly Stanton
Carroll, Elena T.
Cooper, Mary Platt
Dougherty, Madonna Lee
Dowell, Kimiyo Tahira
Eisner, Jill Rabineau
Gupta, Anirma Rakshpal
Harvey, Andrea Ries
Howe, Lisa Michele
Hrdy, Alice Saker
Keiser, Jennifer Rita
Ketterman, Karen Reisinger
Kincaid, Cassandra Lee
Kutler, Joanna Sambrook
Lankler, Tracey Splaine
Lardieri, Cheryl Zak
Lawrence, Kary Beth
Lewis, Jane R.
Majure, Kimberly Tan
Malone, Amy Kathleen
Marculewicz, Anne W.
Margolis, Sharon B.
Marshall, Kimberly Lisa
McShea, Mary G.
Morris, Paige Terry
Murphy, Trudy Voigt
Myers, Kimberly A. Talbert
Panos, Athena A.
Parker, Kim D.
Patton, Diane Chrismer
Penn, Laureen R.
Peper, Jennifer L.
Pergal, Patricia M.
Perry, Denise Michelle
Perry, Mary-Helen
Peyton, Melissa A.
Pineles, Nancy Susan
Pisano, Caroline Suzanne
Pisarchik, Joan Amelia
Plaza, Ann M.
Pleasant, Susan Rita
Poellinger, Allison Kathryn
Pommer, Virginia Rowan
Posa, Margaret Rose
Pratt, Catherine Randall W.
Preston, Diana L.
Price, Lori Hamilton
Primrose-Brown, Donna
Proctor-Williams, Stephanie E.
Pustilnik, Janel Tara
Pyle, Jennifer Mackay
Quash, Michelle Denise
Ramelmeier, Deborah Marie
Renehan, Alexa Ann
Reynolds, Ruthie G.
Rhoades, Anne Louise
Rhodes, Julia Ann
Ricard, Kathryn
Ricciardelli, Paula Ann
Riley, Sandra Ashworth
Roberts, Cheryl Yvette
Roberts, Stephanie A.
Robinson, Sally A.
Rodano, Wendy Rae
Rosenbusch, Arlene Miriam
Ross, Kimberly W.
Ross, Lisa Betsy
Rovner, Laura Lee
Russell, Tonye Michelle
Russian, Sheila Carol
Ryan-Boyle, Lisa Margaret
Sachs, Elisabeth A.
Said, Layla
Sanders, Rhonda Wood
Sandler, Samantha Beth
Santspree, Christine Michelle
Saunders, Michelle Renee
Savage, Jill Pickett

Scafidi, Susan
Schachter, Julie Ellen
Schmidt, Tamara L.
Schneider, Suzanne
Schuman, Mary Elizabeth
Schwartz, Louise H.
Seighman, Susan M.
Sender, Nancy
Shapiro, Ellen Louise
Sharp, Helen Joy
Shemuha, Angela J.
Shock, Mary Kathleen
Shoop, Lyn Goodman
Simmons, Katherine Ann
Singer, Jeanne Forrester
Sinopole, Roberta Clare
Skullney, Kathleen Susan
Small, Lisa Marie
Smedley, Marci Yerman
Smith, Gina Marie
Smith, Jennifer Marie
Smith, Justine DeLoris
Smith, Karen S.
Smith, Michele L.
Sopher, Jane Poland
Sorensen, Heidi A.
Sosland, Esther Abigail
Spellberg, Dianne Sydney
Spiegel, Carol Ann
Spottiswood, Karla Saguil
Steinman, Melissa Landau
Sterling, Debra G.
Stilt, Betty
Stroupe, Joyce A.
Suffoletta, Mary Christine Frances
Summers, Vilecia Cheriece
Sweeney, Bernadette
Sylvester, Jane C.
Tah, Christiana
Taylor, Purshelle Annette
Terhune, Karen Leigh
Theobalds, Elizabeth Dorothy
Thompson, Katherine Kole
Thurtle, Laurie Winkler
Toffenetti, Judith Lynn
Trainor-Fogleman, Dawn Patricia
Travers, Naomi Sandra
Treff, Jennifer Ward
Turner, Leslie Suzette
Uche, Ifeoma Anagam
Vadala, Valerie Victoria
Vadell, Adrienne Teresa
Vazquez, Laura
Venezia, Laura Nicodemi
Vie, Valerie Vanessa
von-Pervieux, Claudia A.
Vora, Sangeeta
Wagner, Ann Louise
Wagner, Jaconda
Walton, Jessica S.
Ward, Carrie M.
Waterston, Marilyn Kay
Waxter, Dixon Gibbs
Weaver, Elizabeth Ellen
Weaver, Traci Klute
Webster, Edith F.
Weishaar, Pamela Jean
Wendt, Cheryl Martha
Whiting, Iris Rita
Wiggins, Dawn Schenke
Wilds, Jeria Bridget
Wiley, Mary Jo
Williams, Elizabeth Zirkle
Williams, Faith Martha
Williams, Kathleen Marie
Williams, Sharlene E.
Wilson, Charlene Adelle
Windsor, Robyn Sommer
Wolfe, Lois Ann
Woodard, Karen Donnella
Worch, Gloria Ann
Wright, Julie Dameron
Yalof, Andrea Pierce
Yaniv, Orlie Natalie
Yontef-McGrath, Amy Lynn
Youn, Susie
Young, Kristin Ann
Zack, Mary Elizabeth

12-17-1993
Brooks-Rodney, Kim D.
Drakopulos, Teresa Erdodi
Frank, Cheryl R.
Paver, Fran L.
Portman, Barbara Lynne
Quinn, Kathleen Terese
Tahmin, Despina Mary
Willis, Kathleen Tenney
Woytek, Mary Elizabeth
Wyre, Myrtle Eugenie

12-20-1993
Schmiedeler, M. Teresa
Young, Jayne Frances

12-23-1993
Karmel, Randi L.

1-3-1994
Palmer, Julie Metzger

1-6-1994
Abbate, Julie Kathleen
Gruber, Moia Tamber
Injeian, Claire Russell
Johnson, Anita Catherine
Martella, Jennifer
Merritt, Yuka Ohashi
Pouliquen, Corinne Marie
Sadove, Elizabeth J.
Seiter, Elizabeth Alice

1-10-1994
Haggard, Loretta K.
Saunders, Kelly Ann
Turner, Ingrid Marie

1-12-1994
Brooks, Michelle Anne Gomez
Sangston, Robin H.

2-3-1994
Shah, Shefali
Vallance, Laura Jean
Wisnowski, Deborah A.

2-14-1994
Hickman, Gwendolyn M.

3-18-1994
Henry, Jeanett P.

4-7-1994
Eger, Esther Anne
McClure, Sarah B.

5-5-1994
Miller, Rachel McClain

5-25-1994
Mazur, Cynthia Stelle

6-2-1994
Forbes, Danielle Marie
Guss, Karen Rose
Hu, Kathryn Rose
Osanloo, Arzoo

6-14-1994
Freeman-Ford, Patricia Ann

6-15-1994
Glushakow-Smith, Frances Sue

6-16-1994
Briglia, Shannon J.
Ochsman, Joanne

6-17-1994
Hairston, Abbey G.
Lord, Sandra

6-20-1994
Finlay, Ellen
Glazer, Sherry A.

6-23-1994
Anderson, Mary Ellen
Angelari, Marguerite
Bailey, Anita Matyi
Baldwin, Deborah Lynn
Baldwin, Mary Coale
Banisky, Sandra Anne
Bazaral, Teresa Tatham
Belendiuk, Lydia Eugenia
Bertoni, Susan Ruppert
Bethel, Thecla
Biberaj, Buta
Biggs, Neda
Bland, Karen LaShann
Bollini, Julia Alessandra
Brandon, Gina Maria
Brown, Danielle D.
Brzezynski, Lora A.
Cabral, Susan Carol
Canton, Denise S.
Cardin, Jan Klinek
Chapman, Kathleen Ann
Cheung, Kathering Ying Kit
Cicone, Linda Marie
Citko, Holly K.
Clark, Geneva Laurence
Cohen, Phyllis Marian
Collins, Jo Ann Petroziello
Collins, Sheri Mariko Lyons
Coons, Margaret Mary
Corcoran, Julia Ann
Corryn-Blessing, Tracey Kathleen
Culberson, Wendy Barrow
Cumming, Isabel Mercedes
Daly, Sarah Dyson
Davis, Ellen Fox
Delahanty, Kathryn Ann
Dellheim, Helen Lee
DeLony, Rieyn
Donovan, Helen Marie
Drain, Aluanda R.
Dravo, Andrea Nora
Eastberg, Kathleen
Evans, Velma E.
Fair, Tressa M.
Fairbrother, Margaret K.
Fondren, Kimberly Lynn
Foreman, Marie Ajali
Freeman, Felicia McGhee
Giblin, Rita McAndrews
Gilbert, Karen Lynn
Gilsenan, Jennifer Marie
Givens, Tracy Riller
Glynn, Jennifer S.
Gonzalez-Scarano, Frances Giovanna
Googins, Linda M.
Gorman, Karen Ponton
Green, Bonnie Ellen
Green, D'Arcy Nicole
Green, Glenda N.
Greene, Shari Elizabeth
Grimes, Suzanne Marie
Guerrin, Mary Ellen
Hall, Lisa Boylan
Hare, Constance M.
Harrison, Elizabeth Ann
Hartmann, Wendy A.
Hoffpauir, Norma Briscoe
Hughes, Dianne Moorehead
Isaac, Peyton Stepney
Janss, Jennifer Lahn
Johnson, Kim Yvette
Johnson, Octavia R.
Johnson-Norman, Karen V.
Jolivet, Kendra Randall
Jones, Lisa Harris
Jorgensen, Setareh Sanjar
Kaplan, Kimberly Melissa
Karlin, Karen S.
Kasemeyer, Pamela Metz
Kaufman, Susan
Kearns, Anne Elizabeth
Kelly, Lisa Michelle
Kelly, Rebecca Adams
Kessler, Laura T.
Koenig, Karen B.
Kohl, Barbara Louise
Kozlowski, Laura Bare
Lantz, Penelope A.
Lawless, Sue
Lawson-Jackson, Edith Aven
Lazarus, Ronna
Lee, Dana Christine
Loane, Cheryl Ann
Loube, Nancy Jane
Lumpkin, Alice Seney
Lundgren, Georgia Campbell
Malan, Janis H.
Mannino, Melissa Blake
Margolis, Donna Pearlman
Marsh, Abigail Hughes
Mason, Wanda Denise
McAndrews Giblin, Rita
McCarthy, Carol M.
McGaughey, Ingrid Johnson
McNeil, Susan E.
Meaney, Deborah Ann
Merritt, Dawana Denean
Mezzack, Janet Lynne
Miller, Fiona Kimberly
Miller, Patricia Beth
Morris, Deborah Lynn
Moseley, Diann Curry
Mtimet, Michelle Darling
Mullen, Lauren Clineburg
Murphy, Susan G.
Nack, Emily Ann
Nacrelli, Renee

Nakhuda, Carol M.
Negin, Alexandra Paradis
Nueslein, Mary Kay
O'Brien-Holcomb, Diane Jeanette
Ordynsky, Eugenia
Palacio, Monica
Pople, Deborah Ann
Price, Anne Ruth
Ralph, Regan Elisabeth
Reilly, Ellen G.
Ricks, DeBora M.
Ricks, Valda G.
Ringel, Susannah Zoe
Roberts, Nancy J.
Robinson, Stephanie Jeanne
Rodriguez, Elizabeth Delgado
Rollman, Sarah Olivia
Rosenblum, Mandy Caren
Sanders, Jennifer Lynn
Schiavo, Mary Fackler
Sell, Nancy Anne
Seto, Tania Manoa
Shoenberg, Dana Lynne
Sinclair, Allyson Clark
Skinner, Sonia Lerlene
Skor, Anita M.
Southard, Kathryn W.
Spencer, Susan Lee
Stancil, Lisa Joi
Stapleton, Carol Marie
Stoudt, Juliet MacMillan
Taylor, Susan Elizabeth
Terry, Andrea Clare
Theodore, Eyphemia Stamos
Thompson, Alexandra
Tippett, Veronica Denise McLaughlin
Tischhauser, Carol Diane
Trujillo, Patricia
Tulloch, Rebecca W.
Turk, Beverly Ann
Turner, Tiffany Faye
van Bergen, Carol
Vick, Vanessa L.
Warning, Kiersten Elise
Wheeler, Sherry J.
Willis, Stacey North
Wilson, Marcella Gragg
Winston-Graham, Mara Pierette
Yang, Barbara Moon
Zachman, Janis Hutchins

6-26-1994
House, Deborah Mary

6-28-1994
Irons, R. Elizabeth

6-29-1994
Ziegler, Ann E.

7-6-1994
Bamberger, Carolyn M.
Binger, Cherie A.
Brown, Lillian M.
Champi, Elaine K.
Dolginow, Angela Tysk
Gardineer, Grovetta N.
Legg, Janet Sue
Payne, Emarie Stock
Purrington, Debra L.
Sacks, Susan Brickerd
Weiss, Lessa N.
Wynshaw-Boris, Diane Elise

7-7-1994
Rottenberg, Julie Beth

7-11-1994
Keenan, Kim Michele
Thompson, Helen Barbara
Walsh, Stephanie Katherine

7-12-1994
Case, Sara Stevenson

7-25-1994
Cox, Ann McCutchan
Kordeleski, Kathleen Mary
Steiger, Patricia Sadler

7-27-1994
Paul, Katherine Larner

7-29-1994
Stern, Deborah

8-4-1994
Farrell, Megan Catherine

8-29-1994
Borell, Caroline Marie
Singer, Jana Beth

8-30-1994
Gomez, Marisa A.

9-6-1994
Creech, Anne Wyant

9-8-1994
Colette, Elizabeth
Flaxman, Lisa J.
Gagnon, Michele Renee
Grant, Kimberly Stefanik
Lane, Lisa Kelly
Leighty, Jody Anderson
Maiden, Stacey Crowell
Quin, Alison Joan
Roemer, Stefanie Frances
Spicer, Patricia Mary

9-14-1994
Kamborian, Lisbeth N.

9-20-1994
Klarman, Marie Elena

9-29-1994
Caldwell, Stacey Turner
Fogarty, Marie

11-3-1994
Sumner, Patricia Ann

12-12-1994
Athay, Margaret Ann
Brust, Jennifer A.
Gayle, Alana Patrice
James, Monica Best
Welch, Melissa Elizabeth

12-13-1994
Adams, Sarah A.
Afsahi, Parisa Michelle
Agee, Danielle Charise
Alderfer, Ruth Ellen
Allen, Karen June
Allen, Rachel Dosseos
Anderson, Alisha Amburgey
Andresen, Judy
Athias, Gretchen Kendall
Baar, Lisa Paulette
Bagby, Kelly Riseden
Bailey, Lyn Anne
Baker, Renata Jeanne
Baker-Battist, Ruth S.
Balaguer, Donna Ann
Baldanzi, Stephanie A.
Barber, Shelley Elizabeth
Barchi, Cathy A.
Bayne, Katherine Anne
Bean, Lori Ann
Bearsch, Laura V.
Beaty, Shari Lynn
Beestman, Joan Ardith
Belasco, Lisa A.
Benson, Barbara Leigh
Binder, Farrell Anne
Bjorklund, Andrea Kay
Blanchard Cook, Carolyn Rae
Blauman, Amy Lynne
Blockson, Taua Jenielle
Borden, Debra Sherise
Bourbon, Margaret Theresa
Bowers, Lynn A.
Bradford, Dana E.W.
Brandel, Abigail Elizabeth
Brandt, Avalon S.
Brown, Shelly Lawon
Bruun, Lori Lyman
Buchanan, Julie Barrie
Burgess, Cindy Lynn
Calia, Lauren Ruth
Caputo, Margaret Ellen McNamara
Carroll, Karen E.
Carroll, Linda Sahid Hudroge
Case, Lauren Elizabeth
Casper, Kelly A.
Cattell, Robin Rice
Chase, Alycia Wojtowicz
Chavez, Maria Ellena
Chiriboga-Roby, Patricia
Chrein, Molly C.
Christmas-DeBerry, Sharon Yvette
Clark, Marjon Monir
Clark, Robin Ann
Claypoole, Kathryn D.
Cleesattle, Jodi Lynn
Conrad, Amy Elizabeth
Cook, Carolyn Rae Blanchard
Coyle, Anna Margaret
Creswell, Jennifer L.
Crittendon, Shari Fawn
Cronan-Yorick, Anne Elizabeth
Crowley, Patricia Carroll
Dailey, Mitzi Elaine
Damelin, Fara
Dandeker, Rebecca L.
Darrow, Susan Elizabeth
Daugherty, Kathleen Diane
Davenport, Lisa M.
Davidson, Jennifer Ann
Davis, Paula Louise
Davison, Gabrielle Giselle
Deegan, Colleen Anne
Delbert, Susan M.
Delivorias, Linda
Demers, Margaret Bass
Diamond, Valerie Frances
Dimon, HelenKay
Djurickovic, Natalija Slobodan
Dobres, Leslie Joy
Doherty, Karen M.
Dorney, Linda M.
Downs, Kirsten Gettys
Dresner, Zita Zatkin
Duke, Nicole Chapin
Dunn, Alexandra Dapolito
Egan, Erin Margaret
Egan, Nancy Jean
Ehlenberger, Carol Lynne
Einhorn, Monique F.
Eisenberg, Jamie Bryna
Emry, Felicia A.
Estrada, Linda Michelle
Evans, Joy Van Blerkom
Evans, Terri Lee
Fanaroff, Carolyn Diane
Farahati, Britta
Fatica, Erin Kathleen
Feghali, Rouda M.
Ferguson, Susan Hunter
Fields, Beverly Ann
Fisher, Maura Christine
Flynn, Deborah Lassman
Fountain, Dorothy Bean
Frame, Tara K.
Freedman, Callista Marie
Freeland, Rebecca Lynn
Futrovsky, Julie Ann
Gaffney, Sylvia Polonsky
Gallagher, Anne Barlow
Gardner, Catherine B.
Garrett, Bridgett Andrea
Garvey, Melissa Jeanne
Gastwirth, Laura-Leigh L.
Gavin, Beth A.
Gilbert, Rebecca Lynne
Girod, Gayle R.
Glickman, Ilene Beth
Goldman, Deborah Beth
Goldman, Elana Natalie
Good, Courtenay Sherrill
Gorman, Ann
Gorman, Debora Ann
Grasso, Jeanne M.
Green, Debra Jill
Green, Valerie Lavet
Greenaway, Karen A.
Hardwick, Maureen Donahue
Hare, Ellen Berkowitz
Hutchinson, Lynn Dymond
Jacobs, Laura Basem
Jacobs, Ruth Margaret DeCoursey
Jennings, Sharon Cizek
Kapani, Manisha Deshmukh
Kendrick, Karen L.
Kerns, Janis Fonda
Little, Miriam Reynolds
Lupo, Robyn Behrman
Moffet, Sandra Grant
Nixon, Belinda Elvan
Philip, Sheila Fay
Poling, Terry Dodson
Ritz, Amy Felice
Ruxton, Katherine Bayne
Saadeh, Catherine M.
Sands, April Juanita
Smith, Susan A.
Steinzor, Rena I.
Storer, Carrie Dove
Sturgess, Beth Burwick
Tanner, Colleen Durkin

12-14-1994
Alexandrides, Athena Katcheves
Alley, Kimberly Ann
Arnquist, Lisa O'Mara
Baynes, Bonnie L.
Colvin, Shannon O'Hara
Cooke, Donna Libretti
Corcoran, Carrie Howie
Crane, Colleen Ann
Culton, Karen L.
Curran, Jennifer Henkle
Duffy, Elizabeth A.
Endries, Karen Holt
Flicker, Mona Lisa
Frazier, Susannah Jones
Gillan, Nona Kaufman LaPlante
Goodman, Ann Karwacki
Gravelle, Anna Katharina Margarete
Groves, Athena Malloy
Guarnero, Lisa Morelli
Gustafson, Suzanne Marie
Gustavson, Karen Ruth
Hani, Tiffany Heitzenrader
Hansen, Mary Lorraine
Harlan, Sarah Pazourek
Harley-Boyce, Atina S.
Harrison, Faith Eidelman
Hayes, Jennifer M.
Heise, Leah Marie
Highsmith, Rhonda Lee
Hildebrandt, Sharon L.
Hines, Shalisha Nanette
Hippen, Sherrilyn Annette
Hoffman, Laura L.
Holman, Monica Tynese
Hoskins, Anne Elizabeth
Hough, Robin Noelle McDaniel
Hubin, Diane Dearman
Huesman, Jennifer Lilore
Hung, Suzy Chan
Hyatt, Randi Klein
Ibarra, Cristina
Jackson, Anne Marie
Jackson, Betsy Grabel
Jackson, Denise Elaine
Jamison, Janice Marie
Johnson, Jennifer Anne
Johnson, Monica J.
Jones, Cynthia Holly
Jones, Debra Ann
Joyner, Alicia D.
Just, Marjorie
Kaufman, Teri
Kazemian, Parisa
Kelley, Carol A.
Kelly, Deanna R.
Kennedy, Linda
Kersey, Laura Lynn
King-Garappolo, Tracey Jean
Koh, Debra
Kolm, Christine Garcia
Koslov, Tara Isa
Kramer, Stacey Beth
Kundra, Chaya
Kunkle, Regina Veronica
Landbeck, Marlise Suzon
Lane, Shannon Valerie
Lee, Gloria Hyun
Leinbach, Susan E.
Leonard, Patricia Anne
Levine, Lisa Lebhar
Limbrick, Kimberly Lynn
Liu, Yan
Lobo, Deborah Evelyn
Loewy, Dina
Long, Karen O'Donnell
Longobardi, Cynthia Jean
Love, Tonya DeLour
Lovoy, Elizabeth Clare
Lubetkin, Beth Andrea
Macht, Alisa Ann
Mack, Kristina Ann
Macon, Ava-Lisa Frances-Ann
Mahallati, Sussan Lee
Mainigi, Enu A.
Mairs, Stephanie L.
Major, Sandra Marie
Mandell, Rachel Batya
Manley, Evelyn
Mann, Laura J.
Manning, Nadine Anne
Marcin Tomalty, Sarah Elaine
Mark, Jeany Chan
Markun, Susan Arlene
Martz-Bowles, Michelle
Mathur, Kamana
McDanial Hough, Robin Noelle
McGill, Paula Jeanette
McHugh, Jennifer Buehler
McKenna, Anne Toomey
McKeon, Shelly Diahn
McLean, Mary Park
McNamara, Jacqueline Mohyla
Meeks, Nicole Marie
Mevorah, Mirjam Karin
Middleton, Laura Delano
Miller, Elizabeth Heath
Miller, Sheryl Rosensky
Moffet, Stacey A.
Montez, Angela C.
Moore, Theresa Lynne
Morgan, Elizabeth Ann
Morris, Gwen Mulberry
Moss, Cheryl Bernadette
Moylan, Lauri McEntire
Muneses, Cecilia Marie Cabatingan
Murphy, Anne
Murphy, Kathleen C.
Murphy, Linell Cristina
Murphy, Lori Michelle
Nassirian, Maura Nicolosi
Nejaime, Nadia Barbara
Nicolini, Maria
Nixon, Lynn Marie
Norris, Denice Renee
Norton, Marci Beth
Nottle, Lorelle Jeanine
Nunziato, Dawn Carla
O'Dea, Catherine Marie
O'Herron, Margaret M.R.
Ohrin, Lisa Marie
Okediji, Adenike Pamela
Oliveri, Susan Lynn
Opgenorth, Joanne Marie
Ortiz, Alexis Antonio
Overton, Amy Elizabeth
Owens, Amanda C.
Owens, Kerry H.
Panos, Cynthia Setien
Parakkal, Kalpana Monika
Patterson, Elizabeth Kay
Quast, Aimee J.
Ringness, Katherine D.
Scarbath, Lisa Marie
Schiller, Tara M.
Seitz, Tracey King
Shorey, Melissa Menkel
Sifford, Lisa Monica
Tomalty, Sarah Elaine Marcin
Valocchi, Beth E. Evans
Ziegler, Victoria E.

12-15-1994
Anguilla, Carol J.
Arnold, Ariana Wright
Arroyo Cochran, Victoria Annette
Belmar, Susan Marie
Beron, Joan D.
Bessin, Sarah Aline
Carmody, Pamela W.
Casaleggi, Lois T.
Clancy, Catherine Rafferty
Cochran, Victoria Annette Arroyo
Cooper, Michelle Perim
Crittendon, Renee Roland
Crunkleton, Rose C.
Depman, Anne Pijar
Desai, Monica Shah
Eisenberg, Deborah Thompson
Ford, Melvina Carrie
Gallagher, Laura S.
Gallo, Kathleen
Gordon, Kimberly Williams
Gottshall, Justine Young
Hardzog, Lisa Anne
Harris, Lee Solomon
Harris, Stacey Winakur
Iley, Brooke Thomas
Ireland, Kathy Davidson
Johnson, Cheryl Sellers
Johnson, Marci Tarrant
Karas, Karen Simonek
Kepple, Cristine A.
Knee, Kathryn
Korrell, Elizabeth W.
Kumar, Mita Shukla
Maged, Jennifer Ann
McKirgan, Tracey Ann
Menschenfreund, Kerry L.
Nemphos, Claudia Ross
Pasekoff, Andrea Jill
Patel, Darshana Dinubhai
Pazak, Cheryl A.
Pellow, Wendy Marie
Penn, Ilene R.
Perry, Kimberly Boulware
Petras, Mary Manning
Phillips, Susana Elena
Phoenix Tildon, Rhonda Fern
Pike, Sandra Gilbert
Pisegna-Cook, Evelyn Deborah
Plummer, Michele Ann
Pokras, Anne
Prangley, Anne Marie Brown
Pressman, Sandra D.
Puckett, Anne Lynne
Puhala, Susan Faith
Quinn, Candida S.
Rafalko, Julia Sara
Raivel, Mary Elizabeth Scannell
Rankin, Jennifer Lee
Ratel, Rachel Singer
Reeves, Marsha Yvette
Regen, Claudia Gabrielle
Reid, Jeannine M.
Reidy, Karen Teresa
Reynolds, Melissa Morgan
Rhee, Helen Ruth
Riccardi, Jennifer Danner
Richardson, Aimee Noel
Richter, Jeanne Holborow
Ridge, Lisa Mills
Robinson, Angele Kimberly
Rook, Mary Grace Riley
Rose, Cheryl Tobi
Rose, Erica
Rosenberg, Samantha
Rosenstein, Jill Ellen
Rosenthal-Goldsmith, Dayna Renee
Ryan, Denise Marie
Sacks, Jamie Heather
Sakalauskas, Lina S.
Saltz, Debra A.
Sandler, Rene
Saunders, Sharon Michelle
Savage, Sarah Elizabeth
Savagner, Mary
Schmid, Julie
Scoville, Tamara Van Antwerp
Seafer, Mindi Debra
Seaton, Elizabeth Ann
Sedlacko, Jean S.
Selover, Linda B.
Shapiro, Julie Kate
Sharara, Norma Meinert
Sharkey, Jennifer Conway
Shomali, Maha Elias
Silber, Stacy Plotkin
Simon, Lisa R.
Simpson, Kathryn Loker
Slamowitz, Christy A.
Smiley, Alison Jill
Smith, Nancy A.
Snively, Susan Hall
Song-Kurlander, Elise
Starbuck, Julie Ann
Steely, Janice Lynn
Strasser, Kimberly Cunningham
Strausser, Kristin Barbara
Street, Sharon Stanley
Strong, Rachel Lisa
Strott, Lynn W.
Su, Jeannie
Sud, Anu
Sullivan, Jean Anne
Sulzbach, Denise Cave
Sun, Grace HaeYoung
Tafro, Angela Virginia
Thompson, Holly Lincoln
Throne, Kelly Ann
Tildon, Rhonda Fern Phoenix
Timberlake, Deana Lateefah
Timpf, Kristen Elizabeth
Toms, Edith Lynn
Tufts, Tamar A.
Tung, Melanie Hsaoyun
Vanderstar, Thankful Townsend
Verveer, Alexandra
Vierra, Donna Christine
Walters, Janet A.
Washburn, Amy Irene
Wasserman, Lori B.
Weathersbee, Lara Christine
Weaver, Rebecca A.
Webb, Deborah Lynn
Weber, Rose Marie

Wecker, Rita L.
Weiner, Tammy G.
Weissman, Jill Amy
Whaling, Elizabeth S.
Whiteford, Meg Bantley
Wilkerson, Chana S.
Williams, Dawanna L.
Williamson, Lynn Clarice
Winograd, Beth A.
Witherup, Margaret M.
Wittenberg, Susan
Wood, Joann M.
Woods, Catherine Field
Yarington, Barbara J.
Yellin, Nancy Sara
Yoon, Suzanne Chi Sook
Zimolzak, Joanne Lydia
Zucker, Irene E.
Zuknick, Rosmary Celia

12-16-1994
Donovan, Priscilla Alden
Fraser, Anne H.S.
Patterson, Mary Burke

12-19-1994
Elkan, Linda Gyrsting
Ng Lau, Ruby T.W.

12-22-1994
Witherspoon, Sharon

12-23-1994
DeMille-Wagman, Deborah J.

1-3-1995
Hawthorne, Ellen L.
Pirsch, P. Elizabeth

1-5-1995
Belmont, Madra Michelle
Delsole, Ellen Page
Gery, Erin Quinn
Greene, Marcy Alice
Litsinger, Karen Miriam
Matonich, Julie
Moylan, Cara Barrett
Petry, Sharlene Elizabeth
Pichney, Valerie Beth
Roberts, Lauren Geralynn
Schweitzer, Michele Lynn

1-9-1995
Force, Melissa K.

1-17-1995
Bridge, Ellen Fishler
Fishler Bridge, Ellen
Miller, Denise Arenth
Peters, Ann Sara

1-18-1995
Abeles, Damaris S.

1-30-1995
Kelly, Arlette

2-2-1995
Moore, Kimberly Ann
Quamina, Lesia H.
Schutjer, Linda Jo
Woodka, Janet Lynne

3-2-1995
Kiely, Elise Porcher Wheeless

3-14-1995
Long, Elisa Ann

3-24-1995
Raman, Elizabeth Pearl

4-6-1995
Reiz, Joyce Esther

4-10-1995
Philipps, Laura Michele

5-4-1995
Feng, Wendy L.
Scott, Melissa E.

5-16-1995
Naas, Lindsay R.

5-25-1995
Small, Kirsten Elena

6-1-1995
Burke, Melissa A.
Shah, Pamira

6-15-1995
Bartlett, Christine Ann

6-19-1995
Leonard, Vally G.

6-21-1995
Abrams, Miri C.
Ahlers, Lynn Zahurak
Akparanta, Helen Ekenma
Alexander, Renee Ann
Almond, Ann Jalynn
Anderson, Laura Elisabeth
Ascher, Margaret Phoebe
Asher, Jacqueline Louise
Bae, Alice Mira
Bahymer, Cheryl Lynne
Bailey, Louise Marie
Baker-Simon, Patricia A.
Bartley, Margaret
Bedore, Elizabeth Noel
Behymer, Cheryl Lynne
Belanger, Terri A.
Benjamin, Jill Marie
Bennett, Patricia Ann
Benson, Susanna Storm
Bhambri, Vandna Wendy
Bjork, Lori Ann
Blatt, Paula Eileen
Blazek, Katherine Merrell
Blumner, Linda Butler
Botts, Tina Fernandes
Branning, Amy Huang
Brinkley Lefkowitz, Ruth Holloway
Brunyansky, Tracey J.
Bullock, Kristina Anne Zimmerman
Butler, Lisa Jeanne
Cahill, Kelly Ann
Calhoun, Erica Chorsie
Caminos Geraghty, Corina P.
Camp, Paula Diane
Campbell, Susan Yvonne
Casula, Denise Marie
Chittick, Stacy Paxson
Chynoweth, Ann P.
Ciccarone, Selma Vives
Clarke, Julia Susan
Cobb, Stephanie Denyse
Cockburn, Vivien Jo
Cohen, Lisa E.
Coley-Lawrence, Natalie Barbara
Coner, Kenyetta R.
Cooper, Kathy Lynne
Cooper, Rhonda L.
Cresswell, Susan Mary
Critides, Elaine Demetra
Crockett, Cynthia Esparza
Cusumano, Leanne
Dacres, Karen Denise
Daniel, Sandra S.
Danoff, Aliza Ann
Davis, Debra Marie
Davis, Lisa Kimberley
Davison, Janice G.
Dawkins, Laura M.
Deardorff, Yvonne Yingling
Devine, Jennifer
Doss, April Falcon
Dumpson, Kimberly Conway
Dursee, Kim Marie
Dutton, Diane J.
Dziadulewicz, Lisa Ann
Englert, Sicilia Si Chi
Fearer, Kathleen E.
Finn, Tamar E.
Ford, Susan Lee
Fortier, Evelyn E.
Gangi, Claudia B.
Garavi, Behrooz
Garber, Julie Ann
Geraghty, Corina P. Caminos
Gianneschi, Lisa Ventresca
Giannino, Sharon Duval
Gidumal, Sonya
Gilfrich, Nathalie Kathleen Hasson
Glass, Laura Anne
Gold, Dina M.
Goodman, Elizabeth Cahn
Gordon, Paula Natalie
Gorman, Erin Eileen
Green, Karin L.
Greene, Katherine
Hadad, Leah
Handman, Martha L.
Hannan, Wendy C.
Hansen, Angela Holliday
Hansen, Kimberly Jurney
Harper, Michele Rene
Harrison, Tara Angelique
Hart, Michele Lynnette
Hasson Gilfrich, Nathalie Kathleen
Hatter, Debra Gatison
Hayes, Gina Clark
Heimlicher, Lisa C.
Heinrichs, Jane Ganz
Henderson, Cynthia Chillura
Henry, Kimberly A.
Hetherington, Kim
Hickman, Kristy Melker
Hoffman, Rebecca E.
Holton, Melissa Anemojanis
Hsu, Amber Wong
Hsu, S. Dana
Hudson, Anndreeze V.
Hurley, Caroline Graves
Hutton, Carla Noel
Jadlowic, Christine R.
Janosek, Diane Marie
Kammel, Carole Renee
Karaganis, Joan Jacqueline
Karkowsky, Nancy Faye
Kataria, Neeta
Kaufmann, Doreen Burns
Keane, Alison Ann
Kim, Angela S.
Kim, Sunny
Kinnett, Rebekah Jane
Kirsh, Rachel Lynn
Kline, Sara Needleman
Koermer, Kelly Ann
Kohn, Karen M.
Kuwamura, Diane Kay
Lefkowitz, Ruth Holloway Brinkley
Leight, Elizabeth Ysla
Lew, Pamela
Lock, Cynthia Alison
Lofton, Yalonda Denyce
Loiseau, Holly E.
Long, Clarisa
MacDonald, Margaret DuFour
Maldonado, Andrea L.
Malefyt, Mary Beth
Manuelides, Kimberly Anne
Marceca, Andrea Rene
Markowitz, Stacy Lynn
Maroldy, Laura M.L.
Maxfield, Melissa
Mayer, Andrea Laura
McComas, Lauren E.
McGillan, Patricia Mary
McInerney, Kelly Ann
McInnes, Hollace Hart
McNaught, Kathleen Marie
Merk, Melinda Sue
Moody, Karen Patrice
Morton, Laura Guadalupe
Moser, Elizabeth Bright
Mullen, Cathleen Anne
Murphy, Erin H.
Neal, Lauren Renee
Nelson, Elizabeth Thayer
Noel, Julie Ann
Officer, Susan Lukecart
Ogebe, Morenike
Orem, Vicky Lynn
Parker, Deborah L.
Parker, Kimberly A.
Parks, Anna Lee
Pegues, Elicia Tamara
Perez-Fowler, Carmina
Pilgrim, Shirleen Marie Elsie
Plagata-Neubauer, Christine M.
Priaulx, Sharmon Veronica
Raphael, Rachelle Hillary
Rico, Lisa M.
Riley, Pamela Kauffman
Rissman, Julie B.
Riviears, Sandra Humphries
Rockwood, Mary Lloyd
Roth, Jeanne Maria
Ruttenberg, Miraim Helen
Salb, Shannon Micah
Sample-Johnson, Paula Danita
Santin, Amy J.
Schaefer, Linda Matisans
Schatz, Julie Pearlman
Scheiner, Toni Renee
Schlesinger, Victoria Alexandra
Schwartz, Keira Lynne
Scofield, Susan Werner

Shapiro, Susan Stobbart
Sheehan, Karen Preset Overly
Shepard, Sara
Simon, Marnie Ellen
Smith, Gwendolyn Chisholm
Smith, Tuwanda M.
Solomon, Dori Beth
Solomon, Gregg Nicole
Srinivasagam, Kamala Marian
Stadler, Linda Louise
Stewart, Jelahn
Strikis, Silvija Anna
Sullivan, Julie Marie
Swaby, Sharon E.
Taler, Gustava E.
Taylor, Rebecca Lynn
Thomas, Debra
Tilghman, Lavertta E.
Toffolo-Cresce, Mary Elizabeth
Turco, Jessica Ann
Walters, Leah Janette
Washington, Pamela B.
Wecker, Kerri A.
Wilkinson, Eleanor Ann
Williams, Gaye Michelle
Wood, Patricia Ann
Woodward, Danae Christina
Wu, Sandra Mo-Har
Wynter, Astrid Helena

6-23-1995
Harrison, Stephanie
Kaufman, Joan Gordesky

6-26-1995
Lewis, Eleanor J.

6-27-1995
Simmonds, Denise Antoinette

6-28-1995
Clay, Michelle Catherine

6-30-1995
Muss, Marguerite Ashlie

7-6-1995
Gamble, Janelle Francis

7-7-1995
Gitlin, Stephanie Marmelstein
Mancusi, Kathy
Marshall, Linda Geisler
Phillips, Alice Anna

7-10-1995
Darmstadter, Celeste Virginia Lagarde

7-14-1995
Artz, Cherie

7-17-1995
Reiskin, Terri Steinhaus
Ruben, Brenda C.

7-18-1995
Grogan, Stephanie J.

7-20-1995
Armbrust, Patricia Moriarty
Gately, Caroline Petro
Hannon, Debra S.
Stafford, Kristie Kunau

7-21-1995
Rosenau, Susan Hansen

7-25-1995
Coe, Cynthia A.
Steele, Shari

7-26-1995
Whitaker, Janet Kay

7-27-1995
Bren, Vicki L.

8-10-1995
Levy, Stefanie Sanders
Semmelman, Karen L.

8-11-1995
Grunberg, Nancy Roberts

8-28-1995
Chung, Won-Kyung Wendy
Nadler, Judith Leenov
Procaccino, Andrea Fay
Voorhees, Virginia S.

9-7-1995
Berthiaume, Laura Vaught Farthing
Carrillo, Maria Mercedes
Hoffman, Bonnie Hope
Sardeson, Nancy Jean

9-11-1995
Chabrow, Claudia Schoenberg

9-12-1995
McDonald, Patricia Lynne

9-18-1995
Smith, Debra A.
Thacker, Connie R.
Throop, Ellen Watts
Weissbach, Carolyn E.

10-5-1995
Preston, Sharon Curran

10-11-1995
Twanmoh, Valerie Hurley

10-13-1995
McGowan, Rachel W.

11-2-1995
Knowles, Kavita Srikant

12-8-1995
Weinberg, Wendy J.

12-12-1995
Ablin, Rachel Beth
Abrams, Adele Lois
Abrams, Anessa
Abramson, Deborah Naomi
Acebal, Maria Laura
Ackerman, Anne D.
Adams, Valerie Denise
Albert, Randi Michelle
Alston, Chrystn Kekealani
Alter, Jamie M.
Apollon, Martine Natasha
Arthaud, Victoria C.
Bailey, Mary Page
Banks, Cynthia Marie
Barkan, Lisa Anne
Barker, Karen Elizabeth
Barnes, Zoa Dolan
Barr, Kimberly A.
Barrett, Bridget M.
Barron, Kathleen Leslie
Becker, Carolyn G.
Bennett, Joan Charlotte
Bernstein, Lara M.
Bittner, Carol Ann
Black, Kimberli Renee
Blair, Elizabeth Towson Prow
Blanchard, Tara Weinstock
Blaya, Robbin K.
Blitch, Susan K.
Block, Leslie Abramsky
Blum, Jennifer Lisa
Bodden, Shirley A.
Boileau, Lynne Jernberg
Boros, Lancey Meredith
Borten, Cathy Greenebaum
Boyd, Stacey Lanel
Bradley, Kimberly Lynn
Brady, Lenore
Brahim, Jacqueline Patricia
Brenner, Jennifer Dolores
Breslow, Julie Rebecca
Bricca, Andrea Therese
Briles, Rita M.
Brooks, JoAnna L.
Brown, Alison M.
Brown, Sandra Lee
Brown, Valentine A.
Buchwald, Julie
Buehler, Lauren Christine
Burke, Sherry Lynn
Calabrese, Kristina Suzanne
Callaway, Claudia
Carhart, Catherine
Carlson, Rachel M.
Cary Williams, Shelore Ann
Caswell, Mary Elizabeth
Catchpole, Tamara Zaida
Chang, Joni Yuk Ying
Chapin, Jennifer Leslie
Chen, Xiu-Fang
Chernosky, Theresa Michelle
Cheung, Denise
Childress, Suzanne M.
Childs-Barnes, Cheryl Denise
Chopra, Marie
Chung, Megan Sue-Anne
Ciota, Andrea Lynn
Clarenbach, Jane
Clark, Charmayne Damara
Clark, Sallye A.
Coen, Shannon Ann
Cohen, Abigail Faye
Cohen, Rachel Susan
Cohen, Susan Jeanblanc
Cohn, Deborah A.
Condos, Elizabeth R.
Conn, Amanda Stakem
Connaughton, Kimberly A.
Connelly, Lisa Paige
Connolly, Donna M.
Coombs, Dianne C.
Cooper, Bari Barton
Cooper, Deena Grodstein
Crellin, Rose Marie
Crewe-Allen, Pamela L.
Croson, Charlotte
D'Souza, Maureen Devine
Daigle, Jessica
Davis, Audre G.
Davis, Tracy DuPree
Dealy, Anne Louise
Deblasi, Ann Marie
deGraffenreid, Jill Marie
Delaney, Linda Anne
Devine, Kathleen S.
Deza, Cecilia Paula Adelaida
Diamond, Claudia A.
DiLima, Marjorie Gabbett
Dillon, Elizabeth J.
Dorsey, DeChane LaRae
Dortenzo, Megan Dowd
Dowd, Jennifer Ann
Duckett, Dione Traci
Dulin, Rebecca Anne
Dwyer, Ami Carroll
Eck, Jennifer M.
Ecklebarger, Terri Anne
Edmond, Donine Carrington
Eilers, Laura Ann
Ellenby, Whitney Lynne
Ellington, Jacqueline Edelen
Faigenblat, Frances Gail
Fallowfield, Linda J.
Farinella, Maria
Favetta, Julie H.
Fenton, Donna Siobhan
Field, Alexandra Margolis
Fink, Stephanie Lynn
Fitzgerald, Kathleen Mary
Fleig, Mary H.
Fonsworth, Janell Penyea
Foster, Elisa Bernadette
Fowle, Cheryl Ann
Frank, Laurie Suzanne
Freifrau von Hollen, Dorothy C. A.
Friedwald, Julie Selene
Friend, Melinda Sue
Gaillard, Robin Rucker
Gary, Keisha Althea
Gazaille, Ruth Ann
Giovannoni, Catherine Marie
Glaser, Amy Beth
Gleason, Susan J.
Glennon, Michelle Brown
Goldberg, Marion Kristal
Goldenberg, Alison Elizabeth
Goldfine, Stephanie Aileen
Gordon-Troy, Tatia Loring
Gould, Stacy Drew
Greenwald, Madeleine Rose
Gumpert, Emily Karen
Guthrie, Sharon Lynn
Guttman, Catherine Rebecca
Haas, Laurie Sevin
Hall, Jennifer Girone
Halligan, Caitlin Joan
Hamilton, Judith Marie
Hamilton, Stephanie Diebold
Hanley, Sheryl Dawn
Hansen, Donna Carol
Harris, Paige Elizabeth
Harris, Patrice Jeanette
Hartman, Jennifer M.
Hayward, Colette Y.
Johnson, Melodie Dawn Edwards
Katz, Cynthia Groomes
La Fiandra, Jacqueline Cohen
Langlieb, Tammara F.
Lenkin, Robin J.
MacDonald, Cynthia Brubaker
Martin, Michelle Marie
Mashkouri, Marie-Nicole Beneus

McLearn, Elizabeth Castiello
Ming, Diane Helms
Moylan, Heidi A.
Nestor, Lauren Casey
Nicoll, Jacquelyn Avin
Pologruto, Kristen Coyle
Ramsey, Kathleen Greenan
Redmond, Barbara A.
Ridgell, Leigh Greene
Schweitzer, Felicia Goldberg
Sidle, Pamela Aud
Simmons, Laura Anne
Slater, Erika F. Daneman
Ware, Ann Doherty
Williams, Shelore Ann Cary
Wright, Shawn Monique
Zois, Laura G.

12-13-1995

Alban, Pamela K.
Alpert, Shara Beth Mervis
Batchelder, Cynthia Ann Jacobs
Beronio, Kirsten Kessler
Blades, Lisa M.
Brodrick, Robin Lynn
Burns, Laura Ann
Clary, Tara Makoski
Connolly, Theresa Mannion
Desai, Urvi Patel
Greiner, Heather L.
Hazard, Leisa Stacey
Higinbothom, Kristal Louvera
Hill, Carrie L.
Hirsch, Andrea E.
Hoffman, Laurie B.
Hogan, Janice Marchiafava
Hostetter, Heather Quinn
Houlihan, Kathy Butler
Howard, Cheryl Lynne
Hughes, Kshama Shukla
Hume, Elizabeth Ann
Jacobs, Cheryl Kelley
Jacobsen, Jennifer G.
Jadwin, Pamela Jill
Jaffe, Suzanne Davison
Jalinous, Shahrzad Heyat
Jarquin, Joanne B.
Jeong, Rosa Seung-Hye
Joehl, Virginia B.
Johnson, Carol Ann
Julio, Alison J.
Kahn, Marta Karin
Katula, Sharon Egan
Kavadi, Manisha Sharad
Keenan, Siobhan R.
Kelly, Heather Jean
Kelly-Judd, Leeann K.
Kendrick, Karin Marie
Kim, Judith Unjin
Kim, Min Jung
Kirby, Jennifer M.
Kirwin, Melanie Jubb
Kline, Lori Elizabeth
Knox, Laura Gail
Kolby, Elizabeth Lee
Korman, Maria E.
Kovacs, Kathryn E.
Kramer, Beth Mikhael
Kramer, Karen M.
Kremer, Kristin L.
Kronenberg, Angela Michele Woodley
Kuehn, Clara Elizabeth
Kuhn, Ellen Lorraine
Kurr, Carolyn Elizabeth
Kutcher, Jennifer Beth
Lachs, Sheila Marie
Lafond, Sally A.
Lafontant, Monique J.
Lamaster, Teresa Kay
Lambrakopoulos, Stavroula Elias
Lavallee, Edie Carol
Lee, Susan
Leffler, Catherine S.
Leitner, Kara B.
Lembo, Ann M.
Leone, Amy Leete
Levine, Heidi L.
Levy, Andrea Lynne
Lewis, Anne M.
Lewis, Meredith Kolsky
Lewonski, Sharon M.
Lim, Esther HyangRan
Lincoln, Sheryl J.
Linden, Page McGuire
Loughney, Erin Elizabeth
Lovelace, Stacy Michelle
Maddux, Lisa Ellen
Maloney, Carol Ann
Mann, Kimberly V.
Mason, Karen Holliday
Mateen, Fatimah Aaliyah
Mather, Cynthia Ruth
Matthews, Elizabeth Ann
Mayor, Heidi Huntington
Mazzone, Martha Ann
McClary, Tonya Diana
McCullough, Jill D.
McGavin, Kim H.
McGowan, Patricia
McGrath, Lisa Jo
McGurk, Cassandra Pagliaro
McHugh, Mary I.
McKenna, Luanne Patrice
McKenna, Suzanne Sumpter
McKinney, Kathryn Marie
McLaughlin, Christine Phinney
McSally, Mary Kaitlin
Mentzer, Susan Lee
Mikhail, Vivian Adel
Millender, Kimberly Ann
Miller, Lisa Alaine
Millman, Dawn Michelle
Mills, Meredith A.
Mir, Shama Diane
Mithal, Maneesha
Mohr, Diane M.
Moon, Hester Kelly
Moran, Judith B.D.
Moskowitz, Amy Sue
Mundt, Michelle Marie
Munoz, Dara Lystra
Myers, Dalhi Nanette
Nagle, Christine L.
Nassab, Rebecca
Natapoff, Alexandra
Nettleford, Leslie Anita
Newby, Narda-Marie M.
Nicoll, Eleanor Carolyn
Norris, Colleen Kearney
O'Berry, Donna Lynn
O'Connor, Nuala
O'Leary, Sheila E.
Oler, Elisa Renee
Oughourli, Diana
Palevsky, Myra
Palmquist, Marie
Pawelski, Victoria Madeleine
Pazniokas, Rita
Peled, Daphna
Pentecost, Diana
Perkins, Karla M.
Polito, Melissa Suzanne
Powers, Kristen P.
Ritter, Elizabeth Jessica
Robison, Katherine Nordhoff
Settles, Lisa Y.
Skok, Stuart Muntzing
Smith, Michelle Dawn
Stern, Kimberly Hope
Thomson, Teresa A.
Wirth, Erin Masson
Wooten, Marjolane Merryweather
Worth, Temple Holland

12-14-1995

Baker, Andrea Saum
Baldwin, Jennifer Shuck
Bavaria, Eloise Quarles
Benefiel, Kelly Reaver
Boggs, Virginia M.
Burns, Lisa Weinstein
Cavey, Jennifer Silver
Coviello, Yvonne Michelle
Cruz, Leslie Sperling
Dietrich, Julie S.
Frantzen, Janelle Williams
Gaarder, Christina Lee
Godine, Corie Williams
Gruendel, Yolanda Ruisanchez
Hastings, Jennifer Lyn
Henning, Alicia
Justice, Erin Michelle
Kathman, Debra Grace
Kearney, Andrea Marie
Kelly, Tadia DeShawn
Krueger, Nicole V.
Kruger, Elizabeth Ann
Kullman, Janice Anne Simons
Levine, Marci Iris Rose
McGeever, Kerry Shanahan
McLindon, Anne Whalen
Melehy, Suvita
Merkel, Sarah Snyder
Mohler, Jean Smith
Omole, Olili Truth
Philburn, Ann Therese
Pinto, Consuela Amalia
Pollard, Nicole Renee
Pomponio, Carol Patricia
Posey, Natalie A.
Possessky, Laura Ann
Prater, Jill Ione
Purvis, Jennifer Ann
Qureshi, Sarah Nafees
Ragsdale, Mary Coleman
Rahilly, Lyn Michele
Rausenberger, Wyndy J.
Raymond, Joanie
Reimer, Patricia Simpson
Remington, Kristi Louise
Reynolds, Catherine Ann
Rhynes, Rhonda F.
Rice, Lorrianne Jeanette
Richardson, Deborah Lynn Sherwin
Riina, Jennifer Lynn Van Lenten
Rising, Wendy Anne
Robertson, Terri Lynn
Robilotto, Nicole F.
Robins, Lena
Robinson, Jennifer Margaret
Robinson, Lisa A.
Robinson, Renee L.
Rosenberger, Francine Judith
Rosenbloom, Deborah Diane
Rosendale, Theresa A.
Rosenstock, Kimberly Lauren
Rothouse, Marla Sherry
Roush, Valerie Granfield
Rubin, Pamela G.
Sabracos, Stella Vavas
Sanders, Deborah Page
Schierling, Tanya Marie
Schminke, Patricia Simmons
Schroeder, Delilah Seroussi
Schulterbrandt, Beverly Stewart
Scott, Stephanie Leigh
Seidel, Heather Ann
Shah, Ami Patel
Shapiro, Julie Heather
Sheldon, Wendy Elizabeth
Sherley, Anne Wilhoit
Siedlecki, Christina Mai Saarlas
Silvain, Allison Leigh Thoburn
Sinelli, Mary Christine
Singer, Lauren Field
Smith, Carla Denise
Smith, Karla Natasha
Song, Soo Cooper
Sonn, Frances Jin
Statesman, Kirstin Aminta
Steel, Lisa Jean
Steimer, Natacha D.
Stevens, Bambi Wilson
Stewart, Jacqueline Marie
Stokes, Tracey Lynn
Stoner, Katherine Waldby Thomas
Strickland, Elyse Lorin
Stringer, Jody Marie
Styers, Kristin Marie
Sultan, Saira
Susalla, Malinda Lee
Swansiger, Erin Reilly
Swiatek, Virginia McDaniel
Thornton, Gayle Louise
Tilney, Lisa Atkins
Tomko, Janet Levis
Tree, Christine M.
Trinh, Linda McAlpine
Tundermann, Karen L.
Tunick, Lisa Amelia
Underwald, Suzanne Marie
Valenstein, Jill M.
Vanneman, Michelle Moore
Vassilovski, Edna
Vergnetti, Beth Stacey
Virnstein, Jill Clare
Vongjaroenrat, Panravee
Waldmann, Christine Cargill
Walters, Christine V.
Walters, Natalie S.
Ward, Melissa Fairley
Ward, Shelly
Wartenberg, Yolanda R.
Washington, Tanya Monique
Watkins, Angela Nicole

Watson, Melanie J.
Webber, Erica Lynn
Wherthey, Kathleen Evelyn
Wilken, Amy Melissa
Williams, Barbara Blake
Williams, Janet Zanobia
Williams, Lisa Antoinette
Williams, Nicole Tenette
Williamson, Nancy Surasky
Willis, Lauren Elizabeth
Willse, Brooke Taylor
Wilson, Jillian
Witter, Kirsten Nan
Wood, Courtney Lewis
Woolfolk, Kelly Camille
Wright, Ginger Ann
Yamamoto, Allison Sumiyo
Yarema, Elizabeth C.
Yelverton, Ann-Kelley
Yi, Jennifer J.
Zaidman, Natalie Fern
Zetwick, Mary Beth

12-15-1995
De Jong, Tracy Barger

12-18-1995
Goodman, Ellen Herman
Lauren, Barbara
Rosenzweig, Linda Edith
Sagner, Dianne Rochberg

12-20-1995
Hughes, Sandra Latham

1-3-1996
Bush, Karen Lee
Cooper, Angela Maureen
Sroufe, Linda

1-4-1996
Arumi, Ana Cristina
Beauchamp, Elizabeth
Betancourt, Julie Lynn
Casale, Karen Elizabeth Dickinson
Chang, Deanna Jen-Yen
Cipriani, Karen L.
Fry, Nancy Dianne
Gallagher, Michele Anne
Glover, Cestaine Francis
Hansson, Leigh Turner
Johnson, Dominique Stanford
Lange, Jennifer Vogdes
Madole, Mercedes Joyal
Monaco, Cynthia M.
Oppenheim, Marlene Peake
Pierson, Barbara J.
Proctor, Michelle A.
Roccanova, Gina M.
Sheridan, Michele Leigh
Snyder, Jill A.
Tadjbakhsh, Shahrzad

1-16-1996
Andrews, Ann-Martha
Birk, Jodi Lynn
Jonas, Judy Diane
Lee, Marietta S.

1-18-1996
Vinson, Carolyn P.

1-25-1996
Lourie, Vanessa Carpenter

1-29-1996
Camet, Lily Arbab

2-1-1996
Ashley, Katherine Downs
Barner, Glenna Elizabeth
Colton, Kimberly H.
Cortez, Linda D.
Hagen, Emily M.
Park, Sharon So-Yun

2-5-1996
Kerr, Dorothy Chamberlin

2-26-1996
Sistrunk, Karen Rene

2-29-1996
Hill, Veronica Renee
LeMon, Erica I.

4-8-1996
Hunt, Pamela Trimble
Wosnack, Karen Marie

5-2-1996
Hildick, Judith Ann

5-30-1996
Zork, Lesley Sue

6-5-1996
Adcock, Eleanor J.
Andersen, Lisa M.
Anderson, Susan Hoscheit
Antonelli, Andrea Patricia
Areizaga Soto, Jaime Ariel
Arrington, Diana Carolyn
Bailey, Julia Kay
Barnes, Linna May
Beers, Elizabeth Rae
Beg, Kimberly Yasmin
Bennett, Melissa Ann
Benton, Debra M.
Berry, Rodella Elizabeth
Berzok, Jennifer Katz
Birk, Diane C.
Blackmer, Rebecca A.
Blythe, Angela M.
Bonds, Adrienne M.
Bouquet, Yun S.
Bradley, Annette L.
Branson, Karen E.
Brantley, Shirene Willis
Brennan, Catherine Margaret
Breuer, Kelly Ann
Brooks, Katherine Michelle
Burns, Nnenna C.
Butler-Truesdale, Tonya M.
Callahan, April Renee
Campion, Susan M.
Canarte, MaryKay
Candler, Elizabeth Gillis
Cannon, Jamie R.
Carty, Alice E.
Cattafesta, Maria Linda
Cavelli, Grace
Chan, Ada K.
Chen, Melinda Elena
Chenault, Susan Lockette
Chicoski, Jennifer Dawn Stiver
Chiriatti, Karyn Meredith
Choi, Yoon Kyung
Cillo, Julie Marie
Clements, Eva M.
Coates, Melanie Diana
Collins, Alicia Phroso
Colton-Bell, Julia L.
Cooley, Jo-Ann Vassallo
Cooper, Yurika Saito
Corpening, LaTanya Y.
Crandall, Joanna Marie
Crews, Belinda Mae
Cummings, Asuncion
Curtin, Caroline Goddard
D'Souza, Gwenlynn Whittle
Dartigue, Natasha Marie
Dean, Angela Christine
Decker, Suzzanne W.
Denice, Patricia Marie
Deppe, Betsy Lee
Domen, Michelle Lynn
Driver, Gayle Marie Brown
Duckett, Tracey Lenhardt
Early, Nicole Michelle
Ehrhart, Amy E.W.
Evans, Martina Deanne
Evert, Sharla Leigh
Falter, Jennifer Ann
Farrow, Olivia Dabney
Feinglass, Susan Beth
Ferguson, Alisia
Fisher, Robyn Jan
Fleetwood, Christine Joy
Fletcher, Kathleen Reardon
Folickman, Pamela Reese
Fonte, Raquel Marie
Foreman, Kimberly Charon
Fowler, Patrina Louise
Fraser, Jennifer
Fuller, Heidi Smeder
Gaines, Rachele Monique
Gallagher, Michele Yvonne
Gatenby, Karin
Geisse, Loreto S.
George, Jodi Tonya
Getz, Lisa Kunitz
Gibson, Amanda Anne
Giles, Susan Lorraine
Glover, Glenda Baskin
Gravell, Kathy S.
Graves, Gretchen Y.
Greene, Nancy Ann DiMauro
Greene, Suzanne Brette
Grise, Jacqueline I.
Hadigian, Dana Gayle
Hagigh, Sara Elizabeth
Hallam, Julie Anne
Handwerger, Stephanie Herbert
Hannan, Catherine M.
Harding, Vanessa Scott
Heerink, Amy Margaret Kamlot
Helfant, Nogah B.
Ho, Jane
Hodges, Tracey Eileen
Hogarth, Joan Dawn
Hoskam, Michelle J.
Hunt, Venus Venay
Hutkoff, Jennifer L.
Ingwersen, Candyce Vana
Israel, Jasmine C.
Izzo, Margaret Scott
Johnson, Nancy Lewis
Jones, Jade Anton
Jones, Kimberley S. Wright
Jones, Kimya I.
Jones, Veronica Patrice
Kamlot Heerink, Amy Margaret
Kauskay, Linda Christine
Kerr, Elisa D.
Khanna, Rita
Kim, Sujin F.
Kimmel, Susan Landay
Klemens, Melissa Lin
Knochenhauer, Natalie
Knowles, Kerry Foley
Kornegay, Mondre Hopson
Kurtz, Leigh
Labson, Courtenay Manes
Lane, Carol Janet
Langley, Tamika Bertini
Lauten, Heather Liddell
Lederman, Pia Rebecca Desiree
Leskovsek, Natasha Veronica
Leventhal, Lisa Ann
Levin, Karen Beth
Lige, Rona Shorr
Lindquist, Karen Elizabeth
Liu, Bo-May
Liu, Carol Benjamin
Long, Elizabeth Dale
Lopez, Margaret Summers
Love, Nicole Denise
Lucchesi, Victoria Lynn
Lytle, Nancy Jean
Mahar, Jennifer Anne
Mahony, Megan Ruth
Majid, Jasmine Avis
Malir, Nancy Jean
Malone, Maura Ruth
Malveaux, Suzette Marie
Marindin, Julie McDonald
Martin, Nicolette B.
Marvin, Barbara Margaret Rewald
Massey, Dimitra Yvette
Mayo, Jennifer L.
McCormack, Megan Clune
McKibben, Tracy B.
Metcalf, Diana H.
Minick, Wendy Sue
Miranda, Veronica I.
Monahan, Mary Kathleen
Moniz, Mary Anne
Morgan, Andrea D.
Morocco, Maria Luisa
Morrison, Mary Lee
Moses, Andrea Marie
Muedeking, Emma Christina
Myers, Jennifer Leigh
Neal, Marcy Lynn
Nelson, April Elizabeth
Neuder, Lisa Robin
North, Karis Lynn
Nurmi, Felicia M.
Nutall, Tracy Brinkley
O'Sullivan, Laura H.G.
Opper-Weiner, Ellen Susan
Page, Jennifer Bassett
Parks, Ann W.
Passe, Michele Arens
Peacock, Kristin L.
Pecora, Christine L.
Penn, Karen Renee R.
Peoples, Charlotte Denise
Perticari, Amy Lynne
Propeack, Kimberley Ann
Radack, Jesselyn Alicia
Ransom, Rainey E.
Rawlings, Stephanie Cole
Reyes, Bella

Richards, Marilyn H.
Richards, Melinda Jeanne
Rosenberg, Cynthia Beth
Roy, Quinn Fisher
Ryan, Alexandra Lynette Elizabeth
Salow, Heidi C.
Sam, Martine
Savage, Meeka
Saxton, Leslie M.
Scanlon, Elise A.
Schad, Deidra Lynn
Schafer, Carolyn
Schuyler, Marilyn Louise
Schwartz, Kay Bittner
Seidleck, Michelle Lee
Sen, Rupa
Shah, Kala
Shamoto, Susan Yoshiko
Shapiro, Joanna L. Armentrout
Sheppard-Walker, Mary Roberts
Shipley, Stephanie Ann
Shortall, Angela L.
Siegel, Robin Joy
Silberman, Judith Gail
Silverstein, Paula S.
Simpson, Sondra L.
Sinclair, Sabrina R.
Sonde-Hawthorne, Andrea M.
Sosne, Pamela Gail
Soto, Jaime Ariel Areizaga
Splan, Heather Carole
Stanley, Joyce Earl Hatcher
Stevenson, Lindsey Jean
Stewart, Susan Vak
Stokes, Lisa M.
Talley, Penelope Thornton
Thompson, Candy L.
Tucker, Erika Schiller
Vinson, Cathy L.
Wagner, Jonya Estelle
Wahlberg, Stacy Beth
Wallace, Bobbi L.
Webb, Hong Le
Weimer, Caroline Fong
Whittaker, Tracy Lynne
Wiegleb, Jennifer A.
Willhight, Andra Jean
Williams, Adelisia Vania
Wink, Victoria Herbert
Winstead, Deborah Leigh
Wong, Natalie Diana
Wong, Yoona Kim
Woods, Christina Gayle
Wrenn, Alison Kramer
Yanofsky, Carole Jill
Yim, Susan S.
Zink, Sharon Anne

6-10-1996
Alberts, Risa J.
Lai, Pearl Chow
McNamara, Mary Joan
Moore, Patricia J.

6-11-1996
Richardson, Sarah Elizabeth

6-14-1996
Blumenthal, Carol S.
Gemmill, Helen Louise
Spring, Milissa Reeks

6-17-1996
Donoghue, Kristen A.

6-19-1996
Krafte, Jill Helaine

6-20-1996
Hart, Melissa

6-24-1996
Kresch, Sandra
McWeeney, Shannon Ailene
Plummer, Pamela J.
Tully, Lisa Kurtz

6-25-1996
Drouet, Suzanne Katherine
King, Cynthia McNeill
Mason, Donna Marie

6-26-1996
Lowery, Sheila Anne
Summers, Kendall Barbara

6-27-1996
Giventer, Lorrie Allyson
Harrison, Ellen Kroll
Helm, Jacquelyn Viorey
Semancik, Caroline Hopkins
Whitmore, Betty Lou

7-2-1996
Dean, Danell Palladine
Dorn, Susan E.
Downing, Donna Marie
Glassman, Margaret Melissa
Jesperson, Joanna
Looper, Valerie E.

7-9-1996
Burke, Elizabeth Clara
Carroll, Courtney Roberta
Molan, Robin Meri
Swaney, Allyson Alaine

7-10-1996
Kruger, Susan Laiken

7-11-1996
Johnson, Wanda Marie
Oleck, Adrienne Lisa
Ross, Julia Lamson

7-15-1996
Gilhooly, Susan Howe

7-16-1996
McLaughlin, Karen Marie

7-29-1996
Newman, Miriam Ann

8-6-1996
Blee, Janette Marie
Spadafora, Peggy Marie Wooley

8-26-1996
Alexis, Agnes K.
Bay, Laurie C.
Berman, Martha A.H.

9-5-1996
Augustin, Genevieve Elizabeth
Baxam, Deanna Lynne
Jackson, Odessa Palmer
Kehoe, Elizabeth Parker
Miller, Kristine M.

9-9-1996
Bernstein, Carolyn

10-3-1996
Hinsch, Claudia Liliana
Rodriguez, Maria Eugenia

10-8-1996
Weich, Cecile Claire

11-25-1996
Murphy, Michele Leah

12-5-1996
McCabe, Sandra Aiko
Pels, Paula Christine

12-17-1996
Abaro, Lorraine Joy
Adams, Michelle J.
Adkins, Jocelyn C.
Adkins, Vivian Lee
Ailiff, Deborah A.
Aistars, Sandra Mara
Alagna, Julie Ann
Alatis, Lisa Jo
Alexander, Michelle Mirian
Allen Godin, Martha
Allston, Monica Roche
Alsobrooks, Angela DeNeece
Anderson, Kristy Kay
Andoll, Michelle C.
Anthony, Teisha Marie
Atkinson, Janet Elizabeth
Bacchus, Sonia A.
Badanes, Lori Jeanine
Bahrampour, Firouzeh Diana
Banker, Elizabeth Ann
Banks, Robin Goldberg
Barber, Sarah DeLaMater
Barbour, Cathy A.
Barney, Melanie Jacobs
Barry, Diana L.
Bassey, Patricia Langan
Beaudreau, Carriellen
Beck, Loretta Christine
Becker, Mila Nerit
Bell, Terry Lynn
Bernstein, Ilisa Beth Goldman
Bernstein, Sandra Joy
Berry, Donna M.
Bieber, Jody Michele
Bisson, Jeannette Louise
Blackwell, Melineh Berenice
Bleam, Roseanne Maria
Bloyd, Melissa M.
Bonaguide, Christine Anne
Boucher, Jamie Lorraine
Boutchyard, Theresa Irene
Bragg, Jennifer Lynn
Branch, LaShanda D.
Brantl, Winafred R.
Branzell, Rebecca Brennan
Brasher, Ingrid Vanessa
Bridgford, Cynthia A.
Briggs, Barbara Lynn
Broder-Feldman, Elena Nicole
Brown, Destiny A.
Browne, Donna Ann Gallagher
Bruckmann, Robin F.
Burkhard, Dianne
Burnett, Darnellena Christalyn
Burton, Nancy Elizabeth
Bush, Robin Zimmerman
Butcher, Catherine Curran
Butterfield, Nagako Isobe
Cacossa, Nicole Andrea
Cain, Erika Alise
Campbell, Cynthia Grace
Campbell, Patricia Lindsey
Canedo, Saundra Kay
Cannon, Jannika E'lan
Carpinteri, Alexis Fogel
Carroll, Amy Elisabeth
Carroll, Catherine
Carter, Candy Lorraine
Caspari, Kimberly Peterson
Cavanagh, Elizabeth Anne
Cellucci, Laura A.
Chakmakian, Alice Anne
Chang, Alyssa W.
Chase, Catherine Babics
Cherry, Risa Beth
Chin, Pamela Elizabeth
Chmielewski, Cynthia Marie
Choi, Heesun Sunny
Choi, Lisa Christine
Chudd, Sharon M.
Chuh, Patricia M.
Chumnanvech, Alyssa
Church, Tomeka Grimes
Clair, Adrienne Elizabeth
Clifford, Sandra Elizabeth
Close, Nalini V.
Cochran, Marie
Coderre, Carol Ann
Collier, Jennifer Duncan
Conway, Caroline Eva
Coogan, Mary I.
Courson, Nancy Jo
Curran, Amy E.
Dabney, Jasmin Ann
Dagustine, Angela M.
Dallahan, Tracey Judith
Dans, Suzanne Elise
Dargan, Latonya Bethann
Davidson, Kelly J.
Davidson Miller, Jessica
Davis, Cecelia Oneathia-Lucenda
Dawkins, Leslie Galyn
Dawson, Jamela Collier
Day, Alice Marie
De Coteau, Pamela Lucine
Deese, Crystal S.
Demopulos, Amelia Hannah
Demouy, Maura Lynn
Dickerson, Elizabeth Brinkley
Dinsmore, Michelle Dawn
DiPietro, Angela Beth
Dixon, Monique LaForest
Donner, Danielle Saba
Duffy, Lisa Anne
Duggan, Lisa Maureen
Eduardo, Amelia Myra
Edwards, Karen Michele
El Guindi-Rosenbaum, Magda
Ellison, Jennifer S.
Embrey, Diana Lynn
Endieveri, Anne Christine
Estafanous, Katherine Elizabeth
Evins, Elizabeth Ann
Exposito, Patricia Ann
Ezrin, Valerie
Fairweather, Donna Marie Alexandria
Fandetti, Elisabeth Jane
Farley, Stacie Free
Favorito, Carolyn A.

Feldman, Miriam Barbara
Fenneman, Rebecca Anne
Ferko, Allison A.
Ferretti, Karen Anne
Fieri-Fetrow, Melissa Susan
Fina, Joan Elizabeth
Fink, Allison
Fisher, Moira Ann
FitzPatrick, Elizabeth Belson
Forness, Mary Pamela
Frieder, Gony
Gaines, Danee Chantelle
Gandhi, Swata Jitendra
Gardner, Juliet Dupuy
Garvin, Terri Theresa
Gaudio, Elizabeth A.
Genton, Regina Ann
Gergen, Jennifer Anne
Gillette, Elizabeth C. Cober
Giuffreda, Eugenia L.
Glasser, Kristine Finis
Goddard, Lydia Ann
Godin, Martha Allen
Goliday, Cheryl Nadine
Goodman, Tracy L.
Goodwin, Kathleen Suzanne
Grant, Davida Marie
Greff, Jacqueline Ann
Grill, Arielle Horman
Gross, Heather Elizabeth
Gundlach, Jennifer Anne
Haber, Jennifer Paige
Haeseker, Lisa Anne
Hahn, Francine K.
Hahn-Burkett, Tracy Robin
Hairston, Belynda Camille
Healy, Samantha J.
Holloway, Gretta Gordy
Junge, Melissa Clarry
Kane, Jill Coleman
Kaufmann, Lynn F.
Kawka, Shane B.
Kleiman, Mary Ellen Fleck
Kupinsky, Natalie Weidener
Lawrence, Kristin Case
Lispcome, Marie-Claire Brown
Maloney, Julie Furst
Manicone, Rebecca S.
Mathias, Lisa DeRosa
McAfee, Karen Brown
Miller, Jessica Davidson
Miller, Monique Choiniere
Myers, Julie Dawn
O'Neill, Holly M.
Pirri, Kathleen S.
Polott, Anita B.
Robidoux, Kimberley Best
Schettewi, Jennifer B.
Sexter, Halley Finkelstein
Shostek, Tara Becht
Stinebower, Cari Nicole
Thomson, Tamara B.
Tini, Leslie Anderson
Trella, Nicole Baines
Wagner, Jennifer Dine
Wilt, Laura Corbett
Wulkan, Donna L.

12-18-1996

Abramson, Stephani Lane
Bober, Leanne Elizabeth Myers
Booth, Brynja M.
Brady, Kathy Kerrigan
Breza, Rachael D.M.
Cawood, Elizabeth Loretta
Collier, Sidney E.
Dale, Mary Margaret
Dinges, Joan Ellen
Drawbaugh, Mary McGuirk
Freiman, Sharon K.
Gates, Angelia Merritt
Grigorian, Christina J.
Hamlin, Machell A.
Hammond, Elizabeth Anne
Hancock, Hope Elaine
Handler, Allyson Brooke
Hardy, Kelly Tubman
Hare, Lisa Lynn
Harlston, Hellen Paula
Harriman, Erin Marie
Hart, Angela Lynn
Haskett, Amber Carol
Hawkins, Lisa Lynne
Hayles, Sheron Althea
Haynes, Dorothy R.
Hellrung, Margaret Cecilia
Henderson, Kamina Aliya
Hill-Midgett, Nannie Doris
Himelfarb, Tacey Nusbaum
Hitt, Denise O'Brien
Hjortsberg, Lara Lidums
Holowinski, Elizabeth Mary
Horowitz, Sharri H.
Howell, Cherie A.
Howell, Marla Lynn
Hoyt, Ayn Valeria
Hsu, Christine Pei-Wen
Huey, Allyson Murphy
Humphreys, Lori June
Hunt, Janine Elena
Jackson, Charla Denise
James, Melvina Yvette
James, Sylvia F.
Jennings, Kelly S.
Jennings, Lynn A.
Jennings, Sandra Alvarez
Jimenez, Melanie Lynn
Johnson, Laura Lee
Johnson, Shubha Kaup
Johnson, Thora Allen
Johnson-Swain, Michele Lynn
Jones, Hilary Markham
Jones, Michelle Annette
Julianelle, Patricia F.
Kahaner, Eileen L.
Kalik, Tracy Ellen Reichman
Karpouzian, Gilda Ohanes
Kauffman, Danna Lubrani
Kaufman, Jessica Berman
Kelman, Abigail J.
Kennedy, Angela Sadie-Edith
Khan, Deborah Veronica
Kilroy, Kelly Gahan
Kim, Susan Hijung
Kisch, Wendy J.
Klasmeier, Coleen Elizabeth
Kluge, Julie Kaplan
Knowles, Kimberley S.
Knuuttila, Kristen M.
Kobrine, Nicole Lynn
Kofman, Mila
Kong-Sivert, Jillian Nicole
Korsower, Rachel Beth
Krumholz, Francine
Kwak, Rosalee J.
Langbaum, Caryn A.
Laux, JoanMarie
Lawson-Davis, Sharon Margaret
Lee, Tara M.
Lenderman, Lisa J.
Lenge, Allison Marie
Letterman, Tracie Dawn
Leventhal, Dinah S.
Lewis, Stephanie
Lieberman, Melissa J.
Lindekugel, Gina Subilia
Littleton, Staci Renee
Lowery, Allison Nicole
Lund, Amy Poskin
Lydia, Kemba Soyini
Lynch, Marilyn Theresa
Lyons, Vicki L.
MacMillin, Emily Kim
Magyar-Socorso, Mimi Leigh
Major, Karen L.
Malinowski, Shana L.
Malloy, Suzanne
Mann, Judy Hwang
Mantoan, Patricia Margiotta
Marks, Michelle Susan
Marthaler, Kathleen Ann
Martielli, Marina M.
Martin, Carmel M.
Martin, Patricia L.
Matlock, Belinda Cooper
Matney, Laura D.
Mazur, Robyn Carie
McAdoo, Leslie S.
McClammy, Erika M.
McCormack, Shalini Sharma
McCormack, Stacy Wiederle
McHenry, Andrea Curtis
McKoy, Denise Andrea
Mego, Diane Michelle
Mehr, Denise Rochelle
Menke, Teri L.
Miles, Gladys Paulina
Mitchell, Heather Ann
Mizel-Goldfarb, Melina Elana
Mobley, Denise E.
Molloy, Monica Shearer
Moore, Donna L.
Moreland, Hallie Ann
Morris, Marcia
Morton, Danielle Carleen
Mulhollan, Erin Finlayson
Musselman, Holly Anne
Myers, Teresa Ann
Myrick, Jill M. McClune
Nabors, Theresa Kovscek
Nee, Dawn Marie
Nelson, Juaria Lenette
Newlon, Jeanne Louise
Newstadt, Jacqueline
Nguyen, Lan Nhouc
Nickel, Ann Harrington
Norris, Nicolle Jacqueline
O'Connor, Kelly Anne
O'Keefe, Erin
O'Sullivan, Judith R.
Oden, Kiyo Dhae
Oh, Cindy Sae Jung
Oldham, Kim Y.
Rhee, Min J.
Rosenberg, Tracy Honors
Saler, Leanna Lynn Morris
Wolff, Heather S.
Zubler, Monica Leimone

12-19-1996

Alvarez, Jennifer A.
Aneckstein, Laura Riley
Becker, Lisa Seltzer
Calabrese, Karen Ann
Carlyle, Shaunia W.
Carson, Sandra T.
Daly, Deadra Whayland
Dry, Maureen Ranney
Ferris, Laura Lynn
Forbes, Lolita Demetris
Glenn, Shelly Stickell
Heitmann, Deborah Wengel
Jacques, Tammy Strange
Keam, Alex Seong
Kearney, Tracey Summers
Lammers, Corinne Allison
Lehner, Tara Kathleen
Loizos, Sheila Ann
Long, Jill Shapiro
Mantell, Hallie Gale
Marsh, Meghan Elizabeth
Matthews, Donna Meredith
McBee, Susan Elizabeth Shaw
McGinn, Kelly S.
McKoy, Letitia Wiggins
Medway, Leah Ellen
Meiser, Jacquelyn V.
Novak, Christina Lynn
Palley, Elizabeth S.
Papa, Nicole Jolie
Pappas, Cleopatra
Pargaonker, Nileema Makrand
Park, Jane Hyo-Sung
Pasciuto, Karen Kelly
Patel, Samia
Patt, Yh
Patton, Lisa Bernadette
Penfield, Leigh A.
Pham, Thy P.
Pharaoh, Jennifer Leigh
Philipose, Nalini M.
Phillips, Olivia Harrison
Phillips-Savoy, Karen Yvette
Poma, Kelly Michele
Pope, Susan Holmes
Price, Mary
Price, Tracy Linkins
Prigge, Anastasia Talbot
Prior, Kimberly J.
Pritchard-Kelly, Ruth Wells
Provencher, Shelby L.
Qayyum, Ayesha
Rajguru, Suvarna Umakant
Ramson, Shanta
Rauen, Kimberly Ann
Redlich, Heidi Faye
Redpath, Susan Jane
Reed, Rebecca Rachel
Reggy, Auma Ngesa Mae Ragwar
Rezvani, Tracy Diana
Ridgeway, Lori Fimmano
Riveira, Diana M.
Robertson, Veronica Marie
Robinson, Laura Marie
Rodgers, Susan Marina
Rojugbokan, Alyce Elizabeth
Rosenbaum, Jessica Tara
Rothschild, Shelley Lynn

Rozsman, Nicole Marie
Rubi, Maria Sequeira
Saenz, Diana Joan
Saindon, Elizabeth H.
Scahill, Patricia Louise
Scanlan, M. Kay
Scanlon, Carrie Anne
Scannell, Courtney Lynn
Schaden, Erin Elizabeth
Schaner Stanley, Amy Louise
Scheingold, Amy J.
Schiminger, Alys Robertson
Schimpff, Kirsten Marguerite
Schmidt, Elizabeth Stewart
Schobel, Diana Magazine
Schrock, Norma J.
Segal, Eden H.
Seiler-Morris, Julie
Shaw, Stephanie Lee
Shaw McBee, Susan Elizabeth
Shearer, Victoria Marie
Shermak, Julie I.
Shimp, Karen Johnson
Sill, Andrea Laurel
Silverman, Cheryl Lynne
Simantov, Leora Rachel
Sims, Dawn Marcia
Small, Audra Joy
Smith, Janene Marie
Smith, Samantha Zanger
Snowden, Alison Welles
Spector, Elaine Papavasiliou
Spielman, Jacqueline
Spurlock, Thomazine Elizabeth
Stanley, Amy Louise Schaner
Stapel, Julie Kathleen
Steinacker, Erica
Stewart, Heather Joan
Stofa, Tamara Vaughn Whelan
Stone, Patricia Carson
Storzer, Leah Mac
Sujono, Dian Angriani
Summerton, LindaBeth Alys
Sweigart, Krista Anne
Swift, Yolanda V.
Talbert-Duarte, Angelia C.
Tennant, Hillary Annan
Thornton, Lisa R.
Threatt, Adrianne Griffin
Thys, Natacha
Tomsick, Mary Elizabeth
Tornatore, Gina Gabriella
Trulove, Jodi
Tsintolas, Suzanne Marie
Turner, Lynae Trista
Tyrrell, Lori Patricia
Vagins, Deborah J.
Valeri, Jodi L.
Varma, Anita
Vidal, Victoria Eva
Villanueva, Robin Hardy
Vona, Hollie Rebekah
Walker, Katrina Demaria
Walpert, Laura Ann
Wascak, Jennifer Marie
Washington, Cheryl Yvette
Watson, Theresa C.
Watts, Lydia Carson
Weglarz, Cynthia R.
Weinryb, Rose-Michele
Weisman, Amy Joelle
Wheeler, Kimberly D.
Whitehurst, Carla Cherlene
Wilkins, Janyce Marie
Williams, Julia Ann
Willis, Sabrina
Winchurch, Susan Anne
Winders, Bonnie Ardinger
Windle, Anne T.
Withers, Theresa J.
Wolff, Sara T. S.
Wolfson, Vicki Beth
Wood, Caroline Elizabeth
Woolam, Kristin Heller
Wright, Julia Elizabeth
Wright, Lori Elizabeth
Yi, Kyong Chun
Yost, Valerie Anne
Zacharopoulos, Melina
Zakes, Deanna Lynn
Zeglin, Mary Patricia
Zeit, Linda Beth
Zemel, Irina S.
Zimmerman, Sarah J.

1-2-1997
Brannan, Patricia A.
Day, Katherine A.
Gowen, Mary Beth R.
MacCarthy, Deirdre M.
Pollock, Deborah Lynn
Russell, Angela W.
Talbott, Catherine Blackwell
Verstegen, Anne-Marie

1-3-1997
Bailliet, Cecilia Marcela
Wolf, Denise Sondra

1-6-1997
Fairley, Trina Lashone

1-7-1997
Douglas, Laura Scruggs
Ricci-Smith, Carrie Frances
Scruggs, Laura A.
Straus, Debra S.

1-9-1997
Brown, Robyn Scheina
Butterworth, Barbara E.
Caroff, Sheryl-Lynn
Chao, Fei-Fei
Civic, Melanne Andromecca
Colyer, Catherine
Gentry, Elizabeth Anne
Haley, Kathleen McGillis
Lee, Bok Soon
Metzgar, Nancy J.
Radich, Rita M.
Rosenthal, Kimberly Anne
Singer, Ellen Rice
Solomon, Deborah A.
Triche, Alicia J.

1-10-1997
Covington, Devorah Lynne
Ittig, Kristen Elizabeth
Johnson, Leslie Diane
Kim, Sandra Chi-Eun
Neubaumer, Lisa Elin
Ting, Rita
Wallace-Booker, C. Diane

1-14-1997
Heetderks, Elizabeth Guckes
Levene, Beth Ann

1-16-1997
Crawford, Michele Lajuan

1-21-1997
Atwell, Grace Ellen
Norkaitis, Paula Dumas
Pave, Margo

1-22-1997
Miller, Monserrat Carmen

1-31-1997
Brady, Surell

2-4-1997
Meleagrou, Eleni

2-6-1997
Banta, Carol Jayne
Fairshter, Robyn T.
Hale, Ellen M.
Kilbourne, Catherine Nina
Lamer, Heidi Haviland
Macel, Leanne Steele
Magee, Kimberly MacLeod
Quill, Carolyn C.

2-7-1997
Hansen, Kristen Maris

2-11-1997
Chaudhry, Neena Kumari
Short, Wendy Lorraine

3-6-1997
Adraktas, Victoria J.

3-25-1997
Herdman, Mary Christine

3-31-1997
Kuo, Susan Shu-Hui

4-10-1997
Ifill, Sherrilyn A.

4-30-1997
Heffernan, Brenda Ann
Kaye, Elizabeth Karen
Powalski, Lynn Marie

5-12-1997
Wiley, Jacquelyne Annette

6-6-1997
Barry, Jennifer Anne

6-13-1997
Asherman, Jeanne
Feldman, Nancy Lee
Griffin, Mary Alice

6-16-1997
Griffith-Lesesne, Ladonna Lynette
Holt, Janet Elizabeth Pitterle
Kohn, Margaret A.
Light, Carol J.

6-17-1997
Pratt, Elina Hum

6-19-1997
Aikens, Linda Anise
Brooks, Terrilyn Elliott
Jackson, Patricia Elizabeth

6-23-1997
Dean, Luana Maria
Hoy, Kelly Montgomery
Schaar, Gina Lee

6-24-1997
Tumlin, Tracy Newcomb

6-25-1997
Ali, Stephanie Davis
Alsup, Tracy Kay
Ames, Nicole Elizabeth
Amzel, Daniela
Arfaa, Dottie Ferris
Armstrong, Anne C.
Aronica, Janice Sue
Atkins, Sheryl D. H.
Ayers, Jessica Rose
Bagwell, Anna Marie
Baird, Rhonda N.
Baker, Teresa Lynn
Balestrini, Lisa Ann
Ballantyne, Michele Suzanne
Barber, Amber Leah
Barrows, Jennifer Lynn
Baskerville, Lisa Celes
Batipps, Joyce Stanley
Beach, Jennifer L.
Beauchamp, Dianne Kassab
Beg, Jill Shameen
Bell, Venetia Darlene
Berick, Ellen Selonick
Berry, Elva Bowden
Betterton, Kimberly Ciccone
Blasingame, Cynthia Pope
Bond-Collins, Rhonda D.
Bonenberger, Jamie Sue
Bordner, Kimberly Lea
Bowman, Sarah Denonn Epstein
Bradley-McBeth, Anna E.
Bronstein, Bayla Cohen
Bryan, Sally W.
Buckler, Beth Anne
Burke, Alison Marie
Burke, Jennifer Derouin
Butler, Andrea Pritsios
Byus, Natasha Monique
Caden, Stephanie Lucas
Calhoun, Candace K.
Canal, Jeanne C.
Chamberlin, Kathleen Marie
Choi, Sun E.
Chong, Alice S.
Christian, Denise Manning
Chuo, Emily Meng-Wei
Ciccone, Kimberly Marie
Clark, Johnine Nicollette
Colbert, Eileen L.
Collins, Christine Marie
Conover, Alison Claire
Cook, Amy Decker
Cottrill, Jody Michelle
D'Anna, Marian L.
Davis, Adrienne Morgan
de Forest, Alicia Tamarh
DeFrancesco, Cynthia Ann
Dent, Suzanne Botts
Dickerson, Melinda Leigh
Donahue, Sharon Marie
Donovan, Constance Ann
Dosunmu, Ona Alston
Dray, Stephanie Hope Accongio
Dubick, Draga Louise
Dunn, Sara Lyn
Ehman, Erin Murphy
Elliott, Jewell Camille

Ellis, Jamellah Leyya
Emerson, Cheryl Jean
Emmer, Susan Cheryl
Engelstein, Allyn London
Engle, Elizabeth Gresham
Ensworth, Laurie A.
Faulk, Page Carrington
Feldt, Judith Amy
Ferrill, Jessica D.
Fiero, Barbara Ann
Fisher, Ilona Mishell
Flynn, Ellen Bryant
Foster, Helen Goff
Francis, Anna L.
Francis, Tricia Dianne
Frazier, Myra Maureen
Friedman, Janet Bertha
Fuller, Barbara Parker
Gardner, Dawna Beryl
Garonzik, Daina Wellen
Gaskins, Tonja Monique
Gasmalla, Tori Danielle
Gergely, Gabriela Susana
Gerken, Heather K.
Gill, Tracey L.
Gillett, Judith Adrienne
Gonzalez, Kate Jesberg
Grant, Arlene Jacqueline Marcelle
Gregory, Christine
Gresham, Colette Romaine
Guerin, Cara E.
Guy, Dorothy M.
Hall, Allyson Christina
Hamlin, Sonya Nicole
Hardy, Lisa Lynn
Harmon, Jewel M.
Harmon, Rachel Ann
Harvey, Clothilda G.
Hayes, Michele Anita
Haywood, Claudia Elaine
Heydon, Beverly Irene
Hlavacek, Valerie Gary
Holman, Cindy Ramirez
Hosey, Tiffany Alexandria
Houck, Carolyn Watts
Huggins, Jasmine Elise
Hur, Livia
Hyde, Dana J.
Imhoff, Sheryl Hurlburt
James, Roberta R.
Jayatilaka, Shireen
Jen, Allynnore Mei-Lin
Jones, Dawn Valleri
Keenan, Elizabeth Campbell
Keith, Kimberly S.
Kelleher, Jennifer A. L.
Kelly, Brigid Attracta
Kemp, Karmen Louise
Kennedy, Kristina Bailey
Kenny, Deborah Elizabeth
Keohane, Laura
Kim, Grace Whang
Knox-Benn, Beverly M.
Kondonijakos, Elizabeth E.
Kripetz, Tanya Marie
Kuhlmann, Katrin A.
L'Italien, Monique E.
Lafontaine, Maribel
Lathbury, Meredith Ellen
LeCraw, Linda L.
Lee, Marianne Jeesook
Lee, Sharon D.
Lester, Laura J.
Levy, Meryl Iris
Lewis, Kimberly Vicena
Liu, Deborah
Livingston, Barbara B.
Logan, Lorryn Daena M.
Ma'Ani-Bruss, Sovaida
Macharia, Lilian N.
Magee, Lori Ann
Mantzaris, Jennifer Gale
Marshall, Lynn Marie
Matthews, Cassandra Yvonne
Maultsby, Katrina Tondalayo
Mays, Simone Belcher
McCann, Kathleen Duckett
McDaniel, Margo Francine
McDermott, Tricia Simone
McGregor, Katherine Mary
McGuire, Lauri Anne
McNeill, Susan Patricia
Meier, Eileen Kochava
Meier, Sharon Adinah
Meisner, Lara S.
Mitchell, Susan Huesman
Moore, April L.
Moore, Diane Preston
Morris-McCormick, Kristin Lynn
Morrissette, Carolyn Marie
Mortensen, Sara
Moxley, Lisa D.
Mulloy, Heather Ann
Mustille, Judith A.
Newhouse, Victoria E.
Nguyen, Lan B.
Norington, Karin Mechelle
Olney, Lisa Anne
Palmer, Phyllis Rae
Pardee, Katherine E.
Parker, Lisa M.
Pasquarelli, Joanne C.
Patrick, Kimberly Yvonne
Patterson, Maria Katherine
Pearson, Debra Bryant
Pendley, Sarah Earlene
Peragallo, Alane Ann
Peralta, Marianela
Pierre, Eunice
Pinjuh, Lori Altorfer
Player, Monica N.
Porges, Hillary Diane
Potts, Glenis N.N.
Pride, Kelly Michelle
Quinn, Jennifer Reynolds
Quinn, Mary Kathryn
Raffinan, Maria Elizabeth
Ray, Cristi Michelle
Raymond, Nia Ama
Reece, Julie Steinman
Reilly, Laura Anne
Rhodes, Tracie Watkins
Rizkallah, Lena Samih
Robinson, Eileen Clair
Roche, Carole N.
Ross, Stacy Lynn
Roth, Felicia Lynne
Rouiller, Danielle
Rudich, Rebecca Goldman
Salamat, Kathy Marie
Sampson, Sherri Annette Braden
Santos, Vanessa Ann
Sarracino, Jaylene Marie
Sehrt-Green, Elaine A.
Sheldon, Elizabeth Torrant
Shepherd, Donna Elizabeth
Shepherd, Monica C.
Shepperd, Sheila Marrissa
Silsby, Patricia Shields
Simmons, Amana Thompson
Sirotkin, Sherri G.
Smith, Juliet B.
Smith, Lila Angelica
Smith, Marie Janet
Snyder, Melanie K.
Snyder, Nancy Olness
Solomon, Robin Mathison
Spicer, Susan Julia
St. Germain, Constance Ann
Stark, Sharon Melissa
Stein, Ellen Dennis
Sterling, Carolyn Anne
Stokes, Gwendolyn Baker
Stokols, Gwen Patricia
Stone, Sally A.
Stup, Carolyn Kalbfus
Sutton, Michelle Renee
Swanson, Jacqueline Petersen
Tabron, Marcheta Y.
Taylor, Cherie A.
Taylor, Stephanie Dorise
Taylor-Phillips, LaQuita Joy
Thompson, Barbara A.
Thornton, Susan O.
Tompkins, Sharon Lewis
Tosini, Jennifer Lynn
Trachtenberg, Jill Lesli
Trotta, Marlo Ann
Trovato, Lisa Rose
Truby, Carolyn Anita
Trueba, Claudia
Venkatraman, Bharathi Anandhi
Villamar, Maria Nenutzka Caymo
Voorhees-Diabate, Martha W.
West, Caroline S.
Whitman, Donna L.
Williams, Louvenia Whitehead
Williams, Tracy Jeanette
Wills, Juanita
Wilson, Annemarie
Winiarz, Kimberlee M.
Woo, Maxine Miyoung
Wuliger-Knee, Amy Angela
Wyckoff, Susan Marie Helen
Wynn, Nicole
Yeung, Lisa Siu Mui
Young, Stacy Marie
Feinberg, Shari Renee
Rourke, Mariclaire Driscoll

7-3-1997

Whitted, Regina

7-7-1997

Grossi, Diane A.
Haines Walton, Diana
Harvey, Lisa Ann
Mendez, Carole McFee
O'Donnell, Mary Anne Busse
Walton, Diana Haines

7-9-1997

Feliciani, Carmel-Ann Constance
Fleischmann, Lisa Ellen

7-14-1997

Maiden, Amber Lisa
Peters-Hamlin, Kristan L.
Walsh, Natalie A.

7-17-1997

Crossley, Lee Ann

7-21-1997

Krygier, Kathleen Marie
Tuttle, Lois M.

7-22-1997

Shubeck, Linda Ann

7-23-1997

Dartez, Kathleen McTeague

7-28-1997

Todd, Kyra Ashbaugh

8-18-1997

Weiss, Jennifer Salzman

9-2-1997

Cessario, Lorraine Christie
Lincoln-Stewart, Kimberly A.

9-4-1997

Buckovich, Suzy Ann
Douglas, Terry
Focsaneanu, Raluca Cristina
Jones, Kristen Susan
Kuffner, Mary Lynn
Lee, Teresa Li-Sien

9-5-1997

Mason, Wallie Helen

9-8-1997

Latimer, L. Patrice

9-15-1997

Tunis, Nancy Deborah

10-6-1997

Strache, Vivian Clara

10-15-1997

Moore-Erickson, Pamela Mary

11-6-1997

Berry, Elizabeth G.

12-4-1997

Ruggieri, Andrea Maria

12-8-1997

Eisenman, Esther

12-15-1997

Carroll, Grace Burke
Evans, Karen Elizabeth
Michaud, Hillary Jane
Piper, Ann HaLarear McLeod
Sachs, Susan D.
Salen, Susan Richards
Shor, Nina
Sloan, Barbara A.

12-16-1997

Ahmad, Aisha
Alfriend, Kimberly Jane
Almason, Allison Louise
Andersen, Stacey Ellen
Anderson-Scott, Karen Lynette
Andrews, Julia
Arthur, Pamela June

Ashby, Tracy Evette
Assatourians, Liza Christine
Atwell-Davis, Carolyn E.
Ayoub, Krista Passmore
Ayres, Mary Elizabeth
Baccus, Nilaya Dara
Bagal, Sujatha
Baltimore, Karin Sandra
Barnabee, Randi Allison
Basham, Christine Affleck
Bautista, Josie Guia Murdoch
Beck, Reagan
Becker, Evelyn Cohen
Bena, Anna Marie
Bennett, Camille Anne
Bennett, Jacqueline Campbell
Berger, Lisa Beth
Berrington, Lacy Diane
Betch, Sharon N.
Bills, Amy Julia
Blakeney, Shellie N.
Bland, Carrie Anne
Bohnenstengel, Robin Knake
Bowe, Cynthia Lenay
Brennan, Suzanne P.
Bresnan Gibson, Paula M.
Briseno, Liliana Ochoa
Broadwater, Stacie J.
Brodie, Katherine Deming
Buchheister, Bevin Ann
Burns, Bethany Moir
Burton, June Kristal
Butler, Holly Drumheller
Butler, Jineki Christina
Butler, Susan M.
Calhoun, Bridget Eng
Callegher, Nancy L.
Cann, Emily Irene
Carlo, Meredith A.
Caro, Luisa
Carroll, Kristy Lee
Cataldi, Elizabeth L.
Chester, Laura Lynn
Christopher, Gina Marie
Ciarrocchi, Katherine Marie
Clagett, Ann Calvert Brooke
Clem, Denise
Coffer, Erin Mary
Cohen, Elana H.
Conlon, Erica J.
Cordier, Mariana C.
Cordish, Melissa Fishman
Cotton, Renee
Covert, Kimberly Lynn
Croissette, Rebecca
Culhane, Shelley R.
Curtis, Michelle R.
Daggett, Kirsten Noel
Dailey, Rosemary Eileen
Darling, Colleen Marie
Davenport, CeCe Cassandra
Davenport, Joan
Davis, Florence K. S.
Davis, Lisa Aimee
Dean, Jennifer Lee
Debry, Kristine
DeFreitas, Maury L.
Deng, Louise
Desai, Bina
DeSisto, Jamie L.
Deutschman, Jolie Starr
Devine, Marie Colette
Dickman, Marjorie J.
Dickon-Matney, Rachel Elizabeth
Diener, Betty Sue
Dixon, Jennifer Hazard
Dombal, Sheila Jean
Doud, Mary Teresa Anastasia
Douglas, Brenda Anna Leah
Dowton, Tamara Y.
Drew, Patricia S.
Drewry, Laura Katherine
Drinkard, Natalie Paige
Dudley, Julie Glass
Elshakhs, Muna Salah
Enemark, Christine Elizabeth
Enos, Katherine Davitt
Entis, Sara Barr
Epstein, Laura Rachel
Fairfax, Jennifer Sue
Fallon, Amanda M.
Feinstein, Deborah W.
Feldman, Jodi Lynn
Fenner, Natalie M. Stroud
Ferrandino, Maya Doane
Ferrari, Alejandra R.
Finch, Edral Laurita
Finch, Nataki Ayodele
First, Patricia Anne
Fischer, Mary Therese
Fishman, Vicki E.
Flaherty, Barbara M.
Flenner, Rise L.
Flum, Sheryl Beth
Forrester, Rosemarie Janise
Fotheringill, Linda M.
Fowler, Rebecca L.
Fox, Mary Josephine
Franklin, Stephanie Suzanne
Freedman, Bess
Friedman, Karen
Gable, Erin Darner
Gallagher, Stephanie Agli
Gallo-Ciscon, Jean Cheryl
Gally, Karen Russell
Gast, Lisa S.
Gauhar, Tashina
Gertner, Heidi Forster
Giantris, Laura Anne
Gibbs, Kirsten Elaine
Gibson, Paula M. Bresnan
Gilbertson, Lisa Marie
Gillespie, Andrea Baldwin
Glaze, Stacie Ann
Goldberg-Kraft, Emily Jane
Goldblatt, Lisa Ann
Goldsmith, Rebecca L.
Gordon, Leza M.
Greenawald, Heather Cameron
Gruber, Victoria Lynn
Jones, Pamela Schwab
Kafetz, Heather Libman
Kaiser, Lisa Kimberly
Keinan, Sarit
Kennedy, Patricia Ann
Kilroy, Kelly Garner
Kolleen, Kenlyn J.
Kulishek, Lisa Maria
Langhorn, Pamela L.
Leib, Gina A.
Lo, Bonnie Gerhardt
London, Robin Dawn
McGonagle, Erin Nugent
Miller, Lisa M.R.
Nathan, Bonnie Dunninger
Oberst, Amy Carrcon
Ornato, Kristen B.
Pardo, Michelle C.
Pashkoff, Dana B.
Pysher, Shannon Marie
Robb, Robin Lynn
Robinson, Johanna Boyle
Shopulski, Donna Kay Campbell
Solan, Andrea Marie
Staley, Allison C.
Thornton, Karen DaPonte
Tompkins, Karen G.
Vartanian, Emily
Vogel, Anne L.
Walsh, Michele Bresnick
Zavakos, Karen T.
Zellweger, Susan Chambers
Zentz, Gina Adams

12-17-1997

Allen, Jennifer Dawn
Bakeley, Avery Johnson
Calderazzi, Kathrine L.
Cheek, Teresa Ann
Clements, Lynn A.
Coleman, Donna Mitchell
Daniel, Terri L.
Eckert, Deborah Krassy
Flam, Anne Kurtz
Frankenhoff, E. Vivian Hamilton
Gil, Kelly Christine
Goodman, Wendy B.
Gordon, Marci Iris
Grannan, Kelly Lynn
Gray, Karen Juliet
Green, Elizabeth Anne
Greer, Felecia Love
Grindon, Tonya Mitchem
Gutrick, Raynette Rose
Hahn, Eva
Hamilton, Heather Dena
Hanback, Brandi B.
Hanna, Tiffany Christine
Hansan, Heidi Ann
Harbinger, Bonny
Hardenbrook, Kristin Amy
Harris, Erin Harper
Hashimoto, Erica Joan
Haskins, Cheryl Yvonne
Hawkins, Ayanna Damali
Healy, Sonya Elizabeth
Hernandez, Melanie Montalvo
Hess, Carolyn June
Heymann, Laura Ann
Holz, Andrea Sansbury
Hopkins, Tammy
Howie, Tami Jeanne
Huerta, Nancy E.
Hultgren, Inger Karen
Immerman, Tracy Jill
Ivers, Melissa L.
Ivey-Colson, Kirsten
Jackson, Carmen Nicole
Jefferson, Anna L.
Jenkins, Lisa-Gail Kingsley
Johnson, Diann Marie
Jolivet, Tina Maria
Jones, Cherie Juliet
Joyce, Kathleen Marie
Judish, Julia Eden
Kaminetz, Cass Laurel Jones
Kaouris, Michelle Denise
Kashatus, Jennifer Myers
Kearns, Shannon Erika
Keniry, Shannon Patricia
Kenniston, Kristi Aasta
Kerns, Alice Fleury
Kessler, Pamela May
Keyes, Mary Helen
Khoury, Andrea Marie
Kimbrell, Stephanie Anne
King, Donna M. Burdyck
King, Elisha Anne
Kisch, Lori Beth
Knorr, Michele L.
Knowles, Tara Beth
Ko, Anita H.
Koehler, Beth Anne
Koerber, Donna Flohr
Konopka, Kathleen M.
Kothari, Rupal Girish
Kovalsky, Laura Gorman
Kraus, Heidi Leah
Krawczyk, Nancy Teresa
La Forge, Amanda S.
Lauerman, Colleen Marie
Lawrence-Whittaker, Lorraine Valerie
Lawton, Julie D.
Layman, Jenifer Amy
Lee, Eileen Cynthia
Letourneau, Rachel Murray
Leveque, Renee Michelle
Levine, Tracy Ellen
Lewis-David, Jennifer Lundgren
Liberatore, Maura
Linde, Selena Janine
Lourie, Linda S.
Lowery, Ruth Ann
Lubinski, Jennifer Sutherland
Lucas, Pamela Reid
Lydic, Karlene M.
Lynch, Dana O.
Mack, Munira Saeeda
Magee, Peggy Ann
Magid, Carol Joanna
Makrodimitris, Pinelopi
Malekzadeh, Ann Hart
Manasseh, Regina Sabrene
Mansoian, Martha Alice
Marshall, Shannon Madden
Martin, Jena Tonice
Martinez, JoAnn A.
Matta, Julia C.
May, Julia Kumpfer
Mayer, Stacy Adele
McAllister, Jennifer Boyd
McCabe, Heather R.
McCotter-Jacobs, Verjeana C.
McCray, Joni Elizabeth
McCullough, Catherine Maureen
McGarry, Jennifer Ellen
McGee, Jennifer Hammer
McGriff, Alison Jordan
McLemore, Mignon
McPhee, Gillian
McQuiston, Cathie Jane
McSpaden, Clare Shea
Mead, Maxine M.
Meade, Allison Marie
Mendelsohn, Jennifer E.
Mensoian, Martha Alice

Merola, Michelle Lynn
Meyer, Maureen A.
Minifie, Margaret Chapin
Monahan, Emmy S.
Morris, Daphne Ann
Morrison, Rebecca Khamneipur
Moss, Aubrey Lynn
Mulroy, Tracy Lynn
Myers, Therese Marie
Nanney, Marysabel Milagros
Napier, Stephanie Lynn
Newcomb, Christine J.
Newlin, Jamyle Katherine
Nieva, Jocelyn C.
Nixon, Donna Marie
O'Donnell, Jill Elizabeth
Ohri, Shaila Lakhani
Raza, Syeda B.
Riley, Kelly McCormick
Rochez, Jo An
Shaw, Regina Hart
Somerville, Amy Elizabeth Hott
Stavlas, Catherine McCallie
Ward, Juanita Hopkins
Zimmet, Gilda Mann

12-18-1997
Agin, Neely B.
Albin, Laurel Anne
Ard, Hannah Anne Stires
Birdsill, Cynthia Stewart
Blumenfeld, Michele Zahner
Borsoni, Jennifer E.
Burton, Emma Katherine
Cape, Omiga C.
Castiello, Cecilia R.
Cogen, Rachel Elizabeth
Conway, Melissa Smith
Deem, Patricia Anne
Dillard, Michele Saba
Edelman, Mira Vayda
Erb, Melissa Margaret
Fetter, Rachel Sternberg
Fleming, Britt Speyer
Grant, Kathy Anne
Hauptmann, Robin Elizabeth
Hersh, Caren S.
Holland, Diana Lynn
Huygen, Julie J. Rim
Kessler, Ida Josefina
Ketchum, Stephanie W.
Lile, Natalie Rae
Lorge, Sonya F.
Lubar, Jessica Rutberg
Margolius, Robye Shaw
Markham, Colleen L. S.
McClure, Elizabeth Stacy
Mester, Antoinette Hope
Mihavetz, Lenora Fanelli
Morales, Manar Sweillam
Moran, Caryn Judith Stoskus
Nash, Suzanne
O'Herron, Suzanne
O'Leary, Jane Marie
O'Rourke, Maria M.
Ogg, Joelle Kay
Oliver, Brenda Jean
Oliver, Margaret Hackett
Ornstein, Chantel Renee
Ouimette, Mary Lorraine
Palan, Elizabeth W.
Pande, Nalini K.
Pappas, Christina Jessica
Parks, Katherine Jennifer
Patton, Sonia Ann
Paytas, Antoinette DeLiso
Pearson, Ericca Loi
Peele, Vernell Yvonne P.
Pell, Deborah Owen
Perkins, Susan Stacy
Perry, Miranda
Perry, Victoria Anne
Petersen, Susan Marie
Pettigrew, Lynne E.
Picou, Ilona Prieto
Pilgrim, Michelle Antoinette
Pistey, Nora Elizabeth
Powers, Melissa
Press, Michelle Lynn
Price, Tracey Michelle
Provencio, Elizabeth Marie
Rath, Erika C.
Rausch, Siobhan Courtney
Ray, Venita Carol
Redd, Alisa T.
Reed, Elizabeth J.
Reed, Johana Arvada
Reed, LaVonda Nichelle
Reichard, Amy Marie
Reichmann, Deborah Andrea
Resnick, Ellen Marie
Resnik, Dana Deisinger
Reza, Sadaf Mona
Ricciardella, Lynn Elizabeth
Richeimer, Gabriela Anita Maria
Richmond, Traci Meakem
Richter, Judith Horowitz
Rives, Kelli Mattiford
Roberts, Carey Shea
Roberts, Christine Sarudy
Robins, Irma Jacqueline
Robinson, Stephanie
Rosen, Candace Jaclyn
Rosenblum, Elyse
Rubin, Allison Epstein
Rulnick, Alisa Tishler
Runte, Christine R.
Rupp, Megan Elizabeth
Ruth, Laura Jeanne
Sanzaro, Karen M.
Sapir, Genevieve D.
Saslow, Julie Anna
Scali, Mary Ann
Scharf, Allison Fainberg
Scherer, Monica Lee
Schoeps, Robin Jeanne
Schowalter, Rachel Lynne
Sendek-Smith, Kristine L.
Shack, Stephanie Lynn
Shaw, Millicent Cheryl
Shearin, Kimberly Maria
Sherman, Stacy L.
Simon, Michelle Jill
Simpson, Christine
Skalaban, Paula Primost
Smalls, Linda Maria
Smith, Barbara Vanessa
Smith, Caroline Carter
Smith, Rachel Elizabeth
Smith, Susan Elizabeth
Snyder, Hilarie Elise
Solomon, Shana M.
Spradlin-Dahn, Linda Theresa
Staley, Mary Jean Reyburn
Stefani, Laura A.
Stein, Christine Collins
Steiner, Tracey Bohn
Stevens, Kathryn E.
Stevens, Mary Harding
Steyer, Bobbie Granville
Strent, Amy Beth
Strimel, Mary Nicole
Subar, Ilana
Swanson, Greta E.
Symoun, Stacey Lynn
Taylor, Jennifer C.
Terrasa, Jennifer Rachel
Tharp, Cathlene Anne
Thomas, Gwendolyn Catherine
Thompson, Deborah Kim St. Lawrence
Thornton, Kenya Ani
Tidler, Cynthia Elizabeth
Trigg, Shari Jenell
Tucci, Elizabeth Olivia
Turner, Wendy Ann
van Beek, Carla Christina
Van Driesen, Jennifer Suzanne
Verhage, Laura Allard
Vierbuchen, Margaret M.
Wales, Michele Makos
Waller, Tonya Louise
Watson, Susan Vanessa
Wein, Olivia Bae
Weiner, Janice Lynn
Weiskittel, Katharine M.
Weiss, Carolyn Peri
Westover, Gail Lynn
White, Carrie Purcell
Whitehead, Kathryn Ann
Whiteman, Nancy Elizabeth
Williams, Heather Shalane
Wilson, Cheryle Lynne
Wilt, Beth A.
Wolf, Margaret B.
Woodard, Kimberly Rochelle
Woung, Simone Marie
Wroblewski, Tamara Devon
Xiques, Gladys
Young, Kimberly Rae
Zell, Nicole Marie
Ziropoulos, Kimberly D.
Zuckerman, Claudia Jeanne

12-22-1997
Giordano, Cynthia Ann
Harris, Ellen
Little, Cathryn MacDonald
Sangree, Suzanne

12-29-1997
Craig, Carol Huston
Mathis, Judith L.

1-5-1998
Rosenberg, Meryl Berger

1-8-1998
Beeson, Mylie A.
Cook, Erica Millicent
Cox, Jaffray Edens
Dierbeck, Robin L.
Heller, Martha E.
Horn, Jennifer Maude
Lester, Laura S.
Martz, Stephanie A.
Xinis, Paula

1-12-1998
Browning, Dawn M.

1-13-1998
Santoni, Cynthia Lee

1-20-1998
Dimmick, Julieann

1-26-1998
Argentieri, Sabrina Marie
Vavrina, Mary R.

1-27-1998
Dennis, Andrea Lesley
Jefferson, Jamila Efuru

1-30-1998
Horne, Lisa Ann
Northrop, Patricia Taibo

2-2-1998
Lonergan, Kelleen McGinnis

2-5-1998
Applebaum, Jill Robin
Murray, Teresa W.

2-23-1998
Jafarnia, F. Allyson Parvizian

3-5-1998
Laro, Marlene Ellen
Murphy, Paula C.
Roig, Julia Anne

4-2-1998
Dominique, Manuelletta Ann
Fox, Pamela S.
Magill, Mary Elizabeth
Vann, Diane Hill

6-4-1998
Lang, Lindsey Bishop
Wilbon, Bernadette Marie

6-8-1998
Amell, Laurie A.
Brodney, Fern J.
Byrum, Lesa Leonard
Clark, Julia Akins
Flatt, Denise Ferguson
Jarva Weiss, Sandra L.
Mair, Julie Samia
Schulze, Katharine Anne
Weiss, Sandra L. Jarva

6-9-1998
Burton, Barbara Lynne
Litwin, Hedda E.
St. Laurent, Ann

6-11-1998
Baran, Tama Vail
Buser, Stephanie Lynne
Campbell, Victoria L.
Chung, Eun Kyung
Liles, Detria Jennell
Murry, Laura L.
Wright, Teresa Burke

6-12-1998
Zinsner, Mary Catherine

6-15-1998
Hand, Laurie A.
Moore, Karen H.

6-17-1998
Camp, Marva Jo

6-18-1998

Dubinsky, Joan Elise
Persico, Deborah A.
Seiver, Dinah Abigail

6-23-1998

Adams, Sylvia Lorraine
Adelman, Joan Patrice
Allen, Mary Ellen
Allen, Vanessa L.
Alvaro, Leith Rochelle
Amitay, Cheryl Aviva
An, Gi Hyun
Andrews, Leslie Dionne
Ardis, Karen S.
Arfaa, Julia Renee
Aronson, Mary
Arrindell, Deborah Jeanne
August, Victoria Rae
Averion-Mahloch, Rowena
Bagby, Melanie E.W.
Bailey, L. Raquel
Bailey, Lorena Cecilia
Balian, Grace Mary
Bare, Susan Elaine
Barr, Nancy G.
Bauer, Carla A.
Benton, Arlene Marie
Bernstein, Michelle Doses
Betts, April Collins
Bierwirth, Margaret van Ekeren
Blades, Tracy G.
Blank, Kathleen Alice
Board, L. Juanita
Boeckman, Ann Mileur
Bondon, Celeste Alaine
Boulay, Corrie A.
Brashers-Krug, Patricia Gail
Bright, Robin Dana Gill
Brody-Brown, Dana A.
Brooks, Annalisa
Brooks, Kimberly Ann
Broten, Lisa Louise
Bull, Tracy Lynn
Burse, LaTina Luvette
Butler, Joann Ruth
Caballero, Theresa
Campbell, Rhonda Lisa
Camper, Deborah Fontaine
Canino, Valerie A.
Cavanagh, Rosemary
Chen, Irene Huei-min
Chen, Katherine
Chettle, J. Anne
Chow, Karen Hsin-Hui
Chu, Belinda Ann
Ciccolo, Angela
Clarke, Idi Aisha
Cockrum, Carlynne Sharma
Coke-Hamilton, Pamela R.
Cole, Tanisha Marie
Cooper, Alfreda Denise
Cooper, Catherine A.
Cover, Danielle Renee
Cover-Huntley, Dawn L.
Curtis, Tina
da Rocha-Afodu, Oluremi Olatokunbo
Dalal, Kosha Kantharia
Dalier, Lauriel Flower
Davis, Charlotte Ecker
Davis, Sylvia Denise
DeCesaris, Annette
Delia, Dawn Marie
DiAntonio, Janet Victoria
DiFilippo, LeeAnne
Dobson, Dana Carolyn
Dornburg, Erica M.
Dougherty, Erin Paula
Drexler, Jessica N.
Edelstein, Michelle J.
Enoch Poling, Diane Kerry
Ezar, Christine Marie
Fall, Camille Blake
Farris, Elaine Lynn
Feeley, Maria Ann
Feinberg, Elizabeth H.
Fidler, Danielle Caroline
Filardi, Maria Frigo
Fischer, Elizabeth Margaret
Fleury, Nicolle Mary
Foltin, Sandra
Forlini, Janet Heald
Gerber, Mary Ann
Gervin, Larmon Rachel
Goldman, Linda Marie
Gonzaga, Maria Cristina Borromeo
Graham, Dorothy Jean
Grant, Lakeisha Belan
Greczek, Elizabeth A.
Green-Brown, Camela Olivia
Guido, Perri Karen
Gulati, Sonia
Hamel, Suzanne Patrice
Handal, Lissette Maria
Hatfield, Lisa Roberson
Hawkins, Cynthia Aleece
Hayes, Latonya Adel Grant
Heifetz, Melissa Tobi
Hemmendinger, Lisa Meredith
Herron, Sharon Renie
Herson-Jones, Lorraine M.
Hochberg, Vera Beatriz Menda
Horton, Elizabeth Duvigneaud
Hou, Hsin-Pin
Hwang-Edwards, Amy Y.
Irish, Rachel B.
Isaacson, Keli Barbara Cunningham
Jarmon, Monique Melisan Adele Foard
Jefferson, Tricia Gail
Jenkins, Lisa Marie
Jones, Diane Ruth
Jones, Kristin F.
Jones, Mary Ann Alexis
Karger, Stacy Lyn
Karpa, Jill Leslie
Kaschak, Leslie Jones
Kasdin, Tovah Marlowe
Kathan, Ann Nicole
Kaye, Carole Penny
Kenney, Teresa Westby
Kenny, Patricia Ann
Kim, Clara Anne
Kim, Gina
Kim, Haekyong Christine
Kim, Mia Sunmee
Klass, Michelle E.
Koch, Robbie N.
Kovacs, Julia Teresa
Krewson, Beth A.
Krips, Cynthia Rachel
Kumbula-Fraser, Mandinema R.
Kwiedorowicz, Laurie Ann
Lee, Jeanny Kim
McGuigan, Kathleen Bauersfeld
O'Connor, Patricia Gieringer
Otis, Laura A.
Penn, Laura Karen Bass
Podger, Sara B.
Poling, Diane Kerry Enoch
Rogers, Jane Saindon
Smollon, Alicia L.
Stewart, Elizabeth A.
Stewart, Joyce E.
Thompson, Delores Gardner
Tuminello, Katherine Ann Mathias
Turner, Leah Darring
Van Bergen, Deborah Grace
Watts, Kimberlee Davis
Wolfe, Marla Rizzo

6-24-1998

Ausby, Kendra Young
Bartko, Norma J.
Brown, Barbara Troffkin
Brown, Heather Allyse Palmer
Cole, Erika Evette
DiPietro, Kimberly Tremel
Dohrmann, Dawn M.
Frederick, Tessa Laspia
Golden, Jennifer Scott
Greene, Arcelia Lillian
Jones, Amy Beth
LaVey, Dina Marie
Lay, Christine Ann
Lazo-Miller, Teresa
Leary, Susan Sween
Lee, Inez
Lee, Jennifer Kyung
Leiby, Lana Lynn
Lemanski, Susan Marie
Lerner, Vivian Diane
Leslie-Miller, Jana Suzanne
Lewandowski, Anne Cori
Liffers, Wendy Ann
Lizas, Rania P.
Llaurado, Mireya Anne Rosa
Long, Alison Boothby
Loughran, Alison Lyn
Ludlow, Marianne Jenean
Lyons-Atwell, Donna L.
Mabanta, Melodie Marie
Madison, Tammara C.
Maleno, Barbara Lynn
Manganaro, Nicole Faith
Mansourkia, Magnolia
Maskol, Cynthia Lee
Mason, Jana Lynn
Masri, Selwa
Maxwell, Susannah Irwin
Maynard, Kathleen Morgan
McBride, Dolores A.
McCarthy, Marcia K.
McDermott, Judith A.
McIntosh, Andrea Stults
McKenzie-John, Koren
McWright, Laura Townsend
Melita, Amie J. C.
Menker, Amy Catherine
Merkle, Jennifer Marie
Merlo, Kathleen Ann
Mertz, Andrea E.
Meseck, Marcia Lynn
Miller, Anne Margaret
Mirshah, Hasti
Mitzel, Sidney Monica
Monroe, Monica Marie
Morinigo, Maria Jose
Moylan, Joyce A.
Mulrain, Lisa Victoria
Nagel, Raenell Leigh
Nelson, Lisa M.
Nicholson, Kristin Elizabeth
Nicholson, May Leah
Nicpon, Dory L.
Novina, Julia Anne
Nwakanma, Uloaku Nkechi
O'Malley, Grace Denise
Oesterreicher, Maria Louise
Owens, Pamela Tarris
Paddack, Stacy Stiffel
Palermo, Nancy Maria
Panarella, Roxane Michael
Parks, Denise Adele
Paskel, Shanetta Julane
Pelaez, Maria Soledad
Pelosi, Samantha Joan
Peoples, Kim Eugene
Perry, Michelle L.
Peterson, Denise E.
Petro-Siraj, Michelle Danielle
Posner, Gerilyn Ann
Powell, Linda Ann
Rancier, Kaitlin T.
Renee, Leane
Richardson, Ami Lynn
Rizk, Rania Ragab
Robinson, Judith L.
Romeo, Jennifer Leigh
Rosenbaum, Tatyana
Rowell, Theresa Ann
Rowthorn, Virginia Mary
Ruderman, Elisa F.
Rudgers, Sarah Beth
Ruff, Katherine Lindsay
Rugani, Jennifer Reusse
Rutenberg, Lisa Michelle
Saint-Amour, Teresa Elizabeth
Sanchez-Aldana, Cristina
Sayles, Crystal D.
Schauer, Teresa Lee
Schuster, Patricia Solomon
Sellers, Melissa Scanlan
Sewchand, Karenina Nadira
Shanklin, Carita Tania
Shaw, Karen Maureen
Sheffield, Joi Elisa
Shelton, Lori Katrine Hansen
Shephard, Kate Harding
Sheppard, Cara Elisabeth
Sheppard, Christle Lynn
Shifrin, Patricia White
Shyr, Linda Summy Jiinwen
Simon, Karen Hannah
Simpson, Christina M.
Sims, Savalle Charlesia
Sims-Taylor, Lynne
Slay, Cheryl Lynn
Snead, Lisa Merchant
So, Jennifer Kwak
Sonnier, Yolanda Florena
Spicer, Erika Elyse
Stateman, Janet Sylvia
Staudinger, Deborah Kim
Stephanos, Ann M.
Storey, Heather Ann
Strauss, Rena Lynne

Stroman, Cynthia Anne May
Sullivan, Kathleen Frances
Sullivan, Terry Kathleen
Swayne, Janet
Tao, Josephine J.
Taylor, Jessica D.
Taylor, Tamela Jacobs
Teiman, Rachel Susan
Terrell-Collier, Tanya N.
Thomas, Amy Elizabeth
Thompson, Diane April
Thompson, Toya Jenine
Tiedeman, Jennifer L.
Timian, Jennifer T.
Tseytlin, Natalia
Urban, Tracey Lynne
Van Horn, Karen Elizabeth
van Stiphout, Monique A.
Vercelli, Patricia N.
Walker, Jill Susan
Washington, Alicia Dorothy
Watkins, Margaret Taylor
Weinfeld, Carrie Beth
Whelan, Helen M.
Williams, Lani LaRue
Williams, Tari D.
Wills, Batina Renee
Woodham, Camella Mercedes
Woods, Deon Marquette
Yackanech, Kristina Denise
Young, Andrea E.
Zuback, Katherine Crotty

6-26-1998

Clark, Jeanette Jackson

7-6-1998

Kim, Heejun

7-8-1998

Burkhart, Mary-Ann Runnels
Casey, Laura Westfall
D'Elicio, Christine Pillsbury
Eichinger, Katja Morgaine
Key, Renee S.
Sotelo, Martha Leary
Westfall Casey, Laura

7-10-1998

Lee, Clarice Parrish

7-14-1998

Bradley, Lorrie A.

7-16-1998

Fincher, Donna Esposito

7-17-1998

Wells, Kathy Bradley

7-27-1998

Jordan, Laura Elizabeth

8-14-1998

Marisa, Suzanne Law

9-4-1998

Oyenusi, Morenike Olaore Euba

9-8-1998

Kang, Seung Oh
McDermott, Dana P.
Pillai, S. Ramani
Waiguchu, Elizabeth M.
Williams, Jennifer Kristine

10-14-1998

Brown, Eilene

10-30-1998

Goldstein, Janet Lyn

11-5-1998

McAllister, Brenda

11-19-1998

Kosaraju, Sheela

12-14-1998

Zimmerman, Barbara A.

12-15-1998

Abbott, Yvonne Renee
Adams, April Joan
Adelman-Snee, Sheryl
Aiken, Deirdre Theresa
Alafassos, Panayiota C.
Albany, Jennifer R.
Albertini, Dana Marie
Allen, Jennie D.
Alt, Nicole A.
Andrews, Mary Kirsten
Anwar, Shazia Nazli
Arnold, Barbara Arlette
Arthur, Bonnie Kay
Avelenda, Saily Maria
Badolato, Michelle Hope
Bakari, Adisa P.
Balbach, Jeanine Koenig
Balliet, Heidi A.
Baraf, Alison Stacy
Barr, Judith Ann
Bartelt, Christen Elizabeth
Barton, Lisa Rose
Bastin, Diane Joanna
Bathersfield, Nizanna
Belouin, Tami Cohen
Benacci, Christina Marie
Bernstein, Tanya Calvelli
Bertsch, Anne Marie
Berube, Anne D.
Bethman, Linda Maya
Biederman, Laura Kim
Bilenker, Stephanie Anne
Bloss-Baum, Linda
Boncutter, Jennifer Rebecca
Boone, Tristi Ann
Bose, Emily Quarles
Bosse, Lisa Staro
Bou, Jennifer Lynn
Boyd, Carmen L.
Bracknell, Rebecca Chesno
Brewster, Ravindra Robert
Brewster-Johnson, Jessica Y.
Brignoli, Barbra Christine
Brinkerhoff, Susan
Bristol, Lynn A.
Brodey, Jessica Mara
Brodie, Lisa Suzanne
Browder, Erica Marie
Brown, Kristen Elizabeth
Brown, Marylou G.
Brown, Zhonette M.
Brukiewa, Melody Ann
Brust, Laura Ford
Bryson, Molly Rebecca
Burrell, Meredith L.
Bushyeager, Amy
Busse, Jennifer Rebecca
Butler, Michelle L.
Calvelli, Tanya Marie
Calvert, Cynthia Thomas
Campbell, Nicole Lefcourt
Carney, Mary Elizabeth
Carr, Jennifer Michelle
Carter, Lisa Coleman
Chan, Linda Elaine
Chasanov, Amy Beth
Choy, Angela Wai-Yuah
Cino, Margaret Joan
Clark, Heather Doherty
Clark, Jeanne M.
Clarke, Jennifer Lynn
Cline, Paula Jean
Colburn, Kathryn Rivard
Cole, Michelle White
Conliffe, Leza Marie
Cook, Susan Margaret
Copeland, Melissa Kaye
Costello, Jennifer L.
Coyne, Jennifer Jean
Crawford, Jennifer Lynn
Cryor, Maisha Fry
Curry, Wytonja L.
Daken, Sarah Beth
Dalzell, Elizabeth M.
Daniels, Kara Lynn
Datta, Veena
Davis, Mary-Denise
de Vastey Jones, Claude
Degraffenreed, Nicole M.
DeHaven, Leesa Alberta
Dekraai, Stephanie Renae
Delaney, Suzanne Patrice
Delgado, Ann-Marie C.
Delk, Patricia Lynne
Demeo, Regina Angelica
Devery, Jennifer Ruth
Dey, Irene
DiDonato, Michelle
Diggs, Francine Chambers
Dixon, Mary M.
Dudderar, Heidi Elizabeth
Duncan, Jayci Shaw
Dunkerton, Kristine June
Duzon, Veronica Anastasia
Ellis, Allison MacDonald
Engleby, Linda Nash
Ennis, Gail Susan
Esposito, Lesli Christine
Evans, Crystal Lynette
Fairfax, Cydonii V.
Ferrando, Catherine E. C.
Field, Ingrid Lorraine Dietsch
Finder, Jodi
Fink, Jeanne Martyn
Fisher, Janet Claire
Fitzgibbons, Amy Steffan
Flanagan, Beverly Meindl
Fleischaker, Deborah T.
Flory, Gillian
Flynn, Brande Allison
Flynn, Kristen
Fontenelle, Christine Clare
Fowler, Elizabeth Jean
Frank, Melanie Ann
Freeman, Katherine H.
Frenkiel, Nora Michele
Fridie, Janice Patricia
Frost, Amanda H.
Gardner, Mary Elisabeth
Gelhaus, Jeanine Marie
German, Teresa Sue
Geyer, Laura Talley
Glaser McCahan, Mara A.
Goffman, Lisa Jill
Goldman, Sarah Hankey
Goldsmith, Therese M.
Goorevitz, Tamara Beth
Gough, Dawn Michelle
Graham, Jessica Carey
Grammas, Carolynn Flowers
Granger, Erin O'Brien
Graves, Tarnisha Antoinette
Gray, Forestine Nicole
Green, Lora Marie
Green, Sheri Nicole
Greenwood, Amy Elizabeth
Griffin-Lawman, Tammy Lin
Grillo, Ann Marie
Gross, Leslie Marie
Gruber, Stacie Lynn
Gully, Pamela Rochelle
Halloran, Colleen Marie
Hambrick, Edith Lorraine
Hamilton, Shelby Gaye
Hammond, Jennifer J.
Howard, Alexis D.
Lyn, Jessica Glick
Lynn, Carolyn Coffey
Maydanich, Zhanna A.
Miller, Larissa N.
Oberbroeckling, Laura J.
Osofsky, Lisa Kate
Paliath, Tracey Cohen
Paskey, Diane Mary
Peterson, Carrie Lynn
Ryan, Patricia Dorothy
Seifert, Jennifer Rae
Thompson, Amy Gibson
Thompson, Christie Grymes
Weltsch, Lisa Cohen
White, Zoe Gillen

12-16-1998

Adkins, Jamie Erin
Bell, Belinda Virginia
Bober, Jennifer M.
Darby, Jennifer Louise
Davis, Jennifer Eleanor
Delp, Tracey Johns
Dickinson, Michelle Jeanine
Downie, Ericka L.
Doyle, Kara Dawn
Harper, Antoinette McIntosh
Harris, Elizabeth Favor
Harris, Kaprice Lynch
Hart, Melissa Danielle
Hartley, Angela Hibbard
Haughton-Denniston, Pamela G.
Heifetz, Kimberly Roeder
Hemelt, Diane Marie
Hertzberg, Elisabeth Miller
Hess, Wendy Noel
Hickey, Anne Therese
Himes, Lisa Norrett
Hirshorn, Rebeca Mayme
Holliday, Melinda Denee
Holloway, Alberta Archie
Hoover, Lydia Belinda
Howe, Amy
Hubbard, Amanda Marie
Hughes, Nicole
Hughes, Shantelle Denise
Imamshah, Nicole Marie

Jalloh, Jeneba
Japp, Jenny Yang
Jimenez, Vanessa Juliette
Johnson, Carolyn Prue
Johnson, Dina Cannariato
Johnson, Jeaneen J.
Johnson, Repunzelle Rachelle
Johnson, Sandra Lynn
Johnson, Sharon
Jones, Allison Mardel
Jones, Dana Lynn
Jones, Darby
Jones, Kimberly Annwyl
Jones, Liza Korsah
Kafele, Heather Lamberg
Kaguyutan, Janice Victoria
Katz, Donna Amy
Keenan, Mary F.
Kemp, Lynne Cameron
Kennedy, Jennifer Jaye Jenkins
Kent, Rachael Dianne
Kessler, Margaret L.
Kidd, M. Elizabeth
Kilgore, Charlane Sue Trautman
Klebasko, Gretchen L.
Kleeman, Jennifer Leigh
Kline, Kimberly Ann
Kline Dubill, Rebecca Leigh
Klohe, Trena Lee
Knox, Anissa Dianne
Kolton, Barbra Marcus
Kraemer, Grace Higbie
Kramer, Anessa Owen
Kronthal, Jennie VanGinkel
Krosnick, Freda L.
Kulynych, Jennifer Jeryl
Lamb, Melissa E.
Larsen, Kerry Elizabeth
Lattin, Stephanie Tara
Lau, Kimberly A.
Leader, Allison B.
Lee, Baotran H.
Levine, Amy Lynne
Levine, Melissa Beth
Levitan, Sandra Lee
Levitt, Marilyn Ruth
Lewin, Genia Stacy
Liberatore, Renee M.
Lieberman, Hannah E.M.
Lindquist, Leigh Ann
Lindsey, Sarah Catherine
Lippincott, Alexandria
Littleton, Cecilia J.
Lostumbo, Rachel
Loubier, Erin M.
Lovett, Kelly Culp
Lutz, Joan
Mabey, Tamara Lynn
Maher, Heather Ann
Mallory, Lark T.
Manculich, Michele A.
Marcuss, Elena Daly
Martinez, Elizabeth Anne A.
Mason, Angela N.
Mason, Nicole Christine
Massengale, Jennifer Lynn
Matthews, Tamarra Dion
Mayer, Linda Anne
Mbye, Neneh
McCann, Cynthia L.
McCormick, Kelly A.
McFadden, Janet R.
McGinnis, Amy Lynn
McGrath, Felicity Ann
McMillan, Kimberly Denise
McRae, Kenya DaNeen
Mead, Anne Martin
Melton, Leigh Roberts
Mendelson, Sondra Tova
Miller, Allyson Blair
Miller, Miriam Dale Sanders
Milner, Aliza M.
Milnor, Cristina A.
Milton, Marisa Lorraine
Mittelstadt, Jill Renee B.
Modhera, Gazal Gulam-Mohmed
Moghadam, Sara Z.
Moran, Stephanie Denae
Morrison, Hillorie Salomon
Morton, Jennifer L.
Motsko, Michelle Mayer
Motz, Catherine Jane
Mowry, Kristin Heim
Muller, Susan Stidham
Myers, Malia S.
Nasrah, Melissa Marie
Nathanson, Kirsten L.
Nee, Susan Margaret
Nelms, Laura Diane
Nemec, Jennifer Alexandra
Ness, Jennifer Amy
Nolin, Christine L.
Noone, Mary-Ellen
Nulty, Erin Elizabeth
O'Connell, Patricia Jean
O'Malley, Melinda Kimmitt
O'Neill, Wendy Sue
Ober, Robin A.
Offley, Susan Christine
Ollie, Leandra Louise
Onorato, Joanna R.
Orenstein, Lisa Faye
Owens, Sabra McDonald
Pahlavi, Yasmine
Palazzolo, Catherine Pauline
Paniker, Anita
Park, Stephanie J.
Parker, Marcia Debra
Patton, Traci Rose
Pollard, Laura Diane
Rubin, Leslie Eden
Schneiderman, Lisa Klein
Shields, Linda Lee
Shrift, Emily Anne
Singh, Preeti
Smith, Irene J.
Smyth, Heather Leigh
Snyder, Amy Landbeck
Varda, Tracy Lee
Vieira, Patricia Kennedy
Williams, Amber Lee

12-17-1998

Ambrose, Candace Keziah
Barkow, Rachel E.
Bellin, Catherine A.
Bolling, Melinda Mills
Bott, Corey Smith
Brown, Anne Margaret
Butler, Evelyn Rubino
Chan, Darcie Ellen
Cleary, Patricia
Day, Gina M.
Dickerson, Tracie
DiMatteo, Julie Yohey
Dincau, Kelly Greer
Duncan, Michelle
Forrest, Latina Shavon
Ghosal, Linda M.
Gill, Tanya
Goldberg, Julie Rubin
Grabel, Jennifer Storm
Guy, Melissa Ann
Hennes, Christine Raub
Jackman, Jennifer Smith
Jaffe, Julianne R.
Johnson, Nina Smallwood
Juergens, Lori Ann
Kovaleski, Amy Schrack
Lazenby, Jennifer Ryan
Martey, Pamela Martekor
Mebane, Pamela Ruth
Nicol, Anna Welch
Patterson-Strachan, Shaunda
Paulding, Marquette D.
Peeples, Brandy Ann
Pekin, Kathleen
Pelly, Maija
Penman, Janis Marie
Peters, Lori-Ann Shastin
Peters, Mary Irvin
Peters, Rachel Anne Vento
Peterson, Sieglinde Talbott
Pettay, Marci Jane
Phan, Loan Kim
Phillips, Brandi Lynn
Pickett, Stacy Stanlee
Piper, Karen Rhoberta
Plotner, Chin-Zen Lin
Poole, Brooke Dana
Pratico, Lynne Marie
Prozinski, Jennifer Gerstner
Rains, Jennifer Bridget
Raysor-Taylor, Sandy Deloris
Rednik, Debra Heather
Reynolds, Alicia Carey
Rhoads, Carrie Aleen
Ringer, Cheryl Melissa Ann
Robinson, Kimberly Yvette
Rohall, Anne Catherine Parrette
Rohr, Jennifer
Rooyani, Rodin
Rose, Yvette Armas
Rosler, Mandee Alahna Stephanie
Ross, Cynthia Ann
Rubenstein, Lauren
Rubino, Laura-Lynne
Rudnick, Elizabeth Sarah
Scarlett, Sophia Dawn Marie
Scher, Malka
Schifferle, Lisa Naomi Weintraub
Schmidhauser, Susan Gail
Schneider, Marci M.
Scott, Janine Angela
Scott, Kristie Wilson
Sege, Jill D.
Shanks, Laurel Elspeth
Sharkey, Catherine Moira
Shaw, Nicole CherElle
Shelton, Deborah Marie
Short, Jennifer E.
Shubert, Leslie Ann
Shuren, Allison Weber
Simmons, Jennifer Annette
Sinkler, Chinita Monroe
Skucas, Ruta Kalvaitis
Smallwood Johnson, Nina
Smith, Linda
Smith, Tiffanie Renae
Snyder, Jo Carol
Solomon, Lisa A.
Song, Patricia Tilley
Spencer, Amy Y.
Sprinkle, Julianne Joan
Sterner, Karen Lynn
Stewart, Penelope Diana
Stoia, Daniela
Strojny, Suzanne Rose
Sullivan, Karen S. VanHoy
Suski, Amy Elizabeth
Szokoly, Robyne L.
Tate, Tshneka Taiyana
Terzaken, Ann Marie
Thomas, Heather A.
Thompson, Ronnette Angela
Thorgeirsson, Sif
Thorpe, Lisa Vanston
Tornatore, Tonia June
Tracy, Maureen Sarah
Trail, Lisa S.
Trasatti, Marisa Anne
Tschernia, Irma Irene
Tsiros, Alexandra Ann
Tucker, Gail R. Harleston
Tucker, Jenifer Sutton
Tucker, Jennifer Marie
Tumidolsky, Rachel
Turner, Nadine Sharisse
Underwood, Jamie Diane
Urban, Judith Ann
Vallandingham, Ann Marie
Vallario, Lisa Beth
Van Voorhis, Dawn L.
VanEmburgh, Sharon Marie
Vaquera, Kristina Helen Szulc
Vargas, Mary C.
Veilleux, Nicole
Vossler, Colleen Kotyk
Waites, Veronique Katherine
Ward, Rachel Lyn
Warden, Kimberley Diane
Warfield, Melanie Wallis
Washington, Kimberly Chante
Watters, Marcia Dawn
Weidenbach, Mary Ledwell
Weil, Jennifer E. Spieler
Welter, Robyn Beth
Wexler, Liza Anne
White, Erica Denise
Whiteaker, Helen Jane
Whittaker, Tiffani K.
Willard, Linda Zeller
Williams, Carol L.
Williams, Deborah Diane Smuda
Wingfield, Alita Tonette
Winston, Wynde Juliet
Wojeck, Lisa Irene
Wong, Amy Reynolds
Wood, Gillian Cara
Woodruff, Leslie Ellen
Wooley, Leslye Evelyn
Wootton, Barbara Helen
Wright, Tiwana Latise
Yeh, Lucinda Tai-ming
Yergey, Amy Lynn
Zack, Erin Kinney
Zeigler-Palmer, Stephanie Lynette

Zelikson, Alexandra
Ziffer, Deborah W.

12-21-1998
Brown, Kay Millicent
Nash, Caroline Marie
Ong, Fiona Whei-jen
Stein, Jennifer Rand

12-23-1998
Houlton, Sabrina A.
Stern, Amy Gabrielle

1-4-1999
Ali, Khadijah Rahshidah
Ford, Kathleen Joan
Martin, Thene Mishon

1-5-1999
Avery-Marguet, Allison Southgate
Ely, Marion J.
Flint, Lara Michele
Flores, Kim Prichard
Hines, Rachel Jean
Mena, Maria E.
Nowezki, Diana Patricia
Schwartz, Lara Hope
Svonkin, Michele Lee
Tyrangiel, Elana

1-7-1999
Aziz, Maisha Lenore Amatullah
Bach, Laura Rebecca
Cinque, Michele Marie
Fitzpatrick, Ivy Bridgett
Johnson, Julie Kirsten
Kim, Penelope Richey
Kuettel, Andrea Corbett
Miller, Lisa Pearson
Milone, Marcie Renee Frum
Nugent, Victoria Stewart
Owens, Angela Lynn
Treanor, Elizabeth Samantha
van den Berg, Muriel Joanne

1-8-1999
Stewart, Dawn C.
Turner, Karen Roberts

1-12-1999
Leotta, Allison Harnisch

1-13-1999
Mitchell, Mary Thursa
St. Clair, Lynetta M.

1-14-1999
Calder, Laurie Finneran
Mattavous-Frye, Sandra

1-25-1999
Azzam, Randa Samir
McIntyre, Jennifer B.
Sinclair, Mary Elizabeth

2-4-1999
Wells, Kristin Deanna
Wetherill, Veronica Moran

2-5-1999
Bupp-Habuda, Heather

2-17-1999
Bowden, Anne Rea

3-4-1999
Hurt, Valerie Elaine
Mango, Andrea Rose
Polk, Stephanie Antoinette
Stubenberg, Melissa Kathleen

3-15-1999
Preston, Diane S.

3-22-1999
Brinkley, Sally LeBlanc
Weintraub, Judith W.

3-29-1999
Williams, Laura Hafer

4-5-1999
Marmoll, Helen Estelle

4-6-1999
Mehta, Sharda

4-8-1999
Jordan, Krystal A.
Melton, Tara Yvette
Wells, Jean Terese

4-13-1999
Martin Ross, Belhia V.
Marvin, Allison Gallaudet

4-15-1999
Riley, Pamela Michigan

6-3-1999
Jezic, Tamara Lee
Master, Maureen

6-10-1999
Kessler, Tamara Jaycox

6-15-1999
Ader-Duncan, Melisse Natalie
Asdorian, Kathleen B.
Belfance, Eve V.
Bramesco, Julienne Wallis
Cooke, Karen Martin
Green, Carol Lynn
Lazzaro, Carol Jeanne
Machado, Lilliam L.
Meiburger, Janet Marie
Walton, Southy Elizabeth
Willman, MaryEllen
Winfree, Katherine
Zanoni, Ruth McLay

6-23-1999
Bahr, Susan Jeanne
Kaplan, Annie P.
Konits, Sharon Cerelle
Mack, Catherine R.
Murphy, Mollie A.
Schlanger, Phoebe
Speed, Leslie B.
Sperling, Megan Anne
Taylor, Erin P.

6-24-1999
Ahlstrom, Susan
Akpan, Zionne
Alexander, Bamidele Burton
Alston, Tracy Chiles
Anderson, Kristi LeFaivre
Andrews, Tara
Arends, Jacqueline Grace
Arroyo, Teresa Maria
Awkard, Veronica Geneva
Bank, Marit Diana
Banks, Daneen M.
Banks, Linda Ann
Barrett, Kristen Milardo
Barton, Rhonda Lynn
Beatty-Arthur, Sherri M.
Berger, Jennifer Leigh
Borno, Karen McCain
Bragunier, Victoria Lynn
Brennan, Mary Kathryn
Brown, Ajile Fernandez
Buchwald, Tamara J. Yakimetz
Bucklew, Andrea Jane
Buntua, Marie Annette
Burch-Rates, Tobi S.
Bustos, Diane Carroll
Byrd, Jacqueline Dean
Canfield, Eileen Ann
Cardenas, Kerri B.
Caudle, Indra R.
Cesarano, Danielle Renee
Chandran, Sharmila Merlynn
Charles, Kathy K.
Clopper, Kelly Leanne
Collins, Stephanie P.
Counterman, Kelley Land
Crandall, Lisa Marie
Criswell, Kimberleigh Jean
Daisey, Carol S.
Dansby, Tonia Michelle
Davis, Christina
Davis, Christine V.
Deoudes, Georgia Mary
Diamondstone, Jessica Charis
DiGrigoli, Julie Alyssa
Do, Ha Thi Thu
Doner, Karen A.
Dorancy-Williams, Jill Deborah
Downer, Ruth-Elizabeth L.
Duobinis, Jacqueline Renee
Durrett, Michelle R.
Eagle, Gwen Gayle
Elliott, Elisha R.
Enderle, Debra McPipkin
Engstrom, Catherine Marie
Estime, Yvonne
Faiks, Janice O.
Feleke, Bethelehem
Fiss, Gina Cohen Rubenfeld
Foley, Heather Deans
Fontello, Paula A.
Foster, Kristin Lenae
Frank, Renee M.
Franklin, Shelley Davis
Frankovich, Jennifer Rachel
Frazier, Marie D.
Freeman, Allison Blum
Freeman, Helen Maria
Funnie, Joscelyn Nicole
Gerstandt, Christine Marie
Goodwin, Ellen Myrick
Gordon, Cheryl F.
Grace, Sandy I-Ru
Graham, Lorie E.
Graham, Lynsey N.
Green, Dawn M.
Guckert, Renee Christina
Hamilton, Jacqueline C.
Hamilton, Tanya Simone
Hammer, Stacey Beth
Harkins, Tanya Elizabeth
Harris, Briana Nicole
Harris, Cristina
Harris, Michele Renee
Hastings, Carol Ann Afrookteh
Hedman, Megan J.
Hentz, Jennifer Michelle
Hernandez-Royer, Mary Ann Celebrado
Hinton, Arielle Fougy
Ho, Diana Chi-Chieh
Hobbs, Diana Kay
Hughes, Kristen Grim
Humphries, Patricia Jean
Hunt, Julie B.
Indrisano, Susan Cupler
Irving, Nayoka LaShawn
Jackson-Taylor, Felicia R.
Jennings, Corey Ali
Jensen, Tracy Elizabeth
Jones, Charlene Virginia
Jones, Lorna Jacqueline
Jun, Gina
Kemnitz, D'Arcy
Key, Alisa Chester
Keyser, Linda Lee
Kierein, Diana S.
Kim, Ki S.
Kincaid, Karin Jennifer Kysilka
King, Cherie Michele
Kong, Hae-Jin Janice Lee
Kreshtool, Shannon B.
Kuhlman, Vanessa LeServe
LaBorde, Patricia Ann
LaPolla, Tonya Michelle
Laxa, Rowena Estanislao
Le, Tai Duc
Leatherwood, Shancethea N.
Lee, Courtney Koo
Lee, Joyce Y.
LeFaivre, Michele Lynne
Leikus, Kerryann Bowen
Leonard-Leach, Alison Yvette
Lightfoot-Walker, Gina
Lisas, Philippa
Lloyd, Kimberley Jon
Logan, Kimberly Marie Taylor
Luong, An N.
Malone, Camille Celeste
Mandl, Donna S.
Marsh, Jennifer Evans
Martz-Fisher, Julia Augusta
Marzullo, Michelle Jacquelyn
Matthews, Jennifer Nicole
McDowell, Gwendolyn Sydney
McGarry, Kimberly Ann
McGowan, Patricia J.
Meadows, Felicia Yvonne
Mehta, Sonal Jawahar
Miers, Sarah Elise
Miller, Carla
Miller, Kristin Caldwell
Morrissey, Ann Duvall
Mosley, Lynnae
Mulligan, Kelly L.
Murphy, Jennifer Michelle Swanhart
Nelson, Julie Ann
Neurman, Beryl Leah
O'Byrne, Mary Erin
Ojeda, Elsa M.
Ortiga, Ramona Fe
Orzechowski, Jennifer S.
Owens, Allyson Harris
Paradise, Alexandra Strubing
Parker, Cheryl Simpson
Perrell, Jacqueline

Peterson, India D.
Pica, Maria Branca
Plant, Marianne DePaulo
Pope-Onwukwe, Karren Jo
Porter, Hope Maria
Pyle, Ellen Louise Stefani
Rein, Lesley A.
Reinhart, Julia Anderson
Rickard, Robin Elizabeth
Roberts, Pamela Anne
Roberts, Schniqua Latae
Robertson, Diane Emily
Rogan, Stacey Ann Willis
Rose, Patricia Healy
Rosenblatt, Shana Lauren
Runyon, Eve LeeAnne-Robbins
Schabacker, Emily W.
Sears, Heather Christine
Semanchik, Rachel Leigh
Shank, Lisa Marie
Shannon-McClellan, Eileen Marie
Shay, Cynthia Ann
Shelburne, Patricia Ann
Shershenovich, Jane
Smith, Sharon Lynne
Snoeren, Margaret Shannon
Sookram, Laila J.
Staber, EunJi Elizabeth
Stawinski, Michelle E.
Straughn, Karen Sue
Strissel, Sandra Lynn
Strutton, Carolyn Ellis
Swanson, Edrei Genet
Tate, Amy Beth
Teague, Pamela R.
Terrell, Mariessa Rebecca
Thayer, Samantha Briggs
Theologou, Diana C.
Thomas, Daria Latice
Thomas-Bellamy, Sandy F.
Thompson, Arlene L.
Turner, Kimberly Martin
Umunna, Dehlia
Urban, Sharon Marie
Valinski, Jennifer Mary
Vipond, Sandra B.
Vitale, Claudia Marie
Walker, S. Symone
Ward, Anne Roberta
Warner-Dennis, Deborah
Washington, Imoni Malaika
Webb, Danielle E.
Weir, Elizabeth J.
Welch, Noreen O'Hara
Westervelt, Deborah Jeanne
Wigfall, Nelida Carmen
Williams, Donna Michelle
Williams, Jocelyn Lang
Williams, Joelle L.
Wiltuck, Katharine Elizabeth
Winarick, Sheryl Corinne
Wolpoff, Sharon Ann
Wrae, Natasha
Wright, JoRhea Nagel
Wyatt, Rebecca Goldman
Xu, Bing
Zappone, Eleanor D.

7-2-1999

Brantley, Sandra Benson
Kim, Hoyun
Langworthy, Nancy Fay
Murray, Melinda Gray

7-14-1999

Capwell, Carrie Nicole
Day, Julie Hottle
Grable, Amy Catherine
Skeith, Terri M.

7-26-1999

Purcell, Pamela
Sarro, Lisa Marie

7-27-1999

Baylin, Bridget Atwell
Robinson, Traci L.

8-3-1999

Morrison, Kathy Weaver

8-13-1999

Westerlund, Ashley Lyn

8-17-1999

Borden, Kathleen Donohue

8-23-1999

Terry, Keeva Lynne

9-7-1999

Canan, Ruth Elaine
Cox, Mary Elizabeth
Eburuche, Patricia A.
Gil, Anna
Hardnett, Charlene Sukari
Reverski, Laura Denise
Sherman, Natalie B.

9-16-1999

Kim, Kay Lee

9-28-1999

Silvera, Colline Mercedes

9-30-1999

Allen, Catherine Manning
Reese, Catherine Mary

10-14-1999

Quagliano, Mary Laura

10-27-1999

Greene, Kia Marie

11-4-1999

May, Allison Noullet

11-22-1999

Goudie, Evangelina A.

12-14-1999

Alexander, Allison Leslie
Allaire, Jennifer Leigh
Allen, Nicole L.
Allison, Bridget Kearry
Alpert, Ruth Siegel
Anastasio, Julia
Anaya, Erica Britt
Anderson, Lisa Nicole
Baker, Phyllis Ann
Barnes, Julie A.
Barton, Katherine J.
Beam, Bethamy N.
Becker, Kristin Lynn
Bellone, Patricia Kelly
Belt, Julie Ann
Bennett, Crystal Michelle
Bernstein, Lisa Alexis
Blalock, Kaija V.
Blasdell, Jennifer L.A.
Block, Patricia L.
Boisvert, Christienne Bethanie
Bond, Tamara L.
Booth, Emily J.
Bovier, Jennifer Johnson
Bowman, Sarah Wicklein
Boyd, Krista Anne
Brannon, Leah
Brannon, Sarah E.
Bremis, Maria
Brennan, Jennifer Ann
Bresso, Gineen Maria
Bright, Sarah Louise
Brinckerhoff, Courtenay Cassel
Brown, Mary Carolyn
Brown, Melanie R.
Brown-Kobil, Nancy Christian
Brunner, Jan Marie
Bruno, Brigid W.
Buchman, Jodie Elizabeth
Burch, Traci Leigh
Busan, Jessica Katherine
Byrd, Vickie Shantel
Byrne, Kathleen Ebersole
Byrne, Marie Michele
Cairo, Deana L.
Cameron, Jennifer Johnson
Campbell, Claudia Adelle
Capozello, Alycia F.
Caravellli, Margaret Elizabeth
Carrington, Karen Maria
Carter, Hope Woodruff
Cendali, Allison
Chanow, Linda Bray
Chapman, Apple
Chappell, Danielle
Chase, Kerri Jeanne
Cheng, Grace I.
Choudhri, Tamanna R.
Chung, Betty Youngwon
Clark, Alexandra Collins
Clayton, Cheryl Annette
Cohen, Jennifer Gazaille
Colby, Amie Virtel
Coles, Amy Fiordalisi
Colofer, Effie
Coltrane, Marcella R.
Colwell, Jessica Lynne
Combs, Rhonda
Connolly, Heather Marie
Connolly, Heidi Anita
Cook, Mary Duden
Cooper, Deborah E.
Corbin, Eve
Coudon, Erin L.
Crossman, Kelly Anne
Curtis, Rena Isabelle
Davis, Christine Spinella
Davis, Lucinda E.
De La Cruz, Zoraya Beatriz
Derr, Lavinia Arpon
DeSarbo, Lynne Celander
Desonier, Margaret Ann
DeWitt, Christine Gollatz
DiGiosia, Lori B.
Dixon, Anjanette Ladelle
Doughman, Janice Burdell
Douthit, Teresa Marie
Du Bray, Katherine Marie
DuBois, Shobita Chakravarthy
duHoffmann, Jessica Anna-Christina
Dunn, Christine
Dupuy, Kathy K.B.
Edwards, Kasey Lykes
Ellinger, Melony Joe
English, Christen Marie
Esquenet, Margaret Aldona
Evans, Gennet
Felker, Jill Elizabeth
Fellabaum, Jennifer Marie
Feudale, Barbara Lynne
Fillpot, Lisa Janet
Fischer, Lynn Marie
Fitzpatrick, Carolyn Dowd
Floom, Kristen Byrnes
Floyd, Angela Therese
Floyd, Eldora Ellison
Force, Rebecca J.
Forestieri, Jennifer Kennedy
Fox, Mary-Elizabeth Swoditch
Franco, Sandra Patricia
Friedman, Francine Elizabeth
Funna, Isatu Mariama
Gaede, Brooke L.
Garrett, Margaret Fletcher
Geroff, Fani Cyd
Goffman, Barbara A.
Gonzales, Robin Freedman
Gordon, Rebecca L.D.
Granadillo, Elizabeth J.
Granrath, Becki S.
Grau, Caren A. C.
Gray, Karen Ellen
Greenwald, Karen Michelle
Griffith, Daniele Creager
Hedges, Margaret D.
Margolius, Jennifer Lynn
Mazarin, Raquel Marie
Merritt, Kristin C.
Miller, Laura Michelle
Muffoletto, Michaela Cavanaugh
Murphy, Ann Vaillant Colville
Nazelrod, Cara Collins
Ocampo, Amy Blank
Phillips, Jennifer Elenbaas
Poteat, Mary Rebecca
Preller, Amanda Cassidy
Rae, Jessica Lynne Cook
Richards, Kay Maureen
Ridgell, Mary Jacqueline
Rodriguez, Jamie Lynn Argento
Rule, Allison Driver
Schwemle, Risheena L.
Sherman, Paula Cagnacci
Speargas, Jennifer B.
Spitulnik, Lisa Susan
Tave, Jessica Aldock
Taylor, Adrienne Beck
Thomas, Lilliane Butzky
Wallace, Gayle Grabow
Williams, Aparna Dasai

12-15-1999

Bernal, Debra Leigh
Bowsher, Marina Kravets
Brown, Amy McNally
Brown, Lori N.
Bush, T. Melindah
Camp, Anna Rachel
Campbell, Mary McCarthy
Craig, Henryka W.

Creighton, Kerry Elizabeth
Crenshaw, Heather J.
Dodge, Hollie Paine
Glaser, Kristina April
Glass, Catherine Martin
Gresham, Christine Levonian
Grove, Valerie Ann
Hamilton, Ann O.
Hammer, Rachael-Anne
Handrigan, Melissa R.
Harkavy, Anne
Hayes, Aquanetta Knight
Healy, Amy Dene
Hendler, Shara Gabrielle
Henline, Misty MaDonna
Henn, Emily Johnson
Henrikson, Kristin Lynn
Hewitt, Nicole Rose
Hinger, Cathy Ann
Hinko, Valerie
Hirselj, Rebecca Allyn
Ho, Christina Sing-Wei
Homsey, Michele Williamson
Hunter, Karlyn Juliet
Idelson, Holly Amanda
Iseman, Haylie Michelle
James, Rosemary B.
Janke, Mendy Mendenilla
Johnson, Heather Lee
Johnson, LaShawn Michelle,
Johnson, Marlene A.,
Jones, Julia Ashley,
Jones, Kelli Karlysa,
Justice, Patricia Sue,
Kamenshine, Wendy Ellen
Karasik, Claudine McCullough
Kassim, Morenike Saskia
Kauffman, Jeannie Pittillo
Kealy, Anne Ravaud
Keeney, Michelle M.
Kelley, Vivieon E.
Kilpatrick, Mary S.
Kim, Soye
King, Susan Hoppe
Kirkwood, Dawn Marie
Klein, Melanie
Koger, Kristin McCabe
Koppel, Chari-Lynn
Kramer, Alexis E.
Kutz, Alexandra Ellen
La Testa, Regan Kreitzer
Lacey, Lauren Elizabeth
Lancaster, Margaret Elizabeth
Langley, Anne Sharon
LaRoche, Jennifer Joy
Leach, Joy Adrienne
Leatham, Erica Allyn
Lee, Dannet Maree
Leiter, Susan Elizabeth
Leonard, Nicole L.
Lester, Kathleen Joann
Leveton, Erin Leigh
Lewis, Stephanie Arlene
Leyrer, Colleen Mary
Liang, Angela Ni
Littlejohn, Shai Aliya
Long, Kathleen Mary
Long, Marie Carolyn Aurelia
Long, Martha
LoPresti, Heather Joy
Mallon, Colleen M.
Marbelstein-Deare, Adriane R.
Marone, Danielle E.
Marta, Mary R.
Martineau, Janet M.
Mason, Sasha Alexandra
McClure, Darla Jo
McGill, Yolanda Dineine
McGoldrick, Lillemor M.
McGregor, Carla M.
McGuinness, Charlotte Marion
McKay, Leslie Megan
McKeen, Michelle Arauz
McKeithen, Piper Faith
McKenna, Anna Alfano
McMullen, Eleanor A.
McTaggart, Kelli Colleen
Miller, Elizabeth Kees
Mitchell, Jennifer
Monroe, Monica Elaine
Mooney, Lauren Marie
Moore, Katrina DiElle
Moore, Tashena Middleton
Moran, Lucy M.
Morgan, Carmen Jerrita
Morse, Christine M.
Mounts, Phoebe
Moutsos, Mary Ellen
Mullikin, Sheri Ann
Myers, Erin Rae
Napier-Joyce, Joy Marie
Neiswender, Jane Ann Roe
Nemiroff, Elisa Ann
Nesbitt, Kristen Nichole
Newton, Elaine
O'Brien, Ann Marie
O'Brien, Michelle E.
Oden, Mary Nicole
Ostrom, Angela Michelle
Pak, Angela Ann
Papagiannopoulos, Aretina
Park, Song E.
Parshall, Sarah Elizabeth
Patel, Jennifer Obray
Patt, Jacqueline Levasseur
Payne, Amy Elizabeth
Payne, Lori Jacqueline Hayman
Reed, Eve Klindera
Robbins, Marcy Wein
Roisman, Natalie Gabrielle
Scivetti, Elaine H.
Sprinzen, Nicole H.
Tate, Gwendolyn S.
Tayman, Alice Isabel Legat
Tosh, Jennifer Martyn
Unglesbee, Cynthia Hatten
Voss, Gerie Ayn
Wohlfort, Jennifer Hook

12-16-1999

Ashbarry, Erin Jeanne
Aslaksen, Julie Palmer
Bailey, Ilene Allison
Becker, Renee Ellen
Benson, Catherine Marie
Bernstein, Alysa Stiefel
Boyd, Melissa Marie
Calleja, Khatereh Razavi
Cameron, Victoria Elizabeth
Clayman, Debra Satinoff
Cohen, Lisa Shimizu
Cole, Ann T.
Cyr, Lila G. Shapiro
Danysh, Laura Grace
Del Negro, Gina Marie
DeSio, Laura C. Yancer
Distler, Jill Schultz
Fagre, Danielle
Gaegler, Ann M.
Gaslevic, Joy K.
Greenspan, Kimberly Simon
Hampton, Lori Nicole
Hopper, Abigail Ross
Hull, Marcy Vonderwell
Isaacson, Tara Steinbok
Jackson, Karen Lacey Wells
Jamieson, Jill Anne Sheldon
Johnson, Shannon M. P.
Knight, Carla Lynn
Kraemer, Gretchen Witte
Lahlou, Shari Ross
Levinson, Sara Ann
McGill, Kelly Lynn
Mrose, Yonina Amy
O'Brien, Melissa Pignatelli
O'Donoghue, Carla Villar
Perez, Patricia Marie
Persico, Jennifer Winter
Pham, Trinh D.
Phillip, Monya A.
Piermattei, Rebecca
Pincus, Jennifer Helene
Pinillos, Georgette
Pompey, Stephanie Marie
Poulon, Christine
Principe, Janet Eileen
Puri, Kavita
Rankin, Jennifer Leigh
Raskin, Frances Marion
Rath, Raina M.
Reeves, Kelly Nicole
Reichmann, Lisa Levin
Reinhart, Meghan McLenahan
Remsburg, Christine M.
Ressing, Amy Loch
Rideout, Lee Gayle
Rife, Brittney Gable
Ripken, Nicole Leigh
Roberts, Rebecca L.
Rodriguez, Janice Marie
Rogers, Amy Smith
Rogers, Beth L.
Rosales, Maria Isabel
Rosenthal, Jessica Nicole
Rouse, Karanja K.
Rozof, Michelle Ilene
Rushing, Elizabeth
Ruttenberg, Kerri Lynn
Ruzz, Jessica S.
Sallerson, Stacy Lynn
Sallis, Yvonne Lesley
Sanders, Cynthia Blake
Sausser, Gail D.
Sawez, Sedica
Schectel, Lori Helene
Schroth, Anne Heesters
Scott, Karen J.
Scott, Marcela Villalta
Sexton, Emily Carolyn
Shah, Amee A.
Shanley, Laura Penn
Shepherd, Camille LaVelle
Sherwood, Lori Lee
Shilling, Synthia J.
Shin, Malissa M.
Small, Tricia Fiona
Smith, Angela J.
Smith, Karen Louise
Smith, Lisa Jane
Smith, Nicole Rose
Soanes, Sherry Denise Therese
Sokol, Erin Lynn
Sosin, Amy B.
Stagliano, Kristen Dorothy
Stasiuk, Teresa Diana
Stearman, Jennifer J.
Steinfels, Alison Barmat
Stephens, Laura Leanne
Steward, Annamaria
Streets, Jennifer A.
Sullivan, Anne Hayward
Teplinsky, Melanie Jane
Terra, Dena Marie
Thom, Janis A.
Tierney, Maura Lynn
Tribble, Kelly R.
Vachher, Eileen M.
van Heuven, Catherine Margot
Vandergrift, Emily Norine
Vaughn, Shelley M.
Verdrager, Kamee Ruth
Vlk, Denise Graham
Vollmer, Jennifer Elizabeth
Wade, Tracy Ann
Wagner, Erlease Maria
Walker, Elinor M.
Webb, Michelle Lynn
Weinel, Jennifer Kristine
Weistling, Ripple L.
Welch, Rachel Callin
Werner, Stacey R.
White, Sydney Marsh
Whittaker-Pion, Angela N.
Whittier, Holly Ann
Williams, Nancy Love
Williams-Bibbs, Mialeeka Cinquann
Wilson, Tammy Leigh
Winter, Jane Kimball
Woodmansee, Jennifer Lynne
Workman, Yvette Renee
Wulkan, Anie Elizabeth
Yerger, Isabelle Puleo
Yodaiken, Ruth T.
Young, Becky Lynn
Zirkelbach, Linda Jacqueline

12-17-1999

Avendano, Ana Luisa
Bielen, Judith Ann
Bledsoe, Monalie Eloise
Enriquez, Jennifer E. Holt
Isicson, Anita
Lippman, Rebecca
Louie, Lily Leong Soohoo
Lucas, Diane G.
MacKinnon, Kathryn D.
O'Reilly, Bernadette Rush
Scherr, Leslie
Weber, Ellen M.

12-27-1999

Alexander, Patience Ann
Kaplan, Lisa L.
Obayashi, Linda Toyo
Pape, Lella Amiss E.
Sosnick, Barbara Ellen
Strom, Elana E.
Wright-Smith, Vickey A.

1-6-2000

Amin, Stephanie Dawn
DeCourcy, Leilani Ann
DiPietro, Diane Clayton
Friedel, Loren Andrea
Gantt, Linda Maxine
Glover, Sandra Slack
Kropf, Sara Elizabeth
Sabo, Kimberly Jennell
Sikes, Cristen Elizabeth
Stoltzfus, Stephanie Lynn
Walker, Genevievette Elvira

1-12-2000

Aleman, Enid Gonzalez
Bellinger-Honig, Charlene Patricia

1-14-2000

Dehn, Negin Nazemi
French, Marcy A.
Walendzak, Christie Marie

1-18-2000

Case-Rossato, Donna M.
Jarvis, Carlotta Pamela

1-24-2000

Bertram, Connie Nora

1-31-2000

Slawta, Kathleen Nealon

2-3-2000

Kinlaw, Beverly Kay
Long, Leslie Janel
Taddeo, Jennifer Darcy
Winston, Aneida Pearl

2-7-2000

Lewis, Jean E.

2-18-2000

Rogers, Laura L.

3-2-2000

Schomaker, Kathleen Cutler
Wilks, Misty D.
Russell, Carolyn C.

3-23-2000

Inagawa, Lisa Kay

3-27-2000

Haine, Susan J.

3-30-2000

Ketchum, Laura J.

4-6-2000

Bailey, Mickie Yolanda
Prejean, Michelle M.

4-28-2000

Parker, Paulette P.

5-2-2000

Montgomery, Meadie Katherine

5-17-2000

Sudik, Gabrielle A.

6-7-2000

Noakes, Gayle Monica

6-8-2000

Rosenberg, Marcia Faye

6-9-2000

Blain, Michelle
Mriscin, Sandra L.
Olson, Beth Jeanne

6-12-2000

Block, Victoria L.
Evans, Virginia Bitzer
Gustavson, Carol Werner
Smith, Patricia A.
Tell, Melinda Gale

6-13-2000

Bourne, Constance Smith

6-15-2000

Daneker, Eva Louise
Fieo, Alyssa Rose
Frank, Gloria H.

6-20-2000

Sargent, Sarah Jeannette

6-21-2000

Adams, Elizabeth Lynn
Albrecht, Melissa M.
Anderson, Lorelle Renee
Anderson, Marcia Ellen
Anderson, Monica M.
Anderson, Vicki Renee
Andrews, Diane M.
Ardinger, Jo Ellen
Asar, Sharon
Bailey, Dori K.
Baker, Hilary A.
Balch-Reno, Karla Anne
Ball, Angela Yvonne
Baptiste, Alana Simone
Baratian, Jacqueline Carberry
Barbieri, Claudia R.
Beach, Barbara N.
Beard, Michelle Lee
Bechberger, Barbara Ann
Beloff, Marcy Suzanne
Bennett, Ruth-Ann
Boehm, Natalie Mazzella
Bonfante, Maricruz Jeennet
Bowers, Christi C.
Brandon, Karen Nicole
Breidenbaugh, Rose C.
Brown, Kristine Dianne
Brown, Monica Joan
Brown, Shadey Turner
Buckley, Tara R.
Buckner, Lisa Michele
Burkholder, Karey
Burns, Rebecca S.
Caballero, Kathryn Pirrotta
Cain, Laura L.
Campbell, Angela Gilless
Campbell, Ayoka Anika
Campbell, Melissa Marie
Casper, Stephanie E.
Caturano, Kristi Malei
Cawood, Kristin deZayas
Cermak, Shelly Guest
Chandler, Cory Marcia
Chang, Elisa Nai-Kwong
Chavis, Kami Nicole
Cheslock, Rosalind Pleet
Chicherio, Christine Marie
Clark-Edwards, Ada Elizabeth
Coakley, Susan Lynn
Coaxum, Monifa Bailey
Conaton, Erin Elizabeth Duffy
Craig, Melleri Renata
Crandall, Deborah L.
Cullen, Erin Mary
DaCosta, Lisa K.
Depo, Rachel Sarah
DePriest, Marcia R.
DeWilde, Leticia Flores
Diamant, Sharon T.
Dodson, Melissa Marie
Drummond, Regina C.
Eagle, Katrina Johanna
Eller, Jennifer Elizabeth Quisqueya
Elsea, Jennifer K.
Emmart, Lisa Karen
Feehan, Christina Gerard
Feiner, Brittany Lynn
Feliciano, Melissa Kathleen
Ferguson, Cassandra Tyiese
Floyd, Mona Karole
Fogel-Bublick, Jennifer L.
Fong, Sue Chang
Forville, Janet Benson
Frampton, Jennifer Wynn
Freedman, Rachel Alpert
Gable, Katrina Michelle
Gaskins, Shannon Renee
Gentile, Karen Cecelia
Giannini, Michelle Freeman
Gioioso, Tina Michelle
Glebocki, Lori Ferguson
Govan, Ronna Marguette
Gross, Amanda C.
Gunawardhana, Sonali Priyangika
Hall, Coleen
Hall, Kristin J.
Hammar, Patricia K.
Harrison, Melissa Mineo
Hawk, Ronna Layne
Hefflin, Denene Khadija Mercedes
Hertz, Lisa A.
Hill, Catherine Adele
Hill, Domiento C.R.
Holloway, Heather Janene
Holloway, Laura A.
Hudes, Nancy C.
Hughes, Layla A.
Hunter, Kelli E.
Ibeneme, Chinyere Millicent
Irvin, Deena A.
Ismay, Jeanie Scherrer
Jemmott, Adriane C.
Jerez, Paulina Loreto
Jones, Alicia Granby
Kang, Jane Chungwha
Kear, Christine Ann
Kelly, Maria G.
Keyser, Jennifer E.
Khalilian, Houri
Kim, Cristine H.
Kleinman, Freda Lukov
Knapp, Aimee Elizabeth
Knight, Joan Ellen
Kralowetz, Nora Margaret Whalen
Kruggel, Yvette
Lacey, Lauren Hong Connolly
Larkin, Sharon L.
Leache, Tammy Michele
Lee, Christine
Leong, Katherine Kitfong
Lewis, Effie Latosha
Lilly, Jennifer Louise
Lowrey, Kerri McGowan
Malhotra, Shibani
Maloney, Kathleen Anne
Markowitz, Rachel Alyse
Martin, Natalie Renea
Martz, Angela J.
Mashhadishafie, Shila
Massengale, Colette Yvonne
Mathis-Barnett, Lisa
Matis, Jennifer A.
Matthews, Deborah Gail
Maumenee, Rebecca Buhner
McAvoy, Maren
McBarnette, Ellen C.
McDevitt, Lisa Lane
McDonald, Robin Yvonne
McDonnell, Cindy A.
McGee, Edith Louise Moore
McGowan, Tracy D.
McKinney, Tanya L.
McLaughlin, Judy Simone
Meiners, Michele Claire
Meta, Jean Danielle
Meyer, Greta A.
Mezan, Laura Callahan
Miles, Jessica
Mitchell, Julia Lorraine
Moloney, Melissa L.
Momeni, Mercedeh
Montgomery, Kelly Lynn
Moore, Nicole Olivier
Moss, Elizabeth Hirshfield
Mozden, Carolyn Dorman
Mullan, Jeannine Marie
Mullins, Deborah Ann
Murray, Kali Nicole
Nepf, Barbara Jean
Nickson, Julie Little
Nimmo, Rachael Wenthold
Noonan, Veronica Anne
O'Malley, Mary Grace Anne
Obot, Theresa Isidore
Onyensoh, I. Sylvia
Pallone, Karen Lynne
Pinnell, Maria Carmen S.
Pitts, Roxanne
Poole, Tiffany Anne
Poplawski, Katrina Lynne
Primo, Helen M.
Quigley, Angela Whitehead
Radix, Stephanie Marie
Rao, Neena
Reed, Margaret Michelle
Retta, Erika Lyn Whelan
Riaz, Tabinda
Roman, Shirley Elaine
Roussos, Maria Janet
Rozenberg, Bella L.
Rubin, Noreen M.
Russack, Camilla Battaglini
Sampson, Katherine T.
Santos-DeJesus, Kellie Jean
Scott, Jennifer S.
Shallue, Lisa K.
Shapiro, Andrea Lisa
Shin, Hee Jung Jenny
Shyovitz, Marcy Eve
Simon, Elizabeth Treubert
Sina, Mujan
Sinclair, Debbie L.
Sinkins, Katherine Margaret

Slovak, Dorothy Cecilia
Smith, Diana Elise
Smith, Pamela Lynne
Smith-McCarrick, Brook D.
Solomon, Angela Goodlow
Solomon, Shari L.
Spalding, Candice Gayton
Steckel, Madeleine D.
Stevens, Dian Patricia
Stockfleet, April R.
Sullivan, Stephanie Erin
Swafford, Rene C.
Swain, Stacy Reid
Swanzey, Genine C.
Talbot, Bizunesh Kiesha-Tanifia
Testa, Susan Rose
Theriot, Dana Glynn
Thomas, Miatta Nyahaleh
Thomas, Shanda Marie
Tolani, Anita Ganpat
Tomlin, Valeria N.
Torres, Eleanor Benjamin
Torres, Jasmin Marie
Train, Amber Alyson
Truesdale, Brenda Louise
Tsai, Nancy
Turner, Deborah Allison
Turner, Heather A.
Tyler, Robyn Coleman
Urick, Diana Marie
Vaval, Geraldine P.
Vecchio, Sally Terese
Walsh, Kathryn Elizabeth
Ward, Anna Emily
Warren, Tracy Anne
Weinstein, Charlotte Kingsley
Weintraub, Rachel Miriam
Werner, Elizabeth Krieger
Williams, Donna F.
Willis, Carol Jean
Wilson, Rachel H.
Wingood, Pamela Lynn
Woods-Podwal, Stef
Wright, Arnettia Smith
Yao, Gretta
Young, Carrie Skye
Zahedi, Nancy Shabnam

7-3-2000
Calhoun, Carol Victoria
Schmidt, Karyn M.
Works, Cynthia Carol

7-5-2000
Toker, Rachel Lee

7-6-2000
Dean, Lisa Harris
Thawley, Barbara Ellen

7-14-2000
Geller, Shannon Haggerty

7-19-2000
Lettiere, Judith Ann Marie Theresa

7-24-2000
Simpson, Phyllis Brown

7-25-2000
Jackson, Suzanne Holly

8-1-2000
Powell, Valerie Elizabeth

9-5-2000
Andrews, Peggy Lisa
Douglas, Katie Lee
Hall, Maria Anne
Sayers, Elizabeth Amanda
Springrose, Linda Jane
Tierney, Heather Elizabeth

9-22-2000
Jones, Jennifer A.

9-27-2000
Abenes, Laura D.

10-5-2000
Hankinson, Kymberly D.
Neagle, Andrea Kochan

10-30-2000
Kinder, Stephanie Dawn

11-2-2000
Jones, Catrina M.
Pagnato, Gina Julia
Vesely, Patricia Ann

11-28-2000
Tennant, Melanie Lynne

12-12-2000
Aceto, Aimee M.
Ades, Renee Bronfein
Ahluwalia, Paramjit Kaur
Allston, Sheelagh Mary
Altice, Edith Kay
Anderson, Aimee Kathryn Marie
Andrews, Natasha Serene
Austin, Katherine Ellen
Babcock, Alexis Bronwyn
Bahar, Mojdeh
Bailey, Amy Lynn
Baker, Heather A.
Baker, Margaret Watt
Barmore, Nicole Kimberly
Basaman, Traci Douma
Batlle, Ann K.
Baylor, Brynee Kyonne
Beasley, Angela L.
Benjamin, Tracy Monique
Berges, Anabelle Virginia
Bernstein, Melissa G.
Biedronski, Beth Ann
Bishop, Samantha
Blanchette, Katherine R.
Bloodworth, Shannon McCartney
Bob, Rachel H.
Bohorfoush, Ada Louise
Bous, Isis M.
Bowers, Catherine Anna
Boyd, Annmarie Holly
Bradley, Sarah Anne
Brannigan, Lisa Deanna
Braveboy, Aisha Nazapa
Brill, Hillary Tova
Brokowsky, Hallie Erica
Brooks, Keisha Lynn
Brooks, Sharon Diane
Brown, Karma Barsam
Brown-Whitfield, Cheryl A.C.
Bruggeman, Jean Marie
Buchner, Claire Evan
Burbach, Cristina
Burton, Dilcy G.
Bushman, Jennifer Marie
Bygrave, Daisy M.
Byrdsong, Latrice A.G.
Carr, Melanie Kathleen
Castner, Maria Daniel
Chambers, Julie Lynne
Cheng, Debra S.P.
Cheng, Yum Yu
Cho, Nam Mee
Ciampa, Aileen Hurley
Clark, Annette Jean
Clark, Catherine Moseley
Clarke, Penelope Anne
Cohen, Erin Paige
Cohen, Stephanie D.
Coleman, Delisa Natasha Adams
Collins, Angela Fay
Connelly, Amy B.
Conyers-Ausbrooks, Melane Arlene
Corwin, Charlotte Klein
Curry, Kimberly Alison
D'Alesandro, Kristine Candura
Daggs, Nicole J. W.
Dale, Kathleen C.
Daly, Karen C.
Daneker, Emily A.
Dariani, Fatema E.
Dash, Jill Felice
Day, Adrianne Elaine
DeLessio, Lisa Crowley
DeMoor, Michelle Ann
Dennis, Marie Sage
Diaz, Amy Sobba
Diedrich, Pamela J.
Domenech, Mildred
Donahue, Justine K.
Dorsainvil, Dolores
Dorsey, Mieka Cherron-Marie
Dubois, Michelle E.
Duvall, Gabrielle Marcus
Egerton Taylor, Nicole
Eiseman, Connie Ellen
Elliott, Mary Nicole
Endres, Jody Michelle
Engel, Dorothy Michelle
Essary, Kimberly S.L.
Evans, Kathleen Eyler
Fano, Katia Ivonne
Farmer, Stacy Marie
Fee, Juliet Albizo
Feiler, Laura M.
Feinstein, Melissa Dupreay
Felix, Korin Ewing
Ferguson, Cynthia Marie
Finegan, Julie Ann
Finger, Shelley Anne
Fischer, Rebecca Claire
Fisher, Melinda Kay
Fleming, Rebecca Ann
Foster, Karen Gail
Frappier, Danielle Marie
Freedman, Abigail G.
Friedman, Emily Renee
Frye, Cara Ann
Fuller, Jessica Aileen
Galvin, Kelley Deline
Gandel, Jennifer Anne
Garment, Suzanne Rose
Garza, Anna-Maria C.
Gascoigne, Tina Marie
Gill, Kristina Hellikki
Gillilan, Mary Laje
Givens, Angela Denise
Glorian, Sarah
Goger, Joanna B.
Goldfrank, Amy Elisabeth
Gordon, Claudia L.
Gorney, Kathrine Amanda
Gray, Jonice Monique
Greatman, Shana Eden
Greer, Carolyn R.
Grimsley, Kimberly Sue
Grogan, Gwen R.
Grossi, Amy L. Hicks
Gunderman, Karen Lynn
Hale, Cheryl Demma
Hanna, Roya May
Hanrahan, Karen J.
Hanson, Kara Elizabeth
Harris, Carole Annette
Harrison, Sherita Danyell
Harvin, Tracey Ann
Hazlett, Christa M.
Hearne, Melissa Anne
Helmes, Jacquenette M.
Hill, Theresa Ladonna
Himmelberg, Mary Carne
Hoerauf, Gwyn Cara
Hoff, Michele E.
Holmes, Tina Renee
Holtz, Allison Anne
Hong, Rosanna L.
Hooper, June Elizabeth
Horowicz, Elizabeth Curtis
Horton, Tonya Dione
Horton-Newell, Amy Eugenia
House, Mary Angela
Ice, Elise Marcela Balkin
Jabara, Kirsten N.
Jacobs, Camellia Javadi
Jacobson, Erica Ruth
Jahromi, Jennifer Fefel
Jaskulski-Tripp, Jennifer Ann
Jaskulsky, Andrea Eileen
Jirousek-Wint, Sarah Antoinette
Johnson, Christine N.
Johnson, Jo Linda
Johnson, Sandra Mary
Kaczka, Kelly Ann
Kado, Carla
Kane, Aisha Maia
Kaye, Cary Berkeley
Kearse, Deborah F.
Keffler, Rosemary J.
Kendus, Michele R.
Keogh, Maureen Derrig
Khalimsky, Ann
Khan, Fizza Ali
Kilbourne, Susan Jean Insley
Kim, Gie Helen
Kim, Hyun Kyong
King, Lynisa Benaires
King, Suzann Marie
Kirwan, Tanya Ilona
Klumpp, Mary J.
Kneeland, Jennifer Larkin
Kolarik, Jana Lyn
Kramer, Holly Ann
Krell, Christine Lea
Krupp, Staci Jeanne
Kulp, Holly Hillary
Landers, Carleigh Anne
Larkin, Vonnette C.
Madison, Siobhan Kelly

Mehigan, Heather Lynn
Mina, Angelike Andrinopoulos
Moseley, Deondra Sue Arko
Much, Amy Kathleen Cavero
Murphy, Carla N.
Nelson, Emily Lam
O'Croinin, Dawn Patricia
Oratokhai, Misty Yvette Johnson
Pequignot, Susanna Fisher
Robinson, Alix Marie
Robinson, Rory A.
Rodriguez, Traci Lynne
Rubenstein, Laura L.
Sager, Jennifer Golub
Samoryk, Michelle Demma
Sclater, Michelle McKim
Shepherdson, Melanie
Spears, Mariama C.
Sullivan, Misty Leigh
Szajda, Heather Hoch
Turnbull, Adele Louise Brockmeyer
Walsh, Rachel Lyn
Waugh, Melissa K.
Weston, Jessica B.
Wilson, Cindy Ball
Wright, Jennifer Ann
Ziembicki, Melissa Ann

12-13-2000

Apenteng, Maryse-Noelle Mills
Barr, Tracy Spriggs
Barry, Kristin Pierce
Berlin, Andrea Lynn Treese
Brewer, Mary Joanne Truchly
Burden, Christina Marie
Burgess, Lori Eden
Butler, Jennifer Olsen
Callander, Leigh Z.
Capati, April Marie Mayo
Colton, Lauren Schultz
Corsaro, Denise V.
Dregier, Katherine Susan
Eisenstein, Stacey Recht
Fassbender, Wendi Erin
Fisher, Emily Sanford
Fisher, Juliet Grace
Fowlkes, Brittany Leigh
Gary, Jennifer Justine Kananionapua Peru
Gibson, Andrea S.
Goodman, Tonya Sulia
Goodwin, Joanna Mary
Hall, Kim T.
Johnson, Shelley Lynn
Kasha, Kelly Lee
Kenney, Kelly Elizabeth Phillips
Klein, Nicole Pastore
Kovacs, Karen Ann
Lambert, Ayana T.
Leasure, Amy Beth
Leatherman, Jennifer Lynn
Lebbos, Aida M.
Lee, Karen M.
Lee, Marie Kalamaras
Lehrman, Julie Sarah
Leonetti, Carrie Suzanne
Leonnig, Ellen M.
Lewellen, Dana Creasy
Lewis, Monica
Lezzer, Lee Ann
Lipp, Shannon Ivy
Littlefield, Bridget Eileen
Lo, Jennifer M.
Logan, Jeaneen M.
Loon, Carla B.
Lowenstein, Katharine Eleanor
Luck, Stacey Kyle
Lyne, Lisa Gay
MacLeod, Lesley Skye
Maddox, Sara L.
Magliocca, Erica Ward
Malik, Joan M.
Marosy, MiaBeth A.
Marshall, Jennifer Lynn
Martin, Rebecca Brand
Martin, Shelly Marie
Martinson, Hilary L.
Mason, Shonita Nicole
Mastracchio, Meghan Michelle
Matricciani, Cheryl Frances
Maynard-Webster, Juliet Janice
McCann, Carrie Lynne
McCarthy, Jacqueline Renee
McDonald, Christina E.
McDonough, Katherine Ann
McFadden, Marion Mollegen
McGovern, Kristin L.
McGuinn, Colleen Elizabeth
McMurry, Ashley
Meekins, Ndenisarya Mona
Michaels, Jacqueline
Mike, Marita K.
Miklasz, Hanan M.
Miller, Alexandra
Miller, Clemence Mary Katherine
Miller, Paula D.
Milner, Susan Rae
Minna, Penny Jeanne
Mitchell, Constance Shaffer
Montague, Rielle Cinese
Moore, Aisha Kai
Moore, Bridget Madden
Morrissey, Lesley-Ann
Moss, Nicole Jo
Mucchetti, Suzanne De Armond
Mukhopadhyay, Anupa
Munro, Nicole Frush
Muratori, Francesca M.L.
Murphy, Julie Anne
Murphy, Rebecca Lynn
Nelms, Brenda F.
Neudorfer, Karin Felicia
Newman, Amy B.
Noorani, Michelle
Nordone, Cynthia
Nowinski, Maryann Elizabeth
O'Conner, Cynthia E.
O'Kane, Jessica
O'Sullivan-Butler, Joan
Odendahl, Jennifer Alison
Ogunye-Raphael, Jacqueline Oluwunmi
Okeke, Loretta Ebere
Olsen, Angela Marie
Otoo, Deborah A.
Padgett, Elizabeth Chu
Pandohie-Johnson, Lisa Patrice
Park, Charlene Lee
Paroutsas, Aspasia A.
Parthemos, Kaliope
Parver, Deborah Gayle
Pastor, Nikita Malhotra
Patel, Sapna C.
Paugh, Jessica Michelle
Payne, Mary-Lee
Pellegrino, Susan M.
Perez, Devon Anne
Perkins, Kimberly Dionne
Perry, Kristen Bowen
Persson, Carol J.
Peters, Deanna Layne
Peterson, Kathleen Ann
Phelps, Lisa Ann
Phelps, Teresa T.
Phipps, Latonya
Placek, Carol Ann
Poling, A. Anne
Pomeranz, Jennifer Leah
Pontell, Devora Wolk
Porter, Stephanie Picard
Posner, Shannon Jacob
Post, Betsy Ann
Potter, Julie Lynn
Powell, Christine Weglein
Pratt, Jennifer Anne
Proctor, Deidra Nicole
Puyang, Mi Martin
Raphael, Tasha Rochelle
Razi, Sara Young
Reik, Jennifer Margaret
Rismiller, Donna Kathleen
Roberts, Joanna L.
Robertson, Jenny Rubin
Robertson, Laura Elizabeth
Robitaille, Lynn Marie
Rogers, Joyce Ann
Roh, Audrey
Ruckman, Kathleen Smith
Rudick, Shayna H.
Rudolph, Jennifer Elayne
Ruffin-Harris, Meeka
Rutherford, Patricia Ann
Salacuse, Maria
Sanchez, Sarah Elizabeth
Saurer, Holly Lynn
Sawyer, Stacie Leigh
Schaub, Ruth Marguerite Marie
Schoem, Cara Beth
Schueler, Veronica
Schulz, Jodi Strauss
Schuster, Kerstin M.
Scott, Lela R.
Serafin, Francine Aurora
Severson, Karen Patricia
Shapiro, Madelyn D.
Shirodkar, Shailaja Madhu
Sibert, Karen Moore
Simon, Jennifer Rachel
Simpson, Carol Elizabeth
Simpson, Erica Sapper
Smallwood, Yvette Williams
Smith, Cathern H.
Smith, Sarah Porter
Somera, Wendy L.
Southall, Alison H.
Spahn, Francie Cohen
Spiegel, Leslie Harriette
Squillario, Jennifer Kathryn
St. John, Anthonia V.
Strohmeyer, Victoria Louise
Sturmfelz, Mandy B.
Styles, Kasandra Robinson
Swindell, Emily Patterson
Sybert, Kathleen Keggins
Tabe, Henrietta Arrah
Tamami, Francesca Ugolini
Taylor, Courtney O'Hara
Taylor, Donna Christine
Taylor, Jennifer R.
Taylor, Kimberly Ann
Taylor, Nichole Germaine
Taylor, Tamika Latoya
Thibault, Shannon Colleen
Thomas, Kimberly Michelle
Thomas, Leahanne Catherine
Thornton, Camille Anne
Threatt, Nerissa Sheree
Tierney, Julia C.
Tippett, Cynthia Lynn
Turner, Susan Elaine
Ungvarsky, Ann Marie
Varma, Anita
Venier, Rachel Alice
Villalobos, Veronica E.
von Natzmer, Joyce H.A.
Wadhia, Shoba Sivaprasad
Wallace, Megan Marie
Walsh, Elizabeth Marie
Walter, Nicole R.
Ward, Roxanne Lynn
Watson, Dionne Marlena
Webb, Kimberly A.
Weidman, Christine
Weiner, Kelly Leigh Shubic
Weiss, Lisa B.
Wells, Ayla Michelle
Weyland, Sarah
Whipkey, Melissa Shane
Wickham, Zenita Ann
Wilkins, Barbara J.
Williams, Marsha Lynette
Williams, Vanessa R.
Wilson, Andrea M.
Wilson, Christina Janee
Wilson, Francine Ana Pierce
Winkle, Anna Nassif
Wirth, M. Heather Lee
Wolff, Janna Elise
Wunderli, Kathy Lynn
Yearby, Ruqaiijah Ayanna
Zaffuto, Annie Tran
Zerner, Loryn Brooke
Zweibel, Patricia May

12-18-2000

Constantino, Pauline A.
Erdman, Laurie Ann
Gulling, Kirstin A.
Herzog, Karen Marie
Lin, Dorothy Henrietta Patterson

12-19-2000

Galindo, Michelle Heron
Treber, Karen Avagliano
Williams, Samantha M.
Wu-Shepherd, Christine Ann

12-22-2000

Bogins, Sharon Anne
Campbell-Smith, Patricia Elaine
Lemken, Deborah Lynn
Turner, Anita Gauhar
Welsh, Barbara Allison

12-29-2000

LoDico, Deborah Marie
Popejoy, Linda B.

Wagner, Eileen Marie Nause
Yehle, Christina Spink

1-4-2001
Bui, Diane
Carroll, Christina M.
Carstens, Anne-Marie Carmen
Dell, Kristina Osche
Hall, Melissa Renee Hersh
Kaczmarczyk, Sandra
Olson, Kelly Annette
Schroader, Janee L.
Vorv, Marlynda Leah
Voso, Lisa Michele

1-10-2001
Carnot, Kimberly Hope
Cartwright-Smith, Lara A.

1-11-2001
Davis, Darragh Jean

1-19-2001
Goodell, Julie
Mann, Martha Collins
Nastasia, Helen A.

1-25-2001
Guinane, Kathleen Marie

2-1-2001
Prather, Tiffany Anne
Rees, Andrea
Ward, Kimberlee Marie
Williams, Risa Dyan

2-5-2001
Bacon, Antoinette Thomas

2-7-2001
Jeffreys, Maureen Ruth

3-1-2001
Castelli, Mary Rose
Hedman, Stacey Ann

3-12-2001
Farr, Karen Tyler
Loveland, Susan Loretta

4-5-2001
Tabor, April

5-18-2001
White, Barbara Ann

5-31-2001
Marcia, Felisa Rodriguez

6-7-2001
Michels, Claudia Anne

6-11-2001
Grill, Andrea S.
Vecchia, Janet A.

6-12-2001
Lawrence, Geralyn R.
McKeegan, Linda Diane
Miller, Sherri M.
Robbins, Aimee C.
Wilson, Donna M.P.

6-18-2001
Manoff, Tracey Carol
Nicholson, Jeanmarie LoCoco
Pembroke, Christine R.

6-20-2001
Allen, Tiffany Drake
Allulis, Rosemary Elizabeth
Ambery, Amy Eileen
Angwafo, Sherry Denien
Atterbeary, Vanessa Elaine
Bae, Rachel S.
Bangert, Beth A.
Barry, Dana Anne
Benedict, Mary Elizabeth
Bohuslav, Kelli Jean
Bourgeois, Jacqueline
Boyle-Lewicki, Edna
Brelsford, Becky S.
Brinkley, Kelly V.
Brown, Alea Marie-Claire
Burdick, Jessica Amanda
Campbell, Alicyn Claire
Carter, Aaronette
Carter, Juina Rana
Chambers, Jasemine Choy
Chapman, Jennifer Noelle
Chopra, Reva
Chu, Lan T.
Clay, Sharon Michele
Cooney, Teresa M.
Cox, Virginia A.
Craig, Ashley William
Crisafulli, Regina Josephine
Cross, Somer Taube
Daniel, Charlene Denise
Dasti, Saamia Haroon
Daugherty, Laura Lewis
Derr, Cara Wittenbach
Durand, Bethany Jean
Earp, Jill Cohen
Ebrahimi, Mariam
Edmunds, Alicia
Farahmand, Bahar
Finkle, Susan Frances
Fisher, Kari Lynn Diersen
Foti, Nancy Lorena
Fox, Kathryn Ann
Fracasso, Amy Kathryn
Freed-Collier, Kathryn Ann
Gardner, Phiona Shirlene
Gascoigne, Gina Maria
Giandomenico, Andrea Rana
Gleason, Rebekah Antoni
Goldstein, Rachel Jeanne
Gonlin, Alice Rebecca
Graves, Lily Ann
Green, Jeanette D.
Hall, Stephanie Summerson
Healy, Susan Ann
Heaney, Elizabeth Ann
Herrington, Jocelyn Johnson
Hill, Leslie Marie
Hindoyan, Lara Mirna
Hochul, Kathleen Courtney
Hoffstatter, Tamara L.
Howard, Catherine Slye
Hughes, Traci LaVon
Hunsberger, Amy L.
Hunt, Yolanda Kathryn
Hylton, Martha Linnell
Jackson, Jocelyn Kay
Jenkins, Erica L.
Jones, Tarsha Lakisha
Jordan, Jo Ellan
Kalishek, Kim Marie
Kane, Mary Deely
Kaplan, Maria Celeste
Katcheves, Konstantina Manjoros
Kedia, Shalini Kumari
Kim, Heili
Kisner, Christy Janelle
Klein, Diana Lee
Kleman, Nicole Anne
Kline, Kimberly Ann
Kornacki, Marci Lee
Kotler, Michelle Suzanne
Kovacic, Kristin Elise
Koya, Oluyemisi Oluyomi
Kushner, Tina Carmelle
Laufenberg, Beth Ann
Lawson, Kimberly E. Connolly
Lee, Christine Yong
Leonard, Nicole Anderson
Lipinski, Nicole L.
Loughlin, Juliet H.
Lynch, Marianne L.
Malmierca-Smith, Montserrat
Martello, Kendra Anne
Mason, Nicole Sherron
Mays, Susan Elizabeth
McKenna, Jennifer M.
McKoin, Claudia L.
McLane, Patricia C.
Meschino, Jennifer Lynn
Miller, Karin Marie
Morrison, Jessona M.
Myers, Erica Waugh
Nash, Fay Furniss
Neill, Lorna Marie
Nicholson, Jennifer K. Michael
Nightingale, Paula Grace
Noonan, L. Jean
Norris, Angela Marie
O'Halloran-Perez, Kimberley Marie
O'Neal, Cerissa Michelle
Orquiza, Dana Denise
Otey, Jania Marie
Owen, Cathleen Rose
Pacheco, Sarah Mayer
Palmer, Tracey D.
Parker, Camille A.
Pauler, Viki Marie
Paulson, Kristin Elizabeth
Plunkett, Deborah Anne
Prasse, Barbara Jane
Price, Sheree Lavell
Rawles, Melisa Darnise
Razor, Jennifer Marie
Reed, Kimberly D.
Reiff, Tiffany A.
Rice, Stacey Burnett
Rico, Mary Catharine
Robinson, Cynthia Renee
Rozenberg, Claudia Francesca
Rubin, Alisha Clare
Salmi, Hallie Wolfe
Sanchez, Michelle
Schmeiser, Susan Rebecca
Schuster, Katharina Wang
Selzer, Michelle Ann
Senft, Donna J.
Setliffe, Caroline C.
Shapiro, Karen N.
Silverman, Tracy
Smeltzer, Katherine Moxley
Smith, Judy Kay
Smith, Tanya Alicia
Stasko, Teresina Anne
Street, Rebecca Elizabeth
Streete, Esther A. E.
Sullivan, Aimee Roth
Sumerwell, Helen Case
Sun-Hoffman, Lin
Sutherland, Marsha Denise
Sykes, Jodie Karen
Terech, Heather Dawn Campbell
Tipton, Hope
Usab, Tricia D.
Valencia, Rachelle Marie
Voisinet, Catherine Mary
Webb, Sandy N.
Weisel, Meredith Renee
Wenzel, Christina
White, Tracy Margaret
Whiteman, Nicola Y.
Whiting, Raquel B.
Wilcox, Anne Loehr
Wilkinson, Lara
Williams, Romanda L.
Winfrey, Jeanine T.
Wisthoff-Ito, Rita Marie
Wohlstadter, Elizabeth Theresa
Yeager, Karen S.
Yoder, Katherine Berman
Young, Kathleen Johnlewis

6-21-2001
Cash, Starr Marshall
Kalish, Ann Sharon
Shepard, Julie Erin Dowler
Szeluga, Mary Therese

6-25-2001
McDonald, Susan D.
Sweeney, Maureen A.

7-6-2001
Silver, Joanna Beth

7-24-2001
Bainum, Rebecca Saybolt
Potter, Lillian Howard

7-30-2001
Privitera, Elizabeth Amy
Theodore-Lewis, Sharon I.

9-6-2001
Becker, Carolyn Elizabeth
Burakiewicz, Heidi R.
Darby, Heidi V.
Dietrich, Karen Barbra
McNair, Paula Dee

10-4-2001
Patel, Komal P.

11-1-2001
Drake, Karenya S.

11-29-2001
Land, Suzannah P.

12-11-2001
Abramson, Rachael Victoria Morgan
Adams, Ama Amoako
Adams, Megan Adkins
Adrian, Nadine D.Y.
Akinbolaji, Omolade R.
Al-Taie, Ferdose
Alsid, Erika Susan
Amos, Julia Catherine
Anderson, Heidi Reamer

Anthony, Jennifer Lisa
Arii, C. Sei-Hee
Askew, Amy Estelle
Baddour, Andrea B.
Bader, Aimee Michele
Baird, Rebecca Ahern
Baldwin, Molly M.
Barack, Brooke Foley
Barbeau, Hali E.W.
Barlotta, Allison Lee
Barnett, Dawn Diggs
Barnett, Renée J.
Belcher, Sherilyn Smith
Bergeron, Diane Marie
Berry, Bibi Mariama
Berry, Katherine Ann
Bhutta, Janet Shamim
Bjork, Rebecca Suzanne
Black, Lea Stanlee
Blank, Janet L.
Blumer, Kristin Elizabeth
Bodendorfer, Molly M.
Bofill, Mariju Libo-On
Bornstein, Katherine B.
Bowen, Joanne Rebecca
Bowman, Donna L.
Briscoe, Kate Bowen
Brisker, Nicole Lynn
Britt, Erika R.
Brooks, Heather Holden
Brown, Ashlea Howard
Buettner, Kathryn Colleen
Burns, Karin Elizabeth
Buzdugan, Maria
Cady, Diane C.
Cafaro, Cindy S.
Calderon, Ofelia L.
Calimano, Karin Elizabeth
Callahan, Jullia Frances
Campbell, Lea Stanlee
Campbell, Lisa Marie
Campbell, Meredith Sarah
Capitos, Lisa Blythe
Caplan, Emily Julia
Capone, Marisa A. Ferraro
Carden, Mary Jo
Carey, Jillian Anderson
Carrick, Stephanie Nicole
Carter, Georgeanne Adele
Carter, Jennifer Marye
Cascio, Amanda Bray
Caseman, Beth Ann
Cavalier, Stefanie Michelle
Chess, Catherine Anne
Chisholm, Barbara Jane
Christopher, Julie Barnett
Cika, Patricia Dolores
Clelan, Courtney Margaret
Close, Raena S.
Cohen, Kerri Bloom
Cohen, Sara Ruth
Coletta, Patrizia Juliana
Colker, Allison Cay
Collins, Crystal Dianne Harris
Connolly, Anne Sheridan
Cook, Jennifer Drugay
Cook, Revella L.
Cooper, Lindsay Cohn
Courtney, Catherine A.
Cowie, Rhonda Marcelle
Cox, Tiffany Lacole
Craig, Jessica Dawn Black
Cribbs, Gia Vassanelli
Crockett, Debbie Sines
Cromwell, Jenifer Alice
Cugle, Christina Lynn
Cunningham, Darcy Hubbard
Cunningham, Karen Elizabeth
Dabo, Miatta Tenneh
Dais, Alyson Jennifer
Daniels, Dee Grace
Darby, Yolanda Lavette
Davenport, Courtney Leigh
De Atley, Melinda M.
Dean, Karen Martin
DeLorenzo, Dana Katherine
Dennis, Chamille Cecilene
Dent, Kelli Ann
Derwart, Melissa Beth
Desaulniers, Kendall Ann
Deuberry, Jamai Alexandra
Devereaux, Kathleen Marion
Dieng, Mary Brown
Dinos, Anthea
Dixon, Susan M.
Dodd, Lynda G.
Dolan, Kristen Adell
Dooher, Carrie Charlotte
Dorsey, Cheri H.
Duff, Grace
Dye, Elizabeth Clare
Dyson, Renee Olivia
Emig, Jennifer Kristin
Englisby, Claudia W.
Enos-Langone, Jennifer
Esworthy, Jennifer Adonizio
Euteneuer, Susan Mae
Farbman, Elizabeth Helen
Farrell, Kelly Jade
Faulkner, Nancy Leigh
Fayed, Rebecca C.
Featherstone, Kerslyn Danise
Ferguson, Tracy Nicole
Firestone, Jessica Michelle
Floeck, Monica
Forbush, Christina Gwyneth
Fortunato, Sallianne
Foster, Courtney N.
Frekko, Katherine Segal
Frickel, Maura Kathleen
Fulton, Laura Marie
Gajwani, Vineeta
Galloway, Mandi W.
Garcia, Vanessa Elizabeth
Garmon, Felisa Carlette
Gartner, Jennifer Ellen
Gasior, Malgorzata Anna
Gates, Katherine Tirrell
Geier, Lisa Langdon
Gerber, Allison Amy
Gibison, Kathleen Carole
Girard, Erin Elizabeth
Girma, Lebawit
Glasgow, Soyini Abena
Goodman, Stacy Marie
Gorham-Oscilowski, Ursula
Gorman, Eileen Mary
Grant, Armada Whitley
Grant, Jennifer Elizabeth
Green, Lesli N.
Gresock, Jennifer Lynn
Griffith, Vater Anika
Grissett, Nycole LaJuan
Guevara, Stephanie L.
Hackett, Jennifer Duncan
Hager, Cheryl Elizabeth
Hall, Sarah Mali
Hall Johnson, Lisa A.
Hambrick, Valerie Diane
Hampton, Colleen Jennifer
Haney, Emeline Michelle
Hargrove, Serena Latoya
Harrison, Belinda Lanette
Hay, Sabrina Lynne
Heda, Anita Harikisan
Helfman, Judith Michelle
Henline, Tracey Lee Ann
Henriques, Lisa Ann
Hershkowitz, Jackie Rene
Herz, Dianne Lynn
Herz, Jamie A. Hochman
Hieb, Jennifer Lynn
Himes, Heather Marie
Himes, Mary Ellen Roy
Hirko, Elizabeth Donahue
Hoard, Jamila Zawadi
Hochman Herz, Jamie A.
Hoffman, Fahryn Elizabeth
Holcomb, Karen Jean
Holder, Elizabeth Kathryn
Holloway, Chandra Walker
Holmes, Essita Raquel
Holmes, Joyette Marie
Howard, Patricia Charise
Howson, Charmaine Aldene
Hoye, Bobbie Lynn
Hulthage, Suzanne Nicole
Hume, Cora L.
Hutchinson, Shoshana F.
Inverary-Wills, Charlene Sattra
Jackson, Tammi Dionne
James, Joycelyn Fae
Jelks, Laura Spencer
Jensen, Robin V.
Johnson, Edith Coral
Jordan, Mary Albrecht
Joseph, Linda A.
Joseph, Stephanie L.
Kaifer, Heather Eve Boardman
Kaiser, Bridgette Lynn
Kaminer, Maggie Ilene
Kane, Bonnie L.
Kaplan, Robyn Stacie
Kardakova, Nelly
Katz, Deborah
Kelsey, Sarah Lynn
Kennedy, Tara Leovna
Kersey, Maureen A.
Knotts, Shannon Anne Graving
Lankster, LaDonne Camille
LaVera, Christina A.
Lazier, Raynell Denny
Love, Carroll Virginia Crumbaugh
McAndrews, Jessica Mary
McClure, Mary Graf
McCray, Danielle James
McElroy, Tara Suzanne
Morse, Patricia Lynn
Ogden, Shannon E.
Oliver, Tonya Esposito
Oxley, Tara L.
Patrick, Suzanne B.
Quigley, Tinna Marie Damaso
Rath, Michele Theresa
Rattan, Mindy L.
Rivera, Elizabeth Bechtold
Roane, Akia F.
Rowe, LaTasha Marina
Sheets, Kathryn Bannister Frost
Shortley, Maura J.
Talbot, Lisa Brindle
Talley, Anne D'Arcy Byrnes
Weston, Kacie McCoy
Williams, Christina Joy Greene
Winbush, Michelle Lynn
Wolf, Stephanie Susanne

12-12-2001

Alexander, Jennifer Michelle
Alford, Alisha Rachel
Antezana, Rebecca Dawn
Barta, Keri Schrader
Barton, Laura Polvinale
Callender, Michelle Renae
Campbell, Michelle Owens
Castor, Jennifer Marie
Chapman, Rashida Jamilla
Chung, Pamela Il Hong
Collins, Johnnie Postell
Daniel, Geeta Valluripalli
De Santis, Sarah Otwell
Derder, Jessica Arline
Dickens, Lydia R.
Gittens, Precious Murchison
Gozycki, Allyson Ann
Greten, Erin Jaislee
Herber, Kristin Pickett
Herring, Jennifer Matthews
Higgins, Demetria McCain
Horton, Heather Lynn
Jenkins, Marcela
Kane, Rita A.
Khajawi, Feiruz Heidi
Kilmer, Melissa Ramirez
Kim, Jennifer C.
Kimbler, Kelly R.
King, Kimberly Ann Nugent
King, Kristen Dawn
King, Marnitta Lanette
Klarquist, Carolyn R.
Kotkin, Diane Sara
Krakovitz, Annette Marlene
Kramer, Melinda Sue
Kramer, Nancy Robin
Kreindler, Marcy Wright
Krupinsky, Kelly Dana
Labriola, Deana A.
Lacoste, Nicole Marie
Lahuti, Isabella
Landeo, Jennifer Vetter
Leader, Robyn Jacqueline
LeBow, Mary Edith
Lederer, Katrina Marie
Lee, Katina W.
Lehmann, Brooke
Levesque, Chistian Alexandra
Lewis, Rosalind Dianne
Lis, Sylwia A.
Lloyd, Amy Marie
Long, Deborah Kay
Lopez, Laina Catherine Wilk
Lowe, Lisa June
Maciel, Kara M.
Maisog, Maria Regina
Mallas, Georgeanne K.
Manchester, Doreen Langa
Mann, Naomi Miriam
Maraviglia, Kimberly Kasberg
Marshall, Melissa April

Martens, Carole Ann
Martinez, Maria Del Rosario
Marvel-Lewis, Kate Elizabeth
Massey, Mary Ann
Maurice, Tracy M.
Maxwell, Lila Ann
McCaffrey, Karen Patricia
McCauley, Marilyn Ginger
McElroy, Donna Burnett
McGinn, Elizabeth Ellen
McGrath, Rhian
McGuire, Meisha Tanaya
McIntosh, Janet J.
McNairn, Denise L.
McQueen, Catherine Huger
Meade, Jennifer Lynn
Michaels, Jill Pogach
Michel, Monique M.
Mielke, Amy
Miller, Karen Stephanie
Minder, Julie Michelle
Moore, Jennifer Kristen
Moreland, Genevieve Lynn
Morgan, Jennifer Lynn
Morris, Elizabeth L.
Morrison, Jessica Erin
Morrison, Katherine Anne
Moses, Joy M.
Mottet, Lisa Ann
Mulkey, Shelly Ava
Murray, Michelle Marie
Nadel, Margot Lynne
Nagarajan, Nithya
Nagpaul, Anjali
Neira, Paula Marcelle
Nelson, Melanie Kate
Nelson, Tonya Lynn
Nemeth, Rebecca Dawn
Netram, Melissa
Newman, Alexandra Ellin
Nguyen, Thu Trang
O'Brien, Alice Ritchie
O'Neill, Caroline Jeanne
Oliver, Debra Gail
Olivieri, Lisa A.
Onwubere, Beverly Marjorie Ngozika
Opel, Cathleen Cogan
Orendorff, Gail Christine
Orr, Kathleen Adele
Owens, Kimberly T.
Owens, Sonia Monique
Palmer, Lyana Gia
Pannell, Jessica Marchegiano
Parikh, Neera A.
Park, Jaime C.
Parker, Tracy Genene
Pestaner, Mitzi Caroline
Pham, Lana H.
Phillips, Jill L.
Pinderhughes, Gayle E.
Piner, Elizabeth Joy
Pirisino, Carolyn M.
Pleasant Kline, Colleen Marie
Quaye, Chandra M.
Rahman, Naureen
Rayman, Ariel I.
Reamy, Julie Marie
Rinaldi, Laura Nicole
Risinger, Susan Stafford
Roberts, Michaela F.
Roberts, Susan Jaffe
Robinson, Angela Stephanie
Robinson, Tiffany P.
Rock, Melissa Savar
Rose, Erika Elizabeth
Rose-McFadden, Jinnah Maria
Rosenberg, Amy Lynne
Ross, Mechelle R.
Sachs, Hope Miller
Sacks, Samantha Brooke
Saggare, Sai Deepa Vittal
Saltarelli, Monica L.
Salter, Jessica Jaye
Saltzbart, Ilana Simone
Saran, Neeta S.
Sartori, Michele Walls
Saunders, Kayin Alphaez
Scates, Robyn Carol
Scharf, Jana Melissa
Scheinberg, Laura Pierson
Schrecengost, Leanne McInturff
Schultz, Kristen Kaye
Schwaber, Calley Renee
Schwartzott, Jennifer Marie
Segler, Florence Hagan
Sekel, Renee Alanna
Self, Katina Beatrice
Shaffer, Regina D.
Shearer, Kimber L.
Showalter, Karla Renee
Shrager, Karen Saks
Sigel, Gabrielle Eve Osman
Simmons, Jennifer Michele
Simmons, Kara Ellice
Sims, Debra Sandra
Singleton, Dawn Star
Small, Charisse
Smart, Kyler Elizabeth
Smith, Kimberly LaShone
Smyth, Catherine Frances
Soares, Antonia Ramos
Sofela, Ifeatu Ifueko
Solomon, Maura Katharine
Sonabend, Heather Eve
Sousa, Bethany M.
Sparks, Lillian Azalea
Spector, Sarah Lichtman
Squires, Cindy Lynn
St. John, Toni Roth
Stein, Meredith S.
Stewart, Abby Thompson
Suh, Julie Joo Yun
Syed, Shehla
Szybillo, Victoria Marion
Tafreshi, Sepidar N.
Tai, Katherine C.
Tardivo, Molly McGuire
Taylor, Dannielle K.
Tetteh-Ocloo, Jonelle Daikuor
Tillett, Melissa Leigh
Tobias, Demetria Titus
Tracy, Lisa A.
Upadhyaya, Shraddha A.
VanderHeijden, Pamela Zo-Yun
Vansickel, Mary Adrian
Varnovitskaia, Natalia E.
Verity, Jade Bristol
Vogt, Alisa Marie
Vosburg, Adriana Rojas
Vossler, Karen
Waniewski, Sandra Margaret
Ward, Myesha Theresa
Washburn, Tenille E.
Weber, Faraza Jehanbux
Weider-Hatfield, Deborah J.
Wheeler, Karen Anne
White, Christine Andrea
Wiggins, Angela E.
Wilkerson, Courtney LaMont
Williams, Carla Michelle
Williams, Denisha Simone
Williams, Hannah Koopmann
Williams, Kamilah Rae
Williams, Kristin Harclerode
Wilson, Monica Denise
Windsor, Jacqueline Nicole
Wood, Claire A.
Worth, Ashley Russell
Wright, Tashia Dionne
Xu, Eva Yahua
Yanak, Heather Nicole
Yasbin, Melanie B.
Yu, Kelli Lam
Yurasek, Holly A.
Zide, Marla

12-17-2001
Donnellan, Rebecca A.
Peery, Donna Ruth Stroup

12-19-2001
Abel, Raquel Avina
Dave, Aparna R.
Hoffmann, Sydney Jean
Hopp, Rachel Mae
Hylton, Maureen L.
Viramonted-LaFree, Vicki

12-27-2001
Gelbin, Ellen Ruth
Lokker, Ellen R.
Miller, Clare Kristin
St. John, Peggy D.

12-28-2001
Caplan, Christina Childs
Primus, Eve Brensike

1-3-2002
Boersma, Cynthia Maxine
Cammack, Olivia Desiree
Davis, Kristin Inez
Funk, Michelle Lura
Garg, Nisha

1-7-2002
Rutledge, Virginia Skidmore
Vogel, Miriam H.

1-9-2002
Davis, Leslie E.

1-11-2002
Caruso, Linda Ann

1-16-2002
Joseph-Daniels, Tiffany C.

1-18-2002
Berlage, Jan Ingham
Buckler, Amy Lynn

2-11-2002
Becker, Judith G.

3-5-2002
Hutnik, Alysa Zeltzer

3-21-2002
O'Toole, Margaret Lynne

4-4-2002
Grundman, Stacey G.

5-2-2002
Dent, Rhonda Maria

6-6-2002
Abrams, Monica Salamon

6-7-2002
Watson, Lisabeth S.

6-10-2002
Blasy, Jill Uhlmann

6-10-2002
Zoller, Danielle Marie Stager

6-11-2002
Elefant, Carolyn
Milloy, Sandra Delores
Siegell, Barbara C.
Waldman, Michelle Toni

6-14-2002
Pozgar, Nina Santucci
Ross, Beverly D.

6-16-2002
Johnson, Lyvette Lyn
Carr, Deborah Meier
Fanaroff, Sheri Van Greenby
Preiss, Valerie G.

6-19-2002
Adams, Tanya Suzanne
Ahmed, Huma Nisar
Ai, Julia
Aita, Anna G.
Archer, Tamika M.
Audain, Linz
Austin, Jennifer Lynn
Baird, Jennifer Jean
Barclay, Lisa
Bartlett, Jessica Simons
Becker, Katherine M. Sutcliffe
Belcher, Teri L.
Berman, Mona Ross
Bhattacharyya, Abanti A.
Bhattacharyya, Deepa
Booker, Ayhanna Tamar
Bowie, Dawn Elaine
Boyet, Valentina A.
Brashear, Monica Bryan
Bristow, Diane Carol
Bungard, Emma Kate
Burke, Christine Louise
Cann, Denise Sandra
Capriotti, Suzanne Lea
Chasan-Sloan, Deborah Miriam
Cheng, Audrey L.
Clark, Lynne Rochelle
Collins, Lynette Arona
Concino, Jennifer C.
Cosca, Rebecca Emily
Cotter, Carol Hollister
Crone, Gretchen Haverback
Currier, Holly Ann
Davis, Leslie Anne
Davis, Monica Shenee
del Toro, Frances Ileana
DePaulis, Sandra Joy
Donniez, Brigid O.
Donovan, Kelly Christine
Edmonds, Courtney Joseph
Eisenberg, Karen Bell

Esch, Valerie Grace
Farinacci, Andrea D.
Files, Sandra Darlene
Forbes, Daphne Turpin
France, Heather M.
Franzblau, Anne
Gardner, Cheri Simpkins
Gaston, Gretchen L.
German, Jennifer Janine
Goecke, Robyn Aronberg
Gold, Rebecca Cheryl
Goldberg, Jennifer Anne
Gorden, Margaret S.
Grzechowiak, Andrea Negron
Hadwen, Deborah Ann
Haglof, Jennifer Kelli
Harth, Stephanie Moore
Hauser, Jane Margaret Traylor
Hesse, Lisa A.
Hidalgo-Rubio, Martha P.
Hill, Michele Renee
Hinojosa, Ikeita Monique Cantu
Homann, Karen Anne
Hughes, Susan Marie
Hunter, Wanda Denisa
Jarmula, Agnieszka Edyta
Johnson, Jennifer L.
Kanyuck, Dawn Marie
Kenny, Heidi S.
Korotkevich, Natalie A.
Lawler, Lisa Marie
Lee, Diana C.
Lewis, Elisabeth Suzanne
Lorenzini, Amy D.
Major, Shanee Therese
Marcello, Stephanie Olympia
Maund, Jennifer
McConnell, Jessica Helena
McCray, Kathryn Nicole
McGallagher, Catherine Louise
McGrath, Melody Ellison
McPhaull, Maria A.
McTaggart, Erin J.
Meade, Veronica Elaine
Mills, Iva C.
Moorer, Laura R.
Morgan, Filia Providentia
Morrison, Jennifer Michele
Munson, Deborah Pincus
Neiswender, Virginia Escobar
Norris, Cynthia Marie
Osborne, Tonya Michelle
Palmer, Sandra Y.
Parvis, Pamela Lindsay
Pavlitsa, Susan Lerch
Perpignan, Cristal C.
Picard, Carissa S.
Picard, Christina Marie
Prichard, Lisa Diane
Rai, Pallavi
Ramirez, Natalia
Ramjohn, Stephanie Ingrid
Rasul, Salma Pir Tillah
Rollins, Suzanne De Haan
Rossbach, Natasha Veytsman
Rudberg, Jacqueline
Saul, Tammy
Schrader, Amy Wilmot
Semko, Jennifer Ancona
Shattuck, Sarah Andrews
Sheppard, Debra Lynn
Shook, Tamiko Sherisse
Sierra, Marianne Aumick
Smith-Valentine, Sonya Anjanette
Sorrentino, Justine Patricia
Staples, Cheri Hance
Themelis-Barberis, Maria Ann
Thompson, Robyn L.
Uba, Vivien Ndidi
Walker, Yvette B.
Waller, Karina Michael
Washington, Rochelle Davina
Webster, Margaret L.
Weedman, Amy Elizabeth
White-Welker, Stacey Elaine
Williams, Charisse Michelle
Williams, Marie Natalie
Womack, April Henderson
Wyatt, Dorothy Katharine
Zhang, Cynthia Hongbing

6-24-2002

Eriksson, Kirsten Marie
Forquer, Jennifer Ann
Mazur, Lori Marie
Reynolds, Pamela Jackson
Simpson, Lisa Bernadette
Walther, Lizabeth Lee

7-1-2002

Belinkoff, Dena Ruth
Mayers, Sheila Bridget Thurmond
Sapin, Barbara Joan

7-9-2002

Weiswasser, Elizabeth Stotland
Yette, Joyce Payne

7-23-2002

Irons, Gloria Frederici

8-29-2002

Bauer, Michele Elizabeth

9-5-2002

Anderson, Natalie Madge
Davis, Andrea DeRusso
Fortsch, Michelle Ione
Jones, Laticia Ines
Zimlin, Pamela Jill

9-18-2002

Henke, Melissa Nicole

10-3-2002

D'Angelo, Sheri Liccioni
Thomas, Nicole Renee

12-17-2002

Abou, Sabitiyu Abiodun
Abrams, Jamie Rene
Adamczyk, Anna D.
Adams, Suren G.
Adams, Susan Dawn
Ainashbekova, Ayauly Saparovna
Akehurst-Krause, Heather Lee
Al-Absi, Jessica Wadih
Alexander, Rachel Merrill
Alfonso-Frank, Stefanie R.
Algarin, Barbara
Alonso, Jennifer Marie
Andreeff, Julie L.
Andronici, Justine Frances
Ao, Terry Meng-Yee
Arnold, Jennifer Elizabeth
Arnold, Kathryn Christine
Ashley, Suzanne Evelyn
At Lee, Kathyrn Elizabeth
Azani, Taraneh
Ballard, Tracey
Balogun, Rukaayat Abolade
Banach, Jennifer Lynn
Baran, Stacy LaSara
Barnett, Crystal D.
Barton, Sheron Andrea
Baskir, Cecily Elizabeth
Batcha, Nadhira
Bates, Karen Cargill
Bauer, Christine G.
Beals, Connie J.
Bell, Christine D.
Benshoof, Anna Rachel
Bentley, Andrea Marie
Bergeron, Emily G.
Berry, Youshea Anika
Blane, Suzanne Malken
Bogicevic, Susan Hughes
Bombach, Kara Megan
Boonshaft, Shara Lynn
Borrello, Stacia J.
Bortz, Ellen Florence
Boyd, Carla L.
Boyle, Allison Jane
Boyle-Donahue, Elizabeth Anne
Bracewell, Clare Donley
Braithwaite, Aisha
Bramble, Jocelyn Cara
Brand, Olga
Bray, Kinley Rae
Bridges, Karissa D.
Brienza, Jennifer A.
Briggs, Valerie Marie
Brino, Amanda
Bromley, Sandra Elizabeth
Brooks, Yvonne K.
Brown, Brandi Oats
Brown, Lasheka M.
Brown, Takisha Vera
Burghardt, Mira Sugarman
Cabrales, Aurora D.
Cahn, Lisa Robin
Calkins, Mary Margaret
Callan, Marie A.
Campbell, Renae Marie
Carr, Jennifer Paige
Carr, Leigh A.
Carter, Adrienne Cox
Cetta, Jennifer Ann
Chaney, Pamela R.
Chang, Joo Yeun
Chapin, Margie Sue
Chappell, Julianne Walker
Charles, Jessica Elena
Chen, Dora V.
Cherian, Meena M.
Cho, Sonia S.
Ciani-Dausch, Jessica Ann
Cimino, Johanna Edith Fortuna
Cinque, Corrin R.
Ciralsky, Jennifer Lynn
Clark, Hillary Ellis
Clark, Kalea Seitz
Clarke, Kathryn Margaret
Clemsen, Kimberly Ann
Clopper, Keitha Lorraine
Cole, Lisa Jacqueline
Coleman, Esther DeAnn
Coleman, Sarah
Collins, Dawn Marie
Connell, Sarah C.
Connelly, Deborah Lynn
Connor, Jennifer Marie
Cooper, Carol Ghingher
Cordero, Rebecca Noel
Cowen, Nataliya C.
Crawford, Rosaline Hayes
Cross, Kerri McGuire
Crump, Anitra Gaye
Dail, Helen Marie
Daley, Thereen Dian
Dang, Harsimran Kaur
Daub, Tammy Renee
Davis, Angela Jewell
Davis, Jacquelyn Beth
Davis, Kara K.
Davis, Stefanie Kay
Dayton, Jennifer Beatrice
De Witt, Tyrona Tiese
Deal, Janet L.
DeBord, Kathryn Reed
Dell, Alexandra Lundy
Deming, Candie Caloia
Devadas, Amy Arathi
Devereaux, Deena Marie
Dill, Jennifer Owen
Doan, Thanh Van Thi
Donaldson, Kara Michelle
Donato, Christina Ruth
Dorsey, Heather Lamar
Dorsey, Jennifer Marie
Dotson, Cybill Lynette
duBois, A. Burridge
DuPuy, Leslie E.
Durham, Laurel A.
Edwards, Danette Rae
Eggleston, Alexa Lenore
Emmett, Laura Spencer
Erwin, Deborah K.
Escalante, Josephine A.
Estano, Wendy Kathryn
Evans, Dawn Patricia
Fidazzo, Dana M.
Filoia, Celeste Barton
Finneran, Amy Knepp
Fisher, Cortney Lyn
Fitzpatrick, Jennifer S.
Flamant, Julie Paul Julia
Fofana, Fatima
Ford, Leah Rebekah
Ford, Mary Catherine
Fortmann, Allison Rebecca
Freeman, Angela Addison
Frentzel-Beyme, Pamela
Galipeau, Erin Anne
Galletly, Marion E.
Galletto, Lori Gabriella
Galotto, Elisabeth Topel
Galvin, Nicole Michele
Geraghty, Mary Katherine
Gerson, Samara Rebecca
Ghei, Nita
Giblin, Margaret Helen Clune
Griffin, Kerri B.
Handel, Lauren Erica
Harms, Monica Garcia
Hengerer, Melodie Hahn
Herwig, Julie E.
Heubert, Katherine Louise Bugbee

Johnson, Mechelle Denise
Kozlowski, Angela Garcia
Kurfess, Victoria J.
MacDonald, Sally Roe
Miller, Lisa Michele Cylus
Mitchell, Heather Louise
Nannis, Veronica Byam
Oliver, Kirsten Borgeson
Patterson, Shelly JoAnn
Pugsley, Allison Dora
Rosado Desilets, Virginia M.
Ruley, Hilary Baldwin
Ruth, Erica Tiffany Davis
Sandmann, Camela June
Scheessele, Jennifer Kate
Shapiro, Melanie Dawn
Siri, Michelle Daugherty
Smith, Brigitte Joelle
Smith, Susan Ann Fales
Spiggle, Anne Dudley
Veigel, Lisa G.
Weaver, Tracie Linne Clabaugh
Rowers, Stephanie

12-18-2002

Ahmad, Shana P.
Andrews, Rajita M.
Ballenger, Katherine Lasher
Campbell, Melissa A.
DeSario, Molly Ann
Dietz, Rebecca Hubbell
Donahue, Lisa Lefante
Felder, Debra Lessin
Feldman, Becky Kathleen King
Finkenstadt, Ivy Ann
Gershberg, Jennifer Kantor
Gilhooly, Colleen E.
Givens, Deborah L.
Glauber, Diane
Gleason, Hannah Jones
Going, Kristin Kendra
Goldfrank, Sarah Alexander
Gomez, Piedad
Gordon, Raquel Yvette
Graybill, Elizabeth Susan
Greco, Kimberly Ann
Griffin, Reagan Leigh
Grimm, Nancy Beth
Grossman, Michelle McKinney
Guttadauro, JulieMarie Myers
Hall, Jessica Marie
Hallein, Katrina Suzanne
Halverson, Andrea Mead
Handwerger, Sarah
Hargrove, Emily Kate
Harney, Carrie A.
Hatcher, Nichole Monique
Hauck, Katharine Edmands
Hausner, Deena
Haussler, Helyna M.
Hawk, Kendra Hagen
Hayduk, Andrea DeFay
Hermann, Caroline B. C.
Herold, Esther Janet Chambi
Heslep, Hilary Todd
Hilliard, Aisha Nicole
Ho, Barbara Janean
Hoffman, Coralee Cole
Holloway, Angela Delola
Hooper, Kelly Anell
Hopper, Jessica Baez
Horn, Christian Lindsey
Huckabee, Jodi Michele
Hudgins, Kristina Nicole
Hunt, Eleanor A.
Iannetta, Christie L.
Iotina, Gergana Emilova
Jaffery, Syeda Z.
Jemison, Lori Michelle
Jesinoski, Jennifer Diane
Jih, Deena S.
Johnson-Noon, Nathalie Isabelle
Jones, Elizabeth Lacey
Jones, Jessica Helene
Kaselonis, Sharon Rose
Katz, Moira Anne
Kelley, Shondriette Danielle
Kendall, Jessica Rachel
Keogh, Nancy Janoske
Keys, Mary Ellen
Kimball, Stanislava
Kinch, Silvia C.
King, Shelley Joy
Kirchoffer, Liza Mee Ling
Klein-Faust, Courtney Anne
Knickelbein, Sabrina Sherry
Kohn, Diane Margaret
Kolb, Pherabe Elizabeth Hardin
Kouroupsis, Lynda Frances Lewinski
Kowitz, Tonya Kelly
Krapels, Helen H.
Kreis, Dana Lynn
Krieger, Robin Christine
Krukova, Elizaveta
Kukla, Heather Eileen Johnson
Kurnot, Stacy Skinsacos
Lee, SoCheung
Lepping, Kavita Battula
Leslie, Heather Carroll
Lewis, Ericka Loretta
Light, Sharon P.
Lignos, Fotini
Limarzi, Megan Davey
Lindley, Ivonne Corsino
Lipkowitz, Michelle Nicole
Lippincott, Kelly Marie
Liu, Jeanne Hui-ching
Llorente, Laura McLoughlin
Logan, Sara Lareen
MacBeth, Kelly Elizabeth
MacCumbee, Kimberly Sue
Mackiewicz, Melissa Lea
Magruder, Angela Diane
Majors, Melanie
Maldonado, Paula Lynn
Manfreda, Mary Elizabeth
Marcus, Danielle Grilli
Marcus, Michelle Meira
Marshall, Karen L.
Marshall, Tracy Pierce
Martellino, Celia Rebecca
Martone-Boyce, Clara Mindy
Mayne, Jessica Lynn
McClain, Amy Marie
McClintick, Ilona M.
McCormack, Shannon Matthew
McDaniel, Christine Marie
McGuane, Melissa M.
McGuire, Margaret Shelley
McIntosh, Nina A.
McLaughlin-Kominsky, Kelly L.
McNair, Melissa Dyan
Mehalick, Lesley Mary
Meriwether, Karyn Ann
Middleton, Caroline Lisa
Miles, Meredith Allsopp
Miller, Eden Ilene
Miller, Kamala Taryn
Mims, Christal Lenise
Mitchell, Andrea Kay
Mitchell, Micah Michele
Moeves, Amy Suzanne
Moisides, Yoanna Xantheppi
Molina, Claudia M.
Montgomery, Bonnie Jean
Mooney, Sarah Elizabeth
Moorman, Felicite D.
Morrison, Rebecca Christine
Mosley-Day, Serena Evelyn
Mundy, Michael-Anne T.
Munson-Ott, Mary Deirdre
Musgrave-Burdette, Nicole Erin
Naqvi, Safia Ali
Nastro, Corinne Michelle
Neal, Tara Stratton
Neureiter, Kimberly Elizabeth
Nicolas, Margarette Bien-Aime
Njoya, Kena Njoya
Nolan, Monique Valerie
Nuckols, Natalia
O'Brien, Michelle Renee
Ochs, India L.
Oliai, Sarah Elizabeth
Oliver, April A.
Onyia, Kosisochukwu Nkenne
Orders, Vonda J.
Orsi, Amy M.
Osinski, Nadine M.
Ours, Leah J.
Petralia, Katherine Anne
Pope, Jean K.
Prendergast, Christy L.M.
Queen, Rashida Lockhart
Roth, Jennifer Jordan
Rothman, Staci Paige
Rumley, MaKara Jackson
Rychak, Laura Newman
Schofield, Rachelle Ann
Steiner, Catherine Kutson
Sweet, Krista Lynn
Wellons, Christine M. H.
Westra, Tara Lynn
Wilham, Michele Brooke
Winn, Logan Helman

12-19-2002

Anderson, Kathleen Harper
Archer, Margit
Atkinson, Yollette Simone
Auzoux, Lydia
Bailey, Rebecca Gage
Bancroft, Jessica Russo
Berge, Ellen Traupman
Betzler, Lauren LaRayne
Bixler, Rebecca Lynn
Brown, Tammy Marie
Burgy, Adriana Leigh
Carney, Daria Ann
Cathell, Audra Trouland
Celeste, Christine Marie
Chandler, Lynne Tucker
Davenport, Kristin R.
Feinberg, Jennifer Wigman
Graham, Robin
Guerin, Toby Treem
Hahn, Erin Nichole
Hammons, Tara Patterson
Hartman, Kimberly Ann
Jones, Lisa Langston
Kaiser, Heidi Lynn
Lake, Mary Stevens
Lederman, Laura W.
Luse, Jaime Walker
Mahoney, Tora A.
Martin, Linda Lee
McLean, Pamela Anne
Morris, Elizabeth Sheree
Pachman, Dayna Sloane
Pachman, Lauren Gayle
Parcelli, Carmen Rose
Parish, Carrie A.
Parker, Charmetra Lynnette
Parker, Dionne A.
Parker, Janice J.
Parsley, Luciene M.
Parsons, Elizabeth Lynn
Pascual, Jocelene Aquino
Pelino, Bridget Elizabeth
Pellettieri, Monica Grace
Peoples, Felicia G.
Perry, Angela K.
Peters, Alexis H.
Phillips, Suzan Alison
Pickeral, Chekevia B.
Pierce, Tanya T.
Pittman, Lucy E.
Policard-Jones, Nadia
Ponton, Ninette Marie
Powell-Bullock, Elizabeth Everett
Pritts, Christa A.
Prout, Megan Becher
Qureshi, Farah Zeba
Radio, Kristy Lynn
Rand, Angela Kimberly
Rasin, Katherine Parks
Rhodes, Kimberly Patricia
Richard, Sybil Marie
Richardson, April Nicole
Richman, Michele Anne
Ridley, Augusta Morgan
Righter, Kimberly B.
Rigney, Amy Claire
Rizek, Anita Louise Horn
Robinson, Jessica Rae
Rock, Deanna Ray
Rollock, Temmi C.
Romero, Jennifer Marie
Rosenkoetter, Darlene Joan
Rothleder, Tamara Beth
Rounds, Anna Mae
Rouse, Veronica Allyson
Ruddy, Lisa J.
Ryan, Patricia Mary O'Brien
Sagerson, Ann N.
Salmon, Erica Lynne
Salvano, Dana Christine
Sanders, Hope Elizabeth
Sanders, Robin M.
Sandler, Kaiya Pontinen
Sappington, Shauna Renee
Sarrat, Robyn Astin
Satiani, Puja
Savedoff, Jill Beth
Savino, Katarina Olivia
Sayers, Allison Michele
Scarlett, Sara Elizabeth

Scaturro, Janeen M.
Schiesel, Erin
Schillings, Rebecca Ann
Schmidt, Tamara D.
Schnur, Rochel Zisel
Schowalter, Regina-Lyn
Scott, Angela J.
Segbefia, Francina M.
Sepehri, Sherene
Shaffer, Kimberly A.
Shah, Sonia Rajni
Shankman, Rebecca Celia
Shea, Jill M.
Shuler, Melodie Venee
Sigmon, Brooke Janene
Simon, Sara
Simone, Kelly Shipp
Simpson, Lisa Jane
Smith, Cheryl Jeanine
Smith, Jen Julie
Smith, Jessica Ann
Smith, Shayon Tylee
Smith, Tonia Rashana
Smothers, Courtney Elizabeth
Splittorff, Shannon Hovis
Steele, Sharon Olivia
Stein, Linda Balon
Steinberg, Helene Susan
Steinhilber, Jessica Stuart
Stewart, Rachel Lynn
Stewart, Stefanie M.
Stobaugh, Amelia Christine
Sudell, Andrea Lynn
Swears, Courtney Elaine
Swienton, Anjali Ranadive
Swize, Jennifer Loraine
Tacka, Christine Gariffo
Taneyhill, Vanessa G.
Tewari, Rita
Themelis, Constantine John
Thibodeau, Jennifer Suzanne
Tilley, Belinda Marie
Torres-Rivera, Sahra I.
Tremble, Kristen D.
Trien, Stacey Eve
Tshibaka, Jean Christian Kanyiki
Tshibaka, Kelly Chaundel
Turner, Leslie Espe
Turner, Tiffany Marie
Tutwiler, Fatimah Al-nisia
Uebersax, Julie A.
Upton, Prudence Avery
Upton, Shelly Ann
Valoy, Miriam A.
Van Bavel, Kimberly Ann
Van Meter, Laura Ann
Varghese, Tracy P.
Vega, Cynthia M.
Vidunas, Vanessa Lynn
Viriassov, Deirdre Amaris Cruickshank
Vishio, Miriam Rose
Wade, Angelia
Waldron, Shannon Taylor
Walker, Melissa J.
Walters, Jennifer Lee
Warfield, Jada Linnell
Warren, Tracey Parker
Wasco, Laura Elizabeth Sutton
Watterson, Stefani Vetter
Webb, Erin L.
Westmoreland, Carol Frances
Wherley, Robin Danielle
Whitlatch, Morgan Kirsten
Widmer, Monique Therese
Williams, Alicia Briana
Williams, Katherine Ann
Williams, Nicole A.
Williams, Sonia M.
Williams, Wendy Webb
Williamson, Christina Marie
Winston, Denise
Wisz, Jamie Theresa
Woodard, Desiree D.
Woodward, April Elizabeth Whitney
Wright, LaTanya D.
Zelenak, Lisa Ann
Zimmer, Julie Rebecca Folkemer
Zito, Mollie Katherine

12-24-2002
Chernof, Alpa Patel
Jones, Cecilia Rochelle
Lee, Soo Jin
McHugh, Kathryn M.
Moses, Gabrielle S.
Payne, Patricia L.
Radcliffe, Michelle Bodley
Solomon, Gloria B.

12-30-2002
Schaefer, Mary Brigid

12-31-2002
Anderson, Sheila
Cohen, Kathy DeVito
Dunlap, Justine A.
Jordan, Cynthia
Murphy, Eileen Marie
Norton, Helen L.
Wallace, Rangeley

1-2-2003
Edwards, Elizabeth LuAnn
Engledow, Lynne Hewitt
Engstrom, Nora Freeman
Griboff, Amy L.
Haley, Elizabeth Ann
Hunter, Mary Elizabeth
Johnson, Tammy R.
Morris, Regina
Perlman, Helaine Rae
Rathbone, Meredith Ann
Richman, Cynthia Elizabeth
Shum, Lucy Wing Yee
Smith, Brooke Gwenvyl
Thornton, Nicole C.

1-6-2003
Park, Marie L.
Perkins, Martha Langley
Trossevin, Marguerite E.

1-7-2003
Bailey, Kathleen Tyger

1-14-2003
Hecker, Karen Lynn
Lauterbach, Kathryn Emily

1-17-2003
Otto, Victoria Anne

1-21-2003
High, Elizabeth Anne
Hochberg, Francine A.

1-22-2003
Wilson, Catherine Schwitter

1-27-2003
Galindo, Sonia

1-30-2003
Oxenham, Ann M.

2-6-2003
Ashworth, Jennifer Kelly
Cohen, Kristin Krause
Daniels, Eileen Frances
Donaldson, Dawn Michelle
Fletcher, Shonte Jurina
Kosh, Talia Victoria
Lueke, Theresa Marie

2-10-2003
Eneas, Kemba Tiombe
Hohos, Danielle Marie

2-12-2003
Min, Kimberly J.

2-13-2003
Brown, Allison Ranelle

3-4-2003
Brunner, Brooke Kathryn

3-6-2003
Casson, Andrea Caryn
Derwin, Christine
Thoms, Laura Anne

3-13-2003
Luneau, Cynthia Marie

3-20-2003
Whitman, Elizabeth Ayres Whiteside

5-1-2003
Ottman, Annmarie J.
Wherry, Tamekia A.

5-15-2003
Houston, Linda Marie
Lippman, Elaine C.

6-5-2003
Crabtree, Jamie Alison
Lewis, Donnaka Darnee Varner

6-6-2003
Megna, Christi L.
Roegge, Jeannette Owen
Wexler, Lesley Michelle

6-9-2003
Fawcett, Myrna L.
Herman, Deborah Kerker
Nixon, Judith Marie

6-10-2003
Hoy, Melissa H.

6-12-2003
Cook, Clarissa W.
Goodmark, Leigh Suzanne
Gustafson, Harriet A. Doheny
Matthews-Harris, Gloria J.
Stack, Laura Barton

6-18-2003
Abbott, Ingrid Josephine
Adams, Chelsie Kathleen
Albrecht, Kathryn Holwill
Allbrandt, Elizabeth Danzette
Allen, Robin Pendleton
An, Youngju
Battaglia, Kimberly Lynn
Bean Clark, Laura Elizabeth
Belaga, Gail
Bellamy, Jennifer Renee
Bender, Steffany K.
Bernardini, Jennifer C.
Bernat, Andi J.
Biaggi-Ayer, Denise A.
Bland, Nicole N.
Blumenfeld, Barbara A. Binzak
Bobes, Lydia Isabel
Boettcher, Toni S.
Bonilla, Isaris
Booker, Lori G.
Breen, Teresa J.
Brown, Ogreta Monifa
Bryant, Deitra Crawley
Bynum, Eboni Ayanna
Camara, Jade T.
Cantu, Christina Renee
Carle, Allison Courtney
Casper, Lauren Diane
Champion, Martha Anne
Chaudry, Tara A.
Chen, Meijiao Sara
Chernack, Andra Roy
Contaoi, T. Deborah VanNewkirk
Cordero, Carrie E. Franklin
Coston, Tiera Shenell
Covington, Cynthia Anne
Cummings, Teresa Epps
Dalichow, Karin
Davidson, Marisa J.
Davis, Simone
DeCesare, Constance Bogh
Dees, Margaret Anne
Delany, Megan Marie
Dews, Terrah A.
DiCesare, Constance Bogh
Dickinson, Julia Hunt
Disharoon, Ella M.
Douglas, Sondra Martin
Doyle, Alice Elaine Dansker
Eisen, Lauren-Brooke
Elguezabal, Teresa Maria
Engle, Donna R.
Etcubanez, Marita Cecilia
Eurgubian, Elizabeth Anne
Everett, LaRai Noelle
Everly, Jennifer Lewis
Felix, Florence Alberte
Field, Anne Lorigan
Frentz, Melissa L.
Gilliam, Virginia Wolf
Gottesman, Shari Esta
Gray, Traci Yvette
Greenwell, Stacie Yolanda
Greer, Schnell Rosette
Hall, Garth A.
Hamilton, Linda Valentine
Hamilton, Lisa Anne
Hancock, Mary Elizabeth
Hartridge, Karen Elaine
Hegazi, Rhonda
Hopkins, Margaret Emma
Jackson, Eugenia M.
Jackson, Janet Thompson
Jackson-Stevenson, Ginina Alexandra

Jahn, Danielle Courtney
Jarkowski, Hope McCormick
Jensen, Tamara Syrek
Joseph, Uchenna Jane
Kadiwar, Meghna J.
Karin, Lori Felicia
Kaul, Meetu
Kessler, Meryl Amy
Kim, Jamie Jungmin
Kim, Jennifer Jung Ah
Kosloski, Jean Marie
Kramer, Tammany Morgan
Krigstin, Dawn Johanna Miriam
Lancaster, Teresa Fidelis
Le Regulski, Cathryn
LeCompte, Tara G.
Lee, Alison Mei
Lee, Elizabeth J.
Lee, Renunda Shea
Lloyd, Jennifer Elizabeth
Lord, Jennifer Gordon
Marcus, Karen Jennifer
Martin, Jill Bailey
Martin, Stacey L.
McFarlane, Patrice
Mecca, Meredith L.
Melton, Angela Buckingham
Mezewski, Amy Lynn
Middleton, Dana Michele
Mills, Kathryn Christensen
Moran, Sha Glynn
Morrison, Patricia Marie
Muroff, Julie Anne
Musalem, Andrea Tania
Muskus, Jennifer Lucille
Naylor, Larissa Marie
Ontaneda-Bernales, Sylvia E.
Paik, Sandra Z.
Paxton, Cara Ann
Petersen, Karen Frances
Pick, Robin N.
Pietragallo, Sarah G.
Powell, Kerry-Ann Theresa
Powell, Sylvia Stewart
Proctor, Candice Nicole
Quinley, Melissa
Quinn, Katherine
Rapp, Allison L.
Re, Lisa Marie
Roberts, Pamela E.
Rollins, Letecia G.
Rothbaum, Monica J. Washington
Rountree, Schwanda Therese
Ryan, Janelle M.
Sarraf, Kiana F.
Scott, Charity Lynn
Seiferas, Luba Rachel
Shaynak, Ariel Heather
Sherrill, Tiffany Renaye
Smith, Jessica Cobert
Sollon, Dafne Despina
Stallmer, Amy Moreland
Stanley, Krishawan N.
Stephens, Kimberly Bowden
Strain, Kristen Hunt
Stup, Elizabeth
Takahashi, Meredith
Tarran, Lynn Marie O.
Teck Seggerman, Patricia Elizabeth
Villa, Loren Rebecca
Walker, Shani Nicole
Washington Rothbaum, Monica J.
Watson, Angela Renee
Whitaker, Misty D.
White, Jennifer Lynn
Wiggins, Ashley Elizabeth
Williams, Guana E.
Wolf, Rachel M.
Woolley, Catherine
Worthington, Catherine C.
Yochelson, Cheri M.
Zaug, Heather E.

6-20-2003

Davis, Virginia S.
Dinsmore, Danielle S.
Roberto, Susan Evelyn
Shaw, Ruth C.
Smith, Elizabeth Childers
Stone, Amy Melissa

6-24-2003

Vanterpool, Samantha Dionne

6-25-2003

Hinson, Diane S.

7-1-2003

McCarron, Katherine E.

7-9-2003

Arnett, B. Teresa

7-15-2003

Scrafford, Jennifer R.

8-11-2003

Kilcoyne, Diane Patricia

8-14-2003

Byrd, Janell M.

8-19-2003

Adams, Jennifer Collesano

8-28-2003

Beygo, Heather Rose
Hall, Mary Theresa

9-4-2003

Lyte, Lauri A.
Ngole, Jacqueline E.
Patti, Meredith L.

9-16-2003

Lee, Sandra Diana

9-25-2003

Kim, Lauren E.

12-4-2003

Berry, Erica Renea
Charpentier, Desiree

12-16-2003

Abbott, Courtney Renee
Abdul-Haqq, Asmaa Safiya
Adams, Harriet F.
Akinola, Elizabeth O.
Akpan, Ubong E.
Alegi, Meaghan Giorno
Alexander, Jennifer Holulani
Allen, Heather S.G.
Almy, Sarah Katherine Wood
Altschuller, Sarah Aylssa
Amick, Regina Frances
Archibald, Sandi Christina
Asfaha, Semira
Baker, Karla Simmons
Balsanek, Kristy Lynne
Barannik, Marina S.
Barnes, Kellie Taitano
Barnhart, Christianna Lewis
Baron, Stephanie Kaye
Barzilai, Malena F.
Bassilly, Caroline
Bastarache, Karen Elizabeth
Batzel, Heather Ann
Baylor Elliott, Tisha Danielle
Bayne, Christina M.
Bedoya, Diana Beatriz
Bell, Wennesa Gaynell
Benfer, Tiffanie Conway
Benjamin Johnson, Dana Renee
Betts, Margaret Collier
Bijpuria, Deepa
Birdsall, Cory Mettee
Biswas, Raakhee
Bizri, Carolyn Rafic
Blackwell-Rudasill, Gwendolyn A.
Blutter, Sarah Canzoniero
Bohle, Kimberly Ann
Boone, Erin Coleen
Bossle, Rebecca Hassinger
Botts, Jennifer King
Bowie, Melissa
Brantley, Jeneen J.
Britton, Christine S.
Brown, Amy Kathleen
Brown, Ava Natalie
Brown, Tina Danielle
Brown, Turkessa Lynn
Bruno, Sarah Long
Bryant, Stephanie Laura
Bukowsky, Katherine Earls
Bupp, Margaret J.
Byrialsen, Jane Holst
Cabrera, Michele Hansen
Cain, Hilary M.
Cameron, Jennifer E.
Cantalupo, Nancy Chi
Caplis, Allison Jill
Carey, Brooke Elizabeth
Carlo-Miranda, Vanessa
Carter, Rebecca Ann
Chang, Sandy Yeh
Chapman, Jennifer Dowling
Cheek, Deirdre Y.
Chernish, Sarah Corrinna
Cianflone, Christina Carroll
Clark, Stephanie L.
Cleary, Bridgid Denise
Cohen, Ilana
Collins, Mary Beth
Connell, Gina Michelle
Cooper, Kinda France
Cornfield, Marcie Beth
Cowell, Lesha Shameka
Cowell, Sharon Strong
Culley, Grace B.
Currie, Angela Erin
D'Wynter, Amanda B.C.
Dalal-Dheini, Sharvari
Dascalu, Diana Michele
Davies, Brooke Alyson
Davies, Kathleen Murray
Davis, Nichole Alexzandrea
Dawson, Shirley M. Marie
Denhardt, Danielle A.
Dennis, Jenelle M.
Didden, Carly Tolchin
Dietrick, Amanda J.
Dimaggio, Toni-Ann
Dorsey, Stephanie A.
Draper, Kristin Elizabeth
Dunlap, Marcy Janelle
Dunlap, Meryle Freiberg
Duos, Laura Ellen
Edwards, Crystal S.
Efeyini, Hope A.
Ehrlich, Dana Alison
Eitzen, Eva E.
Eller, Katherine Brooke
Entin, Alina
Estes, Jessica L.
Farzami, Azine
Feichko, Holli J.
Feinberg, Rebecca Anne
Ferris, Christina Michelle
Ferris, Jamillia Magdalena Padva
Finn, Rebecca Selina
Flannery, Mary Mikel
Fletcher, Carrie F.
Flucas-Cush, LaTrice
Flum, Rachel Price
Foley, Irma
Fonda, Carmen M.
Forker, Krista H.
Foss, Abigail Irene
Fowler, Tillie Anne
Frank, Eve Lynn
Frantz, Rebecca Lynn
Frazier, Leah Ei Wha
Friedland, Miriam Aviva
Fuhr, Althea Izawa
Fultz, Tamika Patrice
Gabriel, Elizabeth
Gammill, Meredith Policinski
Gassler, April Hope
Gastfreund, Sarah Heather
Gee, Kimberlee Joi
Gibbs, Makeba
Gillespie, Shanyn Leigh
Glassman, Kimberly Samantha
Goldstein, Robin Dana
Gomes, Heather Lynn
Gottimukkala, Smitha
Grace, Victoria L.
Gray, Jacquelyn Marie
Grayson, Ariel R.
Green, Erica Adele
Griffin, Rebecca Boba
Gu, Yu
Gudger, Monique L.
Guenther, Megan Elizabeth
Gupta, Jennifer R.
Hall, Suzanne Elizabeth
Hammel, Laura A.
Hao, Victoria Der-Lung
Harrison, Elizabeth Mellen
Harrison, Kristin Leigh
Hartman, Linda Marie
Haskins, Kristen Knight
Hassan, Kim Felica
Hawkins, Bleecker Elizabeth
Henderson, Mada Sunderman
Henein, Karen
Henning, Virginia Helen
Henry, Aisha Elizabeth Rose
Herrington, Jenny Colleen
Hersh, Michelle Guyette
Hitchner, Kristen Elissa
Holley, Brenda Elizabeth
Holmes, Riche L.

Hopkins, Kerry Elizabeth
Hubshman, Melissa A.
Hudnut, Beverly Guidara
Hunter-Ceci, Holly L.
Hwa, Jennifer Reilan
Hwang, Taehee J.
Hyland, Kristyn J.
Ibongo, Irene Njeri
Ifudu, Nnedinma Chineze
Insley, Kathryn Eve
Isbell, Kellie J.
Jasani, Ranak Kanti
Johnson, Kendra Vernelle
Johnson, Megan C.
Johnson, Stephani Leighn
Jones, Rashida Simone
Jones, Shana Campbell
Jones, Tracey L.
Josendale, Erin Marie
Kang, Nancy Haeryung
Kantor, Jayme Beth
Karastelev, Juliet Johnson
Katz, Edythe C.
Keefe, Kirsten Hoffstedt
Keeney, Jennifer Jeanette
Kelly, Dana Felise
Kelly, Heather Lynn
Khoury, Mireille Toni
Khozeimeh, Lili
Kibret, Netsanet
Kil, Huijung
Kim, Janet J.
Knowlton, Myra A.
Konrad, Robin Corinne
Kopelman, Constance Beatty
Kremen, Alexis Roslyn
LaMonte, Jennifer Katherine
Landis, Kristin Hope
Landrum, Tanisha LaToya
Lanz, Jennifer Weinman
Larrabee, Jennifer Ann
Le'I, Candace Lagi Sabado
Lee, Wen C.W.
Leklem, Andrea Elaine
Levy, Catherine Kreindler
Little, Jeannine Michele
Livingston, Nicole Tracewski
Lloyd, Tracy Lynnette
Lo, Laurelle C.
Lomartire, Nicole Celeste
Longsworth, Gaby Lorraine
Lopez-Medina, Lysandra M.
Lovetro, Christine Grace Evans
Lovick, Hillary Renee
Lowe, Cylia Evonne
Lunn-Exinor, Tameika
Lynch, Krista L.
Lyons, Carrie Lynn
Mackrella, Evelyn J.
Manofsky, Catherine Mary
Marsh, Karyn Bergmann
Mehta, Leslie Chambers
Moorhouse, Courtney D.
Niburg, Rebecca Anne
O'Connor, Janet S.
Okubadejo, Olabisi Ladeji
Osimokun, Brandy A.
Owens, Alexis June
Pankey, Lorielle Lyndel
Pickard, Amy Hall
Pilarski, Karen A.
Porwick, Katharine Olivia
Purvis, Dorinda R.
Rossi, Julie Grace
Samman, Amy Krengel
Singh, Anjali Kapur
Smith, Shani S.
St. Clair, Akita N.
Stevens, Jacquelyn
Stratton, Chiarra-May Elayda
Stull, Megan Anne
Sullivan, Anne Elizabeth
Szymanowski, Jocelyn Stephanie
Teper, Jaime R.
Trye, Shauntese Curry
Tupis, Jessica Lee Harnish
Wear, Sabrina Buchsbaum
Westerberg, Megan Kathleen
White, Kristen Klick

12-17-2003

Aiello, Lauren Rabbitt
Beyea, Cynthia Reid
Blitstein, Rebecca Roback
Bouyea, Laura Skowronski
Buck, Bethany L.
Canter, Victoria Matter
Chehreh, Lisa Gail
Chu, Erin Elizabeth-Anne
Dufour, Katherine M.
Eiswert, Julie Anne
Erdmann, Lindsey Kay
Fruman, Tracee Orlove
Gallimore, Jaime Tomhave
Gebhart, Jette Star
Getchis, Kelli
Gordon, Dominique
Hamrick, Erica Stern
Hermecz, Catherine A.
Hewitt, Neha Nagar
Iyer, Jyoti Chidambaram
James, Kelley Margolis
Joniec, Jennifer Marie
Joseph, Chantal Oriental
Kelly, Keri Smolka
Kesler, Amanda Neidert
Kipnis, Dayna Lindsay
Lancaster, Jennifer Anne
Lim, Janet Michal
Lyons, Erin O'Connor
Madden, Erika A.
Maddox, April
Magner, Tara Kathleen
Maker, Melissa Mary
Mancinelli, Ashley
Mantegna, Anna Katharina
Maranzano, Jennifer L.
Marra, Kelly A.
Martinez, Ayana
Marvin, Elizabeth L.
Mayfield, Dionne Knight
McDonnell, Megan Eileen
McFadden, Kelley Spahn
McGarvey, Christina Kalbouss
McGonigle, Maura Elizabeth
McKay, Melissa Brooke
McLamb, Marguerite E.
McNamara, Courtney Sheehan
Meawad, Julie Anne
Mechak, Megan Kathleen
Merrill, Jennifer L.
Metzgar, Mistey L.
Meyer, Lea C.
Miles, Erica B.
Miller, Alexis Reisin
Miller, Amanda Johnson
Minnicks, Jamila Beatrice
Miron, Linnea S.
Mito, Bethany Christina
Molinini, Meaghan Ferrell
Monaghan, Kathleen J.
Monroe, Trisha Marlana
Moorman, Linda Sue
Mortel, Renee Marie
Mosier, Jenny Rachelle
Moskowitz, Laura
Muedeking, Julia Jane
Muhammad, Patricia M.
Munson, Hilma Joy
Murphy, AmyLea Kathryn
Myers, Leah Jessica
Nacos-Saxon, Maria Barbara
Neal, Rotrica Shalice
Neill, Lia Erin
Neville, Cherise Victoria
Newman, Meagan Noel
Nguyen, Martha C.
Nichols, Catherine Suzanne
Nimit, Melissa
Nogueras, Nicolle
Nothstein, Emily H.
Novoa, Sonia Angelica
O'Brien, Kimberly McCormick
O'Connor, Bridget Kathleen
O'Connor, Cynthia E.
Olsen, Megan C.
Olusesi, Tajudeen Abiodun
Onisile, Olabisi A.
Openden, Yona T.
Orhant, Melanie Gabrielle
Oshrine, Sasha Beth
Otieno, Rosalyn Wanjiru
Ottens, Karin Christina
Otum, Peggy O.
Papageorgiou, Phoebe Annette
Parent, Thea
Parikh, Ami B.
Parsons, Kandi
Pate, Mhkeeba LeShare
Patel, Anita B.
Peck, Rachel Levy
Peete, Phillina Erika
Pellegrino, Whitney Marin
Pereira, Amy Beth
Perry, Lindsey Marjorie
Peterkin, Donna M.
Pflug, Amy Jean
Pierre, Melissa Deirdra
Pinnock, Heather Kay Dianne
Potter, Natalie D.
Potter, Susan P.
Radfar, Naheed Emily
Raley, Elisa
Rallo, Jennifer Allain
Regner, Theresa M.
Remaley, Evelyn L.
Reynolds, Lesley Carol
Riley, Erica Simone
Robbins, Katherine DiPentima
Robinson, Tracy Nicole
Rogers, Teresa Michelle
Romanelli, Gloria Rose
Rompf, Kristen Ellen
Rose, Christine Marie
Rosser, Rosslyn R.
Rotan, Kineta A.
Roth, Melinda
Rothschild, Ellen Roman
Ruiz, Nadtya Yoanid
Russell, Racquel Simone
Ryker, Virginia D.
Salzmann, Renee Diane
Sanchez, Hanna Claire
Saxon, Kimberly Ann
Scheinkman, Rena Sandra Levine
Schiller, Julia Christine
Schindler, Alyssa Anne
Schmitt, Addy
Schroeher, Diana Reiley
Schwamlein, Anna J.
Scudder, Traci Renee
Sewchand, Renee Natasha
Shannahan, Melissa Machen
Short, Stacy Lee
Siegle, Linda S.
Silverman, Lauren
Sims, Jane Frankel
Sinon, Brianna Marie
Skopp, Bethany Linden
Slaich, Lucy Light
Sloan, Tiffani Darjan
Sloane, Carla Elizabeth
Snyder, Rebecca Lynn
Sorzano, Tracy Amati
Sprehn, Amanda Chaye
Spurrier, Heather Linn
Steedman, Tracy Lynn
Steinmetz, Stacy Ostfeld
Stewart Hamlin, Dianne M.
Stoller, Sarah Brown
Stotler, Elizabeth Spawn
Stull, Anna Olver
Sullivan, Kathryn Widmayer
Sullivan, Megan Drost
Sunderman, Heather Lynne
Swanson, Colleen Kelly
Sweet, Emily R.
Tabor, Anna-Marie Louise
Tallardy, Erin M.
Taylor, Kiana Iisha
Terenzini, Eden O.
Terry, Stacey LeMarr
Thayaparan, Roshini Sreema
Thayu, Radhi
Thomas, Jennifer Susan
Thompson, Samantha Elaine
Thornton, Bridgette N.
Tockman, Elizabeth D.
Tomero, Leonor Araceli
Trumpbour, Kelly Keenan
Turner, Michelle L.
Upadhyaya, Moxila A.
Ussery, Elizabeth S.
Valdivieso, Jade S.
Vargas, Alexandra
Varghese, Suja M.
Vassallo, Anne Marie
Veerapaneni, Radhika
Velez, Leslie Esther
Vetter, Jami B.
Wachter, Suzanne Stephenson
Wagle, Nisha Christine
Walker, Rebecca Danielle
Walking-Eagle, Karen Panton
Ward, Stephanie Lynn
Watson, Jennafer Brooke
Watts, Tracey Lynette
Webb, Valerie N.

Weintraub Baratz, Raanan Elyse
Wellman, Jennifer B.
Wheeler, Alusheyi J.
Wheeler, Celeste Daise
White, Raquel Simone
Widick, Bethany Claus
Wiley, Lindsay Freeman
Williams, Aprill S.
Williams, Carrie Jennifer
Williams, Lateefah Shari
Williams, Victoria Olivia
Willis, Devin Elyse
Wills, Jessica Jeanne
Wilson, Elizabeth A.
Wilson, Julie Marie
Wilson, Sharon Christen
Winston, Kia Lorren
Wood, Julia Scarpino
Woods, Keirston Rhanel
Woodsworth, Megan Sunkel
Woodward, Carlotta Ann
Wright-Young, Noelle Olive
Wung, Grace C.
Xenakis, Angela Marie
Yang, Alice Karen
Yeh, Patricia Pai-Lun
Young, Kelly Calaway
Yutadco, Maria Theresa Posadas
Zatz, Megan Britton
Zeller, Jessica L.
Zonderman, Mara M.

12-19-2003
Purcell, Laura Lee Potter

12-22-2003
Dworak-Fisher, Sally
Felinton, Mindy
McNulty, Tamara M.
Mitchell, Ethel
Torres, Susan Yoder

12-23-2003
Azeredo, Ruth Ann Grace
Oldak, Regina L.
Sennett, Marie-Ann

12-24-2003
Chagrin, Susan M.
Finkelstein, Lois Rosalyn
Gibbs, Sheila Robin
Kass, Julie Erin

12-29-2003
Burke, Karen
Fath, Alyson M.
Figer, Jeannie Yim

1-5-2004
Crabtree, Kim Marie
Dutra, Amanda Veal
Imtiaz, Saman Rafat
Kave, Jamie Peal
Kertesz, Anna
Lvovsky, Marianna
Pirnia, Kristine
Richardson, Michelle L.
Ritter, Jennifer Warfield
Waters, Jessica Lee
Wiktowy, Andrea Jane Parsons

1-7-2004
Morrel, Ruth

1-8-2004
Stranko, Denise Frances

1-13-2004
Schenck, Carolyn A.

1-14-2004
Augustine, Rene I.
Beysselance, Cherry Joy
Dreher, Patricia Y.

1-20-2004
Tortora, Judith Salzman

1-23-2004
Callender, Arlene Beverly

1-30-2004
Parker, Suzanne M.

2-5-2004
Bralove-Scherr, Alisa D.
Caldwell, Samantha A.
Ewings, Rishaunda Monique
Harper, Alisha Marie
Moon, Danielle Renee

2-9-2004
Sabol, Sherry E.
Taylor, Lora M.

2-11-2004
Lem, Rebecca Elizabeth

2-13-2004
Newberger, Katherine Tang

2-25-2004
Halverson, Candace Nikia White

3-5-2004
Kemp, Patricia A.

3-9-2004
Gschwendtner, Susan M.
Saffo, Theodosia

3-10-2004
Self, Heather M.

3-15-2004
Blass, Bronwen Anne

6-2-2004
McDonald, Loreal Myrick
O'Brien, Linda J.

6-7-2004
Baker, Denise J.
Jones, Melissa Calhoon
Williams, J. Carol

6-8-2004
Fee, Cindy Waeger
Glackin, Maureen
Walker, Vernetta L.

6-9-2004
Davis, Deborah L.
Haaf, Shannon
Pierson, Erika L.

6-10-2004
Brown, Joanne M.
Porter, Jennifer Rebecca
Rubin, Ann C.

6-11-2004
Finley, Renee M.

6-14-2004
Friedman, Barbara A.
Goley, Sharon M.
Harkness, Cynthia Lynne

6-15-2004
Alameddine, Lina Karim
Allis, Carmelina Gomez
Andersen, Janet Katharine
Anderson, Cynthia R.
Anderson-Fintak, Heather B.
Authement, Karen Maria
Badawi, Shirien Kairy
Badders, Jacqueline Gagne
Bak, Suyeun Jacqueline
Ball, Lisa Ellen
Barbarin, Andrea M.
Barczy, Theresa McAuliffe
Barnes, Phnesha Marchette
Barnes, Serena Simone
Battan, Mitra K.
Bawa, Jasbir Kaur
Berhanu, Tsedey
Berry, Mandisa Rebecca
Betts, Aquanetta J.
Beysolow, Jennie M.
Bigus, Kathryn Diane
Bolmarcich, Christina
Bowman, Mary Elizabeth
Brasseaux, Allison Pierce
Brooks, Jamie D.
Brown, Amy Joyce
Brown, Megan L.
Browne, Wanda Donielle
Bulos, Jessica Marie
Burkey-Bridgman, Sarah D.
Bussey, Jill Marie
Cain, Brandi Azra
Carpenter, Heather L. Haverkamp
Cho, Jin
Choi, Juliet K.
Clark, Erin Lea
Cocco, Darlene M.
Colamaria, Angela Farleigh
Collazo-Dingle, Liset
Copsey, Kathleen Hasselback
Dawson, Maria Holbrook
DeLa-Cruz, Sheila Garay
DeLaCruz, Lyzka P.
Delaney, Tracy Michelle
Dempsey, Kathleen Combs
Dennis, Gina Naomi
DeSimone, Cynthia L.
Dolan, Megan Lee
Dominique, Barbara
Donze-Emery, Amy Ellen
Dougherty, Constance Marie
Duff, Karyn A.
Dunkle, Valerie Ann Crane
Edmonds, Tovia H.
Eilers-Bowser, Heather
Etheredge, Anetra Jenee
Fields, Wilma C.
Finlayson, Shelley Kay
Fletcher, Ayrika Grace Meica
Fox, Elizabeth May
Frank, Kimberly Brickell
Goldberg, Janet Cara
Gray, Brandy Jessica
Groer, Sharon Kelly
Halaby, Judy Ann
Hall, Kayla JeTann
Halpern, Eva Elizabeth
Halpern, Meliha Perez
Hamlett, Shahidah Nicole
Hammock, Melissa Cheryl
Harvey, Anika Joanna
Harvey, Travys D.
Hertz, Jamie M.
Hodge, Ivy Samantha
Humphrey, Alecia Rene
Iannone, Lynn A.
Ingram, Anika T.
Ingram, Shelly Maynard
Jarmiolowski, Kathleen Hope
Jean-Pierre, Isabel Domonic
Jeng, Lana K.
Johnson, Emily Scott
Johnson, Erin E.
Jones, Sherri
Katz, Rebecca Ann
Kays, Susannc
Keenan, Carrie Napoleon
Kellermeyer, Tara L.
Kessler, Aimee Therese Hay
King, Dorenda R.
Kinsey, Nicole Erin
Kluge, Kimberley A.
Koch, Sharon M.
Lam, Mon Le
Lamphier, Lisa Charlene
Lane, LaRima Lynn
Lane-Kunz, Renee S.
Law, Erin Kathleen
Lee, Grace H.
Lee, Jung Hwa
Levinson, Rachel Besara
Lewis, Karelle Nichole
Liston, Leah Rachel
Lombardo, Lauri L.
Lucero, Alicia Raquel
Maloney, Meghan E.
Marburg, Monica Rose
Marshall, Genevieve Goodrow
Mayes, Laura Marie
McBride, Luisella Perri
McClellan, Linda V.
McKenzie, Terri-Lynn
McLaughlin, Louisa Content
Mellody, Kathleen Lynch
Meltzer, Abby Lyn
Miller, Tracy Michelle
Monford, Panya Nneke
Naraghi-Arani, Parisa
Nave, Brandi Shanee
Nee, Dawn A.
Onkeles, Lauren Micah
Ortiz, Margarita Lucia
Owens, Amelia Averill
Owens, Cindy S.
Oyewole, Kolade Olufayo
Pair, Lauren James
Parsons, Molly Ann
Pizza, Virginia Ann
Policelli, Maura Ann
Pounds, Alethea Denise
Price, Aaron E.
Raaf, Amy Marie
Reichert, Sarah H.
Reynolds, LaTonya D.
Rich, Seigrid T.
Riley, Margaret M.
Roberts, Mary Elizabeth
Rodgers, Blythe Ilene
Rohrbaugh, Karen Hess
Rosen, Elana E.

Rugg, Julia Lynn
Scarborough, Rhonda Karen
Sharma, Kiran
Shih, Annie Ja-ling
Silverstrim, Karen F.
Slezak, Kimberly Ann
Smith, Helen M.
Smithey, Joyce E.
Song, Soyoung
Suarez, Casandra L.
Tabor, Kathleen Jo Parsons
Tannian, Marcia Ann
Tao, Betsy P.
Taylor, Lisette M.
Thames, Geneau Marie
Thiel, Karen Smith
Titcomb, Lisa Stevens
Tony, Andrea J.
Vaughn, Felina A.
Walsh, Jennifer Mary
Watkins, Jennifer Louise
Watkins, Tammy Renee
Watson, Alison Flynt
Welsch, Meghan M.
Wiggins, Nina
Williams-Franklin, LaShelle Denise
Worthy, Angela Chong
Yoshitani, Rebecca Slade
Young, Marsha R.

6-16-2004
Nunez, Angela Maria
Siegel, Amy Beth

6-21-2004
Aquilina, Carey Ance
Cresta-Savage, Patricia Ann

6-25-2004
Fingold, Helaine I.
Jones, Kristine Roderick

6-28-2004
Scully, Elizabeth Anne
Wagner, Lauren E.
Walker, Kim-Marie

7-2-2004
Brown, Rhonda Rochelle

7-14-2004
Hilmoe, Tatum S.

7-16-2004
Eskay, Jacquelyn Bernard

7-21-2004
Sasser, Tracey

7-23-2004
Podolsky, Susan Rebecca

8-24-2004
Friedgen, Kelley A.

9-9-2004
Cheikh, Julia Mary
Keteku, Anita Adobea
Treaster, Cristin Elizabeth
Wang, Joann Ju-Chuan

9-27-2004
Kim, Ji Eun

9-29-2004
Ruiz, Anita Ahmed

9-30-2004
Krosch, Nola N.
Vadi, Ruth Frances
Walsh, Alexandra Margaret

10-13-2004
Puleo, Theresa J.

10-18-2004
Vestal, Gemma P.

10-22-2004
Davis, Katherine Smith

12-2-2004
Maxwell, Shavonna Monique

12-14-2004
Abrams, Lisa Marie
Adams, Christina Marie
Ajenifuja, Anita U.
Akhter, Saminaz
Akingbade, Ayonife
Akintan, Olajumoke O.
Albertson, Sarah Blackburn
Alcorn, Alicia Clark
Alegi, Karen Hulme
Allan, Theresa Elizabeth
Allen, LaKeecia R.
Amira, Jennifer Lynn
Amunson, Jessica Ring
An, Hei Jun
Andreassen, Kristine Marie
Apostolaros, Maria Andrea
Armas, Nathalie Michelle
Arnold, Jessica M.
Asel, Emily Jourdan
Aubrey, Mandie Kreimborg
Axley, Crea Taylor
Azhar, Marium
Baer, Katherine E.
Baer, Megan Hanley
Baker, Sarah
Ballard, Sarah E.
Bancroft, Rolaine Soril
Barnes, Tara A.
Bashir, Lema
Beck, Sarah Cutchins
Bell, Susan Carol
Belzer, Lydia M.
Berkeley, Catherine Carter
Bickford, Jennifer Anne
Bird, Amy S.
Bonilla, Judith F.
Boyd, Linda Marie
Boyd, Nashiba Finley
Brandlen, Jacqueline R.
Brewer, Rosemary White
Brooks-Williams, Cheryl R.
Browder, Mary Rose
Brown, Kisha Arniece
Brown, Lisa McLennan
Brown, Monica Shenean
Bryan, Teresa J.
Buell, Catherine
Bugel, Kristen Kwiatkowski
Burchell, Kelly Lynn
Burka, Samantha B.
Burke, Kelly Bollinger
Burkhardt, Lentcen M.
Burton, Dawn Marie
Bush, Linda L.
Bush, Sebrina Nailah
Bussom, Deirdre Nicole
Butte, Laura J.
Byrd, Raemona Dene'll
Callahan, Kristine L.
Cameron, Heather Reed
Caputo, Emily Jean
Carrasco, Anastasia Kristina Laou
Carroll, Shannon Anne
Carver, Katherine Jeanne
Chaney, Beth
Chappell, Courtney Ji'Neane
Chawla, Satviner K.
Chen, Laurice Y.
Chesney, Beth Kathleen
Chichester, Lindsay Louise
Chikwelugo, Chioma M.
Chipoco, Jessica Karina
Chou, Jenny Ry-Tyng
Cino, Paula Marie
Clarke, Hyacinth Michelle
Clifton, Ludmila Bussiki Silva
Cole, Kimberly Letecia
Collier, Heather Sue
Collins, Renita Lynne
Compton, Caryn Elizabeth
Connally, Lori Richelle Elizabeth
Connors, Kathleen Marston
Contreras, Andrea Michelle
Cooper, Alana Beth
Cooper, Leslie Combs
Corbett, Rosemary Elizabeth
Cotca, Ramona Raula
Cottle, Selket Nicole
Covarrubias, Erika Virginia
Cowan, Alyssa Burrell
Cowans, Fanta K.B.
Dagostino, Alida M.
Daley, Lisa Marie
Dannels, Jennifer Dee
De Leon, Christina Natividad
DeFontes, June Marie
Delthony, Beth Lara
Dennis, Katrina J.
Deutsch, Ruthanne M.
DiBerardino, Diana
Dinovitz, Shoshana
Donohue, Kelly Anne
Dorsey, Melissia B.
Dorson, Sue Dowell
Douglas, Amy Elizabeth
Droddy, Helen
Drury, Rebecca Raub
Dufresne, Sarah Charlton
Dumas, Jessica Lee
Ebaugh, Donna Davis
Eklund, Karna Anne Johnson
Elbert, Carolyn Elizabeth
Ellis, Elizabeth Kate
Embry, Elizabeth Mears
Epperson, Jennifer Lynn
Erhart, Rina Mariztela
Eyler, Jennifer M.
Faerber, Amanda P.
Falencki, Corinne A.
Faulk, Virginia Terhune
Favretto, Christina Grace
Ferry, Laura Warrene
Fewster, Jaclyn Marie
Fick, Mandy L.
Fields, Dana Cohen
Fine, Heather Rochelle
Ford, Jaclyn Ione
Fox, Jewel Lynn
Francis, Laura DeVeaux
Frank, Kiley Alison
Frazier, April La' Shaun
Frey, Elizabeth Ann
Frisk, Melissa Joy
Frush, Sarah Coffey
Frye, Nneka Aisha Pauline
Fultz, Allison Ishihara
Gardner, Heidi Margaret
Garibay, Deborah Benton
Genovese, Carrie
Georges, Maria
Gerson, Erica Lynne
Giasafakis, Joanna Katheryn
Glatz, Shanna M.
Godsey, Ilene Haynes
Goehl, Angela A.
Goldfrank, Rebecca
Goode, Corlice Ellen
Graeter, Mary Stern
Gray, Jessica Aiken
Green, Emily Elizabeth
Greimel, Jocelyn Wiherle
Gross, Sara Elaine
Gruswitz, Ariel Close
Gutman, Tracy E.
Guzejko, Sharon R.
Guzman, Sandra Veronica
Hafer, Jessica Willow
Hall, Joanna Burke
Hall, Shannon Elizabeth
Hall, Victoria Kathleen
Ham, Tina J.
Hamilton, Kaitlin Alice
Hanes, Njeri S.
Hardy, Chanelle Patrice
Harleston, Shanell Kathleen
Harris, Tatarsha Denise
Hawes, Rebecca Lee
Hayes, Ella Judge
Herrmann, Jennifer Lynn
Hicks, Minisha Camille
Hill, Katherine Bauer Burrows
Hines, Ja-Na Amira
Hoag, Lynn Andrews Howard
Hogan-Burney, Amy F.
Holford, Althea O.
Hollis, Valerie B.
Holloman, Kathryn Lee
Holthe, Serena E.
Houston, Sharon L.
Howarth, Danielle Elizabeth
Hughes, Shannon Simmons
Hung, Elena
Hurley, Stephanie Helen
Jabaily, Annalisa Messing
Jefferson, Patricia A.
Jefferson, René Vañessa M.
Jewell, Neonu Sojourner
Johnson, Alyssa Ann
Johnson, Lisa Alita
Jones, Brandy Nicole
Jordan, Christine Marie
Joseph, Nicole A.
Kahl, Sarah Barr
Kajubi, Elizabeth Nakalanzi
Kaps, Melissa Amy
Kayan, Marianne Renee
Keelty, Gina M.
Kelly, Kari M.
Kelso, Heather Huey
Kelton, Teresa Marie

Kenny, Christina M.
Keyes, Elizabeth A.
King, Amy Marie
King, Nicole M.
Kinsey-Smith, Megan A.
Konyar, Heather Rose
Koss, Lenka Janotka
Kousouris, Alexandra
Kozma, Jennifer B.
Kumar, Chandni
Lane, Tanya Rahael
Langford, Anne Elizabeth
LaPorte, Heather Marie
Larson, Barbara Elaine
Lasco, Chante Marie
Lewis, Brandee Anngellic Dinkins
Lowell, Heather Arpin
Manley, Stacy L.
Medovoy, Lauren Jill
Meisel, Carolyn Dewey
Milam, Mary Cooper
Mosley, Mishonda Monique
Nagji, Elizabeth Fischer
Necessary, Ryane M.
Owings, Megan Bramble
Petty, Kathleen Louise Henley
Porter, Jennifer Rose
Ryan, Kathryn Lynn
Shaivitz, Heather Lynn
Shepardson, Zhiavictoria Louise
Singleton, Shannon M.
Sorisio, Mary Sarah Kelley
Wasylak, Angie B.
Weiss, Bridget M.
Wolson, Stephanie Rachel

12-15-2004

Taylor Carroll, Laura Michelle
Amisano, Angela Marie Zagami
Bagg, Jennifer Phurrough
Ballard, Sherry Ann
Becker, Jennifer Skaggs
Bentz, Tamany Vinson
Bies, Laura Michelle
Borowiecki, Perri Rothemich
Brown, Monise Alexis
Caplis, Mollie G.
Casey, Lindsay Mann
Cirner, Casey Lynn
Culliton, Alyson Catherine
Darwood, Kristina Marie
Dring, Tricia Ryti
Esters, Eyana Jenice
Fahrendorf, Sarah Richardson
Feldman, Rachael Ruben
Flanagan, Abbie Anne
Fogelson, Heather Jill
Grams, Brooke Moore
Greenwald, Elizabeth Mandy
Gronniger, Tracey Thomas
Gundersen, Christine Ann Zack
Hafner, Allisan Sheila
Hammann, Emily Jordan
Hofstatter, Rachel Mindy
Hortie, Ashley Meehan
Howard, Ericka Lynn
Hurson, Abigail Smith
Ives, Margaret E.
Jacobik, Erica Allyson
Johnson, Katherine Elizabeth
Keel, Jennifer Lee
Kletzly, Katrina Elizabeth
Lee, Jennifer C.
Lee, Marian
Lee, Susie
Leftrict, Pamela Denise
Lenchak, Brenna Steinert
Leonard, Jennifer Guste
Lester, Jennifer Bland
Letourneau, Celeste Avril
Lettau, Initia
Leventhal, Rachael Lea
Lichter, Ann M.
Lindberg, Cathlene M.
Lipscomb, Lauren Rachel
Livingston, Erica Leigh
Lor, Rosy Leck
Lord, Lilia C.
Lui, Grace P.
Lukaesko, Becky M.
Mabli, Constance K.
Mack, Eveylon Corrie Westbrook
Madigan, Shana
Mahan, Ashley Rosen
Mahaney, Anna Almon
Maine, Amanda Dawn
Maisano, Clare Marie
Malhotra-Ortiz, Mala
Mallis, Julie Ann
Maloney, Angela
Maltas, Allyson McKenzie
Marbury, Tamara Aswan
Mark, Nicole Renee
Marshall, Sheryl L.
Martin, Kristy Marie
Mason, Meredith Martin
McCarthy, Colleen A.
McCarty, Susan G.
McCarus, Nicole Angelique
McClellan, Sarah Ann Domin
McConihe, Marguerite I.
McCown, Clare
McDonald, Nia Yvonne
McLelland, Sandra Jane
McNeeley, Karen Marie
McNish, Kimberly Sherwood
Mecit, Tuna
Meinhardt, Kristin Beth
Michelich, Susan Elizabeth
Miller, Monica Lisa
Miller, Sara Joy
Minier, Jessie Konala
Minster, Tovah Amanda
Mizrachi, Sabrina
Moffett, Natalie Cater
Montgomery, Megan Wilson
Moore, Whitney Allyn
Moorman, Penelope R.
Morrow, Alexandra
Mufarreh, Jessica Kareem
Naik, Dharma Ravishanker
Nash, AnnaLisa Schmidt
Nazelrod, Carolyn Wees
Neiman-Kelting, Melissa L.
Neville, Jasmine Desiree
Newton, Karen Lynn
Ngoubene, Caroline Raissa
Norton, Anne Balcer
Nwabuzor, Nkechinyem Chukumalobi
O'Grady, Judith L.
O'Neal, Lauri Kramer
Oestreicher, Salima Parmar
Oh, Ju Y.
Olariu, Laura
Olear, Amanda Lesher
Oliver, Leigh Leonard
Olson, Erika S.
Ormiston, Andrea Kirby
Overton, Evynn Marjorie
Owczarek, Marla Stewart
Padley, Andrea Nicole
Palumbo, Amy Shaw
Parker, Ara Danielle
Parker, Jennifer Ann
Parks, Julie Anne
Parroff, Tearyn Julie
Patel, Neha Navin
Patel, Nirali D.
Patel, Purvi
Pechulis, Jennifer M.
Peters, Shannon Erica
Peterson, Kathrina Stone
Pfeifer, Kelly Elizabeth
Piateski, Jennifer Elizabeth
Pierce, Michelle Wirzberger
Pipkin, Staci Lee
Pitcher, Amanda Smith
Podolny, Alexandra C.
Poechmann, Paige Poole
Posteraro, Julie Regina
Power, Sheila M.
Powers, Patricia
Prabhu, Sandhya
Price, Stacy Elizabeth
Proctor, Melissa Anne
Prost, Alison Hooper
Pruitt, Kate Pomper
Ramirez, Kathlynne T.
Rappaport, Anna H.
Raulerson, Anee Patrice
Ray, Jennifer Ellen
Rembach, Kristine A.
Ricchiuto, Rosemarie J.
Richards, Lisa G.
Ried-Barrett, Amber
Riley, Kendra Lynette RaShawn
Robinson Coates, Natasha Camille
Rodgers, Sujata Michelle
Rodriguez, Cristina Maria
Roemer, Kimberly Ann
Rogers, Gretchen Aynsley
Rohde, Alexis Burrell
Romer, Lori Ann
Rooney, Lori Williams
Roose, Rebecca M.
Ross, Carolyn Beth
Rounceville, Amy Katherine
Rudmann, Margaret Walsh
Sailo, Esther R.
Samman, Luna Miriam
Sanchez, Nicola E.
Sanders, Nicola Charlene
Santry, Katy Elizabeth
Sarsenova, Leila K.
Saunders, Tina Hixon
Sawyer, Katherine Anne
Schechter, Rebecca Blodgett
Schneiderman, Sharon Risa
Schollaert, Marisa Renee
Schorr, Kristel
Schramek, Christine Marie
Schultz, Dana Katharine Klahs
Sebor, Jennifer A.
Seesel, Holly Lin
Sentman, Shannon D.
Seshadri, Sheila
Seymour, Anne Elizabeth
Shah, Rina Rajesh
Sharpe, Meridith Lindsey
Sher, Erin
Shorago, Dena M.
Skaggs, Meghan McFarland
Sloan, Tiffany Michelle
Sloane, Tara A.
Smith, Jessica Ruth Bailey
Smith, Rachel A.
Solomon, Catherine Cooper
Song, Cheng Qian
Sorrentino, Julia P.
Spiker, Rachel Beth
Sproule, Christen Anne
Stafiej, Rosanne Elyse
Stansbury, Heather E.
Steel, Alyssa Paladino
Stern, Jodi Ellen
Stevens, Lisa Yonka
Stewart-Hill, Anne Bohen
Stock, Elizabeth Zager
Stone, Leah Mendelsohn
Storch, Tiferet
Sumlin, Ronika Janene
Swan, Heather Suzanne
Taylor, Brenda Nelson
Taylor, Elan D.
Thomas, Alexis Marjel
Thomas, Edith Koke
Timmers, Sarah M.
Toledo, Courtney Erin
Tomko, Carrie Margaret Peck
Trevillian, Rebecca S.
Tseu, Heidi
Turner, Jennifer Lynn
Uhl, Kristen Elizabeth
Valdecantos, Shivohn Quijano
Van Wambeke, Daniela Marie
VandenBroek, Emilia Ward
Varela, Laura Elena
Velasquez, Nichole M.
Vogelstein, Rachel Brauner
Wade, Lecia C.K.
Waicker, Jessica Lea
Wakefield, Laura Ann
Walker, Lauren Brette
Walters, Antoinette McRae
Wang, Sarah Catherine
Washington, Kia Lynnette
Wasserman, Laurie Maier
Wenkman, Kathryn Elizabeth
Westergren, Sarah
Whitfield, Lynette A.
Wickham, Sarah H.
Wilkes, Christina A.
Williams, Cherise Lenore
Williams Rooney, Lori
Wilson, Michelle Keisha
Winters, Tiffany Rae
Wirth, Kristina Ann
Wood, Stephanie K.
Wright, Allison E.
Wu, Clarissa H.
Wyant, Bridget M.
Yeagle, Jennifer Sheff
Zafar, Maryam
Zain, Mila Zarina
Zakir, Nadia
Zhang, Zhen
Zycherman, Lisa Beth

12-28-2004
Cumberland, Michele S.
Fenton, Gillian M.
Hvizdos, Emily C.
Jones, Christina Axa
Montgomery, Stephanie Rene

12-29-2004
Castronovo, Samantha L.

1-3-2005
Garcia, Loretta Jean
Kirby, Wendy T.
Pecuszok, Tina Taylor
Sparkman, Jackie B.
Townsend, Loretta
Washington-Bivans, Angela J.

1-6-2005
Bingaman, Kimberly Ann
Fairbanks, Emilie
Groft, Melanie J.
Heineman, Sarah Beth
Johnson, Kelli Rose
Lothamer, Molly Jo
Madigan, Kelly Beckham
Richmond, LaShunda M.
Talbert, Michelle Yvonne

1-10-2005
Beehler, Kay A.
Corbin, Carmen Forrest
Hogan, Susan Marie
Quattrucci, Ellen Marie
Wood, Laurie Kelleher

1-11-2005
Mantzavinos, Megan Trocki
Saville, Sandra K.

1-12-2005
Mondesir, Glendia D.

1-19-2005
Boice, Lauren Annette
Delaney, Kathleen Marie
Roussel, Christine Fox
Rubenstein, Erin Lewis

1-24-2005
Sher, Daphna R.
West, Pamela S.

2-3-2005
Feit, Traci Shannon
Kamboh, Sonia Mittal

2-4-2005
Dufour, Brooke Elizabeth

2-8-2005
Beckett, Amy Louise
Howard, Amber Dawn

2-10-2005
Beasley, Donna M.
Cones, Maureen E.

3-21-2005
Lunt, Lisa Woodward
Muldoon, Kathleen Ann

3-29-2005
Burg, Ivy Barton

5-4-2005
Warren, Tessa Addie-Lee

5-13-2005
Olesen, Anne Kathryn

5-31-2005
Berlove, Michele Levy

6-6-2005
Dighe, Kristin Wilcox
Kessler, Elizabeth Ann
Marenberg, Roxane Sokolove
Nunez, Vivian
Sims, Priscilla Brown

6-7-2005
Wills, Caroline Emerly

6-8-2005
Cohen, Elizabeth Helen
Luddington, Natasha Renee

6-10-2005
Goldstein, Sonna F.

6-14-2005
Alutto-Schmidt, Teresa Ann
Anderson, Kara Elizabeth
Aning, Effia Akyaa
Atlas, Deborah Eileen
Ballance, Christina Van Breitmaier
Barmon, Jennifer Davis
Bartoshesky, Amanda Elizabeth
Beard, Donna Ruth Fertitta
Beckford, Charlene Elaine
Bednarz, Hilary Abell
Beresford, Carrie Elizabeth
Bhagan, Jessica Gage
Blake, Erica Denise
Bonaparte, Tina Louise
Boyd, Tara Courtney
Bradley, Kardesha Nicole
Bratton, Gwenaelle Michelle
Brodsky, Meredith Barri
Broseker, Carolyn Kern
Brown, Grace Haewon
Brown, Tamika Shaykhia
Bueno, Julia Calvo
Burnell, Mary Elizabeth
Burns, Tracy Arcaro
Cabaday, Amanda Leigh
Chen, Wan
Choi, Yeonu
Chun, Regina
Clarke, Kimberly Ann Jamilah
Danilova, Natasha A.
Davidson, Diana Lynn
Davis, Corinthian Letitia
Day, Kathleen Elizabeth
Dean, Cendoria Yvonne
Deering, Jenikka Joy
Depew, Lona Jo
Deskins, Marva Rashida
Dillier, Sara Beth
DiPietro, Leslie Case
Doherty, Monica Christine
Dykes, Jamie Lynn
Edwards, Rhonda L.
Ekechi, Chinyere Ogazi
Epstein, Joan Stacey
Esposito, Beth Alice
Essien, Shawn Denise
Fagan, Jennifer Glosser
Fisher, Kristen Marie Pali
Foster, Lindsey Brooke
Francoeur-Breeden, Rebecca
Fuller, Fatima Safiyya
Fults, Carla Treseil
Gallagher, Deirdre McCarthy
Gallopin, Colleen Terri
Gange, Heather Elizabeth
Gary, Diana
Gatewood, Nichole Cherie
Gazan, Heather Michelle
George, Sunita Achamma
Gilmore, Karisma Andrea L.
Gloger, Erica Faye
Goldstein, Rachel Eileen
Gonzalez, Eva Elena
Gooding, Sharon H. Fernandes
Gray, Natalie Marie
Green, Carrie Jeannette
Greene, Christine Maria
Grell, Tessa Diane
Grossman, Leslie Ellen
Grossman, Sandra Andrea
Gustave, Tamara Melinda
Hamilton, Dontrice Patience
Harrison, Mikisha Louise
Harry-Bess, Arielle Alicia
Harvey, Sharon R.
Hayward, Kendra Elise
Heath, Gail Lynn
Henry, Sylvie Gabrielle
Herman, Jodi Beth
Herrera, Roselle M.
Hetzel, Dannean J.
Hirsch, Annie Beth
Hopkins, Julie Ann
Hostetler, Heather Christine
Howe, Eva Caroline
Huffman, Angela Dawn
Hutt, Mahoganey Joy
Hyre, Lisa Renee
Jackson, Kimberly Ann
Jennings, Colleen Suzette
Jewell, Karen Foster
Johnson, Gwendolyn
Johnson, Suzanne Christine
Kaizer, Rebecca Woorman
Kanukolanu, Marian Rachel
Karim, Bianca
Khan, Freda Mushtaq
Kilty, Carroll Andrews
Kim, Minyoung
Koerner, Cheri Vera
Koonin, Susan Benita
Koop, Sarah N.
Krause, Tamara Rochelle Hinton
Krivosh, Jennifer Lynn
Krumpe, Kelly Ann
Kubiniec, Joanne Elizabeth
Gilmore, Karisma Andrea L.
Lantz, Jennifer Dillon
Leager, Michele B.
Leboe, Lauren Faith
Lee, Judyann Maureen
Lee, Julia Yun
Leege, Debra Fischer
Llewellyn, Stacy Ann Nicole
Lomax, Gayle McKinney
Longa, Lesly Carmen
Maheridis, Erin Susanne
Marquardt, Carol Anneliese
Maschler, Toni
Mason, Diane Walsh
Mayo, Shereese Diane
McCarthy, Megan Kime
McCarthy, Amy L.
McHenry, Claire Vendla
McKee, Colleen Michelle
Miller, JoAnna Marie
Mills, Stacy Anne
Mister, Katina Shay
Mitchell, Sara Cooper
Moore, Sonji Alise
Muhammad, Aaliyah Rashidah
Naughton, Emily Gooding
Navarro, Delandra Mae
Nelson, Helynn Stephens
Nelson, Rowena Nicole
O'Connor, Shannon Molly
Oladokun, Adejumoke Georgina
Oland, Ashley Marie
Olenginski, Allison
Oswianiecki, Angela Michele
Patel, Jigita
Patrick, Suzanne Marie
Perkins, Anne McFadden
Perry, Leah Nicole C.
Peterson, Katherine Brigid
Polk, Angela E.
Reilly, Christine Anne
Richards, Janelle Natasha
Rickford, Sheryl Ann
Ringgold-Kirksey, La Zette Charnae
Robles, Angel R.
Rodgaard, Katerina
Rogers, Amy Maher
Rosen, Jennifer Cooke
Saberi, Sadaf
Salisbury, Kimberly Lynne
Sanschagrin, Kimberly Ann
Sartorius, Jessica Lynn
Saucedo, Leslie Alexandra
Searfoss, Jennifer Louise
Seward, Jamie Blum
Shannon, Tiffani Nicole
Sidhu, Mehgan
Simpson, Katharine Fay
Sirls, Corrine Jo Ann
Slaughter, Chandria Louise
Smith, Joyanna Sunrise
Sobande, Ibironke
Specktor, Ami Michelle
Sroka, Heather Marie
Sung, Jane Eunjung
Swamidoss, Jana Leialoha Si Yun Fong
Tahmasebi, Golin
Tarkowski, Genifer Maree
Taylor, Era Sherran
Taylor, Samantha L.
Tendall, Kjrsten Marie
Thomas, Lavinia Marie
Thompson, Rosetta Louise
Tinney-Young, Anjanette Karolyn
Tracht, Joeie Elizabeth
Trimble, Susan Clara
Uche, Adaku Nwadiuto
Underwood, Karen Suzanne
Valenti, Michelle Kathryn
Walsh, Carlin Rae
Wells, Robyn Christina Sanders
Welsh, Christy Lee
Whitaker, Nakiya Eva
White, Angela Nicole
Wilkinson-Hagen, Amy
Williams, Tara Shante

Wilson, Celene Coburn
Wissel, Meredith Joy
Wong, Amy Renee
Woodard, Mia Lenee
Wroten, Dana Marie
Young, Stephany Lissett
Zanzucchi, Raemarie
Zorn, Amanda

6-15-2005
Huhnke, Michelle Margaret
Joiner, Marie Antoinette
Yue, Deborah Weiqing

6-16-2005
Mynarski, Jacqueline Anne

6-22-2005
Hazel, Kim Alison
Smith, Mitzie Virginia

6-27-2005
Olson, Patrice Annett

7-6-2005
Archibeque, Amy Glasser
Costin, Sheila Mary
Feierabend, Ruth A.

7-15-2005
Bailey, Regan Monica

8-1-2005
Faibish, Laura Frances
Rodgers, Kerry Ellen

8-2-2005
Bailey, Margaret Malanum

8-31-2005
Guthman, Jillian Allette

9-1-2005
Humphrey, Katina Renae
Pregel, Katherine Ellen Bierma
Sincore, Jacqueline Antoinette

9-15-2005
Seddiq, Mirriam Zary

9-23-2005
Stolasz, Leslie K.

10-6-2005
Greer, Dorothy

11-3-2005
Blackwell, Lisa Wilsonia

12-9-2005
Kuehn, Rebecca Everett

12-12-2005
Burgess, Ursula Koenig
Cramer, Jill Alison
Gruss, Brenda
Mayorga, Lorie Ann
Mezrich, Lisa Beth

12-13-2005
Abreu, Daisy Yesenia
Albert, Sarah E.
Alder, Lauren Jane-Clare
Alexander, Rachel Ann
Alt, Emily Johanna
Ambrose, Jennifer Dorn
Anderson, Abrielle Beaton
Anderson, Shane Candace
Angel, Carole
Angel, Elisa Ann
Arends, Wendy Katharine
Aronson, Hallie Joy
Astrada, Maria Laura
Atkins, Shawnda Tina
Atwell, Anita Elaine
Aubrey, Patrice Gonzalez
Austrie, Wendy Elenor
Axley, Lauren Cole
Azarion, Maryam
Badalian, Kristina
Bagley, Katie Sue
Bair, Cynthia Lynn
Baldwin, Rebecca Jo
Bangudi, Mayabanza Sylena
Barnes, Maura Lynn
Bashaar, Meghan Dawn
Batson, Jamie Elizabeth
Bauer, Allison Kastner
Bechtel, Susan Anne
Begun, Laura Nicole
Behre, Kelly Alison
Bellafiore, Giuseppina Maria
Bellamy, Denise Leona
Bergman, Michelle Lynn Hye-Ri-Won
Bertz, Kristy Layne
Bevan-Dangel, Jennifer Kate
Birdwell, Jodie Allyn
Blankson, Inana Tetsewa
Blauer, Beth Ilise
Bloom, Shayna Michelle
Borden, Meredith Leigh
Bortnick, Tracy Joy
Borzilleri, Keri Lynn
Boussios, Heather Marie
Brennan, Emily Appelbaum
Brennan, Jeanne Marie
Caballero, Khristina Vayda
Callender, Racquel Cheryl
Campbell, Kerrie Alana
Canales, Vicki Renee
Carnes, Stephanie Elizabeth
Casimir, Dominique Liza
Castillo, Alejandra Ybelisse
Caverly, Cassandra Burton
Chesno, Janna Romaine
Chilukuri, Rupa
Chinkhota, Aleacia Lynette Jenkins
Choi, Dinah Lynn
Christiani, Cynthia Eskins
Cieplak, Jenny Elizabeth
Cincotta, Robyn Mitchell
Clark, Jessica Lynn
Clark, Tillena Gregory
Clifton White, Cristyn Danielle
Cohen, Suzanne Gayle
Cohn, Rebecca Levin
Collins, Cristen Eileen
Cooper, Meredyth Sloane
Cooper, Valecia Monique
Cope, Amanda J.
Corlette, Sabrina
Costley, Amanda Lee
Crowder, Patience Adrienne
Cumber, Anishah Aftab
Cuomo, Christina Marie
Cusack, Kathleen Clare
Daigneault, Regan Elise
Daitch, Robin Esther
Das, Maya
Davis, Rebecca Ann
Davis Pratt, Elizabeth Anne Nelligan
Delgadillo, Gabriela Margarita
Denrich, Diana Beth
Desai, Seema Arvind
Dick, Vanessa Lin
Dinger, Erica Lee
Dinneen, Susan Elizabeth
Dlhopolsky, Heather
Donaldson, Jameela Kaneeka
Donis, Ligeia Maria
Doty, Brenda Marie
Douglas, Shana Lizette
Douglas, Vanassa H.
Drogula, Elizabeth Ann
Droz, Shannon Rae
Dudley, Stephanie Nicole
Dugan, Cristina Elaine
Duran, Sarah Kathleen
Edwards, Michele Lynn
Eisen, Faye Neiman
El, Lisa Marie
Elliott-Stevens, Jimma LaJuan
Emenanjo, Olubunmi Ojuolape
Ericson, Ellen Cornelius
Eugene, Wil-Jeanne
Fahrenholz, Kimberly Kay
Farrell, Margaret Mary
Fawell, Elizabeth Barr
Feierabend, Allison Victoria
Feldman, Amy Meredith
Fink, Shannon Michelle
Fisher, Elizabeth Benton
Fitzpatrick, Linda A.
Flanigan, Linda
Flood, Maureen Katherine
Folwell, Mary Grace
Ford, Fiona Amelia Marjorie
Ford, Yaida Oni
Foya, Sylvia Chawana
Franklin, Amanda Hunt
Freed, Samantha Elena
Fribush, Rebecca S.
Frizzelle, Amanda Downs
Gagliardi, Jeanine
Gallagher, Janet Marie
Gallardo, Silvie Ursula
Gardner, Kelli Lynn
Garner, Mary Theresa
Garrity, Sheila Rose
Gielow, Kristine Marie
Ginsberg, Ellen Solomon
Glencer, Kimberly Marie
Glenn, Michelle Rademaker
Glover, Melissa Eagan
Goldstein, Hannah Gillelan
Goodenough, Jennifer Clark
Gosselin, Danielle Caron
Gosselink-Ulep, Nisa Rae
Gowens, Alyssa Joy
Grace-Tardy, Ami Marie
Graditor, Lisa Lawler
Grassi, Maya Desando
Graves, Carmiece T.
Gray, Camille Anthea
Green, Chantelle Monette
Gress, Michelle Renee
Grossi, Tyler Jessica
Johnson, Chelsea Joi
Kidwell, Tracey Ritter
Klein, Sara Ackerstein
Ledbetter, Alexandra M.
Markham, Jessica
McCormick, Gina Beck
Meitl, Michele Marie
Neiderer, Christine Burke
Nichols, Pilar Camus
Pettersen, Donna Charnock
Radz, Stacy Bekman
Resh, Dawn M. B.
Shriber, Christa Ann
Simon, Ellen Ginsberg
Stafford, Rachel Elizabeth
Stouffer, Amy C.
Upadhyay, Clarissa Anne Casaje
Voss, Erin Kathleen
Weber, Julie Goodwin
Weigle, Katherine Connolly
White, Julie M.
Wicker, Denise F. Hamlin
Wiener, Jana Rose
Zawadzki, Meaghan Donovan

12-14-2005
Ashmore, Kimberly Ann
Bedell, Alyssa Meegan
Brown, Nicole Diane
Buckley, Katherine Getty Kiemle
Burton, Meighan Griffin
Collins, Hillary Anne
Dahiya, Valerie Hope
Eisner, Dara Beth
Everest, Christine Caroline
Filo, Maureen Musselman
Freid-Studlo, Laura Ann
Freling, Dara Helaine
Fulton, Katherine M.
Gardner, Helena Marie
Garner, Melanie Joustra
Gibson, Amanda Ellen Hill
Green, Margot L.
Greenberg, Jessica Elise Hay
Grossman, Natalie Lauren
Guest, Roseline Tonia
Guevara, Bettina T.
Guillory, Kristi Carleen
Gupta, Kavita
Gutwald, Season Jo
Hall, Megan Lee
Hampp, Sharon Lankford
Hanrahan, Kathleen Marie
Hansen, Heidi Rachelle
Harding, Kay Natalie
Harewood, Michele Andra
Harley, Keturah Denise
Harnett, Helen Marie
Harrington, Catherine Brady
Harris, Torrie N.
Hart, LeiLani Jo
Hayburn, Mary Katherine M.
Hayes, Katherine Carney
Hecker, Caroline Louise
Hendricks, Marianne Roteany Kim Eng
Herrmann, Christina
Higgs, Laura Marie
Hill, Susan Kathleen
Hines, Christine Michelle DeCicco
Hirao, Risa
Hitt, Amanda Leanne
Hitzelberger, April Joy
Ho-Chen, Angela Rebecca
Hobbs, Mary Terese
Hobson, Anica Jacqueline

Hodes, Lane
Hodgetts, Catherine Anne
Hogan, Stephanie Lynn
Holzapfel, Amy Elizabeth
Horan, Deborah Eleanor
Hoverter, Sara Pollock
Howard, Tara Lynn
Howse, Bernice Lenore
Humphrey, Connie Jean
Hunnicutt, Rachel Kapust
Hussey, Jedidah Mary Boone
Hutson, Kate Emily
Iversen, Julie Marie
Ivory, Alexis Marie
Jackson, Jennifer Renee
Jackson-Boozer, Courtney
Jaron, Patricia Knight
Jessee, Alisa Suzanne
Johnk, Grace Ammer
Johnson, Anitha Wileen
Johnson, LaShanta Renae
Jones, Joyce Elizabeth
Judd, Rebecca Gerber
Just, Amanda Patricia
Kamons, Rachael Amy
Kaplan Rubin, Dana Victoria
Kapoor, Sheikha
Karangelen, Jennifer James
Kaufman, Laurie Rebecca
Kelly, Tara Michelle
Keogh, Sarah Ellen Wertheimer
Kerwin, Courtney Tanis
Kimber, Mary Clare Hazel
King, Caroline Law Miller
Kirlin, Bayly Helene
Klein, Alissa Lynne
Kleinman, Andrea Suzanne
Kobus, Mary Martha
Konstantinova, Nadia Alexandra
Kornblet, Sarah Ann
Krach, Lisa Michele
Kudchadkar, Janardan Vinoda
Kuntz, Emma Elena
Kyriakos, Kristin Renee
Lamm, Marina
Lashley, Emily Kimmitt
Lasky, Jodi Melissa
Laszlo, Reka
Le Goc, Claire Marie Josephine
Lechner, Sarah Louise
Ledford, Laura Marie
Legrain, Hillary Parham
Lentini, Nicole
Leone, Robin Denise
Leshner, Johanna Cohen
Letsome, Allendra
Letsome, Rebecca Elizabeth
Levian, Karen
Linhard, Rachel McGraw
Lipuma, Kristen Michelle
Litchfield, Amber Kaye
Livingston, Emily King
Lloyd, Heather Marguerite
London, Rachel Beth
Lord-Sorensen, Adrianne L.
Luk, Olivia T.
MacGregor, Glenna Yvonne
Madea, Cortney Lynn
Maki, Jennifer Lynn
Malarkey, Emily Claire
Malley, Angela Trang
Maltz, Stephanie T.
Mamdouhi, Lesley Anne Moss
Mandell, Michele F.
Marquardt, Peggy Ann
Marshall, June Marie
Marteny, Katharine Stone
Martin, Stacie Elizabeth
Marzullo, Kelly Marie
Mattson-Sarli, Paula Marie
May, Maureen Fick
McCarthy, Mary O'Neil
McClellan, Kathleen Mary
McCormack, Erin Michael
McCoy, Sheila Rae
McDonald, Dana L.
McDonald, Kelly Burrow
McGrory, Kristin Brianne
McKenzie, Jean Marie
McLaughlin, Jennifer Nicole
Meeder, Jessica Hamman
Messina, Melissa Rose
Michalski, Amanda Lynn
Michiels, Megan Catherine
Mickelsen, Jessica Marie
Middleton, Alice Bonner
Miller, Deni Lyn
Miller, Marina Ivanovna
Mintz, Hillary Cherry
Mitchell, Patricia Annette
Mogil, Marina Ann
Monfried, Melissa Rachael
Montag, Coty Rae
Montesano, Leah Catherine
Moore, Rachel Leah
Morenoff, Dara Joy
Morgan, Tamara Sheree
Morris, Dianna M.
Morrison-Lee, Kelly Rebekah
Moutsatsos, Artemis Gricelda
Moye, Stacey Andrea
Mrazek, Nicola Jean
Mudd, Erica Collier
Muller, Arsima Aileen
Murphy, Christine Helen
Murthy, Priya
Musayelova, Vlada
Napjus, Catherine E.
Neely, Ruthanne G.
Nestico, Amber Csaszar
Niakan, Cameron
Nice-Petersen, Nicole Michele
Nicolaus, Nicole Christina
Noel, Denise Nikeon
Nokes, Sharon Weinberg
Nolan, Erin Mary
Nowak, Jennifer Ann
Oliver, Johanna Liparini
Otero, Vanessa M.
Reichard, Mary Ann
Reilly, Kristen
Releford, Tiffany Murray
Roscetti, Jennifer Howe
Schnabel, Nancy
Serrano, Danae M.
Sheffield, Yolanda Tena
Tierney, Jennifer Marie
Weiner, Heather Kilgore
Willis, Shafanta Denise

12-15-2005

Ayers, Nedra D.
Baker, Abigail Lucie
Benjamin, Sara N.
Bortmes, Davida Ofori
Buenafe, Michele Lee
Carr, Machalagh
Carthens, Shavonnie Renee
Clinton, Erin Troy
Cohen, Yona E.
Connelly, Jennifer Michele
Cornellier, Sasha Hallissey
Douge, Patricia Romulus
Esders, Meredith Louise
Everhart, Sarah Marie
Giles, Charlotte Carolyn
Halloran, Elissa Kathleen
Herbst, Amy Samantha
Jenks, Ulrike Winkler
Johnson, June Phillips
Kelly, Anna Schultz
Kim, Eun A.
Lambert, Michele Bernice
Lloyd, Kathryn Anne
Lyons, Stephanie Pisanelli
McIntyre, Katharine O'Hara
Meadows, Wendy Sare
Mihill, Amanda Michelle White
Miller, Gretchen P.
Miller, Paula Lynn
Moloney, Erin Pearl
O'Connell, Allison Marie
O'Connor, Eileen Mary
O'Hara, Katie Murphy
Oaten, Julia Sarkissian
Oliver, Catherine Anne
Orner, Tali Naomi
Ortiz, Jeanette
Pak, Eleanor Lee
Parrish, Angela L.
Patankar, Anita Jayprakash
Patel, Gayatri Arvind
Paulick, Amy Sette
Perenich, Christine Margaret
Peters, Tamara Catherine
Pezzulla, Mary
Pierson, Elizabeth Ann
Pisanelli, Kristina Marie
Pisano, Lauren Beth
Pitz, Heather Lea
Pogue, Jennifer Ruth-Dougherty
Polley, Carrie Leigh
Powell, Shontell Denise
Purple, Kathryn Baker
Pusin, Sharon Mae
Pyser, Emily R. Pyser
Quade, Stephanie Janel
Radkar, Smruti Vijaykumar
Raj, Shanthala Madhwa
Rea, Kristine Joan
Reddig, Julie Alyce
Reese, Beth Mary
Reese, Debbie-Anne Angelique
Reidy, Megan Michele
Reinard, Meghan Mara
Reynolds, Karen Christina
Richard, Crystal Sewak
Richard, Stephanie Kay
Richardson, Abby Morrow
Richardson, Morghan Leia
Riger, Sarah Louise
Rivera, Cherisse Marie
Rodier, Samantha Protokowicz
Rodriguez, Christina Danielle
Roe, Katherine Alexandra
Rolland, Stacey Lynn
Romig, Rebecca Ann
Rooney, Sarah Elizabeth
Rose, Laura Lynn
Roselle, Avery Ellen Mackenzie
Rosen, Jody Adam
Rosenfelt, Natalie
Rosenthal, Stephanie Krinsly
Ross, Samantha Erin
Ross, Tara Leigh
Roth, Melissa Rubin
Roth, Sara E.
Ruiz Youmans, Aurora
Ruocco, Angela
Ruyak, Carolyn Davol
Ryan, Elizabeth S.
Sadusky, Jessica Shadie
Salsbury, Jessica Meredith
Samenow, Deborah Silver
Samuel, Dodi Penina
Sanchez Fuentes, Zenia
Sanders, Tamara Dawn
Santiago, Melanie Joyce
Saxena, Jaya
Scavello, Catherine Elizabeth O'Connell
Scheydt, Brandy Michele
Schissler, Erika Susan
Schweizer, Staci Danielle
Scott, Ellen
Scott, Jennifer Rae
Scott, Summer E.
Seales, Keela Shanee
Sealy, Karen Anita
Seguin, Debbie Wang
Seldomridge, Lauren Alise
Selmon, Erika Thomas
Servance, Renee La Shonn
Sher, Dena S.
Sherman, Kelly White
Shuey, Kathleen Megan
Sidwell, Heather Lynn
Silva, Sharli R.
Sinapi, Anna Natasha
Siribuo, Augusta
Slattery, Shannon Elizabeth
Smith, Kerri M.
Smith, Kimberly Jameika
Smith, Tazuer Anne
Somerville, Andrea Denise
Sovcik, Anne Elizabeth
Spain, Penelope Jane
Spang, Sheri Ann
Spector, Simone Louise
Spilker, Abby Ross
Stahl, Allyson Melissa
Stair, Jennifer Lynn
Staiti, Lauren Sheppard
Stanfield, Michelle Elise
Stanton, JaCina Nia
Steil, Sigrid Kruse
Stevens, Alice Veronica
Storr, Ghislaine Monique
Stringer, Meghan Meagher
Swan, Sarah Elizabeth
Sweeney, Elise Gabrielle
Sweren, Heather Rochelle
Taylor, Danielle Marie
Teare, Teresa D'Antuono
Thompson, Elizabeth Phifer
Thompson, Lisa Ann
Tomazic, Vlatka Ana
Tranel, Adrienne Martha
Tupper, Elizabeth Michelle

Turnblacer, Nancy Ellen
Turner, Lindsay Leigh
Tuthill, Stephanie Kay
Tzinova, Antonia Ivanova
Vainieri, Emily Allison
Valdetero, Jena Marie
Virmani, Monica
Vogel, Melissa Louise
Vrabel, Ann Marie
Walker, Jennifer Ann
Walters, Cherrie-Ann Esther
Watkins, Dedra
Watson, Zaine Elicia
Webber, Hillary Anne
Weller, Elizabeth Julia
Whitley, Juanita Denese
Williams, Amy Schumacher
Williams, Devon Lorey
Williams, Tiffany Joy Anne
Wong, Iris Lin
Worshtil, Joanna Hollis
Wright, Allie McGrier
Xia, Ang
Yau, Szu-chien
Yonenson, Carrie Ilyse
Zaklad, Jessica Rose
Zamani, Sogand
Zuk, Cary Elizabeth

12-16-2005
Kallal, Mandy S.
Sibley, Mara Jeanne
Williams, Michele Elizabeth

12-18-2005
Hollinger, Jerrietta Ruth

12-20-2005
Hutchins, Renee McDonald

12-29-2005
Brewer, Nancy S.
Dominguez, Linda Anna
Martinez, Heidi Agnes
Walker, Schonette Jones
Yihune, Mizan

12-30-2005
Hatchett, Trina Denise

1-5-2006
Bayisa, Ebise
Brown, Teneille Ruth
Brun, Carmen Lisa
Dziedzic, Bridgette Stewart
Ghahhari, Nowelle Amy
Gieske, Loretta Bridget
Gupta-Kagan, Avni
Guthrie, Karen Rose
Hwang, Jina
Kelly, Erica Lynette
Kurian, Roshni
Lundstedt, Mary Frances Oakley
O'Brien, Jennifer Michelle
Schnabolk, Andra E.
Shepherd, Stephanie Jolene
Walker, Mary Beth
Whisonant, Shani K.
Young, Sandra Caroline
Zangueneh, Sherry Marie

1-9-2006
Wiener, Charlotte Julie

1-12-2006
Hopper, Amanda Beth

1-18-2006
Aylward, Jillian Kindlund
Beam, Cynthia Good

1-19-2006
Zamd, Liza

1-24-2006
Sheer, Margaret Elizabeth

1-26-2006
Hunter, Chakira Teneya
Wolf, Tiffney Carole

2-1-2006
Blanco, Theresa M.

2-2-2006
Berkland, Kristin Kay
Delaney, Susan Elizabeth
Johnson, Kirsten H.
Louis, Camile Anne
Lyon-Collis, Lauren Michelle
Moylan, Leslie Gallagher
Pruitt, Lauren Gaelynn
Sim, Laura E.
Waldstreicher, Joanna Stromberg
Whaley, LaShanda Renee

2-6-2006
R-Ferrulli, Andrea Katelyna

2-8-2006
Davidson, Beth Baskin

2-24-2006
Pimentel, Mayuris

3-2-2006
Highsmith, Lakeshia Nicole
Lawrence, Amanda Jean

3-6-2006
Brown, Cynthia Taleese

3-13-2006
Mundinger, Elizabeth O.

5-3-2006
McCormack, Jennifer Lynn

5-11-2006
McArdle-Phillips, Stefanie

5-31-2006
Santiago, Lisandra Evelyn

6-6-2006
Cluverius, Charlotte Eugenie
Davis, Lucy Gardner
Moschella, Michelle G.

6-7-2006
Page, Helen Tina Louise
Sullivan, Bonnie Alice
Wilson Parham, Alice Witherspoon

6-12-2006
Krauthamer, Lauren D. Burger

6-13-2006
Aaron, Petra Lisa-Ann
Adams, LeDeanna Diane
Ahram, Marni Lefkowitz
Ajala, Jacqueline Taiwo
Armstrong, Lauren Parker
Aucoin, Lauren Jean
Balmforth, Margaret Mary
Banks, Laelia Ugalde
Barnett, Rachael
Bartley, Kathleen Mary
Bianco, Krista Marie Entrop
Black, Kellie Marie
Blackwell, Roxanne Lynn
Bolourchi, Neda
Boston, Johnetta Renee
Brannan, Kathleen Doory
Brodlie, Debra Ellen
Brown, Tabitha Renee
Brown, Wanda Deann
Buie, Sandra Lee
Carpenter, Mona Latesha
Casafranca, Teresa Maria
Casie Chitty, Rozain Elizabeth
Cha, Jessica Byulnim
Chang, Catherine Hyung
Clarke, Melissa Carlene
Coates, Tracey Joy
Collett, Camille Michelle
Corley, Adrienne R.
Crawford, Cynthia Fleming
del Carmen, Rebecca Gollogly
Delambo, Gerardine Majella
Delaney, Danielle Anne
Denihan, Maureen Ann
Diamond, Alizah Zissel
Diener, Elisa Edith
Do, Lynda Anh
Duguid, Regan Kristine
Dunn, Jeannine Elizabeth
Dwyer, Daniela
Edwards, Namha B.
Emmith, Maria Fontan
Faber-Moseley, Christine Lynne
Feldhan, Melissa Ann
Firozvi, Nadia Jahan
Fisher, Ashley Caroline
Foley, Deirdre Elizabeth
Ford, Elisa Rebeccah
Gallucci, Mary Ellis
Galluzzo, Tiffany Paige
Garrison, C. Caroline Rugg
Gayle, Erica Tara
Georgiou, Evridiki
Ghanta, Ulka Patel
Goldblatt, Lisa Merren
Gough, Kathleen Sarah
Gover, Julie Dawn
Green, Allison V.
Greene, Angela Denice
Guley, Allison Suzanne
Gulstone, Ulani D. Prater
Haas, Wendy Couchoud
Halfmann, Rahemoon Husain
Hall McKenzie, Mona Felicia
Harden, Denise Whittington
Hare, Jennifer Elizabeth Fellows
Hassanein, Hebba Magdi
Hayot, Danielle Jeanne
Healey, Alison Marie
Heurich, Alison Mason
Hill, Kelly Starosta
Holland, Angela Erica
Holt, Sandra Maria
Hopkins, Lee Ann
Hudachek, Starla Jean
Huggins, Nadine Rose
Hussey, Susan Elizabeth Wisniewski
Hutchinson, Mary Rebekah
Jackson, Tyree Ayers
Jacobs, Sorella
Jamison, Cheryl Lynette
Jones, Judith Beth
Jordan, Janelle Jennifer
Joshi, Margi Tenya
Kahan, Gail Roberta
Kartha, Pamela Grewal
Keppen, Judith Marie
Keyvan, Shabnam
King, Ericka Nicole
Krause, Suzanne Victoria
Lake, Karen
Lamar, Loretta Michelle
Lang, Victoria Johne
Lauenstein, Leanne Michele
Lawrence, Michele Alia
Le Winter, Andrea Hope
Lee, Monique Latrese
Lee-Camp, Stephanie Michelle
Leighton, Eliza Sarah
Lema, Lisette Ada
Linder, Anne Elizabeth
Linzer, Katharine Allen
Little, Sarah Christina
Lobos, Leslie Eunice
Lukens, Jodi Leigh
Lunn, Tamala E.
Madjid, Aisha
Malhotra, Reema
Mandel, Shannon Noelle
Marcano, Desireé Natalie
Mark, Ilana Calimafde
McBride, Camille Ramona
McBride, Maren Marie
McCaffrey, Katherine Warrington
McDowell, Tara Janet
McGrath-Malott, Maeve Linahan
Milici, Jennifer
Minami, Kristine Miyeko
Minor, Angela Denise
Mitchell, Sabrina Roxanne
Morales, Ryann Bernard
Moscati, Chelsey L.
Murphy, Debra Suzanne
Noel, Yasmin
Nonn, Sharon Kay
Opkins, Nichole Gabriella Blancato
Osorno, Marjorie Rebecca
Otto, Allison Margaret
Overly, Kathleen Blaire
Pamer, Ashley Rose
Park, Laureen Jihae
Parlow, Anita Lee
Plank, Bonnie Elizabeth
Polis, Karen
Portanova, Emily Pertoso
Pride, Erin Elizabeth
Retzer, Elizabeth Orlando
Rhoades, Betty Thurber
Richardson, Angela
Roe, Andrea Ballanfant
Romero Baca, Yohanna Aurora
Rundell, Leila R.
Runge, Holly Daee
Sadler, Jessica Hepburn
Saini, Priti
Samadani, Tahirih Schear

Sandusky, Nicole Marie
Sangmor, Lynda
Scheinfeldt, Anne Heavey
Schnall, Lisa M.
Schneider, Melissa Mary
Sendra, Hope Marie
Sevcik, Victoria Schantz
Simmons, Shanita Karen
Simons, Pamela Denise
Simpson, Chasity Nicole
Sincere, Lisa Marie
Singh, Mamata
Sklar, Maggie Elisabeth
Smith, Aine Fowler
Smith, Eliza Michelle
Smith, Nicole Taylor
Soltow, Tami Lynn
Stern, Andrea E.
Stiffler-Claus, Vanessa Grace
Stokes, Shayla Settlers
Stuger, Tracy Deirdre
Sulerzyski, Victoria Zuchelli
Taylor, Cerise Shaaron
Taylor, Christina Leigh
Torrence, LaVonne Octavia
Toy, Joanna Elizabeth
Turner, Sarah N.
Tynes, Klohver Patrice
Vallar, Genevieve Pidlaoan
van Stone, Maureen Lynne
Varmer, Renee Cherie
Vasbinder, Marie Elizabeth
Walls, Rachel Marie
Weaver, Makita Renee
Wells, Christina Marie
Williams, Desiree Samalla
Williams, Jacqueline R.
Winder, Noelle
Winkworth, Maura Claire
Witlen, Sarah Beth
Woolen, Kisha Lashawn
Wyeth, Wendy M.
Zeilinger, Laura Green

6-14-2006

Fishberg, Lisa Ann Freiman

6-16-2006

Tolbert, Sherece Marie

6-19-2006

Senghor, Sharon White

6-20-2006

Phillips, Susan

6-21-2006

Arnold, Deborah Joan
Spielberg, Sonya

6-23-2006

Maneval, Kristen Orff
Mitchell, Lynndolyn Tippins
Nichols, Lucy Esther
O'Brien, Eileen Marie

6-27-2006

Cook, Adrianne Elizabeth Arnold
Hostetler, Janet Marie
Pappas, Phoebe M.
Robinson, Danielle Nikkol
Simon, Lara Kaye

6-29-2006

Spurlark, Susan Margaret

7-11-2006

Gueh-Thoronka, Kamah Menseleh

7-12-2006

Gorzela, Maura Kathleen

7-14-2006

Battiste, Katherine A.

7-19-2006

Sossamon, Melinda Anne

8-8-2006

Craine Lombardo, Mary Jeanne
DiStefano, Delaney Melissa

8-11-2006

Sydnor, Courtney Renee

8-18-2006

Sallit, Joanne F.

8-22-2006

Sanchez, Roxie Allison

8-30-2006

Eccles, Debra

9-7-2006

Alabi, Kaisha Ladia
Greenwood, Lindsay Edelstein
Hands, Ajeurai Ciara
Jackson, Nicole Farmer
Landry, Claudine A.
Peek, Anne Marie
Wood, Darlene Iva

9-26-2006

Clark, Brianna Sibly-Biers

10-10-2006

Bynum, Alexandra Celia
Kendall, Elizabeth Laybourne
O'Doherty, Lisa Michelle
Rosa, Virginia Grace

10-19-2006

Moodispaw, Michelle Jean

11-2-2006

Edmond, Lesley M.

11-30-2006

DeCostello, Nicole Danielle

12-11-2006

Bender, Melissa Hope
Neptune, Kelli Irvine

12-12-2006

Aber, Olisa Shaina Cofield
Adams, Katharine Margaret Elizabeth
Ademuwagun, Oluwatoyin A.
Admiral, Charmain L.
Ahmed, Araj Fatima
Albarelli, Kathryn Turner
Albrecht, Valerie L.
Albright, Mary Elizabeth
Allen, Amanda H.
Allen, Elizabeth Louise
Allen, Jacqueline L.
Allnutt, Katherine Ellen
Allyn, Vanessa B.
Alvarez, Jessica M.
Anderson, Nicole Lynn
Andrews, Naomi E.
Andritz, Jessica S.B.
Ardito, Laura Rose
Aronson Teitelbaum, Lauren Beth
Atkisson, Kathleen A.
Ault, Katherine Goodwin
Babinski, Laurie Ann
Backus, Jamie J.
Baghai, Shahrzad
Bagley, Sarah Rebecca
Ballute, Jennifer L.
Baltimore, Jewel Angela
Baraloto, Cathleen Frances
Barr, Christine Jane
Bastone, Susan Denise
Batra, Shuchi
Baum, Beth Laurie
Belardo, Tiambe Michelle
Bennington, Jennifer Kathleen
Benson, Hillary Gould
Berger, Jennifer Hari
Beyer, Kimberly Elise
Bina, Rebekah Lara
Birchfield, Jennifer Andrea
Bisset, Darcy Anne Faint
Boettger, Kimberly Garner
Bohl, Kristin Meaghan
Boney, Dbnnoise Yondevia
Bonifant, Kelly
Bonorchis, Kathryn Elizabeth
Boone, Laura Katharine
Bortnick, Abigail Nadine
Bova, Victoria
Brady, Alisa Y.
Brennan, Emily M.
Briggerman, Abigail Clark
Brown, Terese M.
Buffalano, Nicole Alicia
Burda, Cindy Elaine
Califa, Katherine Pearl
Camuti-Carranza, Elizabeth Anne
Canty, Elizabeth Anne
Capps, Meredith Ashley
Carl, Kaethe McClymont
Carolan, Julia Ann
Carroll, Cheryl Elizabeth
Carter, Rebecca Jean
Cassell, Jennifer Ellen Kadish
Castellini, Kerri M.
Cellarosi, Gabriella Vitalina
Chase, Sabrina Elsbeth
Chee-a-tow, Andrea Marissa Francine
Chow, Sonya Minghui
Chung, Sarah K.
Cilento, Kristin Carrie
Cochran, Anita Cheri
Cochran, Patricia Meredith
Cohen, Ellen Connelly
Cohen, Julia Hodapp
Cook, Elizabeth Marie
Cooke, Susan Robyn
Courtney, Brooke
Covolesky, Melissa Ridgely
Coyle, Simone Kiersky
Crooks, Kristina Anne
Custodio, Chantelle Michelle
D'Ambrosio, Leila
Dale, Sarah J.
Dana, Lauren Rachel
Dave, Katherine Atkinson
Davidson, Karen E.H.
Davis, Gwen-Marie A.
Davis, Pawnee Ann
De Jesus, Nicole A.
Deckert, Kathryn Elizabeth
DeJesus, Tracy Marie
Demeroto, Cathy Abrams
Demps-Barrett, Stacey
dePottere-Smith, Madelaine Alexia
DeRose, Jennifer A.
Desjardins, Jamie Lauren
Deutsch, Emily Woodward
Dickson, Katherine Anne
DiLaura, Jillian Lee
Drennan, Elizabeth Ann
Drewry, Samanda Joy
Drexel, Christine M.
Drohan, Kathleen Grace
Dulla, Christine Marie
Eberhart, Christina Lorraine
Eremita, Elizabeth A.
Esposito, Katherine Carr
Farmer, Carmen Leigh
Farrell, Corey Leigh
Farrell, Kristen Astrid
Fay, Caragh Glenn
Feely, Kathleen Marie
Finken, Anne Noelle
Fish, Sloane Lisa
Fitzgerald, Regan L.
Flanagan, Jane Reisen
Foster, Merrill Huse
Foster, Shondell Harriston
Fox, Anne Boro
Fox, Kerry Alexis
Francois, Emmanuelle Regine
Frazier, Adrienne Felecia
Freemire, Alexandra Nicole
Freer, Stephanie Cooper
French, Bethany Sara Katz
French, Dorris Catherine
Fuchs, Miriam S.
Fulwood, Emily Elizabeth
Garfinkel, Lynn
Garrelts, Holly Marie
Garten, Danielle Marie
Georgatsos, Joanna Irene
George, Janel A.
Getty, Alison I.
Gheuens, Judith Anna Gerda
Gibson, Caitlin Wesley
Gibson, Erin Marshall
Giddens, Buffy Nicole
Gill, Sheena
Gillespie, Jennifer Elizabeth
Gilliam, Rebecca Ann
Girmai, Hibret N.
Glover, Donna Marie
Gnall, Johanna Elizabeth
Goldberg, Cori Annapolen
Golden, Linette Frances
Goldthorpe, Sandra Jean
Gonzales, Cherita A.
Gordon, Melinda Ann
Gostomski, Karen Elizabeth
Gould, Dawn Renee
Gould, Ilissa M.
Gousis, Linda Souter
Grafton, Kelly Ann
Grant, Jennifer Linn
Grant Bluechel, Renee Lynn
Grasso, Amy C.H.

Gray, Nakia V.
Grazio, Lori Ann
Green, Nakita L.
Greene, Caprisha Shirvon
Greene, Megan Brennan
Gregory, Rachel Leah
Gross, Akiva Y.
Groudine, Candace J.
Grover, Anne Elizabeth
Guizzetti Hayes, Mia
Haac, Anna Claire
Hackworth, Deanna M.
Haigler, Tiffany L.
Hall, Angela Denise
Hall, Kimmeria Diane Bayton
Ham, Linda Jin
Hamilton-vom Baur, Nerissa
Hammerman, Julie L.
Hammond, Shannon Leigh
Harden, Fatima
Hardin, Niya Joui
Harris, Khalilah Marie
Hatton, Jennifer Lynn
Heithaus, Livya Louise
Herrmann, Carolyn Hurley
Hirsch, Rachel
Holder, Kamilah M.
Holzen, Karen Hunter
Hopkin, Catherine Keller
Horani, Morriah H.
Hostyk, Debra Parel
House, Kamilah Olisa
Howell, Christa
Hurley, Anne Haffner
Hurley, Catherine Ann
Jackler, Hilary Alice
Jacobsen, Arn
Jacobson, Lauri Ellen
Jennings, Veronica Renzi
Johnson, Geneen Nicole
Johnson, Teisha Carmen
Johnston, Trisha Gonitzke
Jones, Annie Blanchard
June, Arian Marjory
Kabaria, Swati A.
Kamara, Yealie Tandiwe
Kannan, Akila
Kaplan, Dana Crespi
Karceski, Rachel E.
Karson, Julie Ann
Kaufman, Bonnie Regina
Kay, Rachel Leah
Keifer, Emily J.
Keipper, Lindsay Anne
Khan, Saima R.
King, Erin Elizabeth
King, Tracey L.
Kinney, Laura
Kiwanuka, Mary Maxensia
Klase, Amanda Elizabeth
Klemt, Amy Rebecca
Knight, Letoria G.
Kochhar, Sonia K.
Lambert, Alison Sutton Friedman
Lawrence, Candace Howard
Lewandowski, Karolyn Blumer
McEvoy, Leianne S.
Merlis, Maura Cahill
Morgan, Shelley Christine
Nobleman, Debbie Kim
Oetting, Angela M.
Oppenheim, Katherine Downs
Osborne, Sha'Donna Michelle
Packard, Adrienne J.
Panda, Moyah Kettle
Perez-Nelson, Monica
Rachlin, Emily Beth
Ridgway, Danie Engles
Risch, Erin Alanna
Roberts, Angela M.
Schneider, Valerie Jill
Sermon, Krista Anastasia
Shaw, Shari Lynn Diener
Silvia, Andrea Lee Curatola
Solomon, Julia Gontrum
Thompson, Valerie Ann
Troiani, Christina Doran
Webb, Shelley Johnson
Williams, Tiese Lovey
Yim, So-Ching

12-13-2006

Berger, Megan Rector
Berman, Jennifer Spiegel
Brooks, Oana A.
Caine, Kimberly Hope
Clark, Ann-Monique Ras
Cordisco, Meredith
Delligatti, Reanna Lee
Dennis, Melissa Rose
Doud, Jennifer Riskie
Erdheim, Rachel Patner
Etheridge, Marcia Murray
Fenton, Carey Anne
Fiorentino, Jennifer Elizabeth
Forsythe, Jennifer Sherburne
Freeman, Carrie McMahon
Gebbia, Emily Saylor
Gussow, Laurie Kathryn
Henley, Camille Melissa Martin
Hudzik, Melissa Ann McCurdy
Iacchei, Emily Alice
Keas, Jennifer M.
Konings, Priya Sharma
Kopelman, Erin Leigh
Kormelink, Karen Anne
Kraft, Elizabeth Thorowgood
Kubick, Danica Charlotte
Kucinski, Melissa Ann
Kunkel, Rebecca Joy
Kurian, Seba P.
Kwiatkowski, Jennifer Lynn
Lam, Hai-Ly Huynh
Latwin, Elizabeth Robin
Leahy, Cheryl Leigh
Lee, Jasmine
Lee, Lynn Marie
Levin, Cecelia Friedman
Levine, Susan Marie
Lewis, Patrice Lenette
Lewis, Rhenelda Helene
Ley, Patricia H.
Liberty, Katherine Zengion
Liotta, Stephanie Marie
Lipman, Isabel
Liu, Qun
Lockshin, Alexis Michele
Loiselle, Margaret Marion
Lombardi, Joyce R.
Long, Fonya Monique
Longford, Kimberly
Lopez, Luisa M.
Mabry, Robyn R.
Madden, Renee I.
Maddox, Paraskevi A.
Malpani, Veena
Mandel, Rebecca Cheryl
Mandycz, Jeannette M.
Marek, Meghan Ritson
Margulies, Jennifer Michelle
Marohn, Rhya
Martinez, Katrina Francesca Rustia
Matini, Lily Monir
McCallister, Erika L.
McDonough, Caitlin Eileen
McGhee, Jasmine S.
McGoldrick, Joline F.
McGrew, Megan Lee
McLeod, Neveen H.
Mehta, Devi
Melchior, Melissa Nicole
Mertens, Amanda Beth
Merwin, Anne Meredith
Mesa, Meredith Bree
Messick, Julia Jane
Messitte, Julia Holman
Millar, Erin O'Brien
Miller, Brigitte J.
Miller, Emily G.
Miller, Letha Ann
Miller, Marilee L.
Min, Hye Joo
Minea, Alison Ann
Miskell, Erin E.
Mojica, Maria de Lourdes
Molseed, Sarah Lynn
Monroe, Nia Marie
Montgomery, Rebecca Dragul
Morisset, Claire Noelle
Morris, Olivia Joan Elise
Morris-Glass, Heather Michelle
Mosby, Marilyn J.
Moshman, Rachael Alexandra Schmid
Moss, Lindsay Victoria Ruth
Mutinsky, Sarah Elizabeth
Neary, Michelle Helena
Nelson, Heather Benson
Nerette, Stephanie M.
Nikakhtar, Nazakhtar
North, Krista Michelle
O'Connell, Jessica Parsons
O'Connell, Monica Ann
O'Donnell, Cherish Ann
Ogunlegan, Adeyinka O.
Older, Stephanie Sherman
Paganini, Lisa Marie
Pallia, Nicole Christine
Palomino, Natalie Cheris
Paton, Margaret Sheeran
Patterson, Earline Nichole
Payne, Terri Bendyna
Perrelli, Amber Marie
Perrick, Tracey Levin
Petaja, Danielle N.
Peters, Sara Elizabeth
Petkovsek, Amy L.
Petticolas, Kisha T.
Pierre-Louis, Natalie
Pierson, Katherine Rossi
Pitts, Jessica Katherine
Podkul, Jennifer Hope
Polk, Lauren Alexandra
Powers, Kelly Ann
President, Lori Evette
Presley, Karen Denise
Preteroti, Kelly M.
Proietti, Tracy Michelle
Protas, Kristin E.
Prucka, Susannah Elizabeth
Pugh, Christine Sindall
Quarfoot, Genevieve Johnson
Randall, April Renee
Rayne, Pamela Schafer
Redlin, Michelle Kae
Reed, Elizabeth Ann
Reidy, Elizabeth Anne
Renner, Joanna C.
Reyna, Jennifer Eileen Schwartz
Ricketts, Peta-Gaye Patrice
Rideout, Brianne Power
Ritchie, Alicia Natasha
Rives, Ann Lawrence
Rizer, Jessica
Roach, Alison Renee
Robbins-Segers, Kim A.
Roberts, Christine Erin
Robinson, Ginger R.
Roddy, Shannon Melissa
Rodenberger, Tiffany Leigh
Rosan, Megan Nichols
Rosenblum, Lilah Simone
Rossman, Mikaela Ivy
Roth, Amy Marie
Rotz, Ann Marie
Ruppert, Jennifer Louise
Russell, Emily Louise
Salcedo Padula, Gloria Maria
Samaras, Amelia Taylor
Samet, Susanna C.
Sanchez, Delora Robin
Sartwell, Danielle Renee
Schade, Rebecca L.
Schaefer, Kristina Marie
Scheib, Megan Susan
Schumacher, Elizabeth Hope
Schwaber, Stacey L.
Schwartzman, Sara L.
Scully, Patricia Evelyn
Shadman Valavi, Mehri F.
Shah, Mona Gulab
Sharma, Indira K.
Sheehy, Kathleen McCarthy
Shelton, Ronica Levette
Shook, Diane Griffin
Shoop, Karen Lynn
Shore-Suslowitz, Rebecca Amelia
Short, Ashley Campbell
Shpak, Anna
Skedsvold, Paula Rhee
Skowronski, Meredith
Sleemi, Saira
Smith, Genetta N.
Smith, Sarah Christine
Snyder, Larna Marie
Snyder, Lauren Brooke
Song, Valerie Marie
Spelhaug, Jesika S.
Spiers, Cindy J.
Stedman, Tiffany Anne
Strippoli, Briena Lorraine
Stump, Kathy L.
Suggs, Qualahnia K.
Sweeney, Regan A.
Sweeney, Soon Ei Elizabeth
Swick, Christina P.
Syquia, Maria-Patricia Tablang
Tabackman, Lauren Beth

Tabatabai, Emily Somers
Tang, Rosalyn
Taylor, Adelicia Cliffe
Tello, Elizabeth Ann
Tenenbaum, Cara Elyse
Terhune, Amelia Adele
Thomas, Anastasia Elena
Thompson, Christine Rose
Thorward, Minda Anya
Torrez, Marya Gassman
Travers, Nicole Ayn
Tsadick, Kristy Bernard
Tucker, Tara Leigh
Turberville, Sarah Elizabeth
Tyrewala, Stacey L.
Urban, April Marie
Vaeth, Kathryn Eleanor
Vaughan, Jennifer Clare
Veltman, Dawn Sunshine
Vitale, Heather Anne
von Spiegelfeld, Maria Cristina Esteron
Wainwright, Katherine T.
Walker, Charlemayne Napoleon
Walthour, Zaneta E.
Ware, Karen L.
Warren, Marietta B.R.
Watson, Rebecca Ann Hoffman
Weaver, Shannon Marie
Webreck, Erin R.
Weeks, Laurie Anne
Wehrle, Johann Paul
Weidner, Laura Elizabeth
Weinberg, Alison Case
Weir, Alyssa Bartlett
Welsh, Lisa Michelle
White, Alyson Stacey
White, Martha K.
Wiethorn, Mary McVaugh
Williamowsky, Jaclyn E.
Williams, Deyka C.
Williams, Sarah M.
Williamson, Sharee Lynn
Windley, Taniya Latrice
Wolf, Liana Gale Turner
Wolkinson, Rachel O.
Wolland, Jessica Lauren
Wolpert, Rachel Ellen
Wolvin, Maria C.
Wright, Emily Teresa
Wucher, Kathleen Elizabeth
Yasser, Rachel Miller
Yates, Lauren Rachel
Ysaguirre, Cassia M.
Yuffee, Emily Nanette
Zachariah, Aswathi
Zadora, Kristy Lynn
Zara, Jane Jule
Zarrella, Jessica Leigh
Zientek, MacKenzie S.
Zilioli, Erica M.

12-14-2006

Seiden, Wendy M.

12-18-2006

Johnson, Margaret E.

12-19-2006

Anderson-Ponzer, Karin Jean
Jacoby, Teri Nelson
Johnson, Eileen Morgan

12-20-2006

Alvarez, Jennifer L.
Faber, Johnna L.
Robokos, Deidre L.
Somer-Greif, Penny L.

12-22-2006

Carlan, Janine A.
Khanna, Roma
Terranova, Jodi Victoria

12-27-2006

Biran, Sarah K.
Carnell, Susanne Harris
Cipollone, Diane Welling
Dean, Andrea Ellyn
Fraser, Amanda Marie Crowley
Loomis, Deborah
Wertheim, Jennifer H.
Zebrowski Tatelbaum, Christine

1-2-2007

Shabo, Victoria Serl

1-4-2007

Brown, Daphne M.
Davis, Dana Rachel
Ireland-Volkan, Keely Marie
Jefferson, Asha Fayola Joseph
Kinslow, Diane Marie
Kosak, Joyce Monica
Minnix, Davina L.
Nappier, Jennifer Alisha
O'Mara, Marsha Joy
Raymond, Kerry Colleen
Tshiteya, Mireille Bilonda
Turmelle, Ashlee Smith

1-9-2007

Davenport, Lynn A.
Schuster, Ruth Brewer
Turner, Teresa Carol

1-19-2007

Emery, Melanie Anne
Sanford, Melissa Potter

1-22-2007

Adler, Jessica Esserman

1-23-2007

Brown, Carla Denette
Chanel, Lisa Danielle

1-24-2007

Johnson, Julie Lee Beth

1-25-2007

Grosko, Tamara Weinstein

1-26-2007

Lane, Jamie Ann

1-29-2007

White, Nancy Ann

1-30-2007

Julian-Arnold, Gianna M.
Mauer, Joanna Aurica

2-1-2007

Carter, Holly Lynette
Kang, C.M.
Nelson, Stefanie M.
Oatley, Zia Cromer
Ogilvie, Claire L.K.K.

2-13-2007

Arzuaga, Patricia
Cobb, Mary Margaret

2-15-2007

Colon, Josephine

2-22-2007

Walsh, Katherine Patricia

3-8-2007

Brandon, Starcinda N.
Burton, Elizabeth A.
Makki, Amanda

3-13-2007

Lockie, Adrienne Jennings
Taylor, LaShanda

4-4-2007

Arnold, Mercia Elayne

4-5-2007

Daniels, Sherell Dolores

4-18-2007

Foti, Jennifer Elaine

5-15-2007

Espinet, Danielle Mary

5-29-2007

Millenson, Debra A.

5-30-2007

White, Erica S.

6-11-2007

Akinfaderin, Tinuade A.
Akintan, Olufunmilola Abosede
Al-Humadi, Bisma A.
Allburn, Megan D.
Armstrong, Cindy Lynn
Baker, Kellee Genean
Bannister, Adonna Jernaye
Barnes, Hasson D.
Basile, Courtenay Allyson
Bellamy, Gretchen Chantelle
Bernhardt, Victoria Coleman
Billingy, Shana Evril
Blavatt, Kelly Joy
Blissett, Kai A.
Boone, Melissa Renee
Brim, India Karissa
Burkhouse, Carrie Elizabeth
Campbell, Catherine Bolton
Cartwright, Suzanne Perry
Cheatham, Demetris White
Cobb, Stacey Maria
Coleman, Maria Natalia
Cook, Kimberly Antoinette
Cowan, Jennie Mayberry
Coyne, Bridget Anne
Crawford, Marisa
Creighton, Emily Jamieson
Curry Newland, Crystal Ardell
Daley, Michelle Renee
Davit, Barbara Myers
DeMarco, Melanie
Denysyk, Adrienne Yvonne
Diamond, Heather Susanne
Diver, Atinuke Oluwatoyin
Douglas, Lauren Kelly
Dozier, Kercena Angelique
Drobnick, Alexandra Scott
Ellis, Kristen Gayle
Emanuele, Victoria Rose
Emrick, Preeti Vijayakumaran
Fabayo, Ifeolu Amaka
Farid, Shaida Shirmohammadi
Gannon, Janine Patrice
Gasper, Brandie Jean
Geddis, Chanekqua Tylania
Gellman, Erin Mea
Ghim, Michelle Hyun Ju
Gibbs, Francesca Bridgette
Gombeski, Kellie Marie
Goodson, Laura Monique
Gouel, Martha Gabrielle
Greene, Aeisha Kym
Griffith, Jennifer H.
Guastello, Catherine Mary
Gurevitz, Jennifer Leigh
Guyer, Julie Marion
Hampton-El, Syeetah Ann
Harvey, Tiffany LeShawn
Hawkins, Kesha Yvonne
Heiser, Nicole Marie
Helbig, Amy Michele
Hodge, Jennifer Lee
Hodgson, Shannon Michelle
Holsey, Heather Harris
Holtzman, Lauren E.
Hondros, Michelle Lee
Hunter Green, Michelle Denise
In, Mi-Young
Jacobsen, Rebecca Bailey
Jassie, Nicole Erica
Jazayeri-Nejad, Sara
Jenkins, Riza Crystal
Johnson, Carlla Y.
Jones, Tracie Nicole
Kassier, Melissa Lee
Kilpatrick, Kathryn Diane
Kim, Claire Jin
Kim, Jeanie H.
Ko, Denice Shana
Koepsel, Kirsten Marta
Laskey-Donovan, Kathleen Keane
Laughner, Nissa Anne
Lea, Lucinda Laurel
Lee, Michelle Joohyun
Lewin, Devorah M.
Liberman, Shanna Charisse
Locey, Michelle Leona
Luong, Shian Tinh-Nhan
Maddox, Leigh Margaret
Man, Lisa K.
Mannette-Blue, Anjanette
McGrail, Mary Ann
McGuire, Erin Elizabeth
McLean, Kimberly Nicole
Mengisteab, Winta
Miliman, Lisa Beth
Millane, Megan McKinley
Mintz, Trudy A.
Mizell, Hasina Dorothea
Modi, Jasleen Kaur
Monroy, Alexandra
Moore, Ronisha A.
Myung, Sookjung
Narasimhan, Sudha
Nath, Sonia Wadhwa
November, Elizabeth Anne
Parish, Margaret Anne
Partesotti, Rebecca Harbour
Pavlick, Elizabeth Erin
Peace, Lynnell Davis
Pierce, Arika Latise
Piontkowski, Vickie

Pokov, Sofya
Purdie, Debyn Wallace
Regmi, Pooja Adhikary
Reinhard, Ellen Courtney
Rennie, Anika Nadia
Rheinhardt, Monica Marie
Richardson, Joy Annette
Robinson, Dajona
Robinson, Ebony M.
Rogers, Camilla Jean
Rosa, Amye Michelle
Scanlon, Susan Christine
Skinner, Darlene Ann
Smalkin, Maria Roxanne Reyes
Smith, Anya Kamara
Smith, Erin Bronwyn
Solomon, Rhonda Rhey
Sterling, Jaymi Kim
Stuckey, Carla Alethea
Stuehrmann, Deborah Louise
Thayer, Erin Chase
Thomas, Erica Christine
Tran, Phan Ngoc
Tyson, Tennille Francis
Vavala, Kristine Marie
Vernon, Christy Noelle
Walker, Jaclyn Kidwell
Waterhouse, Desmarie Mosco
Watson, Joanna Leigh
Woolf, Kristin Leigh
Wooten-Days, Ayanna Lyons
Yates, Shahenaz Y.
Zenkewicz, Kristine Roman
Ziegler, Yvette Marie

6-13-2007
Ferguson, Juanita Fitchett
Kelley, Shelby Jeanne
Knox, Shannon Andra Sullivan
Mahalingappa, Jennifer Rebecca
Nager, Leigh Hyer

6-15-2007
Gohn, Kristi Ann
Meinzer, Heidi Eileen
Randall, Cynthia Lee

6-18-2007
McDonnell, Amy Elizabeth
Morris, Stephanie

6-20-2007
Clemens, Katy Schuman
Herritt, Jacqueline
Shanahan, Marie Roccapriore
Torre, Karen Maria

6-22-2007
Jardine, Georgianna

6-26-2007
Noll, Alison Kenney

7-3-2007
Hoptman, Virginia Whitner

7-9-2007
Baum, Deborah Brand
Tarlow, Elyana
Wellington, Meredith Kays

7-17-2007
Mills, Nygina Tenay

7-18-2007
Mumme, Bettina

7-20-2007
Deng, Amy Duo

7-25-2007
Boivin, Jennifer Moira
Cumberbatch, Allison E-M

7-30-2007
Lundy, Paulette Ann
Stillwell, Earlynn Mae
von Struensee, Susan

8-7-2007
Curtiss, Danielle Arwen

8-20-2007
Ehrlich, Katerina A.

8-23-2007
Mader, Brenda L.

9-4-2007
Wathen, Joan DeChantal

9-6-2007
Dowling, Stacie Marie
Hollis, Sophia Lorain
Livny, Yael Anne

9-14-2007
Butler, Lisa Darlene
O'Regan, Margaret A.

9-20-2007
Pyndell, Leslie Keyes

10-3-2007
Gooden, Donniece Sharee
Lerner, Carrie Anne DeBarr
Ramson, Angela Franceta

10-16-2007
Maslin, Lori Jane Hahn

11-9-2007
Cox, Amy Diane

11-30-2007
Dovodova, Lachina Chariyevna

12-7-2007
Smith, Stacy L.
Weekes, Camille Claudean Logan

12-11-2007
Abrams, Kristen Leanderson
Adcox, Rachel Johanna
Addorisio, Caitlin A.
Albanese, Kelly Walla
Alexander, Maryan
Allen, Lindsey Anderson
Alves, Sarah Ross
Amerkhail, Jennifer Shepherd
Anderson, Jennifer Ann
Ansari-Cobiella, Pamela
Argeris, Priscilla Delgado
Arn, Kimberly Thorn
Arneaud, Roxanne Jeanine
Asike, Sophie Ifeoma
Atencio, Jill Lynn
Aud, Jennifer Officer
Ayers, Angela Tabitha
Bachman, Jennifer Myers
Bailey, Linda Ellen Caisley
Bakker, Sara Ann
Baldwin, Sally Virginia
Ballard, Evelyn Rebecca
Baum, Melissa
Bell, Alison Elizabeth
Bell, Kate M.
Berkowitz, Lauren M.
Berman, Debra Michele
Berry, Brynne Earlene
Betsill, Emily Kirkland
Bhagat, Kay Hannah
Bianchini, Lauren Jennifer
Bibby-Gerth, Jennifer Angela
Bickoff, Alicia Leibowitz
Bill, Carolyn Stewart
Binstock, Lindsey B.
Birckhead, Jennifer Anne
Biswas, Deborah Eve
Black, Briana Liston
Bleimund, Emily Elizabeth
Boas, Heidi Heyward
Bolden, Jaclyn Brandis
Bollini, Subhashini
Bonner, Alice Arcieri
Bonner, Kerri DeWanda
Bosche, Ashley Ann
Bowman, Brooke Hytovitz
Bowman, Jennifer Curry
Boyce, Lauren Elizabeth
Boyd, Marie Carla
Bradford, Chrisandra O. M.
Brady, Jennifer Lynn
Branch, Lori Mechelle
Bregman, Lauren Rachel
Breslau, Jill Havelin
Briley, Siobhan
Brill, Allison Lane
Brinkmann, Vanessa Renee
Brooks, Sandra Ann
Brown, Katharine Elizabeth
Brucker, Kira Nazelrod
Bryant, Amber Lynn
Buck, Mary Catherine Shea
Buckley, Christine Elizabeth
Burkhardt, Amy Jane
Burton, Sarah Martin
Butkera, Jessica Pauline
Campbell, Martha Megan
Cancienne, Erin Hebert
Cannon, Molly Marie
Carmichael, Aimee Joy
Carvino, Leanne Marie
Casuga, Jay-Anne Bautista
Causey, Sara Elizabeth
Cecil, Patricia Lane
Chambliss, Tarica Priscilla
Chan, Jacqueline Jamie
Chapple, Nicole Aguirre
Cheret, Jaime Alison
Chheda, Monica Navin
Christoph, Erica Lynn
Chun, Milin
Chung, Nancy Kyung
Clair, Kathleen M.
Clark, Robin Jessica
Clarkson, Brooke D.
Clifton, Abby Wilhelmina
Cohen, Allison Marie
Cohen, Tammis
Collopy, Dree Kristin
Colvin, Crista Meghan
Conroy, Aindrea Marie
Cooper, Katherine Anne
Correa, Pamela Maria
Costantino, Christine Mary
Costello, Colleen Marie
Crimm, Nina Bafundo
Cuilhe, Diane Genevieve
Curley, Katherine Ann
Dai, Angela Yijun
Dallo, Amanda Khaled
Datiles, Jacqueline Margaret
Davies, Noellyn Kyung Mee
Davis, Kelly Erin
Davison, Jennifer A.
Dedjinou, Adrienne Crain
DeFraites, Meredith Leigh
Deines, Jennifer Anne
DeMaio, Patricia Marie
Dennis, Kia Sherron Johnson
Deriu, Sara Holman
Desai, Khushi Kirtikant
DeSimone, Theresa Ann
Devonshire, Tiffany Anne
DeWire, Kristen Sentoff
Diener, Kathy Elaine
DiGrado, Kelly Allison
Dill, Jennifer Lee
Dinsmore, Jennifer Aurora
Dombrowski, Rachel Anne
Dornsife, Sandra Ellen
Douglas, Jennifer Celeste
Doyle, Erin Elizabeth
Duffy, Arline Patricia
Duvall, Barbara Elizabeth
Edwards, Christal Elizabeth
Edwards, Lauren Kimberly
Englehart, Mary Margaret
Fegan, Jessica Dorothy
Feindel, Alycia Truax
Fine, Joanna Beth
Finkle, Jessica Michele
Finnan, Mollie Lenore
Fletcher, Courtney Rodgers
Flood, Colleen Brigid
Forbin, Viola
Forrest, Rose Marion
Friedman, Joanna Stanford
Froelicher, Katherine Fowle
Gagliuso, Laura Marie
Gallego, Fabiola
Garrett, Edna Denise
Gart, Melanie Fay
Gartee, Naoina Catherine
Gatto, Denise Marie
Gaw, Tamara Karen
Gehman, Andrea Maria
Georg, Mary Elizabeth
Getman, Elizabeth Fletcher
Gibson, Akilah Tulani
Gilmore, Barbara Constance
Gilmore, Dorcas Raejeana
Gilmore, Nancy Michelle
Goldberg, Amory Rainbow
Goldburn, Tricia Deloris
Goo, Christine Oi Jyn
Gooray, Kristin Nirmala
Gordon, Charlotte Lee
Gosney, Amber Farrington
Gott, Lynsay Kaye
Gragert, Sarah Marie
Gross, Rosa
Grunberger, Rachel Cohen
Grunfeld, Rebecca Elizabeth
Guiffre, Erin Rebecca
Haggins, Amber Nicole
Hall, Carisa Ann

Hardy, Marina Taft
Harrington, Jessica Leigh
Harris, Marilyn Jill
Harris, Rachael Abelson
Harris, Theresa Lynn
Harrison, Rea Janqui
Hassler, Laura Marie Kelly
Haun, Ashley Carol
Hawana, Joanne Samir
Hedge, Ashley Fields
Henderson, Heather Marie
Hermosillo, Mary Anastasia
Herrera, Stephanie Marie
Herrington, Jessica Susannah
Hill, Abigail Leah
Hirz, Gabrielle Golda
Hobbins, Margaret Bennington
Holden, Katherine Marie
Huang, Cara Shyng
Huber, Frances E.
Hull, Rachel Lynn
Hupman, Emily Hill
Iacovelli, Corianne
Ingram, Audrey Laning
Jackson, Alexina Guiomar
Jackson, Ashley Latney
Jacoby, Christine Elizabeth
Jester, Amy Elizabeth
Johnson, Alice Booher
Johnson, Eva Wilkinson
Johnson, Marla Yvette
Joice, Veronica Justina
Jordan, Erika Alston
Jorge, Loide Rosa
Juarez, Berenice
Kanner, Rachel Joy
Kaps, Maria Theresa
Kaur, Mini
Kedia, Soma Ranu
Kelly, Jennifer Ellis
Kim, Sue Haksoo
Kim, Yekyung
Kirby, Colleen Michelle
Knowles, Elaine Harrington
Koethe, Alice Margaret
Kologe, Lauren Leigh
Kotula, Sarah Ann
Kpaduwa, Chinwe Omena
Krametbauer, Katherine Seitz
Krause, Emily Irene
Krause, Marisa Giselle
Kunkoski, Victoria Rose
Labiano-Abello, Annette Maggie
Lackey, Laurel Kelley
Laguerre-Brown, Caroline Wendy
Lamptey, Odaale Koshie
Lanigan, Maureen Frances
Lannom, Linda Bean
Lattanzi, Elizabeth Anne
Laventure, Glenda
Lawless, Lydia Eve Dale
Lawrence, Tanya Adrienne
Lee, Jeanette Yeong
Lerman, Leah Victoria
Levenson, Emily Lange
Levesque, Angela Andrea
Levinson, Andi Michelle
Levitas, Daphne Sophie
Lewandowski, Jennifer Lynn
Lewis, Lisa Gayle
Lewis, Megan Amber
Liedquist, Clare Caroline
Lord, Sara Beth
Mackoff, April Birnbaum
Marquardt, Sarah
May, Wendi D. Finch
McConnell, Simona
Morgan, Sharon Oras
Purdy, Erin Brady
Rapport, Adele
Reading, Teresa Garleta
Rollins, Turkessa Bynum
Schopler, Liesel Johanna
Smith, Mary Elizabeth
Spear, Carlie Marie Bloxom
Stover, Christina M.
Straughn, Patricia Barr
Suter, Erica J.
Swift, Nicole B.
Truman, Erin D.
Turner, Alexis Buckhannon
Williams, Jessica Kirsten
Yuzuik, Josaphine Babcox

12-12-2007

An, Sunwook
Ashley, Meghan Lynn
Bacon, Pavitra
Baumgartner, Julie Mumm
Brown, Colleen Theresa
Carr, Callie Jean
Cathell, Emily Ellen
Claassen, Sarah Marie Rempel
Colangelo, Sara A.
Collier, Tara Marie Yutzy
Fisher, Jill Ann
Fitzgerald, Staci Eloise
Forbes, Keesha Pinnock
Gravely, Elizabeth Passyn
Haaf, Kate Elizabeth Stewart
Heiser, Kristin
Hovey, Carrie Timlin
Hughes, Christina Marie
Knauer, Julie Ann
Lange, Kathryn Anne
LoBosco, Julia Ann
Loria, Jessica Wible
Lynn, Morgan Jessica
Lyons, Jessica Bevin
MacKenzie, Amber Lynn
Major, Amy Lynn
Malayaman, Suthima
Malik, Sarah Ilyas
Marenberg, Jill Rombro
Marine, Jessica Frase
Marshall, Michele Anne
Matey, Amanda Witham
Mattonen, Kimberly Ann
Mattson, Courtney Marie
Mazzulli, Tiffany Anne
McCann, Julie Christin
McCarthy, Erin Theresa
McClernan, Kathleen Marie
McCormick, Caitlin Suzanne
McDermott, Mara Beverly Sitzman
McDonough, Kathryn Sharkey
McGeogh, Michelle Marie
McKeown, Alexandra Albinak
McManus, Catherine Mary
McWhorter, Peggie Nichole
Meiser, Verena
Mendoza, Melissa Jeanne
Merrick, Marissa L.
Merryman, Jennifer Dietrich
Metzger, Kedri Anne
Mfume, Melanie Murray
Michalski, Eliza Hull
Migliorini, Lauren Kathleen
Miles, Melody Antoinette
Miller, Pia Janine
Miller, Radhika Meagin Singh
Miller, Rebecca Lee
Mims, Keisha Elizabeth
Misler, Michelle Saffan
Moche, Margalit Alexandra
Mocho, Megan Michelle
Moldenhauer, Meridith Honey
Molina, Heather Kanani
Molpus, Anna Elizabeth
Monahan, Katherine Kay
Moran, Lindsey Julia
Morgan, Sarah Elizabeth
Murphy, Catherine Risdon
Murray, Sarah A.
Narang, Puja Lakhi
Nath, Amala
Neuhaus, Rhonda Sara
Ng, Shirley Yee
Noonan, Katherine Marie
Norris, Lindsay Nicole
North, Bernice Dansoah
O'Brien, Cara Leigh
O'Brien, Meghan Anne
O'Bryan, Rachael Lee
O'Connell, Erin Anna
O'Connor, Sarah Battaile
Obiora, Jennifer AdaObi
Okeke, Darah McCray
Onsager, Erica Welch
Orteza, Audrey Lee
Osberg, Joanne Frances Phillips
Osler, Danielle Marcla
Oza, Rachana Dipak
Pacanowsky, Laura Ann
Pace, Stacy Rebecca
Pacheco, Nubia Nelly
Parraz, Deborah Cooper
Peterson, Christine Nichole
Phillips, Anjali Wagle
Pogranicy, Katherine Janet
Pollara, Jody Renee
Posner, Tara Jane
Powell, Morgan Elizabeth
Pryce, Melissa Alesia
Quinlan, Tracy Ann
Rampulla, Jennifer Christine
Ransom, Angela Jeanette
Ray-Dulany, Naomi
Reece, Emily Callie
Reimelt, Jessica Scott
Renehan, Maureen Megan
Reuwer, Megan Lynn
Reyes, Sioban
Rhodes, Mary Elizabeth
Rice, Sarah Whynne Finnegan
Richardson, Krystin Jane
Richardson, Sabrina Cuthrie
Richardson, Shayna Rene
Riggs, Kate Mary
Ripley, Rebecca Brannan
Robinson, Kristin M.
Rochino, Jennifer Nicolo
Rodriguez, Amaris
Roig, Maribel
Romanoff, Laurie Jennifer
Ronisky, Raquel
Ross, Jennifer
Ross, Kristen Marie
Ross, Shannon Moore
Rothwell, Kimberly Percell
Ryan, Britnie Alicia
Safai, Raeka
Sahaf, Monica Nazira
Saladyga, Meredith Joy
Savage, Taren Kay
Savitz, Gwendolyn McKee
Savoy, Katherine Anne
Sawyer, Christina Abigail
Schneider, Kate Zoe
Schwartz, Abagail Tobiah
Scott, Nikkisha Zodiah
Seabron, Myriem
Seidel, Karyn Lynn
Selwood, Margaret Elena Lynch
Shadle, Leah Teresa
Shah, Anik Ajay
Shah, Nisha Priyavadan
Shah, Reena Kirit
Shanahan, Aileen Marie
Shannahan, Mary Carol
Shapiro, Ariel Ephraim
Shedd, Leslie Catherine
Sherwin, Loni Jean
Shiflett, Rachael Margaret
Shoemaker, Tara Kayte
Shrestha, Ranju Rani
Siehndel, Kathryn Carey
Silverman, Kelly Vanderzell
Simmons, Rachel Claire
Simon, Marcia Jill
Simon, Maria Christina
Skoczylas, Robin Jean
Smith, Karen Elizabeth
Smith, Sakeenah
Snyder, Erin Hayley
Soares, Jeanette Marie
Solomon, Rachel Elizabeth
Southall, Orian Carlena
Spaccarelli, Arianne Michelle
Spangenberg, Malgorzata
Sparks, Lisa Danielle
Spartana, Jessica Leigh
Spoto, Apollina Justina Casal
Srinivasan, Aparna
St. Hilaire, Aimee Beth
Stanton, Taren N.
Steinle, Allison Theresa
Storie, Alaina Lee
Streagle, Sabrina Calice
Stubbs, Margaret Hinkson
Sumner, Deryn Anne
Sutton, La Toya Colette
Sybblis, Nickola Nadia
Tanner, Knia
Tansey, Rachel Gabrie
Teliska, Holly Lisa
Temple, Karmen Juanita
Termini, Jennifer Ann
Thakker, Nisha Ganpat
Thomson, Laura Rackmales
Thornblad, Kristin Anne
Thorpe, Shelia LeVon
Timmins, Megan Nolan Houck
Tobin, Harper Jean
Todd, Jacklyn Marie
Tonsager, Lindsey Lori
Tossell, Elizabeth Ida

Townsend, Melissa Jill
Townsend, Susanne Elise
Trepetin, Yelena
Trinward, Kathleen Jabar
Ulrick, Maeve Zana
Unell, Bela Sarah
Vaughan, Janel Annette
Viglianti, Rachel Ingram
Voss, Kelly Dionna
Wagner, Cecilia Brigid
Walden, Elisabeth Susanne
Walker, Sally Luella
Wall, Annemarie
Washington, Maya Louise
Wasp, Courtney Ann
Watkins, Alison Julia
Watkowski, Kristina Louise
Watts, SaMonna Latay
Webb, Margaret Elizabeth
Wesco, Crystal Davina
Whitehead, DelYvonne Monique
Whitehurst, Jennifer Lynn
Widmayer, Amber Janel
Wiles, Kathleen Marie
Wilkes, Tamiya Nicole
Wilkin, Terri Lee
Williams, Joyce Ann
Williams, Krystal Star
Williams, Natasha Hattie
Williamson, Marot Roelker
Wilson, Alicia Lynn
Wilson, Jennifer Leigh
Winch, Jeannine
Wolszon, Jamie Kujawa
Woolley, Michelle Lynn
Worthington, Maria Nora
Wrathall, Meghan Ryan
Wyant, Michelle Ann
Xenakis, Aileen Brennan
Yaker, Beth Erin
Yasui, Lynne Mariko
Yun, Kerry Elizabeth
Zektick, Barbara Sharon
Zimonjic, Milica
Zwiech Arnouk, Aneta

12-17-2007

Campbell, Patricia Ellen
Castorina, Janine
Weatherspoon, Gladys Minerva

12-20-2007

Donaher, Donna Marie
Holland, Diane Griffin
Maiolo, Tina Marie
O'Brien, Kerry Ann
Person, Cynthia Ranck
Pisano, Anne Marie
Taitano, Victoria King
Teich, Joan Fagan
Tousi, Shaghayegh

1-3-2008

Absher, Martha Rohani
Ademiluyi, April Teniade
Alexander, Jennifer Libby
Ball, Nelisbeth Yariani
Bercovici, Michelle Faye
Bolen, Sarah Rebecca
Cronin, Melody Tagliaferri
Egbuonu, Chizoba Nwamaka
Hanzel, Lauren Faust
Keller-Micheli, Alison Marie
Kim, Grace Hanna
Robinson, Catherine Louise
Scindian, Kelly Marissa
Shapiro, Harriett Wendy
Steiner, Amy Kay
Thomas, Victoria Louise
Tilley, Camille Elise
Wilburn, Frances Charlotte

1-4-2008

Carroll, Priscilla Elizabeth Newton
Clark, Denise Marie
Hughes, Christine Grinde
Knizak, Karen Ann

1-7-2008

Ragan, Maureen

1-8-2008

Puett, Melissa Anne

1-15-2008

Bowers, Phillipa
Stuart, Birgit Dachtera

1-22-2008

Ward, Jennifer L.

1-23-2008

Tien, Wendy

1-31-2008

Harper, Allison Lynn

2-7-2008

Ohtagaki, Johna
Puttagunta, Rupa Ranga
Rhodes, Senta Fiona
Wiseman, Josephine Porter

2-25-2008

Puckett, Tiffany Sharnay
Freeman-Watkins, Cherlyn Francis
West, Felicia Banks

2-29-2008

Johnson, Kathryn Chase

3-6-2008

Allen, Sonja LaVita
Kim, Helen Jung-Eun
Lonergan, Sharon A.A.

3-7-2008

Mitrani, Adriana Leon

3-17-2008

White, Lindsey Anne

4-2-2008

Bergesen, Kristin Lynnette

4-3-2008

Thomas, Christina M.

4-14-2008

Long, Rachell Florence

5-1-2008

Whelton, Cara Joan

6-4-2008

Bennet, Caressa Davison
Darling, Stephanie Lynne
Rush, Regan Lindsay

6-5-2008

Arden, Mary Kathryn
Garver, Claudia Kathleen
Shah, Pooja Ketan Galliara
Veppumthara, Julie Thomas
Wahl, Catherine Elizabeth
Williams, Jillian Aretha

6-12-2008

Isaacson, Virginia Tate
Jones Bosier, Tanya Monique
Marlin, Lesley Pate
Spencer, Jessica DeGroote
Welch, Colleen Suzanne

6-17-2008

Adams, Nyree Michelle
Adler, Stacey Lynn
Amiel, Alexandra Marisa
Aspiazu, Maria
Atkins, Susan Marie
Bader, Jennifer
Bailey, Suzanne
Barnwell, Sarah Ruth
Barr, Melanie Renee
Baum, Ann Slane
Behbehani, Erin Ann
Bergstrom, Lisa Mara Yurwit
Berner, Patricia Anne
Brady, Jennifer Jean
Brown, Alice Elizabeth
Burton, Tiffany Lynn
Cantave, Gabrielle V.
Caspar, Laura A.
Chai, Susan A.
Chandler, Hillary Gordon
Chase, Kelly Victoria
Christian, Kristin Lynn Lewis
Chudnovsky, Robin Leah Rietz
Clarke, Tamika Patrice
Clements, Julie Ann
Cline, Sarah Dawn
Coll, Rachel Elizabeth
Collins, Agnieszka
Dameron, Allison Jo
DeWire, Puja Khanna
Diokno, Vivian Perdomo
Dixon, Tai Aisha
Doane, Devon Cyle
Donaldson, Tiffany Ann
Dorsett, Sarah Renee
Dourney, Katarzyna
Duquette, Donna Marie
Engstrom, Amy Elizabeth
Evans, Janine Marie
Everhart, Lora Tarley
Faust, Whitney Stafford
Ferguson, Savonne Lynn
Field, Sarah Elizabeth
Flynn, Gillian Ann
Flynn, Maria Rebecca
Frierson, Jakisha Ariel
Ghuma, Ranya Abdulmotaleb
Gile, Dawn Danielle
Gilmore, Shannon Amber
Golshani, Leah Frances
Goodman, Diane
Gorelik, Jennifer B.
Gorum, Luciana Marie Evette
Graham, Caroline Preis
Green, Shaloe Tiffany
Hendi, Azadeh Mahoozi
Hill, LaJulia Marie
Hirschmann, Theresa Kathleen
Hobbins, Emily Godwin
Hoffman, Amanda Eve
Houston, Kylean Kariel
Howard, Sarah Downing
Hugh, Margaret Hijin
James, Kelly Elizabeth
Kaleina, Georgene Marie
Kargbo, Mariatu
Kazadi, Kaba-Kabi Ann
Kehinde, Yetunde Bukky
Keller, Amy Lynn
Kelley, Jennifer Anne
Kelotra, Ritu
Kent, Jennifer Lauren
Kern, Jessica Scavia
Kim, Susannah Hy
Kish, Marisa Frances
Kissel, Adriana Laura
Konzman, Eleanor Jean
Kroll, Carrie Anne
Krull, Megan Mary
Kumor, Amber Leigh
Lake, Elizabeth Anne
Lawrence, Anuoluwapo Elizabeth
LeBlanc, Kimberly Sabrina
Lee, Susan Robinson
Litman, Deborah Sharon
Long, Sheila Wiley
Mair, Eva R.
Mayer, Jennifer L.
Mazo, Samantha Lauren
McCurdy, Marisa C.
McDonald, Tracey Nicole
McKay, Natasha Todman
McKinney, Jenifer Eleni
Mellick, Erica S.
Mittra, Megh Milan
Molayem, Susannah
Mondenge, Yvie Maghemba
Moore, Adia Belicia
Moorefield-Shraibman, Adrienne Teresa
Movsessian, Leana Kay
Moye, Michelle T.
Neal, Kimberly Hankins
Niemira, Anneke H.
Novello, Laura Joy
O'Dell, Kerry Clinton
Oduro, Cecilia Olivia
Ohm, Tracey Michelle
Onyango, Caroline Owira
Padmanabhan, Anita
Parikh, Shikha
Peart, Daenia Laureese
Pentecost, Elizabeth Squires
Platt, Terrilynn Dietz
Plunkett, Kaelia Shatana
Primus-Theodore, Sharon Leah
Prud'homme, Arlene Koerber
Rain, Kelly Marie
Ramchandani, Nindiya Gobind
Ramey, Elinor Carson
Sachs, Lesley Bowling
Salaam, Amirah Sabah
Salahuddin, Syeda Saleela
Sandifer, Candace Louise
Schaffer, Karla Lyn
Segal, Jennifer Beth
Serrano-Rivera, Aida
Settlage, Rachel Delia
Shafi, Naseema Begum
Sheikh-Salah, Maya Ahmed
Shepard, Meaghan Leigh
Singh, Harleen Kaur
Smith, Janell Talia

Snead, Ursula Danielle
Sorrento, Christina
Stafford, Hope Lynn
Starkey, Anna Elizabeth
Steele, Heather Rachel
Taylor, Dawn Michelle
Thornton, Courtney Danielle
Tipon, Patricia Valerio
Tran, Carolyn Hong Van
Trento, Andrea William
Varoski, Kaitlin S.
Viola, Rebekah Pearl
Waldrup, Sherrie Marie
Walker de Rodriguez, Amanda Kristen
Wallace, Katrina Lynn
Wallace, Lauren Elizabeth
Walters, Lisa Nicole
Webb, Constance Delorise
Whitehall Wolfe, Keisha Lisette
Williams, Carmen Leeann
Williams, Danielle Nicole
Williams, Sharon James
Wong, Bonny Chong-Wai
Yeluri, Swapna
Yoo, Hannah
Zurowski, Kristin LeClair

6-26-2008
Deligiorgis, Maria
Dietzmann, Elizabeth Moore

7-1-2008
Rodriguez, Lilian

7-2-2008
Miller-Fagan, Lauren Brooke

7-7-2008
Lucas, Tina Louise

7-8-2008
Coventry, Anne Woodbridge

7-9-2008
Flynn, Tara Marie

7-16-2008
Caetano, Christina-Rose

7-29-2008
Cain Gordon, Marilyn Patricia

8-8-2008
DeMarco, Juliane Theresa
Sinclair, Kathleen Hanlon

8-19-2008
Crow, Melissa Ellen

8-22-2008
Shafi, Amina Hamida

8-26-2008
Waddell, Jeri Leeper

9-4-2008
Hassan, Meagan Elizabeth
Herman, Jessica Kusek

9-10-2008
Polozie, Katarina Boer

9-26-2008
Watts, Alissa Anne

10-30-2008
Hite, LaToya Ann
Johnson, Adria Leta
Lucas, Erika E.
Miller, Jo Ann Camm
Mitrenga, Terry Kay

11-12-2008
Sweeney, Susan Beth

12-16-2008
Abbott, Renee Ann
Abii, Ezenwanyi Diane
Adkins, Lauren Danielle
Ahmad, Azizah Yasmin
Ahmadi-Torshizi, Sohair
Alexander, Lory Dione
Ali, Ruhi Fatima
Allen, Gwendolyn Marie
Allen, Janette Louise
Allen, Kayon Karima
Amirthalingam, Vidhya B.
Anderson, Ann-Marie Allison
Anjou, Kanita Elaine
Aracil, Emilie Claire
Archer, Colleen Susan
Arriaga, Kristina Marie
Asher, Simma Miriam
Backus, Alison Brown
Baker, Amanda Yoshiko
Baker, Caroline Lancaster
Bangit, Eliza Navarro
Banvard, Honor Deming
Barber, Tanyka Monét
Barron, Leah Katherine
Bartee, Kenysha Dione
Bartelma, Katy Marie
Baskin, Aeran Nicole
Battersby, Luann Tunison
Batz, Amanda Ann
Beamer, Shannon Elizabeth
Bean, Robin Denise
Beck, Lauren Elizabeth
Becker, Lauren Elizabeth
Becker, Sheena Danielle
Behbahani, Saman
Belgorodsky, Anna
Bell, Janell Nicole
Bennett, Lauren Elizabeth
Bernard, Melissa Elise
Berry-Lewis, Sylvia Annette
Bertumen, Abigail Lynn
Betourney, Chanda Marie
Bhatia, Anita
Billiet, Christina Nicole
Bloom, Heather Alison
Bolter, Michelle Carhart
Boston, Jessica Barnes
Botek, Michelle Marie
Boucher, Lauren Christie
Bourcicot, Yvette Karen Wood
Boyer, Christine Diana
Brady, Erin Marie
Brandt, Catherine Grace
Brannigan, Susan Lynda
Briggerman, Lauren Elyse
Brownley, Holland Catherine
Bruner, Nicolette Isabel
Bye, Catherine Boult
Calvert, Kathryn Elizabeth
Cammack, Ashley F.
Capaccio, Antoinette Christine
Capeloto, Tessa Victoria
Capodilupo, Lindsay Rae
Cardona, Elizabeth Durham
Caron-Moroney, Christina L.
Casadei, Romina Anna
Ceesay, Joy Amienatta
Chaffin, Stacy Marie
Chase, Rosanna Olund Spurr
Chen, Catherine
Chilson, Jodie Lynn
Choi, Mary Jin Kyung
Christopher, Lauren Stephanie
Clark, Jennifer Jo
Clark, Kelly Ann
Clark, Mika Shakiya
Clark, Nancy Stanley
Clark, Patrice Olivia
Clary, Colleen Elizabeth
Cleaver, S. Whitney
Combs, Nancy Lynn
Conkwright, Sarah Elizabeth
Conneely, Nancy Theresa
Coolidge, Melinda Ruth
Crist, Erin Bond Knoska
Cronenberg, Jennifer Elaine
Cuadra, Tabatha Karina
Cubas, Claudia Raquel
Curtin, Julie Farrell
Curtis, Teri Lyn
Dabbs, Hannah Elizabeth
Daly, Sabrina Canfield
Datnoff, Emily Marie
Davis, Diana Marie
de la Piedra, Daniela María
Deady, Anne Meredith
Dennison, Molly Alexandra
Diallo, Aissatou Kesso
Dickerson, Kathryne C.
Dieguez, Pamela Eclar
Dillard, Jennifer Mae Carlisle
Dillingham, Heather Nicole
DiNapoli, Kellie Kai-Yi
Dodrill, Lauren Michele
Dominique, Alesha Monique
Dopplick, Renee Suzanne
Dougherty, Kathryn Anne
Dove, Sylvia Katherine
Downs, Anjali Nilesh Chokshi
Dwyer-Heidkamp, Sarah Elizabeth
Eaton, Melody Khalatbari
Edwards, Teresa Cho
Edwards-Ford, Meghan Cele
Elliott, Amy Silva
Ellsworth, Karen Sue
Eshelman, Suzanne Chandler
Feeley, Cheryl Ann
Feldman, Ellen Belle
Ferrell, Visa Rose
Finney, Amber Keyona
Fionda, Laura Elizabeth
Fitzgerald, Ellen Kay
Forton, Andrea Christine
Foss, Jodi Lynn
Frant, Nina Refowitz
Friedman, Alyssa Sara
Friesen, Tiffany Erin
Gao, Anna Kay
Garcia, Adrienne Mika
Garner, Keisha Ann
Gates, Charisse Yvette
George, Jessica Perry
Getinet, Yadankush
Getty, Meghan Dal
Gill, Celena Pearl
Girma, Tsega
Gitangu, Meredith Loomis
Glasgow, Julie Kathleen
Glassman, Lisa Haas
Gomes, Sonya Olivia
Greenspoon, Marni Sara
Grimm, Jodie Lauren
Hickey, Kathryn Lynne
Huff, Marcia Nicole
Kowalczyk, Tara Elizabeth
Lewis, Alicia Donohue
Lopez, Helena S.
Murray, Cara Chasney
Ornstein, Susan Cecilia Goldhar
Pallozzi, Angela Davis
Salerno, Cara Goeller
Salsbury, Rebecca C.
Sampson, Alexandra Patrice Eikner
Stevenson, Chervonne Colon
Tripplaar, Maria C.
Walsh, Emily Rose
Wilkerson, Gina Elizabeth
Zorc, Bethany Ann

12-17-2008
Akin, Wendi Moy
Arnaoutakis, Hillary H.
Baum, Laruen Elizabeth
Bernstein, Lauren Joy
Bixby, Christina Medzius
Brecher, Lindsay Elise
Brooks, Susan Lehman
Coleman, Megan E.
Duncan, Colleen Rose
Engel, Marlee Miller
Fleming, Shari Hathaway
Good, Tamara Renee
Goodman, Lauren Ross
Greene, Tina Deloris
Greenstein, Ilana Sara
Gresko, Joyce Elaine
Griffin, Amy Lynne
Griffins, Melissa Elizabeth
Grogans, Kathleen
Gupta, Puja
Gutrick, Michele Elaine
Hamer, Jennifer Eileen
Hamilton Evert, Alice Sarah
Hanley, Jennifer Ann
Hardy, Heather Kathleen
Harlow, Britt Elisa
Harvey, Erica Rachel
Hassanali, Sabrina
Hassinger, Kristine Raak
Hatcher, Amy Elizabeth
Haubenreich, Sheerin N. S.
Hawk, Elisha Nicole
Haynos, Elizabeth Ann
Henson, Camille Rogerstine
Henson, Trudy Charlene
Hesch, Jennifer Marie
Hester-Haddad, Allison
Hikel, Natalie Embrey
Hill, Melissa Ann
Hill, Sarah Louise
Hines, Jernita Romaine
Hofmeister, Ashley Elizabeth
Holloway Hill, Deborah Ann
Hopkins, Andrea Kay
Horn, Meghan Colleen
Howell, Veronica Lynn
Huang, Priscilla
Hubbell, Jennifer Megan

Hui, Irene
Hummel, Allison Lee
Hummel, Kathryn Elizabeth
Huyler, Suzanne Elizabeth
Immler, Jessica Marie
Iwarere, Oluseyi Omolara
Jacob, Meredith Williams
Jacobs, Jessica Gail
Jafarzadeh, Razeyeh
Jalbert, Gina Louise
James, Tanisha Ann
Jochim Boote, Christine Adelle
Johnson, Asia Malika
Johnson, Maureen J.
Johnson, Stephanie Louise
Johnson, Zinnaeah Danielle
Johnston, Kristin Ann
Jones, Mary Elizabeth
Jordan, Danielle Elizabeth
Josephs, Serena Claire
Jung, Yuri
Kamphaus, Natalie Grace
Kang, Jennifer Ae-Rie
Kanive, Pratibha Subbaramu
Kashani, Shiva Zeraat
Katz, Jennifer Lynn
Katz, Ruth Orit
Kay, Ashley Devon
Kays, Tammy Nibal
Keegan, Michele Lynn
Keller, Elizabeth Ann
Kernan, Kimberly Tracy
Kim, Lena Yejoon
King, Heather Nicole
Kinnaird, Kendra Claire
Kline, Regina
Kolia, Zeenat Basirmohmad
Kolo, Carly Rayne
Konoshima, Taro
Kravitz, Samantha Hope
Kreisel, Johanna Michaels
Krishna, Anupriya
Krupka, Lauren Jill
Kubicz, Mary Barbara
Kudchadkar, Meagan Vinoda
Kulkarni, Deepti Ashok
Kuperstein, Anna Romaniouk
Laarkamp, Faith Renye
Lacey, Sarah Farrar
Landesberg, Cynthia Diana
Landgren, Celia Elizabeth
Landsman, Jennifer Leigh
Langlois, Christina Renate
Langston, Nicole Elizabeth
Lanham, Jayni Anita
Lau, Linda Chi Yee
Lawler, Katherine Anne
Lawrence, Deliah Dorothea
Leary, Shannon Clare
Lenoci, Kimberly Joy
Leung, Bonita Yuen Hua
Lichtman, Sherri Ellen
Lierman, Brooke Elizabeth
Lim, Mariel Gail
Linebaugh, Melissa Blythe
Livingston, Latoya Alicia
Lizondo, Maria Guadalupe
Locke, Amy
Lucas, Erika Leigh
Lucas, Jennifer Keturah
Ludet, Diana Valeria
Lynch, Erica Noelle
Lynch, Kara Kiminsky
Mack, Virginia Mae
Malinowski, Karen Renee
Mamana, Carla
Mann, Sarah Dorothy
Mann, Tracy Marie
Mannisi, Lisa Marie
Manuel, Katy Michele
Martin, Julia Claire
Martin, Vanessa Elizabeth
Martinez, Melissa Ong
Maskew, Patricia Ann
Mathur, Rachna
Mauro, Amy Constance
Mayor, Mejebi Toritseju
McCarthy, Erin Elizabeth
McCaulley, Erica Anne
McCliggott, Mary Rollings
McCoy, Erin Nicole
McDermott, Meaghan Colleen
McGough, Kristin Leigh
McGowan, Mollie Marie
McNamara, Elizabeth Maeve
McPartland, Amy Elizabeth
McWhorter, Erica Breeon
Mehlman, Dayna Stacey
Meiring, Christina Colleen
Mendez, Michelle Natalia
Mercado, Vashti
Messina, Karyne Constance
Milad, Sarah Selim
Millar, Melissa Anne
Miller, Erin Christen
Minkoff, Dinah Melamed
Mintz, Christine Louise
Mitchell, Heather Kathleen
Mohan, Kavita
Mohla, Abha
Monaghan, Ronni Haertig
Moore, Ashley Candice
Morales, Veronica Wendy
Morris, Jillian Sara
Mulford, Allison Marlo
Mulnick, Gabrielle Anna
Murray, Jolene Kay
Murray, Simyeon Tiffany
Naik, Lina Prakash
Nardone, Nellie Jean
Narsavage, Sarah Lynn
Newman, Johanna Lee
Nicholas, Janelle Nicole
Nitsch, Jeane Teresa
Nolan, Robyn Bari
Norris, Christine Formas
Nowottnick, Kelly Moore
O'Connor, Megan Danielle
O'Shea, Holly Denise
Okoroigbo, Edith Uche
Richards, Elizabeth Meltzer
Ridgeway, Julie Evelyn
Rodgers, Dana Aline
Saler, Mindy Mez
Shpigelman, Viktoriya Mikityanskaya
Stitely, Lila Zoe
Torzilli, Susan Hoppock
Vaira, Tiffany Mead
West, Christine Sachiko Khim
Wikner, Marina Ann Manuson

12-18-2008

Arora, Manali Shah
Beall, Suzanne Sable
Berry, Tiffany Jeanne
Black, Ellen Tallerico
Bowen, Amy
Collins, Tiffani Renee Sterrette
Daniels, Candes Alfie Williams
Datta, Monica Sethi
Fox, Jennifer Tyrrell
Glasner, Ariel Samuel
Klein, Deborah Schabes
Knight, Heidi P.
Kondratyuk, Hana Rose
Larin, Nicole Lauren Zeichner
Levine, Marjorie Rosenfelt
Morentz, Leeann Rosnick
Olatoye, Oyebisi Omolade
Panfil, Sylvia T.
Park, Jennifer Eileen Delong
Pelham, Linda Jean Fletcher
Petroni, Colleen Elizabeth
Pettiquoi, Florence Yamah
Pettway, Elizabeth Burkett
Pfahler, Melissa Ann
Phillips, Lauren Rabouin
Piel, Rita Jennifer
Pisani, Kristen Mary
Plater, Marja Kia
Poff, Lacey Anne
Polen, Melyssa Marie
Popp, Sandra Lynn
Praske, Lauren Anne
Pugliese, Elizabeth Marie
Purcell, Joy Maryel
Quach, Katrina Yujian Pei
Quincosa, Jessica Ann
Racicot, Jaclyn Leigh
Rahamim, Miya Sarah
Rakityanskaya, Galina
Ramos, Roselyn Yvonne
Randolph, Tiffany Diane
Rasmussen, Jennifer Dawn
Raszewski, Melissa Faye
Rauskolb, Melina Amal
Recker, Ashley Louise
Reitter, Breck Ayrn
Remsberg, Loren Andrea
Reynolds, Deena Leigh
Rezvani-Bidgoli, Shahrzad
Rhine, Sarah Spangler
Rice, Courtney Anne
Rich, Teri René
Riemer, Rebecca Phillips
Ringel, Jessica Michele
Rivers, Jacquelyn Linette Antonia
Robinson, Deniece Nicole
Rodibaugh, Jennifer Jei
Roll, Carrie Ann
Rolston, Rani Vanessa
Rook, Julie Elizabeth
Rosenfeld, Sionne Catherine
Ross, Sarah Valenta
Roussos, Markella Joanna
Russ, Sarah Elizabeth
Ryan, Brigid Julia
Ryan, Janice Maureen
Ryan, Nicole Harvey
Ryon-Walthall, Anna K.
Sagri, Alissa Victoria
Sahai, Kavita
Samuelson, Heather Faye
Sanet, Jessica Erin
Santiago, Rowena Cecilia
Sawyer, Michelle Renee
Schandler, Karen Miller
Schichor, Nina Hirschfeld
Schlanger, Lauren Jordana
Schmidt, Amanda Elizabeth
Schmidt, Colby Lee
Schmiedel, Mary Elizabeth
Schuster, Jaime Lauren
Settles, Katrina Belinda
Sevigny, Amy Taylor
Shapiro, Paula
Share, Alison Lowrie
Shea, Ariel Armstrong
Shefter, Frances Lynn
Shepherd, Cori Michelle
Sherman, Sarah Beatrice
Sidhu, Khiran Kaur
Sierra, Laura Elena
Six, Anne Kathleen
Skillman, Jessica Leigh
Skogsberg, Kristen Helaine
Smith, Cynthia Michelle
Smith, Ellen Elizabeth
Smith, Emily Letts
Smith, Jennifer Schoonmaker
Smith, Shontell Melissa
Snyder, Leigh Ann
So, Candice Ada Ching
Staker, Nellie Anne
Stanczewski, Tina Marie
Stepnowski, Elizabeth Marie
Sterling, Stephanie Misty
Stevens, Andrea Michele
Stevenson, Lisa Doup
Stewart-Ponder, Gitana Yvonne
Stinnette, Jennifer Hope
Stopp, Courtney Lynn
Stoudt, Clare Lenore
Stover, Mariah Danielle
Strause, Angela Marie
Strzegowski, Rebecca Woods
Stuart, Kimberleigh Andrea
Stubbs, Jessica Lynn
Sykes, Ranelle Elese
Tadvalkar, Rashmee Ravindra
Tan, Chrisna
Tan-Aquino, Peilin
Thomas, Misty Carin
Throsen, Megan Celeste
Tiedemann, Susan Lee
Tiemeyer, Lindsay Sam
Titford, Kathryn Elizabeth
Tobolowsky, Deborah Marisa
Torain, Melanie Deatra
Toungara, Macani
Travis, Lauren Elizabeth
Troen, Nicole Ann
Tulin, Leah J.
Turner, Christina Elizabeth
Turner, Rita Jean
VanBelleghem, Stacey Lynn
Vaughan, Regan Kelley
Vehar-Kenyon, Katherine Nicole
Velasquez, Pilar Francisca
Vroman-Lee, Ashley Kristin
Vu, Laura Thuy
Wachtel, Melissa Joy
Walker, Joeann Etheline
Walter, Jamie Lynn
Walton, Anne Keith
Wang, Qun
Ward, Kara Michelle
Warnes, Lindsay Nichole

Warrington, Amanda Irene
Watson, Danielle Oriana
Watson, Denisha Arnice
Watt, Jami Michele
Watts, Ambrea Nicole
Weinrich, Kathryn Fitz
Weissman, Naureen Rashid
Welan, Joy Levin
Wells, Tiffany Nicole
Wendt-Taczak, Cheri Patrice
West, Nyasha Augusta
Wetmore, Caryn Siegel
White, Erica Meeks
Whitelock, Julia Kim
Whitlock, Morgan Anne
Wiesner, Laurie Quaife
Williams, Suntrease Wynique
Willis, Tamberneshia Necole
Wilson, Erika K.
Wineholt, Adrienne
Winstead, Beverly Leshea
Wolfe, Mandy Mariah
Wong, Verónica Alvarez
Woodcock, Katrina Ksander
Wozny, Kathryn Jeannine
Wright, Abby Christine
Wyles, Diana Kimberly
Wynn, Bilon Mati
Young, Kate Elizabeth
Yu, Alleen
Zdeb, Sara Schofield
Zinsmeister, Hillary Lane
Zounes, Sherryl Sydel

12-23-2008
Berlage, Tanya Dobash
Brodsky, Renee Kart

12-30-2008
Betsock, Barbara
Cutler, Stephanie Clare
Korte, Robin Danean
Miller, Amy Elizabeth
Miller, Beth B.
Shora, Camille Elizabeth
Skelton, Meghan Suzanne

1-6-2009
Gage, Elizabeth Joyce
Lee, Melanie Marguerite
Matulka, Meghan Anne
Parry, Kim O'Connor

1-8-2009
Basu, Nina
Betkerur, Nivedita Vasant
Carroll, Andrea Elizabeth
Chiu, Candice
Colangelo, Melissa Fay
Collins, Emily Margaret
Cox, Frances Kathryn
Elam, Nicole Antoinette
Figueroa-Rivero, Maria Cristina
Glidden, Elizabeth
Horsey, Kandice Lorissa
Khalfani, Natasha Monique
King, Wendy Paige
Masi, Brina Rose
Parker, Jewell Rocheal
Platt, Meadow Wirick
Reed, Saharie LaShaw
Ritter, Lauren Alexandra
Sakyi, Judith Antwi
Sinicrope, Natalie Theresa
Vazquez Gonzalez, Sasha Magaly
Weaver, Susannah Landes Foster

1-14-2009
Ewert, Elizabeth Lyn
Rosado, Roxanne Feliu
Walton, Cheryl Ann

1-21-2009
Kraai, Megan Messner

1-22-2009
Sadler, Victoria Elizabeth

1-26-2009
Gruver, Judy

2-4-2009
Cohan, June Elizabeth
Mashaw, Nena Easterling

2-5-2009
Chea, Keo Kanhchana
Frost, Jennifer Ann
Garland, Amy Lillian
Mathur, Leigh Mackenzie
McBride Jones, Birdie DeShavette
Stump, Debra Ann
Walker, Petal Pearl

2-9-2009
Brar, Kiranjit Kaur

2-17-2009
Donohue, Kathleen Alicia

2-18-2009
Cooperman, Rebecca Anne

3-5-2009
Healy, Meghan Jo
Kirkbride, Jennika Jane
Miles, Whitney Bayne

4-2-2009
Dunlap, Robyn Elaine

4-6-2009
McClain, Kishka-Kamari Ford

4-24-2009
Dorsey, Kristen Leslie
Fenton, Amalia Louise

5-7-2009
Vosdingh, Rhonda Jean
Webb, Caren Marie

6-4-2009
Dunlap, Amanda Frances
Halbert, Kathryn A.
Rimes, LadyStacie LaChelle
Simpson, Katherine Mary

6-15-2009
Ishak, April Caso
Massengill, Aisha Jorge
Palmer, Karen Antoinette

6-16-2009
Bahrami, Kameh Tahereh
Beall, Patricia Hutton
Boozer, Elizabeth Reese
Boyd, Carrie Cecilia
Brett-Major, Sherry Michelle Williams
Brown, Cheryne Amesha
Brown, Danielle Janine
Burke, Angeline Rose
Carroll, Jennifer Lee
Cherry, Heather Camille
Clitandre, Melissa Kathy
Conyers, Christine Banks
Cox, Fran-Victoria Louise
Dakin, Emily Swann
Daly, Antonette Delee
Danauy, Caroline
DeGan, Brittany Ann
Dixon, Adrienne Nicole
Duvall, Tracy Fell
Elis, Bridget Rossiter
Flowers, Domonique Ajuleigh
Fox, Angela Rene
Frisby, Alecia Brigh
Gallagher, Jamie Michelle
Gelfman, Victoria Faye
Ghosh Ahola, Priya
Gilbertson, Katherine MacGregor
Goetzl, Laura Krevsky
Golkiewicz, Kate Marie
Guha Biswas, Songeeta
Hahn, Keri Anne
Halasz, Kemuel Durham
Harbison, Jeana Maree
Hardy, Lisa Deanna
Harwood, Bridgette Marie
Heegan, Jessica Ann
Heilman, Heather Ann
Hill, Candace Joy
Holland, Angela Avis
Holtje, Rebecca Jean
Holtz, Jennifer Suzanne
Houlik, Elise Anne
Hutton, Caroline Boucher
Jenior, Elizabeth Green
Jones, Jessica Maria
Jones, Stacey Baines
Kamdar, Umber Majeed
Kantartzis, Fani
Kelley, Evelyn Griggs
Khoury, Emily Efrosini
Kushner, Mikhel Angela
Langohr, Mee Soon
Lawrence, Adrienne Jenell
Leamon, Rebecca Elizabeth
Lesko, Teresa Lynne
López Tirú, Lisa Marie
Lyons-Schmidt, Cheryl Lynn
Maguire, Erinn Maureen
Margolese, Jennifer Lynn
McCormally, Niknaz Moghbeli
McLaughlin, Darlyn Rose
Meyers, Christine Marie
Morris, Kathleen C.
Neplokh, Alison Greenwald
Ngaruri, Melissa Kenney
Njogu, Regina Wanjiru
Okasili, Eshigo Philomena
Opdyke, Ellen Cauley
Orme, Helen Marie
Perkins, Kimberly Michelle
Petrosian, Galina
Pinkney, Cynthia Rashalle
Polikov, Hannah Stephanie
Powell, Ashley Catherine
Purvis, Catrina Denise
Reetz, Desiree Maire
Rowlett, Jennifer Lynn
Schaeffer, Amy Elizabeth
Schaeffer, Megan Anne
Schwartzkopf, Amanda Marie
Shields, Amy Beth
Slagle-Peck, Jennifer Ann
Snyder, Amy Kathleen
Sobhraj, Rosa M.
Srinivasan, Seetha
Stein, Mara Andrea
Tah, Michen Marjorie
Teplinsky, Elina
Vakili, Pegah
Valenti, Erin Marie
Voorhees, Claire Sullivan
Wahlgren, Jennifer Kim
Wallace, Audrey Myung Suk Yoo
Williams, Jenelle Renee
Williams, Renee Faith
Wolfe, Frances Elizabeth
Yeo, Myong Hee
Yunkunis, Christiana
Zierler, Aviva Esther Akselrad

6-17-2009
Casserly, Marianne Roach
Collier, Tameka Meshaun
Lawson, Ashley Allison
Merene, Deon Charise

6-23-2009
Feldman, Kiva Keane

6-24-2009
Cabay, Gina Grace Angela
Malmstrom, Jody Lynn

6-29-2009
Lloyd, Mary Margaret

6-30-2009
Finberg, Elizabeth Shattuck

7-7-2009
Bear, Kristin Kay
Daly, Rachel Ellen
Kennedy, Altomease Rucker
Martin, Daphne Nicole
Pastras, Elizabeth Shannon

7-13-2009
Doyle, Aimee Eva
Maldonado, Ellen
Taylor-Heimberg, Amy Alexzandra
Wood, Sheryl Robinson
Magurshak, Jeanine Lynn

8-14-2009
Finn, Catherine H.

8-25-2009
Richards, Jennifer Lynn
Shear, Melissa Gail
Tibebe, Abiye

9-2-2009
Adams, Shanice Tenika
Cherayil, Monisha
Coles, Dana Elizabeth
Franklyn, Heather Margaret
Tyrrell, Lilia Norma

9-14-2009
Cameron, Lisa Marino

10-27-2009
Fefer, Anna

11-5-2009

Balenger, De'Ara Nicole
Hannah, Lynice Jerri

12-3-2009

Embry, Akia Yvonne

12-14-2009

Wilson, Susan Elizabeth

12-15-2009

Abelson, Laura Ginsberg
Abramson, Katherine Margaret
Abreu Medina, Ligia Mercedes
Acuña, Melanie Andrea
Adams, Nedra Shermaine
Ahan, Mary
Airhiavbere, Osasumwen Zoe
Alexander, Sarah Genez
Allison, Tammy Opuiyo
Alpert, Rachel Keen
Alston, Janine Nicole Shari
Ananth, Vinita
Andrea Babington, Tori Denise
Aponte-Rossini, Camille Cristina
Arenas, Christina Marie
Armstrong, Megan Michelle
Arnold, Jesse Digges
Arnold, Lyn
Asiedu, Geena
Auerbach, Erin Dorris
Augustin, Shella France
Baden, Rebecca Caitlin
Baek, Nina Marie
Bakare, Biola
Baldwin, Lindsey Michelle
Ballard, Rachel
Barbour, Danielle Suzanne
Barry, Margaret Frances
Basford, Laura C.
Bashur, Ashley Elizabeth
Batters-Thompson, Vanessa
Baughman, Natalie Ann
Behling, Bridget Keanukapulani Harkins
Beidle, Lyndsey Erin
Beleno Carney, Elena Christine
Bell, Juliana
Bennett, Kimberly Mae
Bento, Andrea Ferreira
Bergen, Sarah Elizabeth
Berland, Katherine Lorena
Berruz, Veronica
Blege, Enyonam Abra
Bloomgarden, Jami Lyn
Bocanegra, Randi Kae
Bokermann, Susan Enderle
Bolton, Stephanie Ann
Bonanni, Lauren Michael
Book, Phyllis Ann
Borowsky, Laura Evelyn
Bowlin, Holly Kathleen
Boyce, Sunita Kara
Braaten, Julia Eva
Bright, Melissa Anne
Britt, Rachel Elizabeth
Brown, Jessica Ivy
Brown-Reilly, Alexis K.
Buchanan-Smith, Henrika Janel
Buckles, Justina Joy
Burch, Melody Malissa
Burgess, Mary Katherine
Burguillo, Malibea Ivette
Burrows, Laura Elizabeth
Caffrey, Jennifer Emily
Callier, Jacqueline Michelle
Calomeris, Patricia Victoria
Cao, Amanda Denise
Cappiello, Elizabeth Jane
Cardy, Emily Arthur
Carouge, Elysha Marie
Cashwell, Morgan Laura
Celli, Michelle Marie
Celotto, Rebecca Kathleen
Chadwick, Gillian Rowley
Chambliss, Cecily Humphrey-Stinson
Chandler, Zakia Yasmeen
Chavez, Maria Chriztina
Choe, Anne Chen
Christensen, Renee Klesmith
Clark, Veronica Renee
Clarke, Shantay Nicole
Clay, Khelani Zakiya Akua
Cloyd, Stacy Braverman
Cobb, Lee Ann
Coffey, Danyele Angelique
Cohen, Nichole
Cole, Stacey Irene
Coleman, Erin Dianne
Coleman, Kerry Justine
Collins, Alice Margaret
Contreni, Maureen Chantal
Cooper, Dana Mariel
Costanzo, Amy Beth
Curry, Laura Theresa
Czajkowski, Katie Elizabeth
Daly, Lindsey Ann
Daniel, Tamica Hasina
Darrell, Leigh Catherine
Dastgir, Ieshah
Dastrup, Lindsey Christine
Davis, Danielle Elizabeth
Davis, Danielle Lynn
De Mar, Candice Marie
DeMar, Jacklyn Nicole
DeMent, Meredith Anne
Denboba, Rahel Hollis
Desaulniers, Angela Jeanne
Diamond, Joanna Leigh
Dickman, Jennifer Louise
Dieck, Brett Michael
Dingle, Ann Elizabeth
Doan, Kim Nghiem
Dohnji, Monica Numbosi
Donayre, Caroll Gisell
Drake, Carly Ann
Dubansky, Emily Connors Chase
Dyer, Kathryn Kitt
El-Amin, Mahasin Shukriyah
Elder, Lisa Ashley
Eliason, Kristin Nicole
Ellick, Jennifer Ann
Ellis, Maia Jalila
Elsbree, Lucy Rial
Epstein, Dina
Ermolaeva, Maria Edouardovna
Evans, Kerriann Marie
Fahrlander, Elizabeth Claire
Ferrero, Suzanne Laura
Finkenhofer, Christina Mary
Finn, Brenna Kathleen
Fisher, Christy Ann
Flohr, Christine Lauren
Foont, Jennie Leah
Forman, Christa Davies
Foster, Emily Michele
Fox, Alexis Curry
Frank, Carlendra Aisha
Franzonello, Anna Rachel
Frazee, Erin Nicole
Fuentes, Monica Maria
Galbo, Julie Lee
Gao, Hang
Garcia, Kari Elizabeth
Garvin, MacKenzie Rae
Geisser, Lauren Monica
Gibson, Kimberley Kay
Gilgenbach, Dana Michelle
Gilius, Lauren Larkin
Gill, Elaine Quinta Stocks
Gillis, Ieesha Marquay
Glasgow, Katie Christine
Glasser, Dara Joy
Gleeson, Maryellen Johanna
Gloth, Erin Marie
Goitom, Mahlet
Goldberg, Sandra Michelle
Goldscher, Allyson Brooke
Goldstein, Laura Suzanne
Goodman, Allison Jill
Goodwin, Alisa Michelle
Gordon, Alexandria Kara
Gordon, Lindsay Erin
Gordon, Tori Beth-Anne
Gore, Britton Lee
Gorman, Meghan Larkin
Graf, Melissa Anne
Graham, Sherifat Bolanle
Grant, Marie Louise
Graubard, Rachel Gittel
Hoppmeyer, Melissa Elizabeth
Howard, Julia Eva
Kaminer, Joan M. Easterbrook Gibson
Kaplan, Lindsay Eyler
Koenig, Elizabeth C.
Maier, Jamie Black
Makris, Elizabeth Rena
Marlin, Megan Eisenman
Monto, Tayyaba Chaudhrey
Murray, Julie Dietrick
Nagode, Christine Duggan
Stack, Alycia Ellwood
Sullivan, Laura Meredith
Thomas, Kimya B.

12-16-2009

Anderson, Ashley B.
Berman, Jacqueline Rachel
Byers, Karen Rebecca
Caplan, Jamie Francine
Gable, Sarah Michelle
Gavril, Jessica T.
Gregory, Candace Wynette
Griffin, Heather Christine
Grossberg, Rachel Elizabeth
Grossman, Lauren Ilene
Grupp, Amy Nicole
Gunn, Marissa Lynne
Gunzburg, Noelle B.
Guzman del Real, Pamela Yee
Hafey, Elizabeth Anne
Hagedorn, Rosa Lynn
Haines, Lynn Ann
Han, Jeanie
Han, Kay Heekyung
Handy, Alicia Anne
Hansen, Courtney Lynne
Hanshaw, Lois Antonette
Hanson, Tiffany Renee
Hantson, Katherine Grealy
Harada, Julie Suzanne
Harris, Rachel Blevins
Harrison, Erin Shea
Hawley, Carson Michelle
Heeb, Natalie Angela
Hennen, Amy Pearson
Henry, Shanelle Alyse
Higgins, Kia Latrice
Hill, Susan Corts
Hirsch, Lucy Rose
Hochman, Meredith Teresa
Hoffman, Molly Patricia
Holbeck, Kristin Valentine
Hoover, Ashley Marie
Howard, Kristen Michelle
Hu, Lydia Shih-ying
Hughes, Alexandra Michele
Hughes, Sheree Sena Kpodo
Hung, Chee-Yuen
Hussmann, Katrin Almut
Hyman, Carissa Messimer
Jang, Anne Jahee Lee
Januszkiewicz, Jennifer Caroline
Jawade, Rashi Mohan
Jennings-Howard, Ragin Monique
Joe, Phyllis Leann
Jones, Alison Elisa
Jones, Chervonti JaRay
Jones, Lauren Fay
Jones, Millicent Marie
Jordan, Elizabeth Katherine
Jorgensen, Kimberly Anne
Joyce, Mary Christine
Joyce, Mercedez Michel
Justilien, Wiline
Kabaklian-Slentz, Salpy Ofelia
Kafshi, Sara
Kanatas, Catherine Elaine
Kanner, Valerie Blair
Kapell, Sara Jessica
Karamloo, Reza
Katouzian, Mojgan
Kaufman, Jacqueline Rachel
Kehl, Jennifer Janice
Kelly, Katherine Leigh
Kessler, Elise Lena
Khan, Farah
Kim, Sohyun Esther
Kim, Yeojin
King, Sheree Danielle
Klemans, Pillar G.
Knepper, Jaime Kaylene
Knepper-Stephens, Kelly Susan
Kon, Hannah Weisman
Konstantopoulos, Melanie Demetra
Kontak, Kristina Louise
Kovacs, Talley Hollings-Scroggs
Koya, Oyinade Olufoyeke
Kranz, Erika Barnes
Kraus, Shannon Leigh
Krevor, Diana Michelle
Krigman, Yael
Kuester, Jessica Elizabeth
Kuspa, Julie Beth
Lack, Adele Helen
Lakowski, Terri Ann

Larson, Julie Marie
Latin, Colle J.
Lee, Angela Min
Lee, Cherlena Celesté
Lee, Esther Chung-Min
Lee, Jessica Ming-Lun
Lee, Na Rae
Lego, Kellie Nicole
Lele, Pratima Pramod
Lenahan, Mary Monica
Levine, Cheryl Robin
Lewis, Ameenah
Liaw, Stephanie Nicole
Lilly, Gunella Yvonne
Lin, I-Chun Jenny
Lindhard, Krista Marie
Lindo, Katherine Elizabeth
Lombardo, Evelyn Carol
Loyd, Lauren Elizabeth
Luoma, Jeffrey Stokes
Lusk, Rebekah Damen
Lutz, Elaine Kristen
Magil, Lisa
Maguire, Annise Katherine
Maloney, Natalie Dawn
Manfreda, Lisa Keefe
Mann, Kimberly Danielle
Manon, Maria
Marable, Lindsey Daniel
Marcusse, Katie Michelle Bailo
Maril, Robin Suzanne
Mason, Montez Deantee
Mason, Susan
McDonnell, Melissa Marie
McFarlane, Camilla Isylen
McGinley, Kathleen Allie
McIlvaine, Jennifer Lynn
McKenzie, Jocelyn Patricia
McKoy, Dana-Marie
McMillan, Joyce
McMiller, Jessica Layli
McNair, Saundra Michelle
Mech, Carolyn Estella
Meinken, Gretchyn Gay
Melvin, Christina Marie
Mendocilla-Navarrete, Nataly Clara Lyz
Methner, Cameron Ashley
Meyer, Sarah Elizabeth
Mikha, Natasha Nadette
Miller, Dana Lynne
Miller, Jasmine-Simone
Miller, Marialisa
Mills, Stacie Yavon Lewis
Mitchell, Michelle Adria
Mitchell, Taryn Louise
Moore, Elisa Christine
Moore, Katherine Leigh
Moore, Meghan Kathryn
Moorstein, Amelia Chase
Moylan, Alexandra Patricia
Murtaugh, Christina Lynn
Myers, Kimberly Marie
Myers, Krystle Ishika
Nadolny, Sarah Lynn
Najhram, Cindy Gita
Nakhla, Beth Zarkin
Napolitano, Amber Nicole
Narimatsu, Julie Keiko
Navarro, Angela Louise
Nesbitt, Sarah Novak
Newcomb, Kristina Gwendolyn
Newland, Laura Se-Jin
Nguyen, Christina Giang Thu
Nguyen, Kimberly Phu
Norton, Sarah Alison
Nottingham, Kara Devonne
Noukelak, Marie-Claire
Nunez, Anna Maria
Nyakweba, Jeannette Kwamboka
O'Barr Decker, Shannon Colleen
O'Donnell, Caitlin
Park, Nicole J.
Powers-Heaven, Jessica Natalie
Preston, Anne Legg
Stewart, Katherine Rose
Stoll, Jessica Leah
Summers, Lonni Kyhos
Suttenberg, Elana Sara
Tanenbaum, Phyllicia Michelle Hoffman
Tracey, Claire A.P.
Tucker, Katherine Louise
Tyndell, Katy Jackman
Vaughan, Courtney Moore
Walsh, Caroline Murray

12-17-2009

Andrews, Andrea Silvestri
Appelbaum, Amanda Lauren
Bennett, Lisa Lynn
Calmus, Diane Reta
Capelle, Lauren Slevin
Drake, Jessica Sheer
Grace, Kristy Naomi
Hielke, Rebecca M.
Ignozzi, Marie J.
Malykin, Dora
Marshall, Wendy Rose
Martinez, Elizabeth Ryan
Odierno, Jill Marie
Oladapo, Jumoke Funmilola
Oleszczuk, Erica Nicole
Oliver-Zhang, Julie Teresa
Olsen, Megan Lynn
Ordun, Elizabeth Anne
Osseo-Asare, Afua Agyepoma
Oveissi, Emily Rapoport
Parks, Octavia Rachel
Pasciuto, Amanda Yellon
Pealer, Shaina Elias
Perkins, Kelly Ann
Peter, Katalin
Petrusek, Marissa Leigh
Pham, Uyen Ho Van
Philipp, Meredith Ryan
Phillips, Nancy Ann
Pierson, Claire Amy
Plenge, Alison Jo
Podolny, Erin Victoria
Pouyes, Nydia Manouchka
Powell, Caroline Lears
Powell Shulman, Octavia Seneka
Powers, Tanya Marie
Powers-Heaven, Hiram Kistler
Prizeman, Jennifer Elizabeth
Procoffie, Sherri Lee
Pruger, Heather Robyn
Pulliam, Laurie Durham
Purcell, Emily Corcoran
Quander, Katherine Alicia
Queen, Lauren R.
Rasputnis, Jebby Florence
Ratliff, Merrilyn Elise
Records, Jennifer Angel
Reichlin, Michele Anne
Reifke, Inga
Resnikoff, Lisa Schopler
Rhudy, Kathryn Anne Rezabek
Riewerts, Pamela Kayatta
Roberts, Heather Schilling
Roberts, Ibidun Olawunmi
Robey, René Marie Parks
Rockhill, Cara McKinney
Rodgers, Chelsey Sophia
Rogers, Erin Elizabeth
Rogerson, Sarah Frances
Rohrer, Alison Christine
Romanenko, Victoria Olegovna
Romeri-Lewis, Natalie Wright
Romig, Devon Elizabeth
Rothfarb, Lisa Anne
Ryan, Suzanne Dawn
Saifollahi, Banafsheh Elizabeth
Sakoh, Mayumi
Salomon, Amy Elizabeth
Sanders, Tiffany Delgado
Sanford, Courtney Nelson
Santos, Diana Marie
Schaeberle, Dianna Kate
Schafer, Julie Anne
Scharf, Mira Aviv
Schell, Teresa Ann
Schiffer, Jennifer O'Neill
Schlick, Josephine Nichole
Schonewald, Stephanie Lynn
Schoppert, Christina Lynn
Schultz, Vanessa Marie
Schwarz, Laura Marie
Scialpi, Errin Rae
Scop, Deborah Ann
Scott, Samara Marie
Seader, Melanie Ann
Seitz, Rebecca Anne
Senger, Molly Trustman
Sewell, Christen Nalley
Shahabuddin, Jennifer Shifat
Shank, Katrina Nason
Shirole, Pallavi Subhash
Shyr, Sarah Jean
Silberman, Mallory Brooke
Silvestri, Lauren Kathleen
Simon, Sarah Mae
Simpson, Lacie Beth
Sincell, Miriam Renae
Skiouris, Elena
Skroejer, Aylin Melisa
Slater, Gretchen Anna
Smith, Calisa Michelle
Soares, Kelly Eulalia Viana
Sperr, Andrea Marie
Staley, Danielle Monique
Steffes, Maryann Elizabeth
Steinnerd, Tara Elizabeth
Stevenson, Ruth Buslepp
Stewart, Alicia Dawn
Stone, Lauren Ann
Stuckey, Caleisha Nicole
Sue-Ling, Kelly Chalisse
Sullivan, Sharon Lin
Swanston, Kelly Lorimer
Sweeney, Nichole Ellis
Sybenga, Katherine Claire
Szelc, Rebecca Marie
Tang, Angela Jacqueline
Taylor, Candas Chonn
Thibodeau, Jessica Kane
Thomas, Barbara Elaine
Thomas, Jennifer Ward
Thompson, Julia Autumn
Tibbitts, Adriana Verleysen
Tinoco, Anne Carey
Torrontor, Cheryl Leslie
Townes, Cecelia Nicole
Trego, Genevieve Nicole
Vignarajah, Krishanti
Vladeck, Karen Shafrir
Walters, Amy Elizabeth
Wang, Diana Marie
Warren, Samantha Marie
Waters, Gwendolyn Ruth
Watkins-Esuke, Sherawanda Arlene
Weekes, Dana Tenille
Wehrenberg, Brooke Erin
Weigelt, Michelle Rei
Weiner, Adrienne Aileen
Westby, Ashley Owen
Whelehan, Katherine Renee
White, Tyechia LaShauna
Wieker, Amanda Flynn
Williams, Ria Maria
Williamson, Flavia Monique
Wilson, Diane Bruce
Wilson, Kimberly Ann
Wolf, Andrea Brem
Wong, Helen Pei Ying
Woodard, Michele Elizabethe
Wreathall, Cordelia Louisa
Wyss, Sarah Marie
Yang, Chunlian
Yanker, Hsing Lan
Yeh, Chengyu
Yi, Jane
Zlatkus, Christy Anne
Zychowicz, Emily Lauren

12-23-2009

Bond, Mayrav Judith
Bonner, Michelle Renee
Hanson, Michelle Ann
Holt-Charles, Teri Joyce
Jameson, Susan
Lang, Kathryn Rose
LaRue, Michelle Lamdanski
Maxman, Melissa Helen
Posner, Jane Sarah
Tausend, Rachel Marcia

12-29-2009

Sargeantson, Sara Marie

1-5-2010

Lyons, Laurie Heather
McLaughlin, Lauren Pacelli
Rowinski, Lauren Marie

1-6-2010

Kling, Rachel Ann

1-7-2010

Brown Hanks, Vanessa Laura
Dodds, Ciji Shawandra
Gayapersad-Chan, Daniella Abimbola Sarian
Giannetti, Erin Appel
Holben, Natasja Danielle Croft
Huls-Simpson, Natalie Miranda
Kaplan, Kayla Stachniak
Kelley, Gail Sandra

Kerwood, Adrienne Rose
McCullough, Elizabeth Kidd
McGough, Maureen Quinn
Mueller, Leah Nicole
O'Donnell, Evann Christine
Orsinger, Rachel Riordan
Pyle, Ashley Susanne
van Leynseele, Anne M.
Zielinski, Anjali Tara

1-12-2010
Gambale, Roberta Lynn
Guarnieri, Elizabeth Carolyn
Maxwell Fox, Marie Elaine

1-14-2010
Preis, Sarah Marie

1-19-2010
Moore, Beverly Carol

1-20-2010
Campbell, Elizabeth Ruth
Pak, Yoora

1-27-2010
Shelton, Summer Ashley

2-4-2010
Bradley, Elizabeth Marie
Dorsey, Pamela Marie
Jacobs, Robin Lee
Kumar, Sonia
Liu, Yue
Peterson, Emily Ristine

2-16-2010
Latour, Stephane Joseph
McAsey, Christine
Taff, Jennifer Suzanne

2-17-2010
Shams, Suzanne Taher

2-18-2010
Beth, Corinne Shelov

2-22-2010
Hitzel, Cheryl Lynn

3-1-2010
Lee, Min K.
Stasio, Renée Lee

3-4-2010
Chedekel, Tabitha Felice
Gray, Rebecca
Kircher, Ashley Susan
Moore, Jaida Althea
Sherman-Presser, Kala

3-10-2010
Mulholland, Jennifer Lynn

3-19-2010
Phillips, Katrina Lynn

3-25-2010
Javitt, Gail Hannah

4-1-2010
Byrd, Courtney Claire
Rhodes, Shauna Alicia
Singer, Kelley Elizabeth
Winston, Rachel Leslie

4-12-2010
Vaughn, Andrea Joie

4-15-2010
Smith, Elsa Elizabeth Waite
Whitted, Eunice M.

4-20-2010
Novins, Lisa Sally

5-5-2010
Collins, Valerie Lisa
Moriatis, Peggy Stavroula
Mpela-Thompson, Dineo
Wenzel, Kara Ann

5-21-2010
Thomas, Alexandra Nicole

6-2-2010
Khonsari, Niloufar
Nelson, April Elaine
Smith, Jacqueline Vella
Wagstaff, Brandy Lynn

6-8-2010
Henninger, Sarah Elizabeth
Zettler, Laura Lee Dailey

6-10-2010
Fancher, Bridget Snyder
Freeland, Kimberly Suzanne

6-16-2010
Weisz, Cynthia Marie

6-17-2010
Ali, Amrana
Amarsingh, Kusmin Linda
Archie-Burton, Melissa Nichole
Asfaw, Yodit
Azar, Julie Rima
Baehr, Malinda Marie
Balum, Britta Elisabeth
Banks, Bernice Tiara
Barr, Debora Regina
Bennecoff, Amy Lynn
Benneh, Nana Abena Ohenewaa
Booher, Kimberly Dempsey
Bosken, Katherine Marie Royal
Boveja, Namrata
Brandon, Catherine Alexandra
Bryce, Shauna Celestina
Burk, Eileen Susan
Burns, Carolyn Perozzi
Carmichael, Toya Shelley
Carr, Robin Merissa
Chacko, Lisa McClurkin
Chaconas, Sara Anne
Chen, Alice Chung-Ann
Chen, Cecille Hilario
Clark, Christine Anne
Clark, Stacy Ann
Clarke, Tara Kate
Conklin, Suzanne Howell
Cook, Surena Bonds
Crow, Elizabeth Erin
Crowell, Dawn Kelly
Daniel, Fei Guo
Denson, Shaketta Ayana
Dent, Jennifer Dwyer
Duke, Nsagha E.
Eaton, Diana Leigh
Edwards, Ashley Danene
Englander, Itta Channa
Fardshisheh, Erin Nicole
Finney, Jenifer Victoria
Franc, Tiffany Stacey
Gallagher, Angela Monique
Garrott, Erika Renee
Gibson, Caroline Elizabeth
Gilbert, Leslee Koch
Granlund, Stephanie Russell
Haalboom, Kirsten Noel
Haggerty, Kathleen Erin
Hall, Megan Kathryn
Han, Jean Chang
Hargrove, Sherine Blagrove
Harmon, Megan Elizabeth
Harris, Radiance W.
Herr, Rebecca Anne
Hoffpauir, Jennifer Jenine
Howlett, Erin E.
Hutchison-Cass, Kathy Tonya
Ivanov, Ashley Willis
Jacobs, Anna Loraine
Jacobson, Cary Caroline
Jean, Martine Andrelle
Jones, Terri-Ann
Jung, Miri
Jupiter, Carla Lavonne
Kabongo, Veronica Annie
Kaja, Vanessa Chiebonam
Kaleem, Farheen
Keiser, Lauren Sandra
Keller, Danielle Leigh
Kiel, Julia Anne
Koehler, Claire Elise
Koshy, Ann Elizabeth
Kreloff, Lori Beth
Kushlan, Kristin Frohring
Lamm, Elizabeth Ellen
LaPonzina, Falen Marie
Larson, Lisa Marie
Lawrence, Catherine Ruth
Loeb, Ellen Ruth
Loncarich, Kathryn Elizabeth
Longaker, Kelcie Lee
Loy, Tamara Joann
Mariner, Ashley Michelle
Marshall, Sharon Marie
Martinez, Mary Deyanira
Maschal, Colleen Marie
McBeth, Melinda Quinn
Meeks, Brandy Kathleen
Miles-Hare, Lindsy Ann
Miller, Jessica Lauren
Min, Dorothy Hae Eun
Morgan, Dana Amber
Morris-Frazier, Jerica Monique
Moss, Kathryn Elisabeth-Dolan
Murdoch, Alexandra Alferieff
Nelis, Brenda Susan
Nghiem, Nancy
Nightengale, Gwendolyn Keleigh
Nussbaum, Lydia Renee
Nussenblatt, Valerie Rosine Leah
Opoku-Asare, Jennifer Twumasi
Parks, Kathleen Marie
Pastrikos, Nomiki M.
Payne, Debbie Flowers
Pesin, Elizabeth Miheikin
Pickrell, Christina Lynn
Price, Alicia Victoria
Price, Kathryn Lynne
Ram, Natalie Ruth
Reed, Jwyanza Ajene
Reifsnyder, Teresa Marino
Robinson, Kimbery Anne
Rodrigues, Ana Mafalda Morgado
Roeper, Maria Ann
Roth, Sharon Diane
Sadler, Chelsea Mae
Sala, Heather Mae
Sanchez, Joellie Lorraine
Sarkar, Shaoli
Saylor, Erin Marie
Schieke, Wendy Little
Scott, Rabihah
Selway, Jessica Dawn
Shields, Candace Mary
Shisler, Pamela Renee
Silbaugh, Toscha Louise
Skrenczuk, April Nicole
Smith, Harper Alice
Spess, Emily Ann
Stevens, Kenya Lisette
Sudakow, Kimberly Rose
Sweetman, Karlyn Amanda
Taylor, Ashlei Coit
Telfer, Jeanine Myra
Toney-Thomas, Andrea Freda
Townley, Kristin Anne
Trinh, Jessica Chieu
Turnipseed, Danielle Patrice
Upchurch, Michelle Janell
Uram Mubangu, Justina Marie
Vetter, Suzanne Kathleen
Vollmer, Jessica Anne
Waldman, Jennifer Gann
Wassef, Courtney Lynn
Westry, Erika Ann
Woodward, Donna Ostlund
Wu, Nina Sandy
Yerkes, Jessica Ann

6-18-2010
Koss, Natalie Marie

6-25-2010
Brady, Michelle Ann
Speyer, Debra Gail
Thomas, Michelle Candíce

6-30-2010
Sarvadi, Jennifer Leigh
Stevens, Linda Marie

7-7-2010
Haller, Julia Zsuzsa
Li, Kathleen O'Neill

7-13-2010
Drelichman, Natalia

7-14-2010
Shumaker, Kate G.

7-20-2010
Barker, Gretchen Marie

7-26-2010
Hibsch, Kimberly Megan

8-3-2010
Beardsley, Meghan Allen

8-24-2010
Mihok, Susan Amanda Baumann

9-1-2010
Jacque, Laura Marie
Lokshin, Maria Lev
Love, Rhonda Kornegay
Miller, Pamela Anna
Pondexter, Rosmatine M.
Sturdivant, Elice Nicole

9-3-2010
Holmes, Candace Michelle

9-9-2010
Blonder, Suzanne Marya

10-7-2010
Lantz, Cristin Danielle

11-4-2010
Collins, Stephanie Sue
Lemon, Nicole
Watford, Yoshika Myesha
Webb, Jennifer Mary

11-17-2010
Falk, Brooke Sands
Nelson, Amy Elizabeth

12-2-2010
Moore, Yonelle Andrea
Weaver, Ashley Jean

12-14-2010
Abbasi, Sharifa
Abboud, Maureen Murphy
Ablorh-Odjidja, Awuraakua Larko
Acoraci, Rose Carol
Adams, Kelly Nicole
Ahern, Jennifer Anne
Albert, Michelle Dara
Albright, Anastasia Lauren
Alexander, Angela Antionette
Allen, Jacquelyn Pearo
Altum, Julia Donata
Alvarez, Jennifer Lynn
Anderson, Brin Thaxton
Andes, Caroline Elizabeth
Anukem, Jennifer Adaugo
Bachowski, Kitciu Soraya Zinat
Bakhtiary, Katrine Homa
Balogh, Lindsey Marie
Banks, Cathrin Stephanie
Barr, Margaret Elizabeth
Batler, Anna
Bautista, Andrea Abigail Barranda
Bearden, Mary Elizabeth
Beaver, Jessica Sinclair
Bechtel, Laura Eaton
Bedard, Natalie Rose
Benczik, Sarah Anne
Bennett, Tamara LaVerne
Bergin, Moira Ellen
Bin-Humam, Yasmin Klaudia
Black, Sarah Elizabeth
Blackfield, Anne Pauline
Blum, Jade Allison
Borgeson, Kathryn Mannix
Bosken, Sarah Elizabeth
Bostick, Christina Julianne
Bowen, Rachel Kathleen
Bowman, Marva LaWand
Boylan, Kathryn Meghan
Brady, Crystal Ann
Brewington, Erica Nicole
Brooking, Christina Michelle
Brooks, Lindsey Elisabeth
Brown, Nicole Katharine
Brown, Raichell Savoy
Brown, VaLiesha Marie
Burke, Katie Denise
Burnett, Grace Maral
Burs, Danielle Marie
Burton Stalzer, Sandra Renee
Byrd, Carmen Alexis
Callahan, Elizabeth Marie
Canterbury, Crystal Rachélle
Cao, Qi
Carey, Christine Carol
Carlisle, Jennifer Alyson
Carrano, Julia Lucille
Cathell, Caroline Biden
Chen, Cindy Helen
Cheung, Yi Man
Chilcote, Kira Elizabeth
Chin, Yue Pui
Church, Pamela Christina
Cirincione, Maria Rosa
Ciurca, Lauren Elise
Clark, Jennifer Marie
Clinton, Rebecca Kimberly
Cocce, Heather Ann
Cockett, Kiesha Noelle
Colaiuta, Angela Sue
Colandreo, Lauren Elizabeth
Coleman, Rebecca Jean
Conners, Sharon Elizabeth
Cooper, Suzanne Rebecca
Corace, Jessica Dawn
Cornetto, Sarah Catherine
Cornwell, Ashley Zena
Corso, Scarlett Marcella
Costantino, Mary Joy
Cowan, Elizabeth Watson
Craig, Lindsey Mae
Crowley, Katherine Gamelin
Cumberland, Emily Caitlin
Dadlani, Priya Sabrina
David, Ioana
Davidson, Brianna Rae
Day, Erin Elizabeth
Day, Tiffany Lee
Dayhoff-Brannigan, Eleanor Maurine
Days, Loren Ashley
Deckert, Heather Anne
Dempsey, Leah Conway
Desai, Kusha Atulkumar
DeSmyter, Krista Nicole
Diehm, Elizabeth Ann
Diouf, Sarah Elizabeth
Doiron, Lynn Esther
Donahue, Margaret Maureen
Doory, Elizabeth Lowe
Dorch, Adina Iman
Dorélien, Astrid Marie
Dorsey, Arnette Marie Lang
Doty, Kelsey Beth
Duke-Olinick, Pamela Lynn
Duley, Cye Marie
Dunmire, Melinda Dawn Lee
Dunn, Heather Marie
Duszczyszyn, Danielle Andrea
Eagen, Molly Kathleen
Edler, Emily Ann
Ehrenfried, Mindy Lenore
Einik, Daniella Adar
Ellis, Ebony Latoya
Epperly, Ingrid Alicia
Epstein, Eve Esther
Escudero, Marisa Carla
Famili, Aminah
Farrell, Caroline Lindsay
Fawcett, Kathleen Anne
Feldman, Sarah Elizabeth
Ferguson, Meghan Anne
Fernández, Jennifer Renée
Ferraioli, Molly Erin Grace
Fields, Alverta Simone
Fischer, Kara Lynn
Fisher, Katherine Colt
Fitzsimmons, Mary Davern
Foreman, Rachel Beth
Forester, Amanda Katherine
Franceschi, Helena Stephanie
French, Jennifer Bryden
Fry, Taryn Michele
Furo, Rukayya Dawuda
Garcia, Oxalis Bianca
Garneau, Carolyn Ann
Geiger, Sonya Rachel
Gelinas, Elise Monique
Gershowitz, Suzanne Beth
Ghosh, Anita
Gibson, Adriana Francesca
Gibson, Alexis Elizabeth
Gillis, Diana Lynne
Glasgow, Adrianne Eva
Glass, Courtney Danielle
Goldberg, Lindsay Sharon
Goldmeier, Melissa Esther
Goldstein, Jean Spirt
Gomes, Lisa Marie
Gomez, Camille Yolande
Goon, Laurie Beth
Gordon, Inna
Gordon, Waverly Lakeam
Graf, Kristen Cannon
Grant, Bridget Elizabeth
Grant, Caitlin Culhane
Jolicoeur, Emily Duvall
Magette, Sara
Murphy, Renee S.
Palazzolo, Anne Marie
Reschovsky, Allison L.
Shirley, Gabrielle D.
Sprague, Emily Brant
Tang, Mabel Duguies
Zinsli, Fay Mara

12-15-2010
Bandzwolek, Lindsay Greer
Cook, Erica Lee
Duggan, Amber Rachel
Green, Candace Nicole
Grobowski, Eve Muriel
Gross, Karen Andrea
Grunstra, Lydia Ruth
Haaga, Bethan Mair
Hackett, Tracee Nicole
Hager, Janet Marie
Hagermann, Courtney Jewel
Han, Marianne Tzu-Chwen
Hantman, Irene Amy
Harbor, Rachel Esther
Harner, Lauren Ashley
Harrell, Lindsay Elizabeth
Haskins, Megan Paula
Hawks, Ann Woods Isaacs
Healy, Katharine Lintot
Heilman, Kathleen Roth
Henson, Fatima Renee
Henson, Shaneka Tarae
Herrington, Alyse Leigh
Higgins, Brenna Kate
Hightower, Kelly Marie
Himelfarb, Allyson Tracey
Hoagland, Lindsay Janelle
Hockaday, Layne Turcan
Hodges, Katlyn Lee
Hood, Renée Elizabeth
Hopkins, Holly Noel
Horowitz, Sarah Feldman
Horska, Katerina
Hough, Amy Lynn
Houston, Dallas Elana
Hu, Tian Tian
Hudson, Jenna Adrith
Huff, Erynn Alexis
Huff, Mary Carmen
Hurtt, Portia Imani
Ifon, UduakAbasi Ekwere
Iheme, Nkechinyere Delphine
Ivanowski, Jennifer Liv
Izadi, Lily
Jacobs, Courtney Elizabeth
Jacobsen, Alisha LeeRae
Jaimes, Jennifer Evelyn
James, Ashley Gwendolyn
Jamshidi, Arezoo
Johnson, Tiffany Jewel
Joly, Tiffany Monique
Jones, Angelina Delores
Jones, Stephanie Kristen
Joyner, Kristina Danielle
Kalaria, Kristen M.K.
Kamenas, Lauren Marie
Kane, Anastasia Rose
Kane, Kristin Allison
Karch, Alison Suzanne
Karram, Alexandra Mariam
Keefer, Danielle Lori
Kellagher, Lauren Nicole
Kelley, Catherine Hinckley
Kenderdine, Elizabeth Ennis
Kersey, Christianna Josepha
Khaing, Hnin Nu
Kiefer, Rachel Melissa
Kim, Jung Woo
King, Alexandra Juliet
Klein, Lauren Amanda
Knapp, Kristen Alexandra
Knauff, Abigail Sarah
Kohler, Adriana Damien
Kroehl, Meredith Jessica
Kuntz, Mary Elizabeth
Laptosky, Jill Megan
Larkin, Jessica Kristen
Larson, Meredith Nicole
Latta, Laura Lynn
Laux, Jessica Lea
LeBow, Ashley Megan
Lee, Allison Lauren
Lee, Jennie Sewon
Lee, Jung Hyun
Lee, Paula
Legaspi, Tracy Marie
Leibowitz, Lori Renée
Leiby, Michele Langevine
Leigh, Laila Enid
Lesker, Katherine Virginia
Levy, Jayme Lynn
Lewis, Cara Yvonne
Lewis-Bosley, Nicole Elizabeth
Lipps, Emily Rachel
Lobato, Quinn Breece
Löfgren, Ingrid Marie
Loloei Marsal, Anahita
Lucas, Kendall Ashley
Lynch, Victoria Noel
Lynn, Ashleigh Jessica Framm

Lyons, Margaret Jessee Schnurrenberger
Mackowiak, Stephanie Lee
MacMillan, Anne Cannon
Mann, Jessica Susan
Manners, Trenna Laurel
Manohar, Revathi Lalitha
Marino, Angela Ann
Martin, Mallory Anne
Masumi, Mariam
Mathew, Fenn Cherian
Mathioudakis, Stephanie Maria
McCarthy, Megan Louise
McChrystal, Lynne Kathryn
McCormack, Jacqueline Marie
McCrory, Lindsay Shea Lewis
McCulloch, Meghan Elizabeth
McDonald, Priya Chhugani
McGuinness, Mary Caitlin
McKeever, Marissa Irene
McLeod, Michelle Andrea
Melcher, Megan Leigh
Mildenberg, Samantha Anne
Miliman, Mandy Lyn
Miller, Katheryn Rebecca
Miller, Kelley Kathleen
Miller, Kerstin Marie
Miller, Westra Bea McKetney
Mills, Kymberly Shannon
Mohr, Amber Mary Nicole
Mollett-Gaumer, Sarah McKelvey
Montgomery, Melissa Rose
Monyei, Allison Chidi
Moon, Michelle Mina
Moore, Ashley Revée
Morrissette, Megan Cifrese
Mountenay, Elizabeth Ann
Mouta-Bellum, Carla Alexandra Saraiva
Mowell, Heather Talley
Mueller, Megan Lucille
Mukherjee, Sukanya
Mumm, Jennifer Ritter
Munitz, Jessica Rose
Murray, Claire McCusker
Murray, Jessica Lynn
Mwaniki, Mwaafrika-Mbili Namibia
Neuman, Nicole Brooke
Nguyen, Thy Hoang Anh
Nica, Alexandra
Nicholl, Caitlin Kelly
Niles, Lyndsay Ayanna
Noncent, Karine Anne
Noravian, Andrea
Nuñez-Bellamy, Consuelo Beatrice
Nuon, Buthany
O'Boyle, Colleen Bailey
O'Fallon, Kelleen Kane
O'Neill, Kerry Anne
Oleszewski, Megan Elizabeth
Oudia, Jacqueline Brejite
Oyedele, Nancy Olatokunbo
Selba, Lindsey Kiddoo
Sinfield, Lani Martinez
Soraruf, Nicole Marie Necklas
Vranian, Danielle Marie
White, Lisa Marie

12-16-2010

Browning, Theresa Jo
Capellán, Andrea Pestone
Fitch, Charissa Thornton
Flanders, Bethany Lynn
Hylton, Christine Lynn
Kang, Anne Akhila Rubins
Kemper, Lauren Elizabeth Pagano
Lericos, Gia Nicole
Minton, Jenna Wilkes
Pachikara, Melissa Anne
Palmer, Nina Lee
Parekh, Jaymin Narendra
Park, Soyoung Michelle
Parks, Debra Marie
Parsi, Pegah Kamkar
Parsi, Shireen Hannah
Patel, Shiwali Govardhan
Patente, Maria Teresa
Patkin, Debra Joy
Paul, Rachel Elizabeth
Pearlstein, Lisa Cheryl
Peightel, Anne Lauren
Peloso, Brooke Courtney
Pepinsky, Elizabeth Romney
Perry, Jamie Brinkmeyer
Petros, Joanna
Pham, Ngoc Tien
Phillips, Catherine Lytton
Pichler, Judith Sara
Pike, Elizabeth Anne
Price, Michelle Anne
Prose, Sara Jo
Quan, Helen Marcela
Quijano, Allyson Lalere
Raafat, Dina Ahmed
Randall, Élise Reneé
Ray, Amanda Jean
Reid, Erin Margaret
Rhodes, Lindsay Harris
Rickard, Nantz
Riley, Samantha Jean
Roberts-Satinsky, Megan Marie
Robinson, Laura Jill
Rokosz, Jessica Kay
Rosenbaum, Debra Beth
Rottschaefer, Maureen Lynn
Runels, Sarah Margaret
Ryan, Sara
Sack, Jamie Jessica
Safai, Shaida
Sala, Emily Marie
Salerno, Brianna Denise
Sanchez, Nancy
Sasarak, Stephanie Ann
Savory, Jennifer Lauren Humphrey
Sawhney, Piya
Sawhney, Vintee
Schiebelhut, Alison Meeker
Schleh, Caroline Jeanne
Schmidt, Lauren Elizabeth
Schulman, Tamara Hope
Scott, Regina Nicole
Seiferth, Jill Catherine
Severson, Chelsea Savoy
Shackelford, Courtney Erin
Shad, Vimi Harindar
Shapiro, Jenna Nicole
Shapiro, Rachel Ann
Sickenberger, Rebecca Ann
Siegel, Julie Surell
Siegel, Sylvia Katherine
Sigler, Heather Jeanne Christine
Silber, Alison Faye
Silvestri, Lisetta Jane
Simak, Christina Maria
Simon, Stacie Michelle
Sims, Tiffany Nicole
Skelton, Anna Zappulla
Skubikowski, Anna Elizabeth
Smith, Callie Louise
Smith, Cara Marie
Smith, Lindsay Nicole
Smith, Nicole Aimee
Smith, Nicole Renee
Smith, Rayna Monique
Smith, Sharnae Lashaun
Smith, Tehma Hallie Stanton
Sokolower, Heather Gilhooly
Stahl, Melissa Renee
Stefanski, Kimberly Beth
Stillman, Rona Barbara
Stoll, Jessica Marcus
Storey, Alexis Pauline
Stubbs, Delia Ann
Swain, Sarah Katherine
Sweeney, Meghan Mary
Taib, Rama Mwaffak
Taylor, Hilary Holbrook
Taylor, Shannon Denise
Teague, Amber K.
Terry, Natalie Nicole
Thompson, Jessica Michele
Ticer, Amy Lee
Tiffany, Talia Rossell
Tornabene-Velez, Wendy Lynn
Turner, Sabrina Johnson
Tyson, Elizabeth Marie
Ung, Melissa Mei
Urizar, Nancy Lissette
Van Buskirk, Kelly Marie
Vandevander, Caitlin Quinn
Vayner, Milana
Videnieks, Lindsay Anne
Villarivera, Alison Marie Mibale
Wagner, Ashley Elizabeth
Wagner, Carolyn Wade
Waicker, Elizabeth Louise
Waldrop, Sarah Rachel
Walters, Dana Lee
Watkins, Mary Elizabeth
Wayne, Bryn Mayes
Weatherly, Whitney Zacchetti
Weaver, Christie Marie
Webster, Elizabeth Murray
Wehner, Amanda McCallister
Weiss, Kristen Winterling
Welch, Heather Marie
West, Dondi Sanchez
White, Elizabeth Genevieve
Wiggins, Ashleigh Lauren
Wiley, Shanna Alexandra
Wilkinson, Sara Covington
Williams, Jessica Jenee
Williamson, Tara Lynn
Winkles, Devon Elisabeth
Witriol, Rachel Medwin
Wright, Laura Ruth
Wroten, Ashley Elizabeth
Wylin, Bethany Ann
Wyman, Katherine Maeve
Yakubu, Beatrice Oluwayemisi
Yao, Ron-Wen
Yoon, Connie Kanghee
Young, Tia Marshell
Zander, Morgane Marcelle
Zax, Sara Marie
Zegeye, Meti
Zenzinger, Robyn Elaine
Zgoda, Elizabeth Ann
Zhang, Sufen
Zohorsky, Jennifer Eileen

12-17-2010

Bacsardi, Shari Beth Domow
Braucher, Anne Elizabeth
Ekekwe, Olekanma Arnnette
Hawkins, Lynn Eisinger
Koenig, Elisabeth Angelica
Lantz, Chandra Doré
Tenney, Amy Bliss
Topper, Nicole Rory

12-29-2010

Green, Kim Angela

1-5-2011

Goldstein, Elizabeth Jan
Harlan, Elizabeth Ann
Mullen, Kathleen Ann
O'Rourke, Katherine Anne
Roover, Melissa Ann

1-6-2011

Bartmann, Amanda King
Beras, Melissa Ellen
Blackwell, Katy Elizabeth
Chengappa-Astrada, Ganga Palecanda
Coughlin, Johanna
Hernandez, Meghan Dalton
Hoffman, Laura Gayle
Isak, Sonila
Khan, Fasiha Halim
Klein, Jennifer Ann
McNamee, Victoria Margaret
Miller, Angela Janet
Phillips, Jennifer Elmezzi
Richman, Patricia Louise
Sackin, Jessica Simone
Stewart, Jessica Lee
Wallace, Renée Odilia
Zepeda, Elizabeth Greenlees

1-7-2011

Bruce, Janelle Nichole
Corkran, Christine Marie
Dansereau, Sarah Rose
Houle, Suzanne Rose
Kim, Diana Shin
Mitchell-Tombras, Katharine S.
Noel, Elizabeth Victoria
Queen, Crystal Michele
Rao, Smita Ashok
Rhee, Caroline
Root, Katie Anne
Schoenfeld, Nancy Lynn
Sekhri, Rajni Kumari
Vahey, Megan Suzanne
Vora, Reema Rajesb
Watkins, Barbara Patricia
West, Rasheedah Taliah

1-10-2011

Glosser, Deborah Beth
Petrova, Angela

1-14-2011

Boardman, Deborah Lynn
Fungaroli, Joanne Mary
Menkes, Lauren Dale
Roberts, Jenny Misao

1-20-2011
Blaeuer, Maria Evangeline
Largie, Laverne Marie

1-24-2011
Chang, Sandy Shu-Yu

1-25-2011
Dumouchel, Katherine Shannon

1-31-2011
Brown Gaines, Eden Joanna
Steil, Marybeth Lenkevich

2-3-2011
Fisher, Courtenay Clarke
Hatef, Bethany Kate
Omoruyi, Edoghogho Dominica
Owens, Danielle Dionne
Samuels, Nicole Patricia Ruth
Sprowls, Leigh Nicole
Sullivan, Rebekah Joy Henn
Tsotakos, Alexis Nicole
Wells, Shanelle Celeste

2-7-2011
Burnette, Lauren Marshall
Drykerman, Rikki Susan
Tomasello, Beth

2-16-2011
Levine, Jennifer Perry

2-22-2011
Ford, Megan Jean

2-23-2011
Deane, Heather Shoaf

3-3-2011
Burgan, Genelle Alyse
El-Shammaa, Mary Anne
Ortega, Sharyn Marie
Spero, Navah Chaya
Stockhausen, Megan Bridget
Usova, Georgeanne Michelle
Wagstaffe, Leslie Mills

3-23-2011
Gonzalez Gallego, Catherine

3-29-2011
Post, Julia Finkel
Shin, Dongbin Christina

4-5-2011
Seabrook, Robyn Nicole
Simpson, Elizabeth Anne

4-6-2011
Van Saanen, Marisa Bronwyn

4-7-2011
Carr-Lambert, Rebecca Allison
Gray, Trish Lenae
Taylor, Kathryn Elizabeth
White, Cheryl Denise

5-4-2011
Gilman, Amanda Burrell
Yakren, Sofia

5-16-2011
Fitzgerald, Meaghan McCabe

6-1-2011
Cohn, Jaime Alexadra
Ryan, Bridgette Elizabeth

6-13-2011
Rabb, Katherine Anne
Small, Sandra Graffley

6-15-2011
Abdul-Majid, Mujadala Mumtahina
Adams, Amanda Sue
Adams, Dana Nicole
Adams, Danielle Duvall
Afkhami, Sadaf
Alexander, Elizabeth Evans
Anderson, Lindsay Marie
Baden, Deborah Solano
Bauman, Lisa Weill
Beasley, Mary Elizabeth
Berman, Karen Beth
Bertrand, Amal Amelie
Bey, Tiana Afrika
Blount, Natasha Cara
Blundell, Laura Marie
Bond, Jocelyn Patricia
Borenstein, Sylvia Fait
Boursiquot, Victoria Mulenga
Boyland, Ashley Marie
Britton, Pamela Jean
Brown, Alexis Yolanda
Burch, Katie Marie
Byron, Margaret Kinsey
Carlin, Sarah Catherine
Case-Herron, Sarah Elizabeth
Cassell, Melissa Leona
Chancellor, Carroll Ashley
Cheikh, Erin Marie
Churchyard, Lori Jo
Claywell, Erin Marie
Cogswell, Leah Lynnette
Collins, Maudisa McSween
Craddock, MyEsha Ruth
Dailey, Jenna Kay
Dao, April
Daramola, Bisola Oluwatoyin
Deckelbaum, Amy Cheryl
Dickerson, Tiphany Baker
Dwyer, Elizabeth Ann
Earle, Lauren Grace
Evans-Sendall, Sharon Ann Elizabeth
Fithen, Melinda L.
Ford, Caroline Elizabeth
Frate, Christine Marie
Fuchs, Jacqueline Fay
Gantt, Jana Michele
Gardner, August Martina
Genco, Allison Marie
Glover, Crystal Jesselyn
Godoy Brito, Diana Cecilia
Goitein, Hannah Rose
Goldberg, Betty Ngoc
Gorney, Mollie Danielle
Gregory, Maggy Lewis
Habtemariam, Abeba Emnetu
Hamilton, Lauren Rebekka
Harding, Jennifer Irene
Harlin, Daria Marie
Hasan, Nida
Hatfield Yanacek, Meghan Renee
Heidari, Natasha Jeyran
Hendrix, Kemba Ayanna
Heyliger, Victoria Lyn
Holcombe, Olivia Rebekah
Hollis, Princess Jaynece
Honarpisheh, Rosa
Hopkins, Gabriela Quercia
Huang, Lu
Hughes, Deandra Marie
Hurst, Jessica Lana
Ibidapo, Ima-Nkoyo Chioma
Inderfurth, Ashley Ann
Iqbal, Zeenat Asra
James, Denise Nicole
Jarvis, Camille Janette
Joe, Amoree Nika
Johnson, Charlene Annette
Joshua, Aimee
Joshua, Jamie
Kalwa, Suzanne Renee
Kang, Se Hoon
Kang, Soo Yong
Katrivanos, Nicolle Eleni P.
Khazra, Leila
Kim, Elizabeth Sun-Young
Klecan, Pamela Candice
Klepper, Jennifer Eilers
Kornilova, Anna Guermanovna
Kranias, Anastasia Theodora
Lambert, Amanda Michelle
Lavis, Amanda Jean
Lee, Ha Jeang
Lee, Youme
Lee Bathgate, Susan Kyong
Lentz, Shannon Marie
Levinstim, Ann Elizabeth
Locke, Lisa Jimmelle
Lui, Sai Cheong
Lunsford, Nancy Marano
Mah, Angie Siu Yee
Makris, Eleni Dimitrios
Marengo, Kristen Koterwas
Mathew, Lisa Sara
Mattingly, Amanda Dawn
Metz, Felicia Anne
Meyer, Cynthia Liu
Middleton, Myshala Emunah
Mikoy, Danielle Michelle
Milan, Pamela
Mir, Sarah Hamid
Moore, Zeely Omi
Morris, Marianne Elizabeth
Murphy, Erin Lynn
Nesbitt, Lauren Theresa
Noah, Sadia Isha
Nwankwo, Gift Uchenna
Okura, Aguri Christina
Paine, Trisha Lynn
Patel, Divya Aswin
Perna, Maria Sakavich
Phillip, Maliaka Stacey
Poirot, Thomasina Esmee
Razzaque, Jhumur
Reid, Stephanie Susan
Riggins, Lisa Marie
Rinaldi, Cynthia Youko
Ro, Priscilla Young
Roberts, Haley Michelle
Roberts, Lisa Jane
Rose, Lanarka Lydia
Rothwell, Suzanne Louise
Ruiter, Stephanie Marie
Rushing, Claudette
Scott, Kathryn Meyer
Scott, Tedra Tenille
Sesana, Laura
Shaffer, Maili Kim
Shannon, Ivy Nichole
Sharma, Varsha Mathur
Silverman, Davida Michelle
Sincavage, Alyson
Smith, Kristin Nicole
Smith, Rebecca Leigh
Stampfer, Amy Lisa
Stevenson-Smith, Sahmra April
Strausner, Erica Marie
Sullivan, Bruke Hope
Sullivan, Caroline Granum
Talbert, Cailin Jean
Tarr, Ashley Lynn
Taylor, Maureen Yvonne
Thomas, Alexi Carlos
Thomas, Andrea Louise
Thornton, Maureen O'Hara
Tirocchi, Sheryl Ann
Tong, Julie Vinh
Torch, Jessica Hope
Valencia-DeWitt, Pamela Dawn
VanCleef, Ashley Shanna
Veltre, Brenna Loring
Waldrep, Arren Taylor
Wander, Mollie Lynn
Warner, Emily Elizabeth
Weber, Jessica Paulie
Wessel, Diane Elizabeth
White, Dartania Whitney
Whittingham, Natalie Elizabeth
Williams, Abena Yakini Dede
Williams, Carol Ann
Wingo, Shereen
Woodley, Carmen Lynette
Wu, Melissa Anne
Yang, Kimberly Fu-Jia
Zadjura, Jessica E.
Zhang, Mingya

6-17-2011
Boardman, Ellen Ozga
Connolly, Helenanne
Duston, Laura Dawn
Hart-Edwards, Angela Denise
Lefevre, Margaret Lunger
Thompson, Melissa Moore
VuLe, Sandra Phuong
Zech, Kristin Anne Martin

6-21-2011
Woldemariam, Wintta Mekonnen

6-23-2011
Ewart, Andrea M.
Landon, Jana Michelle
Ochsenhirt, Lisa McGuinn
Tennen, Sara Bresnick

6-27-2011
Cassie, Jane Elizabeth Tommay

6-28-2011
Bergeron, Jennifer Lynn
Sheehan, Kathleen Gabrielle
Sznyter, Judith Ann

7-1-2011
Beckman, Emily Rose Ritvo
Hancock, Manuella Wainwright
Kadagathur, Sheila Jaya

7-11-2011
Andrascik, Kimberly Sue
Balint, Rebecca Teale

Lee, Jaime Alison
McMillan, Charlene Hardy
Portis, Bonnie Lynn
Prakash, Anjali Parekh
Scott, Sara Shon
Seeburg, Whitney French

7-25-2011
Grace, Kathryn Anne

8-24-2011
Peskin, Lisa Kaye

8-31-2011
Allen, Rosica Popova
Anderson, Alexes Erlene
Ayala, Ana Sumei
Broughton, Grace Michelle
Delgado, Tatyana Estybaliz
Fialkowski, Elizabeth Mary
Lewis, Jane Hannah
Lewis-Blagrove, Neisha Petra
McFarland, Ashley Elaina
Ross, Ebony Joyran
Smith, Nefretete Amelia
Stance, Donnika Danéa

9-6-2011
Murdock, Alison Rebecca Stein

9-13-2011
Whatley, Arcola Anne

9-26-2011
Robinson, Virginia Ellen

10-6-2011
Aiyepola, Lydia Oluranti Omotayo
Driscoe, Lara Marin
Hurtado, Jessica Adriana

11-1-2011
Ibe, Chinyere Valerie

11-29-2011
Hershkovitz, Stephanie Yael

12-1-2011
Katz, Lauren Shane
O'Connell, Caitlin Eagen

12-9-2011
Koenig, Elizabeth Joanna

12-13-2011
Abend, Katherine Ann
Adams, Erika Rae
Adcock, Kathleen Dilley
Adegbuyi, Rafiyat Damilola
Adejumo, Simisola Morenike
Ali, Salima Jamal
Allen, Kimberley Kay
Alman, Arielle Cherise
Alonso-Yoder, Ana Corina
Amick, Michelle Anne
Anchors, Lindsay Malle
Anderson, Keleigh
Anderson, Sara Elizabeth
Andrews, Katherine Nora
Anello, Erin Elizabeth-Rose
Angel, Emily Michelle
Apol, Tasnima
Aquilino, Catrina Celestine
Arnold, Briana A.
Ashar, Monica Marie Glockner
Ashkeboussi, Leila
Assefa, Cassandra Charie Valdez
Atas, Laura Harger
Atta, Saiqa
Aybar, Jennifer Lynn
Ayd, Jessica Jendrek
Azocar, Kara Leibin
Balkum, Erica Joy
Barnes, Khaliah N'cole
Barry, Amy Diana
Basin, Mariya
Baum, Sarah Elinor
Beauheim, Alice Diana
Belfon-Valentine, Joi Sharonda
Bell, Lisa Meghan
Bellamy, Yonné Sylese
Ben-Zev, Juliya
Berkey, Shannon Marie
Bertinelli, Alexa Elena
Bidinger, Elizabeth Marie
Bisig, Brynne Cory
Blackmon, LyTia Nichelle
Blank, Avery Morgan
Blegay, Walakewon Massaquoi
Blondell, Nicole Marie
Bona, Andrew Vernon
Bonifant, Nancy Elizabeth
Boppana, Sravya
Boston, Kristen Schrock
Boudouris, Kathryn Lee
Boyd, Sandi Pessin
Bradbury, Jennifer O'Connor
Branch, Leah Lynn
Brassell, Courtney Elizabeth
Brenha, Christina Barradas
Brockmeyer, Katherine Mary
Brondi, Heather Nicole
Brooks, Paula Jean
Brooks-Gelling, Patrice Nicole
Browne, Rita Gayle
Brunner, Margaret Louise
Brunsdale, Shaleen John
Buck, Alexandra Jane
Bucy, Dana Renee
Buettner, Courtney Kaye
Burns, Christine Ann
Caiazza, Amy Beth
Calomeris, Jeannette Linda
Campbell, Sheree Briana
Campbell, Sheri Danielle
Campion Samueleis, Jennifer Barrett
Cane, Nicole Alexis
Cappuccio, Laura Ann
Cardozo, Julia Louisa
Carothers, Christin Cahli-anne
Carter, Melissa Alaina
Cascio, Virginia Marie
Chado, Cheryl Lynn
Chaffatt, Abby-Gail Shannon-Lee
Chance, Antoinette Nicole
Chang, Wei Chieh
Chiarizia, Emily Mary
Chin, Jessica May Yee
Choe, Soyoung
Clark, Helen Torsella
Clarke, Jessica Barbara
Cole, Jessica Lee
Cook, Shelby Jill
Cooke, Brec Allison
Cooke, Elizabeth Ashley
Cooper, Carla Kallman
Cooper, Dayna Chimere
Copeland, Stacy Deidre
Cornwell, Judith Gibson
Cortemeglia, Cheryl
Cotten, Christin Elizabeth
Cruz, Marisa Frances Likar
Cuffee, Antonia Lynn
Cugelman-McMahon, Tara Lindsay
Cuneo, Carolyn Jane
Cuomo, Gina Marie
D'Alessio, Mariela Christine
D'Andrea, Lindsay R. D.
Dahl, Stephanie Michele
Dalphonse, Helen Yoon-Mee Marie
Davies, Kathleen Megan
Davis, Megan Elizabeth
Davis, Michelle Antonette
DeAngelis, Kate McErlain
Dechter, Anne Wallace Howard
Deere, Molly Margaret
Dein, Jennifer Dara
Delawter, Meaghan L.
DeLeon, Katherine Malia Malie
Dembeck, Barbara Jean Callegary
Denison, Katelyn Diane
Dent, Shannon Abell
Denton, Michelle Nicole
DeSalvo, Bria Nicole
Desloover, Kelsey Allemang
Di Salvo, Anne Elizabeth
DiPadova, Nina Elizabeth
Dittamo, Tara Lindsey
Dobbs, Kristin Elizabeth
Dodrill, Andrea Nicole
Dolan, Danielle Ashley
Doran, Erin Eileen
Doyle, Shannon Mary
Drake, Kristin Louise
Drew, Nicole Yvette
Droste, Meghan Alexis
Drumm, Kaelyn Marie
Dubin, Ashley Picker
DuBois, Kelly Esgen
Duker, Maame Vivian
Earley, Katherine Marie
Eden, Amanda Claudette
Eisenmenger, Jessica Anne
Eisner, Marina
Elkins, Sarah Margaret
Emery, Margaret
Essama, Lydie
Evans, Beth Patricia
Fairman, Leah Sebastiane
Farquhar, Margaret Jennings
Farris, Alexis Marie
Fattahi, Parva
Feldman, Dena Lynn Wigder
Feldman, Yana Iosifovna
Ferner, Stephanie Rae
Ferrine, Alexis LaToya
Fersh, Rachel Ilana
Figueira, Julie Rose
Finstein, Eve Rebecca
Fitzgerald, Erin Page
Flanagan, Krista Miquel
Flores, Linh Tran
Flowers, Arija Morgan
Fogarty, Meghann Rose
Follick, Julia Solway
Foltz, Madeleine Nichol
Forde, Jennifer Margot
Fowlkes, Elena Aceves
Fox, LaKeeshia Austin
Foxworth, Ashley Manning
Francis, Susan Kay
Francis-Williams, Latoya Andrea
Frison, Teresa Louise
Frohman, Jennifer Lynn
Fuller, Elizabeth Anne
Galan, Juliana Marie
Gandal-Powers, Mara Kressin
Gandhi, Mahvash Latif
Gannon, Kathleen Claire
Garman, Holly Annette
Gaudiano, Ashley Nicole
Gaughenbaugh, Alison Catherine
Gawronski, Jennifer Lin
Gelmann, Emily Beth
Gemmell, Elizabeth Killian-Marie
Genvert, Lauren Catherine
Geyer, Hannah Rae
Gibson, Misty Phillips
Gilliland, Alexandra Victoria
Ginsburg, Shana Rae
Glaze, Kelly Albright
Goff, Marie-Therese Perry
Goldsmith, Jennifer Susan
Goodman, Rachel Miriam
Gordon, Shari Knollisia
Gottshall, Adrian Barbara
Grabenstein, Sarah Maria
Grace, Maggie Teresa
Gray, Crystal Lee
Green, Sandina Lenina
Grier, Lark Yaa Asantewaa
Grimball, Megan Michelle
Gross Guinan, Gabriela Lucia
Grossman, Elyse Rachelle
Grossnickle, Jacquelyn Marie
Grzech, Erinn Frances
Haghshenas, Parisa
Hallmark, Sara Albert
Halyard, Tashira Shawntae
Lowy, Jessica
Martie, Meghan Dimond
McClelland, Shanice A.D.
Parker, Allison Mae
Pollack, Alison F.
Skinner, Jocelyn Eskow
Thorin, Catherine Jeanne Cravath

12-14-2011
Hama, Sali
Hansford, Masha Godina
Hanson, Emily Rachel
Harada, Satoko
Hardley, Keisha Monique
Harne, Kathleen Haley
Harrell, Tiffany Noelle
Harwin, Alexandra Dianne
Hashmi, Hera Syed
Hawes, Christine Brittany
Haynes, Tameka Daniele
Heide, Crystal LeiAnne
Herendeen, Rosalind Heyroth
Herman, Cara Lynne
Higgs, Emily Alice
Hoffman, Taylor Christine
Holtz, Elizabeth Cabrera
Hosseinzadeh, Kristin Roya
Hottle, Ashley Marie

Howell, Amanda Beth
Huang, Joanna Mengya
Huey, Ashanti Sartor
Hulsey, Sarah Katherine
Hung, Lang My
Hunn, Selena Nicole
Hunter, April Nicole
Hunton, Bernadette Marie
Huo, Ivy
Hussain, Hina Zehra
Hutchison, Linda Sigillito
Hutson, Courtney Metz
Imbimbo, Erica Stephanie
Inman, Kelley Megan
Ito, Emi Julia Elizabeth
Izzo, Anne Nicole
Jackson, Brett Joann
Jackson, Sharonda Rakia
James, Denesha Patrice
Jaskot, Emily Catherine
Jehn, Erin Gannon
Jenkins, Megan Marie
Jewell, Elizabeth Anne
Johnson, Anne Elizabeth
Johnson, Candace Renee
Johnson, Lucrecia Patrice
Jones, Amanda Carol
Joy, Melissa Jane
Kafka, Sarah Elizabeth
Kalinina, Maria Evgenievna
Kannapel, Amanda Christine
Karr, Laura Pierson
Kearns, Elizabeth Ann
Keefe Singer, Jenilee
Kelly, Leah Mary Angelica
Kemerer, Ashley Lynne
Key, Candace Iman
Khanzode, Sonia Satish
Kim, Jennifer Sumi
King, Brittany Leigh
Kirkwood, Heather Jean
Klein, Amy Elizabeth
Klemm, Sara Helen
Klocko, Caroline Hancock
Knell, Rachel Elizabeth
Knoll, Molly Grace
Knolle, Evelyn Fay
Kogan, Hadass
Kostakos, Carly Michele
Kotch, Kristin Marie
Krishna, Meera
Krohn, Jesse Lynn
Kujda, Melissa Lauren
Kurtz, Jessica Caryn
La Mell, Samantha Brooke
Lakhany, Sonia Fatima
Lamasa, Sarah Emily
LaPier, Angela
Lawton, Katherine Jean Hanley
Lederer, Anneliese
Lee-Chun, Lillian Dee
Lenehan, Maureen Catherine Meyer
Levine, Allison Rachel
Levy, Katherine Heather
Levy, Lauren Fusillo
Lewis, Dionna Maria
Lewis, Taylor Nicole
Licorish, Khalilah Sade
Lindberg-Aganga, Amanda Marie
Lindenbaum, Dara Sircus
Lohmann, Stacey Michele
Lohmeyer, Kristen McManus
MacVittie Kpetigo, Rebecca
Maier, Krista Rachel
Maiorino, Roz
Malloy, Breana Michelle
Mansbach, Rebecca Eve
Marini, Lauren Elizabeth
Marinzel, Alexandra Jean
Marucci, Ashley Lynn
Maslikova, Ioulia Sergeevna
Mastrogianis, Helena Christina
Matese, Victoria Anne
Matthews, Cheryl L.
Maul, Laura Louise
Mayo, Natalie Nicole
Mayo, Nola Mondesir
Mays, Tianna Jade
McCarthy, Meghan Alison
McCrary-Dennis, Alexandra Leonettie
McDowell, Jaimee Chaveed
McInturff, Elizabeth Joan
McIntyre, Kristen Ann
McKnight, Erica LaVerne
McManus, Jennifer Caragh
McNeal, Patricia Ann
McQuillen, Robyn Anne
Medina, Melanie Ann
Mehta, Shetal Mithani
Mehu, Natasha Edwine
Mendiola, Sarah Catherine
Meyer, Lauren Sydelle
Millard, Alexandra Elisabeth
Miller, Gina Kristol
Miranda, Christine Elizabeth
Mobley, Brittany Monique
Montanez, Marissa Ann
Moody, Anna Katherine
Morgan, Emily Josephine
Morrow, Lindsay Elizabeth
Morse, Theresa Catherine
Morton, April Meredith
Moses, Jana
Moy, Laura Michelle
Muenzfeld, Danielle Kidd
Mullen, Ashley Erin
Murray, Heather Ann
Muschett, Bonnie Michica
Myers, Jennifer Rachel
Neely, Clynnetta Kimberly Patricia
Ng, Connie May-Ting
Nielson, Katherine Hogan
Nnoli, Eileen Chiamaka
Nonaka, Melissa Olivia
Norcross, Diane Elizabeth
Norton, Tamica Cadisha
Norwood, Kendra Perkins
Nunez, Jasmin Adrianne
O'Brien, Colleen Kennedy
O'Connor, Shakisha Ayana
Oberhausen, Jennifer Lindsay
Oliphant, Kamilah Shani
Olive, Jessica Marie
Orthner, Monika Frieda
Owen, Meredith Lauren
Owens, Clarisse Ann
Tyrrell, Katherine Schuyler
Wolf, Ariel Seth

12-15-2011

Davis, Shauna Lynn
Feeney, Jessica Wenny
Lee, Samantha Shinsato
Medvedev, Katerina Dorothy
Pappas, Katherine Elizabeth
Paraguya, Reena Pastrana
Pardo, Anna
Parry, Caitlin Emelia
Patterson, Sydney Marie
Paul, Rachel Lauren
Pava, Mindy Beth
Pensyl, Heather Rae
Peters, Rebecca Nicole Bloomfield
Phillips, Jessica Laine
Pike, Jennifer Lindsay
Pillai, Vineetha
Posten, Lauren Ann
Pourhosseini, Sarah Mariam
Preston, Julia Eve
Pugh, Catherine Lucille
Ramsey, Amy Nicole
Ramudo, Patricia Ann
Randall, Lindsey Farrah
Raquin, Isabelle Roxane
Ray, Alta Marlynn
Rebarber, Jessica Ann
Rescigno, Maria Eugenia
Resurreccion, Jamie-Lynn Alerta
Rettammel, Lia Sumitra
Reynolds, Alison Rosholt
Ricci, Patricia Anne
Rice, Heather Ann
Richardson, Orriel LaShae
Richter, Ena Juvardo
Roberson, Sydney Elyse
Robinson, Melissa Marie
Rohm, Emily Ann
Rothschild, Jennifer Michelle
Rungfarsangaroon, Ann
Rusin, Courtney Micole
Ruthven, Marisa Elise
Ryf, Colleen Mary
Sakai, Laurel Mikie
Saladino, Julia
Salomon, Michelle Amy
Samu, Dianne Zemnaan
Santella, Amanda McLaurin Boote
Santora, Alexa Ariana
Sarti, Erica Laura
Schantz, Melissa Ann
Schlanger, Serra Jessica
Schuster, Margaret Frances
Schwarcz, Aniko Rebecca
Seifert, Elizabeth Ann
Shaffer, Kristin Eriika
Shaner, Elizabeth Moody
Sharma, Arushi
Shea, Emily Elizabeth
Shea, Katherine Baird
Sheckleford, Michale Alecia
Shelton, Ashley Nicole
Sheppard, Rebecca Jean
Sherry, Nishamarie Bose
Sheth, Mona Yogesh
Shovlin, Katherine Elizabeth
Shutinya, Mariel Whitney
Sidorova, Anastasiya
Siedell, Emily Fairchild
Silverstein, May Olivia
Silvestri, Kathryn Hall
Simmonsen, Rachel Anne
Simpson, Sarah Lynne
Sitapara, Roshni Arvind
Slattery, Catelyn Elizabeth
Smith, Amanda Leigh
Smith, Rachel Sarah
Smith, Sarah Louise
Smokler, Alexia Nicole Baba
Smoluchowski, Jessica Anne
Snavely, Rachel Cara
Soderberg, Eve Christina
Soles, Maureen Berard
Sorathia, Sadia Ruby
Southerland, Janel Asheley
Spiering, Emily Jo
Spooner, Ashley Regina
Starkey, Miranda Rae
Stenlake, Katherine Anne
Stephenson, Andrea Lynn
Stevenson, Elinor Olga
Stewart, Ellen Renee
Stone, Pamela Jill
Straight, Alyson Anne
Studer, Carolyn Olivia
Studt, Christina Michele
Sullam, Jennifer Malia
Sussman, Sara Rebecca
Swaney, Julie Marie
Sweet, Jocelyn Anna
Szafran, Tammie Louise
Tam, Jennifer Lena
Tarlecki, Michelle Lynn
Taylor, Allison Whiteman
Taylor, Brandi Ann
Taylor, Lisa Marie
Taylor, Shari Amanda
Teitel, Adriana Ruth
Tellock, Michelle Maria
Theodore, Elisabeth Susan
Thomas, Laura Lynn
Thompson, Blair Erin
Thompson, Katherine Parkman
Thompson, Lauren Nicole
Thompson, Savannah Elizabeth Schram
Tiv, Prachin Sam
Traini, Cecilia Grace
Travanty, Constance Elizabeth
Tung, Mary Beth
Turner, Lauren Ashley
Tushe, Nadine Bahia
Valle, Diana Carolina
Venkatesh, Soumya
Virtue, Ashley Allison
Vlasova, Anna Alexandrovna
Wallace, Lauren Elizabeth
Walters, Caitlyn Kelly
Walters, Revée Michaela
Ward, Ernestine Jallaya Zahir
Wargo, Amanda Lynn
Warner, Blair Christina
Weaver, Janeé Claressa
Webb, Tiffany Louise
Weber, Joy Kenawell
Weeks-Titus, Makeda Maria
White, Danielle Frances
White, Emily Elise
Whitney, Caroline Elizabeth
Wilcox, Kara Michelle
Wilkinson, Ashley Ann
Willcox, Kathleen Carolyn
Williams, Heather Leigh
Williamson, Danielle Antoinette
Willis, LaRita Mae
Wilson, Jennifer Lynn

Wilson, Jennifer Marie
Wilson, Kristen Nicole
Wilson, Nichole Catherine
Wisner, Jessica Kathleen
Wolf, Megan Louise
Wolfsheimer, Amy Beth
Wood, Portia Marguerite
Wyman, Christine Glendenning
Yates, Brittany Danielle
Yohannes, Sidon Yemane
Young, Katherine Alice
Youngblood, Charlotte Megan
Ziegler, Lauren Banaszewski
Zubair, Sarah Meagan

12-21-2011
Burke, Rachel Denger
Calem, Andrea Rae
Kling, Virginia A.S.
Whyte, Megan Kathleen
Barry, Kathleen Mary
Perry, Stephanie L. Terry
Prentiss, Gail Randolph
Sweeney, Carolyn Maria

1-3-2012
Celestin-Antonin, Lynn Michele
Cohen, Leslie Ruben
Feld, Tamara Shari
Heimann, Robin Adele
Hopkins, Jacqueline Denise
Lebowitz, Donna Sue
Nazareth-Phelps, Natasha Marina
Robins, Ann
Swank, Sarah Elizabeth

1-5-2012
Abrams, Tanya Marie Newhouse
Childress, Jessica Nicole
Dinkin, Victoria
Estrada, Emily Lauren
Fonner, Gina Frezzo
Hao, Grace
Hirsch, Rachel Ann
Hung, Alice
Levin, Anna Tova
Lieberman, Eve Susan
Lopez, Mara Rebecca
Maier, Gloria Kathleen
McKitty-Griffin, Esther Arlene
Moore, Jennifer Marie
Panza, Lucía
Pavlik, Mary Elizabeth
Pinkrah, Jessie Ama
Wickwar, Amanda Jill
Yordanova, Milena Stefanova

1-6-2012
Blackledge, Morgan Leigh
Cantrell, Constance Helen
Guy, Sally McMillan
McDougall, Courtney LeighAnn
Mollock, Shakaira Simone
Prease, Lauren Carole
Russell, Tangela Carrie
Shepley, Cara Ann
Shippey, Sydney Justine

1-9-2012
Flaherty, Reneé Denise

1-11-2012
Rembert-Carroll, Devon Grace
Trimmer, Cynthia Kay

1-12-2012
Bennett, Jamie Michele
Munasifi, Dina Samar
Vernet, Ruth Janet

1-27-2012
Mitchell, Tabitha Nicole

1-30-2012
Austin, Page Insley
Morris, Jennifer Rose

2-2-2012
Ahmad, Aasma
Allen, Rachel Diane
Boffen, Christina Nicole
Hunter, Denise Marie
Jones, Blaire Glover
Newman, Megan Cunnion
Smith-Scott, Arlene Adasa
Terrill, Katherine Alice

2-6-2012
Reed, Shaterra LaFaye
Wright, Sarah Christine

2-9-2012
Clapman, Alice Joanna

2-17-2012
Singleton, Crystal Melissa

2-22-2012
Brown, Julia Mehr

2-23-2012
Gold, Sara Ellen

2-29-2012
Roy, Priya

3-1-2012
Berry, Susan Charmaine
Chandrasekher, Rekha
Clark, Rena Adonica
Nwankwo, Raluchukwu Eziafakaego
Steward, Rosalyn Clarisse

3-15-2012
Maleck, Marisa Christina

4-5-2012
Boring, Amy Renee
McDowell, Zila Domenica

4-19-2012
Hill, Eve Lynne

5-2-2012
Coleman, LaTosha LaVette
Lee, Peggy Po-I
White, Jana Dolores

6-4-2012
Broderick, Catherine Emily
Ferrette, Chelsea Philippa

6-6-2012
Dolan, Stephanie Renée
Elledge, Caitlin Flannery
Watson, Leah Monique

6-8-2012
Lasher, Patricia Johnson
Miorini, Yahne Yvonne Denise
Okun, Joleen Roslyn
Taylor, Teresa Nicole

6-12-2012
Duncan, Adrianne Claire
Schott Murray, Catherine Faye
Simms, Gina Laurie

6-14-2012
Clary, Allison Grace
Habl, Nicole Kathryn

6-19-2012
Ladle, Julie

6-20-2012
Adams, Stephanie Ann
Adaramola, Ilesanmi Olaseni
Ash, Brandes Shenée Gabrielle
Augustin, Charnay Danielle
Awusah, Daria Chinedum
Bacon, Jennifer Alice
Banihashemi, Sheva Michelle
Barlow, Aleia Nikena
Barry, Alison Marie
Bartek, Alice Bernadette
Bender, Kristen Michelle
Berhane, Yodit Ghebreab
Berry, Britney DeAnn
Bingham, Dana Cassandra
Broomfield, Catherine Lucille
Brophy, Stephanie Renee
Brown, Cheryl Underwood
Brown, Rachel Renee
Calderón, Layla Tamara
Capoccia, Nancy Cantarilho
Capunitan, Elizabeth Ann
Carr, Abigail Grayson
Cheung, Melody Ce-won
Chowdhury, Keya
Clarke, Carla Nadine
Clunk, Kara Marie
Cohen, Cori Morgan
Coleman, Lisa Monique
Combe, Holly Elizabeth
Conway, Molly Elizabeth
Cooney, Amanda Jane
Cooper, Natalia Roxana
Corco, Katarina Elida
Cornish, Amber Ninell Moss
Derakhshani, Delara Manda
DiBella, Erica Lindsay
Dimyan-Ehrenfeld, Jane
Dixon, Kertisha Laceria
Doyle, Katelan McKenzie
Driver, Melissa Joy
Elavia, Jasmine Sean
Emmett, Shelby Susan
Estrada, Kathy Mariana
Ferguson, Candice Nicole
Fernley, Melissa Ann
Fesche, Camille Guevara
Fluellen, LaToya Katrice
Fuchs, Neena Sarada
Gentry, Michelle Maureen
George-Wheaton, Amanda Dawn
Gilkeson, Nicole Suzanne
Gordon, Fay La Frossia
Grason, Catherine Elizabeth
Gude, Sara Lynn
Guilarte, Monica Marie
Hamilton, Megan Elizabeth
Harkavy, Brenda Allison
Hayes, Serena Marilyn
Heins, Amanda Jill
Henderson, Vanessa Leigh
Hendrick, Leah Isadora
Hicks, Brandyn Julia
High, Koryn Nichole
Hilton, Sarah Louise
Hobson, Natalie Monique
Holsey, Adrienne Marie
Hulme, Catherine Donnell
Hyland, Kathleen Patricia
Jacobson Faulb, Samantha Erica
Jardine, Fiona Mary
Jesada, Rebecca Alice
Jones, Erica Michelle
Karalevicz, Sarah Kim
Kearney, Mary Catherine
Kinner, Meredith Leah
Kuksova, Kseniya Alexandrovna
Kwashnik, Gretchen Elizabeth
La Rue, Stephanie Altamirano
Lay, Sakhouy
Liao, Leslie Chang
Luethans, Emilie Anne
Maddin, Stephanie Danielle
Maldonado, Nadya Denise
Malloy, Molly Mae
Manne, Caroline Judith
Marciani, Karina Rebecca
McCartney-Green, Ludeen Antonette
McLean, Miya Iman
Meier, Jamie Lynn
Memon, Aisha Elizabeth
Meshkin, Catherine Campbell
Miliman, Jamie Diane
Miller, Shalonda Renee
Mitchell, Danielle Elizabeth
Mohan, Megan Elizabeth
Mojallal, Partmiss
Moses, Audia Fanesha
Myers, Sherry Kay
Nasserghodsi, Sahar
Nelson, Kristin Leigh
Ng, Connie Kwan Yee
O'Donnell, Claire Leslie
Owusukoko, Kimberly Mprengo
Pfeifer, Anna Winslow
Philip, Golda Georgia
Pollock, Leslie Nicole
Potdar, Divya
Pourkarim, Javaneh
Predeoux, Shawnielle Davette
Prokop, Kelli Ann
Roque, Rachel Erica Dahlen
Salim, Debra Ruff
Salu, Shari Ayokuti
Sanders, Shannon Iman Sandra
Sauer, Elizabeth Passapae
Scholten, Hillary Jeanne
Schuessler, Danielle Kathleen
Sedlacek, Keisha Marie
Shea, Stephanie Wright
Simmons, Ivey Lucette
Siracusa, Kristen Melissa
Smith, Danielle Nicholson
Smith, Susannah Eaton
Steedman, Cheryl Athene Steele
Stehle, Katherine Marie
Sussman, Rachel Faye
Tallinger, Kelly Elizabeth
Terrot, Marianne Simone
Thaler, Sabina Bunt
Thomas, Christina Lyn

Tonello, Angela Michelle
Tucker, Richelle Jones
Ukpai, Nneka I.
Unger, Julie Christine
Valadez, Allyson Breech
Van De Mark, Tara Lee
Van Derslice, Elisabeth Rappold
Vasta, Elisa Maria
Venanzi, Amber Rose
Villella, Karen Eileen
Walker, Susan Jessica
Walton, Trina Mathews
Whitten, Dana Huger King
Wimberly, Sade Latrell
Witherow, Michele Dawn
Wood, Kirsten Kelly
Wootton, Kathleen Elizabeth
Yacoub, Maya Gabrielle
Yeh, Teresa

6-22-2012

Gappen, Tamara Lynn
Weiner, Emerald Erickson
West, Melanie Mayo

6-29-2012

Ehiawaguan, Justina Omon
Haiber, Jayne Therese

7-3-2012

Adelman, Leslie Jean
Batie, Marianna
Battle, Sasha Elizabeth H.W.
Huang, Shirley May

7-10-2012

Desai, Bindi Kishor
Kommuru, Caitanya Gopalrao

7-12-2012

Braxton, Cathy Ann
Ferrante, Teresa Anne
Lambert, Denise Ann

7-17-2012

DeCoster, Rebecca Ann

7-19-2012

Thompson, Julie Parker

7-26-2012

Benno, Deetza Galeet
Cobb, Nancy Chrissinger
Sanders, Stenise Rolle

8-1-2012

Leighton, Ashley Marion

8-3-2012

Biggs, Ambika Joline

8-10-2012

LeGrand, Rebecca Suzanne
Parson, Vietta Elizabeth

8-13-2012

Gaztambide-Arandes, Laura Judith

8-21-2012

Ewert, Michelle Yvonne

8-27-2012

Ballenger, Laurie Grace
Renaud, Ellen Kyriacou

9-6-2012

Cooper, Jacques Lee
Hampton, Kelley Anne
Holness, Toni Elizabeth
Hosain, Anna Asra
Jennings, Sharita Donte
Moore, Danielle
Pittman, Elizabeth Michelle Wagner
Salguero, Rosemarie
Santerre, Julia Bridget
Williams, Keisha Elaine

10-3-2012

Roberson, Camilla Louisa

11-1-2012

Glass, Nancy Caroline
Shelley, Naza Nicole
Stinson, Joycelyn Romanetta

12-7-2012

Donaldson, Dorothy Lee
Gorelik, Dana Allison

12-10-2012

Hall, Klaudia

12-11-2012

Agboola, Yewande Ajoke
Ahmad, Hajrah
Alejandro, Hannah
Alencherry, Luica Mary Johnny
Aljinovic, Katherine Ilsa
Alkebsi, Zainab Abdulwahab
Altema, Irnande Marie
Amato, Natalie Rose
Ambush, Whitney Alexis
Amelga, Liya
Anderson, Sharifa Akanke Netifnet
Anderson, Rose Erin
Anderson, Karen Elizabeth
Archung, Kelly Ann
Arkwright, Amanda Leigh
Arnold, Shalonda Gayton
Autrey, Chanell Denise
Ayalew, Mahlet
Aygun, Serra
Bagley, Katherine Sarah
Baldwin, Carol Noel
Baldwin, Jennifer Louise Petty
Ball, Jamila Patrice
Barnes, Felicia Hope
Barteld, Leah Elizabeth
Basso, Samantha Marie
Baugh, Sarah Allison
Baust, Donna Carol
Bayly, Elizabeth Catherine
Bayus, Kristy Lee
Beach, Meredith Lee
Beaghler, Mary Elizabeth
Beech, Tara Marie
Bensky, Stacy Lianne
Berkson, Allison Jessica
Berman, Emily Anne Goldberg
Bernal, Carli Rae
Berndtson, Ellen Dana
Beuchler, Alexandra Kathryn
Beuhler, Elizabeth Ann
Biddings, Verlene Minneva
Biggs, Melissa Lynn
Binau, Anna Noelle
Bird, Lindsay Elizabeth
Blackwell, Michele Nicole Gates
Blake, Jillian Nicole
Blemur, Jennifer Ashley
Blumberg, Jessica Susan
Boening, Emily Ann
Bohbot, Jescie Lynn
Bohrer, Carrie Virginia
Boluda, Jessica Noelle
Boone, Elizabeth Ann
Borges, Deborah Nadine
Boyd, Marianna Lonice
Boyle, Kara Lacy
Boyle, Suzanna Lynne
Bracho, Raquel Gislea
Bramble, Emma Alicia
Braslow, Kimberly Denise
Brecher, Marcie Lynn
Breen, Rachael Elaine
Breese, Danielle Gertrude
Brooks, Catherine Margaret
Brooks, Jourdan Elise
Brooks, Shaneequa Yvette Bourne
Browder, Rachel Anne
Brown, Alyssa Ladona
Brown, Lesley Taylor
Brumfield, Shanika Meshae
Brunner, Michelle Anne
Bruyere, Brandy Lynn
Bryant, Casey Laura
Bullard, Alice
Burke, Janine Marie
Burniske, Jessica Sara
Caldwell, Catherine Henrietta
Cameron, Kelsey Welch
Caplan, Lauren Rebecca
Carfora, Debra Jean
Carmack, Freda Jacqueline Fox
Carmean, Monica Whitted
Chiang, Sarah Ping Hsuan
Cho, Charlene
Choi, Sun Hee
Chu, Meng-Wei Peggy
Clarke, Heather Leigh Allison
Clarke, Patrice Meredith
Clausen, Elsa Lucia
Cockerham, Eva Christine
Cohen, Erin Michelle
Colwell, Theresa Mae
Conner, Abre Leann
Cook, Lindsey Michele
Cooper, Channing Marie
Cornejo Suarez, Daniela Ximena
Costabile, Amanda Sedriks
Craine, Khyla Danielle
Cramer, Brittany Paige
Cronin, Lindsay Elizabeth
Curtis, Jeanette Madeline
Cynn, Young Ah
Czanecki, Michelle Patricia
Dachelet, Whitney Danielle
Dachman, Pauline Toby
Dankner, Margot Sarah
Darnell, Kelsey Michelle
David, Tatiana Suren
Delisio, Christine Straub
Demedis, Katherine Arrianna
Denholm, Mary Lynn
Denny, Laura Kathleen
Desaulniers, Courtney Leigh
Desperes, Michelle Marie
Devan, Emily Kathryn
Devaser, Holly Holmes
DiBiasio, Amy Jennifer
Dickey, Ruth Eleanore
DiMauro, Jennifer Megan
Disque, Lila DeViverios
Dolin, Elizabeth Katherine
Donohue, Laura Ann
Douthat, Lacey Anne
Drake, Elizabeth Lee
Dubick, Emily Alexa
Dunn-Reid, Ann-Marie Carol
Eisenrauch, Emily Marie
Elfner, Lauren Marie
Ellwanger, Brittany Laine
Estoesta, Ivy Clarice Celestial
Evans, Tamara Lynn
Evens, Lauren Elizabeth
Fagbohoun, Morolake Beverley M.
Falb, Alison Forslund
Farrar, Elizabeth Ann
Feldman, Kiri Lee
Fisher, Grey Brant
Fisher, Juila Mariko
Fisher, Nicole Marie
Ford, Brianna Marie
Ford, Madelaine Virginia
Forton, Jessica Marie
Frank, Lindsey Nicole
Freimuth, Emily Jean
Fujioka, Lauren Kyoko
Fujisaki, Alexandria Soleil
Ganvir, Malini Hyacinth
Garcia, Melanie Louise
Gardner, Casey Elizabeth
Gardner, Mary Melissa
Gehringer, Jennifer Marie
Genevich, Kelsey Anne

12-12-2012

Foehrkolb, Kristina Vladimirovna
Gawnyalla, Feh Kafuh
Ghuma, Rayyan Abdulmtaleb
Gibbons, Lauren Marie
Giblin, Katherine Mary
Gibson, Malia
Ginsburg, Jennifer Blair
Glass, Megan Christine
Godwin, Katherine Elizabeth
Goldberg, Jaclyn Michelle
Goldich, Meredith McIsaac
Goler, Kellyn Marie
Goluskin, Chiara Tattiana
Gonsalves, Stacie Lynn
Goodman, Kathryn Rose
Goodman, Shaina Leah
Gordan, Rachel Mara
Gosselink, Jill Suzann
Graham, Beverly Jo
Grant, Wanda Lafaye
Gray, Elissa Anna
Green, Megan Elizabeth
Gregory, Tierra Roberta
Grove, Callyson Taylor
Grunberg, Jessica Kim
Gujral, Rasneek
Gutierrez, Llamilet
Guy, Erica Marie
Haghani, Shadan Ebadollahzadeh
Haimovitz, Erica Hope
Hall, Stephanie Renee
Hamilton, Lisa Michelle
Harris, Sara Anne
Harrison, Jennifer Lynn

Hatcher, Jessica Christine
Healy, Meredith Burns
Heesch, Meghan Elizabeth
Heim, Maggie Arina
Helmes, Rebecca Ann
Hendricks, Melissa Ann
Henry, Lorna Maria
Henson, Maryam Nissa
Hernandez, Dinora Aracely
Hernandez, Jenny Reed
Hershey, Rachel Ganong
Hession, Jennifer Leigh
Hodge, Ashlee Victoria
Hoidra, Shirareh Borhani
Holgate, Heather Rochelle
Holmes, Devon Rae
Hong, Ji-Min
Horne, Deborah Ruth
Horwitz, Julia Ann
Hubbard, Alyson Gayle
Hughes Niazy, Bridgette Summer
Hussain, Aiysha Sultana
Iames, Karen Ann
Ignatowski, Elizabeth Anna
Irvin, Traci Janelle
Irving, Brooke Elyse
Issac, Raquel Ann
Ivey-Crickenberger, Jennifer Lynn
Izevbigie, Osasumwen Natalie
Jackson, Caroline Elaine
Jackson, Catherine Alicia Seward
Jackson, India Ashley
Jaffee, Kathryn Lauren
Jasiukaitis, Marianna Mileiko
Jenkins, Julia Anne Geradine
Jenkins, Angelica Denetra
Jentzen, Kelly Elizabeth
Johnson, Andrea Nicola
Johnson, Caroline Elizabeth
Johnson, Muhtarat Iyaboh
Johnson, Jennifer Okema
Johnson, Kathryn Reynold
Johnson, Andrea Lynn
Jones, Cheryl Ann
Jones, Elizabeth Coleman
Juambeltz, Maria Eugenia
Kahn, Alyssa Jonas
Kai-Lewis, Chantal Benedicta
Kalmar, Eva Nicole
Kane, Sabrina Ramsey
Kates, Rena Stern
Kattan, Illana Rachel
Kaufmann, Jennifer Lauren
Kayi, Varsha M.
Keller, Emily Elizabeth
Kendzia, Carolyn Jane
Kerlick, Bridget Kathleen
Kershaw, Gretchen Ellis
Kertesz, Kata Marta
Khirallah, Anne Taylor
Kight, Stacey Ellen
Kilic, Sarah Perron
King, Amy Catherine
Kleiza, Lynette Teresa
Klemm, Lauren Elizabeth
Kling-Quintana, Ines Maria
Klosko, Deborah Kaye
Kociuruba, Alysa Nicole
Kohler, Rachel Joan
Kohler, Krystél Monique
Koloup, Elisabeth Michelle
Koshgarian, Samantha Matthews
Kotey, Samantha Adei
Kramer, Alexis Stephanie
Krasna, Vered Esther
Kugel, Diana
Kuhls, Erin Elizabeth
Kularni, Neesha Radha
Kurland, Allison Gail
Kutzer, Ellen Marion Mays
Lalwani, Pooja Haresh
Lanaux, Marguerite Elise
Landis, Alexandra Elizabeth
Lane, Kimberly Brooke
Lauderdale, Katrina Wagner
Lawson, Andrea Maureen Cole
Leatherman, Amanda Kay
Lechner, Emily Clancey
Lechuga, Jessica
Lederberger, Lisa
Leidich, Anne Renee
Lenes, Victoria Ann
Lennon, Lindsay Hope
Lett, Erin Marie
Levin, Carly Serena
Lewis, Marquisa Latia
Lewis, Sarah Ann
Lindsay, Tiffany Nicole
Lineman, Nancy Catherine
Litman, Leah Mihalchick
Livaditis, Alisa N.
Locklear, Lauren Elizabeth
Loew, Kimberly Ann
Lookadoo, Rachel Elizabeth
Lopez, Jessica Ross
Lustila, Kirstin Michele
Lynch, Laura Ann
Mac Gabhann, Lucy Gibson
Mack, Shakira Nicole
Madavo, Emily Tendai
Madden, Molly Keturah
Mallett, Eyvonne Renne
Marberg, Sarah Christine
Marcus-Wenger, Elizabeth Ann
Markwood, Colleen Elizabeth
Marlow, Christina Ashley
Marnik, Christina Ann
Martell, Lana Nicole
Martin, Denise Adams
Martirano, Maria Ann
Marzec, Megan Leigh
McCarthy, Mary Elizabeth
McCombs, Alexa Brittany
McCulley, Lindsey Nicole
McCullough, Megan Alyssa
McCurdy, Lindsey May
McDermott, Wendy Joy
McFadden, Allison Maria
McIlroy, Leslie Jennings
McMahon, Laura Elizabeth
Meeks, Julie Ann
Mendrinos, Nikoletta Sara
Mervis, Lindsey Cloud
Messina, Kristen Jean
Metelitsa, Olga
Mettam, Anne Elizabeth
Miller, Lauren Michelle Searcy
Miller, Tracy Celeste
Minaya, Mariana Catalina
Mirvis, Margot Lucinda
Mitchell, Sierra Brooke
Mohammed, Aisha Oluwakemi
Molina, Vanessa
Moll, Mary Sheppard
Mongeon, Camille Christian
Moore, Emily Suzanne
Moreau, Justine Marie
Morrell, Vanea Alyce
Morris, Rachel Diane
Morrison, Jacquelyn Renee
Mount, Jodie Michele
Murali, Supraja Tennoor
Murch, Daniela Miriam
Murray, Kasey Kendra
Nable-Juris, Nikola Elizabeth
Narrow, Annais Catherine
Nasir, Sheza
Neubauer, Jennifer Elizabeth
Neuhausen, Emily Elizabeth
Newhart, Lauren Elaine
Newman-Blount, Sheba Michelle
Nguyen, Minh-Tam Le
Nicholas, Amy Lynne
Nichols, Courtney Ann
Nichols, Tiffany Marie
Nowrouzi, Shabnam
Nunley, Kate Nicole
O'Brien, Annie Mahoney
O'Connell, Tamara Adriana
O'Connor, Megan Renee
O'Meara, Megan Fisher
O'Toole-Loureiro, Melissa Mae
Ochoa-Truszynski, Christina M.
Ognibene, Adrienne Lee
Onken, Laura Cielle
Ortega, Chelsea Rebeka
Oshineye, Adetutu Adeshola
Packman, Iris Gillian
Palazzolo, Katherine Anne
Palmer, Jennifer Ordelt
Pang, Lin
Pascual, Rosalinda
Paslick, Marissa Grace
Peddicord, Audra Marie
Pedersen, Cynthia Marie
Pelletier, Pauline Marietta
Pennington, Kathleen Faye Donovan
Perez, Christine Marie
Pergola, Julia Lawrence
Perry, Samantha Lynn
Peters, Mandi Marie Gordan
Peterson, Amanda Brittany
Petty, Tanesha Matthews
Philips, Tracy Elizabeth
Philips, Aliyah Morgen
Plewes, Andrea Kristine
Podzius, Megan Elizabeth
Polansky, Hayley Elizabeth Evans
Pollack, Jennifer Robyn
Ponczak, Jana Lindsay
Posner, Samantha Britney

12-13-2012

Dension, Amanda Blair Sallee
Owens, Kelley Umberger
Preer, Shaunte' Marie
Priddle, Laura Jane
Priolo, Nichole Francesca Maria
Quaile, Leah
Qureshi, Sarah Umbreen
Raba, Jessica Marie
Radke, Amanda Marie
Ragwar, Achieng Rosa Otieno
Rana, Yasmine Ibrahim
Rapp, Stephanie Lynn
Razdan, Neerja
Redmond, Erica Ann Ritchie
Reek, Kristen Nicole
Regan, Kelley Patricia
Retta, Tsehaitu Girma
Reyes, Marianne Angelica
Reynolds, Megan Jo
Reynolds, Lillian Lane
Reza, Jabeen Zehra
Rice, Elizabeth Anne
Rice, Jamie Joan
Rider, Rachael Elizabeth
Riedl, Ellyn Marie
Ritter, Sarah Evelyn
Roark, Christine Trufant
Robel, Michele Lynn
Robins, Sima Gavriella
Robinson, Syritha Leann
Robinson, Tamiesha Captora
Rodgers, Rebecca Juliet
Rogers, Emily Claire
Romagnino, Kara Dawn
Romanosky, Theresa Lee
Romeo-Stuppy, Kelsey Ann
Romero, Alexandra Martin
Rosen, Elizabeth Morehouse
Rosenthal, Sloane Kuney
Ross, Jennifer Jane
Roundtree, Portia Marie
Roussil, Jennifer Megan
Rowe, Elizabeth Cordeiro
Rowe, Elizabeth Lathrop
Royce, Amelia Anne
Royer, Lauren Marie
Ruhl, Christina Marie
Ruiz Garay, Jennifer
Russell, Jessica Lynn
Rusz, Shannon Elka
Sadanandan, Seema
Sager, Rebecca Caroll
Saikh, Jesmin Parveen
Samakow, Rachel Witt
Sambataro, Laura Christina
Sanger, Sarah Rice
Schiller, Sabina Suzanne
Schloss, Leah Selma
Schmaedick, Agatha
Schmitt, Genevieve Claire
Schopick, Abigail Jo
Schramm-Strosser, Meredith Lynn
Schreibfeder, Elaine Meredith
Schuller, Mary Clare Cooch
Schultz, Jana Christina
Severance, Rachel Marie
Shaheed, Jahaan Akilah Ruth
Shanklin, Jan Renee
Shay, Caitlin Eileen
Shea, Jinni Xie
Shearer, Stephanie Lynn
Sherertz, Alexandra Barrett
Sherman, Laura Elizabeth
Shmerling, Bryna Shmerling
Siad, Hodan
Simanski, Catherine Anne Boone
Simon, Amy Michelle
Singelmann, Olivia Sealey
Sites, Heather Brooke

Skinner, Erin Will
Slacter, Ann Rachel
Small, Rebecca Michelle
Smith, Kaitlin Reilly
Smith, Kerri Lee
Smith, Lisa Kaitlyn
Smith, Tiffany Nicole
Smith-Kaprosy, Jessica
Smola, Susan
Snowberger, Amy Marie
Solomon, Bari Rachael
Sorenson, Julie Ann
Spigel, Kelley Margo
Stanley, Sarah Virginia
Stedman, Anna Marie
Steers, Nicole Marie
Stohr-Hendrickson, Whitney Grace
Stubbs, Jennifer Michelle
Swann, Julie Ann
Swick, Ellen Andrea
Tajammul, Shuaa
Taury, Angela Joy
Thaker, Kanan Nitin
Thelusma, Sophia
Thompson, Daria Nichole
Thompson, Elizabeth-Ann Smith
Thomsen, Martha Sawyer
Thorn, Jelena
Thuell, Mary Whitney
Tomar, Shivani
Torggler, Lauren Ashley
Treger, Rachele Mira
Trevisan, Lauren Elizabeth
Troy, Alice Alberta
Tucker, Michelle Lynn
Turkel, Sarah Beth
Tussey, Sara Nicholson
Uchegbu, Uchechi Onyinyechi
Uwanaka, Vivian Ahunnaya Ijeoma
Vayo, Elizabeth Ann
Veenstra, Latham Taylor
Vekstein, Julya Erica
Veney, Tiffany Renee'
Vindell, Aida Del Carmen
Vishnuvajjala, Radha Ranjani
Vogel, Rachel Jean
Wade, Ebony Alere
Wade, Jamille Imena
Wagenheim, Jamie Michelle
Wahed, Lailuma
Wainwright, Laura Elizabeth
Walker, Jessica Tyler
Wallace, Autumn Tonya
Wallat, Katherine Sarah
Walsh, Sara DeSales
Wang, Arianne
Ward, Ashley Jachin
Waring, Christina Marie
Warren, Anne Addison
Waryck, Natalie Ann Tammi
Washatka, Jenna Rose
Waugaman, Mary Brummond
Weatherford, Katherine Ann
Weinberger, Jessica Leigh
Weisflog, Sheryl T. Ntsame
Welsh, Marie Elizabeth
Westveld, Amanda Sue
Wexler, Sara Lynne
Whetsell, Maureen Holly
White, Brittany Amber
Whitman, Hannah Minor
Wiggins, Jennifer Marlene
Williams, Jennifer Noelle
Williams, Krystal Jamila
Williams, Veronika Joy
Wilmarth, Catherine Marie
Winston, Pia Mercedes
Wise-Graham, Sage Catherine
Wisniewski, Melissa Joy Ritmiller
Witri, Sarah Elizabeth
Witt, Rebecca Lundberg
Wohl, Sarah Elizabeth
Wolfson, Kate Elissa
Wrenn, Shannon Dawkins
Wright, Kathleen Lynn
Wyman, Alyson Leigh
Yahyavi Azad, Homa
Yamat, Maribel
Yeh, Nicole Katherine
Yelamanchi, Maheeta
Yi, Deborah Mill
Yoon, Samantha Ahreum
Young, Bethany Janese
Young, Ashley Nicole
Young, Jeanine Denise
Yourougou, Catherine Beket
Zabihi, Sara
Zeman, Shira Renee
Zoghlin, Rachel Claire
Zotos, Katherina Maria

12-14-2012
Juncker, Eva Nicole
Luckett, Melissa Cocci
Mcintee, Sarah Courtney Reimers

12-18-2012
Carr, Maureen Elizabeth
Chapin, Michelle Jacobs
Clark, Elizabeth Ann
Cohee, Bridget Marie
Ramapuram, Christine Stephanie
Selton, Marguerite Leary
White, Marilyn Joyce
Casado, Stephanie Kathryn
Kautz, Larysa Maria
Manseau, Gwenann Seznec
Muttamara, Doungamon Fon

12-19-2012
Wilson, Zenia Gabriel

12-27-2012
Jordan, Kelly Lynn
Marshall, Alina Ionescu
McAuley, Beth Kathryn

12-28-2012
Brogan, Kathleen Ann
Baykan, Deniz Mary
Boronow, Clare Marie
Cornley, Jennifer Hargett
Enyeart, Kali Alexis
Handler, Marcia Susan
Jackson, Amber Nicole
Kim, Im Han
Lee, Amanda Ting-Ting
Lilly, Bethany Jo
Mozaffar, Nadia Shabnam
Roldan, Joyce Maramot
Zaslavsky, Kristen Calvin

1-8-2013
Bortnick, Yael
Campise, Cynthia Patrica
Levy, Michelle Cohen

1-11-2013
Boyce, Sarah Gardner

1-16-2013
Satorsky, Leah Vivian

1-17-2013
Barnes, Crystal Elizabeth
Dixon, Tyeesha Ishell

1-23-2013
Andreen, Christina Margaret
Everson-Donnelly, Wanda Yvette

1-30-2013
Clarkson, Karalyn Marie
Mullins, Alison Rachelle
Nagel, Laura Louise

2-5-2013
Lichtler Carson, Jennifer Marie
Plutnick, Beverly Ann
Pomeranz, Diana Jill

2-7-2013
DiFonzo, Monica Rose
Dudley, Lauren Rochon
Greene, Mary Barclay
Lotlikar, Régine Mondé
Picard, Jamie Michelle
Sauter, Rachel Elizabeth
Sharrock, Lauren Christina

2-8-2013
Bardot, Heather Kathleen
Reimert, Gretchen Carol
Stevens, Taylor Alexandria
Wickersham-Edson, Gillian Eve

2-20-2013
Earls, Danielle Leigh
Tramontana, Christine Kelley

2-22-2013
Mishler, Karen Lynn

2-26-2013
Helford, Bella
McCord, Beth Marie

3-11-2013
Beier, Amy Joanna

3-12-2013
Peirce, Lara Marie

3-13-2013
Beglin, Lauren Elizabeth
Mason, Katrina Theresa

3-20-2013
Massey, Kimm Hudley

3-27-2013
Evans, Danieli Guinevere

4-3-2013
Barrolle, Senchal Dashiell

4-15-2013
Grace, Jennifer Johnson

4-22-2013
Geiser, Cheryl Ann

5-1-2013
Middleton, Sheereen Elizabeth
Vest, Ayanna Nikiah

5-30-2013
Qadeer, Saman

6-5-2013
Lawrence, Rachel Maria
McCarl, Lindsay Irene
Olumide, Adetoun
Shirk, Meaghan Marie
Tellawi, Manal Rana
Whitney, Jessica Marie

6-6-2013
Donahue, Jennifer Lynne
Klis, Deborrah Ann

6-10-2013
Alpert, Sara Louise
Chun, So Alexandria
Dery, Janet Marie
Earnest, Robin Michael
Gold, Andrea Rifka
Martin, Ganesha Michelle
Rhoads, Melissa Lynn
Underwood, Jessica R.

6-12-2013
Keller, Kathleen Mary
DePasquale, Megan

6-18-2013
Davis-Niles, Regina Augusta Maria

6-19-2013
Adkins, Alexandra Hussein
Anderson, Folashade Ama Olubunmi
Anderson, Sopanha Te
Armstrong, Allison Burr
Aziz, Dyana Ramiz
Baldwin, Esther Elizabeth Mae
Barker, Adessa Akela
Belimenko, Galyna
Benedetti, Tara Colleen
Benko, Lauren Karina
Berger, Kerry Elizabeth
Bessicks, Amanda Marie
Blair, Nicole Anoinette
Bourne, Sara Naggar
Bratz Williams, Francesca Magaly
Braz Williams, Francesca
Brown, Leah Nichole
Brown, Rebecca Ann
Buckle, Shavonne Charice
Burlington, Elizabeth McDowell
Burt, Janet Hughes
Campbell, Robin Elizabeth
Campbell, Stacey Helen
Castillo, Jennifer
Cates-Bristol, Jessica
Chang, Ellen Erie
Chimah, Bernadette Uchenna
Chod, Jessica Leigh Rosenthal
Clark, Marissa Ann
Connell, Christen Moire
Costas, Nadya Karina
Crane, Catherine Elizabeth
Damato, Samantha Stokes
Dastvar, Farisa

Davisson, Laura Cook
del Pozzo Darnell, Maria Daniella
Demchenko, Leslie Ward
Desroches, Lyne-Robert
Dorfler, Christy Marlene
Edwards, Courtney Denia
Eikenberry, Diane Christine
El-Shall, Sara Mohamed Samy
Epres, Christine Nagrampa
Esche, Caroline Imola
Esedebe, Adanwimo Beatrice
Fahmy, Sherin Mohamed
Fairchild, Sydney
Fallahian, Saviz
Fernandez, Cristina
Findlay, June Cynthia
Fleisher, Stephanie Lynn
Fleming, Allison Leigh
Forgie, Lauren Elizabeth
Garcia, Laura Danielle
Garcia-Ulloa, Veronica Beatriz
Geiger, Amy Sarah
Ghoston, Stephanie Le'Chele
Gladney, Jamila Amanda
Glaspie, Tara-Yetive Stacey
Gowhari, Kowsar Jamshidi
Griffin, Tamika Chanelle
Gupta, Parul Hemanth
Hall, Alisha LaNea Dorothy
Harsley-Dean, Veronica LaTrice
Hazelwood, Alyssa Kristine
Hillman, Tisha Sherrell
Hogan, Christine Rebecca
Hotz, Heidi Kohler
Howard, Kelly Lynn
Hubbard, Mason McNulty
Humphrey, Kimberly Rose
Jeremiah, Onyinyechi Onyebuchi
Jones, Catherine Denise
Kalutski, Vlada
Kaufmann, Ann Helen
Keith, Katherine Mary
Kim, Catherine Borahm
Kite-Stone, Anneliese Marie
Kobi, Ashley Laura
Kondowe, Angela
Kovarovic, Kate Eileen
Kumarachandran, Kumudha Nadine
Kuntz, Marcia Beatriz
Labuz, Susan Marie
Lacey, Jeanah Daun
Lainez, Claudia Patricia
Lattimore, Kue Miyo
Lau, Elisia Mayling
Lee, Shauna Edana
Leifert, Lilian
Leone, Arianna
Lewis, Sonrisa Marie
Leyba, Tracy Lynn
Lim, Christina Songeun
Linville, Bonnie Alison
Loomba, Namrata
Lubow, Abigail
Lyster, Heather Marie
Maloney, Lorna Elise
Manchester, Meaghan Elizabeth
Mason, Toi Monique
McAndrews, Caitlin Elizabeth
McCulloch, Lauren Cary
McDowell, Tonet Shebree
McNamara, Colleen Marie
Megias, Eileen
Monahan, Laurie Elizabeth
Morales Ford, Nery
Nagaraj, Renuka
Neelbauer, Juliana Celeste
Noh, Pa Ra
Ntiri-Reid, Boatemaa Afua
Obiesie, Nwamaka Stephanie
Okolo, Ijeoma Adaobi
Otvos, Judit Katalin
Owens, Elizabeth Adele
Parmley, Cynthia Jill
Parran, Monica Reve
Patel, Archita Niranjan
Patel, Misha Rajendra
Pavolillo, Shalyn Marie
Payne, Kimberly Elizabeth
Phares, Mallory Ann
Pleake-Tamm, Amalia Maria Pearl
Poppenhouse, Kristen Dyan
Robinson, Courtney Kristina
Rodriguez, Adrianna Christina
Rodriguez, Paola
Rollins, Nicole Marie
Ross, Andrea
Ruffin, Sheila Brittany
Rupinta, Aubrey Sabrina
Saint-Louis, Vanessa
Saleh, Azita
Salter, Stephanie Lynne
Salvatore, Julia
Schnitzer, Samantha Leigh
Schwartz, Casey Michele
Scott, Carly Indigo
Scott, Lanet Renee
Scott, Mia Shantee Renie
Sellers, Tanya Sue
Shebaya, Sirine
Shuford, Andrea Blonder
Siegel, Jennifer Ivy
Skinner, Sakinda Lenice
Smith, Meredith Camille
Staropoli, Alexandra Ferrara
Stearns, Wendy Jane Beveridge
Steege, Sarah Gabrielle
Steier, Gabriela
Stemple, Hillary Muir
Stevens, Jamie Wellman
Summers, Jessica Buonaccorsi
Szeliga, Nicole Elaine
Tang, Jenny Jing Jing
Taylor, Laura Ann
Teng, Kay Jillian
Tice, Arianne Elizabeth
Torres, Johanna Margarita
Turlington, Margaret Eva
Uy, Margaret Ngo
Vample, Erica Patrina
Westbrook, Viviana
Whelton, Natalie E.
Williams, Alana Michelle
Williams, Christina Nesarany
Williams, Eriade Demaree
Williams, Jaclynn Nicole
Williams, Tina Clarice
Wilson, Michele-Ann Coleen
Wurst, Leonice Ann
Yanagihara, Ann Masae
Yasin, Alisa N.
Young, Sarah Elizabeth

6-24-2013

Barrett, Katherine Margaret
Kitchel, Allyson Chilton
Lopez, Elizabeth

7-1-2013

Clark, Joanne
Danner, Tracee Alayne
Debevec, Christine Marie
Flax, Margaret Jacobs
Geraghty, Pamela M.

7-11-2013

Paulus, Penelope Maria

7-12-2013

Dumais, Laura Marie Colangelo

7-15-2013

Berman, Keri Lane
Geller, Rebecca Rose
Hassett, Megan Elizabeth

7-19-2013

Hoffman, Lindsay Jones

7-30-2013

Akinshola, Tinuade Sarah
Macias, Lucia Carmen

7-31-2013

Carter, Abigail Virginia

8-8-2013

Smith, Stephanie Mari

8-9-2013

Brandenburg, Stacey Michelle
Tadros, Mariam Wagih

9-3-2013

Miller, Rachel Ellen

9-4-2013

Johnson, Tiffany Monique
Noorishad, Kiana
Oliver, Essence Latoya
Sykora, Katherine Collins

10-31-2013

Didow, Katherine Cole

12-5-2013

Burnett, Christina Renee
Reynolds, Katherine Ann
Rigamonti, Eva Vittoria
Robinson, Rhonda Obelia

12-13-2013

Silva, Loni Diane
Sim, Mariah Namoseub

12-17-2013

Abid, Nabeela
Abraham, Elsa Anna
Abramat, Alyssa Megan
Abramson, Sarah Jane
Acquaviva, Megan Elizabeth
Acquie, Yodeski Yazari
Agiri, Morenike
Ahn, Kathy
Aiken, De'Ericka
Ailloud, Marlene Shays
Alicea-Cambel, Debra Alia
Almaraz, Rachel Elizabeth
Anderson, Katheryn Elizabeth
Anthony, Katherine Dara
Applestein, Rachel Lynne
Arora, Reena
Arthur, Susan Monich
Atkinson, Rachel Christina
Aubrey, Amanda Christine
Aurelien, Gueter
Axton, Renee Marie
Ayazi, Awista
Azebu, Lauren Michelle
Babalola, Deborah O.
Babheri, Sheila
Babik, Gizelle Genevieve
Baker, Amanda Jessica
Baker, Laura Jean Mitchell
Bardales, Emily Mavila
Barnoon, Yaara Zeeva
Barratt, Christine Marie
Barreto, Rachel Deborah
Barron, Molly
Batey, Kathryn Bosse
Baxter, Sikenah Tranai
Bazik, Nicole Ann
Belanger, Emily Frances
Bell, Avonne Shara
Bell, Lauren Maune
Bennett, Rachel Allison
Bensman, Jodie Adar
Benson, RaShaunda Yvonne
Bevis, Kelley Christian
Bhat, Radhika Uluvana
Bieber, Michelle Alysia
Bitencourt Emilio, Anna Paula
Bitonti, Lindsay Elizabeth
Black, Sarah Louise
Blinstrub, Christine Nicole
Bonventre, Mary Catherine
Bordas, Veronika
Breen-Portnoy, Ceala Eloise
Breslow Boyd, Joanna Pei
Brockmeyer, Lauren Nicole
Brown, Amy Holman
Brown, Lauren Michele
Bruce, McKayle Davison
Buckner, Lindsey Austin
Buenavista, Adrienne Susan Lyon
Buford, Tina Rechelle
Burguieres, Genevieve Marie
Burroughs, Robin Lynn Stevenson
Burton-Bragg, Stefanie Lee Ann
Bush, Lauren Constance
Callanan, Bridget Eileen
Campbell, Laurielle Camille Ann
Campbell, Nekeisha LaVonne
Campbell, Sarah Vickery
Cannon, Brandy Raquel
Caplan, Claire Rasin
Cardin, Courtney Carlyle
Cardin, Danielle Nicole
Cardona, Luisa Fernanda
Carney, Tiffiney Frances
Carpenter, Lindsey May
Cartwright, Hannah Charissa
Casey, Meghan Christine
Cassel, Kaitlin Ann
Catucci, Francesca Angela
Challender, Megan Marie
Chihos, Victoria Leigh
Cho, Mi Your
Choe, Linda
Cimino, Sara Nicole
Cissel, Kimberly Brooke
Clark, Caroline Deneault
Cobun, Heather Grace

Coffman, Colleen Nicole
Cohen, Elizabeth Shaftal
Cohn, Diana Rachel
Colonese, Courtney Rose
Colvin, Lashawnda Renee
Comstock, Margaret Mary
Cooper, Katherine Hamner
Cooper, Meagan O'Brien
Cornwell, Jennifer Armstrong
Cossman, Jenna Nicole
Cramer, Anna Lauren
Crist, Nina Marie
Crouch, Megan Renee
Crupiti, Amy Patricia
Cuff, Charlye Victoria
D'Antonio, Natalie Claire
Danilenko, Elena Gennady
Daubach, Ashleigh Rene
Dawson, Sarah Rose
Daya Korkor, Christine Marie
De Lozier, Emilie Marie
DeHaven, Rebekah Louise
Delia, Cydney Deanne
Demougeot, Isabella Charlotte
Deutch, Lauren April
Diana, Keelan Foster
Dirzuweit, Rachael Lee
Divertie, Adrienne Chase
Dixit, Indraneela Amol
Dollar, Lauren Ilene
Donahue, Kristina Elizabeth
Donlin, Alexis Marie
Dorian, Katherine Ann
Dorr, Kara Abbey
Douglas, Kelly Nichole
Douglas, Mia Brittani
Downs, Caitlin Elizabeth
Drabkin, Sarah Beth
Du, Haixia
Dubin, Yaira S.
Duckworth, Emily Megan
Dunning, Sydney Ann
Dupee, Jennifer Mary
Duson, Lctam Precious Anthonia
Dykstra, Erin Lindsay
Earlbeck, Jessica Nichole
Edwards-Ransom, Julianne
Elessie, Sylvaine
Emerson, Jessica Elayne
Epstein, Mindel Carla
Epstein, Tamar Silton
Erb, Melanie Carol
Erickson-Muschko, Sarah Elaine
Evans, Caitlin Elizabeth
Evans, Grace Anne
Evans, Paula Bailey
Farmer, Jessica Lynn
Farmer, Meghan Kathleen
Fedorova, Julia Valeryevna
Fernandez, Marina Carin
Fields, Caroline Anne
Fine, Stephanie Ilana
Fisher, Jessica Lynnetta
Flanzer, Samantha Campbell
Flynn, Kaitlin Noreen
Foroutan, Mojan Banou
Foster, Janet Maria
Freedman, Leah Cristina
French, Crystal Antonia
Friscia, Alexandra Elizabeth
Fritz, Tjasse Lee
Fryer, Leanne Ewing
Fuller, April Lyn
Fuller, Lisa Graham
Fusting, Emily C.
Gant, Portia Elaine Shizuyo
Ganvir, Serena Lakshmi Natasha
Garth, Jessica Lowell
Geare, Elizabeth Catherine
Gentile, Angela Mary
Gentry, Christine Elizabeth
George, Adedamola Olunfunmilayo
Georgiev, Katerina M.
Gervasi, Christina Noelle
Gibbs, Virdina Stephanie Fabiola
Gill, Ruchi Gugliani
Gipe, Alicia Jennepher
Girard, Jennifer Frances
Gitomer, Madeline Himmel
Gleason, Christina Kate
Gohlke, Melissa LeAnn
Goldblatt, Monica Nicole
Goldstein, Beth Lauren
Gonzalez, Catherine Moore
Gottlieb, Sarah Helen
Graae, Hannah Mitchell
Grady, Karima Ani
Graham, Jhanelle Alexia
Gray, Tifanny Renee
Green, Karin Virginia
Grosnoff, Nicole Shawna
Gruesbeck, Michelle Ann
Gumbs, Hazel Shermel
Hagerty, Elizabeth Marie Frances
Hailu, Hellina Yirga
Haley, Jennifer Marie
Hall, Rebecca Noël Wizeman
Hall, Spencer Margaret
Hambleton, Stephanie Patrick
Hammelman, Melanie Suzanne
Hardwick, Margery Thayer
Harris-Crest, Nicole Ebony
Hauser, Leah Marie
Havemann, Anne Elizabeth
Haymon, Leslie Caroline
Hecker, Elizabeth Ann
Heffernan, Amanda Therese
Hein, Christine Frazier
Heitt, Melissa Sidman
Hendrick, Amber Modestine Steele
Hernandez, Vivian
Hernandez Araujo, Marta Julia
Herodotou, Katerina
Herzfeld, Karin Nicole

12-18-2013

Fisher, Meghan Ann
Hildreth, Sophia Louise King
Hillman, Megan Christine
Hodges, Brittani Lea
Hoffman, Kathryn Opal
Holden, Allison Marie
Holmes, Tanya Dawn
Hong, Marie Shau-Ying
Horton, Laura Erin
Huang, Tiffany Ru-Shuan
Hutchinson, Nzinga Johari
Hynum, Natalie Marie
Igbokwe, Olivia Ugonma
Ighedosa, Ese Rene
Iliff, Jarett Blaike
Ingraham, Elizabeth Mae
Ingram, Caroline
Inniss, Blair Marie
Ives, Alison Michelle
Janet, Carin Ellen
Jara, Ana Lorraine
Jbaili, Nadine
Jiang, Fu-Mei Chao
Jiang, Michelle Ying Chiu
Joe, Yeana Sarang
Johnson, Brittany Sheree
Johnson, Mallory Ann Morell
Johnson, Nana Yaa Adoma
Johnston, Anna Elizabeth Sidney
Jones, Kimberly Caddie
Jones, Chelsea Marie
Jones, Laura Jessica
Kahng, Esther Jee-Eun
Karimi, Najeela Candace
Kass, Rebekah Eva
Kastellorizios, Ioana
Kay, Jamie Elise
Kazam, Elizabeth Toba
Keller, Jill Rebecca
Kellogg, Martha Lynn
Kemmerzell, Kerianne Patricia
Kennedy, Kathleen Patricia
Kerner, Kathleen Rose
Khan, Amira Erin
Kidwell, Jennifer Lee Heald
Kilbert, Angela Mae
Kim, Rosa
King, Lauren Frances
Kohler, Kate Elizabeth
Kolas, Emily Patricia
Kollecas, Lauren Emily
Konstantinova, Slavena Iulianova
Kosman, Mary Anne
Kosmerl, Amanda Lauren
Kramer, Madelaine Amanda
Kuczynski, Rebecca Hasbrouck Wise
Kukaj, Antigona
Kumar, Akshaya
Kylis, Kelly Sullivan
Ladeau, Rachel Adams
Lagomasino, Leslie Ann
Lansell, Allison Marie
Lanza, Emily Marie
LaRiccia, Ashely June
Lavan, Morgan Renee
Lee, Michelle Chia-lin Ruth
Lee, Heain
Leeson, Meredith Pepper
Lefebvre, Celine Sonia Anselmina
LeFevre, Cynthia Teresa
Levick, Rachel Gayle
Lewis, Holly Kathryn
Lewis, Nora Catherine
Lewis-White, Gabriella Marie
Liang, Xiao
Lilja, Marissa Kai
Lim, Melissa
Lincoft, Gabrielle Ann
Lindemann, Bonnie Vi
Lindley, Carolyn Field
Lindner, Genevieve Hayner Reynolds
Ling, Vivian
Lipshultz, Jennifer Rachel
Litovitz, Erica Lee
Lobel, Hannah Justine
Lockshin, Diana Michelle
Lofton, Brandi Mishon
Long, Sari Michelle
Lookabill, Jami Julia Ann
Loring, Inna
Loughner, Kaitlyn Ann
Luebke, Yasemin Kasim
Macek, Susan Lynn
Maddox, Rebecca Sarah
Mainen, Allison Mara
Malcolm, Stephanie Renee
Manganaro, Samantha Nicole
Mapp, Muriel Patrice
Markuski-Fabac, Christina Marie
Martinez, Ariel Ann
Massaro, Stacey Lynn
Mathias, Joan Castleton
Matzye, Jennifer Lynn
Maury, Meghan Julia
McBrien, Claire Durante
McCarthy, Angie
McChesney, Lauren Dalton
McClain, Nicole Emmalee Evelyn
McComiskey, Kathleen Mary
McGee, Christa Dawn
McIntyre, Geraldine Rose
McPartland, Kimberly Eve
Meade, Catlin Marie
Medeiros, Erin Frances
Melody, Lindsey Marie
Menachery, Anne Rose
Mendoza, Maria G.
Messick, Heather Dawn
Meyers, Jennifer Lynn
Miles, Samantha Alexandria
Miller, Kristina Laura
Miller, Erin Elliott
Miller, Giovanna Aritha
Milo, Caitlin McPartland
Missouri, Natalie Olga
Mokhtari, Vida
Monson, Courtney Marissa
Montes de Oca, Julianne Merrie
Morgan, Erin Elaine
Mpasi, Patricia-Joy Kimanga
Mugmon, Sarah Michelle
Munn, Astrid Gabriela
Murphy, Haley Winn
Murray, Allison Scates
Nangia, Mala
Nash, Kristina Marie
Nassar, Shaba Nazarine
Nasuta, Angela Marie Wisniewski
Ndou, Livhuwani
Nelson, Sylvia Claire
Novak, Taylor Leigh
Nowrangi, Priya Mala
Nyarko, Nana Alice
O'Neill, Meaghan Mary
Ofosu, Afua Quaye
Ohanesian, Lilyanne
Okafor, Ebele Pamela
Okojie, Ebosetale Violet
Olusada, Oluwayemisi Nicole
Omps-Botteicher, Lara Kay
Ondeck, Katherine Carol
Ooi, Maura Mei-Lee

Oputa, Chioma Nwabata
Ortega, Windy Rhea
Owen, Rachelle Marie
Page, Ashley Nicole
Pappas, Natalie Kane
Pariser, Jana Robin
Parker, Blair Deana
Parnes, Naomi Esther
Patel, Gayatri Mahesh
Patterson, Emily Michele
Paugh, Brianne Elaine
Payne, Barbara Elizabeth
Peak, Bethany Jennene
Schroeder, Kathleen Oprea

12-19-2013

Bobongi, Laticia Sanchez
Klenicki, Erica Trachtman
Moran, Mackenzie Rae
Pelta, Rikki
Persin, Vlatka
Peyton, Joycelyn Sari
Poindexter, Porschia Nicole
Polasko, Cynthia Lynn
Poonai, Miranda
Pope, Jennifer Stanley
Pryor, Lisa Michelle
Qadir, Lala Rukh
Qu, Katherine Tianyue
Quashie, Christina Louise
Queri, Nicole Marie
Quill, Elizabeth Ann
Quinn, Alyssa Nicole
Quinn, Kelly Anne
Quinn, Anne Showel
Radcliffe, Dalene Agnello
Raswant, Maansi Kumari
Ratzkin, Sarah Jacqueline
Reddy, Vasanthi Guduru
Reese, Kelsey Jae
Reina, Josephine Ana
Reutter, Susan Annette
Reyher-House, Caelyn Arlene
Reynolds, Christine Alice
Rigney, Rebecca Marie
Rininger, Kristin Lynn
Roberts, Elizabeth Lorelli
Roberts, Lindsay Marie
Robinson, PaTricia Ann
Rodgers, Jane Libert
Rodriguez, Hina Luz
Rodriguez, Carleigh Trappe
Romero, Stephany Gissel
Rosenblatt, Alexandra Judith
Rosenstock, Coryn Giles
Rosenthal, Carolyn Krinsly
Rouse, Josephia Elease Georgetta
Ruch, Lauren Michelle
Rudy, Zhi Lily
Rush, Danielle Lynn
Sackman, Brenna
Salaheldin, Maram Taher Shokry
Salgado, Suzanne Marguerite
Samadnejad, Farnoush
Sandler, Elysse Paige
Sapia, Jamie Lou
Schefkind, Melissa Lynn
Schenker, Julie Rapoport
Schlie, Lynn Christina
Scott, Abigail Beryl
Scott, Kathleen Elizabeth
Scown, Samantha Leeann
Scruggs, Alyssa Dominique
Scurto, Natalie Lynn
Seidelman, Eva Susan Chazin
Selvy, Amanda Lynne
Sentman, Maureen Elizabeth
Sferrazza, Lisa Regina
Sharif, Sahar Ashley
Sheehan, Hanna Marie Connelly
Shelton, Jacquelyn Marie
Shemer, Brooke Jaclyn
Shepard, Maude Browning
Shergill, Jasmine Kaur
Sherman, Mackenzie Ann
Sherman, Valeriya
Shumsky, Emily Anne
Siddiqui, Sonia Sadat
Sidhu, Rebekah Elizabeth
Sievers, Miriam Hadass
Silveiro-Allen, Emily Laura
Silver, Shari Heather
Simon, Eliza Hahn
Simpson, Rebecca Oliver
Simson, Emma Page-Riley
Singh, Sarita Maude
Singh, Anisha
Skullestad, Randi Aileen
Slan, Erica Lauren
Slattery, Kathleen Marie
Slaughter, Nicole Andrea
Smith, Jacia Terez
Smith, Shannon Nicole
Smith, Julie Christine
Smith, Amanda Chartier
Snow, Sydney Ra'shan
Snyder, Rachel Natanya
Sonko, Fatoumata
Sorensen, Kim Elizabeth
Sowls, Ashley Nicole
Spencer, Cara Jo
Stach, Jenifer Roe
Steiner, Elizabeth Ebeling
Stelfox, Ashley Michele
Stevens, Melanie Ann
Stewart, Kimberly Ann
Stewart, Rebecca Lynn
Stolar, Julia Robin
Stone, Victoria La Salle
Stone, Devin Goldsborough
Storus, Mallory Brooks
Subramaniam, Sasika
Sultan, Jamilah Nafeesa
Summerville, Jennifer Lee
Swan, Cara Michelle
Swift, Stefanie Gustin
Tamburello, Hayley Elise
Tan, Kim Lam
Tanenbaum, Rebecca Joan
Taylor, Xin
Teague, Elizabeth Kate
Thaniel, Casiya Yvette
Tharps, Revae Marie
Thind, Ravneet Kaur
Thomas, Karen Marie
Thompson, Ebony Monet
Thompson, Elizabeth Helen
Thompson, Jennifer Lindsey
Thornton, Kathleen Marie
Tinnell, Ashley Odessa
Tokar, Erica Lynn
Tolliver, Kei Shionoiri
Tonnesen, Sara Elizabeth
Toth, Kayleigh Ann
Totman, Elizabeth Anne
Treadwell, Chelsea Bittner
Triebwasser, Suzanne Kivel
Trower, Sara Nicole
Truax, Jacqueline Cynthia
Truppi, Samantha Susan
Tullia, Kirsten Elise
Tunis, Jamie Lauren
Ullah, Hafsah
Ulman, Marissa Renee
Umeh, Kaosy Nwamaka
Vallandingham, Rebekka Jane
Van Treuren, Naomi Praveen
Vanselow, Annie Danielle
Vasudevan, Divya Manga
Vaughn, Amanda Rose
Ver Ploeg, Emily Joan
Vieder, Rachael Anna
Villareale, Catherine Patrice
Vissichelli, Allison Marie
Vlacich-Ceppetelli, Adrianna Stanka
Wack, Claire Elizabeth Carey
Wahabzadah, Rema
Walker, Kristen Nicole
Walker, Anna Davis
Ward, Sherri Vauls
Ward, Bridget Kimberly
Waring, Katherine Fiscus
Washington, LaSheena Monicque
Webb, Krissa Love
Webster, Amanda Paige
Wedderburn, Patrice Alecia
Weil, Sonia Louise
Weinberger-Divack, Hannah
Weiss, Ayelet Rena
Weitzman, Carly Blair
Wenzel, Elyssa Lacson
West, Marisa Sara
Wete, Danielle Ymanuelle Tatsa
White, Teza Mishon
White, Danielle
White, Christine Ellen
Whitehurst, Emilie Alexandra
Wilkes, Lindsey Warren
Wilkins, Elizabeth Wood Claytor
Williams, Jasmine Anais
Williams, Cathleen Valda
Wilson, Caitlin Elizabeth
Winters, Jennifer Susan
Withrow, Mary Ellen
Wolf, Helen Kathleen
Woods, Jessica Frances
Wright, Tiffany Regina
Wright, Thelma Bernice
Wyse, Rexanah Philippa
Yoder, Alison Dorit
Yu, Veronica Kristen
Zacuto, Erin Elisabeth
Zadrozny, Sarah Ashley
Zaleski, Cassondra Ann
Zhuravitsky, Maryam
Zorbaugh, Crystal Michelle

12-26-2013

Adelson, Lisa Anne
Borden, Rebecca Anne
Brown, Carole Dominguin
Burke, Susan Laura
Dorfman, Elizabeth Graff
Erhardt, Elizabeth Treas
Haar, Mona Suhayl Kalash
Hanan, Margaret Eve
Hill, Rachelle Elizabeth
Hornfeck, Lane Christine Mills
Johnson, Sarah Moore
King, June Bridget
Levi, Deborah Katz
Levin, Sari Mandel
McDonough, Yuchong Connie
Mitchell, Tara Newberry
Schaefer, Courtney Botts
Spencer, Deatrice Monique
Wabeke, Karen Elizabeth
Wadhawan, Sheena

12-30-2013

Boorman, Paige Elizabeth
Faust, Joanna Lee
Hughes, Lisa Marie
Polley, Gina Elizabeth

1-3-2014

Lendino, Danielle Kimberly
Mayberry, Laura Deanne

1-7-2014

di Marzo, Giulia Maria
Kaiser, Emily Zivanov

1-9-2014

Cacchio, Christina Ann
DeCoursey, Brigid Collen
Egan, Jennifer Lyn
Geevarghese, Anupa Iyer
Hilger, Alicia Ann
Klem, Lisa Jeanette
Longville, Catherine Helen
McCarthy, Megan Rodgers
Moran, Elizabeth Noelle
Russell, Alexandra Isadora
Shen, Valerie Yahan
Thompson, Alyce Wilyn
Walker, Cady Helen
Warner, Carolyn Ann
Whelan, Amanda Colleen

1-10-2014

Birmingham, Marisa Christina
Bogsted, Allison Clare
Bruton, Anna Michelle
Deisher, Kandace Ann
Feagles, Amy Winter
Jenkins, Lauren Anne
Kelly, Kathryn Marie
Young, Jessica Ellen

1-14-2014

Glickson, Melanie Lisa

1-16-2014

Royal, Stephanie Lynn
Wright, Cheryl Ann

1-28-2014

Osberg, Carson Marie

1-29-2014

Saas, Heidi Tindall

2-6-2014

Buchanan, Jayme Michelle
Dawson, Megan Elise

2-7-2014

Smith, Suzanne Rebecca
Smith, Raquel Melody

2-10-2014
Wolhowe, Catherine Gloria

2-11-2014
Gurkin, Danielle Melanie

2-24-2014
Singley, Andrea Michelle

3-20-2014
Leete, Anne Kingsley
Rambsy, Phillis Hegmon

3-28-2014
Stokes, Deirdre Dwyer

4-3-2014
Brasher, Kelsey Anne
Heyd, Brittany Thatcher

4-4-2014
Hannon, Mary Frances

4-16-2014
Bauknight King, April Celeste

4-24-2014
Walker, Onikki Tennel

4-29-2014
West, Brittany Lynn

5-9-2014
Mah, Ashley Michelle
Escobar, Rosana Marie

5-20-2014
Melton, Amber Nicole

5-27-2014
Ahmadzai, Brittany Antoinette

6-2-2014
Cohen, Rebecca Hannah
Mogetz, Amy Beth

6-4-2014
Chitiga, Yevedzo Rufaro
Harrison, Janet Elaine
Nordberg, Erica Susan

6-6-2014
Kelly, Kristi Cahoon
Manne, Beverly Weiss

6-13-2014
Foster, Morgan Elizabeth
Pickersgill, Dianne Stewart
Rosenstock, Paula Amy

6-14-2014
Sellers, Amanda Leigh

6-16-2014
Charintranont, Tharinee

6-17-2014
Abadi, Parisa
Acosta, Iyen Abdon
Agarwal, Meena
Agbim, Ogenna Dionne
Akinfolajimi, Omolola O.
Akpan, Idara Emmanuel
Allen, Lauren Marie
Altamirano, Alicia Vanessa
Alvarado-Taylor, Jamie L.
Anderson, Sarah Jane
Anoriscat, Elienne
Ashe, Jaclyn Faulkner
Bajaj, Sarah Monawar
Barber, Katie Lynn
Barile, Jessica Elizabeth
Bartlett, Juanita Sandra
Baxter, Brennan Richelle
Beauchamp, Allyson Bradshaw
Benesh, Melanie Megan
Bonsall, Ashley Ann
Bouffard, Theadora Shihadeh
Boutsikaris, Constance
Braden, Rachel Felice
Brewer, Brittany Gail
Brown, Christina Margaret
Callahan, Brett Anna
Callanan, Molly N.
Cervantes, Jennifer Lynn
Clark, Megan Frances
Cobb, Hope Alexandra Place Coppage
Collison, Kristin Curley
Cowell, Sunny Hazel
Cox, Mary Catherine
Croft, Heather Marie
Cruse, Rachel Jeanne
Culpepper, Mercedes Aleah
D'Adamo, Kathryn Lynne
Dash, Laura Ann
Davis, Adriene Marie
Davis, Caroline Anne
Dawson, Hannah Marie
Ditto, Brittany Alexandra Anne
Dixon, Safiya Latrice
Dow, Susan Kornegay
Duncan, Laura Grace
Einstein, Joy Catherine
Ellenberger, Gabriel Lewis
Emery, Elizabeth Marie
Fejka, Silvia
Fitch, Tresa Lucille
Folus, Morgan Brittany
Ford, Lauren Ashley
Foster, Ebony Joy
Foster, Katherine Ruth
Frick, Alexandra Barbara
Fussell, Priscilla
Gaffney, Jennifer Burton Gervais
Garg, Anjali
Gehring, Caitlin McCall
Gibbons, Leslie Allison
Gluck, Melissa Elyse
Godfrey, Kristal Michelle
Good, Misty Annette
Goodlander, Emily Catherine
Greene, Megan Marie
Hamidullah, Rasheedah Denise
Hanna, Courtney Ashley
Harris, Cherie Niasha
Harris, Trish Celeste
Harris Souvannamethy, Amanda Nicole
Hatton, Holly Lynn
Healy, Samantha Geddes
Heldreth, Allison Elaine
Hemphill, Athena
Hernandez, Ana De la Hoz
Hoffman, Courtney Dianne
Iannatuono, Maria Louise
Irungu, Betty Wanjiru
Johnson, Shanelle Alease
Jones, Heather Leigh
Josey Ward, Kristin Einera
Kim, Ann
King, Angela Camille Yaminah
Kronfli, Yasmin Rashad
Kuo, Yu-Hua
Laperouse, Alexandra Gibbons
Laroche, Natalie
Lazas, Amy June
Le, Sophie Loan
Leese, Kasha Maria
Little, Paulette Cecilia
MacDonald, Lora Elizabeth
Mack, Barbara Kristina-Nicole
Maddox, Natalie Lynn
Maizel, Beatriz Eugenia
Makris, Stacy Lynn
Malone, Erin P.
Manoharan, Ruby Amutha
Martin, Anna Beth
Mathis, Meredith Samantha Maria
Matthews, Kerry Allison
Maye, Tamara Marie
Mc Nicolls, Mikhaila Miriam
McNeal, Alicia Marie
McWilliams, LaNita Lee
Minhas, Dilpreet Kaur
Molter, Connie Marie
Moore, Alyssa Marie Ruth
Moskos, Danielle Marie
Moskowitz, Samantha Jacqueline
Myers, Dawn Nicole
Nash, Dempsey Dasalla
Norton, Ashley Anne
Norton, Valerie Barbara
Oliver, Rebecca Lee
Ottesen, Dorothea Annette
Parker, Stefanie Jamela
Perrone, Maria Anne
Peterson, Elizabeth Louise
Phillips, Janeé Clovis
Philogene, Ritchie Djenane
Pickens, Carmen Dionne
Plitt, Caitlin Christine
Pollin, Samantha Helaine
Portillo, Alisha Ann
Pradhan, Grishma
Pressley, Hanifa Alisha
Puhl, Emily Anne
Pye, Natalie Amelia
Quinn, Christina Paige
Raheen, Laila
Ravenell, Christia Hope
Reese, Amanda Carmen
Reimer, Stacie Elizabeth
Richardson, Nicole Audet
Rosen, Rachel Catherine
Rucker, Tanya Denise
Saba, Saman
Sakinedzad, Sara
Sanders, Lauren Nichole
Sandul, Alyson Kimberly
Sarowitz, Lindsey Blair
Schifanelli, Gordana
Sealing, Erika Marlo
Shank, Emily Paige
Shuman, Lauren Danice
Simmons, Nicole Lindsay
Simon, Chantel C.
Smith, Andrea Danielle
Smith, Krystil Elan
Snyder, Caitlin Elizabeth Meehan
Stevens, Amanda Marie
Stotler, Stephanie Erin
Sutler, Eliot Leila
Telfer, Stacy-Ann Tamika
Thomas, Katherine Frieder
Trowers, Terron Latoya
Umbrino, Tara Lee
Uzupis, Abby Vexler
Valente, Melanie
Velez, Yaritza
Viscomi, Tiziana
Waymel, Marie Francoise Therese
Weidel, Alicia Andrea
Weiler, Jamie Fisher
Whitaker, Lauren Alexis
White, Amanda Rhea
Wilkerson, Laurie Mitchell
Williams, Enita Ann
Wilson, Cheronne Renee
Wilson, Molly Megan
Wilson Ambrose, Jillian Slater
Woods, Kristin Nicole
Yates, Amani Chenoa
Yeh, An-mean
Young, Meghan Elizabeth

6-19-2014
Anderson, Corinne Christine
Gohng, Eunhae Mary
Montgomery, Malaeika Eyitemi
Talley, Kathleen Elizabeth

6-23-2014
Gusky, Leigh Ann

6-24-2014
Bell, LaToya Renee

6-25-2014
Brown, Margaret Ann
Crites, Allison Joann
Guyton, Helen Gerostathos
Marks, Margaret McCallum
Molitoris, Megan MacKay
Sow, Amanda Gilbert

6-27-2014
Burke, Christine Michalopoulos

6-30-2014
Book, Christa Marie
Freeman, Sarah Katherine
Funsten, Allegra Little

7-3-2014
Burford, Lola Annie

7-8-2014
Lysaught, Judith Gayle
Stagliano, Liza Ann

7-11-2014
Brown, Laura Anne

7-12-2014
Colangelo, Laura Marie

7-15-2014
Gibson, Rosanna Edith

7-28-2014
Buckner, Angela Nichole

7-29-2014
Roth, Pamela Hope
Stamoulas, Maria Apostolos
Wettstein, Nadine Kae

8-1-2014
Smith, Shavon J.

8-5-2014
Gude, Tayrn Lee

8-29-2014
McNett, Keria Marie

9-3-2014
Christmas, Elaina Antoinette
Mwangi, Hilda Waithira
Roberts, Megan Renee
Silvious, Elaine Susanne
Smith, Alice Curtin
Wase, Alana Michelle
Willingham, Jacquelyn Kay Hutson

9-12-2014
Philip, Meagan Meehan

9-13-2014
Kennedy, Elizabeth Jane

9-24-2014
Herbig, Rebecca Sayrd

10-9-2014
Jandrain, Kimberly Jane

10-23-2014
Hennessy, Patricia Ann
Robinson, Catherine Rebecca

10-24-2014
Aburam, Nancy Akua Biraa Addae
Patterson, Christine Steffen

11-5-2014
Royal, Priya Prakash

11-6-2014
Buhay, Mariestela
Bui, Ly Yen
Kim, Michelle Meejung
May, Lauren Marie

11-24-2014
Teitgen, Katherine Elizabeth

12-5-2014
Melloni, Alessandra

12-11-2014
Hickey-Warren, Patricia Mae
Joelson, Marissa Beth
Podlesni, Julie Dillon
Rexroat, Lauren Rae

12-12-2014
Martinez, Sarah
Read, Emily Brittain

12-15-2014
Kennedy, Carly Everett
Ramanathan, Radha

12-16-2014
Acevedo, Krystle Ann
Achuko, Ogechi Cynthia
Adeoye, Beatrice Abinbola
Adetobi-Folawiyo, Victoria Tolulope
Adkins, Cyndi Nicole
Agbai, Nnenne Udumna
Aiken, Ella Rachel
Akhtar, Syeda Sarah
Alatorre, Jessica Cristina
Ali, Sadia
Alpino, Heather Nicole
Alt, Emily Kate
Ameli Grillon, Leila Julie
Amelung, Courtney Blair
Amerson, Ally Merrill
Amos, Amanda Eleanor
Amos, Theresa Lynn
Anderson, Stephanie Antoinette
Archer, Lauren Ashley
Arredondo-Santisteban, Laura
Ashrafi, Safa
Atkins, Eleanor Brooke
Avrine, Iryna V.
Ba, Aminata Jude Andreasan
Bailey, Angelica Camille
Baker, Shannon Marie
Ball, Kaitlin Marie
Bansal, Lucy Brierly
Barbo, Allison Rose
Barnard, Nicole Marie
Barnaskas, Shauna Marie
Barnes, Valerie J.
Bartz, Kathryn Elizabeth
Batenhorst, Cara Marin
Bello, Kafiyah Idera
Bendoraitis, Kathryn Marie
Berihun, Hiwot
Best, Caitlin Leigh
Beyda, Samantha Jean
Biggins, Caitlin Marie
Bindelglass, Julie Rachael
Bitar, Mallory LaRue
Bittner, Magaly Delisse
Blanchard, Nicole Lynn
Bland, Tonya Marie
Blaser, Emma Rose Wischusen
Blevins, Kathryn Louise
Bokey, Jillian Jean
Bondra, Petra
Bookwalter, Elizabeth Mead
Bosley, Pilar Marie
Boyce, Kristen Michele
Braafladt, Katarina Elizabeth
Branson, Tiffany Nicole
Bronson, Jessica Anne
Broughton, Dana Lasha
Brown, Claire Walsh
Brown, Dorothy Nicole
Brown, Kelsey Lynn
Brown, Saudiee Marie
Brunot, Rochelle Odette
Buchanan, Maggie Jo Poertner
Buck, Andriani
Burnett, Megan Brianna
Burnworth, Kristin Sarah
Burroughs, Jennifer Lauren
Callahan, Virginia Regis
Callaway, Kirby Lee
Camacho, Audryana Marivi
Campbell, Margot Melissa
Campbell, Sarah
Cardwell, Jacquisha Racquel
Carliner, Angelica Ashley
Carliner, Leah Judith
Carty, Amalia Mariah
Cassidy, Jenica Erin
Chang, Stephanie Lo-yin
Chavez, Daniela Midori
Chavez, Rosana Esperanza
Chieppor, Jillian Rebecca
Chuka-Obah, Zuka Joy Ogosi
Chuney, Alayna Dionne
Clement, Gypsy Avery Meghan Elizabeth
Clyburn, Naoka Yolanda
Coates, Caroline Patterson
Cobb, Ellen Elisabeth
Cobo, Diana Elizabeth
Collins, Sabrina Reneé
Concepcion, Albania
Connell, Elisabeth Regan
Coonin, Sara Danielle
Cooper, Kelly Jean
Correa, Lyra Gayle
Costantino, Claire Victoria
Costelloe, Sylvia Grogan
Cottrell, Shamia Renee
Cunningham, Jessica Marie
Dailey, Kathleen Theresa
Dane, Rachel Elaine
Dang, Melanie Anh
Davis, Gobriella Monqiue
Davis, Rosalba Novoa
Day, Kristina Lynn
Deegan, Kristen Nicole
Demps, Darra Danielle
DeVoll, Marguerite Lee
Dexter, Erin Elizabeth
Dietz, Kristine Leigh
Doerflinger, Maria Christina
Donahue, Christina Elena
Donohue, Corinne Elizabeth
Dorsey, Heather Anne
Downs, Brittni Ariana
Dunn, Laura Lynette
Eanes, Amber Ray
Ebrahimi Eftekhari, Pegah
Ecklund, Mary Katherine
Eddy, Amanda Colleen
Edwards, Deanna Elizabeth
Edwards, Lilit Sheymajash Konobush
Eisenberg, Hilary Lauren
Ervin, Femila
Espinosa, Jamilah Liz Giraud
Evans, Nancy Ruth
Fahsel, Stacie Marion
Falade, Adetokunbo Amdalat
Falk, Sara Lynne
Fan, Wei
Felder, Katie Lauren Voller
Feldman, Jennifer Lauren
Fernandez, Wandaly Esther
Ferrell, Adrienne Janelle
Finch, Cameron Blair
Findley, Kaitlyn Rae
Finn, Mallory Ann
Firippis, Irene Angelica
Fisher, Jasmine Maria
Flack, Christine Michelle
Fletcher, Elizabeth Ward
Floyd, Laura Elizabeth
Forman, Jenna Lynne
Foster, Kelly Ann
Fox, Stephanie Leann
Fradette, Jacquelyn Erin
Freedman, Samantha Rae
Frezza, Amanda Claire
Friedlander, Anna-Claire Olson
Friedrich, Lauren Michele
Fullerton, Kimberly Lee
Furlong, Katherine Elaine
Gallagher, Cathleen Phyllis
Gallagher, Kathleen O'Neill
Gardner, Michelle Lynne
Gartland, Claire Theresa
Geewax, Allison Grace
Gelburd, Mollie Elizabeth
Gellatly, Amy Malia
Gerhart, Susan Marie
Getty, Katherine Trenholm
Gevorkian, Ani
Glaubach, Julie Anne
Gleiberman, Nina
Glenn, Christen Lauren B'anca
Goerlich, Emma Lee
Gold, Lauren
Goliver, Christine Anne
Gonnella, Danielle Elyse
Gorsky, Jessica Michelle
Governski, Meryl Conant
Graber, Abigail Alice
Graham, Alison Hope
Grant, Marita Lyn
Grant, Nicole Antoinette
Green, Megan Kimberly
Green, Noelle Sadé
Greene, Rosemary Carol
Greenwell, Patricia Jane
Grimes, Saidah Akilah
Gurok, Galina
Hailey-Granderson, Samantha Denay
Halleck, Olivia Mei
Hamilton, Cheri Monique
Hankin, Emily Gordon
Hanna, Shaundria Adina
Hanson, Julia Kaye
Harden, Anjelica Nicole
Hardin, Carolyn Lee
Harris, Dana Marie
Hart, Danielle Natasha
Hasselbarth, Nikki Jauane
Hassett, Kari Elizabeth

12-17-2014
Healy, Mary Katherine
Heidebrecht, Erin Shannon
Hellwig, Elisabeth Maxwell Horsey
Hendriksen, Patrice Elizabeth
Herman, Jennifer Lynn
Herold, Patricia Mercedes
Hickey, Amanda Jayne
Hickey, Sarah Michelle
Highsmith, Courtney Anne
Hill, Christine Michelle
Hindle, Megan Irene
Hollingsworth, Marcia
Horevay, Anna Caitlyn
Horn, Alyson Tamara
Horn, Amanda Catherine
Hosmer, Heather Anne
Howard-Nicolas, Diona Fay
Hudnet, Julie Lynn
Hudson, Alicia Denise
Hughes-Parry, Caitlin Mary
Humphrey, Kathryn Gordon
Hunt, Laura Ann
Imhoff, Sarah Jean
Iversen, Emily Himes
Ix, Megan Elizabeth
Jacobson, Jamie Ruth
Jagadish, Lavanya
Jakhelln, Samantha Grover
James, Sherica Bruinelda Helena

Janofsky, Robin Jody
Ji, Tianyun
Johnson, Frances Anne
Johnson, Janell Robin
Johnson, Lynsey Rae
Johnson, Stephenie Alana
Jones, Margaret
Jones, Samantha AnnaJeane Meier
Joseph, Jennifer Reed Doran Klein
Jung, Elizabeth Rae
Kahn, Melanie Lynn
Kane, Christina Joy
Kaplan, Elizabeth Anne
Kaplan, Jessica Lily
Kappler, Jacqueline Frances
Karimian, Yasmin
Kavanagh, Stefanie Elizabeth
Kawecki, Victoria Anne
Kearsley, Christine Hunt
Keller, Catherine Spencer
Kelley, Tiffany Patrice
Kerner, Ilana Mika
Kerns, April Marie
Kessler, Rachael Clair
Kestle, Sydney Rochelle
Khan, Nadia
Kikani, Rima Amulkumar
Killeen, Jessica Ruth
Kim, Jinly Joy
Kim, Soojin
Kim, Soyeob
Kim, Stephanie Haewon
Kinoshita, Mana
Kirkland-Mercedes, Corinne Venita
Kitzmiller, Lauren Elizabeth
Kleinman, Jessica Vesselinovitch
Kleinschmidt, Katharynne Marta
Klint-Gassner, Emmanuel
Kokot, Amy Paula
Kole, Allison Ursula
Kozlowski, Mary Claire Santana
Kramer, Shauna Meryl
Krohn, Dana Miriam
Krueger, Kaitlyn Ann
Kuhn, Alana Beth
LaMontagne, Laurel Elizabeth
Lane, Cassidy Meghan
Larson, Kimberly Beth
Laudick, Abigail Michelle
Laws, Jessica Miller
Leibfarth, Esther Neuwirth
Leibold, Meghan Alexandra
Lenaghan, Julie Ann
Levandusky, Whitney Clare
Levin, Hannah Ilene
Lewis, Melinda Rose
Lewis, Sheena Latisha
Liebeskind, Abigail Lauren
Lietz, Elizabeth Ann
Lim, Kristen Fon Lei
Limsky, Jacquelyn Lehecka
Lindenberg, Elisabeth Claudine
Livas, Megan Elizabeth
Llanso, Laura Cheek
Logue, Hannah Elizabeth
Loveland, Lauren Elaine
Luxenberg, Sara Michelle
Lynch, Jacqueline Nicole
Lynch, Kelly Elizabeth
Lynch, Meaghan Brittni
Mahoney, Lisa Ann
Maiden, Christian Joy
Makar, Zina
Mao, Coreen
Markert, Freyae Kellean
Martin, Leah Suzanne
Mason, Beth Marie
Matavich, Margaret Elizabeth
Maus, Emily Jean
May, Orly Tamar
McClease, Tiffany Nicole
McClurkin, Stacey Chenelle
McCrea, Amanda Claire
McCurdy, Caitlin Grace
McDaniels, Portia Alexandria
McGinley, Christie Lynn
McGinnis, Megan Jeannette
McGullam, Karen
McNaughton, Caitlin Adele
Menezes, Marisa Elise
Mennona, Jenna Nicole
Mersky, Sarah Nell
Michaloski, Sara Ann
Migliorini, Alicia Marie
Mikailova, Milena
Miles, Kasey Megan
Miller, Alexis Kahn
Miller, Emily Katherine
Mirkin, Aubrey Elise
Mitchell, Christine Elizabeth
Mody, Pari Rashmi
Moir, Diane Elizabeth
Moloney, Angela Lynn
Montgomery, Mallory Lynn
Morgan, Yuripzy Abigail
Morisi, Alejandra de Lourdes
Moses, Sarah Elizabeth
Moss, Ashley Ineas
Mossovitz, Arin Hotchkiss
Mullen, Sara Maffei
Murray, Kimberly Ryan
Myers-Duncan, Jasmine Elena
Naguib, Iten Tarek
Nathan, Megan Rachele
Navarrete, Alyssa Ann
Nelinson, Brenna Danielle
Nelson, Kirsten Rose
Nelson, Rachel Wendy
Nelson, Sable Kathleen
Nguyen, Flora Win-Cheung
Ngwashi, Marthe Jane Bwalya
Noethe, Katherine Marie
Nolley, Amber Nabre'
Novak, Natalie Elise
Nunez, Adilene
Nuss, Kristin Michelle
Nussbaum, Lauren Michelle
Nyman, Jessica Thi
Obler-Grill, Leigh Madeline
Odusami, Oluwakemi Kehinde
Ojo, Temitope Oluseyi
Okasi, Obianuju Urewunwa
Omojola, Abigail AraOluwa
Opoku, Evonne Serwaa
Orenstein, Renee Beth
Orie, Chinyere Ekemma
Orris, Karissa Michelle
Ortega, Victoria
Ortiz, Dorothy Elaine Farley
Pagan, Hannah Cari
Pak, Jessica Etta
Pak, Kristen Marie
Pal, Navneet
Palasik, Jessica Michele
Pan, Shirley Shiang-Jiun
Papale, Lisa Anne
Park, Yoon Ha

12-18-2014

Parraway, Alexius Elaine
Pasternak, Sharone
Patterson, Kelsey Taylor
Pearson, Allison Christine
Pearson-Farrer, Natalia Nichole
Perpignano, Christina Mattia
Peters, Samantha Lynn
Peterson, Corey Samantha
Petry, Megan Lindsay
Pfenson, Elizabeth Ashley
Phillips, Ashley Latoya
Piccinini, Lisa Marie
Ponard, Jennifer E.
Power, Stephanie Burgess
Prawde, Alyse Lauren
Prezioso, Emily Maria
Pride, Felichia Tiara
Queen, Anisha Shanae
Queirolo, Jacquelyn Alexis
Quinn-Matute, Andrea Elizabeth
Rabon, Anna Cecile
Ragany, Meredith Ann
Rajasekhar, Anjali Lakkaraj
Ram, Regina Veronica
Ramirez, Shannon Lee
Ranel, Shaundricka Monique
Ravindra, Tara Rao
Redinger, Mika Jane
Reed, Virginia Lynn
Regan, Kimberly Elizabeth
Reinbold, Jennifer Catherine
Retka, Jessica Joana
Rhoden, Tavia Vandian
Riaz, Syeda Mehveen
Richardson, Ashley Chin
Richardson, Leanna Marie
Rill, Abby Elizabeth
Robertson, Kathryn Alicia
Robinson, Anne Cole
Robinson-McElroy, Sarah Anne
Roby, Errin Kathleen
Rojas, Kelly Marie Lange
Romero, Lylian
Rose, Durriyyah Monique
Rosenzweig, Mollie Quinn
Rossi, Elizabeth Anne
Roth-Gormley, Shana
Rouhanian, Anoosha
Rounds, Rebekah Gay
Rowan, Danielle Marie
Rupert, Julia Simone Gagne
Russell, Miranda Dale
Russo, Rachel Lyn
Rutherford, Chelsea Marissa
Rutkowski, Lauren Nicole
Sagar, Gina
Sami, Arooj Tariq
Sautter, Stephanie Meryl Lipkin
Sawyer, Sarah Michelle
Scarpelli, Leah Nichole
Schick, Suzanne Murphy
Schindel, Kimberly Ann
Schroeder, Crystal Diane
Schur, Jodi Kramer
Schurick, Alison Cate
Scott, Sarah Louise
Seger, Michelle Denise
Sessa, Rachel Elizabeth
Sessions, Carly McRae
Shaffer, Kelly Jo
Shanklin Roberts, Maia Nzinga
Shcherbatyuk, Jessica Mei Fong
Shechtel, Bethany Gayle
Sheldon, Laura Day
Shelton, Alicia Leigh
Shimshoni, Hilla
Sholl, Anna Susan
Sibblies, Lisa Simmone
Sirois, Christina Pauline
Sita, Zarena
Skeabeck, Shelby Suzanne
Slowen, Margaret Anne
Smith, Alana Bryant
Smith, Allegra Blythe Ziller
Smith, Beverly Lynn
Smith, Cheri Danielle
Smith, Kristin Lloyd
Solloway, Joanna Clare
Spates, Kathryn Elizabeth
Spencer, Samantha Perry
Spielman, Ellen Ashley
Springer, Brighton Leigh
Squire, Deidra Renee
Steinfeld, Michelle Lynn
Steinmetz, Lyndsay Elizabeth
Stepanek, Meghan Ann
Stewart, Emily Danielle
Stortini, Kristin Leigh
Subasinghe, Nisa Charmaine
Sullivan, Mary Eileen Hogan
Surdokas, Maria Viktoria
Taraban, Laura Kristen
Tawes, Megan Elizabeth
Taylor, Lauren Michelle
Thacker, Kathleen Joyce
Thomas, Lesli Suzanne
Thomas, Lindsey Ann
Thomas, Tasha Marie
Thompson, Abigail Kane
Tijerina, Anna Alyssa
Tillman, Sakinah Lateeda
Timbers, Melissa Anderson
Torstveit Ngara, Emily Claire
Tremaine, Anita Cherie
Tuchman, Lindsay Sullivan
Tucker, Ashley Jean
Turco, Kimberly Michelle
Ulan, Kristen Olivia
Uliano, Christina Maria
Unger, Jacqueline Kate
Utterback, Amanda Surchi
Valdes, Yisel
Van Schaik, Kathleen
Van-Tull, LieAnn Tru
Vanderbilt-Mathews, Marie
Vasa, Sabrina Vashti
Vassil, Emily Jean
Ventresca, Jenna Angela
Villanueva, Brenda De La Cruz
Vining, Jessica Rose
Vogelmann, Constance Lynn
Vollmer, Adrienne Rae
Vora, Amee Rohitkumar
Wagner, Karen M.
Wakefield, Megan Rachel
Walker, Abigail Post
Walsh, Amanda Elizabeth

Ware, Dawn Davina
Wei, Deborah Miranda
Weissman, Jennifer Nicole
West, Brittany Grace
Whelden, Emily Elizabeth
Whitaker, Nicole Marie
White, Melissa Marie
Wilder, Whitney Elizabeth
Willard, Colleen Marie
Willetts, Sarah Joelle
Williams, Charlene Mary
Williams, June Anita
Willoughby, Kristal Darchele
Wilson, Caitlyn Marie
Wilson, Emily Catherine
Wilson, Julie Christie
Wilson-Williams, Abeni Ife
Witz, Erica Marie
Woizesko, Chelsea Nicole
Wolf, Rebecca Jean
Wolf, Stephanie Lynne
Wood, Robin Williams
Woolums, Viola Anna
Wright, Katherine Marie
Wright, Lauren Michelle
Wyatt, Lauren Lyndsie
Xu, Wenning
Yarborough, Connie Alease
Zhao, Emily Xuwen
Zhou, Ming Yuan
Zick, Rebecca Marie
Zuber, Kira Elizabeth
Zumwalt, Thea Felicia

Indistinguishable

Abrams, Yehuda Hillel
Alvez, Aguida
Ashutosh, Anu
Bosely, Corey Lee
Bulluck, Jesse Artis
Burgess, E.H.
Callard, Francis Jacobus
Chen, Wei-Chen
Choi, Young Hwan
Choi, Young Il
Chun, Yeo Jin
Evan, Jinu M.
Frenkel, Tally
Goldsberg, Yakenya
Hemphill, A.L.
Hines, Jan Allen
Kim, Eun Chung
Kim, Minchan
Kim, Soo Hyun
Knight, J.G.
Lee, Sunny Yoo
Mullins, J.G.
Nanz, C.H.
Nnabuihe, Obiageli Ada
Norrington, Frances Taylor
Panh, Ratha L.
Park, Ji Won
Park, Sung S.
Ponnamperuma, Gayathri Wijeratna
Richard, Dana Francis
Rousi, Cameron H.
Russell, Hsin-I Chow
Schiffman, Jess G.
Soegeng, Jemy
Sung, Tak Ki
Swagerty, Jo
Tran, Quynh dao Nhu
Tsai, Hui-chuan
Tu, Anh-Huong Thi
Turner, L.H.
Vadlamudi, Venkataratnam
Voss, Terri L.
Waheed, Rehan
Ward, E.L.
Weiss, L.H.
Williamson, Lindsay
Williamson, Stacy L.
Wilson, C.C.
Wodajo, Tizeta M.
Wolf, Leslie
Worthen, J.H.
Yamada, Towako
Yu, Chengzhi
Yu, Hyunjong
Yum, Chris Chulho

Appendix D: List of Donors

Everyone who is affiliated with the *Finding Justice Project* is indebted to those who have given so much to make this endeavor possible.

Publication Grants

Maryland Women's Bar Association Foundation
University of Baltimore Foundation, Inc.

Donations by Organizations

Ain & Bank, P.C.
Andalman & Flynn, P.C.
Artemis Group
Bouland And Brush, L.L.C.
Chen, Walsh, Tecler & Mccabe, L.L.P.
Colon Tsaknis Law Offices
Conti Fenn & Lawrence, L.L.C.
Diana H. Metcalf, Esq., L.L.C.
Emma Twigg Clarke Attorney At Law
Genn & Murphy, L.L.C.
Gordon, Feinblatt, Rothman, Hoffberger & Hollander, L.L.C.
Jack B. Rubin, P.A.
Kerr McDonald, L.L.P.
Kramon & Graham, P.A.
Law Offices of Angelia Rowe Garner & Associates
Law Offices of Debora Fajer-Smith, L.L.C.
Law Office of Marc G. Hall, P.C.
Law Offices of Sally B. Gold
LexisNexis
McGuire Woods, L.L.P.
Miller, Miller & Canby, Chartered
Neuberger, Quinn, Gielan, Rubin & Gibber, P.A.
O'Malley, Miles, Nylen & Gilmore, P.A. (John P. Davey)
Pitterich & Snedegar, P.C.
Proctor & McKee, P.A.
The Raker Group
Rebecca Nitkin Esquire, P.C.
Saul E. Kerpelman & Associates, P.A.
Shipley, Horne & Hewlett, P.A.
Thyden Gross and Callahan, L.L.P.
Womble Carlyle Sandridge & Rice, PL.L.C.

Donations by Individuals

Alison L. Asti
James B. Astrachan
The Honorable Mary Ellen Barbera
The Honorable Lynne A. Battaglia
William and Constance Beims
Gregg L. Bernstein
Ava Lias-Booker
Kristen Brinster
Diane Carol Bristow
Wanda G. Caporaletti
William J. Chen, Jr.
Harriet E. Cooperman
Kathleen A. Costlow
Lynn Jones Day
Mary Malloy Dimaio
Suzanne L. Duclos
Kathleen Dumais
Charles and Carol Eaton
Susan Carol Elgin
Carol Freeman
Melanie Shaw Geter
Marci Gordon
Nancy Grasmick
Peter H. Gunst
Warren and Anne Hamel

Arielle A. Harry-Bess
Nina Rodale Houghton
Deborah E. Jennings
Jennifer E. Keyser
Teresa K. Lamaster
Julie Ellen Landau
Vincent J. Leahy
Andrea Leahy-Fucheck
Cynthia Leppert
Ronald M. Levitan
The Honorable Cheryl McCally Lester
Deborah Luxenberg
M. Natalie Mcsherry
Neil A. and Sayra Wells Meyerhoff
Erin C. Miller
Charles F. Morgan
William J. Murphy
Judith Mustille
Theresa A. Nolan
Susan Oldham
The Honorable Elaine Patrick
Charles J. Peters
Kathleen Pontone
Lisa Diane Prichard
Julie Rubin
Nikkisha Z. Scott
Margaret Lynch Selwood
Kathleen and Daniel Shemer
Wendy L. Shiff
The Honorable Andrew L. Sonner
Rebecca Newman Strandberg
The Honorable Ann N. Sundt
John Parker Sweeney
Carolyn and David Thaler
Donna M. D. Thomas
Mayda Tsaknis
Margaret Fonshell Ward
Olive and Thomas Waxter
T. S. Woodward and A. R. Arthur
Women of Achievement in Maryland, Inc.

In-Kind Donations

The Afro-American
Amarle Web Designs, L.L.C.
American University's Washington College Of Law
Astrachan Gunst Thomas, P.C.
The Baltimore Sun
Calvert Fine Wine & Spirits
Catholic University, DuFour Library
Fastspot, L.L.C.
Goucher College
Historical Society of Frederick County
Historical Society of Talbot County
The Honorable Anne K. Albright
Leahy & Desmet, L.L.C.
Maryland Historical Society
Maryland State Archives
Maryland Women's Heritage Center
Maryland Women's Law Center
Miles & Stockbridge
National Philharmonic Orchestra
Neil Pain of Pain, Moulden & Associates
Neuberger, Quinn, Gielen, Rubin & Gibber, P.A.
The Maryland Daily Record
Susan Oldham
University of Baltimore School of Law
University of Maryland School of Law
Venable, L.L.P.
Washington County Historical Society
Women in Leadership Project

NOTES

Foreword

1. "Commission on Women in the Profession," American Bar Association, www.americanbar.org/groups/women/initiatives_awards/margaret_brent_awards/pasthonorees.html. Two Maryland female lawyers have brought the award home: Jeanette Rosner Wolman (admitted to the Bar in 1924), who figures prominently in this book; and the Honorable Irma S. Raker (admitted to the Bar in 1973), the second female judge of Maryland's highest court, the Court of Appeals.

2. Virginia Drachman, *Sisters in Law: Women Lawyers in Modern American History* (Cambridge, MA: Harvard University Press, 2001), 251. By 1878, women were admitted to practice law in the District of Columbia, Illinois, Iowa, Maine, Minnesota, Missouri, Michigan, North Carolina, Ohio, Utah, and Wisconsin.

3. "Women Lawyers: Mrs. Lockwood is Denied Admission to the Maryland Bar," *The New York Times* (October 19, 1878): 3.

4. Drachman, *Sisters in Law*, 251–52.

Introduction

1. The question, "Where is justice?" was posed in 1647 by Margaret Brent. Brent is Maryland's most well-known female attorney-in-fact, and one of the first, if not the first, in the state. Brent's exclamatory inquiry was her now-storied response to the legislature's denial of her right to cast a vote as a female landowner regarding the colony's financial operations. Ironically, when she was denied the right to vote on the basis of her gender, Brent was serving as the executrix for the estate of Governor Leonard Calvert and attorney for Lord Baltimore, a dual and historic designation granted her by the Provincial Court. It is important to note that Brent's status as a female landowner and respected attorney-in-fact were exceptionally rare for her time. She was a single woman (and therefore not subsumed within the legal identity of a husband) of considerable wealth who had access to Maryland's proprietor, who was her cousin. Although the importance of her historic public inquiry is in no way diminished by this context, a student of this book and its subject should appreciate that Brent's experiences and access to opportunity were in every way rare and unrepeated across the female population in colonial Maryland, and perhaps in all of the colonies. Whatever opportunities privilege may have afforded her, Margaret Brent seized them with courage and intelligence. Her demand for justice for women—one imagines it was nothing short of a demand—finds apt application in the title of this book.

2. *Bradwell v. Illinois*, 83 U.S. 130, 141, 21 L. Ed. 442 (1872).

3. "Portias" is a term for women lawyers derived from the character of Portia, a woman who acts as a lawyer, in William Shakespeare's play *The Merchant of Venice*.

4. Although the women succeeded in delaying Colledge's execution until October 18, 1671, the records are silent as to whether she was ultimately executed or pardoned by Governor Charles Calvert; she is not, however, listed among the names of those pardoned for their crimes.

5. *Stuart v. Board of Supervisors of Elections of Howard County*, 266 Md. 440 (1972). The Women's Law Center filed an amicus brief in support of the Petitioner. Also of note is the amicus brief filed by the American Civil Liberties Union, on which, among others, Ruth Bader Ginsberg (future U.S. Supreme Court Justice) and Elsbeth Levy Bothe (future judge of the Circuit Court for Baltimore City) appeared on the brief.

Chapter 1

1. The term "attorney-at-law" is reserved for one formally admitted to the Bar. Sophie H. Drinker, "Women Attorneys of Colonial Times," *Maryland Historical Magazine* 56 (1961): 335. The Provincial Court Proceedings reflect the use of the terms "attorney" and "attorney at law" to distinguish an agent without formal legal training from those formally admitted to the Bar; see Archives of Maryland Online, 11: 336 (available at http://archivesofmaryland.net).

2. Drinker, "Women Attorneys of Colonial Times," 335–36.

3. Ibid. Hereinafter, the circumflex has been omitted from feme to reflect current usage.

4. Ibid.

5. Ibid., 349.

6. Ibid.

7. Historian Dr. Lois Green Carr indicated that Margaret Brent arrived in Maryland with her brothers, Giles and Fulke, as well. See Lois Green Carr, "Margaret Brent—A Brief History," Maryland State Archives, February 7, 2002, http://www.msa.md.gov/msa/speccol/sc3500/sc3520/002100/002177/html/mbrent2.html. Drinker, "Women Attorneys of Colonial Times," 349. Lord Baltimore issued a letter to Leonard Calvert, his brother and agent in Maryland, which he gave to Margaret Brent; see Carr, "Margaret Brent—A Brief History."

8. Margie H. Luckett, "Margaret Brent," in *Maryland Women*, Volume 1 (Baltimore, MD: King Brothers Press, 1931), 45.

9. Drinker, "Women Attorneys of Colonial Times," 349. As a propertied woman of noble descent, Brent may have found greater legitimacy as an attorney-in-fact than other similarly situated women: "Mistress Margaret Brent, kinswoman of Cecil Calvert, Lord Baltimore, the Proprietor of Maryland, and of his brother Leonard Calvert, the first governor of the colony.... Margaret and Mary Brent, who were cousins of the Calverts." Caroline Sherman Bansemer, "A Colonial Dame. Neglected Records of the Life of Mistress Margaret Brent, The Earliest American Woman to Demand the Right of Suffrage," *Harper's New Monthly Magazine* (July 1898): 229. According to Dr. Carr, Brent "was active in importing and selling servants and lending capital to incoming settlers," and often appeared for herself in court to collect her debts and handle her business affairs "as a man would have done." See Carr, "Margaret Brent—A Brief History." Drinker, "Women Attorneys of Colonial Times," 349.

10. Ibid. According to Drinker, Brent worked for the "good of the colony, looking after the welfare of children and Indians, assigning acreage to the men in her employ."

11. Ibid.

12. Ibid., 349–50.

13. Ibid., 350.

14. Carr, "Margaret Brent—A Brief History."

15. Archives of Maryland Online, 1: 215. Brent's declaration, "Where is justice?," alternatively noted as "Is this justice?" spawned the Finding Justice Project, dedicated to uncovering the history of Maryland's women lawyers, and is a fitting title for this work. See Lynne A. Battaglia, "'Where Is Justice?' An Exploration of Beginnings," *University of Baltimore Law Forum* 42 (2011): 1, n.2; and Ann Jenson, "'Is this Justice?' A Woman's Plea in Colonial Maryland Puts Margaret Brent Ahead of Her Time," *Annapolitan* (June 1990): 47.

16. Archives of Maryland, 1: 239; Bansemer, "A Colonial Dame," 231 ("The Assembly (that of 1649) defended her actions… in a letter written to Lord Baltimore.").

17. Jenson, "'Is this Justice?,'" 49. Brent died on her Virginia property, "Peace," in 1673.

18. Archives of Maryland, 10: 104.

19. Drinker, "Women Attorneys of Colonial Times," 337–39. The practice dated from feudal times when the English Courts maintained that it "is an indisputable law that a wife can act as attorney to her husband." Ibid., 336.

20. Archives of Maryland Online, 66: 204.

21. See Dr. Lois Green Carr, St. Mary's City Men's Career Files: John Barnes, Maryland State Archives, http://www.msa.md.gov/megafile/msa/speccol/sc5000/sc5094/000001/000247/html/sc5094-0247-01.html (noting that John Barnes is last referenced in the St. Mary's records in 1681).

22. Archives of Maryland Online, 717: 211.

23. See Dr. Lois Green Carr, St. Mary's City Men's Career Files: John Hammond, Maryland State Archives, http://www.msa.md.gov/megafile/msa/speccol/sc5000/sc5094/001000/001784/html/sc5094-1784-01.html; and Archives of Maryland Online, 41: 266.

24. Ibid., 10: 443, 538–39.

25. Ibid., 10: 16.

26. It was not until 1867 that women were formally excluded by statute from serving on juries. Chapter 329 of the Maryland Laws of 1867 required the Clerk of the County Commissioners for each county to provide the Clerks of the Circuit Court in that county with "a fair and complete list of the white male taxable inhabitants or residents of the said county…." Before 1867, the selection of possible jurors was made by the sheriff, according to common law. *Cooper v. State*, 64 Md. 40, 45 (1885).

27. Archives of Maryland Online, 10: 457-58.

28. Matthew P. Andrews, *The Founding of Maryland* (Baltimore, MD: Williams and Wilkins, 1933), 201.

29. Ibid.

30. Marilyn Geiger Wichers, *The Administration of Justice in Colonial Maryland,* 1632–1689 an unpublished Ph.D. thesis (Lawrence: University of Kansas, May 1979), 28–29.

31. Ibid., 181. In 1669, Fendall attempted a rebellion to overthrow the Proprietary government and replace it with a republic, of which he would be the leader and "virtual dictator." He renounced his governorship commission from Lord Baltimore, announced his intention to make Maryland a "commonwealth," and accepted a new commission from the Assembly. Fendall was ultimately released, upon "pleading illness and giving security for good behavior." Andrews, *The Founding of Maryland*, 249.

32. Drinker, "Women Attorneys of Colonial Times," 345.

33. Ibid., 346.

34. Archives of Maryland Online, 53: 148.

35. Ibid., 326.

36. Ibid., 262.

37. Ibid.

38. Drinker, "Women Attorneys of Colonial Times," 346.

39. Ibid., 348.

40. Ibid.

41. Dr. Lois Green Carr, St. Mary's City Women's Career Files: Mary Larkin, Maryland State Archives, http://www.msa.md.gov/megafile/msa/speccol/sc4000/sc4040/000001/000947/html/sc4040-0937.html; see Proceedings of the Provincial Court, 1666-1670, 57 Archives of Maryland Online, 598-99, http://www.msa.md.gov/megafile/msaspeccol/sc2900/sc2908/000001/000057/html/am57--598.html.

42. See notes 14-15, above, and accompanying text.

43. Peter Charles Hoffer, *Law and People in Colonial America*, Revised Edition (Baltimore, MD: The Johns Hopkins University Press, 1998), 92–93.

44. Ibid., 94.

45. 54. Ibid., 82.

46. 55. Ibid., 81.

47. Ibid., 82.

48. Ibid., 103.

49. Archives of Maryland Online, 30: 252.

50. Ibid.

51. Ibid.

52. Hoffer, *Law and People in Colonial America*, 94.

53. Karen Berger Morello, *The Invisible Bar: The Woman Lawyer in America: 1638 to the Present* (New York: Random House, 1986), 40.

54. Ibid., 39.

55. Ibid., 41.

56. Ibid., 43.

57. Ibid., 43–44.

58. Portia was the beautiful, highly intelligent, wealthy heiress, and heroine of Shakespeare's *The Merchant of Venice*. In the play, Portia disguises herself as a man and appears in court as a lawyer representing (successfully) a friend of the man she wants to marry. William Shakespeare, *The Merchant of Venice*, Act 4, Scene 2. Morello, *The Invisible Bar*, 37–38.

59. Joseph A. Ranney, *In the Wake of Slavery: Civil War, Civil Rights, and the Reconstruction of Southern Law* (Westport, CT: Praeger, 2006), 114.

60. *Bradstreet v. Baer*, 41 Md. 19, 23 (1874).

61. See Richard H. Chused, "Married Women's Property Law, 1800–1850," *Georgetown Law Journal* 71 (1983): 1399.

62. Chapter 293 of the Maryland Laws of 1842, enacted on March 10, 1843, provided:

> Section 1. *Be it enacted by the General Assembly of Maryland,* That from and after the passage of this act, an married woman may become seized or possessed of any property, real or of slaves by direct bequest, demise, gift, purchase or distribution, in her own name, and as of her own property; provided the same does not come from her husband after coverture.
>
> Sec. 2. *And be it enacted,* That hereafter when any woman possessed of a property in slaves, shall marry, her property in such slaves and their natural increase shall continue to her notwithstanding her coverture, and she shall have, hold and possess the same as her separate property, exempt from any liability for the debts or contracts of the husband.
>
> Sec. 3. *And be it enacted,* That when any woman during coverture shall become entitled to or possessed of slaves by conveyance, gift, inheritance, distribution or otherwise, such slaves, together with their natural increase, shall enure and belong to the wife in like manner as is above provided as to slaves which she may possess at the time of marriage.
>
> Sec. 4. *And be it enacted,* That the control and management of all such slaves, the direction of their labour and the receipts of the productions thereof, shall remain to the husband agreeably to the laws heretofore in force, all suits to recover the property or possession of such slaves shall be prosecuted or defended as the case may be, in the joint names of the husband and wife, in case of the death of the wife, such slaves shall descend and go to her children and their descendants, subject to the use of the husband during life without liability to his creditors, and if she die without leaving children living, or descendants of such children living, they shall descend and go to the husband.
>
> Sec. 5. *Be it enacted,* That the slaves owned by a feme covert under the provisions of this act, may be sold by the joint deed of the husband and wife, executed, proved and recorded agreeably to the laws now in force in regard to the conveyance of real estate of feme coverts and not otherwise.
>
> Sec. 6. *And be it enacted,* That a wife shall have a right to make a will and give all of her property or any part thereof to her husband, and to other persons with the consent of the husband subscribed to said will; *provided always,* that the wife shall have been privately examined by the witnesses to her will, apart and out of the presence and hearing of her husband, whether she doth make the same will feely and voluntarily and without being induced thereto by fear or threats of or ill usage by said husband, and says she does it willingly and freely; provided that no will under this act shall be valid unless made at least sixty days before the death of the testatrix.

> Sec. 7. *And be it enacted,* That from and after the passage of this act it shall be the duty of every man whose wife shall have either property in slaves in possession, or shall receive the same in any way property by this act, to record the same, their names and ages upon the records of counties in which he may reside.
>
> Sec. 8. *And be it enacted,* That any married woman who by her skill, industry or personal labour, shall hereafter earn any money or other property, real personal or mixed to the value of one thousand dollars or less, shall and may hold the same and the fruits, increase and profits thereof, to her sole and separate use with power as a *feme sole* to invest and re-invest, and sell and dispose of same; *provided* that such money or property shall be liable for the payment of any claim or debt incurred by such married woman, and may be liable to be proceeded against by attachment from the county court to compel such payment upon petition and proof of claim according to the circumstances of each case, according to the court of the attachment law.

Chapter 293 was part of a larger trend of "debt-free laws," or laws enacted to protect the property of married women from the creditors of their husbands, or a means of protecting wives "from husbandly improvidence." For a description of the legislative history of Mississippi's debt-free law, see Ranney, *In the Wake of Slavery*, 116.

63. Chused, "Married Women's Property Law, 1800–1850," 1400–01.

64. Ibid.; Karen A. Weyler, "John Neal and the Early Discourse of American Women's Rights," in Edward Watts and David J. Carlson, eds., *John Neal and Nineteenth-Century American Literature and Culture* (Lewisburg, PA: Bucknell University Press, 2012), 241.

65. Norma Basch, *In the Eyes of the Law* (Ithaca, NY: Cornell University Press, 1982), 37–38.

66. According to Professor Chused, the phrase "sole and separate use" is "break-through language" originating in Mississippi's Married Women's Property Act in 1839. Chused, "Married Women's Property Law, 1800–1850," 1411; Richard H. Chused, Symposium, "History's Double Edge: A Comment on Modernization of Marital Status Law," *Georgetown Law Journal* 82 (1994): 2217.

67. *Neale v. Hermanns*, 65 Md. 474, 477-78, 5 A. 424, 425-26 (1886).

68. *Baker v. Hedrich*, 85 Md. 645, 661, 37 A. 363, 365 (1897).

69. Md. Const. art. III, § 38. A life estate is "[a]n estate held only for the duration of a specified person's life, usu. the possessor's." *Black's Law Dictionary*, Ninth Edition (St. Paul, MD: West, 2009), 628.

70. David A. Thomas, ed., *Thompson on Real Property*, Volume 2 (New Providence, NJ: LexisNexis, 2000) 19.07, 773.

71. 1853 Md. Laws 323.

72. Ibid.

73. B. Zorina Khan, "Married Women's Property Laws and Female Commercial Activity: Evidence from U.S. Patent Records, 1790–1895," *Journal of Economic History*, 56 (1996): 361 (stating that the provision of separate estates for married women was a response to the increase in "commercial uncertainty [and] the potential for fraud by debtor households towards creditors").

74. *Schindel*, 12 Md. at 313.

75. Ibid.

76. Md. Code (1860), Art. 45, Sec. 2.

77. Joel Prentiss Bishop, *Commentaries on the Law of Married Women* Volume 2 (1875), § 724, at 524 (quoting *Hall v. Eccleston*, 37 Md. 510, 521 (1873)).

78. 1867 Md. Laws, Chap. 223.

79. *Worthington v. Cooke*, 52 Md. 297, 307–08 (1879).

80. See *Armstrong v. Kerns*, 61 Md. 364, 367 (1884): "When a married woman acquires property in any of the modes prescribed by the statute, *without any declaration or limitation to her separate use*, and without any special mode or power of disposition annexed to the estate, the statutory use attaches, and the statutory mode of disposition exclusively applies and controls." [Emphasis added.]

81. Section 5 of Chapter 457 of the Maryland Laws provided:

> Married women shall have power to engage in any business, and to contract, whether engaged in business or not, and to sue upon their contracts, and also to sue for the recovery, security or protection of their property, and for torts committed against them, as fully as if they were unmarried; contracts may also be made with them, and they may also be sued separately upon their contracts, whether made before or during marriage, and for wrongs independent of contract committed by them before or during their marriage, as fully as if they were unmarried; and upon judgments recovered against them execution may be issued as if they were unmarried; nor shall any husband be liable upon any contract made by his wife in her own name and upon her own responsibility, nor for any tort committed separately by her out of his presence, without his participation or sanction.

Augustus C. Binswanger, *Married Women in Maryland: Property and Contractual Rights* (Baltimore, MD: M. Curlander, 1903), 36.

82. In addition to placing the *feme sole* and *feme covert* on equal footing, the 1898 Act sought "to put the husband's and wife's property rights on an exact equality":

> The purposes of the recent legislation seem to be to put the husband's and wife's property rights on an exact equality, both during life, and after death, and to give the wife the right to engage in business, sue and be sued, and contract, as a *feme sole*; and to relieve her husband from liability for her contracts, and for her torts not committed in his presence or with his sanction.... The Acts of 1898 are the culmination of a series of enabling statutes, starting with the Code of 1860; the outcome of this recent legislation is to place the feme covert, as to her property and contractual rights, on the same footing as a *feme sole*.

Ibid., 1–2.

83. "Married Women's Property Act (1848)," in Jeffrey D. Schultz & Laura Van Assendelft, eds., *Encyclopedia of Women in American Politics* (Phoenix, AZ: Oryx Press, 1999), 136.

84. Ibid.

85. "The Legislature: Proceedings in Detail in Each Branch of the General Assembly of Maryland," *The Baltimore Sun* (February 9, 1898): 8.

86. Mary Ross Walsh, *Doctors Wanted: No Women Need Apply* (New Haven, CT: Yale University Press, 1977), 107.

87. Charles O'Donovan, M.D., Professor of Diseases of Children, "Address at the Opening of the Woman's College for the Session of 1895–96," *Bulletin of Medical Society of Woman's Medical College of Baltimore*, Vol. 1, No. 5 (October 1, 1895).

88. Ibid.

89. Rand Jack and Dana Crowley Jack, "Women Lawyers: Archetype and Alternatives," *Fordham Law Review* 57 (1989): 937.

90. Virginia G. Drachman, *Sisters in Law: Women Lawyers in Modern American History* (Cambridge, MA: Harvard University Press, 2001, 1998), 24.

91. Ibid.

92. *Bradwell v. State*, 83 U.S. 130, 141 (1873) (Bradley, J., concurring).

93. In the eighteenth and nineteenth century in Maryland, the bar admissions process was decentralized, so that the authority to admit lawyers was vested in "the Justices of the Severall Courts." Archives of Maryland Online, 30: 252.

94. Lockwood wrote:

> I have never been able to enter into the prejudices of the centuries past, that have had no foundation in reason, in nature, or in nature's laws, nor to discover that the limitations of woman's sphere as heretofore dictated by the customs of society were worthy of serious consideration. My only thought was to do those things which in the nature of human affairs seemed the things to be done, and to do them in the best and most expeditious manner. Hence I was not careful as to the nature of my work, so that it was means to an end, and never for a moment stopped to consider whether the labor was such as women were accustomed to do, but only whether I had the ability to perform it.

Belva Lockwood, "My Efforts to Become a Lawyer," *Lippincott's Monthly Magazine* (February 1888): 215.

95. Virginia G. Drachman, *Women Lawyers and the Origin of Professional Identity in America* (Ann Arbor, University of Michigan Press, 1993), 242.

96. Jill Norgren, *Belva Lockwood: The Woman Who Would Be President* (New York: New York University Press, 2007), 3, and Lockwood, "My Efforts to Become a Lawyer," 216.

97. Ibid.

98. Norgren, *Belva Lockwood: The Woman Who Would Be President*, 4–5.

99. Lockwood, "My Efforts to Become a Lawyer," 217.

100. Ibid., 217–18.

101. Ibid., 220–21.

102. Ibid., 221–22. Columbian College is now George Washington University. "History," *About GW*, http://www.gwu.edu/history; accessed September 10, 2012.

103. Norgren, *Belva Lockwood: The Woman Who Would Be President*, 23.

104. Lockwood, "My Efforts to Become a Lawyer," 222.

105. The National University Law School merged with the George Washington University Law School in 1954. "History," *GW Law*, http://www.law.gwu.edu/School/Pages/History.aspx; accessed September 10, 2012. Lockwood, "My Efforts to Become a Lawyer," 222–23; Drachman, *Sisters in Law*, 243.

106. Lockwood, "My Efforts to Become a Lawyer," 223, and Drachman, *Sisters in Law*, 243.

107. Jill Norgren, *Belva Lockwood: Blazing the Trail for Women in Law, Prologue Magazine* (Spring 2005); available at http://www.archives.gov/publications/prologue/2005/spring/belva-lockwood-1.html.

108. Lockwood, "My Efforts to Become a Lawyer," 223.

109. Ibid., 224; Norgren, *Belva Lockwood: The Woman Who Would Be President*, 50–51.

110. Lockwood, "My Efforts to Become a Lawyer," 224, and Norgren, *Belva Lockwood: The Woman Who Would Be President*, 85.

111. Ibid., 227–29.

112. Norgren, *Belva Lockwood: Blazing the Trail for Women in Law.*

113. Ibid.; 131 U.S. 187 (1880).

114. Jill Norgren, *Belva Lockwood: Blazing the Trail for Women in Law, Part 2, Prologue Magazine* (Spring 2005), *available at* http://www.archives.gov/publications/prologue/2005/spring/belva-lockwood-2.html.

115. "Letter from Upper Marlboro, Md.," *The Baltimore Sun* (October 11, 1878): 4.

116. Ibid.

117. Ibid.; "Letter from Washington," *The Baltimore Sun* (October 18, 1878): 4.

118. "Women Lawyers: Mrs. Lockwood is Denied Admission to the Maryland Bar," *The New York Times* (October 19, 1878): 3.

119. "Minutes of the Carroll County Circuit Court (May 9, 1881)," *Maryland State Archives*, http://www.msa.md.gov/megafile/msa/speccol/sc3500/sc3520/015800/015841/pdf/msa_sc5458_51_5098_1.pdf.

120. "An Able Opinion," *Democratic Advocate* (May 14, 1881).

121. Jeriah Bonham, *Fifty Years' Recollections with Observations and Reflections on Historical Events* (Peoria, IL: J. W. Franks and Sons, 1883), 257.

122. "Woman's Rights in Frederick," *Daily Times* (March 9, 1880).

123. "Women at the Bar," *The Washington Post* (October 17, 1892): 4. Prior to reapplying for admission to the Prince George's County Bar, Lockwood gained national attention as the first woman to run a full-fledged presidential campaign in 1884. She campaigned as a suffragist, although her candidacy was not accepted by all suffrage leaders, some of whom thought her a "Barnum." Lockwood believed her bid for the presidency would help women gain the right to vote and acceptance into partisan politics. She told reporters that although she could not vote, nothing in the Constitution prevented men from voting for her. She received less than 5,000 votes. When Lockwood ran a second time in 1888, she told reporters, "Men always say, 'Let's see what

you can do.' If we always talk and never work we will not accomplish anything." Norgren, *Belva Lockwood: Blazing the Trail for Women in Law.*

124. Ibid.

125. 1898 Md. Laws 599–601.

126. Ibid.

127. Ibid.

128. "To Dismiss All Contests," *The Baltimore Sun* (March 5, 1902); "Admits Miss Maddox," *The Baltimore Sun* (September 25, 1902): 7 ("Change In The Law So As To Admit Women To The Bar Was Largely Due To Her Effort").

129. "Physicians and Lawyers," *The Baltimore Sun* (March 30, 1893).

130. "Admitted to the Bar," *The Baltimore Sun* (April 13, 1893).

131. "She Must Be Examined," *The Baltimore Sun* (June 25, 1902).

132. Ibid.

133. "Shade of Blackstone Weeps: Women Excluded from Baltimore Law School," *The Baltimore Sun* (September 27, 1907): 7.

134. "Run Down by Engine Horses," *The Baltimore Sun* (February 5, 1904): 6; "Negro Attacks Woman: Woman Lawyer's Purse Snatched On Guildford Avenue," *The Baltimore Sun* (November 10, 1911): 14.

135. Maryland Laws of 1900, Chapter 699, Section 16A.

Chapter 2

1. The actual year of her birth cannot be verified. See Hollis Atkinson, *Etta Haynie Maddox: Maryland's First Woman Lawyer* (Baltimore, MD: Women's Bar Association of Baltimore City, 1950), 1. Her death certificate lists her date of birth as January 6, 1866; Census reports, however, indicate that her date of birth was between 1859 and 1860. See Eighth U.S. Census: 1880.

2. Margie H. Luckett, "Etta H. Maddox," in *Maryland Women* (Baltimore, MD: King Brothers Press, 1937), 239. See, also, Atkinson, *Etta Haynie Maddox*, 1 (characterizing Etta's ancestors as having a "lively interest in Colonial affairs").

3. "[M]ost of the first women lawyers grew up in families that enjoyed middle-class status, or at least aspired to middle-class values, families in which women's education was encouraged," Mary Jane Mossman, *The First Women Lawyers: A Comparative Study of Gender, Law and the Legal Profession*, (Oxford, UK, and Portland, OR: Hart Publishing, 2006), 281–82.

4. "Justice Maddox's Funeral," *The Baltimore Sun* (December 29, 1892): 8.

5. See "Miss Maddox is a Lawyer," *The Baltimore Sun* (June 7, 1901): 10.

6. Atkinson, *Etta Haynie Maddox*, 1.

7. Margie H. Luckett did author a brief biographical sketch of Etta Maddox, which was published in 1937 in *Maryland Women*, but that, too, was a posthumous account with no first-person accounts of her life.

8. John Van Camp, "Legal Eve Honored," *The Bal-*

timore Sun (February 23, 1950): 12.

9. Apparently, due to the lack of known living relatives of Etta Maddox, the Maryland Archives accepted, on her behalf, the mementos for her induction into the Maryland Hall of Fame (a certificate and a silver bowl) in 2002. Although *The Baltimore Sun* reported that a "Niece Attends Ceremonies" at the Maryland Bar Library, it is believed that the niece was actually a relative of Dr. J. William Funck, and not a direct blood relative of Etta's. "Bar Library Given Picture," *Baltimore Sun* (February 21, 1950): 12; see "Pioneer Feminist of Maryland Dies," *The Baltimore Sun* (March 22, 1940): 28 (listing one niece as the sole survivor of Etta's sister, Emma Maddox Funck).

10. "Died," *The Baltimore Sun* (February 8, 1916): 6. It is reported that single women attorneys chose to be single due to their belief that "marriage imposed too many domestic obligations on women and therefore, was incompatible with a serious career." See Virginia G. Drachman, *Women Lawyers and the Origins of Professional Identity in America* (Ann Arbor: University of Michigan Press, 1993), 26. See, also, Virginia G. Drachman, *Sisters in Law: Women Lawyers in Modern American History* (Cambridge, MA: Harvard University Press, 1998), 99–100, 178 (noting that the 1890 Census found that only twenty-one percent of practicing woman lawyers were married). While an intention to remain single cannot necessarily be ascribed to Etta, she does fall within the noteworthy statistic for early women lawyers.

11. Mal Hee Son Wallace, "Emma J. Maddox Funck, Maryland Suffrage Leader," in Winifred G. Helmes, ed., *Notable Maryland Women* (Cambridge, MD: Tidewater Publishers, 1977), 145.

12. Etta's estimated age of forty would be based on U.S. Census data from 1880. See note 1.

13. Atkinson, *Etta Haynie Maddox*, 1–2.

14. Etta Maddox graduated from the Eastern Female High School on June 26, 1873. For academic achievement, she was awarded the Peabody Gold Medal at her graduation. See Atkinson, *Etta Haynie Maddox*, 1. If the commonly used date of birth for Etta (1860) is correct, she would have graduated from high school at age thirteen.

15. Ibid., 1.

16. See ibid., 1–2.

17. "Local Musical Matters," *The Washington Post* (November 27, 1882).

18. See Atkinson, *Etta Haynie Maddox*, 2; see, also, Van Camp, "Legal Eve Honored," (recalling that there was family opposition to a singing career); "The Bischoff Concert Last Night," *The Washington Post* (February 10, 1883): 9.

19. Luckett, "Etta H. Maddox," 239; Atkinson, *Etta Haynie Maddox*, 1–2; see, also, "Miss Maddox is a Lawyer," *The Baltimore Sun* (June 7, 1901), which characterizes her as a well-known vocalist, having sung in the choirs of several local churches.

20. See Atkinson, *Etta Haynie Maddox*, 1.

21. See "She will Graduate in Law," *The Baltimore Sun* (June 6, 1901); "Shade of Blackstone Weeps," *The Baltimore Sun* (September 27, 1902): 7. As mentioned in the preceding chapter, in 1893, Miss Otto Hunckel became the first woman to receive her diploma from a law school in Baltimore City. Ms. Hunckel applied to the Supreme Bench of Baltimore in 1902, but was refused admission.

See "She Must be Examined," *The Baltimore Sun* (June 25, 1902). Nearly a year after Etta's law school graduation, Ms. Hunckel wrote the Baltimore Sun to "record her claim of being Maryland's first woman lawyer." See "Society News," *The Baltimore Sun* (May 15, 1902).

22. See notes 104–133 of this chapter and the accompanying text in the section "Sisters for Suffragists," below.

23. Jen Hafner and Alicia Brooks, "Etta Haynie Maddox," March 9, 2006, http://www.msa.md.gov/megafile/msa/speccol/sc3500/sc3520/012400/012464/html/12464bio.html.

24. "Is Anxious to Practice Law," *The Baltimore Sun* (June 8, 1901): 12; see, also, Mary Katherine Scheeler, "Etta Haynie Maddox, Pioneer Lawyer and Suffragist," in Winifred G. Helmes, ed., *Notable Maryland Women* (Cambridge, MD: Tidewater Publishers, 1977), 225.

25. The Baltimore Law School was chartered by the Maryland Legislature in 1900; it merged with the Baltimore University School of Law in 1911 under the name the Baltimore Law School; it then merged into the University of Maryland in 1913. See "Law Schools Consolidate," *The Baltimore Sun* (January 5, 1911): 4; and "Law Schools Now One," *The Baltimore Sun* (July 16, 1913): 3. At the time Etta attended law school, there were three law schools in Baltimore: The University of Maryland, Baltimore University, and Baltimore Law School. See ibid. Overall, higher education for women in Maryland was limited. For example, the Johns Hopkins University did not admit women until 1893, and, even then, it was only as a condition for receipt of $500,000 from the "Women's Fund." See Wallace, "Emma J. Maddox Funck," 143. Additionally, in 1907, the Baltimore Law School reversed its policy and no longer admitted woman until 1920. See "Shade of Blackstone Weeps," *The Baltimore Sun* (September 27, 1902): 7; and Atkinson, *Etta Haynie Maddox*, 2.

26. "She Will Graduate *in Law*," *The Baltimore Sun* (June 6, 1901): 7.

27. Ibid.

28. See Scheeler, "Etta Haynie Maddox," 229.

29. "Miss Maddox is a Lawyer."

30. See "Shade of Blackstone Weeps," *The Baltimore Sun* (September 27, 1907): 7.

31. See Drachman, *Sisters in Law*, 85–86.

32. See ibid., which quotes Marcus Reed, "Is Portia Possible?," *MacMillan's Magazine* (March 1906): 377.

33. See Drachman, *Sisters in Law*, 222 (in which a 1904 article that appeared in the *American Lawyer* is discussed).

34. "Is Anxious to Practice Law," 12; see, also, Scheeler, "Etta Haynie Maddox," 225.

35. Mrs. Edward Addison Greeley appears to have referred to herself vis-à-vis her husband's name; her full name was Miriam Pearson Mason. See National Society of the Daughters of the American Revolution, *Directory*, 88. Apparently, Mrs. Greely was visiting a friend in Baltimore near the time of Etta's graduation and "heartily congratulate[d her] on her well-earned distinction." See "Women as Lawyers," *The Baltimore Sun* (June 24, 1901): 7.

36. Ibid.

37. Ibid.

38. "'Him' Includes 'Her,'" *The Baltimore Sun* (June 26, 1901): 10.

39. Ibid.

40. Ibid.

41. See Atkinson, *Etta Haynie Maddox*, 4.

42. Ibid., 5.

43. Professor Howard Bryant, as one of the creators of the Baltimore University School of Law, read the mandate ordering the graduation of the class at Etta's graduation ceremony in 1901. See "Miss Maddox is a Lawyer"; "Howard Bryant Dies Suddenly at Hospital," *The Baltimore Sun* (September 19, 1930): 28. Mr. Bryant served in the House of Delegates from 1916 to 1918 and was later elected as Baltimore City Council President for two terms, from 1923 until his death in 1930. He was actively involved in women's equality issues not only related to bar admission, but also to other women's causes including the suffrage movement.

44. Brief for Petitioner at 13, *In re Etta Maddox*, 93 Md. 727, 50 A. 487 (1901) (No. 110).

45. Ibid., 7–8; see, also, *In re Etta Maddox*, 93 Md. 727, 727–28, 50 A. 487, 487 (1901).

46. Brief for Petitioner, 4-5, *In re Etta Maddox*, 93 Md. 727, 50 A. 487. Etta also referenced the states which either utilized gender neutral terms, such as "every person" or "any citizen" in its statutes, or expressly mandated that no person would be refused a license to practice law on the account of sex. Ibid. (referring to Indiana, New Hampshire and Illinois, respectively). See, also, Drachman, *Sisters in Law*, 36 (stating that, "between 1888 and 1923, twenty of thirty-one state courts had admitted women to practice either independently or by court decision").

47. Prior to its amendment in 1898, the Bar Admission Statute was codified at Article 10, Section 3 of the 1888 Maryland Code (amended, 1892 Laws of Maryland, ch. 37). Section 3 provided: "Upon ever such application for any male citizen of Maryland above the age of twenty-one years..." The 1898 Laws of Maryland, Ch. 600, amended Section 3 to provide, "All applications for admission to the bar shall be referred by the Court of Appeals to the State Board of Law Examiners, who shall examine the applicant, touching his qualifications for admission to the bar."

48. Brief for Petitioner, 6, *In re Etta Maddox*, 93 Md. 727, 50 A. at 487.

49. Ibid., 10.

50. Ibid.

51. Ibid.

52. Ibid., 8.

53. Ibid.

54. Ibid., 11–13.

55. In retrospect, the only area lacking in her brief was any reference to an Equal Protection claim under the Fourteenth Amendment of the Constitution. Notably, it was Myra Bradwell's decision to include a Fourteenth Amendment argument in her brief to the Illinois Supreme Court that preserved her ability to appeal to the United States Supreme Court in 1873. Drachman, *Sisters in Law*, 17–18.

Although the *Bradwell* decision in 1872 held that women were not entitled to privileges and immunities for admission to the state bar, perhaps, thirty years later, such position would have been revisited by the U.S. Supreme Court.

56. See *In re Etta Maddox*, 93 Md. 727, 50 A. 487 (1901)

57. Ibid. at 487–88.

58. In 1888, eleven years after *In re Charles Taylor*, 48 Md. 28 (1877), the General Assembly amended the Bar Admission Statute to remove reference to race. 1888 Md. Laws at 316.

59. *In re Etta Maddox*, 93 Md. at 728, 50 A. at 488 (quoting *In re Charles Taylor*, 48 Md. at 33).

60. Ibid. at 730, 50 A. at 488.

61. Ibid.

62. Ibid. at 732-33, 50 A. at 489.

63. Ibid. "To abrogate a longstanding and heretofore uninvaded and unquestioned doctrine of the common law merely because a rule of interpretation, adopted more from a superabundance of caution or as a matter of convenience than from any real necessity, declares that the masculine shall include all genders, would attribute to the Legislature an intention which we find nothing to indicate ever existed." Ibid., 732, 50 A. at 489.

64. Ibid., 735–36, 50 A. at 490.

65. Ibid., 736, 50 A. at 489.

66. Ibid. This notion is reflective of what one author characterized as the tenacious clinging "to the principle of jurisprudence of separate spheres," wherein admission would only be permitted via legislative action not judicial fiat. See Drachman, *Sisters in Law*, 36. While Etta's request to take the state bar examination was denied by the Court of Appeals, "[t]he Court however, did invite the General Assembly to enact legislation if it believed that the citizens of Maryland wanted women to practice law." See John Carroll Byrnes, "Histories of the Bench and Bar of Baltimore City," *University of Baltimore Law Forum* Vol. 27, No. 5 (1997): 98.

67. "Bars Woman Lawyer," *The Baltimore Sun* (November 22, 1901): 10.

68. Ibid.

69. See Atkinson, *Etta Haynie Maddox*, 7. Senator Moses introduced Senate Bill No. 30 on January 23, 1902. See 1902 Md. Laws at 566.

70. See Scheeler, "Etta Haynie Maddox," 226.

71. Etta was accompanied by: Mrs. Ellen Foster (who had been admitted to the Bar of Iowa in 1875), Miss Laura Clay (President of the Equal Rights Society of Kentucky), Miss Gail Laughlin (an attorney in New York), Mrs. M. B. Thomas (Maryland), Dr. H. B. Blackwell (Massachusetts), Dr. Cora Eaton (Minnesota). See Atkinson, *Etta Haynie Maddox*, 8; Carolyn B. Stegman, *Women of Achievement in Maryland History*, (University Park, MD: Anaconda Press, 2002), 376. One woman artfully characterized the process as "not a revolution, but evolution." Ibid.

72. "Women as Lawyers," *The New York Times* (February 23, 1902): 13. See "Memorial Proceedings in Honor of Deceased Members of the Bar," *The Daily Record*, of Baltimore (January 8, 1934): 3,

in which it was reported that strenuous efforts were made to kill the Bill in committee, to which Etta purportedly responded, "It will never die while I live."

73. "Grinding out Laws," *The Baltimore Sun* (February 11, 1902): 9.

74. "Women as Lawyers," *The Baltimore Sun* (February 21, 1902): 8; quoting Miss Laura Clay, President of the Equal Rights Society of Kentucky, whose father was a Marylander so was "no stranger to the methods of Maryland thought."

75. Ibid.

76. Ibid (reporting on Miss Gail Laughlin's speech).

77. Ibid.

78. Scheeler, "Etta Haynie Maddox," 226.

79. "Women as Lawyers," *The New York Times* (February 23, 1902): 13.

80. "Grinding Out Laws," *The Baltimore Sun* (February 11, 1902): 9.

81. "Women at the Bar," *The Baltimore Sun* (February 21, 1902): 4.

82. See Atkinson, *Etta Haynie Maddox*, 9. See, also, "To Dismiss All Contests," *The Baltimore Sun* (March 5, 1902): 9 (reporting on the Senate's passage of the bill to admit women to the Bar and the anticipated passage by the House).

83. Francis Mooney, "Biography of Etta Maddox," in "Memorial Proceedings in Honor of Deceased Members of the Bar," *The Daily Record*, Baltimore (January 8, 1934).

84. 1902 Md. Laws 566, Ch. 339, § 3A, codified as Md. Code (1904), art. 10, § 3. Section 3A was inserted as a part of Section 3 of Article 10 of the Code, which governed the ability to practice law in Maryland.

85. See Atkinson, *Etta Haynie Maddox*, 11; "59 Passed Law Examination," *The Baltimore Sun* (July 17, 1902): 9.

86. See Atkinson, "Etta Haynie Maddox," 11–12; see, also, "Suburbs and County: Woman Lawyer Creates Mild Sensation At Towson," *The Baltimore Sun* (July 31, 1902): 9.

87. See "Admits Miss Maddox," *The Baltimore Sun* (September 25, 1902): 7.

88. Atkinson, *Etta Haynie Maddox*, 12.

89. Ibid., 12.

90. See Drachman, *Sisters in Law*, 218.

91. Ibid., 218.

92. See Atkinson, *Etta Haynie Maddox*, 12 (noting that Maddox's first law office was located at 509 Law Building, at the corner of St. Paul and Lexington streets; after the 1904 Baltimore Fire destroyed that building, her office was relocated to 223–225 Courtland Street).

93. Ibid.

94. "Said No to Miss Maddox," *The Baltimore Sun* (May 14, 1902): 12.

95. The "writ de lunatico inquirendo" originated from the common law of England as a means of determining whether an individual was men-

tally ill and thereby incapable of managing his or her own property. If the writ was granted, "A jury of twelve men would inquire into the matter; and if they found that the man was a lunatic or an idiot, he would be committed into the care of a relative or friend, called his committee. While it fell to the king to protect the property of the lunatic, care of the person of the non compos mentis was committed to his friends or family. To prevent 'sinister practices,' the next heir, having an interest in the lunatic's property after his death, was seldom permitted to be the committee of his person." Joan L. O'Sullivan & Diane E. Hoffmann, "The Guardianship Puzzle: Whatever Happened to Due Process," *Maryland Journal of Contemporary Issues* 7 (1995): 14–15.

96. Atkinson, *Etta Haynie Maddox*, 12–13.

97. See Scheeler, "Etta Haynie Maddox," 226. See, also, "Miss Maddox Tries a Case," *The Baltimore Sun* (December 15, 1904): 7.

98. "Miss Maddox Tries a Case." Quite tellingly, the reporters appeared as interested Miss Maddox's chosen attire as in her prowess as a litigator, commenting not only on the coat and hat she wore into the courtroom, but her "white shirtwaist and blue skirt" that she wore under the coat. Ibid.

99. "Another Orphans' Home," *The Baltimore Sun* (January 26, 1906): 10.

100. See Scheeler, "Etta Haynie Maddox," 228.

101. See Atkinson, *Etta Haynie Maddox*, 14.

102. Ibid.

103. Ibid.

104. See Van Camp, "Legal Eve Honored," 12.

105. See Scheeler, "Etta Haynie Maddox," 227. See, also, Suzanne Ellery Green Chapelle, et al., *Maryland: A History of Its People* (Baltimore, MD: The Johns Hopkins University Press, 1986), 215.

106. See Stegman, *Women of Achievement in Maryland History*.

107. See "Suffragist Protests," *The Baltimore Sun* (January 22, 1916): 12 (reporting that Etta Maddox had been at each legislative session for the last twelve years). See Scheeler, "Etta Haynie Maddox," 227 (stating that her annual attendance began in 1908 rather than 1904).

108. Ibid.

109. See "Plead for Suffrage," *The Washington Post* (February 16, 1906): 2.

110. See Luckett, "Etta H. Maddox," 239. The bill was introduced by Delegate William Harry Pairo, a lawyer and ardent Republican. "Women Plead for Votes," *The Baltimore Sun* (February 24, 1910): 11; "Mr. Pairo Addresses Suffragists," *The Baltimore Sun* (April 7, 1911): 10.

111. See "Maryland Suffragists Predict State Victory," *Woman's Standard* (Waterloo, Iowa), Vol. 22, No. 12 (February 1910).

112. "Women Plead for Votes," *The Baltimore Sun* (Feb. 24, 1910). Scheeler, "Etta Haynie Maddox," 227–28; see also "Women Plead for Votes," 14; "Equal Rights for All," *The Evening Capital and Maryland Gazette* (February 23, 1910).

113. "Equal Rights for All," *Evening Capital and Maryland Gazette* (February 23, 1910).

114. “Women Plead for Votes.”

115. Ibid.

116. Ibid.

117. Ibid.

118. Ibid.

119. Ibid.

120. Ibid.

121. Ibid.

122. Ibid.

123. See Scheeler, “Etta Haynie Maddox,” 228.

124. Ibid.

125. Ibid.

126. “Suffragist Protests,” *The Baltimore Sun* (January 22, 1916): 12. See, also, Atkinson, *Etta Haynie Maddox*, 15.

127. Ibid.

128. “Samuel Brown—‘Mossback,’” *The Baltimore Sun* (January 21, 1916): 2. “Suffragist Protests,”[12].

129. “Suffragist Protests,” 12; see, also, Atkinson, *Etta Haynie Maddox*, 16.

130. “Suffragist Protests,” 12; Atkinson, *Etta Haynie Maddox*, 17.

131. Ibid.

132. Ibid.

133. Despite steadfast efforts by both Etta Maddox and her sister, Emma Funck, the Maryland Legislature failed to ratify the Suffrage Amendment to the United States Constitution; thus, Maryland women obtained their constitutional right to vote *in spite of* their own elected leaders by virtue of other states ratification of the Suffrage Amendment. See Wallace, “Emma J. Maddox Funck,” 145.

134. Margaret Ann Maddox died on February 5, 1918, preceding her sister, Etta, in death by twenty-two years. “Died,” *The Baltimore Sun* (February 8, 1916): 6.

135. See Wallace, “Emma J. Maddox Funck,” 142.

136. Ibid. Dr. Funck was a charter member of the Men’s League for Woman Suffrage. See Scheeler, “Etta Haynie Maddox,” 227.

137. Emma was President of the Baltimore Suffrage Club from 1897–1920. See Wallace, “Emma J. Maddox Funck,” 142. In 1904, the Maryland Woman Suffrage Association was formed, and Etta became its president, also serving until 1920. She was also President of the Woman’s Suffrage Party for two years. Ibid., 143 and 145.

138. Ibid., 144–145 (explaining that “[t]he years 1896–1910 have been called “the doldrums” for the suffrage movement, a time when relatively little was accomplished across the country partly due to lack of dynamic leadership at the national level”).

139. Ibid., 142.

140. Ibid., 145.

141. Ibid.

142. Maddox was asked to enter the field of candidates to run for President of the Women's Democratic Club in 1925 when then-President, Mrs. S. J. Poe's continuation as leader was strongly opposed. See "Baltimore Woman Identifies Youth as Robber," ("Would Oust Mrs. S. J. Poe"), *The Washington Post* (February 7, 1925): 8. See, also, "Miss Maddox, Leading State Feminist, Dies," *The Baltimore Sun* (February 20, 1933): 14.

143. See "Miss Maddox, Leading State Feminist, Dies," *The Baltimore Sun* (February 20, 1933): 14. See, also, "Certificate of Death of Etta Haynie Maddox," Maryland State Archives, http://www.msa.md.gov/megafile/msa/speccol/sc3500/sc3520/012400/012464/pdf/deathcert.pdf, accessed October 8, 2012. Her death certificate lists her age at death as sixty-seven years. This must be incorrect, as that would have put her birth year as 1866, meaning she would have graduated from high school at age seven.

144. "Miss Maddox, Leading State Feminist, Dies," 14; See Atkinson, *Etta Haynie Maddox*, 18.

145. See Estate of Etta Haynie Maddox, Baltimore City Register of Wills, Estate no. 17887, Maryland State Archives.

146. See *The First and Final Administration Account of Emma Maddox Funck, Administratrix of the Personal Estate of Etta Haynie Maddox, Late of Baltimore City, Deceased*, Orphans' Court of Baltimore City. See, also, Atkinson, "Etta Haynie Maddox," 19. At the time of her death, Etta owned six properties, four of which were jointly owned with Emma. Presumably, these were the Maddox family's properties that continued to be leased and managed by the sisters.

147. See "Miss Maddox, Leading State Feminist, Dies"; see, also, Atkinson, *Etta Haynie Maddox*, 18.

148. See Mooney, "Biography of Etta Maddox," *The Daily Record* (January 8, 1934): 4.

149. Ibid.

150. Atkinson, *Etta Haynie Maddox*, 19.

151. Contemporaneous with this honor, a biography of Etta Maddox was written by Hollis Atkinson, which is referenced extensively herein. See note 1, above.

152. See Margaret Dempsey, "Women Bar Members will Honor Pioneer," *The Evening Sun* (February 21, 1950), http://wlh-static.law.stanford.edu/articles/honormad.htm. See, also, Van Camp, "Legal Eve Honored."

153. Hafner and Brooks, "Etta Haynie Maddox."

154. Mossman, *The First Women Lawyers*, 16.

155. Ibid., 14–15. In fact, after accounting for several different factors to explain the relative simultaneity of women's admission to the legal profession in Europe, including levels of modernization among the countries, different systems for legal education, and differences between Protestant and Catholic countries, "there was no consistent explanation for the timing of women's admission to European legal professions." Ibid. (citing James Albisetti, "Portia Ante Portas: Women and the Legal Profession in Europe, ca 1870–1925," *Journal of Social History* 33 (2000): 825–26).

156. Ibid., 57 and 239. Louis Frank published a comprehensive review of women and the legal professions in 1898, entitled *La Femme-Advocat*,

in which he advocated support of legal reforms to achieve equality for women.

157. Mossman, *The First Women Lawyers*, 58–59 (emphasis added). Mary Anne Green grew up in Rhode Island but entered Boston University Law School in 1885. She graduated *magna cum laude* in 1888 and subsequently became the second woman admitted to the Massachusetts Bar, the first woman to argue a case before the Supreme Court of Rhode Island, and the first woman contributor to the *American Law Review*, which she used this forum to advocate for wives' legal rights. See Drachman, *Women Lawyers and the Origins of Professional Identity in America*.

158. Mossman, *The First Women Lawyers*, 65, citing "Women Lawyers," *Leslie's Illustrated Weekly* (1896): 363.

159. "Is Anxious to Practice Law," 12.

160. Ibid.

161. Ibid.

162. Those states included Colorado, Connecticut, Indiana, Iowa, Kansas, Maine, Michigan, Missouri, Montana, Nebraska, New Hampshire, North Carolina, Ohio, Pennsylvania, Utah, and Washington, in addition to thc District of Columbia. See "Bars Woman Lawyer," *The Baltimore Sun* (November 22, 1901): 10. The first woman admitted to the Pennsylvania Bar was Carrie Burnham Kilgore, who was admitted in 1886 after she petitioned the Pennsylvania General Assembly three times. See ibid. (referring to Indiana and Pennsylvania); and http://womenshistory.vermont.gov/?TabId=61&personID=210.

163. Those states include: California, Illinois, Massachusetts, Minnesota, Mississippi, New York, Oregon, and Wisconsin.

164. Karen Berger Morello, *The Invisible Bar: The Woman Lawyer in America, 1638 to Present* (New York: Random House, 1986), 37–38.

165. Ibid., 43.

166. Ibid. See also Drachman, *Sisters in Law*, 37.

167. See Drachman, *Sisters in Law*, 37–38.

168. For example, after years of accepting women in the legal profession as attorneys-in-fact, when California opened its Hastings College of Law in 1878, it was closed to women until that position was challenged by two women, Clara Foltz and Laura Gordon. See Morello, *The Invisible Bar*, 61–63.

169. See Morello, *The Invisible Bar*, 66. While some acknowledge a pattern of greater resistance to the admission of women to the Bar in the East versus the Western states, that does not explain the divergence between those Eastern jurisdictions wherein upwards of a thirty year gap exists; for example, Washington, DC (1872) and Maryland (1902).

170. Sec Morello, *Thc Invisiblc Bar*, 37 38; Drachman, *Sisters in Law*, 26.

171. The Maryland Constitution of 1864 mandated a statewide system of public schools; Maryland, however, lagged behind most states in public education, as many of the local towns and counties chose not to collect taxes to fund education. See Chapelle, et al., *Maryland: A History of its People*, 195. In fact, in 1900 in Baltimore City,

only forty-three percent of those aged five to nineteen were enrolled in public schools. Ibid. See Morello, *The Invisible Bar*, 66–67.

172. See Drachman, *Sisters in Law*, 39. See, also, Robert Stevens, *Law School: Legal Education in American from the 1850s to 1980s* (Chapel Hill: University of North Carolina Press, 1983), 109.

173. See Drachman, *Sisters in Law*, 39. Indeed, the American Bar Association was established in 1878, in part to raise the standards of the profession.

174. See D. Kelly Weisberg, "Barred from the Bar: Woman and Legal Education in the United States 1870–1890," *Journal of Legal Education* 28 (1977): 495.

175. "Women Lawyer's Timeline," SC Women's Lawyer's Association, http://www.scwla.org/timeline.asp; accessed October 10, 2012.

176. "North Carolina Women's History Timeline," North Carolina Museum of History, http://ncmuseumofhistory.org/workshops/womenshistory/timeline_hndout.htm; accessed October 8, 2012.

177. Ellen A. Martin, "Admission of Women To the Bar," *Chicago Law Times* 84 (Catherine V. Waite, ed., 1887), http://wlh-static.law.stanford.edu/articles/chicagotimes.pdf; C. Sleeth, *First Women Lawyers in the United States*, Bar Assoc., July 18, 1997, *available at* http://wlh-static.law.stanford.edu/papers/sleeth.pdf.

178. See Drachman, *Sisters in Law*, 118.

179. Ibid., 173.

180. Ibid., 148–49 and 174.

181. See Hedda Garza, "Barred From the Bar: A History of Women and the Legal Profession," (1996) publication at www.naderlibrary.com.

182. See Mossman, *The First Women Lawyers*, 34.

183. See Drachman, *Sisters in Law*, 73–74.

184. See Drachman, *Sisters in Law*, 65 and 71 (discussing the topics of debate in the Equity Club, including how women attorneys could balance their gender and professional identity).

185. See Tricia D. O'Neill, "The Emergence of Women on the Legal Profession," *Maryland Bar Journal* (1996): 39.

186. See Mossman, *The First Women Lawyers*, 13 (referencing C. Bolt, *The Women's Movements in the United States and Britain from the 1790s to the 1920s*, (Amherst: University of Massachusetts Press, 1993)). See, also, D. Kelly Weisberg, "Barred from the Bar: Women and Legal Education in the United States 1870–1890," *Journal of Legal Education* 28 (1977): 485.

187. See Drachman, *Sisters in Law*, 23.

188. Ibid.

189. Ibid., 27, citing *Lelia J. Robinson's Case*, 131 Mass. 376 (1881).

190. Mossman, *The First Woman Lawyers*, 40–41.

191. Ibid., 41, arguing that, because successful women lawyers adopted a professional identity as lawyers, they increasingly distanced themselves from other women activists.

192. Drachman, *Sisters in Law*, 12.

193. As with bar admission, the Western states were more favorable to women's suffrage than the Eastern states. In fact, by the time the Nineteenth Amendment was ratified in 1920, almost every state west of the Mississippi River had already, on their own accord, granted full suffrage to women. In some states, such as Wyoming, women had already been voting for nearly fifty years. See Sandra L. Myres, *Western Women and the Frontier Experience, 1800–1915* (Albuquerque: University of New Mexico Press, 1982), 232.

194. On a national level, the end of the Civil War in 1865 was followed by passage of what is known as the Reconstruction Amendments, which include the Thirteenth Amendment (ending slavery), Fourteenth Amendment (equal protection of, and privileges and immunities of, citizens), and Fifteenth Amendment (guaranteeing African Americans the right to vote). While geared toward ensuring the equality of African Americans in the post-Civil War era, the Reconstruction Amendments stopped short of changing the status of women from a constitutional and equality perspective. Additionally, the U.S. Supreme Court's decision in *Bradwell* also forced women to battle the issue of practicing law at a local level. The *Bradwell* Court effectively refused to consider a woman's right to admission to a state bar one of "privileges and immunities" under the Fourteenth Amendment of the U.S. Constitution and instead considered it a licensing issue within the control of each state's legislature. Incidentally, although *Bradwell's* counsel made a cursory "equal rights" argument, it was virtually ignored in favor of arguments on the privileges and immunities provision. See Mossman, *The First Women Lawyers*, 45. As a result of the failure of Congress to act to protect women during the Reconstruction Amendments and the Supreme Court's failure to act to protect women's rights during the *Bradwell* case, women were left to battle the issues of the right to practice law and the right to vote on a state-by-state basis. More often, given the damning precedent in the post-*Bradwell* world, women were forced to seek amendments from state legislators to gain admission to the Bar, rather than achieve that same end through the courts. See Mossman, *The First Women Lawyers*, 50.

195. See Mossman, *The First Women Lawyers*, 53. Other women, such as Phoebe Couzins, the first woman to graduate from the Washington University Law School, chose not to practice law in order to devote her career to suffragist work. Ibid., 60.

196. Ibid., 55, discussing several early female lawyers who enjoyed successful legal practices and did not strive to push down other barriers for greater equality.

197. See Drachman, *Sisters in Law*, 168 (noting that it wasn't until Beatrice Doerschuk's publication of *Women in the Law* in 1920, where Doerschuk trumpeted the "birth of the new woman lawyer in America" as a result of the shift in the underlying rationale for women in the legal profession "from the woman lawyers movement to the idea that women were equally as capable as men in succeeding in law."

198. Chapelle, et al., *Maryland: A History of its People*, 223.

199. Connecticut, however, actually ratified the Nineteenth Amendment within a month of national ratification in 1920; Vermont did so

on February 8, 1921, and Delaware on March 6, 1923. The remaining nine states took more than sixty years to ratify the amendment; those states included Maryland (March 29, 1941, but not certified until February 25, 1958), Virginia (February 21, 1952); Alabama (September 8, 1953); Florida (May 13, 1969), South Carolina (July 1, 1969, but not certified until August 22, 1973); Georgia (February 20, 1970); Louisiana (June 11, 1970); North Carolina (May 6, 1971) and Mississippi (Mar 22, 1984). The underlined states shared the distinction of being the last states to admit women to the Bar as well.

200. Chapelle, et al., *Maryland: A History of Its People*, 206–07 and 210; and Frank Richardson Kent, *The Story of Maryland Politics*, 228; see, also, Bernard C. Steiner, "The Southern States of America: The History of Maryland" (Chapter III), found at http://www.electricscotland.com/history/america/south/south11.htm.

201. Robert J. Brugger, *Maryland: A Middle Temperament* 1634–1980 (Baltimore, MD: The Johns Hopkins University Press, in association with Maryland Historical Society, 1988), 407.

202. Justin Haas, "State of Maryland vs. Louis Hyman: Did Progressivism, Concern for Public Health, and the Great Baltimore Fire Influence the Court of Appeals?" *Building Baltimore* (Fall 2010): 26–27, http://www.digitalcommons.law.umaryland.edu/cgi/viewcontent.cgi?article=1023&context=min_pubs; accessed October 8, 2012.

203. Brugger, *Maryland: A Middle Temperament*, 407.

204. Chapelle, et al., *Maryland: A History of Its People*, 206–07. For further discussion of the socio-political environment that existed in Maryland during Etta's battles with the General Assembly, see, also, Chapter 3 of this book.

205. Ibid., 208; Brugger, *Maryland: A Middle Temperament*, 406.

206. Chapelle, et al., *Maryland: A History of Its People*, 206–07.

207. Ibid., 210.

208. Ibid.

209. Frank Richardson Kent, *The Story of Maryland Politics* (Baltimore, MD: Thomas and Evans Printing, 1911), 330. When the Democrats regained control of the General Assembly, they made plans to prevent another Republican victory; given that African American votes contributed to the strength of Maryland's Republican Party, the Democrats plans largely involved attempts to disenfranchise blacks. See Chapelle, et al., *Maryland: A History of its People*, 210. In fact, in 1903, Democrats ran on the platform that "political destinies of Maryland... should be shaped and controlled by the white people of the State." See Brugger, *Maryland: A Middle Temperament*, 420. Thus, reform bills took a back seat to these attempts.

210. See, for example, Brugger, *Maryland: A Middle Temperament*, 420; Chapelle, et al., *Maryland: A History of Its People*, 210.

211. Ibid. This theory is supported by the fact that the states that opposed ratification were all from the South. See note 195, above.

212. "Women as Lawyers," *The New York Times* (February 23, 1902).

213. *Bradwell*, 83 U.S. 130, 141 (Bradley, J., concur-

ring). Justice Bradley's sentiments were echoed when Ms. Goodwell applied for admission to the bar in Wisconsin: "There are many employments in life not unfit for female character. The profession of the law is surely not one of these. The peculiar qualities of womanhood, its gentle graces, its quick sensibility, its parity, its delicacy, its emotional impulses, its subordination of hard reasons to sympathetic feeling, are surely not qualifications for forensic strife. Nature has tempered woman as little for the juridical conflicts in the court room, as for the physical conflicts of the battle field." See *In re Goodell*, 39 Wis. 232, 245 (1875).

214. "Is Anxious to Practice Law," 12.

Chapter 3

1. Carol Sanger, "Curriculum Vitae (Feminae): Biography and Early American Lawyers," review of *America's First Woman Lawyer: The Biography of Myra Bradwell* by Jane M. Friedman, *Stanford Law Review* 46 (1994): 1257.

2. Barbara Ann White, "Traversing 2nd and 3rd Waves: Feminist Legal Theory Moving Forward," *University of Baltimore Law Forum* 39 (2008): iv. The term "first wave" generally refers to the first wave of feminism which began with the Seneca Falls Convention and faded after World War I. The movement was focused on gaining the right to vote, to contract, and to own property, as well as to gain legal and political independence. I use it here to describe Maryland's own first wave—the first group of women admitted to the Maryland Bar, most of whom might be considered feminists and who shared an interest in securing equal rights for women, particularly the right to vote. See, also, Barbara Allen Babcock, "Clara Shortridge Foltz, First Woman," *Valparaiso University Law Review* 28 (1994): 1285 (concluding that, "[b]y virtue of their efforts to join the profession, all of the first women lawyers were, in effect, members of the women's movement").

3. See notes 134–35 and the accompanying text.

4. See note 150–52 and the accompanying text.

5. See notes 160–64 and the accompanying text.

6. Joan Jacobs Blumberg and Nancy Tomes, "Women in the Professions: A Research Agenda for American Historians," *Reviews in American History*, 10 (1982): 275–76.

7. Martha Minow, "'Forming Underneath Everything That Grows': Toward A History of Family Law," *Wisconsin Law Review* 819 (1985): 821.

8. Faith Jaycox, *The Progressive Era: Eyewitness History* (New York: Facts on File, 2005), 5. The population of the United States grew from 31,400,000 to nearly 63,000,000 between 1860 and 1890.

9. Ibid., 6–7. The cities with populations of more than 1,000,000 were New York City, Chicago, and Philadelphia; those with more than 250,000 were Baltimore, Buffalo, Cincinnati, Cleveland, San Francisco, and St Louis.

10. Isabel Wilkerson, *The Warmth of Other Suns: The Epic Story of America's Great Migration (New York: Random House,* 2010), 244.

11. Isabel Wilkerson, interview by Terry Gross, *National Public Radio* (September 13, 2010), http://www.npr.org/templates/transcript/php?storyID=1298274444.

12. Jaycox, *The Progressive Era*, 9.

13. Jacob Riis, *How the Other Half Lives: Studies Among the Tenements* (New York: Charles Scribner's Sons, 1890), 13. See, also, Andrew S. Dolkart, *Biography of a Tenement House in New York City: An Architectural History of 97 Orchard Street* (Santa Fe, NM: Center for American Places, 2006).

14. See *Bradwell v. Illinois*, 83 U.S. 130, 132 (1872) (Bradley, J., concurring.): "God designed the sexes to occupy separate spheres of action and... it belonged to men to make, apply, and execute the laws...." Linda Waite, *U.S. Women at Work* (Santa Monica, CA: The Rand Corporation, 1981): 2, http://www.rand.org/pubs/reports/2008/R2824.pdf; accessed October 12, 2012. In 1890, approximately twenty percent of women worked for wages outside the home. Most worked in domestic services, factory work, or the "new white collar occupations" in retail, offices or telephone operators; see Jaycox, *The Progressive Era*, 30.

15. See, generally, Carl Degler, *At Odds: Women and the Family in America from the Revolution to the Present* (New York: Oxford University Press, 1980), 26–30; and Nancy Cott, *The Bonds of Womanhood* (New Haven, CT: Yale University Press, 1977).

16. Brumberg and Tomes, *Women in the Professions*, 285.

17. Jaycox, *The Progressive Era*, 28. The women's suffrage movement began in the mid-nineteenth century but gained strength when two organizations, the National Woman Suffrage Association and American Woman Suffrage Association, merged in 1890 under the leadership of Elizabeth Cady Stanton. For further information on these organizations and others led by women during the Progressive Era, see http://www.nwhm.org/online-exhibits/progressiveera/introprogressive.html.

18. Emmanuel Sampath Nelson, ed., *African-American Authors, 1745–1945: Bio-bibliographical Critical Sourcebook* (Westport, CT: Greenwood, 2000), 380. Terrell was an activist, writer and leader for both women's rights and African Americans. She was the first African American woman to sit on a school board in the United States. She wrote about her struggles and achievements in her autobiography, *A Colored Woman in a White World* (Washington, DC: Randsell, 1940).

19. "100 Years of History," NAACP, http://www.naacp.org/pages/naacp-history; accessed October 17, 2012. Jaycox, *The Progressive Era*, 11, citing Walter I. Trattner, *From Poor Law to Welfare State,: A History of Social Welfare in America* (New York: Simon and Schuster, 2007). Although official policy of many settlement houses reflected a desire to serve the poor regardless of race, segregation of neighborhoods resulted in both a system of "white" and "black" settlement houses. Although the black settlement movement did not start in earnest until the post-World War I era, a number of prominent African American women founded community organizations similar to the Settlement Houses during the Progressive Era, including Janie Porter Barrett, the founder of Hampton House in Virginia, Rosemary Skinner Keller, Rosemary Radford Ruether, and Marie Cantlon. *Encyclopedia of Women and Religion in North America*, Vol. 3 (Bloomington: Indiana University Press, 2006), 1066.

20. 20. Walter I. Trattner, *From Poor Law to Welfare State: A History of Social Welfare in America*,

Sixth Edition (New York: Simon and Schuster, 2007), 171.

21. Jaycox, *The Progressive Era*, 13. In the Settlement House movement, for example, more than ninety percent of the women were college educated, and more than half had done graduate work. See, also, Judith Ann Trolande, "From Settlement Houses to Neighborhood Centers: A History of the Settlement House Movement in the United States," The International Federation of Settlements and Neighborhood Centers, http://www.ifsnetwork.org/LinkClick.aspx?fileticket=oX-%2FGcHlAzQE%3D&tabid=481&mid=1303; accessed August 2, 2012. "The feminist movement influenced the development of settlements. The first generation of women college graduates felt a special obligation to do something useful with its education."

22. One commentator has talked about the impact of the cooperation of black and white women on the Progressive Movement: "Particularly in the late 19th century to 1910, black women succeeded in urging racial cooperation… "See Elisabeth Lasch-Quinn, *Black Neighbors: Race and the Limits of Reform in the American Settlement* 1890–1945 (Chapel Hill: University of North Carolina Press, 1993), 150.

23. Claudia Goldin, "The Work and Wages of Single Women, 1870–1920," *Journal of Economic History*, 40 (1980): 82. Most worked in domestic services, factory work, or the "new white collar occupations" in retail, offices or as telephone operators. Brumberg and Tomes, "Women in the Professions," 282: "By the 1840s, the spread of the public school system had brought middle class women into teaching. During the late nineteenth century, the proliferation of urban welfare services, hospitals, and public libraries led to the entry of women into social work, nursing, and librarianship. In all of these areas, the need for a cheap, abundant labor force harmonized with prevailing notions of 'innate' female abilities."

24. Ibid., 16. In 1869, Arabella Mansfield, of Iowa, became the first woman to be admitted to the Bar in the United States.

25. Ibid., Appendix I, Table 1.

26. "Portias of To-day," *Illustrated London News* (November 13, 1897).

27. Between 1870 and 1890, 288 women were admitted to the Bar in the United States. From 1900 to 1920, about 2,400 were admitted. But, even with the increase by 1920, the number of women admitted in each state were relatively small and lagged behind other professions. See Virginia G. Drachman, *Sisters in Law: Women Lawyers in Modern American History* (Cambridge, MA: Harvard University Press, 2001), 2: "By 1920, women made up 86 percent of all school teachers, 66 percent of all social workers, 5 percent of all doctors 4.7 of all scientists and only 1.4 percent of lawyers."

28. Richard Woodworth, "Some Influences on the Reform of Schools of Law and Medicine, 1890 to 1930," *The Sociological Quarterly* 14 (1973): 496–516. Some have argued that, while training for medicine improved as a result of these changes, training for lawyers actually was weaker under the new system.

29. James F. Schneider, *A Century of Striving for Justice: The Maryland State Bar Association* 1896–1996 (Baltimore: Maryland State Bar Association, 1996), 20 (noting that the Maryland State Bar

Association was founded in 1896, because "There was a perception that the public image of the legal profession had sunk to its lowest level because of the misdeeds of certain members of the bar, those that were unfit because of a lack of moral, ethical or legal training. Reform was in the mind.").

30. For a general discussion of the role of the "professionalization of law," including the development of formal legal education, in the admission of women to the Bar in the United States and abroad, see Mary Jane Mossman, "The First Woman Lawyers: Piecemeal Progress and Circumscribed Success," *Osgoode Hall Law Journal* 45 (2007): 379.

31. *Bradwell v. Illinois*, 83 U.S. 130, 141 (U.S. 1872) (Bradley, J., concurring): "The constitution of the family organization, which is founded in the divine ordinance, as well as in the nature of things, indicates the domestic sphere as that which properly belongs to the domain and functions of womanhood. The harmony, not to say identity, of interest and views which belong, or should belong, to the family institution is repugnant to the idea of a woman adopting a distinct and independent career from that of her husband."

32. See, for example, Minow, "Forming Underneath Everything That Grows: Toward A History of Family Law," 881–82. (Re-examining, inter alia, how the social context of *Bradwell v. Illinois*—the founding of the juvenile court, Prohibition, protective labor laws for women and children, sanitation codes, and other social welfare programs, as well as women's suffrage—as extensions of their domestic roles and concluding that women's own contributions to legal change, particularly admission to the Bar, included "their struggle not only for their own rights but also for domestic virtues on a public scale.")

33. See, for example, Anthony Platt, *The Child Savers: The Invention of Delinquency* (Chicago, IL: University of Chicago Press, 1977), 139. Ellen Ryerson, *The Best-Laid Plans: America's Juvenile Court Experiment* (New York: Hill and Wang, 1978), 4–5: "One question is whether the movement for which it is named was peopled by an old middle class acting out status frustrations, or by a new middle class acting out its professional ambitions, or by a business elite seeking a predictable environment in which to pursue its own interests. A variant of the question is whether progressivism was a movement of humanitarian reform that failed or a movement of capitalist conservatism that succeeded."

34. Elizabeth Scott and Laurence Steinberg, *Rethinking Juvenile Justice*, (Cambridge, MA: Harvard University Press, 2010), 93.

35. See Brumberg and Tomes, "Women in the Professions," 287: "Women found their 'golden opportunities,' so to speak, in the massive social dislocation caused by immigration, poverty, economic uncertainty, and labor exploitation." While Brumberg and Tomes focus on women's development of "helping professions" like social work, public health nursing, and teaching, the Progressive Era reforms expanded the opportunities for "helping" within the legal profession and thus drew women to this work.

36. Virginia G. Drachman, "Women Lawyers and the Quest for Professional Identity in Late Nineteenth-Century America," *Michigan Law Review* 88 (1990).

37. Robert J. Brugger, *Maryland, A Middle Temperament, 1630–1980* (Baltimore, MD: The Johns Hopkins University Press, 1996), x.

38. James B. Crooks, *Politics and Progress: The Rise of Urban Progressivism in Baltimore, 1895–1911* (Baton Rouge: Louisiana State University Press, 1968), ix.

39. Brugger, *Maryland, A Middle Temperament*, 306 and 387.

40. Ibid., 340–43.

41. Ibid., 347–51 (describing the influx of blacks, women, children, and immigrants in the labor market).

42. Ibid., 412–14. *The Baltimore News* described Southwest Baltimore at the time as a place in which "Foul streets, foul people in foul tenements filled the foul air." Ibid., 401, citing *The Baltimore News* (September 20, 1892): 20.

43. Brugger, *Maryland, A Middle Temperament*, 416.

44. Bureau of Census, Twelfth Census of the United States, Vol. 1: Population, Pt. 1. By 1910, the urban population (50.8%) exceeded the state's rural population (49.2%) for the first time. Suzanne Ellery Greene Chapelle, Jean H. Baker, Dean R. Esslinger, Whitman H. Ridgway, Jean B. Russo, Constance B. Schulz, and Gregory A. Stiverson, *Maryland: A History of Its People* (Baltimore, MD: The Johns Hopkins University Press, 1986), 180.

45. Brugger, *Maryland, A Middle Temperament*, 387.

46. Ibid., 363.

47. Ibid., 351.

48. Chapelle, et al., *Maryland: A History of its People*, 206–07.

49. Brugger, *Maryland, A Middle Temperament*, 386.

50. Crooks, *Politics and Progress*, 156.

51. Brugger, *Maryland, A Middle Temperament*, 398.

52. Crooks, *Politics and Progress*, 11.

53. Brugger, *Maryland, A Middle Temperament*, 25.

54. The Hon. James McSherry, President of the Maryland Bar Association, "Annual Address," Transactions of the Second Annual Meeting (Baltimore, MD: Maryland State Bar Association, 1897), 64.

55. Crooks, *Politics and Progress*, 25. Among these groups were some of the leading male Progressives in Maryland.

56. Brugger, *Maryland, A Middle Temperament*, 411.

57. Joan Marie Johnson, *Southern Women and the Seven Sister Colleges: Feminist Values and Social Activism* (Athens: University of Georgia Press, 2010), 11; Staff Writers, "10 American Colleges that Paved the Way for Women," *Online Colleges News* (May 9, 2011); Julia B. Morgan, "The Question of Coeducation, 1874–1877," in *Women at the Johns Hopkins University* (1986), http://old.library.jhu.edu/collections/specialcollections/archives/womenshistory/chapter1.htm; accessed October 14, 2012.

58. Brugger, *Maryland, A Middle Temperament*, 411. For example, Mary Ellen Richmond served as Assistant Treasurer and later as Secretary. Edward James, et al., *Notable American Women, 1607–1950: A Biographical Dictionary*, Volume 2 (Cambridge, MA: The Belknap Press of Harvard University Press, 1971), 152; Brugger, *Maryland, A Middle Temperament*, 411. See, also, Jane Cunningham Croly, *The History of Women's Club*

Movement in America (Ann Arbor: University of Michigan Library, 1898), 583 (discussing the Club's "municipal housekeeping"); and Crooks, *Politics and Progress*, 79.

59. Brugger, *Maryland, A Middle Temperament*, 411.

60. Ibid.

61. Ibid. In a letter from President Taft to the 3rd Annual Congress of the Children's Playground Association in 1909, he reflects on the focus of the group and expresses his support for the Association: "I do not know anything which will contribute more to the strength and morality of that generation of boys and girls compelled to remain part of the urban populations in this country, than the institutions of in their cities of playgrounds where their hours of leisure can be occupied by rational and healthful exercise." From *Proceedings of Annual Meetings & Annual Report* By Children's Playground Association of Baltimore City, 3 (1907). See, also, Brugger, *Maryland, A Middle Temperament*, 411; Theda Skocpol, *Protecting Soldiers and Mothers: The Political Origins of Social Policy in the United States* (Cambridge, MA: Harvard University Press, 1992), 391 (crediting Maryland's chapter, among others, for working effectively to pass labor legislation in 1912 regulating women's work hours).

62. Bobbie Sorrill, "Southern Baptist Laywomen in Missions," *Baptist History and Heritage*, 22, (1987): 23.

63. Chapelle, *Maryland: A History of its People*, 190.

64. Minow, "Forming Underneath Everything That Grows: Toward A History of Family Law," 827. See also, Mary L. Clark, "The Founding of the Washington College of Law: The First Law School Established by Women for Women," *American University Law Review* 47 (1998): 640-41. "These voluntary associations served as springboards for women's nascent political activity. First, many of the associations were organized around particular political and social issues. Second, joining these associations to advocate certain causes often led to other political activity, and, ultimately, to the women's suffrage movement."

65. See, for example, Mary Katherine Scheeler, "Emilie A. Doetsch, 1882–1969, Suffragist and Lawyer," in Winifred G. Helmes, ed., *Notable American Women* (Centreville, MD: Tidewater Publishers, 1977), 107–08.

66. Erin M. Masson, "The Woman's Christian Temperance Union, 1874–1898: Combating Domestic Violence," *William & Mary Journal of Women and the Law* 3 (1997): 166. Eventually both Stanton and Anthony just focused on suffrage, leaving the Women's Christian Temperance Union to other women leaders.

67. "Women's Christian Temperance Union of Maryland History," http://www.wctumd.org/History.html; accessed October 15, 2012. But see Edgar Leigh Venzke, "The Temperance Movement in Maryland, 1825–1918," (Baltimore, MD: Ph.D. dissertation, The Johns Hopkins University, 1947), 34 (noting that, despite their "enthusiastic" support for the cause, the power of women in the temperance movement in early-twentieth-century Maryland was limited by their inability to vote).

68. Masson, "The Woman's Christian Temperance Union 1874–1898," 164. See, also, Ruth Bordin, *Woman and Temperance: The Quest for Power and Liberty*, 1873–1900 (Philadelphia, PA: Temple University Press, 1981), 3–4; JoEllen Lind, "Symbols, Leaders, Practitioners: The First Women

Professionals," *Valparaiso University Law Review* 28 (1994): 1353–54.

69. See "Prominent Maryland Women Organize Dry Reform Group," *The Baltimore Sun* (December 17, 1929): 28 (detailing efforts of a group of Maryland women to repeal prohibition after its implementation led to a variety of unintended consequences).

70. Crooks, *Politics and Progress*, 83: "Though some advocates undoubtedly looked to political reforms as an end in itself, increasingly Baltimoreans saw it as a means to social ends.... [W]omen's suffrage was a means to improve schools, playgrounds and sanitary conditions."

71. For example, in 1910, the Equal Suffrage Association and the Maryland Women's Suffrage Association introduced two separate measures to the General Assembly, with the former "permitting women to vote only in Baltimore elections." Brugger, *Maryland, A Middle Temperament*, 450. See, also, Crooks, *Politics and Progress*, 80–81. In 1906, the Maryland Suffrage Association, a branch of the National American Suffrage Association, hosted the annual meeting of the national organization in Baltimore. It was an opportunity for the political and social establishment of Maryland, including leading women in the Progressive Movement, to meet national figures like Susan B. Anthony, Jane Addams, Florence Kelly, and Clara Barton. "Demand Right to Vote: National Convention of the Woman's Suffrage Association to be Held in Baltimore—Leading Local Representative," *The Baltimore Sun* (January 7, 1906): 8.

72. Drachman, *Sisters in Law*, Appendix 1, 255.

73. For additional analysis of the issue of Maryland's delayed acceptance of women to the Bar, see Chapter 2.

74. Drachman, *Sisters in Law*, Appendix 1, 251–52. North Carolina, Louisiana, and Florida were the only southern states to admit women to the bar before 1900.

75. Jane H. Pease and William H. Pease, *Ladies, Women, and Wenches: Choice and Constraint in Antebellum Charleston and Boston* (Chapel Hill: University of North Carolina Press, 1990), 24: "The elite men of the Antebellum South ran a patriarchal society that allowed them to dominate over the women of their lives. Men controlled the lives of the women in his life to protect his own place in society."

76. Brugger, *Maryland, A Middle Temperament*, 451.

77. William Gillette, *The Right to Vote: Politics and the Passage of the 15th Amendment* (Baltimore, MD: The Johns Hopkins University Press, 1969).

78. Chapelle, *Maryland: A History of Its People*, 210–11.

79. Ibid.

80. Ibid.

81. Brugger, *Maryland, A Middle Temperament*, 450–51. They were concerned that it would lead to a "Doubled black-Republican vote."

82. Crooks, *Politics and Progress*, 82: "That the suffragists found persuading the legislature a difficult task was not surprising. .. The struggle to prevent Negro disenfranchisement undoubtedly took time and energy from democratic efforts to refine the instruments of self-government."

83. Crooks, *Politics and Progress*, 75: "In 1898, each Baltimore delegate represented 5,891 voters; each rural delegate represented 1,980 voters. The disparity in representation was at a ratio of 3 to 1. In the state senate, it was 5 $^1/_2$ to 1."

84. Ibid., 82 (noting the limited "political reform phase" of the progressive movement in Baltimore). Brugger, *Maryland, A Middle Temperament*, 424 and 426 (describing the "ambiguity of progress" in Maryland and the difficulty in balancing "public and private interest" to achieve the Progressive Era's political and social reform agenda"). Chapelle, *Maryland A History of its People*, 214 (concluding that despite some victories, "Maryland fell short in several areas" in accomplishing the reforms during the Progressive Era).

85. "... [I]t is possible that the establishment of law schools (whether professional or university-based) may have been *the* important factor in encouraging women to seek access to the bar in Canada (and in a number of other jurisdictions)." Mossman, "The First Woman Lawyers," 382.

86. Drachman, *Sisters in Law*, Appendix 1, Table 1, 251.

87. Ibid., Appendix 1, Table 5, 255.

88. Ronald Chester, *Unequal Access: Women Lawyers in a Changing* America (Westport, CT: Bergin and Garvey Publishers, 1984), 12–17 and 53–86. Massachusetts, Ohio, Pennsylvania, and Washington were among the first states to admit women, and they were admitted in relatively high numbers there. Ibid., 93.

89. D. Kelly Weisberg, "Barred from the Bar: Women and Legal Education in the United States 1870–1890," *Journal of Legal Education* 28 (1977): 485.

90. Catalog and Announcement, "University of Maryland School of Law," 1914, http://www.law.umaryland.edu/marshall/schoolarchives/documents/Catalog1914.pdf, 9. Today, Maryland has two law schools, the University of Maryland and the University of Baltimore School of Law (UB). Although both are now public law schools and are part of the University System of Maryland, UB was founded as the Mount Vernon School of Law in 1925 and always admitted women.

91. See Appendix A, Table 1 at 165.

92. For a full discussion of Etta Maddox's advocacy to open the practice of law to women before both the courts and the legislature, see Chapter 2.

93. Interestingly, most of these men and women, involved in Progressive Era causes in Maryland were also middle to upper class. In answering the question, "Who were the Baltimore Progressives?" James Crooks describes both the men and women in this group as 'elite' in terms of social standing and education. Crooks, *Politics and Progress*, 196 and 198.

94. Heather Garms, *Etta Haynie Maddox*, Women's Legal History Biography Project, Stanford University Law School, 13 (February 28, 2003), http://www.law.stanford.edu/library/womenslegalhistory/papers0203/MaddoxE- Garms03.pdf.

95. Ibid., 3.

96. Ibid.

97. Margie H. Luckett, *Maryland Women* (Baltimore, MD: King Brothers, 1937), 88.

98. Ibid.; see, also, "The Scheib School of Zion," Zion History: The Virtual Tour, http://zionbaltimore.org/vthistory_1800s_the_scheib_school.htm; accessed October 16, 2012.

99. Letter from Emilie Doetsch to the "Girls," dated September 31, 1936, found at http://meyerhoff.goucher.edu/library/robin/1936/9-31-ED.htm.

100. Washington College of Law, "Persons to Whom Degrees Were Awarded," 1899–1932, Washington College of Law Archives.

101. "Miss Helen Hill Admitted to Practice by State Tribunal," Washington College of Law Archives, accessed August 29, 2012. She was also a generous donor as an alumna but may have funded those contributions from her own earnings.

102. Samuel R. Gerber, M.D., *The Encyclopedia of Cleveland History*, modified July 16, 1997, http://ech.case.edu/ech-cgi/article.pl?id=GSRM.

103. Ibid.

104. "Emily R. Dashiell Dies, Had Been Law Librarian," *The Baltimore Sun* (February 9, 1983): A13; see, also, "They Lived in Somerset: 17th Century Marylanders," last modified July 22, 2012, http://www.rootsweb.ancestry.com/~mdsomers/tlis/tlis1_d.htm.

105. "Death of Chas. W. Dashiell," *The Baltimore Sun* (August 17, 1898): 7.

106. Ibid.

107. Ibid.

108. Fourteenth Census of the United States: 1920 Population.

109. Thirteenth Census of the United States: 1910 Population.

110. Etta Maddox, Emilie Doetsch, Anna Grace Kennedy, Marie Coles, and Mary Meushaw were the only women in their law school classes. "Miss Maddox Is A Lawyer: Will Try To Have Law Amended So She Can Practice," *The Baltimore Sun* (June 7, 1901): 10 (Etta Maddox); "Another Woman Lawyer," *The Baltimore Sun* (June 12, 1906): 7 (Emilie Doestch); "Another Woman Lawyer," *The Baltimore Sun* (May 19, 1907): 6 (Marie Elizabeth Kirk Coles); "She Took Two Prizes," *The Baltimore Sun* (June 14, 1905): 12 (Anna Grace Kennedy); "Many Get Diplomas," *The Baltimore Sun* (May 22, 1907): 7; "Doctors, Lawyers, Dentists," *The Baltimore Sun* (May 22, 1908): 12; and Andrews, *Tercentenary History of Maryland* 477 (Grace Rebekah Gerber).

111. "Women Students Barred: They Had Captured All the Prizes At Baltimore Law School," *The Washington Post* (September 17, 1907), (suggesting that Baltimore Law School closed its doors to women in response to a petition by male students angry the women got all the prizes at graduation).

112. "Another Woman Lawyer," *The Baltimore Sun* (May 19, 1907): 6; and "She Took Two Prizes," *The Baltimore Sun* (June 14, 1905): 12.

113. "Many Get Diplomas," 7.

114. "Doctors, Lawyers, Dentists," 12.

115. See Appendix A, Table 1 at 165. Death certificate for Emilie Doetsch, 8 June 1969, Reg. No. 695885, Baltimore City Health Department (copy in possession of the author); death certificate for Helen F. Hill, 14 March 1966, Maryland State Department of Health, Division of Statistical

Research and Records (copy in possession of the author); death certificate for Emily Dashiell, 8 February 1983, Reg. No. 830314, State of Maryland Department of Health and Mental Hygiene (copies in possession of the author).

116. "Pair's Romance Goes From Courts to Altar," *The Washington Post* (June 26, 1930).

117. Ibid.

118. United States Census: 1940 population (indicating Seth was eight years old in 1940).

119. Ibid.

120. To Wed After Long Delay," *The Baltimore Sun* (August 20, 1921): 7.

121. "Wife Sues for Maintenance," *The Baltimore Sun* (April 3, 1924): 11. There is also ample evidence that he had a lively and diverse law practice and shared Grace's interest in politics. "Lawyer Reported in Scuffle with Woman in Courthouse," *The Baltimore Sun* (January 30, 1934): 22; "Lawyer Asks $10,000 for Assault," *The Baltimore Sun* (February 4, 1917): 15; "Many Ward Meetings Held," *The Baltimore Sun* (October 25, 1911): 10.

122. "Funeral Services," *The Baltimore Evening Sun* (December 30, 1965): C10.

123. Transactions, Maryland State Bar Association, 1960: 65th Annual Meeting (Baltimore, MD: Maryland State Bar Association, 1960), 104–05.

124. Maryland State Bar Association, "Report of the Committee on Admissions," 104–105; "Section of Insurance, Negligence and Compensation Law," American Bar Association 1961 and 1962, accessed August 1, 2013.

125. For a discussion about the number of women who chose to balance careers and families among early female admittees around the nation, see Drachman, *Sisters in Law*, 98–112.

126. Drachman, *Sisters in Law*, 99.

127. Ibid., 99–100.

128. Ibid., 245, citing the Bureau of Vocational Information questionnaire 150 (March 1, 1920).

129. Prior to the Progressive Era, women who had to work were left with few alternatives for caring for their children. Indeed, many were forced to give up their children, on a temporary or permanent basis. See *Encyclopedia of Children and Childhood in History and Society, Orphanages* at http://www.faqs.org/childhood/Me-Pa/Orphanages.html: "[O]rphanages at the end of the nineteenth century were considered the best method of care for dependent children; their popularity increased and single poor parents often regarded them as places they could leave their children temporarily until circumstances improved, or as places where their children could get a good education."

130. Women In the Progressive Era, http://www.nps.gov/nr/travel/pwwmh/prog.htm: "Over time, the hundreds of settlements that opened in cities all over the country routinely offered day care and kindergartens for the children of working parents… " Interestingly, an article describing a lecture on motherhood at Washington College of Law in 1912 notes that early admittee Helen Hill presided over the meeting. One of the panelists, Ellen Spencer Mussey, Dean of Washington College of Law, is quoted as saying, "In the double standard of morality women are supposed to be innocent because ignorant…." Another panelist discusses "statistics of what is being done by the

17. "Jeanette Wolman," *Daily Record* (100 Years Issue, June 1988).

18. "Attorneys Kerpelman Present Son Leonard to Bench Today," *The Baltimore Sun* (December 3, 1949): 7; see "Woman Attorney Given Divorce for Desertion," *The Baltimore Sun* (April 14, 1933): 7.

19. "Obituaries," *Baltimore Jewish Times* (July 21, 2006); "Baltimore University Coed to Be Fifth Lawyer in Family," *The Baltimore Sun* (June 7, 1935): 4.

20. "Baltimore University Coed to Be Fifth Lawyer in Family."

21. "Jeanette Wolman," *Daily Record* (100 Years Issue, June 1988); "Mrs. Proser, Lawyer, Teacher, Dies," *The Baltimore Sun* (September 4, 1973): A9; and Putzel, "Jeanette Rosner Wolman, 1902—Lawyer and Civic Leader," 409.

22. Nationally, during the period up to 1920, single women's employment grew with a decline in employment for women after marriage, but "the 1920's appear to mark a turning point in the declining employment of married women," as, in the period between 1920 and 1940, employment by married women slowly rose. In 1920, forty-six percent of single women and only nine percent of married women participated in the labor force. By 1950, the percentage of single women in the labor force had risen only five percent while the percentage of married women in the labor force had risen thirteen percent. The number of married women in the labor force continued to rise over the next three decades to reach fifty-one percent by 1980. Claudia Goldin, *Understanding the Gender Gap: An Economic History of American Women* (New York: Oxford University Press, 1990), 10–12. During the 1920s, there was a marked increase of women wage earners in the business and professional workforce who were married, as combining career and family was "a novel, modern goal." Woloch, *Women and the American Experience*, 388 and 394.

23. Additionally, only one woman from the first group of women lawyers discussed in the previous chapter, Grace Gerber, had a child. See Chapter 3 of this book.

24. Charles V. Flowers, "Making a Case for Women," *The Baltimore Sun* (December 5, 1982): 281–90; "Obituaries," *The Baltimore Sun* (December 29, 1992): 4B.

25. Flowers, "Making a Case for Women."

26. "Obituaries," *The Baltimore Sun* (December 29, 1992): 4B; and Flowers, "Making a Case for Women."

27. "In Memoriam," *Women Lawyers Journal* 73 (Winter 1987): 13. Eleven years later, her son, Melvin Jack Marshall, joined her in practice, becoming one of the first mother-son teams to practice law in Baltimore. Ibid. Her other two sons followed in the footsteps of their father, George J. Marshall, and went into merchandising. "First Mother, Then Lawyer, Now High Court Candidate," *The Baltimore Sun* (April 14, 1956): 16. Melvin Marshall also served as his mother's campaign manager when she ran and was elected for a judgeship on Baltimore City's Orphan's Court. "Fair Play Urged in Judge Race," *The Baltimore Sun* (May 7, 1962): 11.

28. "Jeanette Wolman," *Daily Record* (100 Years Issue, June 1988); and Flowers, "Making a Case for Women." During the early part of the 1900s, the rise in number of women in professional careers was primarily in the clerical sector. Many offices

maintained policies preventing women from taking positions with promotional possibilities and with widespread unemployment during the Great Depression of the 1930s, many employers claimed that it was "public-spirited" to deny women jobs in favor of their male counterparts. Goldin, *Understanding the Gender Gap*, 106, 110–12; and Karen Morello, *The Invisible Bar: The Woman Lawyer in America, 1638 to the Present* (New York: Random House, 1986), 203.

29. "Jeanette Wolman," *Daily Record* (100 Years Issue, June 1988).

30. J. S. Bainbridge, Jr., "Pioneer Applied to Join State Bar for 20 Years," *The Baltimore Sun* (April 22, 1984): C3.

31. Ibid.

32. Virginia G. Drachman, *Sisters in Law* (Cambridge, MA: Harvard University Press, 1998), 88–89.

33. Ibid.; "Baltimore Woman Attorney Helping to Defend Niemoth," *The Baltimore Sun* (June 19, 1930): 26; "Move is Made to Free Man in Lynching Case," *The Baltimore Sun* (November 24, 1933): 26; Morello, *The Invisible Bar*, 179–80; and Hedda Garza, *Barred From the Bar: A History of Women and the Legal Profession* (New York: Franklin Watts, 1996), 101.

34. "Move is Made to Free Man in Lynching Case"; "Bar License Denied to German Group," *The Baltimore Sun* (January 20, 1938): 24.

35. Helmes, *Notable Maryland Women*, 47; and "R. P. Ingram, Lawyer, Dies," *The Baltimore Sun* (March 28, 1966): 11.

36. Fred Rasmussen, "Sarah Burke, Pioneering Lawyer," *The Baltimore Sun* (March 20, 1994): 4B. Although she gave up the practice of law in the 1930s to start a family, Burke continued to actively advocate for women's rights and was one of the founding members of the Women's Bar Association. Ibid. Katharine Thurlow, "Women in the Law," *Maryland Bar Journal*, Vol. 19, No.[5] (1986): 24; "Sarah Rosenberg Burke."

37. "Miss Ida Claire Lutzky Weds Bernard U. Proser," *The Baltimore Sun* (August 29, 1932): 3; "Mrs. Proser, Lawyer, Teacher, Dies."

38. "Lawyer, Women's Advocate, Jeanette Rosner Wolman: A Soldier in the Fight for Women's Rights," *The Baltimore Sun* (The Anniversary Issue, May 17, 1987): 107.

39. Ibid. "Jeanette Wolman," *Daily Record* (100 Years Issue, June 1988). Ben Wolman became head of the Criminal Injuries Compensation Board and served until 2003. "Benjamin R. Wolman, 74, Dies; Lawyer, Teacher, Police Advocate," *The Washington Post* (June 11, 2004). Paul Wolman was a World War I veteran, having enlisted in 1917 during his final year at the University of Maryland School of Law. "Wells Appoints Paul Wolman Assistant State's Attorney," *The Baltimore Sun* (January 30, 1938): 18. He graduated in 1920, established his own practice, and gained prominence in Maryland as Assistant State's Attorney and, later, as Chairman and Director of the State Board of Parole and Probation and, nationally, as National Commander in Chief of the Veterans of Foreign Wars. "V.F.W. Parley Ends, Wolman is Commander," *The Baltimore Sun* (September 6, 1930): 20–21; "Wells Appoints Paul Wolman Assistant State's Attorney"; "New Parole Head," *The Baltimore Sun* (September 24, 1961): 12.

40. In 1949, Fannie Kurland Kerpelman's son, Leonard Kerpelman, joined his aunt, Helen Sherry, in practice. "Attorneys Kerpelman Present Son

Leonard to Bench Today." In 1929, Louis Sherry left the family, and, in 1933, Helen Sherry was granted an absolute divorce on grounds of desertion and custody of her two children. "Woman Attorney Given Divorce for Desertion."

41. "United Railways Wins Verdict In $30,000 Suit," *The Baltimore Sun* (October 17, 1928): 28; "Man Jolted off Ladder is Given $3,000 Verdict," *The Baltimore Sun* (October 17, 1935): 22; "Glenn L. Martin Co. Sued for $175,000," *The Baltimore Sun* (June 22, 1939): 26; and "Divorcee Acquitted in Fatal Shooting of Man on Visit to Her," *The Baltimore Sun* (October 28, 1941): 26.

42. "Baltimore Woman Attorney Helping to Defend Niemoth"; *Elliott Bldg. & Loan Ass'n of Baltimore City v. Karopchinsky*, 156 Md. 302, 144 A. 254 (1929).

43. "Niemoth Verdict Upheld on Appeal," *The Baltimore Sun* (March 21, 1931): 4.

44. "United Railways Wins Verdict in $30,000 Suit"; Henrietta Dunlop Stonestreet, "The Women Lawyers in Maryland," *Women Lawyers' Journal* 15 (1927): 8.

45. Emilie Doetsch to the Goucher College Class of 1903, Sept. 31, 1936, *Round Robin Letters*.

46. Ibid.

47. Fred Rasmussen, "Rose Zetzer, 94, Founded 1st All-Female Law Firm in Md," *The Baltimore Sun* (April 9, 1998): 11B.

48. "Officers of the Year," *Women Lawyers' Journal* 30 (1944): 20 and 21.

49. Bainbridge, "Pioneer Applied to Join State Bar for 20 Years."

50. "First Woman Bar Member Scoffs at 'Men Only' Idea," *The Evening Sun* (October 22, 1946).

51. Although the firm survived during the tenure of Zetzer, Carton, Friedler, and Parke, the firm ultimately closed when its youngest member Carton retired from the practice of law in 1964. See Gerri Kobren, "Mothers & Daughters: Why Some Choose Similar Careers," *The Baltimore Sun* (May 9, 1982): E1–E3; "Obituaries: Anna W. Carton: Lawyer-Activist," *The Baltimore Sun* (December 29, 1992): 4B.

52. Gilbert Sandler, "Blazing Trails: Rose Zetzer Was a Jewish Pioneer on the Frontier of Maryland Law," *The Baltimore Sun* (February 25, 2005).

53. Ibid; "Rose Zetzer, 94, Founded 1st All-Female Law Firm in Md."

54. "Portias May, But Don't, Wear Their Hats in City's Courts," *The Baltimore Sun* (April 9, 1947): 26.

55. Ibid.

56. Ibid.

57. See Jill Norgren, *Rebels at the Bar* (New York: New York University Press, 2013), 188.

58. Hon. Lynne A. Battaglia and Evelyn C. Lombardo, "Investing in the Future of Maryland Women," *Maryland Bar Journal* 44 (July 2011): 14.

59. Battaglia and Lombardo, "Investing in the Future of Maryland Women," 14; and "Women Lawyers Organize Club and Name Officers," *The Baltimore Sun* (March 24, 1927): 26.

60. Battaglia and Lombardo, "Investing in the Future of Maryland Women," 14.

61. Stonestreet, "The Women Lawyers in Maryland," 8; Joan Bossman Gordon, "Women of the Baltimore Bar," in *Histories of the Bench & Bar of Baltimore City* (Baltimore, MD: Baltimore Courthouse and Law Museum Foundation, 1997), 97 and 99; Battaglia and Lombardo, "Investing in the Future of Maryland Women," 14; and Stonestreet, "The Women Lawyers in Maryland," 8.

62. Stonestreet, "The Women Lawyers in Maryland," 8.

63. Gordon, "Women of the Baltimore Bar."

64. "Lawyer, Women's Advocate Jeanette Rosner Wolman: A Soldier in the Fight for Women's Rights."

65. Stonestreet, "The Women Lawyers in Maryland," 8. After the meeting, Dean Riley invited some of the women to a luncheon in Washington, DC, to meet members of the Washington Bar Association, including Mrs. Burnita Shelton Matthews, who would become the first female U.S. District Court Judge. Norgen, *Rebels at the Bar*, 211. Burnita Shelton Matthews attended law school in Washington, DC, and passed the bar in 1920. After facing rejection in applying to be a lawyer for the Veteran's Administration, she opened a law firm with two other women. Ibid., 210.

66. Stonestreet, "The Women Lawyers in Maryland," 8.

67. Ibid.; Battaglia and Lombardo, "Investing in the Future of Maryland Women," 14; and Gordon, "Women of the Baltimore Bar," 99.

68. "Bar Association Rejects 4 Women," *The Baltimore Sun* (October 25, 1928): 3; "Women as Members of Bar Body is Aim," *The Baltimore Sun* (December 12, 1928): 3.

69. "Bar Association Rejects 4 Women."

70. Henrietta Dunlop Stonestreet, "Women Lawyers vs. the Baltimore Bar Association," *Women Lawyers' Journal* 19 (1931): 18.

71. Ibid., 19.

72. Ibid.; "Lawyer, Women's Advocate Jeanette Rosner Wolman: A Soldier in the Fight for Women's Rights"; and "History of the Women's Bar Association of Maryland," http://wba-md.org/history.aspx; accessed September 13, 2013.

73. Bainbridge, "Pioneer Applied to Join Bar for 20 Years"; and George J. Hiltner, Jr., "Bar Group to Admit Women; Upsets 50-year Precedent," *The Baltimore Sun* (June 30, 1946): 24–25.

74. "We Shall Try Again Come 1950," *Women Lawyers' Journal* 32 (1946): 147.

75. "First Woman Bar Member Scoffs at 'Men Only' Idea," *The Evening Sun* (October 22, 1946).

76. The Baltimore City Bar Association did not have a formal policy excluding women and minorities from membership, but, until the Association's members voted on June 17, 1957 to admit both groups, "for 78 years it had been tradition that they were not considered acceptable" to apply. "Baltimore Bar Votes to Open Member List," *The Washington Post* (June 18, 1957). In contrast, the Maryland State Bar Association's policy required an amendment to the organization's constitution, approved by vote of the majority of members, be-

fore women could be considered for membership. "Women as Members of Bar Body is Aim."

77. "Bar Association Votes to Admit All," *The Afro-American* (June 29, 1957).

78. Morello, *The Invisible Bar*, 117.

79. Although the Nineteenth Amendment passed nationally in 1920, Maryland refused to ratify it until 1941. See Suzanne Ellery Greene Chapelle, et al., *Maryland: A History of Its People* (Baltimore, MD: The Johns Hopkins University Press 1986), 225–26; Calvin Gabriel, "I remember… the Fight for Woman Suffrage," *The Baltimore Sun* (November 2, 1958): M2; and Woloch, *Women and the American Experience*, 356. The refusal to ratify the Nineteenth Amendment was apparently grounded in the belief that a state held "the fundamental right... to define its political community" and the "authority to decide its own domestic course." Robert J. Brugger. *Maryland: A Middle Temperament,* 1634–1980 (Baltimore, MD: The Johns Hopkins University Press, in association with Maryland Historical Society, 1988), 453. It was not until 1941 that the General Assembly finally ratified the Nineteenth Amendment. Burnita Shelton Matthews, "The Woman Juror," *Women Lawyers' Journal* 15 (1927): 15. As of 1927, nineteen states—Arkansas, California, Delaware, Indiana, Iowa, Kansas, Kentucky, Louisiana, Maine, Michigan, Minnesota, Nevada, New Jersey, North Dakota, Ohio, Oregon, Pennsylvania, Washington, and Wisconsin—all recruited women for jury service. Ibid.,

80. "Many Lawyers Favor Women for Jury Duty," *The Baltimore Sun* (January 6, 1921). Proponents argued that the Nineteenth Amendment abrogated the provision of the city charter which mandated that jury service applied only to men. Opponents argued that the issue should be determined by the State, that women should not be subject to hear about certain subject matter, that jurist conditions could not accommodate women, and that the majority of Maryland women did not want to serve on juries. Ibid.; "Jurists Will Consider Calling Woman Juries," *The Baltimore Sun* (January 5, 1921): 18.

81. "Jurists Will Consider Calling Woman Jurors," *The Baltimore Sun* (January 5, 1921):18.

82. "State Clubwomen Plan Fight for Jury Bill," *The Baltimore Sun* (January 23, 1931): 20; "Want Ritchie's Aid for Woman Juries," *The Baltimore Sun* (December 18, 1930): 5; "Women Make Plea for Jury Service: Delegation of 200 Appears Before House Committee Favoring Farrington Bill," *The Baltimore Sun* (February 26, 1931): 24; and "Jury Service Bill Opponents Heard," *The Baltimore Sun* (March 5, 1931): 4.

83. See Chapter 2 of this book.

84. Holly J. McCammon, "Maryland: Intermittent Activism," in *The U.S. Women's Jury Movements and Strategic Adaptation: A More Just Verdict* (New York: Cambridge University Press, 2012), 103.

85. "Jury Service Bill Opponents Heard"; and "Women Make Plea for Jury Service: Delegation of 200 Appears Before House Committee Favoring Farrington Bill."

86. "Women Make Plea for Jury Service: Delegation of 200 Appears Before House Committee Favoring Farrington Bill."

87. Helen E. Brown also drafted "Jury Service for Woman," a brief that was "widely quoted throughout the United States and is something of a standard work on the subject." "Southerner Wants Women in Jury Work," *Christian Science Monitor* (October 29, 1942); and Helmes, *Notable Maryland Women*, 47.

88. "Women Make Plea for Jury Service: Delegation of 200 Appears Before House Committee Favoring Farrington Bill."

89. "Jury Service Bill Opponents Heard."

90. McCammon, *Maryland, Intermittent Activism*, 101; and "Jury Service Bill Rejected in House," *The Baltimore Sun* (February 27, 1933): 8.

91. See Ibid.; and "Women's Service on Juries is Urged," *The Baltimore Sun* (February 16, 1935): 20.

92. "Making a Case for Women."

93. "Ruling Lacks Effect Here," *The Baltimore Sun* (December 11, 1946): 14; and "300 Women Cheer, Clap, Boo to Support Jury Service Bill," *The Baltimore Sun* (February 2, 1939): 22–23.

94. "Bars Women Anew From Jury Duty," *The Baltimore Sun* (March 14, 1941): 16.

95. The other women's organizations represented in the Maryland Committee for Women's Jury Service included the Maryland Business and Professional Women's Clubs, Federation of Republican Women, Maryland Federation of Women's Clubs, Maryland League of Women Voters, Maryland National Women's Party, and United Democratic Women's Clubs of Maryland. McCammon, *Maryland, Intermittent Activism*, 106.

96. Ibid., 106–07.

97. Ibid., 108.

98. The only woman who spoke in opposition was Mrs. Reuben Ross Holloway of the Woman's Constitutional League. N. T. Kenney, "Jury Service Hit by Mrs. Holloway," *The Baltimore Sun* (February 19, 1937): 26–27; "Jury Service Bill Opponents Heard." Quotation from David Stickler, "Women Campaign for Jury Service," *The Baltimore Sun* (January 30, 1947): 30–31.

99. Stickler, "Women Campaign for Jury Service."

100. McCammon, *Maryland, Intermittent Activism*, 108.

101. "Women to Begin Jury Tests Today," *The Baltimore Sun* (June 2, 1947): 4.

102. Ibid.

103. "Eleven Women Like Jury Duty," *The Baltimore Sun* (September 27, 1947): 6.

104. Women lawyers likely valued the synergistic relationship with women's increased presence across various professional fields. While they did not use their legal degrees to practice, Marie Presstman regularly spoke to women's groups to encourage women to aspire to professional careers despite opposition and to seek the highest offices in national, state, and city government and B. Olive Cole, Professor of Economics and Pharmaceutical Law and a graduate of the first University of Maryland School of Law class to admit women, inspired students and encouraged women to pursue higher education. See "Woman Movie Censor is Campaign Speaker," *The Baltimore Sun* (October 21, 1920): 20; "About Our Women in Maryland: Dr. B. Olive Cole, Phar. D., L.L.B.," *The Mercury* (June 1936); and Carolyn B. Stegman, *Women of Achievement in Maryland History* (University Park, MD: Anaconda Press, 2002), 205.

105. Helmes, *Notable Maryland Women*, 108; "Women Voters Break Record," *The Baltimore Sun* (May 9, 1923): 2.

106. Emilie Doetsch to Goucher College Class of 1903, Updated 1925, *Round Robin Letters.*

107. Helmes, *Notable Maryland Women*, 108.

108. Ibid., 48; Her later campaigns, also unsuccessful, included the Republican Primary for Governor and Attorney General. Ibid.

109. "Woman is Urged as Magistrate." *The Baltimore Sun* (December 11, 1934): 4.

110. Ibid.; "The Housing Court Magistracy Under Helen E. Brown," *The Baltimore Sun* (September 15, 1951): 8.

111. Helmes, *Notable Maryland Women*, 48 and 51.

112. "Obituaries," *The Baltimore Sun* (December 29, 1992): 4B.

113. "North, East, West, South," *Women Lawyers' Journal* 28 (1942): 18; and Doris Nohren Murison, "Lawyers Seek Bar Primary," *The Baltimore Sun* (May 14, 1943): 4.

114. Burnita Shelton Mathews to Rose Zetzer, September 13, 1951, Jewish Museum of Maryland. In her correspondence to Judge Matthews, Rose Zetzer suggests that the State's Attorney for Baltimore City, Anselm Sodaro, was reluctant in considering Zetzer for an Assistant State's Attorney position, due to "the matter of religion." She later wrote: "I think that argument is just an alibi." Rose Zetzer to Burnita Shelton Matthews, March 21, 1952, Jewish Museum of Maryland.

115. Ibid.

116. "In Memoriam," *Women Lawyers' Journal* 73 (1987): 13. She was later defeated in 1956, 1960, and 1962 but continued private practice until her retirement in 1968. Ibid.

117. "Woman Eyes Senate Seat: Judge Nellie Marshall to Run Next Year," *The Baltimore Sun* (October 27, 1957): 25; and "Nellie Marshall, 1st Woman to Win City Office, Dies," *The Baltimore Sun* (December 7, 1986): 14B.

118. Ibid.

119. Helmes, *Notable Maryland Women*, 410.

120. Ibid., 51.

121. "Cook Will to Aid Women," *The Baltimore Sun* (January 31, 1961): 13.

122. Elize A. Braase, "Rose S. Zetzer—A Pioneer Who Cleared the Path for Women," June 1991 (on file with The Jewish Museum of Maryland, Rose Zetzer file).

123. Helmes, *Notable Maryland Women*, 51–52.

124. Michael J. Clark, "Would-Be Voter Finds a Supporter," *The Baltimore Sun* (April 26, 1972): A9.

125. Ibid.; see, also, "Voter Challenges Registration Rule: Judge to Decide What's in a Name," *The Washington Post* (April 27, 1972); "A Court of Appeals of Maryland Time Capsule: Six Historic Arguments in the Nation's Oldest Appellate Court," *University of Baltimore Law Forum* 30 (1999): 26.

126. Clark, "Would-Be Voter Finds a Supporter."

127. "The Right of a Married Woman to Use Her Birth-Given Surname for Voter Registration: Stuart v. Board of Supervisors of Elections," *Maryland Law Review* 32 (1973): 409.

128. *Stuart v. Bd. Of Supervisors of Elections for Howard Cnty.*, 266 Md. 440, 295 A.2d 223 (1972).

129. Kevin Smokler, "Jeanette Rosner Wolman on 75 Years of Women's Suffrage," *The Baltimore Jewish Times* (August 25, 1995).

130. Erin Cox, "Women Gain Majority on Md.'s Highest Court: Barbera Named Chief Judge, Watts Joins Bench," *The Baltimore Sun* (July 3, 2013): A1.

Chapter 5

1. Kenneth Walter Mack, "A Social History of Everyday Practice: Sadie T.M. Alexander and the Incorporation of Black Women into the American Legal Profession, 1925–1960," *Cornell Law Review* 87 (2001–2002): 1405–06.

2. J. Clay Smith, Jr., *Emancipation: The Making of the Black Lawyer*, 1844–1944 (Philadelphia: University of Pennsylvania Press, 1993), 182, n. 216. Although admitted to the Maryland Bar, Lucas never practiced in the state, choosing instead to teach at Howard University's Law School in Washington, DC, before leaving Maryland for New York. J. Clay Smith, Jr., ed., *Rebels in Law: Voices in History of Black Women Lawyers* (Ann Arbor: University of Michigan Press, 2000), 88–89; and Taunya Lovell Banks, "Setting the Record Straight: Maryland's First Black Women Law Graduates," *Maryland Law Review* 63 (2004): 758.

3. Smith, *Emancipation*, 635–36 (Table 13). By 1940, Massachusetts, Michigan, Ohio, Pennsylvania, and other states had at least one African American female lawyer, while most Southern states lagged behind—including Maryland, which had none.

4. Banks, "Setting the Record Straight," 757; University of Baltimore, *The Reporter* (1928): 52. Anna A. Tully is listed in the 1928 *Reporter* for the University of Baltimore School of Law, noting that "[n]one of us were particularly keen about having women classmates, but Miss Anna has won all hearts and now we don't know what we would have done without her." Ibid.

5. 169 Md. 478, 182 A. 590 (1936); and Banks, "Setting the Record Straight," 758.

6. University of Maryland, *Catalogue* 1942–1943 *and Announcement for* 1943–1944: *The School of Law*, 20. Orchard (as "Orchard [*sic*], Emily V.") is listed as a first-year evening student for the 1942–1943 school year, but her name does not appear under any class in the following year's catalogue. University of Maryland, *Catalogue* 1942–1943 *and Announcement for* 1943–1944: *The School of Law*, 18–21. The March 1944 announcement of her marriage, however, describes her as "a University of Maryland law student." Lula Garrett, "Emily Orchard, Babe Jones Married in Montclair, N.J.," Gadabouting in Baltimore with Lula Jones Garrett, *The Afro-American* (March 11, 1944): 11.

7. University of Maryland School of Law, *Yearbooks and Catalogues,* 1939–1973.

8. Ibid. While the University of Baltimore School of Law had yearbooks with photos, the University of Maryland School of Law did not; therefore, the only way to identify women of color at the University of Maryland was by clearly Asian or Hispanic last names or by graduation from a historically black college. Both indicators are unreliable. Because some African American women earned degrees from Columbia University, the University of Pennsylvania, New York University, and other Northern schools, our method of relying solely

on graduation from known black colleges and universities may underestimate the actual number of African American women who enrolled. There are a variety of other reasons why women graduates of color might remain invisible under our metrics. For example, there are many Spanish-speaking South Americans with English and Italian last names. Additionally, a married Latina or Asian woman using a non-Latino or non-Asian husband's last name would not be counted; neither would a Latina, Asian, or American Indian adopted by a family with an Anglo last name. Similarly, we might mistakenly include white women with racially ambiguous last names.

9. Yuriko Sata graduated in 1967, University of Maryland, *Catalogue* 1966–1967 *and Announcement for* 1967–1968: *The School of Law*, 33, and Rai Saint Chu in 1971, University of Maryland, *Catalogue* 1970–1971 *and Announcement for* 1971–1972: *The School of Law*, 16. Mercedes Casado Samborsky graduated in 1969, University of Maryland, *Catalogue* 1969–1970 *and Announcement for* 1970–1971: *The School of Law*, 44; though her name suggests that she might be Latina, her ethnicity is unknown.

10. Although in this book the authors have focused on women who have passed the bar examination, it may be that the Bar itself created barriers for women.

11. J. S. Bainbridge, "Lawyers Debate Benefits of Women's Group," *The Baltimore Sun* (April 22, 1984): C1; and Garrett, "Emily Orchard, Babe Jones Married in Montclair, N.J.," Gadabouting in Baltimore with Lula Jones Garrett.

12. Mack, "A Social History of Everyday Practice," 1407–08.

13. Mari J. Matsuda, introduction to *Called from Within: Early Women Lawyers of Hawai'i*, Mari J. Matsuda, ed. (Honolulu: University of Hawaii Press, 1992), 3.

14. See Jerold S. Auerbach, *Unequal Justice: Lawyers and Social Change in Modern America* (New York: Oxford University Press, 1976), 3, which states explicitly that it is a "social history of the professional elite" and that its subject is "the response of elite lawyers to social change in the twentieth century." Mack, "A Social History of Everyday Practice," 1409.

15. Ibid., 1410; Mari Matsuda introduced this concept as part of critical race theory. Mari J. Matsuda, "Looking to the Bottom: Critical Legal Studies and Reparations," *Harvard Civil Rights-Civil Liberties Law Review* 11 (1987): 323.

16. Matsuda, introduction to *Called from Within: Early Women Lawyers of Hawai'i*, 2.

17. Ibid.

18. University of Maryland, *Catalogue* 1942–1943 *and Announcement for* 1942–1943: *The School of Law*, 20.

19. J. Clay Smith Jr., introduction to *Rebels in Law: Voices in History of Black Women Lawyers*, (Ann Arbor: University of Michigan Press, 2000), 2.

20. The University of Maryland School of Law admitted two black men in 1887, but it did not admit any women until 1920. The Maryland Bar removed racial restrictions in 1888, but women were not admitted to the Bar until 1902. Banks, "Setting the Record Straight," 753–57.

21. In 1802, blacks were barred from voting. C. Fraser Smith, *Here Lies Jim Crow: Civil Rights in Mary-*

land (Baltimore, MD: The Johns Hopkins University Press, 2008), 48. Slaves could appear in court only to testify against free blacks, the right of free blacks to assemble was restricted, and free blacks visiting the state could remain no longer than two weeks. George F. Bragg, *Men of Maryland* (Baltimore, MD: Church Advocate Press, 1925), 13–17.

Maryland's large population of free blacks resulted from several interlinking factors, most of which relate to Maryland's slaveholding culture, which differed in a number of ways from that in the rest of the South. Emancipation was more common in Maryland than elsewhere, beginning after the American Revolution (1776–1781) and continuing, despite efforts to discourage and limit manumission. Furthermore, when Maryland masters freed their slaves, they tended to do it en masse, emancipating most or all of them rather than a favored few, as was typical in the Lower South. These large-scale emancipations resulted from political and religious beliefs as well as economic pragmatism. See Christopher Phillips, *Freedom's Port: The African-American Community of Baltimore,* 1790–1860 (Urbana: University of Illinois Press, 1997), 37–38. It was also relatively common for slaves to purchase their own freedom or for friends and relatives to purchase a person's freedom, as Daniel Coker's friends did. Term slavery, wherein a slave would become free at a certain age or after a certain number of years, was common in Baltimore. Ibid., 46–47 and 131. The end of a term, however, did not instantly bring freedom from bondage: there was often a gap between the end of a slave's term and actual manumission. Furthermore, the fact that an adult was freed did not mean that his or her children were emancipated as well. The status of a child born to a term slave was determined by the mother's deed of manumission, which typically required that the child would be a slave until a certain age, usually twenty-five for males and twenty-one for females. In 1809, the General Assembly of Maryland decreed that, if a term slave's deed of manumission was silent on the status of her children, those children would be slaves for life. Ibid., 44–45. Slaves and free blacks often intermarried, and the free spouse would sometimes live with the slave spouse. Thus, black families typically intermingled with free individuals, slaves for life, and family members subject to a variety of types of term slavery. It was also common for a master to hire his slaves out—far more common, in fact, than sale, despite Maryland's high-volume slave trade. This practice allowed slaves some degree of autonomy, though the amount depended largely on the slave's level of skill and the employer's location: the higher the skill and the more urban the environment, the more independence a slave might have. The hiring system was not a panacea for slavery's hardships: Frederick Douglass's hire arrangement, for example, essentially estranged him from his mother. The practice of hiring and the tangles of legal status within families meant that many slaves in Maryland and, particularly, in Baltimore had close and frequent contact with free blacks. These practices carried their own host of problems, but the exposure to free blacks gave the slaves living examples of existence outside of slavery. Ibid., 39. See Barbara Jeanne Fields, *Slavery and Freedom on the Middle Ground: Maryland During the Nineteenth Century* (New Haven, CT: Yale University Press, 1985), 24, 27–32, and 39.

22. Matthew A. Crenson, "Roots: Baltimore's Long March to the Era of Civil Rights," in Richardson Dilworth, ed., *The City in American Political Development* (New York: Routledge, 2009), 206; and Barbara Mills, *"Got My Mind Set on Freedom": Maryland's Story of Black and White Activism,* 1663–2000 (Bowie, MD: Heritage Books, 2002), 10.

23. Women comprised fifty-four percent of the total population of free black adults, though the gender ratio in the adult slave population was approximately equal. Fields, *Slavery and Freedom on the Middle Ground*, 29–30. In northern Maryland, fifty-seven percent of the free adult blacks were women, while, in southern Maryland and on the Eastern Shore, women were only fifty-one percent of the free black population. Ibid., 29. There appear to have been two likely causes for this imbalance: First, women tended to be freed at earlier ages than men, usually at twenty-one rather than twenty-five. Phillips, *Freedom's Port*, 42. Second, the 1808 ban on international slave trade drove up the domestic market for slaves, particularly in the heavily agrarian states to Maryland's south and west. Ibid., 46 and 55. Many slave owners kept their skilled male slaves, whom they could hire out or use as field hands if necessary, but sold the unskilled ones, causing a gender imbalance among the remaining black population. Ibid., 55.

24. Phillips, *Freedom's Port*, 145.

25. Mills, "*Got My Mind Set on Freedom*," 11; Robert J. Brugger, *Maryland: A Middle Temperament*, 1634–1980 (Baltimore, MD: The Johns Hopkins University Press, in association with Maryland Historical Society, 1988), 211. Free blacks lived in all wards of the city; see William George Paul, "The Shadow of Equality: The Negro in Baltimore 1864–1911," Ph.D. dissertation (Madison: University of Wisconsin, 1972), 14. Before 1850, most were concentrated in the central, southern, and eastern sections. See Harold A. McDougall, *Black Baltimore: A New Theory of Community* (Philadelphia, PA: Temple University Press, 1993), 34. Their types of housing varied depending on their financial situations, but the majority lived in run-down buildings on side streets or in alleys. See Paul, "The Shadow of Equality," 14.

26. Bettye C. Thomas, "Public Education and Black Protest in Maryland, 1865–1900," *Maryland Historical Magazine* 71 (Fall 1976): 381.

27. Mills, "*Got My Mind Set on Freedom*," 21.

28. Ibid., 86. *The Afro-American* was probably not Baltimore's first black newspaper—Everett Waring, discussed *infra*, edited a paper called the *Star*, apparently during the late 1880s—but it is the longest-running such paper, and still exists today. John J. Oliver, Jr. is the current publisher and Chairman of the Board of Directors. See Thomas, "Public Education and Black Protest in Maryland," 386; and "Contact Us," AFRO, http://www.afro.com/contact-us.htm; accessed June 15, 2012. Karen Olson, "Old West Baltimore: Segregation, African-American Culture, and the Struggle for Equality," in Elizabeth Fee, et al., eds., *The Baltimore Book: New Views of Local History* (Philadelphia, PA: Temple University Press, 1991), 67–68; and Mills, "*Got My Mind Set on Freedom*," 86–88.

29. Olson, "Old West Baltimore," 118 and 144.

30. Ibid.; Mills, "*Got My Mind Set on Freedom*," 14.

31. Crenson, "Roots: Baltimore's Long March to the Era of Civil Rights," 206–07; and Mills, "*Got My Mind Set on Freedom*," 14.

32. Phillips, *Freedom's Port*, 170–72.

33. Mills, "*Got My Mind Set on Freedom*," 75; and Jo Ann E. Argersinger, *Toward a New Deal in Baltimore: People and Government in the Great Depression* (Chapel Hill: University of North Carolina Press, 1988), 14. Though this commitment was especially prevalent among the black middle class, it extended throughout every social class:

homeless groups collaborated with one another, sometimes interracially, and black public-housing tenants launched an extensive network of community services, including nursery schools, men's and women's clubs, dramatic and literary societies, and more. See Mills, "*Got My Mind Set on Freedom*," 75; and Argersinger, *Toward a New Deal in Baltimore*, 14, 106–07, and 172–73.

34. Tera W. Hunter, To 'Joy My Freedom—Southern Black Women's Lives and Labors After the Civil War (Cambridge, MA: Harvard University Press, 1997), 69.

35. Phillips, *Freedom's Port*, 171. When a member died, the Free African Civilization Society provided for "his widow and children, or relatives." Ibid. These types of organizations, also known as secret societies, were quite popular in black communities throughout the South during the nineteenth century. See Hunter, *To 'Joy My Freedom*, 70. Some secret societies outside Baltimore included both men and women, and a few featured an even gender balance in leadership. Ibid.

36. McDougall, *Black Baltimore*, 50.

37. *In re* Taylor, 48 Md. 28 (1877).

38. David S. Bogen, "The Forgotten Era," *Maryland Bar Journal* 19 (1986), 10.

39. Ibid.; Mills, "*Got My Mind Set on Freedom*," 51. Waring also became a member of Union Baptist, Rev. Johnson's church counsel to the Brotherhood of Liberty, and President of the Lexington Savings Bank. Ibid., 51; Bogen, "The Forgotten Era," 10; and Antero Pietila, *Not in My Neighborhood: How Bigotry Shaped a Great American City* (Chicago, IL: Ivan R. Dee, 2010), 27. Though Waring's career in Maryland was at first stellar, it came to an ignoble end when Waring lost the bank's money and skipped town. In 1892, W. Ashbie Hawkins, who would go on to have a distinguished career in Maryland, became the first African American to be admitted on examination to the state's Bar. Ibid., 27 and 74; and Mills, "*Got My Mind Set on Freedom*," 51.

40. Smith, *Here Lies Jim Crow*, 55–56. A portrait of Dean John Prentiss Poe is still displayed prominently on the fourth floor of the University of Maryland's Carey Law School.

41. Ibid., 56.

42. Ibid., 88–89. The correspondence between the school's registrar and dean regarding Seaborne's application is truly eye-opening. Smith's account does not make clear whether Seaborne had an attorney or threatened legal action, but it seems that none was taken. Ibid.

43. Smith, *Here Lies Jim Crow*, 91–92; and Crenson, "Roots: Baltimore's Long March to the Era of Civil Rights," 217.

44. Smith, *Here Lies Jim Crow*, 92–93. Shifting attitudes toward civil rights within Baltimore also mediated a positive judicial outcome, for which Baltimore's NAACP head, Lillie Mae Jackson, deserved at least partial credit. Ibid.

45. Crenson, "Roots: Baltimore's Long March to the Era of Civil Rights," 94–97. When the verdict was announced, Clarence Mitchell, Jr., then still a journalist, ran the twelve blocks to the offices of *The Afro-American* to write the story. Ibid.

46. Ibid., 98; *Murray v. Pearson*, 182 A. 590, 169 Md. 478 (1936). Murray then had to come up with money for tuition; ultimately, Carl Murphy

loaned it to him. One professor refused to call on Murray until the Court of Appeals issued its ruling. See Smith, *Here Lies Jim Crow*, 98.

47. Smith, *Here Lies Jim Crow*, 147.

48. Murphy, William H. Jr., "A Son Remembers; Judge William H. Murphy Sr. 1917–2003," *The Afro-American* (June 13, 2003).

49. Mills, "*Got My Mind Set on Freedom*," 84–85.

50. Ibid., 85 and 87.

51. J. Clay Smith, Jr., "Black Women Lawyers: 125 Years at the Bar; 100 Years in the Legal Academy," *Howard Law Journal* 40 (1997): 365.

52. Phillips, *Freedom's Port*, 166–67; Smith, *Here Lies Jim Crow*, 6–7; and Bettye C. Thomas, "Public Education and Black Protest in Maryland, 1865–1900," *Maryland Historical Magazine* 3 (Fall 1976): 382. More than twenty-five years before *Plessy v. Ferguson*, Maryland's governor, Oden Bowie, declared "separate but equal" education in Maryland, with the result that black schools received shabby buildings, hand-me-down books, shorter school years, overcrowded classrooms, and lower pay for their teachers.

53. Ibid., 37–40.

54. Dana Z. Sutton, "Juanita Jackson Mitchell (1913–1992)," Archives of Maryland (Biographical Series), last modified October 2001, http://msa.maryland.gov/megafile/msa/speccol/sc3500/sc3520/002300/002306/html/2306bio.htm; accessed January 24, 2012; l; "Charm and Brains Combined," *The Afro-American* (June 20, 1936): 19; and "Funeral Rites Held for Housing Official," *The Afro-American* (March 17, 1962).

55. Louise K. Hines, "20 Attending University of Maryland Law School," *The Afro-American* (October 19, 1946): 20; and Catherine Pugh, "Blacks in the Boardroom," *The Baltimore Sun* (May 8, 1986): 8.

56. "Mrs. Elaine Davis Gets Study Grant," *The Afro-American* (August 6, 1957): 12.

57. Juanita Jackson Mitchell, at age thirty-three, was working for the NAACP when she enrolled at Maryland. Banks, "Setting the Record Straight," 758–59. Elaine Carsley Davis was twenty-five but a teacher at Douglas High School. See Hines, "20 Attending University of Maryland Law School"; and "Elaine Carsley Davis," *Who's Who Among African-Americans* (Farmington Hills, MI: Gale Group, 2009). Lena King Lee, thirty-seven, had been teaching for more than ten years in Baltimore. Hines, "20 Attending University of Maryland Law School," 20. Only Joan Sessoms Ford, twenty-two, came to Maryland Law immediately after graduating from the University of Maryland at College Park. See note 204, interview with Joan Sessoms Ford.

58. Pauli Murray and Mary O. Eastwood, "Jane Crow and the Law: Sex Discrimination and Title VII," *George Washington Law Review* 34 (1965): 232.

59. Banks, "Setting the Record Straight," 759.

60. Katherine Kenny and Eleanor Randrup, *Juanita Jackson Mitchell: Freedom Fighter* (Baltimore, MD: Publish America, 2005), 41.

61. Catherine Pugh, "Blacks in the Boardroom," *The Baltimore Sun* (May 8, 1986): 8.

62. "U.S. Government Manual—Department of Labor," U.S. Department of State, http://infousa.

state.gov/economy/finance/docs/dept_labor.pdf; accessed January 23, 2012.

63. Frederick N. Rasmussen, "'She stood very tall' Educator Was One of First Black Women in General Assembly, Lena K. Lee 1906–2006," *The Baltimore Sun* (August 26, 2006): 1B.

64. Michael A. Fletcher, "Juanita Jackson Mitchell Dies at 79: Civil Rights Leader Battled Bias in Court," *The Baltimore Sun* (July 8, 1992): 1A.

65. Phoebe A. Haddon, "Education for a Public Calling in the 21st Century," *Washington Law Review* 69 (1994): 574.

66. Hines, "20 Attending University of Maryland School of Law."

67. Ibid.

68. University of Maryland School of Law, *Catalogue* 1946–1947 *and Announcement* 1947–1948.

69. Mills, "*Got My Mind Set on Freedom*," 75; and Smith, *Here Lies Jim Crow*, 108.

70. Ibid., 82. Keiffer Jackson continued to travel, showing movies, many of which he made himself, which depicted black people in a positive light, a rarity at the time. Ibid., 82–83.

71. Kenny, *Juanita Jackson Mitchell*, 11–12.

72. Ibid., 12.

73. Prudence Cumberbatch, "What 'the Cause' Needs Is a 'Brainy and Energetic Woman,'" in Dayo F. Gore, et al., eds., *Want to Start a Revolution? Radical Women in the Black Freedom Struggle* (New York: New York University Press, 2009), 47 and 54.

There are some indications that Jackson was not an ideal landlady: Willie Adams called her "a very poor landlord" with "all kinds of violations on her properties." See Andrea Appleton, "Seen & Heard: Maryland's Civil Rights Era in Photographs and Oral Histories," *City Paper* (February 22, 2012), http://citypaper.com/news/em-seen-heard-maryland-s-civil-rights-era-in-photographs-and-oral-histories-em-1.[127]4626); accessed December 28, 2012.

74. Smith, *Here Lies Jim Crow*, 83. In several photographs of Lillie Mae Jackson, she stands or sits with the non-disfigured portion of her face to the camera. George H. Callcott, *Maryland and America, 1940 to 1980* (Baltimore, MD: The Johns Hopkins University Press, 1985), 147.

75. Smith, *Here Lies Jim Crow*, 82 and 84; By the mid-1930s, Lillie Mae Jackson was receptive to the suggestion of Carl Murphy, her former classmate and a national NAACP board member, when he suggested she run for president of the Baltimore chapter. "I don't want anybody to give me love," she is reported to have said; "just give me my constitutional rights." Cumberbatch, "What 'the Cause' Needs," 47.

76. Smith, *Here Lies Jim Crow*, 84; and Mills, "*Got My Mind Set on Freedom*," 76.

77. Mills, "*Got My Mind Set on Freedom*," 76.

78. Fletcher, "Juanita Jackson Mitchell Dies at 79"; and Cumberbatch, "What 'the Cause' Needs Is a 'Brainy and Energetic Woman,'" 54.

79. Fletcher, "Juanita Jackson Mitchell Dies at 79"; and Kenny, *Juanita Jackson Mitchell*, 22. She later observed:

> Here at Penn, I was able to lose my fear of white people, I made friends across the board. Gradually, I shed the shell I had brought with me to Pennsylvania, which had made me reticent, afraid to venture, afraid to speak up because of anticipated insults (which were not forthcoming), expected rejection (that did not happen). I have feared no man since.
>
> Again at Pennsylvania, in this first-class educational environment, I developed the security that comes from competition with the best and being able to meet it. It gave me confidence in my own ability. It did something for me that has lasted all my life. I might be denied equality of opportunity but I knew I was not inferior.
>
> I believe that what happened in Philadelphia ought to happen in Baltimore—my home. Exposure to democratic practices in Pennsylvania strengthened my faith that democracy could work in Baltimore.

Denton L. Watson, *Lion in the Lobby: Clarence Mitchell, Jr.'s Struggle for the Passage of Civil Rights Laws*, Revised Edition (Lanham, MD: University Press of America, 2002), 62 (quoting Juanita Mitchell from an interview and *The Daily Pennsylvania*, Penn's student newspaper).

80. Cumberbatch, "What 'the Cause' Needs Is a 'Brainy and Energetic Woman,'" 54; and Sutton, "Juanita Jackson Mitchell (1913–1992)."

81. Cumberbatch, "What 'the Cause' Needs Is a 'Brainy and Energetic Woman,'" 49; and Genna Rae McNeil, "Youth Initiative in the African American Struggle for Racial Justice and Constitutional Rights: The City-Wide Young People's Forum of Baltimore, 1931–1941," in John Hope Franklin and Genna Rae McNeil, eds., *African-Americans and the Living Constitution* (Washington, DC: Smithsonian Institution Press, 1995), 69.

82. Cumberbatch, "What 'the Cause' Needs Is a 'Brainy and Energetic Woman,'" 49.

83. Ibid., 47.

84. Smith, *Here Lies Jim Crow*, 84; and Mills, "*Got My Mind Set on Freedom*," 76–77. In 1931, Clarence Mitchell, Jr. had just graduated from Lincoln University, a historically black college in Pennsylvania, and become the chief lobbyist for the national NAACP. They met at a dinner given by the socialist socialite Elizabeth Coit Gilman. Mills, "*Got My Mind Set on Freedom*," 76.

85. McNeil, "Youth Initiative in the African American Struggle for Racial Justice and Constitutional Rights," 56 and 59–60; and Cumberbatch, "What 'the Cause' Needs Is a 'Brainy and Energetic Woman,'" 55.

86. McNeil, "Youth Initiative in the African American Struggle for Racial Justice and Constitutional Rights," 60; and Mills, "*Got My Mind Set on Freedom*," 77.

87. Ibid., 78; Cumberbatch, "What 'the Cause' Needs Is a 'Brainy and Energetic Woman,'" 55; McNeil, "Youth Initiative in the African American Struggle for Racial Justice and Constitutional Rights," 64–66; Cumberbatch, "What 'the Cause' Needs Is a 'Brainy and Energetic Woman,'" 56; and Andor Skotnes, "'Buy Where You Can Work': Boycotting for Jobs in African-American Baltimore, 1833–1934," *Journal of Social History* 27 (1994): 742–43.

88. Watson, *Lion in the Lobby*, 66–67.

89. Sutton, "Juanita Jackson Mitchell (1913–1992)."

90. McNeil, "Youth Initiative in the African American Struggle for Racial Justice and Constitutional Rights," 76; and Watson, *Lion in the Lobby*, 83.

91. McNeil, "Youth Initiative in the African American Struggle for Racial Justice and Constitutional Rights," 76; and Watson, *Lion in the Lobby*, 83.

92. Cumberbatch, "What 'the Cause' Needs Is a 'Brainy and Energetic Woman,'" 56.

93. After her election in 1935, Jackson built a coalition with the Interdenominational Ministerial Alliance and used her family and social connections to bring more women into the NAACP, which saw a resulting surge in female leadership. Ibid., 88, and Cumberbatch, "What 'the Cause' Needs Is a 'Brainy and Energetic Woman,'" 57. She filled the chapter's board with activists, labor leaders, and longshoremen and involved the NAACP in issues such as fair housing. See Callcott, *Maryland and America*, 146; and McDougall, *Black Baltimore*, 53. Jackson's leadership, characterized by one historian as "ironfisted," was not without conflict. See Cumberbatch, "What 'the Cause' Needs Is a 'Brainy and Energetic Woman,'" 52. Several important members left, and critics complained of nepotism and exclusivity. Ibid., 52–53.

In response to egregious overcrowding in African American neighborhoods during World War II, Jackson and the NAACP, Murphy, and the Alliance organized a 2,000-strong march on Annapolis in 1942. McDougall, *Black Baltimore*, 53. By the war's end, there were 6,000 new public housing units for blacks.

By 1946, Baltimore had the largest NAACP chapter in the nation, with more than 20,000 members. Ibid., and Olson, "Old West Baltimore," 68.

94. *Pearson v. Murray*, 169 Md. 478 (1936) (affirming the Baltimore City Court's decision in 1935); and Watson, *Lion in the Lobby*, 70–72.

95. Watson, *Lion in the Lobby*, 79. See, also, Cumberbatch, "What 'the Cause' Needs Is a 'Brainy and Energetic Woman,'" 59.

96. Cumberbatch, "What 'the Cause' Needs Is a 'Brainy and Energetic Woman,'" 60; and Watson, *Lion in the Lobby*, 95.

97. Watson, *Lion in the Lobby*, 102; and Cumberbatch, "What 'the Cause' Needs Is a 'Brainy and Energetic Woman,'" 60.

98. Ibid., 60–61: "Mitchell's status as a 'volunteer' changed after she was asked to lead Baltimore's fall membership campaign in 1940. She insisted that she would only return as a paid organizer.... [S]he valued her labor as a wife and mother, insisting on a pay rate of fifty dollars per week, nineteen more than her initial salary at the NAACP. Mitchell successfully reentered the field as a contract worker with a salary from the national office that legitimized her professional activities."

99. Ibid., 60–61; Watson, *Lion in the Lobby*, 109 and 113.

100. Denton Watson, "Juanita Jackson Mitchell and the Civil Rights Dynasty," *The Baltimore Sun* (July 12, 1992): 4.

101. Sutton, "Juanita Jackson Mitchell (1913–1992)"; McNeil, "Juanita Jackson Mitchell (1913–1992)," 804; and Cumberbatch, "What 'the Cause' Needs Is a 'Brainy and Energetic Woman,'" 61.

102. Watson, "Juanita Jackson Mitchell and the Civil Rights Dynasty."

103. Ibid.; Watson, *Lion in the Lobby*, 545–46. Much later, Mitchell's son, Clarence III, remembered "those week nights from 1946 to 1950 when his

father bundled him and his brother Keiffer into the car to take Mrs. Mitchell to her law classes." Watson, "Juanita Jackson Mitchell and the Civil Rights Dynasty."

104. Cumberbatch, "What 'the Cause' Needs Is a 'Brainy and Energetic Woman,'" n. 79 (quoting from an interview with Mitchell).

105. Mark V. Tushnet, *The NAACP's Legal Strategy Against Segregated Education,* 1925–1950 (Chapel Hill: University of North Carolina Press, 1987), 54.

106. Mitchell was first listed on the editorial board in the third (summer) issue of the 1948 year and all issues of the 1949 year; see *Maryland Law Review* 9 (1948): 261. The other African American was Robert B. Watts, who went on to found the first major black law firm in Baltimore and the first African American appointed to the Municipal Court of Baltimore City. Frederick N. Rasmussen and Dennis O'Brien, "Judge Robert B. Watts, 76, dies," The Baltimore Sun (October 9, 1998): 1C.

107. Banks, "Setting the Record Straight," 760.

108. "Unenforceability of Racial Restrictive Covenants," *Maryland Law Review* 10 (1949): 263 (no author listed but anecdotal evidence shows Mitchell claimed credit for this article, see Banks, "Setting the Record Straight," 760).

109. "Templeton's Stand Lauded by Leaders," *The Afro-American* (January 17, 1953): 14.

110. Kenny, *Juanita Jackson Mitchell*, 41.

111. Ibid., 38 and 41. Mitchell, in an oral interview in 1991, attributed this quotation to Charles Houston. Bruce A. Thompson, "The Civil Rights Vanguard: The NAACP and the Black Community in Baltimore, 1931–1942," Ph.D. dissertation (College Park: University of Maryland, 1996), 239 (on file with the University of Maryland College Park McKeldin Library).

112. "Battle for the Beaches," *The Afro-American Red Star* (October 13, 2007): 13.

113. Even in her last semester of law school, Mitchell was a board member of the local NAACP branch; a group of construction trade union officials led by her husband, then Labor Secretary of the NAACP's Washington office, asked the Baltimore City School Board to prevent racial discrimination in contracting and hiring for school construction. "School Building Bias is Charged," *The Baltimore Sun* (January 20, 1950): 32.

114. "Univ. of Md. Board Opens School to All," *The Afro-American* (February 10, 1951): 1.

115. Ralph Matthews, Jr., "U. of Md. Draws New Color Line," *The Afro-American* (March 8, 1952): 7.

116. Ralph Matthews, Jr., "Maryland NAACP Plans: Suit to Test Barriers at Friendship Airport," *The Afro-American* (August 4, 1951): 14. Mitchell recalled Carl Murphy's role in getting Jackson to take the lead in revitalizing the Baltimore NAACP. See Cumberbatch, "What 'the Cause' Needs Is a 'Brainy and Energetic Woman,'" 62, n.40; Murphy was the chair of the legal redress committee by June 1951. The committee did back but did not direct or subsidize the 1951 airport integration lawsuit, unlike its leadership of the Sandy Point cases starting in 1952. See "Governor Hears NAACP Police Brutality Complaints," *The Afro-American* (June 28, 1951); Matthews, "Maryland NAACP Plans"; and "Pre-Trial Legalities in Sandy Point Case Begin," *The Afro-American* (November 29, 1952): 14.

117. "Governor Hears NAACP Police Brutality Complaints," *The Afro-American* (June 28, 1951): 12.

118. *Lonesome v. Maxwell*, 123 F. Supp. 193 (D. Md. 1954), *rev'd sub nom.*, *Dawson v. Mayor of Baltimore City*, 220 F.2d 386 (4th Cir. 1955), *aff'd*, 350 U.S. 877 (1955) (Fort Smallwood, Sandy Point, municipal swimming pools); and "New Claims of Job Bias Hurled at Curtis Bay Yard," *The Afro-American* (October 11, 1952): 8.

119. Kenny, *Juanita Jackson Mitchell*, 43; Ollie Stewart, "Report from Europe," *The Afro-American* (August 25, 1951): 4; Juanita Jackson Mitchell, "French Station at Cherbourg Cleaner Than American Station," *The Afro-American* (September 1, 1951): 20.

120. Juanita Jackson Mitchell, "The Jacksons Abroad: On Tour of Southern Italy Hotel Looks Like Movies; Free From Segregation; Letter From Home; Baltimoreans Should Give Mayor D'Alesandro, State's Attorney Sodaro Trip Back Home," *The Afro-American* (October 13, 1951): 20.

121. "Monumental Bar Association Drops Its Jane-Crow Policy," *The Afro-American* (November 22, 1952): 12; "Monumental History," http://www.monumentalcitybar.com/history; accessed May 11, 2012. Along with her legal work for the NAACP, she also took cases as a solo practitioner or as the member of a team with other lawyers, especially W.A.C. Hughes, Jr. Her work included representing a black real estate investor bilked by an unscrupulous real estate agent, a suit seeking to ban segregated union lodges, as well as liquor board, zoning, and criminal cases. See, for example, *Taylor v. Brotherhood of RR. & Steamship Clerks*, 106 F. Supp. 438 (D.D.C. 1952); *Snead v. State*, 234 Md. 63 (1964) (appeal of drug conviction); *Bird v. State*, 231 Md. 432, 190 A.2d 804 (1963) (criminal case); *Sharpe v. Maryland*, 375 U.S. 946 (1963); *Snowden v. Mayor of Baltimore*, 224 Md. 443, 168 A.2d 390 (1961) (zoning); *Kennard v. McKamer Realty Co.*, 224 Md. 490 (1961); *Good Citizens Cmty. Protective Ass'n v. Bd. of Liquor License Comm'rs*, 217 Md. 129, 141 A.2d 744 (1958); *Aaron v. Mayor of Baltimore*, 207 Md. 401 (1955) (zoning); *Suttleman v. Bd. of Liquor License Comm'rs*, 209 Md. 134, 120 A.2d 388 (1956); *Payson Street Neighborhood Club v. Bd. of Liquor License Comm'rs*, 204 Md. 278 (1954); *Kappelman v. Bowie*, 201 Md. 86 (1952) (real estate investment). Mitchell represented her former black classmate at University of Maryland School of Law, Virginia Jones, in her criminal case for disturbing the peace by refusing to cede her taxicab to a white woman. "Taxi Service Difficulty Aired at Social Worker's Trial," *The Afro-American* (April 11, 1953): 14. Since most of her private cases involved black victims of racial discrimination, her private and NAACP work blended together, especially in claims of police brutality and illegal police raids. Many of these cases received high visibility. See, for example, "U.S. Attorney General Gets Wilkins Case," *The Afro-American* (March 28, 1953): 14; "Morganite Shot By Cop: $50,000 Damage Suit Filed Against Officer," *The Afro-American* (April 12, 1952): 22; "Grandmother Wins Suit Against Cop: Arrest In Home Without Warrant Declared Illegal," *The Afro-American* (April 18, 1953): 8; "NAACP Raps House Search, Asks Investigation by Commissioner," *The Afro-American* (August 4, 1953): 14; "Broadus Case Probe Asked," *The Baltimore Sun* (May 23, 1954): 26; and "Rehak Is Held for Killing War Veteran," *The Baltimore Sun* (June 16, 1954): 40.

122. *Brown v. Bd. of Ed.*, 347 U.S. 483 (1954); "Mergenthaler Bars Negroes: School Board Refuses 4 Boys Printing Courses Admission," *The Baltimore Sun* (February 6, 1953): 23.

123. "Public to View New High School," *The Baltimore Sun*, April 14, 1953, 23; and "Negroes File School Suit: Seek Admission of 2 Students At Printing Institution," *The Baltimore Sun* (June 6, 1953): 14.

124. "Negro Girls Are Barred at Western," *The Baltimore Sun* (June 24, 1953): 38; and "Western High Suit Is Filed: N.A.A.C.P. Asks U.S. Court to Act on Negro Girls," *The Baltimore Sun* (July 16, 1953): 23.

125. *Brown v. Bd. of Ed.*, 349 U.S. 294 (1955); "School Board Adopts Policy Erasing Racial Basis for Registration," *The Baltimore Sun* (June 11, 1954): 38; McNeil, "Juanita Jackson Mitchell (1913–1992)," 804; and Watson, *Lion in the Lobby*, 268; "Sandy Point Segregation Ban Sought," *The Baltimore Sun* (May 29, 1954): 24.

126. "Sandy Point Segregation Ban Sought," *The Baltimore Sun*.

127. "Race Issue Bars Sandy Point Use," *The Baltimore Sun* (July 3, 1953): 6; and "State Holds Out For Jim Crow Beach," *The Afro-American* (July 11, 1953): 22.

128. *Mayor of Baltimore v. Dawson*, 350 U.S. 877 (1955) (affirming *Dawson v. Mayor of Baltimore*, 220 F.2d 386 (4th. Cir. 1955)); Sutton, "Juanita Jackson Mitchell (1913–1992)." The author writes: "Also during the early 1950s, Mitchell filed lawsuits, which led to the desegregation of Sandy Point State Park, Fort Smallwood Municipal Park Beach, and Baltimore City swimming pools. Three years after her victory with Sandy Point State Park the Supreme Court upheld a decision that segregation of state facilities was unconstitutional. This set another legal precedent in the United States. This decision extended the 14th amendment to state beaches and other recreational facilities."

129. Kenneth D. Durr, *Behind the Backlash: White Working-Class Politics in Baltimore, 1940–1980* (Chapel Hill: University of North Carolina Press, 2003), 114.

130. "Segregation Challenge is Deferred," *The Baltimore Sun* (August 25, 1954): 32.

131. St. Mary's County: *Robinson v. Bd. of Ed.*, 143 F. Supp. 481 (D. Md. 1956); *Groves v. Bd. of Ed. of St. Mary's Cnty.*, 164 F. Supp. 621 (D. Md. 1958), *aff'd*, *Bd. of Ed. of St. Mary's Cnty v. Groves*, 261 F.2d 527 (4th Cir. 1958). Harford County: *Christmas v. Bd. of Ed. of Harford Cnty.*, 231 F. Supp. 331 (1964), *Moore v. Bd. of Ed. of Harford Cnty.*, 152 F. Supp. 114 (D. Md. 1957), *aff'd*, *Slade v. Bd. of Ed.*, 252 F.2d 291 (4th Cir. 1958); *Moore v. Bd. of Ed.*, 146 F. Supp. 91 (D. Md. 1956); *Pettit v. Bd. of Ed. of Harford Cnty.*, 184 F. Supp. 452 (D. Md. 1960). Charles County: *Hart v. Bd. of Ed. of Charles Cnty.*, 164 F. Supp. 501 (D. Md. 1958). See Watson, *Lion in the Lobby*, 269.

132. *Brown v. Bd. of Ed.*, 349 U.S. 294, 301 (1955); Juanita Jackson Mitchell, "Front Line Soldiers In the Struggle For Freedom," *The Afro-American* (July 2, 1955): A9.

133. She succeeded in ending the segregated seating policy at the privately-operated Marva Theater, because it was owned by the City of Frederick, but lost the attempt to bar Montgomery County from enforcing the segregation of the private Glen Echo amusement park by arresting protestors. *Jones v. Marva Theatres, Inc.*, 180 F. Supp. 49 (D. Md. 1960); *Griffin v. Collins*, 187 F. Supp. 149 (D. Md. 1960). In the midst of the protests against segregation in Cambridge, which led the Maryland National Guard to occupy the city for almost two years, Mitchell successfully represented two black minors who were committed to juvenile reform facilities for daring to

participate in a sit-in. See Smith, *Here Lies Jim Crow*, 198–204; Frederick Rasmussen, "'Glorious Gloria' led the battle," *The Baltimore Sun* (February 23, 1997): 6J; *Ex parte* Cromwell, 232 Md. 305, 192 A.2d 775 (1966); and *In re* Cromwell, 232 Md. 409 (1963). Mitchell lost her initial challenge to the 1961 arrest of twelve black students conducting a sit-in in a segregated Baltimore restaurant but prevailed in her appeal to the Supreme Court three years later. See *Bell v. State*, 227 Md. 302 (1961), *vacated and remanded*, *Bell v. Maryland*, 378 U.S. 226 (1964). The defendant Robert M. Bell, then a student at Morgan State, later became Chief Judge of the Court of Appeals of Maryland. John Carroll Byrnes, "Commemorative Histories of the Bench and Bar: In Celebration of the Bicentennial of Baltimore City 1797–1997," *University of Baltimore Law Forum* 27 (1997): 17. Robert Charles Murphy and Lawrence F. Rodowsky, two of the prosecutors of the case, later served with Judge Bell on the Court of Appeals. Ibid. Mitchell also served on a NAACP team that victoriously litigated two companion sit-in cases from South Carolina decided by the Supreme Court that term. See *Barr v. City of Columbia*, 378 U.S. 146 (1964); and *Bouie v. City of Columbia*, 378 U.S. 347 (1964).

134. McNeil, "Juanita Jackson Mitchell (1913–1992)," 805.

135. "NAACP Cites VA Discrimination," *The Afro-American* (July 30, 1960): 8; and "Housing Complaint Spurs VA Probe," *The Afro-American* (October 15, 1960): 6.

136. Watson, *Lion in the Lobby*, 572. Lillie Mae Jackson was still the president in July 1962, but, by June 1963 Mitchell was identified as the president. See Cliff Mackay, "Thurgood Given Runaround Again," *The Afro-American* (July 21, 1962): 1; and Adam Clymer, "Shift in Schools Race Policy Is Seen," *The Baltimore Sun* (June 14, 1963): 44.

137. The law was flawed: it exempted three Eastern Shore counties, and segregationists forced a referendum on it in November 1964, but it addressed the concerns of Attorney General Robert Kennedy and other federal officials who were alarmed that hotels and restaurants on U.S. 40 refused to serve black foreign diplomats. Smith, *Here Lies Jim Crow*, 206 and 209; and Frederick N. Rasmussen, "Racial Bias Revealed Along U.S. 40 in 1961," *The Baltimore Sun* (October 8, 2005): 2B.

138. Fletcher, "Juanita Jackson Mitchell Dies at 79."

139. Sutton, "Juanita Jackson Mitchell (1913–1992)"; and Nicholas Lemann, "The Myth of Community Development," *The New York Times* (January 9, 1994).

140. Juanita Jackson Mitchell and Archie D. Williams are listed as attorneys for Carl J. Murphy and others as intervening plaintiffs in *Maryland Citizens Comm. for Fair Congressional Redistricting, Inc. v. Tawes*, 253 F. Supp. 731–732 (D. Md. 1966) citing *Westberry v. Sanders*, 376 U.S. 1 (1964).

141. *Lankford v. Schmidt,* 240 F. Supp. 550 (D. Md. 1965), *rev'd*, *Lankford v. Gelston*, 364 F.2d 197 (4th Cir. 1966); and McNeil, "Juanita Jackson Mitchell (1913–1992)," 805.

142. "Action Urged On Brutality," *The Baltimore Sun* (March 2, 1966): A11; and Sutton, "Juanita Jackson Mitchell (1913–1992)."

143. Sutton, "Juanita Jackson Mitchell (1913–1992)"; "Freedom House Honors Outstanding Policemen," *The Afro-American* (April 14, 1973): A8.

144. *Morton v. Charles Cnty. Bd. of Ed.*, 373 F. Supp. 394 (D. Md. 1974), *aff'd*, 520 F.2d 871 (4th Cir. 1975), *cert. denied*, 423 U.S. 1034 (1975).

145. Fletcher, "Juanita Jackson Mitchell Dies at 79."

146. "Civil Rights Lady," *The Afro-American* (April 18, 1981): 6.

147. She pursued cases such as oppression of black activists. "From the suits for desegregation of the Baltimore schools and municipal swimming pools, which she won in the 1950s, to her representation of student activists convicted of criminal trespass while demanding civil rights and African American residents in the 'Veney Raid' cases of the 1960s, her use of the law for the disadvantaged and oppressed was consistent and exemplary." Genna Rae McNeil, "In Memoriam: Juanita Jackson Mitchell," *Maryland Law Review* 52 (1993): 512.

148. "Keiffer J. Mitchell for Delegate," *Meet Keiffer J. Mitchell, Jr.*, http://www.keiffermitchell.com/page/biography/; accessed July 18, 2012. Two of her sons, Clarence and Michael, became civil rights leaders and Maryland state senators but were later convicted of, respectively, obstructing a federal grand jury investigation and theft. Fletcher, "Juanita Jackson Mitchell Dies at 79." Mitchell nearly bankrupted herself paying their legal fees, and her house on Druid Hill Avenue, where she had lived since she and her husband bought it early in their marriage, was scheduled for foreclosure and sale at auction. A community fundraising drive, however, was able to gather the funds needed to save it and Mitchell was able to stay in her home. Ibid.

149. Interview with Elaine Carsley Davis, conducted at her home on March 19, 2013, by Jane Wilson, Director of Public Relations at the University of Maryland Francis King Carey School of Law.

150. "Elaine Carsley Davis," *Who's Who Among African-Americans* (Farmington Hills, MI: Gale Group, 2009).

151. "State Scholarships Cut in Half Due to Fund Shortage," *The Afro-American* (June 9, 1945): 16; "Pritt Retires, Reckling In," *The Afro-American* (June 30, 1945): 17.

152. They were married in May or early June 1945, as she was described as "Miss Elaine Carsley" in early May ("Stanley Carsley Buried Thursday," *The Afro-American* (May 5, 1945): 17) but as "Elaine C. Davis" a month later ("State Scholarships Cut in Half Due to Fund Shortage," *The Afro-American* (June 9, 1945): 16).

153. Hines, "20 Attending University of Maryland Law School."

154. "Davis, Urban Official, Dies," *The Baltimore Sun* (March 8, 1962): 15. Clarke Davis enrolled in the first year evening class in 1946–1947; the second year evening class in 1947–1948; and as an unclassified student in 1948–1949, while Elaine went on to the third-year evening class. Clarke Davis did not enroll again at the University of Maryland School of Law. University of Maryland, *Catalogue* 1946–1947 *and Announcement* 1947–1948, 23; and University of Maryland, *Catalogue* 1949–1950 *and Announcement* 1950–51, 30.

155. Lena Lee credited her husband for pushing her to consider law school as a means of resolving the Baltimore City Public School system's refusal to promote her to principal. "Oral History (Recorded 1988)," Thurgood Marshall Law Library, African Americans in the Law Collection, http://www.law.umaryland.edu/marshall/specialcollections/lenaleepapers/; accessed December 31, 2012. Two other women who attended the Law

School around the same time, Verda Welcome and Helen Estes Baker, were married to doctors who provided financial security for their wives. "Verda Welcome, Maryland Women's Hall of Fame," http://msa.maryland.gov/msa/educ/exhibits/womenshall/html/welcome.html; accessed December 27, 2012; and "A Guide to the Papers of Helen Estes Baker," http://ead.lib.virginia.edu/vivaxtf/view?docId=vsu/vipets00014.xml; accessed December 27, 2012.

156. Interview with Elaine Carsley Davis, conducted at her home on March 19, 2013, by Jane Wilson. In the interview, Davis explicitly stated that she did "not plan to practice" but "to gain a general working knowledge of law."

157. Telephone interview with Elaine Carsley Davis, conducted on March 19, 2013, by Jane Wilson.

158. Banks, "Setting the Record Straight," 759.

159. The Johns Hopkins University granted its first degree to an African American, Reginald James, in 1946. (He started his M.P.H. in 1944.) Johns Hopkins did not admit women to its undergraduate program until 1970. The first black student at John Hopkins, Kelly Miller, had enrolled in 1872 but was forced to leave before graduation when a dire financial crisis at John Hopkins forced a twenty-five percent tuition increase. "Chronology of Johns Hopkins University," http://webapps.jhu.edu/jhuniverse/information_about_hopkins/about_jhu/chronology/index.cfm; accessed December 31, 2012; Adam Lovett, "Voices for Change: The History of Black Student Activism at Johns Hopkins University," an unpublished senior thesis (Baltimore, MD: The Johns Hopkins University Press, 2008), 7, available at https://jscholarship.library.jhu.edu/bitstream/handle/1774.2/32779/history%20of%20black%20student%20activism%20at%20jhu.pdf. Johns Hopkins's closure to blacks and women may also explain Lee's decision to earn her M.Ed. from New York University, although the University of Maryland, as part of its efforts to remain "lily-white," arranged for fellowships for black students at Johns Hopkins and St. John's College, in Annapolis, in 1948. George Streator, "Maryland Paying Negroes' Tuition: $60,000 Is Allotted for Study at Private 'White' Colleges—Ban at State University," *The New York Times* (December 7, 1948).

160. Davis received a George Peabody fellowship in 1956–1957 and a John Hay Whitney Fellowship and American Association of University Women Fellowship in 1957–1958. "Fellowship Is Given to Mrs. Elaine Davis," *The Baltimore Sun* (August 8, 1957): 22; "Mrs. Elaine Davis gets study grant," *The Afro-American* (August 6, 1957): 12; B. M. Phillips, "If You Ask Me," *The Afro-American* (August 17, 1957): 18; and "Phi Beta Kappa," *The Afro-American* (May 24, 1958): 16. The John Hay Whitney Foundation (1946–1983) was founded to fund "innovative educational and minority-directed projects." Judith Ann Schiff, "John Hay Whitney," *Yale Alumni Magazine* (2002), available at http://archives.yalealumnimagazine.com/issues/02_04/old_yale.html; Edgar Logan, "Would You Be Interested in a Year of Study on Full Pay?" *The Clearing House* 32 (1957): 86–88 (describing the John Hay Whitney fellowships).

The History of African Americans at the Johns Hopkins University's Website dates the first Ph.D. to an African American woman in 1970 ("Miriam DeCosta-Willis," http://afam.nts.jhu.edu/people/decosta_willis/decosta.html; accessed December 31, 2012).

161. B. M. Phillips, "If You Ask Me," *The Afro-American* (May 10, 1958): 16; "Mrs. Elaine Davis gets

study grant," *The Afro-American* (August 6, 1957): 12.

162. Ibid.

163. Adam Clymer, "Board Fills School Posts After Row," *The Baltimore Sun* (June 20, 1963): 54.

164. Ibid.; "Principals for Three New Schools On List Appointed," *The Baltimore Sun* (June 20, 1963): 39; Lowell E. Sunderland, "Board Asks Phasing Out of Dunbar," *The Baltimore Sun* (June 18, 1965): 44; Roger Nissly, "School board approves two tax plans," *The Afro-American* (March 23, 1968), "Area Directors Listed in School Promotions," *The Afro-American* (March 30, 1968): 17; and "Feminists, school aides to meet on 'sexist' books," *The Baltimore Sun* (July 5, 1972): D22.

165. "College trustees pick Dr. Davis," *The Afro-American* (January 13, 1973): 20 ("Educational Assistant" to Patterson); "School administration airs reorganization data," *The Baltimore Sun* (April 13, 1973): C17 ("top aide"); and "'Brass Tacks' to focus on education," *The Baltimore Sun* (May 8, 1973): B7 (one of three public representatives of school system's proposed changes— with Patterson and the associate superintendent of curriculum and instruction). Grayson Mitchell, "White School Board Members Try to Ax Black Head," *Jet* (November 28, 1974): 44–45; and "School Chief Patterson Out; Sizemore Hearings Set," *Jet* (August 7, 1975): 25.

166. Howell S. Baum, *Brown in Baltimore: School Desegregation and the Limits of Liberalism* (Ithaca, NY: Cornell University Press, 2010), 166; and Frederick N. Rasmussen, "John L. Crew Sr.," *The Baltimore Sun* (November 21, 2011): A10.

167. "Dr. Davis gets top Hopkins slot," *The Afro-American* (July 27, 1974): 8; "Mrs. Davis leaves city schools," *The Baltimore Sun* (July 27, 1974): B3; and "Education: The Public is Being Badly Stung," *The Baltimore Sun* (September 2, 1974): A8. Davis appears to have become director of the education division of the evening and summer programs by 1978. "Personnel changes," *The Baltimore Sun* (February 15, 1978): A13.

168. "Education Bill Signed," *The Baltimore Sun* (February 27, 1963): 25; "Tawes Hails His Record on Education," *The Baltimore Sun* (September 29, 1966): C24.

169. "Interim Report of the State of Maryland Advisory Council for Higher Education" (1965) 31–32, http://www.lawyerscommittee.org/admin/education/documents/files/interim-report-of-the-state-of-maryland-advisory-council-for-higher-education-1965.pdf; accessed December 31, 2012.

170. Maryland Advisory Council for Higher Education, "Supplement [to the Second Annual Report]" (1966), xvi; Maryland Advisory Council for Higher Education, "Report" (1967), xvii. In the 1966 report, she is listed as Dr. Elaine Davis Johnson. Chapter 130 of the Laws of Maryland of 1968 renamed and changed the membership of the Council. 1968 Md. Laws 162.

171. Stephen E. Nordlinger, "Curlett Plan Gets Support; Morgan Asks Exemption," *The Baltimore Sun* (January 25, 1963): 38; Charles Whiteford, "Renominations Mark Green Bag," *The Baltimore Sun* (February 19, 1965): 42; Gene Oishi, "Trustees Agree to Discuss Control of Morgan College," *The Baltimore Sun* (April 11, 1967): C7; and Gene Oishi, "Trustees Agree to Discuss Control of Morgan College," *The Baltimore Sun* (April 11, 1967): C2.

172. "Education Bill Signed," *The Baltimore Sun* (February 27, 1963): 25; and Gerald W. Clarke, "Colleges and Boards, All Kinds," *The Baltimore Sun* (January 13, 1964): 14.

173. Adam Clymer, "Delay Looms on Takeover of Morgan," *The Baltimore Sun* (July 26, 1963): 40.

174. Gerald W. Clarke, "Higher Education in Maryland: Colleges and Boards, All Kinds," *The Baltimore Sun* (January 13, 1964): 14; Janetta Ridgely, "For and Against—II: A Branch University for Baltimore" *The Baltimore Sun* (February 26, 1963): 18 (quoting Morgan State president Jenkins as supporting only a graduate branch in the Baltimore region); Gerald W. Clarke, "U. of M. Policy on Graduate Students Hit," *The Baltimore Sun* (January 12, 1964): 32; and Gerald Clarke, "County Campus Purpose Defined," *The Baltimore Sun* (February 4, 1964): 42. Verda Welcome, a fellow graduate of Morgan State, was a key supporter of Morgan State in the Assembly and called for the university to hold up on establishing its UMBC branch until the council completed its study of the "tripartite system of higher education." Gerald W. Clarke, "Data Urged on U.M. Site," *The Baltimore Sun* (January 16, 1964): 31.

175. "Morgan is Urged to Seek Whites: Jenkins Says College Cannot Continue Segregated," *The Baltimore Sun* (January 17, 1964): 38; Gerald W. Clarke, "Integration Plan Backed For Morgan," *The Baltimore Sun* (January 19, 1964): 32; "Morgan to Push Recruitment of White Students," *The Afro-American* (March 28, 1964): 14; and Gerald Clarke, "Morgan Gets More Whites: But Slight Gain Is Called No Test Of Program," *The Baltimore Sun* (October 18, 1964): 10.

176. "State Board Take-Over of Morgan Set," *The Baltimore Sun* (June 30, 1967): C24.

177. Gene Oishi, "Morgan Head Greets Board," *The Baltimore Sun* (July 21, 1967): C13; *Stovall v. Sec'y of State*, 252 Md. 258 (1969); "Dr. Davis named to college board," *The Afro-American* (August 5, 1967): 3.

178. Davis joined Judge Robert Watts, one of the original members. *Maryland Manual* 1965–1966 (1966), 62; *Maryland Manual* 1967–1968 (1968), 63. Davis, along with Mrs. Thomas W. H. White, Jr. and Elizabeth Cole, a distinguished woman lawyer and strong integrationist as general counsel for the Commission on Civil Rights' Public Education Section, was one of the first female trustees. "Mrs. E. E. Cole Dies at Age 63: Prominent In Education, Rights Movement," *The Baltimore Sun* (March 18, 1966): A11. Davis was appointed in time for the official 1967 group portrait. The trustee that appears to have filled Cole's spot in 1966, Mathias DeVito, shared Cole's experience of being a government attorney dealing with education. Adam Clymer, "Delay Looms on Takeover of Morgan," *The Baltimore Sun* (July 26, 1963): 40; "Big College Plan Pushed," *The Baltimore Sun* (June 28, 1966): C7; and "Schools Plan Money Pool," *The Baltimore Sun* (March 30, 1967): 12. Davis shared Cole's background in law and educational administration and experience with desegregation.

179. *Maryland Manual* 1965–1966 (1966), 62; *Maryland Manual* 1967–1968 (1968), 63.

180. "Mrs. E. E. Cole Dies at Age 63," *The Baltimore Sun* (March 18, 1966): A11.

181. "Dr. Davis named to college board," *The Afro-American* (August 5, 1967): 2; and "Zarfoss Leaves W. Md. For Key B&O Post," *The Baltimore Sun* (July 20, 1966): C9.

182. Mary Cordory, "Coppin Role is Continued," *The Baltimore Sun* (May 6, 1969): C24; "Coppin Lives

On," *The Baltimore Sun* (May 11, 1969): PK4; Mary Cordory, "New Salisbury State President Chosen," *The Baltimore Sun* (May 14, 1970): A13; and "Dr. King B. Cheek New Morgan Prexy," *The Afro-American* (September 5, 1970): 19.

183. H. Joost Polak, "Integration Held Failure," *The Baltimore Sun* (September 10, 1968): C7.

184. Neil D. Rosenberg, "Bowie State Conditions Deplored," *The Baltimore Sun* (November 4, 1969): C24.

185. Callcott, *Maryland and America*, 64–66.

186. "New Morgan President: Dr. King Check is Made Official," *The Afro-American* (September 26, 1970): 2; "Elaine C. Davis To Chair State College Trustee Panel," *The Baltimore Sun* (January 15, 1973): A10; "People," *Jet* (February 15, 1973): 48; and "Gerry Major's Society World," *Jet* (April 26, 1973): 36.

187. G. Jefferson Price, 3d, "4 Ok'd for Jail Board," *The Baltimore Sun* (October 3, 1972): C24; and "New trustees named at Goucher College," *The Afro-American* (September 9, 1972): 21.

188. "Personnel changes: Two Rouse Directors Named," *The Baltimore Sun* (February 15, 1978): A13. Baltimore voters approved Rouse's planned Harborplace in November 1978. "Important Dates During the History of Harborplace," *The Baltimore Sun* (July 1, 2010), available at http://articles.baltimoresun.com/2010-07-01/business/bs-bz-harborplace-timeline-20100701-11_1_light-street-pavilion-tall-ships-rouse.

189. Unless otherwise indicated in endnotes, the information in this paragraph comes from "The Lena Lee Collection—Biographical Sketch," Thurgood Marshall Law Library African Americans in the Law Collection, http://www.law.umaryland.edu/marshall/specialcollections/lenaleepapers/#bio; accessed February 15, 2013.

190. Banks, "Setting the Record Straight," 760.

191. Frederick N. Rasmussen, "'She Stood Very Tall,' Educator was One of the First Black Women in the General Assembly," *The Baltimore Sun* (August 26, 2006): 1B.

192. Following the 1935 decision in *Murray v. University of Maryland*, 169 Md. 478, 182 A. 590 (1935), which ruled that the university must provide access to graduate law education for blacks and which resulted in Donald Gaines Murray's admittance to the Law School, the university created a scholarship program to pay black graduates to attend graduate schools outside of the state in order to keep College Park white-only. See "An Illegal $2,800,000," *The Afro-American* (August 3, 1957): A12. The program paid not only tuition, but also travel and living expenses at out-of-state schools, many of which were private and very prestigious. See Mike Bowler, "Brown vs. Board of Education: 50 Years Later; Black Students Sent Away; Scholarships: To Keep Them Out of College Park, Maryland Subsidized the Graduate Education of its Black Teachers Out of State," *The Baltimore Sun* (May 16, 2004): 6G. The University of Maryland also entered into a compact with other Southern states to maintain segregated graduate schools by reciprocal agreements to admit blacks from states without a particular graduate program for blacks. For example, Maryland had no veterinary program for blacks. It sent black Marylanders seeking a veterinary degree to study in black programs in other Southern states. In 1950, the Court of Appeals barred this practice, a decision which integrated the University of Maryland's graduate programs in College Park. (*McCready v. Byrd*, 195 Md. 131, 73 A.2d 8 (1950).) Donald Murray was one

of McCready's attorneys. The Supreme Court decision several months later in *Sweatt v. Painter*, 339 U.S. 629 (1950), provided further support for integration, although Towson Normal School (now Towson University) still refused to admit blacks. "Total of 233 Students Now in Dixie Colleges," *The Afro-American* (November 17, 1950): 20.

193. "Oral History (Recorded 1988)," Thurgood Marshall Law Library African Americans in the Law Collection, http://www.law.umaryland.edu/marshall/specialcollections/lenaleepapers/; accessed December 31, 2012.

194. "The Lena Lee Collection—Biographical Sketch," Thurgood Marshall Law Library.

195. In 1948, Welcome enrolled in the first-year day class at the University of Maryland School of Law, likely as a way of gaining knowledge to further her activist work. University of Maryland, *Catalogue of Law Students During the Year* 1947–1948, *XXIX Bulletin* 1948–49, 29. Like many of the early African American women students, she did not finish; her name does not appear in the records for any successive year. University of Maryland, *Catalogue of Law Students During the Year* 1948–49, *XXX Bulletin* 1949–50; Banks, "Setting the Record Straight," 761.

196. Ibid., 763.

197. Ibid., 765.

198. Housing and Urban Renewal, The University of Baltimore, http://ubalt.libguides.com/content.php?pid=123245&sid=1104686; accessed March 28, 2013. "In 1956, Mayor Theodore R. McKeldin abolished the Baltimore Redevelopment Commission and combined its functions with elements of the City Planning, Health and Welfare departments into a single agency: the Urban Renewal and Housing Agency (BURHA)." Jesse Glasgow, "R.L. Porter Is Named To Cohen's Job," *The Baltimore Sun*, June 14, 1955, 38; "J. N. Curlett Will Head School Unit," *The Baltimore Sun* (January 3, 1957): 36.

199. Stephen E. Nordlinger, "Groups Named in Curlett Plan," *The Baltimore Sun* (July 3, 1963): 40.

200. "The Lena Lee Collection—Biographical Sketch," Thurgood Marshall Law Library.

201. Banks, "Setting the Record Straight," 766; "George Mahoney, 87, Maryland Candidate," *The New York Times* (March 21, 1989) observed: "In the 1966 contest Mr. Mahoney campaigned on the slogan 'your home is your castle—protect it,' a statement that was considered aimed at those opposed to open housing and other civil rights goals. Many Democratic groups withheld their support."

202. "The Lena Lee Collection—Biographical Sketch," Thurgood Marshall Law Library.

203. Ibid.

204. All information in the Joan Sessoms Ford profile, unless otherwise cited, is taken from a telephone interview with Joan Sessoms Ford, conducted on June 19, 2012, by Rachel W. W. Granfield, and email exchanges from February 7, 2013 to August 28, 2013 between Jane Wilson and Joan Sessoms Ford, who reviewed, revised, and added language to this and earlier drafts.

205. Ibid.

206. For anecdotal evidence, see Bernard D. Meltzer, "The University of Chicago Law School: Ruminations and Reminiscences," *University of Chicago Law Review* 70 (2003): 239–40.

207. Neither the University of Maryland Office of the Registrar, nor the University of Maryland Francis King Carey School of Law Office of Registration & Enrollment have detailed records on the Maryland Law Class of 1971. Research has disclosed that the class of 1971 was composed of twelve graduates from the fall of 1970 who received their degrees on January 25, 1971, and 123 graduates from the spring of 1971who received their degrees on June 4, 1971. Information on the demographics of the Maryland Law Class of 1971 is unavailable.

208. See interview with Joan Sessoms Ford.

209. Ibid.

210. Ibid.

211. Ibid. During law school, Sessoms was the Student Bar Association's Law School Division Representative, served as Managing Director of the Community Teaching Project, helped create the first Association of Law Women at the law school, was awarded a Reginald Heber Smith Fellowship in 1971, and was one of the first women at the law school to become a member of the Phi Alpha Delta Law Fraternity. Bettye Moss, "IF YOU: Ask Me," *The Afro-American* (June 19, 1971): 5.

212. See interview with Joan Sessoms Ford.

213. Ibid.

214. Ibid.

Chapter 6

1. Paula Gaber, "'Just Trying to be Human in this Place': The Legal Education of Twenty Women," *Yale Journal of Law and Feminism* 10 (1998): 215.

2. Ibid.

3. Carolyn B. Stegman, *Women of Achievement in Maryland History*, Suzanne Nida Seibert, ed. (University Park, MD: Anaconda Press, 2002), 378 n.2.

4. "History of Women's Bar Association of Maryland," Women's Bar Association of Maryland, http://www.wba-md.org/history.aspx; accessed July 18, 2012.

5. Ibid.

6. The Honorable John Carroll Byrnes, "Commemorative Histories of the Bench and Bar: In Celebration of the Bicentennial of Baltimore City 1797–1997," *University of Baltimore Law Forum* 27 (1997): 20.

7. "History of Women's Bar Association of Maryland."

8. Ibid.

9. Alice Steinbach, "Lawyer, Women's Advocate Jeanette Rosner Wolman: A Soldier in the Fight for Women's Rights," *The Baltimore Sun* (Anniversary Issue, May 17, 1987): 107.

10. The Honorable Lynne A. Battaglia, "'Where is Justice?' An Exploration of Beginnings," *University of Baltimore Law Forum* 42 (2011): 34.

11. The Honorable Kathleen O'Ferrall Friedman, interview by Ellen Cobb, February 27, 2012.

12. Stegman, *Women of Achievement in Maryland History*, 378.

13. "History of Women's Bar Association of Maryland."

14. "Commission on Women in the Profession," American Bar Association, www.americanbar.org/groups/women/initiatives_awards/margaret_brent_awards/pasthonorees.html; accessed July 17, 2012.

15. "mentor, n." OED Online. June 2012. Oxford University Press. http://www.oed.com/view/Entry/116575?rskey=d61mTB&result=1; accessed July 20, 2012.

16. Janet Stidman Eveleth, "Raker Honored With ABA's Prestigious Margaret Brent Award," Maryland Bar Bulletin (August 2007), http://www.msba.org/departments/commpubl/publications/bar_bult/2007/aug/raker.asp.

17. Johnathon E. Briggs, "Mary Arabian, 1st woman Municipal Court judge, dies; Served almost 30 years on bench in Baltimore," *The Baltimore Sun* (August 26, 2002): 10B.

18. Ibid.

19. Ibid.

20. "History of Women's Bar Association of Maryland."

21. Stegman, *Women of Achievement in Maryland History*, 405.

22. Battaglia, "Where is Justice?" 34; "Mary Ann Saar," Maryland Archives, http://www.msa.md.gov/msa/mdmanual/22dpscs/former/html/msa11915.html; accessed July 21, 2012.

23. Mary Ann Saar, "One Hand Helps the Other: Why Women Need to Make Good Connections and Use Them to Help Other Women up the Career Ladder," *Corrections Today* (October 2005), http://www.aca.org/fileupload/177/prasannak/saars_web.pdf.

24. Stegman, *Women of Achievement in Maryland History*, 402.

25. Ibid.

26. Ibid.

27. "Rita C. Davidson Award," Women's Bar Association of Maryland, http://www.wba-md.org/RCDaward.aspx; accessed July 21, 2012.

28. "Rosalyn Blake Bell," Maryland Women's Hall of Fame, http://www.msa.md.gov/msa/educ/exhibits/womenshall/html/bell.html; accessed July 21, 2012.

29. Battaglia, "Where is Justice?" 27.

30. Ibid., 5.

31. Steinbach, "Lawyer Women's Advocate Jeanette Rosner Wolman."

32. Battaglia, "Where is Justice?" 32–33.

33. Ibid., 29.

34. Ibid., 30, quoting Fred Rasmussen, "Rose Zetzer, 94, Founded 1st All-Female Law Firm in Md.," *The Baltimore Sun* (April 9, 1998): 11B.

35. Ibid., 31.

36. Ibid.

37. Ibid.

38. The Honorable Diana Motz, interview by Ellen

Cobb, June 20, 2012.

39. Marcia Myers, "Diana Motz Joins Federal bench Today," *The Baltimore Sun* (July 22, 1994): 1.B, available at http://articles.baltimoresun.com/1994-07-22/news/1994203116_1_motz-diana-court-of-special.

40. Motz, interview.

41. Ibid.; Myers, "Diana Motz Joins Federal bench Today."

42. Motz, interview.

43. Ibid.

44. Ann Turnbull, interview by Ellen Cobb, May 23, 2012.

45. Ibid.

46. Natalie McSherry, interview by Ellen Cobb, February 6, 2012.

47. See Chapter 2 of this book.

48. McSherry, interview.

49. Ibid.

50. "Kathleen O'Ferrall Friedman," Archives of Maryland, Accessed February 25, 2012, http://www.msa.md.gov/msa/mdmanual/31cc/former/html/msa11781.html; The Honorable Kathleen O'Ferrall Friedman, interview by Ellen Cobb, February 27, 2012.

51. O'Ferrall Friedman, interview.

52. Ibid.

53. The Honorable Ellen L. Hollander, interview by Ellen Cobb, February 21, 2012.

54. Ibid.

55. Eleanor M. Carey, interview by Ellen Cobb, May 24, 2012.

56. Ibid.

57. Ibid.

58. The Honorable Deborah K. Chasanow, interview by Ellen Cobb, June 13, 2012.

59. Ibid.

60. Stegman, *Women of Achievement in Maryland History*, 411.

61. Motz, interview.

62. Ibid.

63. Turnbull, interview.

64. Ibid.

65. Ibid.

66. The Honorable Ann S. Harrington, interview by Ellen Cobb, February 15, 2012.

67. Ibid.

68. Ibid.

69. McSherry, interview.

70. Ibid.

B. Cavanaugh, Judge Deborah S. Eyler, Estelle Fishbein, Jo B. Fogel, Major Rose Forrest, Nancy Forster, Tiffany Franc, Carol Garfiel Freeman, Judge Kathleen O'Ferrall Friedman, Dorcas R. Gilmore, Sally B. Gold, Monica M. Haley-Pierson, Judge Ann S. Harrington, Deena Hausner, Cheryl Hepfer, Kristin Herber, Kathi Hill, Barbara Loveless Holtz, Judge Barbara Kerr Howe, Julie Landau, Judge Diane O. Leasure, Elizabeth G. Loggia, Barbara A. Maher, Judge M. Brooke Murdock, Christyne Neff, Judge Theresa Nolan, Sandra A. O'Connor, Anne C. Ogletree, Master Rita Rosenkrantz, Naima Said, Mary Roby Sanders, Reena Shah, Ann Rhind Sparrough, Nell Strachan, Master Joanne Suder, Mayda Colón Tsaknis, Anne M. Turnbull, and Linda Woolf.

Appendix A

1. See *Court of Appeals of Maryland, Test Book: 1851–1916*, Volume I, 240.

2. Death Certificate for Emilie Doetsch, 8 June 1969, Reg. No. 695885, Baltimore City Health Department. Copy in possession of author.

3. Death certificate for Helen F. Hill, 14 March 1966, Maryland State Department of Health, Division of Statistical Research and Records. Copy in possession of author.

4. Death Certificate for Emily Dashiell, 8 February 1983, Reg. No. 830314, State of Maryland Department of Health and Mental Hygiene. Copy in possession of author.

5. "Pair's Romance Goes From Courts to Altar," *The Washington Post* (June 26, 1930).

Table 1.1

1. Dr. Lois Green Carr, St. Mary's City Women's Career Files: Katherine Hebden Marshall, Maryland State Archives, http://msa.maryland.gov/megafile/msa/speccol/sc4000/sc4040/000001/000741/html/sc4040-0741-01.html.

2. Dr. Lois Green Carr, St. Mary's City Women's Career Files: Ann Johnson Dorrington, Maryland State Archives, http://www.msa.md.gov/megafile/msa/speccol/sc4000/sc4040/000001/000852/html/sc4040-0852-01.html.

3. Dr. Lois Green Carr, St. Mary's City Women's Career Files: Ann Danby (Dandy), Maryland State Archives, http://www.msa.md.gov/megafile/msa/speccol/sc4000/sc4040/000001/000411/html/sc4040-0411-01.html.

4. Archives of Maryland Online, 10:553.

5. Dr. Lois Green Carr, St. Mary's City Women's Career Files: Agatha Morris Langworth, Maryland State Archives, http://www.msa.md.gov/megafile/msa/speccol/sc4000/sc4040/000001/000927/html/sc4040-0927-1.html.

6. Dr. Lois Green Carr, St. Mary's City Women's Career Files: Martha Lashley Bogue, http://msa.maryland.gov/megafile/msa/speccol/sc4000/sc4040/000001/000144/html/sc4040-0144-01.html.

7. Dr. Lois Green Carr, St. Mary's City Women's Career Files: Martha Lewger, Maryland State Archives, http://www.msa.md.gov/megafile/msa/speccol/sc4000/sc4040/000001/000950/html/sc4040-0950-1.html.

8. Dr. Lois Green Carr, St. Mary's City Women's Career Files: Sarah Benton, Maryland State

Archives, http://www.msa.md.gov/megafile/msa/speccol/sc4000/sc4040/000001/000131/html/sc4040-0131-01.html.

9. Dr. Lois Green Carr, St. Mary's City Women's Career Files: Mary (Marie) Lindsey Mackloughlin, Maryland State Archives, http://msa.maryland.gov/megafile/msa/speccol/sc4000/sc4040/000001/000957/html/sc4040-0957.html.

10. Dr. Lois Green Carr, St. Mary's City Women's Career Files: Elizabeth Stockes Large Morgan, Maryland State Archives, http://www.msa.md.gov/megafile/msa/speccol/sc4000/sc4040/000001/000935/html/sc4040-0935-1.html.

11. Dr. Lois Green Carr, St. Mary's City Women's Career Files: Rose Gerrard, Maryland State Archives, http://www.msa.md.gov/megafile/msa/speccol/sc4000/sc4040/000001/000584/html/sc4040-0584-01.html.

12. Dr. Lois Green Carr, St. Mary's City Women's Career Files: Hester Lecompt Cordea, Maryland State Archives, http://www.msa.md.gov/megafile/msa/speccol/sc4000/sc4040/000001/000365/html/sc4040-0365-01.html.

13. Dr. Lois Green Carr, St. Mary's City Women's Career Files: Katherine Lewis Shore, Maryland State Archives, http://www.msa.md.gov/megafile/msa/speccol/sc4000/sc4040/000001/000953/html/sc4040-0953-1.html.

14. Dr. Lois Green Carr, St. Mary's City Women's Career Files: Ann Evans, Maryland State Archives, http://www.msa.md.gov/megafile/msa/speccol/sc4000/sc4040/000001/000499/html/sc4040-0499-1.html.

15. Dr. Lois Green Carr, St. Mary's City Women's Career Files: Rebecca Clocker Askins Dayley Simmons, Maryland State Archives, http://msa.maryland.gov/megafile/msa/speccol/sc4000/sc4040/000001/000043/html/sc4040-0043-01.html.

16. Dr. Lois Green Carr, St. Mary's City Women's Career Files: Mary Evans Lamb, Maryland State Archives, http://www.msa.md.gov/megafile/msa/speccol/sc4000/sc4040/000001/000504/html/sc4040-0504-1.html.

17. Dr. Lois Green Carr, St. Mary's City Women's Career Files: Julian Legitt Powell Whittor, Maryland State Archives, http://www.msa.md.gov/megafile/msa/speccol/sc4000/sc4040/000001/000946/html/sc4040-0946-1.html

18. Dr. Lois Green Carr, St. Mary's City Women's Career Files: Audrey O'Daly Cocks Llewellin Taylard, Maryland State Archives, http://www.msa.md.gov/megafile/msa/speccol/sc4000/sc4040/000001/000965/html/sc4040-0965-01.html.

19. Dr. Lois Green Carr, St. Mary's City Women's Career Files: Abigail Thomas Lewis, Maryland State Archives, http://www.msa.md.gov/megafile/msa/speccol/sc4000/sc4040/000001/000952/html/sc4040-0952-1.html.

20. Dr. Lois Green Carr, St. Mary's City Women's Career Files: Anne Bankes, Maryland State Archives, http://www.msa.md.gov/megafile/msa/speccol/sc4000/sc4040/000001/000065/html/sc4040-0065-1.html.

21. Dr. Lois Green Carr, St. Mary's City Women's Career Files: Ann Abington, Maryland State Archives, http://www.msa.md.gov/megafile/msa/speccol/sc4000/sc4040/001000/001701/html/sc4040-1701-01.html.

22. Dr. Lois Green Carr, St. Mary's City Women's Career Files: Katherine Bevin, Maryland State Archives, http://www.msa.md.gov/megafile/msa/speccol/sc4000/sc4040/000001/000132/html/sc4040-0132-1.html.

23. Dr. Lois Green Carr, St. Mary's City Women's Career Files: Elizabeth Carberry, Maryland State Archives, http://msa.maryland.gov/megafile/msa/speccol/sc4000/sc4040/000001/000252/html/sc4040-0252-1.html.

24. Dr. Lois Green Carr, St. Mary's City Women's Career Files: Mary Heard Tant Ford, Maryland State Archives, http://www.msa.md.gov/megafile/msa/speccol/sc4000/sc4040/000001/000534/html/sc4040-0534-1.html.

25. Dr. Lois Green Carr, St. Mary's City Women's Career Files: Annastatia Langham (Langhorn), Maryland State Archives, http://www.msa.md.gov/megafile/msa/speccol/sc4000/sc4040/000001/000924/html/sc4040-0924.html.

26. Dr. Lois Green Carr, St. Mary's City Women's Career Files: Moor Langley, Maryland State Archives, http://www.msa.md.gov/megafile/msa/speccol/sc4000/sc4040/000001/000926/html/sc4040-0926.html.

27. Dr. Lois Green Carr, St. Mary's City Women's Career Files: Elizabeth Daft, Maryland State Archives, http://msa.maryland.gov/megafile/msa/speccol/sc4000/sc4040/000001/000406/html/sc4040-0406.html.

28. Dr. Lois Green Carr, St. Mary's City Women's Career Files: Dorothy Leigh, Maryland State Archives, http://www.msa.md.gov/megafile/msa/speccol/sc4000/sc4040/000001/000947/html/sc4040-0947.html.

29. Dr. Lois Green Carr, St. Mary's City Women's Career Files: Elizabeth Herbert Daft, Maryland State Archives, http://msa.maryland.gov/megafile/msa/speccol/sc4000/sc4040/000001/000408/html/sc4040-0408.html.

30. Dr. Lois Green Carr, St. Mary's City Women's Career Files: Mary Little Baley Fear, Maryland State Archives, http://www.msa.md.gov/megafile/msa/speccol/sc4000/sc4040/000001/000960/html/sc4040-0960-1.html.

INDEX

ABOUT THE EDITOR AND THE CONTRIBUTORS

Lynne A. Battaglia was raised in Silver Creek, New York. She received her B.A. in international relations in 1967 and her M.A. in International Relations in 1968 from American University. After having been awarded an NDEA Title IV Fellowship, Judge Battaglia entered Georgetown University in 1968 to embark on her doctoral studies in American government. Before receiving her doctorate, Judge Battaglia entered at the University of Maryland Law School, where she received her Juris Doctor degree in 1974; she was Articles Editor of the Law Review and graduated Order of the Coif. She continues to teach as an adjunct faculty member at the University of Maryland Law School and the University of Baltimore Law School. Judge Battaglia began her legal career in 1974 at the Baltimore law firm of Semmes, Bowen & Semmes. In 1978, she was recruited to serve as an Assistant United States Attorney for the District of Maryland, a position she held for the next four years. In 1984, Judge Battaglia became Senior Trial Attorney within the Office of Special Litigation in the Department of Justice. In 1988, she was chosen by Maryland Attorney General J. Joseph Curran to become Chief of the Criminal Investigations Division and, within three years, was recruited to become Chief of Staff to U.S. Senator Barbara A. Mikulski. She was appointed and confirmed by the U.S. Senate to serve in the position of United States Attorney for the District of Maryland, serving from August, 20, 1993, to January 26, 2001. Judge Battaglia is currently a Maryland Court of Appeals Judge from the Third Appellate Circuit. She was nominated by Governor Parris Glendening, confirmed by the Maryland Senate, and was sworn-in on January 26, 2001.

Judge Battaglia has received numerous honors and awards during her distinguished career. In November 2007, Judge Battaglia was elected to membership in The American Law Institute, an elite group consisting of judges, practicing lawyers, and legal scholars from all areas of the United States as well as some foreign countries, who are selected for membership on the basis of professional achievement and demonstrated interest in the improvement of the law. Most recently, she was inducted into the Howard County Women's Hall of Fame in 2010. She is also a model leader and mentor, having served on and chaired numerous committees and boards. She currently serves as Chair of the Professionalism Center and Chair of the Women Lawyers in Maryland Project.

Phoebe A. Haddon was born in Washington, DC, and grew up in Passaic, New Jersey. She received her B.A. in government from Smith College, her J.D. from Duquesne University School of Law, and her LL.M. from Yale Law School. Haddon is currently Chancellor of Rutgers University–Camden. She previously served as Dean of the University of Maryland Francis King Carey School of Law, where she was instrumental in securing a $30,000,000 gift to the law school—the largest in the history of the school and one of the largest in the history of the University System of Maryland—

from the W.P. Carey Foundation. She also was on the faculty of the Temple University Beasley School of Law for nearly thirty years. She has co-authored and edited numerous books, including *Tort Law: Cases, Problems, Perspectives* (Ashgate, 2007), *Constitutional Law: Cases, History, and Dialogues* (LexisNexis, 2006), *First Amendment Law: Cases, Comparative Perspectives, and Dialogues* (Anderson, 2003), *Tort Law: Cases and Materials* (LexisNexis, 2002), and *A Constitutional Law Anthology* (Anderson, 1997), and has contributed many law review articles and essays to such publications as *Temple Law Review*, *St. John's Law Review*, *Litigating Medical Malpractice Claims*, and *Maryland Journal of International Law*. She currently is a member of the American Bar Association's Commission on the Future of Legal Services. Haddon received the Great Teacher Award from the Society of American Law Teachers in 2011, and was named one of the "Top 100 Women" in Maryland by *The Daily Record* in 2012, and one of the "25 Most Influential People in Legal Education" by the *National Jurist* in 2012 and 2013.

In 2014, Haddon was an invited speaker at the 91st annual meeting of the American Law Institute, where other invited speakers included U.S. Supreme Court Chief Justice John Roberts and U.S. Supreme Court Justices Stephen Breyer and Ruth Bader Ginsburg; that same year, she was named among the "Women of Distinction" to be honored by the *Philadelphia Business Journal*. Her judicial appointments include the Court of Appeals for the Third Circuit Task Force on Equal Treatment in the Courts and the Pennsylvania Supreme Court Committee on Racial and Gender Fairness in Court System. She has served on numerous boards and governing bodies, including the executive committee of the Association of American Law Schools, the Delaware Valley Community Reinvestment Fund, the Women's Law Project, the William Penn Foundation, the Samuel S. Fels Fund, the Philadelphia Education Fund, and the Baltimore Leadership School for Young Women.

Andrea M. Leahy was born in Baltimore, Maryland, and raised in Prince George's County, Maryland. She received her B.A. in music and politics from Catholic University and her J.D. from American University, Washington College of Law. She is currently a member of the Maryland Court of Special Appeals. Leahy has served as an Assistant United States Attorney from 1999 through 2001, Chief Counsel to the Governor of Maryland from 1995 to 1999, and Associate County Attorney for Prince George's County from 1989 through 1992. Prior to her appointment to the Court, Leahy was Of Counsel to Whiteford, Taylor & Preston, L.L.P., and, in 2006, became the founding and managing member of the firm of Leahy & DeSmet, L.L.C., in Calverton, Maryland. She has served as a member of the Prince George's County Trial Courts Judicial Nominating Commission, the Prince George's Hospital Authority, and the Maryland State Ethics Commission. Leahy has also served on numerous private, nonprofit, and public boards, including the Baltimore-Washington Chamber of Commerce Board of Directors, Pallotti High School Board of Directors, and Maryland WBA Foundation Board of Directors, for which she also served as Chair of the *Finding Justice Project* until her appointment to the bench.

Leahy has received the Leadership in Law award from *The Daily Record* and was selected as one of *The Daily Record*'s Top 100 Women three times, culminating in her induction into The Circle of Excellence. She was named one of Maryland's Top 50 Women Lawyers by *Baltimore Magazine* in January 2013, and her firm, Leahy & DeSmet, LLC, was recognized among the Top 100 Minority and Women Owned Businesses in the Mid-Atlantic region in 2010.

Diane O. Leasure was born in Cumberland, Maryland. She received her B.A. in human behavior and development from Rowan University, her M.S. in Human Behavior and Development from Drexel University, and her J.D. from Rutgers University-Camden. Judge Leasure is now retired from the 5th

Judicial Circuit, where she served as the Fifth Circuit Administrative Judge and the County Administrative Judge for the Circuit Court for Howard County for nearly ten years. Prior to her sixteen years as a Circuit Court judge, she was a Principal of Fossett & Brugger, Chartered. After her retirement from the bench, she was appointed by Governor Martin O'Malley to serve as Chair of the Maryland State Commission on Criminal Sentencing Policy and to serve as a member of the State Advisory Council on Administrative Hearings. Judge Leasure was a member of the Conference of Circuit Judges and served as its chair from 2008 to 2010, a member of the Judicial Cabinet and the Judicial Council, and an Inaugural Science and Technology Fellow in The Advanced Science and Technology Adjudication Resource Center (ASTAR). In addition to being certified by the Court of Appeals for recall in the circuit courts and to serve as a mediator for the Court of Special Appeals, she is a Senior Adjunct Faculty Member at the University of Maryland's Francis King Carey School of Law and has a private mediation and arbitration business. Judge Leasure was selected as one of *The Daily Record*'s Top 100 Women three times, culminating in her induction into The Circle of Excellence in 2011, and has received the Leadership in Law award from *The Daily Record* in 2004, the Anselm Sodaro Judicial Civility Award from the Maryland State Bar Association in 2008, the Beverly Groner Family Law Award from the Maryland State Bar Association's Family and Juvenile Law Section Council in 2012, and the 2013–2014 Outstanding Adjunct Faculty Award from the Student Bar Association of the University of Maryland Francis King Carey School of Law.

Michelle R. Mitchell was born and grew up in North Dakota. She attended the United States Naval Academy and received her B.A. in government and politics, M.A. in public policy, and J.D. at the University of Maryland. Mitchell is currently a shareholder in Wharton Levin Ehrmantraut & Klein, a law firm based in Annapolis, Maryland. Mitchell served as Articles Editor for the *Maryland Law Review* and has contributed articles to *Doctors RX* and *Maryland Law Review*. She was named as a Rising Star in *Baltimore Magazine*'s Top Attorneys list for 2014.

Jane C. Murphy was born in Freeport, New York, and has lived in Maryland since 1983. She earned her B.A. in English and Political Science from Boston College and her J.D. from New York University School of Law. She is currently the Laurence M. Katz Professor of Law at the University of Baltimore School of Law, where she has been a faculty member since 1988 and served as Associate Dean for Academic Affairs from 2008 to 2010 and Holmes Professor of Theory and Practice from 2006 to 2011. Murphy has also taught law at Georgetown University Law Center and was a visiting professor at the Washington University School of Law. In 1988, she co-founded, with Jane Schukoske, the University of Baltimore School of Law's Clinical Program. Murphy is the co-author of *Divorced from Reality: Reimagining Family Dispute Resolution*, with Jana Singer, (New York University Press, 2015) and *Family Mediation: Theory and Practice*, with Robert Rubinson, (LexisNexis, 2009), and as co-editor, with Jana Singer, of *Resolving Family Conflicts* (Ashgate, 2008). She has also contributed law review articles to numerous publications, including *Cornell Law Review*, *Hofstra Law Review*, *North Carolina Law Review*, and the *Notre Dame Law Review*. She is the recipient of numerous awards, including the 2011 Legal Aid Bureau Champion of Human Rights and Justice Award, the University System of Maryland's 2004 Award for Faculty Excellence, the first University of Baltimore's Presidential Faculty Award in 2004, *The Daily Record*'s 2004 Leadership in Law Award, the 2003 Benjamin L. Cardin Distinguished

Service Award, and being named one of Maryland's Top 100 Women in 1999.

Julie R. Rubin was born and grew up in Baltimore, Maryland, where she graduated from Bryn Mawr School. She received her B.A. in history and Spanish from Mount Holyoke College and her J.D. from the University of Maryland School of Law. Since 2013, Rubin has been an Associate Judge for the Circuit Court for Baltimore City and, since 2003, an adjunct professor at the University of Maryland School of Law. In 1998, she served as an Asper Fellow with the Honorable Marvin J. Garbis of the U.S. District Court for the District of Maryland. Rubin has been on the Board of Trustees of the Bryn Mawr School since 2006 and served as Chair of the Board from 2011 to 2014. She has been on the Board of Directors of the College-Bound Foundation since 2008, the Board of Directors of the Maryland Society for the Prevention of Cruelty to Animals since 2013, and the Board of Trustees of the Baltimore Educational Scholarship Trust since 2014. Rubin was a columnist for SmartCEO (from 2008 to 2012) and Citybizlist.com (from 2006 to 2007) and has contributed articles to the *Maryland Bar Journal*, *The Daily Record*, and *The Business Lawyer*. She co-hosted, with Dan Rodricks and Jim Astrachan, *Midday on the Law*, a bi-monthly legal news radio program aired on WYPR 88-FM, the local National Public Radio affiliate in Baltimore. Rubin has been named an American Bar Fellow and has been honored by *The Daily Record* as one of the "Top 50 Women in Maryland Under 40," a "Very Important Professional" (for professionals under 40), and one of "Maryland's Top 100 Women.". Rubin serves as a Representative of Maryland's 8th Judicial Circuit on the Maryland Circuit Judges Association.

ABOUT THE BOOK

Finding Justice: A History of American Lawyers in Maryland since 1642 was brought to publication in an edition of 1,000 hardbound copies. The text was set in Minion, the paper is American Eagle White, 70 lb. weight, thirty percent post-consumer recycled, and the book was professionally printed and bound in the United States of America.

Editorial note: Out of respect for some readers, the hyphen that usually appears in compound adjectives has been omitted in proper names such as African American and Asian American.

Publisher: George F. Thompson

Manuscript Editor and Research Assistant:
Mikki Soroczak

Proofreader: Purna Makaram

Book Design and Production:
John Cole and David Skolkin

Special Acknowledgments: Joseph S. Wood, Provost of the University of Baltimore, was instrumental in making this book possible, as were three remarkable law clerks to the Honorable Lynne A. Battaglia who helped develop and prepare the manuscript: Hannah Levin, Alicia L. Shelton, and Diane E. Feuerherd.